THE CROSSMAN DIARIES

Selections from the Diaries
of a Cabinet Minister
1964–1970

RICHARD CROSSMAN

THE CROSSMAN DIARIES

Selections from the Diaries
of a Cabinet Minister
1964–1970

Introduced and edited by
ANTHONY HOWARD

BOOK CLUB ASSOCIATES
LONDON

This edition published 1979 by
Book Club Associates
By arrangement with Hamish Hamilton Ltd,
and Jonathan Cape Ltd

Printed offset litho in Great Britain by
Cox & Wyman Ltd,
London, Fakenham and Reading

Contents

Illustrations

Introduction

Dick Crossman was one of those meteors that occasionally lighten the British political firmament. He was never quite a politician of the first rank; even in his own life-time his fame was easily outshone by such contemporaries as Harold Macmillan, Aneurin Bevan and Hugh Gaitskell. But he was still one of that select group of politicians (Iain Macleod and Tony Crosland were other recent examples) who fleetingly bring a glow to the normally grey and dingy skies of British politics.

Of course, in the eyes of many of his colleagues Dick Crossman is today very much a fallen star—considered 'neither a comrade among his friends nor a gentleman by his enemies'. The principal reason for that is to be found in these *Diaries*—a posthumous memorial to a politician who not only refused to recognize the normal rules of collective (and, therefore, generally non-existent) cabinet responsibility but was resolutely resolved to smash them if he could as well. There has latterly been a tendency among some of those who worked most closely with Crossman to suggest that the *Diaries* represent, as it were, an aberration—a departure from the norm of accepted conduct that he would never have sanctioned had he been fit and well and lived long enough to supervise their entire publication. Nothing could be further from the truth.

The most familiar charge brought against Crossman even while he lived was that of 'inconsistency'. Yet in one area, from the days when he was a young Oxford don, he was as constant as the Northern Star. His first, and favourite, book *Plato Today*[1] wrestles with the problem of to what degree British parliamentary democracy is a sham, a fraud or a hoax: and it was a question that Crossman continued to tussle with until the day he died. It made him a highly unusual, not to say unorthodox, politician (his fellow practitioners of the craft being more generally noted for conveying complacency rather than betraying disquiet about a system that at least had had the merit of recognizing their own talents). Crossman, however, as well as possessing 'the bump of irreverence' that he was much given to boasting about, had throughout his career a passionate—and at times inconvenient —commitment to the notion of making democracy actually work. His haunt-

[1] London: Allen & Unwin, 1937.

ing doubt—and this is as apparent in his last public lecture[1] as in his first book—was that in some way the British electorate was being fobbed off with what Plato called 'the noble lie': in other words that the British voter, while encouraged to believe that he was part of a self-governing democracy, was in effect—through the device of so-called 'representative institutions'—enduring government by oligarchy. The guilty secret at the heart of the British governmental system, Crossman came increasingly to believe, was that it was deliberately designed not to give ordinary people their heads but rather to tame the demon of democracy before it did too much damage.

This conviction, strengthened rather than weakened by his six years as a Cabinet Minister, offers the key not just to his attitudes but to many of his actions (including the decision not only to keep these *Diaries* but his personal determination to fight, if necessary, to get them published). They would provide, Crossman became more and more convinced, his lasting contribution to British politics—and provide it for the very good reason that they would give to the ordinary voter what he most lacked, knowledge. His deliberate aim, in fact, was (as he put it in his own Introduction to the First Volume)[2] to disclose 'the secret operations of government', thereby enabling the humblest elector to cut his way 'through the masses of foliage which we call the myth of democracy'.

For to Crossman, if ignorance was impotence, knowledge was power. How could the citizen fully exercise his democratic rights if he was not even allowed to know which were the working parts of the British constitutional mechanism and which the purely decorative ones? Next to Plato (whose conclusions he repudiated while accepting a large part of his analysis), Walter Bagehot probably had the strongest influence of anyone on Crossman's political philosophy; and, just as he borrowed the language of the 'Guardians' and 'the noble lie' from Plato's *Republic*, so he took the notion of the 'dignified' and the 'efficient' elements of government from Bagehot's *English Constitution*. Yet which were which? Part at least of the zest which Crossman brought to his voyage of discovery through the inlets of Whitehall—after a nineteen-year wait stranded on the shores of the rival Kingdom of Westminster—lay in his realization that at long last he was going to find out. It has become fashionable to claim (or at least Sir Harold Wilson has done his best to create the fashion)[3] that Crossman had made up his mind about British government long before he arrived in the Cabinet and that anything he discovered thereafter was bound to be used simply to reinforce his already pre-ordained prejudices. Again, nothing could be further from the truth.

[1] *The Role of the Volunteer in the Modern Social Service*: Sydney Ball Memorial Lecture (Oxford: Clarendon Press, 1973).
[2] *The Diaries of a Cabinet Minister, Volume One: Minister of Housing 1964–66* (London: Hamish Hamilton and Jonathan Cape, 1975).
[3] Harold Wilson, 'A Desire to Educate', *Listener*, January 5, 1978.

If anything, indeed, Crossman, once past the safety curtain that separates the backbencher from the Minister, comes across rather as the Queen of Sheba contemplating the wisdom of Solomon: 'behold, the half was not told me'. It is impossible to mistake the genuine astonishment with which he gradually discovers the full extent of the power of the civil service—a power, he eventually concludes, that rests on two time-honoured Whitehall customs (neither of which—perhaps surprisingly for a relatively active back-bencher—he had known anything about before entering government). The first arises from the civil service's role as 'keeper of the muniments': the fact that, through the cabinet secretariat, the civil service not merely records the discussions of cabinet but also minutes its decisions bestows on permanent officials, Crossman argues, a tremendous discretionary prerogative. Only what is recorded officially ranks as precedent: and, therefore, precedent very soon becomes that to which the civil service—and in particular the cabinet secretariat—gives its approval.

Probably, however, the second civil service 'reserve power' came as even more of a shock. When he entered the Cabinet in October 1964, Crossman knew, of course, of the existence of individual influential civil servants—indeed one of the most influential of all (Dame Evelyn Sharp) was to be his own Permanent Secretary at the Ministry of Housing and Local Government. But what he does not appear to have reckoned with was the ease with which such individually influential, non-elected figures in Whitehall could (and would) combine in order to impose what, perhaps revealingly, is always called 'the official view'. Civil servants can do this, Crossman points out, at two levels. First, there is the insistent, 'official' advice that a Minister gets within his own Department; but, on top of that, there is always 'a cohesive, inter-Departmental view' to be pressed on the Minister's own colleagues once any disputed question goes to Cabinet. Little wonder that within six months of being in the Cabinet he had already concluded that, unless a Minister has the Prime Minister or some other extremely important colleague backing him to the hilt, 'the chance of prevailing against the official view is absolutely nil'.

It would be quite wrong, however, to give the impression that Crossman was wedded to any 'conspiracy theory' of politics. If he collided with the civil service, it was because he was an upholder of open government, whereas officials tend to think of the task of public administration as something best conducted well away from the vulgar gaze. That apart, Crossman was not a natural opponent of the civil service, least of all at the ground level in places like local social security offices; indeed, he was himself a planner—even a democratic centralist—by nature and by instinct. His enemy was never bureaucracy itself but rather the secrecy in which it insisted on transacting much of its business—something that he vividly demonstrated by perhaps the bravest political action of his career, his resolute decision in 1969 to publish in full, in face of all 'official' advice, the report (written by a political opponent) on the scandals attending the administration of the Ely Mental Hospital just outside Cardiff, for which he himself as Secretary of State at the D.H.S.S. was constitutionally responsible.

In fact, second only to his passionate allegiance to democracy came his positive loathing of unnecessary secrecy in any form. It was not merely that he never felt at home with it—one of the most endearing passages in his unpublished diary covering the beginning of his *New Statesman* editorship comes in the entry in which he reflects on the enormous sense of relief that he feels at no longer having to worry about blurting something out that he shouldn't have done. His dread of inadvertently giving something away must stem, he explains, from his period in 'top secret security' during the war; but his instinctive resentment of the whole English tradition of 'least said, soonest mended'—or, as he once put it in the *New Statesman*, his reflex rejection of the maxim 'Not in front of the children'—almost certainly went back far beyond that to the days of his own childhood.

Those apt to reflect on how slow the pace of social change is in Britain should perhaps recall that only just over seventy years ago, when Dick Crossman was born (in 1907), it was still the habit in upper-middle, professional class families for family prayers to be held every morning. In the only piece of straight autobiographical writing he ever attempted[1] Crossman once vividly described the ceremony that would regularly take place every morning of the year in his own home:

My first memory of my father is at the assembly of the household at 7.55 precisely for morning prayers. He sat at one end of the breakfast table and my mother at the other, while the children were ranged on their special little chairs in front of the fire; then the bell was rung and the maids and nurses filed in to their places with their backs to the window. Attending morning prayers before breakfast, and changing into evening dress for dinner, were practices my father required of his family until he died.

It was perhaps a Victorian, Forsyte household lingering on after its time; but its influence on Crossman—if only in terms of offering something to react against—was continuous and strong. Indeed, in that same fragment of autobiography (written when he was already fifty-four) Crossman confessed that he had long since resolved that 'the most useful contribution I can make to public life is to expose the cowardice of conformity wherever I detect it and challenge the organized hypocrisy of the Establishment'.

He certainly started doing that from an early age—and in private just as much as in public. Crossman's father was a Chancery barrister who later became a High Court judge: apart from his wife and six children (one of whom, his youngest son, was killed in the war and was then, incredibly, omitted from his *Who's Who* entry), the two loves of his life were the law and

[1] 'My Father' by R. H. S. Crossman, *Sunday Telegraph*, December 16, 1962.

his old school, Winchester—whither Dick Crossman, the cleverest of his children, went at the age of twelve, winning a scholarship and a place in College, just as his father had done before him. It was Winchester, Crossman was ever afterwards to proclaim, that first made him into something that he was constantly accused of being all his life—'an intellectual bully'. He would sharpen his dialectical skill and his debating ability at the family dining table—laying intellectual booby-traps for his mother into which 'the poor woman would always blunder'. In later years he was to display some remorse over that—but he was never able to lose his contempt for his father's cowardice in keeping a timid (and not even chivalrous) silence while his own and his wife's most sacred values and principles were being brutally attacked.

The pugilistic temperament, which caused Crossman throughout his life to enjoy nothing so much as what he used to call 'a jolly good set-to', was thus given full rein from an early age—perhaps too early for his own good. For though Mr Justice Crossman was never particularly politically minded (he voted Conservative as a matter of course, only suffering anxiety when so dangerous a figure as Winston Churchill became the candidate he was expected to vote for in Epping in 1924), he did have one friend who was a politician, and a Labour one at that. A frequent guest at the Crossman home and on the family tennis court at Buckhurst Hill, Essex in the 1920s was that most strait-laced and conventional of all Labour politicians, Clement Attlee. He it was who became the reluctant and resentful witness to all Crossman's bullying and baiting of his own family—bear-garden exhibitions, no doubt, made worse in his eyes by the fact that the fellow was, dammit, not just a public schoolboy but actually head of his school as well. Crossman himself never wavered in his belief that his failure to attain any form of office in the Attlee governments of 1945–51 was at least partly due to the fact that, in the Prime Minister's eyes, he was responsible for bringing his father's grey hairs down with sorrow to the grave.[1] And there is at least some evidence that his belief may have been accurate. In 1950, when Hugh Gaitskell was Chancellor of the Exchequer, he went to the Prime Minister to plead Crossman's cause and to draw attention to his great and wantonly overlooked ability—only to be rewarded with the Attlee-esque comment: 'Not a question of ability at all. Question of character—that's the trouble there.'[2]

But long before that, of course, Crossman's storm-trooping tactics with his own family had gone well beyond words to actions. An exemplary career of scholarship at both Winchester and Oxford brought him in 1929 the offer of a Fellowship at New College where he had been an undergraduate winning a Double First in Mods and Greats (again, as his father had done before him). But the transition from being a junior member of the college to being a

[1] Mr Justice Charles Stafford Crossman died in 1941, four years before Mr Attlee became Prime Minister.
[2] Hugh Gaitskell: interview with A.H.

member of the Senior Common Room was considered too abrupt to be taken at one leap: Crossman was, therefore, encouraged to spend a year abroad—and he chose Germany. It turned out to be a fateful choice: not only was Crossman able to witness the preliminary stages of the rise of Hitler but he actually brought back home with him a German-Jewish girl as his fiancée.

That, to its credit, was not even a cause for mild concern in what, as we have seen, was a strictly conventional Christian family: indeed Crossman's fiancée, Erika, soon charmed his parents. The scandal arose only with their discovery that she had already been married twice and that she was in Crossman's own words 'a *morphiniste*' (or morphine addict)—something that he had not troubled to warn them about beforehand. They forbade the marriage and—disregarding his own brusque instruction: 'You're supposed to be Christians. *You* look after her'—threw her out of the house, thereby insuring that he did in fact marry her.

Fortunately, despite the shock and outrage caused to the family's friends (including, no doubt, the Attlees), it did not prove to be a lasting arrangement. Within six months the first Mrs Crossman had announced that she had fallen in love with someone else (she was, in fact, ultimately to marry a total of seven times) and Crossman was able to abandon the converted barn in which he had started married life and move into his bachelor rooms at New College. In later life he was always to speak of his first wife with a certain flamboyant pride—explaining, with a dash of schoolboy daring, that she had 'solved my sexual hangups'. These, one was given to understand, had been of a homosexual variety—though, apart from an Oxford friendship with W. H. Auden and a life-long enmity with Sir Maurice Bowra, the surviving evidence from this phase of Crossman's life is suspiciously slight. The nearest perhaps he ever got to supplying any actual detail came one evening when he described at length a railway journey that he and Wystan Auden had taken from Oxford across the Midlands and into Yorkshire—all to watch a gilded youth from the university playing football at Sedbergh School. Despite Crossman's own best efforts to lend the episode an air of raffish adventure, the impression—alas—left on his hearers was that even in the 1920s there must have been more exciting things to get up to than that.

And in the more public aspects of life in Oxford—at least in the 1930s—there naturally were. As an undergraduate Crossman had played little or no part in politics—concentrating on poetry (he wrote a little of it at the time—none of it apparently preserved) and literary magazines. But as a don he soon rectified that—throwing himself not just into the incestuous politics of the university but into the rather more extrovert ones of the city as well. Spurning the then reserved and supposedly 'independent' university seats, he got himself elected as a Labour councillor for Cowley and in 1934 became leader of the, admittedly, small Labour Group. He also formed a friendship with that great patron of bright young men in the Labour Party, Hugh Dalton (whose then lonely view on the need for British rearmament he fully endorsed), and, partly through Dalton's influence, secured for himself in 1937 while still only twenty-nine the by-election candidature for the constituency of West Birmingham. He did not win the seat—but a by-product of that contest was his first meeting with George Hodgkinson, Secretary-Agent for Coventry, and his adoption later in 1937 as prospective Labour candidate for what was then that city's one Parliamentary consti-tuency held in 1935, if only marginally, by the Conservatives.

Frequently afterwards Crossman would recall the frustration and im-patience he felt, with a potential Labour seat under his belt, at having to wait eight long years to get into the House of Commons. The wait, however, may have had its conveniences. For one thing, it gave him a solid six-year background in local government—something he would often reproach his young colleagues on the *New Statesman* of the early 1970s for lacking. And, more immediately, it also enabled him to escape what otherwise might have been, at least in the 1930s, the awkward public repercussions of the second great convulsion in his private life. By 1937 Crossman had become one of the dominating academic figures of Oxford University—the debunker of the Platonist school of philosophy, a lecturer who could draw an audience to the examination schools at nine in the morning, even one of the first dons to acquire an outside fame through broadcasting (principally on the subject of Germany and the Nazi threat). His seven-year Fellowship at New College was in 1937 drawing to its end but there was certainly no reason to believe it would not be renewed: indeed he had recently been appointed Dean of the College. It was precisely at this moment that Crossman's capacity for outrag-ing orthodox bourgeois values betrayed itself once again. He formed an attachment to, and eventually ran away with, not merely the wife of another don but one who was his own colleague in the New College Senior Common Room. The consternation thereby caused may today seem comic—the rooms in New College in which Crossman was placed under virtually close arrest are occasionally pointed to with a *voyeur*'s relish even today—but the crisis posed for Crossman's career was none the less real.

There is some reason to believe that both he and his second wife, Zita (who, to make matters worse, already had two young children), hesitated before taking the plunge into actual matrimony, knowing full well what the consequences would be. In fact twenty-five years later—and a decade after Zita's own death in 1952—Crossman wrote in the *Guardian*[1] how at a moment of crisis in his personal life he had gone to 'a remote and uncomfort-able eyrie' on the South Downs to seek the counsel of that humanist oracle, Bertrand Russell, and had been given advice that he had never regretted taking. Within New College itself the Warden (H. A. L. Fisher) seems to have given similar advice—though in his case based rather more on grounds

[1] May 25, 1962. According to Crossman, displaying a view of himself that not everyone would share, Russell urged him on to 'a most uncharacteristic recklessness and disregard for common prudence that brought me years of enduring happiness'.

of public usefulness than private happiness. Without naming the subject of
the story, Crossman in 1947 related in a *New Statesman* book review[1] how 'a
young don' had once gone to Fisher to seek his advice on whether to stay in
Oxford or to launch forth into the world outside. The Warden, according to
this account, first said officially that he was prepared to recommend the
renewal of 'the young don's' Fellowship which, given the background (not,
incidentally, spelt out by Crossman in his 1947 book review), was certainly
an act of liberal courage; but, as a former politician, indeed Lloyd George
Cabinet Minister, he proceeded, on a personal basis, strongly to urge
Crossman to burn his boats:

> I stayed in Oxford too long and I went into politics at the top. That was the
> cause of my failure. Go in now while you are young. I can see you have the
> desire for it which I had at your age ... I would like you to avoid my
> mistakes.

Crossman took Fisher's advice—though at that stage there was, as we have
seen, no chance of his getting into national politics at least until 1939 or 1940
when most people then assumed the next general election would come.
Instead, having married and suffered the necessary sentence of exile, he
retired from Oxford to a country cottage in the Chilterns and managed to
eke out an existence by combining the earnings of a W.E.A. lecturer with
those of being 'a dogsbody' (his own phrase—later to be used to irritate other
young men thirty years later)[2] on the *New Statesman*.

Crossman was to remain—apart from a five-year gap from 1940–5 spent
entirely in psychological warfare first in England and then with Harold
Macmillan in Algiers—with the *New Statesman* for the next seventeen years
(combining his editorial duties from 1945 onwards with the scarcely arduous
ones of being a backbench M.P. to a Labour Government at first at least with
a solid majority). He was acknowledged even by the paper's editor, Kingsley
Martin (who did not like him), to be easily the most brilliant member of the
staff: 'the best leader writer I've known in a long experience apart from H. N.
Brailsford' ... 'has a quality of fertility which I've never seen equalled' ...
'the best book reviewer I've ever known'.[3] Why, then, did he not become
Kingsley Martin's successor—which was, at least until 1960 when John
Freeman got the job, the peak of his ambition? The brief answer is that
Kingsley Martin—whose moral disapproval of Crossman was, ironically,
scarcely less than that of Clement Attlee—was determined at all costs to
prevent that happening; and when, in fact, Crossman attempted an abortive
coup in the summer of 1955 by threatening to leave the paper for the *Daily
Mirror*, unless some guarantees were given as to his ultimate prospects of the

[1] 'The Charm of Politics', *New Statesman & Nation*, August 2, 1947. Also the lead essay in
R. H. S. Crossman's book of the same title (London: Hamish Hamilton, 1958).
[2] See 'Mr Crossman's Dogsbody' by James Fenton, *New Review*, November 1976.
[3] Kingsley Martin, Private (undated) Memorandum.

succession, his 'take-over bid' was effortlessly repulsed by both the editor and John Freeman with relief and without regret.

It remains, however, a perfectly arguable view that, had Crossman been permitted to take control of the *New Statesman* in 1955, he would have made a very great editor indeed (certainly a much better one than he, in fact, made when he returned to the paper as editor after being a Cabinet Minister at the age of sixty-two in June 1970). For one thing, he had already by the mid-1950s (with his new power-base as a member of the party's National Executive Committee, to which he was elected on the 'Bevanite' ticket at Morecambe in 1952) displayed to both the Right and Left of the Labour Party that no one was ever going to intimidate him out of his independence. If his kicking over the traces on the Anglo-American Palestine Commission of 1946 served notice on the Party Establishment that he was never going to be anyone's man but his own, then his lonely support among the Party's Left-wing for Harold Wilson's action in taking over Aneurin Bevan's seat in the 'shadow' cabinet in 1954 equally reminded the enraged 'Bevanites' that in his political conduct he would never owe allegiance to anything except his own (often unpredictable) judgment.

Later on, that was a lesson that even Hugh Gaitskell himself was to learn. It is sometimes said—indeed it was occasionally put about by Crossman himself—that, until Harold Wilson became leader of the Labour Party in February 1963, he had never made a speech in the Commons from anything but the backbenches; but that is not strictly true. During the October 1959 general election, in which Crossman acted as chairman of the campaign committee always established at election times by the National Executive, the association between him and the party leader naturally became much closer than it had been in the past (they had been at school at Winchester and at New College, Oxford together—but that is not always a guarantee of future comradeship).

There was, however, no doubt that by 1959 Hugh Gaitskell had firmly persuaded himself that it was possible to harness Crossman's undisputed talents to the service of the official leadership. It had, in fact, been he who, against some reservations among his own normally most loyal supporters, had pressed for his appointment as chairman of the campaign committee and, though the election was a bad disappointment for both men, the result in no way affected their growing warmth for each other. Accordingly in the new Parliament Crossman—who had had a great personal success presenting a new pensions policy[1] to the party conference two years earlier—found himself the party's official spokesman on pensions. He was not a member of the 'shadow' cabinet since that required election and he had not yet

[1] 'National Superannuation: Labour's Policy for Security in Old Age', a policy document passed by the 1957 Brighton Labour Party conference. Crossman was to live off-and-on with the subject for the next ten years but no Labour Superannunation Bill reached the Statute Book in his lifetime.

sufficiently lived down his 'rogue elephant' past to command the total confidence of his staider parliamentary colleagues; but he was a member of, as it were, Hugh Gaitskell's 'alternative government' and had at long last got—at least when pensions were being discussed—his feet safely up on the Despatch Box.

They were not to stay there long. Before six months had passed a sharp exchange of letters marked the end of Crossman's excursion under the Gaitskell regime into 'responsibility'. Once again it was his insistence on being allowed to act according to the sovereignty of his own conscience, rather than in a way other people considered was prudent, that caused the final break. A pained and plainly exasperated Hugh Gaitskell was to be found writing to him by March 10, 1960:

> Dear Dick, I am writing to confirm what I said to you this afternoon regarding your position as official Front Bench spokesman of the party on pensions and national insurance. Should it be your intention persistently and publicly to oppose the official policy of the party on defence—or, for that matter, on any other issue as decided by the party meeting—I do not consider this would be compatible with your continuing to be one of our official party spokesmen.

One day later a totally uncontrite Crossman was replying:

> My dear Hugh, Thank you for your letter which, as you no doubt realised, makes it quite impossible for me to remain on the Front Bench. May I say that I very much regret having to give up the job of official spokesman on pensions? But the terms in which you write leave me no alternative.

Considering the amount of effort Gaitskell had made, it was not perhaps surprising that he was (temporarily) exasperated; or, indeed, that Crossman ever afterwards remained (wrongly)[1] convinced that he would never get a Cabinet job in a Gaitskell administration and that he might just as well pack up politics and make his long way back to teaching at Oxford.[2]

That would not, in fact, have been as large a sacrifice as it might have appeared to his parliamentary colleagues. Not only had Crossman always had the ability to earn a living by his own pen; he had also now established himself as a Man of Property in a rather grand way at Prescote Manor Farm, near Banbury, within easy driving distance from Oxford. Even more to the point, he had in 1954 (or two years after his second wife's death) married for the third time—and on this occasion had two children of his own. There is almost a fairy-tale *motif* to this final Crossman marriage, as those eventually

[1] Baroness Gaitskell to A.H.

[2] I decided to find some academic post where I could write my books and resume the teaching which I enjoyed better than anything else. But, as Harold Laski used to remind us, in British politics while there is death there is hope. Gaitskell died and Harold Wilson succeeded him. My prospects were transformed'. R.H.S.C., Introduction, Volume One of *Diaries* (op. cit.).

able to study the *Diaries* in the original at Warwick University will discover. His bride, Anne—thirteen years younger than himself—was the daughter of one of the few anti-Tory landowners in Oxfordshire: as a young girl of fourteen she had watched the dashing young don stride up to visit her father in their seventeenth-century manor house and had resolved there and then that he was the man she would ultimately like to marry. Nearly twenty years later she did. She brought into Crossman's life not only an entirely new kind of financial security (her father, when he died, left the farm to them jointly) but also a contentment and serenity, quite apart from the life of politics and journalism, that he had never known before. Once their children were born,[1] the family home became Prescote Manor—and no one reading even these abridged *Diaries* can possibly doubt the degree of solace and happiness Crossman derived from returning to it as a haven even at the most turbulent of political times.

For the rest, one can only say with J. G. Lockhart on Sir Walter Scott 'he shall be his own biographer'. These *Diaries* provide not just an unprecedented perception into the life of politics at the top but also an insight into the character of a man who was an extraordinary, exciting and exceptional politician. Shortly after Dick Crossman died on April 5, 1974—and when there was still a considerable legal dispute over whether such revelations were entitled to be published—Sir John Hunt, the Secretary to the Cabinet, told me on the telephone that it would be 'a tragedy for his reputation' if they ever were. On the contrary, I maintained at the time (and would argue even more confidently today) they represent the vindication of all Dick Crossman ever strove for—and will continue to stand for many years as the kind of triumph against 'the organised hypocrisy of the Establishment' that few radical democrats enjoy, even posthumously.

July 1978   ANTHONY HOWARD

---

[1] Patrick and Virginia. Patrick died at the age of 18 in 1975 – one year after his father's death.

Editor's Note

Some note of explanation is perhaps needed on the methods, or guidelines, I have followed in reducing a published three-volume diary of some 1,060,000 words to a one-volume version of just over 300,000 words. It was inevitably in many ways a forbidding task and there were moments when I was consoled only by the knowledge that Dr Janet Morgan had trod an even more rugged path before me. She faced the far more formidable challenge of reducing an original transcript, taken from dictated tapes, of some 3 million words—preserved in its raw form at Warwick University—to a more manageable (or publishable) total of just over 1 million. But, though the ratio of reduction may have been roughly equal between us, the quantity of work certainly was not; and I must begin by acknowledging my debt to Dr Morgan, on the back of whose three-volume work this one-volume edition necessarily rides.

There was no single overriding principle by which I decided what to cut and what to retain. Broadly, my aim throughout was to preserve the narrative element of the original diary: thus, when a particular story starts, the reader may normally assume (give or take a trimming here or there) that it will be carried through to completion. Inevitably, since Crossman was rather given to side-road excursions off the main thoroughfare, this has involved some substantial excisions along the way. Many were made simply in the cause of economy; others, I dare to hope, may actually aid the cause of clarity. For the rest, I have tried as a general rule to preserve (apart from the mustier examples of Departmental detail) the various episodes in which Crossman himself was closely involved—at the cost, admittedly, of ditching those parts of the political history of 1964–70 at which he was a mere spectator. Unlike Dr Morgan's three-part work, this slimmer (if still bulky) volume cannot, therefore, pretend to give a comprehensive picture of the domestic politics of the years 1964–70, still less of events abroad to which Crossman himself would often react as nothing more than an interested newspaper reader. On the other hand, I believe it does offer a striking self-portrait of the life of a senior politician—as well as a view, certainly no less impressionistic than Sir Harold Wilson's own, of the 1964–70 Labour Government.

July 1978   ANTHONY HOWARD

1964

Thursday, October 22nd

I was appointed Minister of Housing on Saturday, October 17th, 1964. Now it is only the 22nd but, oh dear, it seems a long, long time. It also seems as though I had really transferred myself completely to this new life as a Cabinet Minister. In a way it's just the same as I had expected and predicted. The room in which I sit is the same in which I saw Nye Bevan for almost the first time when he was Minister of Health, and already I realize the tremendous effort it requires not to be taken over by the Civil Service. My Minister's room is like a padded cell, and in certain ways I am like a person who is suddenly certified a lunatic and put safely into this great, vast room, cut off from real life and surrounded by male and female trained nurses and attendants. When I am in a good mood they occasionally allow an ordinary human being to come and visit me; but they make sure that I behave right, and that the other person behaves right; and they know how to handle me. Of course, they don't behave *quite* like nurses because the Civil Service is profoundly deferential—'Yes, Minister! No, Minister! If you wish it, Minister!'—and combined with this there is a constant preoccupation to ensure that the Minister does what is correct. The Private Secretary's job is to make sure that when the Minister comes into Whitehall he doesn't let the side or himself down and behaves in accordance with the requirements of the institution.

It's also profoundly true that one has only to do absolutely nothing whatsoever in order to be floated forward on the stream. I have forgotten what day it was—indeed, the whole of my life in the last four days has merged into one, curious, single day—when I turned to my Private Secretary, George Moseley, and said, 'Now, you must teach me how to handle all this correspondence.' And he sat opposite me with his owlish eyes and said to me, 'Well, Minister, you see there are three ways of handling it. A letter can either be answered by you personally, in your own handwriting; or we can draft a personal reply for you to sign; or, if the letter is not worth your answering personally, we can draft an official answer.' 'What's an official answer?' I asked. 'Well, it says the Minister has received your letter and then the Department replies. Anyway, we'll draft all three variants,' said Mr Moseley, 'and if you just tell us which you want ...' 'How do I do that?' I asked. 'Well, you put all your in-tray into your out-tray,' he said, 'and if you put it in without a mark on it then we deal with it and you need never see it again.'

I think I've recorded that literally. I've only to transfer everything that's in my in-tray to my out-tray without a single mark on it to ensure it will be dealt with—all my Private Office is concerned with is to see that the routine runs on, that the Minister's life is conducted in the right way.

Now, how have I spent my time in this first week? It's been almost entirely spent in seeing, in series, the top officials. At each of these meetings, which have taken about one-and-a-half to two hours, I have been able to use the seminar techniques I'm used to: I ask questions to drive them on, to find out what's on in the Department. Of course, all through I've had an underlying anxiety caused by my complete lack of contact (thank God they can't quite realize it) with the subjects I'm dealing with. It's amazing how in politics one concentrates on a few subjects. For years I've been a specialist on social security and I know enough about it. Science and education I had picked up in the months when I was Shadow Minister.[1] But I've always left out of account this field of town and country planning, how it's organized, what it does, how planning permissions are given—all this is utterly remote to me and it's all unlike what I expected. And every now and then I wake up early in the morning and I think how can I possibly cope? Won't I be detected in my first speech? And all the time at the back of my mind I am getting ready for that first time in Parliament when I have to make a speech. I suppose it will be on housing policy in the debate on the Queen's Speech.

The person who dominates all the proceedings is, of course, Evelyn Sharp. She's been Permanent Secretary now for ten years, she is aged sixty-one, one year past retirement age, and she is only in the Department now because she can't bear to leave. She is a biggish woman, about five feet ten inches, with tremendous blue eyes which look right through you, a pale, unmade-up face, uncoloured lips. She is dressed as middle- or upper-class professional women do dress, quite expensively but rather uglily. She is really a tremendous and dominating character. She has worked with a great many Ministers before me. She was under the 1945–51 Labour Government in the Silkin Ministry of Town and Country Planning and in the Reith Town and Country Planning Ministry. She comes from the planning side of things. She is rather like Beatrice Webb in her attitude to life, to the Left in the sense of wanting improvement and social justice quite passionately and yet a tremendous patrician and utterly contemptuous and arrogant, regarding local authorities as children which she has to examine and rebuke for their failures. She sees the ordinary human being as incapable of making a sensible decision. Practically everybody I ask her about, when I hear of somebody who is some good, she dismisses as utterly worthless. Of course she is devoted to her Department and has the Civil Service's deference to her Minister. What will she make of me? Well, the truth about Dame Evelyn is that in one sense I am lucky: the first moment she met me was a moment of crisis when her Department was in danger.

Last Saturday, when I was appointed, she drove back from her country cottage at Lavenham and told me the moment she got to London that, largely owing to me, the Department had been sold down the river by Harold Wilson's decision that Fred Willey should be in charge of planning and that I

[1] Until 1963, when Harold Wilson became Leader of the Labour Party, Crossman had only held front-bench office very briefly between 1959 and 1960; but after Gaitskell's death he became Shadow Minister of Education and Science and fully expected to be offered this Department when Labour won the 1964 election.

should do housing.[1] When Harold told me of this decision my main feeling was one of relief that if Fred Willey took on planning I shouldn't be responsible for the appallingly complicated Bill on the Land Commission.[2] However, the Dame explained to me that what I had unconsciously done was to demolish the whole basis of her Department, because in her view—which I now suspect is correct—it's quite impossible to give physical planning, the land policy, to a new Ministry without giving it all control of housing. If I was to accept what Harold told me, Fred Willey would run all the land policy, Charlie Pannell, as Minister of Works, would run all the materials and labour side of housing, and I would be left titularly in charge.

As soon as she realized this Dame Evelyn got down to a Whitehall battle to save her Department from my stupidity and ignorance. That battle was waged through Saturday, Sunday, Monday and Tuesday, and was really only finally decided this morning. I had imagined that the final decision had been taken after a personal talk I had with Harold on Sunday morning by telephone, when I explained what Dame Evelyn had told me. He assured me that I was to lead the housing drive and that everything was perfectly all right. On Monday morning I talked to him again and he again assured me all was O.K. On both occasions he rebuked me and Dame Evelyn for the way she had been waging her Whitehall war; and he said, 'You don't know what she is like, going behind my back to the civil servants.' I knew quite well what she was like and I knew she had gone to the head of the Civil Service, Helsby, and to Eric Roll, head of George Brown's new D.E.A. Regardless of anything that Harold had said, she continued the war, capturing Fred Willey and putting him in a room by himself in our Ministry while she got hold of his new Permanent Secretary, Mr Bishop, and lectured him. Yes, she fought and fought. When on Wednesday afternoon at a meeting I turned to her and said, 'Well, Dame Evelyn, you've won,' she replied, 'It's been the worst two days of my whole life.' 'Yes,' I said, 'but you have saved physical planning for us.' And she said, 'Of course, I always win. But it was exhausting.'

During this period—Monday to Thursday—of my first week there have been two Cabinet meetings. The first was a mere formality only concerned with the economic crisis and, honestly, we were told as little about it as the National Executive of the Party is ever told. It really was an absolute farce to have George Brown saying, 'Naturally you won't want to be told, for fear of the information leaking, how serious the situation is. You won't want to be told what methods we shall take but we shall take them.'

The main interest in this Cabinet meeting was arriving in Downing Street,

[1] The Prime Minister's original intention after the election had been to give the planning functions of the Ministry of Housing and Local Government to a separate Ministry of Land and Natural Resources. Fred Willey served as Minister until August 1967. See Harold Wilson, *The Labour Government 1964–70, A Personal Record*, p. 9 (Weidenfeld & Nicolson and Michael Joseph, 1971), hereafter cited as *Wilson*.

[2] This body would purchase land for local authority use. The Government also intended that it should exact 'Betterment Levy', a tax on the profits from land sold for development.

pushing through the herd of photographers and entering No. 10, where I have only been once or twice before, and walking down that passage with the busts standing on the left-hand side and looking along to the left to a little room inside which were Marcia Williams and Brenda Dew, Harold's other secretary, and George Wigg,[1] all looking rather blue now because they feel they are being squeezed out and contracted by the Civil Service.

The second Cabinet meeting, which took place this morning, was much more serious. The agenda was first of all the crisis in Rhodesia, then steel, then the Queen's Speech, and then the economic crisis. On the first of these the threat that the Rhodesians would declare themselves independent was the main thing we had to deal with.[2] We received the minute describing it last night from the Defence Committee. And in my red box I found a draft by Arthur Bottomley,[3] written before he flew out to Zambia, in which he tried to browbeat the Rhodesian Government for threatening revolt, saying that this would be a terrible thing. I was able to ask why it was that he talked of rebellion and revolt whereas in the minutes of the Defence Committee this was called a unilateral declaration of independence. That was my first intervention in Cabinet and I made this very simple point: that it surely was unwise for us to use language which implied we would take action that we couldn't and never would take, i.e. to treat them as rebels. As I say, this was my first actual Cabinet intervention and I was commended by Harold and I think the point was taken.

Then we moved on to Fred Lee's paper on steel, in which he urged that for various technical reasons nationalization should be postponed to the second Session. The moment I heard the proposal I knew it was hopeless. George Brown weighed in, saying this was absolutely fatal. Steel must be taken early in the first Session. This view of George Brown's was reflected in speech after speech, everybody realizing (a) that it was impossible to drop steel, and (b) that if we had to keep it in the programme we ought to get it through as early as possible so that when we do go to the country or when we are defeated it will be on the Land Commission or rent control or pensions, on anything except steel. This was our first real Cabinet discussion. Most people took part. Harold sits there in the middle, facing out towards the Horse-guards, and on the extreme left of the long thin oval table there is Barbara and at the extreme right-wing end there is myself and Fred Lee. We are the junior members of the Cabinet; the senior members of the Cabinet are towards the middle of the table. There is Harold in the middle on the near side and there is George Brown opposite him, flanked by Gerald Gardiner,

[1] Paymaster-General, with special responsibility for security 1964–7. Made a life peer 1967.
[2] Before granting independence the British Government insisted on certain guarantees; the principle of unimpeded progress towards majority rule and the end of the discriminatory system of land apportionment were two of the most important. The Rhodesian Cabinet threatened to declare independence unilaterally.
[3] Labour M.P. for Rochester and Chatham 1945–59 and for Middlesbrough since 1962. Secretary of State for Commonwealth Relations, 1964–6.

the Lord Chancellor. I notice that Harold, who sits chewing his pipe, is very careful, like Attlee; says nothing at first and lets us all make the decision. There wasn't anybody really, except Douglas Houghton, who gave the faintest sympathy to Fred Lee. When he had been absolutely trounced and defeated Fred turned to me and said, 'I got the best of that.'

After that we turned to the Queen's Speech. This has been my chief preoccupation in the Department in the last four days. I've been aware from the start that my main job in the first instance in the legislative programme, and that is what the Queen's Speech is about, would be to introduce a big measure for reasserting rent control. Characteristically enough, I find that though the Labour Party has been committed for five years to the repeal of the Henry Brooke Rent Act,[1] there is only one slim series of notes by Michael Stewart[2] on the kind of way to do it in the files at Transport House. That's all there is. Everything else has to be thought up on the spot. Now, the Dame felt very strongly that that was quite enough for us in the first Session. She had been glad to get rid of the Land Commission Bill to Fred Willey. She had briefed me to go to Cabinet to say that the third inordinately complicated measure, leasehold enfranchisement,[3] should be postponed to the next Session; and it was my job in Cabinet at all costs to resist the effort to suggest that this leasehold enfranchisement (which still remains the job of our Department) should come in this Session. But it is of great interest to Welsh M.P.s and to a lesser extent to Birmingham M.P.s, and in Cabinet I found myself under enormous pressure to agree that leasehold reform should be added to the Queen's Speech. It was only thanks to the previous decision to take steel this Session that I was able to ensure that we didn't have to do this.

The formal tone of Cabinet proceedings surprised me. It is really determined by a very simple thing. We don't call each other Dick and Harold and George as we do in the National Executive. We address each other as 'Minister of Housing' or 'First Secretary' or 'Prime Minister', and this, corresponding to the House of Commons technique, does have a curiously flattening effect and helps us to behave civilly to each other.

As for Cabinet as a decision-taking body, my first impression is that it's a much more genuine forum of opinion than I had been led to expect or than I had described in my Introduction to Bagehot.[4] On the other hand it's quite clear that the preparations for dealing with the economic crisis, the item

[1] This Act, brought on to the statute book by Henry Brooke as Conservative Minister of Housing, came into effect in October 1958 and freed from rent control over half the houses in Great Britain previously affected by rent-restriction legislation; it also raised the rent limits on most of those remaining subject to controls.

[2] He had been Shadow Minister of Housing when Labour was in Opposition.

[3] This measure would give tenants on long leases the right to eventual purchase. It had originally been a Private Members' Bill sponsored by Denis Howell, Labour M.P. for Small Heath, Birmingham. The issue was especially vital in Birmingham and South Wales.

[4] Crossman's Introduction to W. Bagehot, *The English Constitution* (London: Fontana, 1963), sets out a description of Cabinet Government.

which followed the Queen's Speech, had been entirely done by Harold Wilson himself with the help of James Callaghan, George Brown and—I imagine—Douglas Jay at the Board of Trade. The crisis programme was just imposed on the rest of us. I didn't much like that. We were given the draft of the Statement due next Monday on the crisis and the measures to meet it. Personally, I didn't think very highly of the draft but Cabinet as a whole had no advance notice so we simply had to accept the *fait accompli* or resign. To judge from this first meeting the Prime Minister can consult whomever he likes in a crisis and once he has consulted, Cabinet must really go along. The contrast between this and the way Harold handled the steel issue was interesting. There is, I think, more possibility of decision in Cabinet than I realized as well as more possibility of Prime Ministerial dictatorship.

I continue to have this curious sense of fiction, the feeling that I am living in a Maurice Edelman[1] novel. All this business of being a Cabinet Minister is still unreal to me. And this feeling has been particularly strengthened by the fact that every time we left Downing Street or moved along Whitehall there was always a crowd of people watching, cheering, clapping as we went in and out—it's as if we are taking part not in real life but in a piece of reportage on the British constitutional system.

Undoubtedly the most fantastic episode in this novel was the kissing hands and the rehearsal. It took place last Monday when we new Ministers were summoned to the Privy Council offices to rehearse the ceremony of becoming a Privy Councillor. I don't suppose anything more dull, pretentious, or plain silly has ever been invented. There we were, sixteen grown men. For over an hour we were taught how to stand up, how to kneel on one knee on a cushion, how to raise the right hand with the Bible in it, how to advance three paces towards the Queen, how to take the hand and kiss it, how to move back ten paces without falling over the stools—which had been carefully arranged so that you did fall over them. Oh dear! We did this from 11.10 to 12.15. At 12.15 all of us went out, each to his own car, and we drove to the Palace and there stood about until we entered a great drawing-room. At the other end there was this little woman with a beautiful waist, and she had to stand with her hand on the table for forty minutes while we went through this rigmarole. We were uneasy, she was uneasy. Then at the end informality broke out and she said, 'You all moved backwards very nicely,' and we all laughed. And then she pressed a bell and we all left her. We were Privy Councillors: we had kissed hands.

Wednesday, October 28th
I woke up with a terrible cold today and after breakfast I went off to Transport House for the first meeting of the N.E.C. since the general

[1] Colleague of Crossman's as a Labour M.P. for Coventry, he was also the author of a number of political novels of which *Who Goes Home?* (London: Hamish Hamilton, 1953) is perhaps the best known. He died in 1975.

election. We started with a kind of desultory discussion of the election results during which I managed to read through my Ministry papers and prepare myself for the day. So I sat in the Executive and digested the views which Dame Evelyn had given me about the line I should take at the Cabinet meeting at 3.30 this afternoon.

So I come to this afternoon's Cabinet meeting. What happened is really only intelligible in terms of the Cabinet Committee on the financial implications of the Queen's Speech which I went to yesterday. This was chaired by the Chancellor and he had with him all the Ministers concerned with expenditure. We had a frank discussion about old-age pensions, prescription charges, subsidies for mortgages, all the claims for money which had been in the manifesto and which might have been covered in the Queen's Speech. It was clear that whereas we all wanted a 12s. 6d. increase in the old-age pension and the abolition of prescription charges, the Chancellor would only go as far as 10s. and no abolition of prescription charges. At this Committee meeting I had made it clear as Minister of Housing and Local Government that I was not pressing at the moment for any concessions to mortgagors or to the ratepayer since it was important to get our priorities right. Indeed I argued we should make a virtue of necessity by saying that we should give everything at present to the old, the sick and the unemployed and ask everybody else to hold back.

Now we were in full Cabinet and the whole argument was rehearsed once again. This time it was started with a paper by James Callaghan insisting that 10s. was all he could afford and nothing else. After he had made his case Douglas Houghton made a speech saying why he wanted 12s. 6d. (Douglas Houghton as Chancellor of the Duchy of Lancaster was the representative in the Cabinet of two social service Ministers, Peggy Herbison, the Minister of Social Security, and Kenneth Robinson, the Minister of Health. Douglas was therefore an old-fashioned overlord, i.e. a Minister without departmental responsibility but responsible for two Ministries.*) Peggy Herbison and Kenneth Robinson were both present at this meeting though they were not members of Cabinet. Peggy Herbison supported Douglas on the 12s. 6d. and then Kenneth Robinson gave the case for abolishing prescription charges. The Cabinet slowly warmed up and it was soon clear that the overwhelming majority took the view that a 10s. increase and nothing else was neither one thing nor the other. It would not be enough to dam the tide until national superannuation was introduced: there would have to be a second flat-rate concession at incredible expense. As for prescription charges, our package wouldn't impress anybody if we failed to abolish them right at the beginning. Those were the two main arguments employed. I was absolutely staggered at what happened because I am used to the idea that the Cabinet doesn't discuss a budget before the budget takes place. Yet here we

* As usual the arrangement worked very badly indeed. [All asterisked notes are Crossman's own.]

were discussing budget secrets, considering what concessions should be made and to some extent discussing the taxes by which we should raise them, in full Cabinet — although Harold warned us about leaks which had occurred over the weekend. I thought he conducted this meeting in the most extraordinary way and shouldn't have allowed all this to happen. I should be amazed if some of it doesn't leak into the press and it might even leak out that only Frank Longford supported the Chancellor in the end—Harold Wilson, having waited, sided with the rest of us. Like us, no doubt, he remembered Hugh Gaitskell in 1951 and how he made the saving of the £11 million on teeth and spectacles a matter of principle when his calculations were actually £300 million out.[1]

All this occurred in full Cabinet with Harold Wilson chatting away, adding up the figures himself, and the Chancellor adding up the figures himself. It was staggering, as I said to Frank Longford who was sitting next to me; he also, with his experience of Cabinet, said he had never observed anything so extraordinary as this way of conducting business. By the end we had almost decided that this must be the policy even if it means raising enormous sums by further taxation in an autumn budget. And it was at this point that Harold brought in the idea that sacrifices must be imposed on private enterprise as well as on public enterprise and that one sacrifice would be the cutback in ostentatious office building in London. He turned to me and said this was something *I* was responsible for.

When I got back to the Ministry I warned them what was on and said I must have another paper on building controls. They weren't very pleased because they had briefed me firmly against them. I hadn't told the Dame that I had discussed this idea on the telephone with Harold Wilson on Sunday and suggested it as an example of the kind of tough measure that we should introduce quickly, or that I had gone on, on Monday, to discuss with Douglas Jay the practical methods of doing it. Nevertheless, by the time I got back to the Ministry on Wednesday the Dame's line had changed, the Whitehall grapevine had worked, she knew that building controls had to come in, and she said she would get me a paper ready for next morning.

Thursday, October 29th

Since the main item of Wednesday's Cabinet agenda, the Queen's Speech, had been squeezed out by the economic crisis we had to take it this morning at 11.30. We were pretty busy at the Ministry because we were discussing building controls; already by the time I got there the Dame had the paper showing the practicability of the method Douglas Jay had suggested to me on Monday and which she had told me was totally impractical. So then I went on to the Cabinet meeting on the Queen's Speech.

It was just like a meeting of the National Executive. There we were,

[1] It was on this issue that Aneurin Bevan, Harold Wilson and John Freeman resigned from the Labour Government in April 1951.

twenty-three people, sitting down as a drafting committee, taking the Queen's Speech line by line. It was fantastic to see the Prime Minister sitting there, doing the drafting, and other people joining in. The meeting with its interminable amendments, redraftings and incompetence drooled on and on. I got so bored that I went in to talk to Marcia and Brenda in the little room behind, and waited there for Harold who was due to have lunch with me at the House of Commons that afternoon. At 1.25 he came through rubbing his hands, saying what a splendid Queen's Speech we had got, and I was just thinking what an appalling performance the morning had been.

When Harold asked me to lunch he said, 'We have to go over to the Commons,' and as he sat down in the corner of the Members' dining-room he said to me, 'The cook at Downing Street is ill so we can't manage it there.' I thought, 'My God, here is a Prime Minister who can't eat in his own house because his cook is ill.' But Harold was obviously pleased with everything. In the course of my report to him on what was going on in the Ministry he said, 'Well, you people must be desperately busy. I'm having an easier time now than for ages because I am no longer a one-man band. I've got my staff and advisers.' He also added that he was going to leave us all to run our Departments pretty freely. All he wanted was to know what was going on and he hoped that when he got Chequers going we would come down with our wives and spend the day with him and he would acquaint himself with all the details of the departments.* I said to him that it was a little too early for us to be able to say much about housing but I thought the press conference I had held the day before, to judge by the morning papers, had been a modest success.

Sunday, November 1st
I was hoping for a fairly free day today but I found the whole morning pretty well engaged over problems of the Protection from Eviction Bill. The draft Bill was sent down to Prescote late last night and I was asked to confirm the paper, which the officials obviously thought was a mere formality. But when I looked at it I was worried about it, especially when I found that there was no kind of protection for tenants during the period between publication of the Bill and its being made law, which might be five or six weeks. I was anxious to find some way of making the Bill retrospective or at least effective on the day of publication. I rang up first of all the Under-Secretary at the Ministry, who said no lawyers were available on a Sunday, and I then tried to get the Attorney-General, Elwyn Jones, who was not available. And finally I rang Arnold Goodman.[1] That resourceful man was once again full of ideas and by the end of the morning I had got a number of these clear in my head

* This idea never in my experience materialized.
[1] Senior Partner Goodman, Derrick and Co. (solicitors) and friend of Crossman since the days of his libel action against the *Spectator* in 1957.

and I talked them over with the Ministry and at least had worked out a possible device for filling the gap. It was rather a thing, I suppose, for a new untried Minister to intervene at this late stage in the drafting of the Bill and clearly the Ministry didn't expect it. I dare say I shall find some difficulties tomorrow morning when I get back.

Monday, November 2nd
I've been learning some of the problems of ministerial responsibility. This started at the railway station where we were met by the station-master and all the other people were looking at us and saying, 'Why does the confounded fellow need a whole compartment to himself?' The explanation is absurd. The security people have laid it down that if we are to open our red boxes and read our documents in the train this can only be done in a reserved compartment; a reserved seat will not be sufficient. However, having made a big fuss about national security to George Wigg I have decided to be extremely careful in everything I do personally so I've had scramblers and big safes installed in London as well as here at Prescote and I have agreed to reserve a whole compartment despite the fury of the commuters.

It was a bit nerve-racking on Monday morning because there had been a thick fog and I wondered whether I would be late for my first Cabinet Committee. This was on economic development and I was able to see the relative performances of George Brown and James Callaghan, George in the chair as the First Secretary and Minister in charge of the D.E.A. and James Callaghan as Chancellor of the Exchequer. It was pretty clear from the first that George is the man of action. He decides, he does things, and James sits beside him sort of bleating amiably what he feels.

That brings me to the next thing I am beginning to discover about the life of the Minister. He is very largely concerned with public relations and with the fight inside Cabinet for his share of legislation and publicity. I can now see the job of a Minister from the civil servants' point of view. It is not merely to fight successfully at Cabinet, which I can do. It is not merely to get himself across in the House of Commons, which I am still not sure I can do. He is also required to sell himself to the public with announcements and pronouncements which, though they are not making any new policy, give a sense that he is doing something. And so I see around me in Cabinet all my colleagues struggling and pushing to get in and speak on the Queen's Speech, putting up papers in Cabinet Committees which really say nothing but which are intended to get the Minister on the map.

Strangely enough, whatever else may be said about my thrustingness and self-assertiveness, in these ways I am a very poor pusher. I am not a political shover. Then I am also deeply inexperienced on the front bench and therefore reluctant to plunge in at the House. And as for making pronouncements, or getting things put on the agenda of Cabinet Committees in order to get on the map, I have a snobbish aversion from doing anything as phoney as that. I want to do what it's good to do; and for my Ministry now, frankly, the only thing I have got to do immediately is to deal with rent control.

I should add here that my behaviour last week over the anti-eviction Bill had caused Dame Evelyn absolute consternation. This evening she stayed behind to talk to me about other things, then said she had never been so insulted in her life and had very nearly resigned when she heard of my conduct. The very idea of consulting Arnold Goodman when she should have been consulted was intolerable. I said I was angry with her because I thought the Ministry had let me down very badly. The Bill was entirely un-satisfactory. Since I tried everybody around and there was no legal advice available I had to go outside and she would have to get used to the idea that I would always regard Arnold Goodman as an invaluable adviser and be bound to use him. She said nothing except that she would have to have a quiet talk with me about her future. I am not sure what her future will be.

Tuesday, November 3rd
Cabinet was almost entirely devoted to the secret plan George Brown and I had worked out for stopping all office building in London. This was suddenly presented to Cabinet. George spoke. I gave details on the factual case for doing it, and despite the predictions in my Ministry that there would be tremendous opposition there was none at all. Nobody in a Labour Cabinet is going to object to an action which is extremely popular outside London and which will only ruin property speculators; actually, it probably won't even do that because a lot of them will make money out of the rising rents paid now for offices already in existence. It all went with a bang, and we got it through comfortably. They all went off to the State Opening, and I went back to my Ministry to report, and then at 12.30 I went down to the D.E.A. to work out the details with George Brown of the actual text which we thought was due on Thursday afternoon.

Wednesday, November 4th
Today we suddenly found George Brown was to speak this afternoon and not on Thursday, and everything had to be prepared for the great declaration on office building. We had another work-over of our brief in my Ministry because I was due to take a Lobby conference with George Brown after-wards. Then in the afternoon I went and sat beside him, the first time I had really taken my place on the front bench. At the Lobby conference after-wards George took the main brief and did very well. When he had finished I filled in with a number of details which I had collected very carefully. While I was doing this George said laughingly, 'Don't give away the whole of my Second Reading speech.' But I was sure I was right that the time to put out the justification is on the morning after you have made the announcement. In fact this was a terrific success. It gave a tremendous sense of the Hundred Days, to have the press giving this sensible account of what we had done and

to have no criticism of it at all. I got no credit outside, though I may have got just a little inside the Cabinet.

Saturday, November 7th
This is the most perfect autumn I can remember—on and on, lovely warm sunshine, mists in the early morning, the farm amazingly dry. This afternoon we and the children had our splendid Saturday walk. I've never seen a more beautiful crescent moon rising in the sunset behind the dairy. Coming to Prescote isn't running away from work but a way of doing it. I bring down all the stuff I have to reflect on, all the planning permissions, for example, because there is so little writing involved. And I shall look forward more and more to loading myself with boxes and coming down here as early as possible each weekend.

That is, of course, if we have more than a few months before the election or if *I* have more than a few months as Minister. I'm not at all sure yet whether I am a born Minister, not at all sure whether I shall come off in the House or even want to. In a curious way I'm not fully engaged in the work. Yes, I am engaged on rent controls already and maybe that is the one thing I've got to do in this Session, to put the Rent Bill on the statute book and make a job of that.

Monday, November 9th
After the morning's work in the office I went home to give lunch to Bob Mellish and Jim MacColl, my two Parliamentary Secretaries, with whom I have now arranged a weekly meeting at 1 p.m. to check things through and see how they are going. Jim MacColl is my prim, prissy, high-church expert on local government. I think he is fairly happy with me though he dislikes being number two to Bob Mellish. Bob, breezy trade unionist, is a typical product of the London Labour movement, one of the men who were most anti-me when the trade unions took umbrage at my remarks in the *Daily Mirror*, made when we were in Opposition, that there were only four of them capable of being useful members of a Labour Cabinet. Now he has got a job in my Ministry, and as long as I am successful and my success is something he depends on he is going to be loyal to me. Certainly he now goes round saying what a wonderful chap I am. He is doing a jolly good job himself in keeping contact with the London boroughs. I don't think I like him any more or any less than I did when he treated me as a dirty bastard. I think I really prefer MacColl, though I don't know whether I am getting any closer to him.

Having diverged a bit about the Ministry personalities, let's get back to Monday. The *New Statesman* held one of its big parties in Stationers Hall in the evening. It was the first important party I've gone out to since becoming a Minister. Harold was there, the whole Left establishment was there. And I found it quite pleasant to be one of the people courted and talked to with interest and respect while I held my glass of champagne in my hand. From there I went back to the House for dinner with Eddie Shackleton.[1] While we were sitting together Harold Wilson came in to dine with Frank Cousins. As I was going he called me over and said, 'Why on earth are you giving dinner to Shackleton?' I said, 'He was my old lodger,' and we went across and sat down with Harold and Frank for twenty-five minutes. It's the longest time I've been with Harold informally since we lunched together. He talked absolutely without a break, with enormous self-confidence. The main thing he said was, 'Well, now I can sit back and study strategy and leave you chaps to do the tactics and the detailed work in your Departments. My strategy is to put the Tories on the defensive and always give them awkward choices. Now, for instance, they have an awkward choice on the budget. They have an awkward choice voting for or against the pension increase. We have given them an awkward choice on office building and, Dick, you'll be giving them an awkward choice with your Bill for preventing evictions. Whatever we do we must keep the initiative and always give them awkward choices.' He was also full of the possibilities in foreign affairs. I only had half an ear for his long talk about the tremendous chance he now has to become a mediator in the deadlock in the Western alliance over nuclear weapons. The main impression I got was of enormous exuberance, self-confidence. He felt that the Government had been established and we could continue like this for as long as we liked and then have the election at the moment of our own choosing.

Tuesday, November 10th

At 9.30 we had a crucial meeting, for me, of the Legislation Committee where the revised version of my anti-eviction Bill was being considered. Once again I had taken a great deal of trouble and sweat over it. I was delighted when the Bill got through with virtually no change. I went straight on to the Cabinet on the budget. This was extremely interesting. Callaghan read aloud the budget proposals, which I felt straight away didn't make a budget at all. There was only one proposal in it, the tax on petrol, which was imposed straight away. Everything else either had been already announced in the Government's first week or was a pre-announcement of something to come next April, i.e. new scales of social security benefits, the new capital gains tax, and new corporation tax and the increase in the standard rate of income tax. There we were. I said rather bluntly that I wondered if this budget was tough enough for the crisis; if we were going to have a budget at all shouldn't we ensure all the imposts, all the unpopularities were got into it, and I asked this particularly in view of Callaghan's remark that his budget was the very minimum we could afford to do. 'Why should we be doing the

[1] Lord Shackleton (made a life peer in 1958) was Minister of Defence for the R.A.F. October 1964–January 1967. He was a former lodger at Crossman's London home, No. 9 Vincent Square. He was leader of the House of Lords 1967–70.

minimum?' I asked. We should be doing the maximum now. Harold replied that we must take care not to do a stop–go–stop budget and not to make the mistake of creating deflation. Production wasn't going forward very well; we had to raise production and we must be extremely careful not to depress the economy. He thought it just about right.

It may be so. But I must say, looking back from now I feel that my comment wasn't too bad. However, it wasn't confirmed when we got to the budget speech next day.

For the rest of the day I found myself virtually unemployed as far as the Ministry was concerned. There were quite literally no engagements for me. George Moseley said the only thing to do was to go off and sit in Parliament and listen to the debate on the Address. I had been increasingly uneasy about the absence of work and this was too much. I sat around in a fury and listened to a knock-about debate with Ted Heath and George Brown getting themselves into a terrible tangle at the end, and I felt deeply depressed that evening.

Wednesday, November 11th
The first thing I did was to ring up Harold Wilson and explain to him that work was being kept from me and that I had had enough of the Dame. I then went and saw Dame Evelyn at 10.30 and told her this was an impossible situation. Straight away she said, 'I haven't seen anything of the real office work either. I have been entirely diverted from my real responsibilities by the great battle for the future of the Department,' to which I said, 'Well, that may be so. But I'm not sure we've done very well in fighting the battle during these last weeks. The main job was to get your Minister into his work and see that he was taking over responsibility. That you've failed to do. I insist on having regular staff meetings, regular decisions put up by you to me and I insist on having it done in the way I want it done.' She said she knew it was her fault and we must work out a system. And I found as one often does that I couldn't ask her for an explanation that day because she was so busily pleading guilty to all the crimes but also pleading extenuating circumstances. And I daresay the circumstances were extenuating, because it's true that the eruption of Wilson into Whitehall, the creation of the new Ministry, the uncertainties of the future of planning and land sales must all have been vastly disturbing to any mandarin, particularly to someone like Dame Evelyn who does really care passionately about her subject. Whereas most of the Permanent Secretaries move from Ministry to Ministry and feel professional in them all, she stayed twelve years in Housing and she is a dominant character within this field. It's quite clear to me now that in the Ministry, especially in the planning section, there are many who feel her era of despotism should be brought to a close and would like to see her go. But I don't think they would want to see a person as ignorant and as out of touch with planning as I am get rid of her.

Thursday, November 12th

I was due to go to the theatre to see *The Boy Friend* in the evening but I found myself taking Dame Evelyn out to dinner at the Farmers' Club because she had invited herself in order to discuss the crisis between us. Directly we sat down she put the situation to me with her usual bluntness. 'Well,' she said, 'you are a lucky Minister. You've the choice either of keeping me or getting rid of me. Which do you want?' I knew this was a trap and I couldn't possibly say 'Get rid of you', so I said, 'I want to have you working for *me* for a change,' and I again put it very bluntly that I wanted her to treat me as a chief of staff treats his general, to prepare things for *me*, and see that I really was taking charge of the Department. I also told her I thought she mishandled our relations in Whitehall by fighting too hard (this is something George Moseley himself said to me the other day), and I thought in some things I could do better than her since a word in Wilson's ear at the right time might be worth five of her stormy meetings with her fellow mandarins. The fact is that throughout these three weeks her personal battle for the future of her Department has antagonized most of the Civil Service and a number of my colleagues, particularly George Brown and Fred Willey. Even worse for me, it's made everybody say, 'There is Dame Evelyn running round, but what is her Minister doing?'

As dinner went on, I came to see that though I had convinced myself on Monday and Tuesday that I was going to insist on getting rid of her and though she had convinced herself she was ready to go if I wanted it, neither of us was actually likely to do it in this particular year of grace 1964 or in this particular week of November 1964. We weren't prepared to break, partly I think because we really do quite like each other and regard each other as exceptions to a dreary rule; we are two people who know their own value and know the other's value. And on my side there is another reason. Dame Evelyn stands high in Whitehall and if I were to throw her out and make an enemy of her, if it were on my initiative she were expelled, I know quite well (Harold warned me when I rang him up on Wednesday morning to say how impossible life had been) the whole of the Whitehall hierarchy would be against me. There would be Questions in Parliament and a hell of a row. So I came to the conclusion that what I needed was to get on with her as well as I could, and to use her as far as I possibly can. Then if she feels she can't fit in I will make it possible for her to go. By the end of the evening I was clear that we were working quite well together and she had given a good deal to meet my point of view and would try to give even more. In fact since last Tuesday she has already tried to work the way I want her to work.

Monday, November 16th

I went up as usual by my morning train and found myself just in time for a meeting of the Economic Development Committee on Concorde. This was almost the first subject put to Cabinet at our first meeting; we were told that something dramatic must be done and Concorde should be scrapped because of the economic crisis. Since then, more cautious counsel has prevailed. It has been found impossible to scrap it without tearing up not merely a commercial contract but a treaty, so possibly making ourselves liable to pay bigger compensation to the French than the cost of going ahead. It has also been found that the French are delighted to make it as difficult as possible for us and at this meeting Roy Jenkins (he is not in the Cabinet and at a grave disadvantage for that reason) put forward a paper on what should be done.

I think this was the first time that a really important issue had been put to a Cabinet Committee since we took office. What it means is that Harold Wilson has decided that if he can get an agreed solution in the Cabinet Committee he won't have to waste his time dealing with it in Cabinet. The paper of Roy's we were discussing offered us five alternatives ranging from cancelling completely to trying to interest the Americans in a tripartite project. It was soon obvious that our two main economic Ministers, the Chancellor and the First Secretary, were determined to cancel the contract at any price and to pooh-pooh the Attorney-General, Elwyn Jones, when he gravely warned them about the effects of treaty-breaking. On the other side it was clear that Douglas Jay, who as President of the Board of Trade had had a terrible time defending the 15 per cent surcharge against the infuriated members of EFTA, was appalled at the possibility of breaking another treaty. Here we had the two sides lined up, the brutal economizers on the one side and the more internationally minded people on the other, including the Foreign Secretary. Between them the rest of us were watching and carefully considering what should be done. I found myself rather on the side of Tony Crosland. Both of us thought George Brown was pretty free and easy about the cancellation of the contract and also unduly defeatist in writing off Concorde completely. On the other hand, he was strongly supported by Frank Cousins who said that by concentrating all our technological resources on to aircraft the contract was distorting the economy and everything would be gained technologically by getting rid of it altogether. Perhaps the most interesting feature of the meeting was Roy Jenkins's performance. He had quite strong support from Douglas Jay and one or two others, including Tony Crosland and myself, for a moderate view. If he had been prepared to propose that we should produce the two prototype aircraft, I think he could have got a firm commitment from the Committee. As it was, he went away with instructions to negotiate from an almost impossible position.

After this I went out to dinner with George Weidenfeld.[1] I had been invited to the Lord Mayor's dinner but since I haven't got a white tie and a tailcoat I had refused to go. And I must admit that this has been noticed already on the television by more than one commentator. However, I did

[1] Chairman of the publishing house of Weidenfeld & Nicolson, and noted for his literary and political parties.

have an extremely pleasant evening. I sat next to Noel Annan's[1] wife, Gaby, and altogether it was the kind of party I enjoy. If I am going to relax that's the company I prefer to keep.

Tuesday, November 17th

I stayed at Vincent Square and Jennie Hall, my secretary, came; together we prepared the first part of my speech. I had just about completed this when I went off to lunch and afterwards to the House of Commons where I had to be at 3.15, for Questions. Once again my Questions weren't reached.

Then I went across to the office where I had asked George Moseley to have a shorthand-typist and Jennie available to get the speech done. We started off at about 7.15 and we finished at about 1 a.m. while the discussion on immigration was still taking place on the Expiring Laws Continuance Bill.[2] It took a great deal longer than I thought to prepare the speech because all the passages drafted by the Department were totally useless with one minor exception. Though I had assumed, for example, that someone could write for me a clause-by-clause description of what was in the Bill, when the draft actually came up it was exactly like the memorandum from which it was drawn and I had to do the whole thing myself. I did it.

Wednesday, November 18th

When I got to the office at eleven o'clock the draft was ready and I knew that I had got a speech I could deliver. The process had been an object lesson. The fact is that a Minister who relies on a departmental brief is going to have a very dull exposition of his Bill.

My Second Reading went fairly satisfactorily. I planned a half-hour speech but as I was interrupted seven or eight times it ran to forty minutes, which was a bit too long. Neverthelesss, it was about the right mixture: it ensured that the Bill was non-controversial and accepted by the Tories and yet gave our own back-benchers some feeling that the Minister was on their side. I don't think a single Cabinet Minister waited to listen to me. George Brown had been there at the end of Question Time and said, 'You can hardly expect me to wait for this, my dear brother,' and I said, 'Of course not.' In fact all my colleagues were too busy, though it would have been nice to have some support because I was extremely nervous. This was virtually a maiden front-bench speech. The fact is I've been almost totally absent from the House recently and have less front-bench experience than any other Cabinet Minister. That was why I was so nervous and why I had written out the speech in full, every word. I much prefer speaking ad lib and I always did on the back benches, but I think I shall have to do this in future on any

[1] At this point Noel Annan was Provost of King's College, Cambridge. In 1965 he was created Lord Annan and in October 1966 became Provost of University College, London before being elected Vice-Chancellor of London University in 1978.

[2] This renewed, each Session, legislation in force for one year only. Though unhappy with the Conservative 1962 Commonwealth Immigrants Act, the Government continued it as a holding measure.

complicated Bill because a written script does enable one to get everything in, which is certainly something one can't guarantee when one ad libs.

There was also the alarm that in dealing with a subject which I've only been looking at for a few weeks I might be caught out by the questions. So it was an enormous relief that I got through and Tam Dalyell[1] after a round of the House said there was no doubt our side had thought it a good show, although they had taken this for granted. Most of the rest of the debate seemed to be maiden speeches and Bob Mellish wound up with a really rumbustious, knockabout speech that went down extremely well. Then I took Bob and his wife and Jim MacColl home to Vincent Square and we all felt the kind of enormous exhilaration one does feel when a first night is over.

Friday, November 20th
I spent the whole day on departmental affairs, starting with a meeting of the Home Affairs Committee where I put forward a paper on leasehold reform. It outlines a way, suggested to me by one of the Welsh Whips, to pacify the Welsh lobby while not introducing the actual Bill. The pacification would come from a statement that leaseholders whose leases run out before the Bill's enactment would be able to receive all the advantages of the Bill. Characteristically enough, the moment I put forward the proposal the lawyers began to find all sorts of difficulties in the draft statement, but I finally got what I wanted—permission to call a meeting of the Welsh group to put this statement to them and to say that I was willing to make it if they felt that it didn't cause more perturbation than it allayed fears.

The other important meeting that Friday was a long-delayed meeting on local government, which the Dame has been very keen to hold. She had presented me with a long official paper which I had studied the night before. The more I looked at it the more I realized that this is one of my most important responsibilities. The problem is roughly this: for some eight years now the Local Government Boundary Commission (which was reconstituted after Aneurin Bevan tore it up) has been at work, going round the country making specific recommendations for revising local government boundaries, mostly those of boroughs and county boroughs, leaving the counties fairly well alone. Some of their most ambitious work has been done in the West Midlands conurbation and in Tyneside. They have also recommended the revision of the boundaries of Leicester city and of Nottingham city as well as my own city of Coventry. All these proposals are now coming up to me, because in the last period before the general election my predecessor, Keith Joseph, found an excuse for postponing any decisions.[2] So

---

[1] Crossman's Parliamentary Private Secretary, who also used the top floor of No. 9 Vincent Square as his London home.

[2] The Minister of Housing was responsible for adjudicating on the reports of the Local Government Boundary Commission. The directive to the Parliamentary Boundary Commission (the Home Secretary's responsibility) meant that local government constituency arrangements affected parliamentary constituencies.

suddenly I have a whole series of extremely important decisions to make—in each case I have to decide whether to carry out the recommendation of the Commission or whether to modify it in any way. Dame Evelyn is naturally concerned to get me to make these decisions as soon as possible. On the other hand, I soon discovered that as a Labour politician these are for me not merely decisions about the boundaries of *local authorities* but decisions which will influence the boundaries of *constituencies*. The reason for that is simple: constituency boundaries are drawn broadly in conformity with the boundaries of county boroughs; that is to say, the Parliamentary Commissioners try as far as possible to keep Coventry a unit divided up into two or three constituencies and to avoid having constituencies which are partly Coventry and partly Warwickshire. This fact means that every time, as Minister in charge of local government boundaries, I alter a county borough boundary I may affect the fate of the M.P. sitting for this borough.

Very soon after I became Minister I had been approached by Bert Bowden, Lord President of the Council, and told that if the reform of the boundaries of Leicester went through, at least two of the Labour seats would be in danger, including his own. I also discovered that in Coventry there were risks involved, but that I could by a minor amendment make practically sure that Coventry remains our way. So I find myself as Minister of Housing a powerful politician in my own right. Of course, it's a little improper to see these local government boundary changes in relation to parliamentary divisions and we must remember that the Parliamentary Boundary Commission responsible to the Home Secretary won't be reporting until five or six years' time, i.e. after the next election.[1] Nevertheless, my colleagues are bound to consider the impact of local government boundaries on their constituency boundaries; and I also have to consider what general attitude I should take to the Local Government Boundary Commission as well as how I shall handle these particular decisions. Frankly, the more I looked at what the Commission has been doing the more futile I found their work. I had a very challenging meeting with the local government section of the Ministry at which I said that I would like to see genuine local government reform on the agenda of the next Government with a big enough majority, and that we should now prepare for that as a real possibility.

Sunday, November 22nd
Life here at Prescote gets lovelier the longer it goes on. Really, the more I am a Minister the better I feel physically, the more stimulated I feel. Work doesn't exhaust me at all. It feels far lighter in a way and it's far easier work than the arduous strains of writing for popular papers. Life personally for me is going magnificently. I'm not being a particularly successful Minister in the sense of throwing my weight about or getting known, but I think I am settling

[1] James Callaghan (by then Home Secretary) managed to delay the implementation of the recommendations. This was to be a constitutional *cause célèbre* in 1970.

in to the Department. With so few weeks behind me it is almost incredible how quickly I have got into the Ministerial swing, become accustomed to the tempo and style of the work, with motor-cars and Cabinet Office and Private Office. It's a routine which moves so smoothly and envelops one so completely that it's difficult to remember I have ever done anything else. Of course, this doesn't mean that I'm not aware of how inexperienced I am in the politics of the Cabinet and the intrigues of Whitehall. There is an enormous lot to be learnt about running the Department and handling the House and putting one's case in Cabinet. But it still remains true that the routine has now got into my system. After twenty years of journalism I don't feel it strange that I am not writing anything, or that I hardly read the newspapers apart from the subjects I am interested in, or that my work consists of office work, administration, decision-making, conferences. Indeed, in all of this I feel perfectly at home now and far less tired than I did in what you might call my free independent life as a working journalist.

What about the Cabinet? I notice there is some talk in the press about an inner Cabinet, no doubt partly occasioned by the Chequers weekend which is now taking place with all the Defence people to brief Harold for his visit to Washington. I don't think there is really any evidence of the existence of an inner Cabinet. What is clear is that Harold himself is taking a predominant interest in foreign affairs and defence and George Brown is becoming the Deputy Prime Minister, in charge of the home front. That suits me perfectly well. But there is a very delicate relationship between George Brown and myself because he, as head of the D.E.A., is interested in developing economic planning and I, as Minister of Housing, am in charge of physical planning. Almost inevitably there is a collision between my well-established job and George Brown's new ideas. I have been trying for a long time to persuade him that he and Willey and I should sit down together without officials for a couple of hours and ask where we are. I rather suspect that if I do, I shall find that on the whole subject of regional planning and regional organization he has left Bill Rodgers to do the job[1] and that he really knows very little about it. And that's typical of Cabinet, too. It's now a specialist Cabinet. We haven't any conflicts which have lined us up into Left and Right groups. We've had two tremendous arguments, one about pensions and the other about the budget, and we've had the disagreement about M.P.s' salaries. But in each of these cases there seemed to be a line-up of realists against gesture-makers, and in each case the P.M. failed to get his way. No, I can't now say that Harold is a presidential Prime Minister. On the contrary, he has done what he said he would do, genuinely delegated so that each Minister can run his own Ministry without running to him for assistance. As long as I carry on satisfactorily and don't cause trouble he will be satisfied

[1] M.P. for Stockton-on-Tees since 1962. Parliamentary Under-Secretary at the D.E.A. 1964–7.

with me. The difference for me of course is that I see him much less, even less than I did when he was leader of the Opposition. He is now very remote indeed.

This evening Nicholas Davenport[1] and Olga have come over to see us from Hinton. He rang me up this morning to tell me he wasn't going to support Harold's Tory budget, and I said on the spur of the moment, 'Why not come over and see us,' and they turned up at six o'clock. And before I knew it we were in a furious argument. Nicholas's theme was a simple one. The City, he said, have lost confidence. After all, Callaghan threatens the City daily with the corporation tax and the capital gains tax, and the City feel they don't know what to fear; then they lose confidence. 'You are heading', said Nicholas, 'straight for devaluation.' And then something happened to me. For the first time since I became Minister I woke up out of my departmental seclusion and looked at the world round me and realized that in the Cabinet I had been as far removed from reality as Olga sitting painting a picture in Chelsea. I went up to town that evening by the nine o'clock train uneasy for the first time and wondering whether we had come unstuck. It was pretty clear from what Nicholas said that Callaghan's budget speech really had been a flop. Confidence had not been restored, at least not in the City; and with heavy selling and speculation in Zurich we were in the kind of classical financial crisis socialist governments must expect when they achieve power and find the till empty.

Monday, November 23rd
And, sure enough, when I got to my office I had a message that the Chancellor wanted to see me before the meeting of the Economic Development Committee. I went round to No. 11 and there was Callaghan, heavy and gloomy as ever. 'I am the Selwyn Lloyd', he said, 'of this Government.' He was obviously overawed by the situation and full of self-pity. There was to be an announcement of a 7 per cent bank rate at eleven o'clock, he said to me, and he wanted to warn me of it. He was in a terrible state and couldn't really tell me anything. We walked across to the Economic Committee where he gave the announcement again to the whole Committee before we got down to our ordinary business.

In the afternoon I sat on the front bench and heard Callaghan making the announcement to the Commons and emphasizing that he would try to mitigate the effect of the bank rate on housing and in particular on public-sector housing. What he meant by this God only knows. I thought it was quite unnecessary, and if he had asked me I would have told him not to say it. I gathered that Harold Wilson and George Brown had also been going round pacifying the comrades in the tea-room and trying to take the edge off the measures designed to soothe or at least to reassure the City and the Zurich bankers.

[1] Distinguished financial journalist writing for the *Spectator*.

Tuesday, November 24th

Cabinet day. After a brief account by Callaghan of the reasons for the 7 per cent bank rate we had a long discussion about pensions, which revealed a great deal about what was wrong with our Cabinet. The previous week we had been under great pressure from the back-benchers, who wanted the pension increase backdated at least to Christmas. Last Thursday's Cabinet therefore decided to pay out £4 a head to everyone on national assistance, something I personally protested would do a great deal of damage since millions of pensioners aren't on national assistance and would keenly resent getting nothing. Cabinet had instructed Peggy Herbison to work out a scheme of back-payment. I was very much against this, too, since I thought we had done quite enough for the pensioners. The whole mood of the Cabinet last Thursday had been one of readiness to surrender and appease the back-benchers, but now, between the two Cabinet meetings, we had been faced with a sudden economic crisis and we could hardly fail to realize the obvious fact that if we implemented our decision of the previous Thursday we might well have a 9 per cent bank rate or a devaluation.

So what was really striking was the difference between the mood of the two Cabinets. Peggy Herbison had worked out a backdating scheme as instructed but she got nothing but almost universal hostility. She was extremely angry at this and said she wouldn't explain it to the P.L.P. meeting this evening.

This was really the first Party meeting of the new Parliament under the new Labour Government. It was an alarming experience. It revealed once again the utter weakness of this Government. Really there are two weaknesses. The Government is very weak on foreign affairs—its three foreign representatives, Patrick Gordon Walker, Douglas Jay and Arthur Bottomley, are really all pretty hopeless. The second weakness—the one which concerns me chiefly—lies in the relation between the Cabinet and the Parliamentary Party, for which the Chief Whip, Ted Short, and the Lord President of the Council, Bert Bowden, are responsible. As far as I can see, these two men are really little disciplinarians with no idea of imaginative leadership and no real contact with the back-benchers, and as a result a great deal of ill will has crept in between the Cabinet and its supporters. We've been there five weeks. Yet not one of the Party groups has yet been re-established. I think I'm the only Minister who has got hold of his interested back-benchers and started them working.

Well, it was a packed meeting and Douglas Houghton, in his usual rather pedestrian, pedantic way, gave an elaborate speech about Peggy's plan and what the difficulties were, and then he referred to the Cabinet decision and told the Party that despite the fact that the plan for backdating was technically possible the financial situation forbade it. After this questions were allowed for ten or twelve minutes and Douglas then made a lengthy reply. It was pretty obvious that the Party was out for major concessions, and that the danger outside, the danger of devaluation, wasn't real to that packed, smoky Party meeting. I was sitting on the platform, and as George Brown came in he said to me, 'The situation is desperate. It's the worst we've ever had.' Then Jim Callaghan came in and sat down on the other side of me and he said the same thing, and I sat there realizing that we were absolutely on the edge of devaluation while the Party talked about getting more concessions for the old-age pensioners.

It was a fantastic situation when one realized that the whole major crisis had been caused by the Government's attempt to do justice to the pensioners. The situation was grim. George Brown got up and did magnificently. He rallied the Party, he indicated the danger without actually describing it in so many words, and he pulled the back-benchers round and made them feel they had to drop the idea of any further concessions to the pensioners.

After this meeting I took Anne[1] in to dine alone with me in the Strangers' dining-room. When we had finished I looked into the other part of the room and found Harold and Tommy Balogh[2] and I went to have a chat with them. This was really a fascinating occasion. I had hardly said a word to Harold before he gave us all brandies twice round. He seemed cool and collected and we discussed the situation we were in. Then the bell rang for the division and as we were walking along the corridor he said, 'You know, Dick, in any great campaign like the Peninsular War the commanding general has to know where to retreat to. He has to have his lines of Torres Vedras.' 'Well,' I said, 'a number of people want devaluation now.' I had been talking to Thomas who, like Nicky Kaldor[3] and Robert Neild,[4] felt that devaluation was the only thing left and should be got over as quickly as possible. But Harold Wilson would have none of it. 'You're talking nonsense,' he said. 'Devaluation would sweep us away. We would have to go to the country defeated. We can't have it. No, I have my lines of Torres Vedras which I am retreating to, and I'm popping off now along the lobby to carry out the retreat.' And along the lobby he popped.

Wednesday, November 25th
I had been asked by George Brown to see him yesterday evening at 10, but I had Anne there and I didn't feel like going. I know now that during that period from 11 at night till 1.30 in the morning George and Harold, with the Governor of the Bank of England, worked out a magnificent appeal which rallied £3,000 million to our aid and really saved the Labour Government as well as saving the pound.

I went to see George today at 9.20; at 9.35 he turned up, bleary-eyed. I thought at first this was because of drink, but no, he had of course been with

[1] Crossman's third wife whom he had married in 1954.
[2] Economic Adviser to the Cabinet 1964–7. He became a life peer in 1968.
[3] Special Adviser to the Chancellor of the Exchequer 1964–8. Created a life peer 1974.
[4] Economic Adviser to the Treasury 1964–7.

Harold and the Governor the night before and he told me that he wasn't yet sure the trick had worked. Fred Willey came in and we got down to talking about planning. I explained what my Ministry wanted; I don't think George Brown had fully realized before that the creation of the Land Commission was a major factor in the whole planning operation for which he at the D.E.A. should be responsible.

From there George and I drove across to Smith Square to the N.E.C. meeting which we found three-quarters empty and absolutely flat, a long post-mortem on the election to which nobody was paying any attention. This is another of the dangerous weaknesses of our Party today. If we as a Cabinet have neglected our relationship with the Parliamentary Party we have equally neglected our relations with Transport House and the Party outside. Frankly, Transport House is dying on its feet because we are not facing up to the problem of giving it a job to do. What that meeting of the National Executive proved was that there really wasn't a function for the Party. Half the members who are Ministers weren't there, the trade unionists had their little chats and the whole situation was dead and, for that reason, dangerous.

Thursday, December 3rd
I went to Cabinet at eleven o'clock. Nothing of interest there. Harold Wilson was just off to Washington; and we had some discussion about the 700th anniversary of the Parliament of Simon de Montfort. There was a general sense of finishing, winding up, with Harold going off. Again I had the uneasy feeling that we weren't grappling with central problems. To make Cabinet government work as against Prime Ministerial government, Cabinet should really discuss general policy. Whereas in our case all that happens is that twenty-three of us come, each with his particular pressures and problems, trying to get what we want. And we do avoid any collective discussion of general policy except perhaps on defence and foreign affairs. On the essentials of the home front there doesn't seem to be any general discussion at all—general issues just aren't raised.

Sunday, December 6th
What do I feel on reflection over this last week? First of all, my own Ministry. We don't argue too much and at last I think they are accepting leadership as far as I can give it. As for the House of Commons, I've got the anti-eviction Bill through the Committee Stage. I've not done particularly well, but well enough. I've also had to deal during these first five weeks with the whole question of the Local Government Boundary Commission. I mentioned this subject since discussing this at length with the Dame some days ago, I've talked to my colleagues about it and I've got them to agree after a great deal of humming and hawing that I can't delay my decisions on the recommendations of the Commission any further and that I am bound to make and announce these decisions in the near future. They are my personal decisions.

Not even the Prime Minister can influence me in them. My colleagues know this and this gives me an odd detached power in dealing with them. After all I can make or mar George Brown at Belper, Bert Bowden in Leicester, Bill Wilson in Coventry, Ted Short in Newcastle; each of them now knows that as Minister of Housing the decision I make may be life or death for them in terms of representation at Westminster.

What about the Cabinet? Well, the pound is still being nibbled away and I feel the Cabinet isn't very firm or very stable because the central leadership isn't there, the sense of priorities, the sense of grip that you need. Yes, we've got a remarkable man in Harold Wilson and a good man in George Brown, and both have already got some tremendous individual achievements to their credit. But what we still lack is that coherent, strong control which is real policy. Least of all do I feel that our legislative programme makes any sense whatsoever. I know now we shall be able to formulate a decent rent reform which will do us credit, but Fred Willey's Land Commission Bill is laughable. He hasn't done any basic thinking and if he puts the Bill forward in its present form and it becomes law it will get unstuck. As for Fred Lee's steel nationalization, that's got to be postponed until March because it has run into difficulties too. In these major reforms we are suffering from sheer lack of brains and imagination. And then of course there is the quite unsolved problem of handling the Parliamentary Party on the one side and Transport House and the Party in the country on the other. I'm beginning to wonder whether I shouldn't become a Cabinet Minister, organizing some kind of movement in Cabinet to ensure that we do face up to our problems before they overpower us in a smash and sweep us away.

Wednesday, December 9th
I had a meeting at Transport House, a confidential discussion with Len Williams on the Local Government Boundary Commission. Len Williams[1] confirmed that if I implemented the recommendations of the Commission, we were likely to lose Herbert Bowden's seat in Leicester, two seats in Nottingham, and Bill Wilson's seat in Coventry South. Lose them, of course, not in the next election but in the next but one election, after the Parliamentary Boundary Commission has revised the constituency boundaries.

Back from there through the Christmas shopping scrum, to see the Local Government Boundary Commission itself. Fussy old gentlemen, full of themselves, somewhat disconcerted by meeting a Minister with strong ideas of his own where they have been used only to dealing with the Permanent Secretary. Then along to the Chancellor's room to discuss the building societies' rate of interest. Since the economic situation is still not very good and there is continued lack of confidence, there is, of course, pressure on the

[1] General Secretary of the Labour Party 1962–8.

societies to raise the rate and the Chancellor had to plead even more strongly with them to hold back and to urge them at least to postpone the decision until after Christmas. It was obvious that we were fighting against the tide.

After the building societies had left I sat with Callaghan and had a chat. I didn't feel that his heart was in his job. Indeed, I thought he was thoroughly unhappy and I tried to stiffen him and to discuss the kind of fighting, back-to-the-wall speeches we should make to the Party Conference at the end of the week. It's a good idea to cultivate Callaghan; I find he tells me a good deal.

Friday, December 11th

We started with a Cabinet at which Harold Wilson reported on his Washington visit. It doesn't show up much in my diary but in fact the week has been dominated by news of this first visit of the Prime Minister, the Foreign Secretary and the Defence Minister to Lyndon Johnson in Washington. They had flown back on Thursday and were coming to Cabinet to report to us in full. On this occasion I took notes at Cabinet and I am going to put down here my summary of his initial address. It will be interesting to compare what I recorded as having been said and what the Cabinet Secretariat said he said.

He started by saying there were two conferences, one which took place and one which the British press reported. And he rebuked the *Sun* for sending back fictitious reports, in particular for suggesting that he had already sold out on the issue of the M.L.F. He also said it was quite untrue that a pistol had been put to his head on Vietnam. The conference, he said, was more like an onion being peeled; the outer leaves came off and you gradually reached Europe at the centre. The most encouraging fact about the conference was America's emphasis on Britain's world-wide role; this line had been taken in particularly moving terms in a talk Denis Healey had had with McNamara on the plane to Omaha. McNamara had gone out of his way to emphasize the importance of Britain's role east of Suez. Harold went on to say that the whole conference moved away from any inward-looking worry about the alliance to positive discussions on peace-keeping and new disarmament proposals.

Then he turned to the economic problems. The Americans, he said, had shown much understanding of the point he himself had made about the danger of our over-commitment. President Lyndon Johnson had shown himself deeply concerned about our situation and virtually promised us all aid short of war. He also expressed an appreciation of the help which we had given him in the election and all that Harold Wilson's speeches had meant for him. (I found this extremely funny but I fear the humour was entirely unconscious.)

Harold said that he himself had made no request for a fresh loan, that he had discovered that the Americans were ready to help, that they were cutting their own defence costs and were therefore not unsympathetic to our doing the same. So Harold then turned to the problem of reducing costs by pooling. This he said was the most fruitful possibility, pooling weapons, pooling research and development; we must have a really constructive Anglo–American rationalization of defence budgeting. Broadly speaking, they led on air-frames, we led on air-engines, and that gave us a chance of useful co-operation.

Turning to Europe, he said the atmosphere was different from what he expected. The President feels as strongly as we do the danger of proliferation of nuclear weapons – and then Harold made a long reference to the problems of China and India, saying that the great watershed of proliferation would be if India were compelled to make a nuclear weapon under threat from China. The Indians, he said, could become a nuclear power in eighteen months once they had decided to do so. That is a very real danger.

Harold then turned to Vietnam and said that the President himself is deeply committed to Vietnam and asked him outright for a British military commitment. Harold had resisted, apart from offering the use of our jungle training team in Malaya and also our teams for anti-subversive activities. He didn't think the Americans really expected him to concede; they wanted not so much the presence of British soldiers as the presence of the British flag. He had persuaded the Americans not to embarrass our Foreign Secretary who, with the Russians, is co-chairman of the Geneva Conference. He ended up by referring to the importance of the communiqué and drawing attention to the last paragraph, emphasizing continuing discussion at all levels so that we, the British, are to be in on all the transatlantic conferences. 'They want us with them,' Harold said. 'They want our new constructive ideas after the epoch of sterility. We are now in a position to influence events more than ever before for the last ten years.'

Well, that's the end of my note on what happened in Cabinet. It's quite interesting to compare what Harold told us in confidence with what I could read next day in John Freeman's account of the Washington conversations in the *New Statesman* or Henry Brandon's in the *Sunday Times*. Harold has told nothing to Cabinet which hasn't been told to the press.

I picked up Anne at Vincent Square and we drove to Victoria to catch the 4 p.m. train to Brighton for the Labour Party Conference.[1] We got down there in lovely weather but that was the last we saw of the sun. From then on the wind blew and for the next two days we were in a sea mist.

By 6 p.m. we were plunged into a terrible row with the union members of the Executive as the result of Harry Nicholas retiring from the Treasurer-ship. The details don't matter. But this does show one how the old conflict of trade unions and intellectuals still carries on.

[1] Because of the general election the Labour Party's annual Conference had been postponed from October to December. It was held over a weekend, rather than the usual week.

Saturday, December 12th

Filthy weather and a dreary morning in the conference hall. But I found myself seated on the platform between Barbara Castle and Jim Callaghan and as a result I was able to get quite a lot of information about what was going on in the Treasury and in Overseas Development. While the Young Socialists' discussion dragged on James was telling me of the seriousness of the economic situation. Poor James, he is off to Paris to try and get some more money and I think he told me (I heard this always against the noise of the speeches) that the reserves would only last ten days and if the wound can't be staunched by then, we shall be forced to have a devaluation and a general election straight away. All these were bits and pieces which came out during the session. Anne and I lunched with Sydney Jacobson,[1] Harold Hutchinson and Pam Berry.[2] I warned Harold Hutchinson how critical Wilson had been at Cabinet of the *Sun* and how angry he was. I came out of the lunch and Harold met me and said, 'So you've been dining in the enemy camp.' I thought he was laughing but he wasn't, which shows how passionately he objected to the criticisms of the press.

All this became more intelligible when I went down to the Conference and heard his speech that afternoon. There is no doubt it was a brilliant Conference performance. He had only had a day to prepare it since returning to London. He did extremely well. But it was a grievous disappointment to me because it *was* just a Conference performance, a lightweight affair with a great attack on the *Evening Standard*, quite unworthy of a Prime Minister. It didn't seem to me that he struck the right Prime Ministerial note and he certainly didn't steel our people for the difficulties ahead. As Minister of Housing I know quite well that I've got to explain the fact that the local authorities aren't going to get the money to build the houses. They will have to cut back their housing programme; and the building societies are going to charge 6¾ per cent and deter private building. The fact is, deflation is really starting. That's what I feel in my bones. But it hasn't been said and Harold Wilson blithely denies it. That's what I found unsatisfactory in his speech.

Sunday, December 13th

I must say I expected a pretty miserable debate this morning but to my surprise it was a great success. I won't record it because from my point of view what really happened was that Callaghan went on talking to me during the speeches about the terrible situation. When I wasn't listening to that, I was talking to Harold Collison, the General Secretary of the Agricultural and Allied Workers, about a way of resolving the problem of the tied cottage. The only other thing I remember is watching Harold Wilson climb-

---

[1] Editor of the *Sun* 1964–5 and afterwards Editorial Director of I.P.C. He became a life peer in 1975. Harold Hutchinson was political correspondent of the *Sun*.

[2] Wife of the Hon. Michael Berry (created Lord Hartwell 1968), Editor-in-Chief of the *Daily Telegraph* and *Sunday Telegraph*.

ing up to the platform and standing like a little Napoleon while being photographed. In fact he talked to me for three or four minutes on the steps while we were photographed together. 'You got your £20 million off Callaghan,' he said. 'You are pleased about that, I suppose; a big victory for you. And your anti-eviction Bill is pretty popular, isn't it?' I said, 'Yes, that's true, but I'm in trouble about getting money from the building societies and I want you to make quite sure I can get some money for local-authority building apart from housing,' and he replied, 'Well, Tommy Balogh and Robert Neild said the budget wasn't deflationary enough but I told them that by April we shall need some reflationary expenditure. So it looks as though you will be able to have your public-sector housing financed after all, my dear Dick.'

What a contrast between the attitude of Harold Wilson during those four minutes on the steps and that of James Callaghan, his Chancellor! When I said something about Callaghan, he said, 'Yes, I'm having to hold his hand. His nerve isn't very good these days.'

The morning ended with a magnificent speech by George Brown in which he did all the things which Harold Wilson should have done. George Brown DID talk about the difficulties, he did warn people, harden them, and the Conference ended up in pretty good form.

After that Anne and I lunched with Liz and Peter Shore and the Croslands and Wedgwood Benns, and we all came back in the train together. Conference this year was more enjoyable than I had ever known it and really we all needed it. I think it made us realize how isolated we have become in our Ministries and how much we needed a sense of getting together, of good humour, of companionship which really we don't get in our Ministerial lives.

The fact is we are a fragmented Government. In the middle there are Harold Wilson and George Brown, each giving us a lead in his own way and often in his own direction. And around them are the rest of us, each on his own, not working as a team but working in towards either Harold or George Brown. Our relations with the Party in Parliament are already very bad and our relations with the Party in Transport House and outside are much worse. What we really need is somebody whole-time in the Cabinet—as a Tory Government always has—dealing with the Party, dealing with the presentation of Cabinet policy. One of the things I shall have to do, and Tam Dalyell is prodding me to do it, is to try to put over to Harold and George the need for integrating our Cabinet policy with Transport House policy and through Transport House getting it across to the Party outside and to the general public.

Looking back on this first stage of the Labour Government—from our election victory to our victory conference—I would say that on the whole the Government has established itself extremely well in terms of departmental efficiency. On the other hand, I'm not sure we have done very well in terms of our own socialist strategy or of our integrated leadership. I don't think

Harold has really established himself as the leader we need. But he has certainly grown a great deal more Napoleonic. The trouble is one never sees him except when one needs to. He is therefore getting more and more apart from us all, relying more and more on his own ideas, and I think Tommy is probably right in saying that he is more and more in the hands of his civil servants. Indeed, I get the impression this Government isn't running itself in but just running along; maybe it's doing this for the reason Callaghan gave. Maybe until we know whether we are going to have a devaluation and election before the spring we shan't get very settled.

Difficult for me, therefore, to believe that the work I am doing in my Department has any very enduring value. I'm learning my job; I've got a certain amount of praise for the anti-eviction Bill; all that is useful. I don't feel I've sunk many roots, and I still feel a sense of unreality when I make my speeches in the House, when I answer my Questions, when I hold a press conference, when I sit on the platform at Brighton; I still feel I am taking part in a book I've written about the constitution and not actually playing a real part in real politics.

1965

Sunday, January 3rd

I have had my first Christmas and New Year break as Minister. Rather to my surprise I found that the Ministry and I agreed that they didn't want to see me for the whole of the first week after Christmas. So I had a complete break until last Thursday when Jennie Hall came down for a light day's work.

Reflecting on the Ministry after ten days' absence, I find that distance doesn't increase my respect. No, the personnel is second-rate and unimpressive. They are extremely good at working the procedures of the Civil Service. What they lack is a constructive apprehension of the problems with which they deal and any kind of imagination. Also they are resistant in the extreme to the outside advice which I think it is my job to bring in. So the battle between me and the Ministry will go on as I try to get these admirable officials, conscientious and thorough people, somehow widened, and a little blood pumped into their veins by people from outside who know the realities which they handle in such an abstract and aloof way.

So much for the Ministry. Now what about the Cabinet and the Government's record? Looking back to October, I am impressed by our extraordinary innocence when we took over. We proceeded to do a number of things by almost instantaneous decision, all of which seem to me now to have been ill-judged, and of which Harold and George and Callaghan, the three men chiefly concerned, failed to foresee the consequences. For example, the 15 per cent surcharge, which is still causing us the most appalling trouble in Europe, was blatantly a flagrant violation of the EFTA treaty; and Douglas Jay at our first Cabinet warned us of all the trouble it would bring. Yet it was pushed through by George Brown and Harold Wilson. Then there was our innocence in insisting on the 12s. 6d. increase in the old-age pension and the abolition of prescription charges, despite the warnings of the Treasury. In both these cases, if I remember aright, Harold Wilson and James Callaghan were overruled. Cabinet wanted them and was allowed to carry out its wishes without anybody seriously warning us of what would happen. As I recall it, nobody expressed the fear that by carrying out these increases in pensions and announcing the tax increases which would pay for them we should unloose a crisis of confidence, provoke a 7 per cent bank rate and upset the foreign bankers. Harold Wilson was so experienced and shrewd and calculating throughout the election; yet when he actually entered No. 10 and tried to show himself a man of action and tried to vie with Kennedy's Hundred Days, he became unstuck on the very subject where he should have been expert—on economics.

But there is one case where he has had a stroke of luck. We came into office full of doubts about George Brown. Harold had said to me more than once before and more than once after the election that we would have to get rid of G.B. within six months. Actually, his leadership has been outstanding. He has created the new D.E.A. and got a number of excellent people into it;

he has done a tremendous job on the prices and incomes policy in getting
the employers and trade unions to sign the Declaration of Intent; and there
is no doubt that as First Secretary and Deputy Prime Minister he is absolutely dominant over poor old James Callaghan who trails along as number
three.

Of course, Harold himself has been good, above all in his handling of the
Rhodesian crisis. He called Mr Smith's bluff brilliantly. I think he has also
been extremely successful on his visit to Washington in convincing the
Americans that Britain is a loyal junior partner. By getting Lyndon Johnson
firmly on his side he has convinced himself at least that we can get through
without the devaluation of the pound because we are now built into the
American system. But here again we have to pay a price for our success.
There's no doubt about it that one of the things we really hoped for when we
came to power was a substantial cut in defence expenditure. Yet as we have
looked at each of our overseas commitments—at Hong Kong, at Malaya, at
the Maldive Islands, the Persian Gulf and Aden—the Defence Ministers
have been overwhelmed by the advice of their experts, who say 'Oh, Minister, you can't cut that.' As a result we are moving up to the period of the
Defence Estimates without any serious cut being carried through by Denis
Healey and his staff. Indeed, it now looks as though in 1964 Harold Wilson
was responsible for an over-commitment in overseas expenditure almost as
burdensome—if not more burdensome—than that to which Ernest Bevin[1]
committed us in 1945, and for the same reason: because of our attachment to
the Anglo-American special relationship and because of our belief that it is
only through the existence of this relationship that we can survive outside
Europe. And here is something we have to remember. While we have been
establishing our Labour Government here, tremendous events have been
taking place in Europe, including the final agreement on grain prices
between Germany and France, which creates the foundation for the common agricultural policy. I think we are going to find that the European
Community will now forge ahead and there will be no place for Britain in it.
Our last chance of joining has gone unless some convulsion were to follow
General de Gaulle's death.

So much for Harold Wilson's handling of foreign affairs. We have yet to
see how good he is on the home front. So far he has shown a singular failing in
dealing with general economic policy. Nor do I think he has been doing very
well in the great upheavals in Whitehall. Though George Brown is a great
success, the division of power between the Treasury and the D.E.A. is a
development for which we are having to pay a heavy price in divided
authority and dissension in central planning. I have some grave doubts about
the new Ministry of Technology under Frank Cousins and Lord Snow. As for
the new Ministry of Land and Natural Resources, carved out of my Ministry
as a separate creation, it is purely unnecessary. There's no doubt that if the

[1] When he was Foreign Secretary in the post-war Labour Government.

Land Commission had been handled by M.H.L.G. with Fred Willey as a Minister of State, we could have got a far better Bill prepared in time. Another equally idiotic creation is the Department for Wales, a completely artificial new office for Jim Griffiths and his two Parliamentary Secretaries, all the result of a silly election pledge. No! I don't think Harold Wilson has done too well in Whitehall. Certainly he has caused an enormous strain on the staff, which poor Dame Evelyn curses every day.

Monday, January 4th
As I have said before in this diary the Whitehall grapevine is an extraordinary phenomenon. When I got into the office this morning I saw the Dame about a mass of business (my first day back after ten days of Christmas holiday). She told me at once that the Prime Minister had asked that Sir Laurence Helsby[1] should see me about my agreement to take Bruce Fraser[2] and kick her out. She said all this in perfect good temper. After all, she was past resignation age and on the point of going when the election took place. She is merely waiting in order to find a good replacement. She told me that Helsby would be coming to see me in a day or two. In return I told her I was going to discuss her future with the Prime Minister and insist that she should wait and only leave in the summer, giving me plenty of time to find a suitable replacement. Dame Evelyn said that I would find the Prime Minister a bit more pressing than that. It was a good day to go since he was just back from the Scillies, there was no Cabinet, and no Cabinet Committees, and he had nothing to deal with until Indonesia at four o'clock.

So there I was at three o'clock, sitting beside him. When he receives you he is standing alone in the big Cabinet room. I started off on the green belt[3] and asked him whether he was worried about it. 'No,' he said. 'I only thought this was a job which Fred Willey should have had, not you. I wanted him to get all the bother I knew there would be about green belt decisions. That's why I originally wanted to shift planning to him and leave you only with housing.'

This confirmed something that I have often noticed about Harold. He never really changes his mind. He is a Yorkshire terrier and having got his teeth into an idea he worries at it and never gives it up. Originally, he had been determined to split housing and planning and still that is his *idée fixe*.

Then we turned to the problem of Dame Evelyn's successor and he indicated once again that he wanted Bruce Fraser to succeed her within a few weeks. 'We must find Dame Evelyn a good job,' he said, 'she's a fine

[1] Joint Permanent Secretary to the Treasury and Head of the Home Civil Service 1963–8.
[2] The second Permanent Secretary at the Department of Education and Science whom Crossman had heard the previous month the Prime Minister wished to succeed Dame Evelyn Sharp.
[3] Crossman had run into some noisy opposition over planning decisions concerning the green belt, notably at Hartley in Kent.

woman.' 'Well,' I said, 'it's not as easy as that. I don't want to have some cast-off Permanent Secretary imposed on me with all Whitehall knowing what has happened. I'd rather keep her till the summer and give myself time to look at Bruce Fraser carefully, and also to take a look at Philip Allen, whom the Department would prefer. You know the Department rather resents first having a politician with no knowledge of housing like me being palmed off on them and then being given a Permanent Secretary like Sir Bruce Fraser.' 'Philip Allen?' said Harold. 'Yes, he's Helsby's number two, he's possible. Yes, I can see the chances of a shift round. All right, my dear Dick, you try and do that.'

Wednesday, January 6th

Punctually at ten thirty Sir Laurence Helsby arrived to have the expected conversation with me. When I looked at him I suddenly realized I had been at Oxford with him where we had both done Greats. He's a curious character, amiable and apparently pleasant, but with veiled eyes. He came straight to the point. He wanted to announce Sir Bruce Fraser as my next Permanent Secretary, though he was prepared to let Dame Evelyn stay on for a few months of transition. I said I was interested in Sir Philip Allen. He told me that Allen was more suitable for the Home Office and Bruce Fraser for my Department—though he didn't say the latter very convincingly. We sparred a good deal and I finally said I was prepared to give dinner to both men and then to give Helsby my opinion. He said I must appreciate that a Permanent Secretary would last longer than a Minister and that therefore he was concerned to find one who not only got on with me but who was suitable for the Department. I said that if he was not concerned to appoint someone who got on with me, I had to be even more concerned than ever to get someone who suited me. We then had some talk about the Prime Minister's views on planning, where Helsby clearly sided with Dame Evelyn, and we also had a useful chat about the Land Commission, where I primed him about the alarm we felt. I found we had had quite a decent meeting together by the time he left at eleven.

Sunday, January 17th

This last week I have been outside the mainstream of politics.[1] The papers were full of reports about the TSR2 and discussion of whether we are going to cancel it or not. Day after day I read this in my morning paper but as a member of the Cabinet I know *absolutely nothing* about it. Even on Thursday when we had Cabinet the issue wasn't discussed. I read in the papers that it is being discussed at Chequers this weekend, with George Wigg and his pals present and people like me completely excluded. So much for Cabinet responsibility. Actually, I am not against what is going on and I shan't complain; but it is true that when the issue comes up to Cabinet for final

[1] Crossman had been on official Ministerial visits in the North-West.

decision, those of us who were not departmentally concerned will be unable to form any opinion at all.

Wednesday, January 20th

I went down to Nuneaton for the eve-of-poll meeting in Frank Cousins's[1] by-election. Of course, I had known for a fortnight while the by-election campaign was going on that there had been difficulties. It wasn't so easy to find two constituencies whose Members were even willing to consider going to the House of Lords in order to make room for Frank Cousins and Patrick Gordon Walker. Finally two old stalwarts, Sorensen of Leyton and Frank Bowles of Nuneaton, were put under tremendous pressure. Both of them are loyal Members and both are rather on the Left. Each in his own slightly sulky way finally agreed to go to the Lords and leave room for the two Cabinet Ministers. I assumed the majorities were so big that there was no conceivable chance of their not being elected, though there might be a small drop in the majority. As the election campaign developed the impression I got was that whereas things were going very well at Nuneaton, things were going very badly indeed at Leyton. Having taken the taint of Smethwick[2] with him into this gloomy North London suburb, of which a quarter of the population is old-age pensioners, Patrick Gordon Walker was doing a thoroughly dreary job of putting himself across.

Arriving at Nuneaton, I had a pleasant dinner with Frank Cousins and found him in an elated mood. He told me there had never been an election campaign where there had been such a tremendous response. I did just notice that the agents were not over-enthusiastic—they stayed quiet while Frank talked in this way, and so did Norman Pratt, the miners' agent. And when I got to the meeting I was extremely disconcerted to find that only about a hundred people were in the huge school hall and they were just Party stalwarts. I did my best, but it was an extremely flat meeting. I went back to London thinking, 'Well, it isn't very bright at Nuneaton but Frank seems to have done quite well.'

Thursday, January 21st

Tam suggested that I should stay up and listen to the *Gallery* programme on B.B.C. television. I thought that marginally it would be worth it and so I undressed and then went into the sitting-room and there were the TV cameras at Nuneaton showing Frank Cousins looking somewhat grim. When the result was announced with a 6,000 slump in the Labour vote,[3] I realized something was pretty wrong and thought I had better stay up and see what had happened at Leyton.

[1] Frank Cousins, General Secretary of the Transport and General Workers Union, had joined the government as Minister of Technology in October 1964 but without a seat in Parliament.

[2] Patrick Gordon Walker had been defeated at Smethwick after a campaign largely fought on local racial resentments.

[3] Frank Cousins held Nuneaton but the majority was reduced from 11,702 to 5,241.

It was one of those occasions when TV really does bring the viewer right into the event. I could see the Tory candidate not really believing his ears and watch Gordon Walker acting with melancholy dignity—and also revealing his deep inner defeatism.[1] It was an awful evening. I felt an epoch had ended—ironically enough this was the ninety-ninth day of Harold's famous Hundred Days. It was a shattering of our complacency and also a shattering of our Government's authority. I rang George Wigg and found he was still round at Downing Street. But, no, wiser not to try and talk to him.

Friday, January 22nd

So I waited till next morning and then spoke to Wigg on the phone. We agreed there were really probably three factors at work. First of all the resentment in the constituencies at having a Cabinet Minister foisted on them and a respected senior Member turned out. Secondly, we are as a Government in a very bad patch owing to the unpopularity of our mortgage programme, our attack on the aircraft industry and so on. And thirdly, the smear which Gordon Walker had carried with him from Smethwick probably accounted for the fact that the swing at Leyton was 8 per cent, whereas it was only 4·5 per cent at Nuneaton.

The main thing we agreed was the need for the Government to establish its authority, and I had to go to the Ministry to do my share. This wasn't so easy. Jennie Hall described to me how, sitting in the Private Office, she had seen the extraordinary supercilious detachment of the other officials. On the night before, I had had them in for a session on the organization of the Private Office and again insisted that I wanted to sign my own letters. Finally I had lost my temper and had said, 'You bloody well do what I tell you. Get out and do it.' That was what had happened on Thursday evening and there they were today looking at Jennie rather smugly and smirkily. The confidence that we could carry on despite our slender majority which had been building up in the previous weeks was suddenly no longer there. Now they were hedging and feeling 'They'll be out soon.' I knew I must reassert my personal authority in the Department.

The trouble was that I had to spend the whole morning on a Party speech. While I talked to George Wigg I suddenly remembered that I was speaking in Coventry on Saturday evening and that I might be able to be useful there. George agreed I must get something drafted as rapidly as possible, so I scrapped my lunch and everything else, knocked off a press release and sent it round to Harold at 2.30 in the afternoon. This is not the kind of conduct which Ministry officials like, particularly since I had to scrap the business they had planned for me, but that couldn't be helped—I rushed over to the Commons and walked straight into Harold's room where he was standing

[1] Gordon Walker was defending a majority of nearly 8,000 but the Conservatives won the seat by 205 votes. Wilson would have to find another Foreign Secretary.

with Marcia, Percy Clark[1] and George Wigg. They had already prepared two drafts of speeches which were to be handed over to Ray Gunter and Tony Greenwood. I then produced mine. Harold glanced through it and told me to delete a passage in which I referred to racialism and Smethwick. Otherwise he seemed to like it. Then he said, 'Stay behind a moment. I want to talk to you.'

When Marcia and Percy had gone out he turned to me and said, 'Look, Dick, we have decided on Michael Stewart for Foreign Secretary and he has accepted. He and his wife are quite pleased.' He didn't ask my opinion. I said that I realized that he couldn't do what I would have liked and make Denis Healey Foreign Secretary and Roy Jenkins Minister of Defence. 'No,' he said, 'I wouldn't trust Healey in the Foreign Office with all those professionals. And anyway we can't let him run away from the Defence job. It's something he has to wade through. No, we can't do that. That's why I chose Michael Stewart. You'll laugh, Dick, but when I talked to him he said he felt like crying at having to leave Education.' I looked at Harold and said, 'Well, I would actually have cried if I had lost M.H.L.G. owing to this shemozzle.'

He then said, 'Who shall we put at Education? We could of course take Reg Prentice ... No, it's too big a job for the boy, though he made an excellent speech last night.' Then George Wigg said, 'What about Fred Willey?' looking at me. And I said, 'God, not on your life. That would be a nightmare—though from my own point of view I would be glad to get Fred out of Land and Natural Resources.' Then Harold said, 'What about Tony Greenwood?' And I said, 'Frankly, you know he's not up to it.' Then George came up with Anthony Crosland, and he said immediately, 'That's the right choice. If we can't have Roy Jenkins, let's have Crosland.[2] He's got a good brain, he's written well about education and he will be a positive addition to the Cabinet.' We all agreed that if George Brown would release Tony Crosland this would be the right solution. The Prime Minister didn't show much sign of any personal agony at Gordon Walker's plight. He obviously felt, as I did, that he really had been no good as Foreign Secretary and no great strength in the Government.

That forty minutes I spent with him, drinking a glass of brandy, was really like going back to old times. It was the first time since we took office that he and George Wigg and I, the old gang, had been on the job together. As I left Harold said to me, 'After such a long time it's been really exhilarating,' and I too felt exhilarated, keener, more excited than I had been for some weeks. Outside the door I found Sara Barker, the national agent, nearly crying because she had been down at Leyton the night before. For the right wing and the staff of Transport House this defeat had been the most ghastly blow, far worse than for Harold, George and me. I went back to the Ministry and

[1] Head of the Publicity Department at Transport House.
[2] Wilson had already offered the job to Roy Jenkins, who had turned it down.

found I could do no more than hand the draft speech over to be corrected and typed by Jennie because I had to rush to catch my train at Paddington.

Sunday, January 24th

Yesterday, Saturday, I had to get to Coventry at 9.15 a.m. for my first official visit to the city. This went pretty well. Coventry were nice to me in an unenthusiastic way and gave me a pleasant lunch. To be frank I think they would have entertained me more regally if I had been the Minister of Housing but not their local Member. They don't like their M.P.s hogging the limelight. At the lunch I made the big speech in which I gave an official Government reaction to the defeat at Leyton.

To my great embarrassment, later that afternoon I found that the *Coventry Evening Telegraph* had taken the odd relative clause out of my press release and made it their main lead by announcing that I was preparing legislation on mortgage payments. This might well be difficult since no Cabinet Minister is allowed to announce legislation in advance. I got hold of my press officer at the Ministry and instructed him to issue a correction. But I very much doubt whether he did so because I find today, Sunday, that most of the papers have given this announcement very great prominence.

However, that difficulty may be eased by the death of Winston which was declared this morning at eight o'clock. It has of course been macabre that his illness, which lasted for ten days, went on so long that the bulletins finally faded out because people got bored or sick or embarrassed by the whole affair. At Cabinet on Thursday the Prime Minister told us that this would be like the death of a monarch and that every Prime Minister in the Alliance would come and there would be important conversations for which we must all be ready and at their disposal. And he warned us that we would virtually have a week of respite from party politics for the funeral and the state mourning.[1] Well, the respite should make things easier for me in this mortgage affair. If we had had the debate on Wednesday I should have had some explaining to do.

Looking back on this week I have no doubt that this was the biggest crisis we have had and Harold Wilson came out of it as well as we could possibly hope. He was tough, he was exhilarated by the unexpected disaster and he handled it as thoroughly as anyone could.

Monday, January 25th

In the afternoon Parliament met for tributes to Sir Winston. By then I felt we had already had enough tributes, but here they came, Wilson, Douglas-Home, Jo Grimond. I sat on the front bench squeezed between Barbara Castle and Tony Crosland and fell into a quiet slumber while the lugubrious

[1] Parliament customarily adjourns for the day on the death of a former Prime Minister; but in this case the Prime Minister, Leader of the House and Chief Whip had decided to adjourn for the period until Churchill's funeral.

1 The Rt Hon. Richard Crossman, M.P.

2 The official Cabinet photograph, 1964. Left to right (standing): Fred Lee, Frank Cousins, Douglas Houghton, Anthony Crosland, Douglas Jay, Barbara Castle, Anthony Greenwood, The Earl of Longford, Richard Crossman, Ray Gunter, Frederick Peart, Thomas Fraser and Sir Burke Trend. Left to right (seated): William Ross, Sir Frank Soskice, Michael Stewart, Lord Gardiner, George Brown, Harold Wilson, Herbert Bowden, James Callaghan, Dennis Healey, Arthur Bottomley, and James Griffiths.

3 With George Brown and Harold Wilson, talking to Her Majesty the Queen at the 75th Royal Anniversary reception of the County Councils Association in November 1964. Michael Stewart is in the background.

process went on. In the evening I had dinner with Richard Llewelyn-Davies, and found Nicky Kaldor there. They spent most of the evening talking about a Lib–Lab pact, and I found the whole argument pretty futile. What mattered to me was that at eleven o'clock I was due to meet Fred Willey, who had asked to see me about the Land Commission Bill. At once he said to me straight out that he wanted my support for his paper. I replied, 'Let's agree to put a paper to Cabinet in which we indicate that there is a major political decision to be taken. They must decide whether they want the Land Commission with monopoly powers right now, or whether they are prepared to have a much more modest Bill at the beginning.' Willey found no difficulty in agreeing to this—at least so I thought—and I reported to Dame Evelyn that it was now all right for the officials of both Departments to draft the Cabinet paper presenting the issues to be decided.

Tuesday, January 26th
At our first Cabinet since Leyton we were ostensibly discussing Winston's funeral arrangements; actually we were discussing the Leyton defeat. Harold made a very long and not very persuasive *plaidoyer*. I don't know quite what he was trying to achieve, but at least he did one thing that George Wigg and I had insisted on when he emphasized the need for contact with Transport House and communication with the Party in the country. I backed him up on both points and did it all the more confidently because my Saturday speech at Coventry had had a very big press, not only on Sunday but also on Monday, and was being treated as the dominant Government speech on the crisis. As I have mentioned in this diary, it had been headlined with firm promises to mortgagors and so I had expected fierce resentment in Cabinet. Not at all. Not one word was said—presumably because everybody was so frightened by Leyton.

Thursday, January 28th
This was my critical day with in the morning Cabinet—at which I had been told by Dame Evelyn that James Callaghan was to launch an attack on my housing programme—and in the evening the crucial meeting about the Land Commission. Just when Cabinet was starting I got a note from Harold Wilson congratulating me on agreeing to accept Bruce Fraser as Dame Evelyn's successor,* and concluding by saying that he was going to back my housing programme. So there it was. The row was over before it started, which was satisfactory for me! The evening meeting was also satisfactory. I found myself in the Cabinet room, Harold in the chair, with the Attorney-General (I had insisted on our lawyer being present) and Fred Willey.

* What I'd actually done was to put up to Helsby the proposal that if Fraser was to come to the Ministry of Housing he should spend the next six months working on local government finance at the Treasury while the Dame stayed on until the end of July; this was the condition on which I accepted Fraser. Harold was pleased with this.

George Brown came in for a moment and walked out again. That left four of us to have the most vague informal discussion. After a couple of hours it was decided that Willey should draft a White Paper defining the policy he believed in for the Land Commission. O.K. by me!

Saturday, January 30th

Winston's funeral. All through the week London had been working itself up for the great day. The lying-in-state in Westminster Hall had taken place on Wednesday, Thursday and Friday. I went on all three evenings, taking Molly and our doorman, Arthur, on one night, and Anne and Tommy Balogh the second night, and then on the third night Mr Large who cuts my hair. Each time one saw, even at one o'clock in the morning, the stream of people pouring down the steps of Westminster Hall towards the catafalque. Outside the column wound through the garden at Millbank, then stretched over Lambeth Bridge, right round the corner to St Thomas's Hospital. As one walked through the streets one felt the hush and one noticed the cars stopping suddenly and the people stepping out into the quietness and walking across to Westminster Hall. We as Members of Parliament could just step into the Hall through our side door.

I really hadn't wanted to go to the funeral. But it was obvious that I couldn't be known to have stayed away and I was a bit surprised, but also relieved, when Anne finally rang up and said she would like to go too and would come up on Friday. My chief memory is of the pall-bearers, in particular poor Anthony Eden, literally ashen grey, looking as old as Clement Attlee. And then of the coffin being carried up the steps by those poor perspiring privates of the Guards, sweat streaming down their faces, each clutching the next in order to sustain the sheer weight. As they came past us they staggered and they weren't properly recovered when they had to bring the coffin down the steps again to put it on the gun carriage to be taken to Tower Bridge. My other chief memory was the superb way the trumpets sounded the Last Post and the Reveille. The trumpeters were right up in the Whispering Gallery, round the inside of the dome, and for the first time a trumpet had room to sound in a dimension, a hemisphere of its own. But, oh, what a faded, declining establishment surrounded me. Aged marshals, grey, dreary ladies, decadent Marlboroughs and Churchills. It was a dying congregation gathered there and I am afraid the Labour Cabinet didn't look too distinguished either. It felt like the end of an epoch, possibly even the end of a nation.

Sunday, January 31st

I came down to Prescote with Dame Evelyn because I wanted her to see the place. I have used the opportunity of her being here to discuss housing policy. This is something which has been formulated in the Ministry throughout the week and we are now safely committed to my ideas of differential interest rates. The Dame, of course, was keen on the policies of the Department and has her own plan for reorganizing the housing subsidies. At Prescote I think I managed to persuade her that we should try to fix the interest rates for housing across the board and have a subsidy which prevents the rate paid for building council houses rising above 4 per cent whatever happens. Then on top of this one could have special subsidies for high-rise building and so on. Each year (and this is my second main idea) I think we have to fix the total volume of houses we build by agreement between the Government, the industry, the building societies and the local authorities. I have a concept here of a house-building review rather like the annual farm-price review. Dame Evelyn sees a thousand administrative difficulties. She is a good civil servant but she knows I am set on this, and I think we shall work out something constructive and have it ready for Harold pretty soon.

Monday, February 1st
Straight from Prescote to the Cabinet which had been called on a Monday because it was necessary to get clearance for a provisional Statement on aircraft which Harold Wilson wanted to make in his reply to the censure debate tomorrow.

This was the first time Cabinet had discussed defence. I took virtually no part because it was clear that once again a postponement of a decision on the TSR2 was to be announced. I found the discussion as unilluminating as usual except in that James Callaghan revealed that he had already made up his mind firmly against the TSR2. It was also clear that the Prime Minister was against *him*.

Friday, February 5th
The day started with a visit to Douglas Jay in his office in the new Board of Trade building at the corner of Great Peter Street and Victoria Street. He really has a magnificent view, and you can see the dome of St Paul's behind the tower of Big Ben.

When I got back to the Ministry I found that George Wigg had rung up asking urgently that when I went to Stoke at the weekend I should do a hand-out on immigration. We have been having sittings of the Cabinet Committee on Immigration for week after week under Frank Soskice's chairmanship—poor Frank Soskice with his arthritis and his twisted shoulder and his amiability and his self-centredness. He is a disaster as Home Secretary and he has to deal with the hottest potato in politics—the problem of immigration. As the Committee has proceeded under his chairmanship he has been gradually dragged out of his purely liberalistic attitude to a recognition that we have to combine tight immigration controls, even if it means changing the law, with a constructive policy for integrating into the community the immigrants who are there already. This has been my line as a Midland M.P. and here I really do represent my constituents. Ever since the Smethwick election it has been quite clear that immigration can be the greatest potential vote-loser for the Labour Party if we are seen to be permitting a flood of immigrants to come in and blight the central areas in all our cities. I told George I would certainly try and draft the speech for Stoke and I worked away at frantic speed during my lunch. I only just got it done and round to Frank Soskice, with a copy to Harold, before I went into the big Cabinet Committee on the Ministry of Technology, which was a pretty good waste of time but which I had to sit out before catching the Pullman for Coventry.

It was the night for my surgery and I found a long queue and sat there for two and a half hours, seeing finally a delegation of aircraft workers from Armstrong-Whitworth. They represented the 8,000 workers at the factory, which is now threatened with total closure by the announcement Harold Wilson made at the end of Tuesday's debate.

This was the first occasion on which I found a real conflict between my responsibilities as Minister and my responsibilities as a constituency M.P. I was interested to see how I could handle this split, all the more because ever since the first day of this Session Maurice Edelman has been taking the lead in organizing the aircraft workers and becoming the spokesman of the aircraft industry in protest against any kind of closure. He had quite a success when we all thought Concorde was due for cancellation, because he stood up for Concorde and, through his close contact with the French, made a great impression on the Coventry workers. And now once again, with the threat of the closure of Armstrong-Whitworth, he has been leading the workers' marches—10,000 were in procession last week—and proclaiming his readiness to die with them on the barricades. Naturally enough, he has not done anything to help the other M.P. for Coventry—the Minister in whose constituency the A.W.W. factory is and who has so far been unable to open his mouth in public.

Well, they all filed into the big room at Coundon Road and I had a good rough meeting with them while six or seven journalists waited outside along with photographers in order to get a picture of the row. I thought the only thing to do was to talk pretty frankly and so I started, 'You understand that I am in favour of drastic defence cuts. It's impossible to buy British planes if they cost twice as much as American planes and if they are not ready at the right time. On the other hand, I will fight like a tiger to see that if any unemployment does take place, Coventry doesn't get more than its share.' I think—though I am not sure—that I managed to get through a very difficult meeting; though it is quite true that when A.W.W. closes down—as I think it will—I shall be in an impossible position. The truth is that one loses votes by being in the Cabinet because one has to keep one's trap shut. In the last general election the Conservative Ministers by and large did worse than the back-benchers because the back-benchers were able to talk more freely and say the things their constituents wanted to hear. And though my own particular job should give me some popularity, it certainly prevents me from making the kind of hearty, calculated indiscretions which I had been able to indulge in as a back-bencher for twenty years.

Saturday, February 6th
In the afternoon I did a Labour Party regional conference in Hanley Town Hall, where I used to give my local government W.E.A. classes in 1936. There were some 250 delegates there and I tried to raise their morale with a fighting speech, telling them frankly of the difficulties of the Government, of the legacy we inherited from the Tories, explaining how we couldn't reveal the worst of that legacy for fear of destroying the value of the pound, and saying that the time had come now to fight back and to put the blame where it really belongs. I was amazed and relieved to find that morale, which I thought had been shattered, was still very solid indeed. These people were quietly and placidly discussing with me how to strengthen their support for their Labour Government, and none of them seemed unduly alarmed. The Young Socialists were bleating but there was no shriek from them, and even the old-age pensioners weren't shouting their complaints.

The value of going out into the constituencies, as I did today, and talking to our people is that one tests grass-roots morale. Provided we can carry the Chancellor with us and provided Harold can get some strategy and coherence into our policy, there is no reason why we shouldn't get through this very bad patch and settle down to do a decent job. What we need now (and this was the lesson of this regional conference) is to use the Labour Party as our main instrument of communication with the rest of the electorate. That's now George Wigg's main job as the person who is doing the liaison between the Cabinet, Transport House and the constituencies, one of the most important jobs in the whole Government.

Monday, February 8th
The first Cabinet meeting of the week was quite unexpected. When I got to London in the morning I was told it was on at eleven, because a new factor had suddenly turned up in the defence problem. Outside the Cabinet door I met Roy Jenkins, the Minister of Aviation, who said to me, 'I'm afraid I'm not going to please you.' And he quickly informed me what I had half guessed—that Hawker Siddeley had suddenly, after three days' and three nights' unbroken work, come up with a new proposition—a proposal for a hybrid plane which did provide a real alternative to the American plane. I had heard about this Hawker Siddeley proposal when the delegation came to see me in Coventry last Friday evening. In Cabinet the discussion was started by Roy Jenkins, who described the firm's offer, saying that it was almost embarrassingly good and that Hawker Siddeley had now cut down its price, cut down the period of manufacture and put themselves really in a position comparable to that of the Americans. It was only because the delivery date

was two years later than the Americans' that on balance he recommended rejection of the firm's offer. Roy was then supported by Denis Healey, who put the issue rather more crudely. He just said that if we wanted the American package we couldn't go back on it and start thinking about making one British plane which would upset the whole deal. It was obvious from the start that Harold Wilson, George Brown, Denis Healey and Jim Callaghan, whatever their disagreements, had made up their minds on the American package and wanted to be authorized by the Cabinet to turn down this embarrassing Hawker Siddeley offer. There were only two people prepared to ask for it to be seriously considered—Frank Cousins and myself, who, of course, are two local M.P.s for Hawker Siddeley workers. Against us was ranged practically the whole Cabinet. I remember Barbara Castle made a very high-minded speech telling us that we must face the need to cut back the production of British planes. I couldn't help wondering what she would have said if the plane concerned was manufactured in her constituency and her biggest factory was due to be closed down and could have been saved if we had accepted this last-minute offer. Nevertheless, I didn't really fight hard because it was quite clear that all that was being asked for was formal Cabinet consent to a package which had been signed, sealed and delivered well before Christmas.

Thursday, February 11th
Today we had a second exciting Cabinet. I think it was the most dramatic meeting we had had and it revealed for the first time the way this Labour Cabinet splits on a really important socialist issue. The whole discussion centred on the proposals for expanding the housing programme. In these last weeks various Ministers—Kenneth Robinson, for instance, and Anthony Crosland at Education—have come forward pleading for small supplementary estimates. Each Minister has been told that he is only allowed the increased estimates allocated to his Department by the Tory White Paper last year. This means that over the next four years, if we keep the priorities unchanged, Transport would get an increase of 30 per cent, Education 30 per cent and Housing only 10 per cent. The reason is simple. In order to win votes in that last period before the election the Tories were prepared to announce a rapid expansion of higher education, a huge hospital-building programme, a huge road-building programme. The one social service they felt it was popular to cut back was public-sector housing—the construction of rented houses by local authorities, in contrast to the construction of owner-occupier houses by building society mortgagors. As a result of their policy, though council-house production was somewhat bigger than in the previous year, in 1964 it was still far less than it had been under Nye Bevan in 1949.
    It was my contention that whereas the other Ministers could fairly be asked to be content with the amount of money in the Tory estimates, this was

quite unreasonable in the case of housing where we were pledged to reverse the Tory policy and expand council-house building. I was therefore putting forward at this Cabinet a modest proposal. In 1964 the Tories had budgeted for 135,000 council-house approvals and the actual number of approvals was 144,000. I proposed to raise 144,000 to 156,000—the figure Harold Wilson had privately suggested to me. I spoke extremely moderately. I was followed by Callaghan who in a long, violent harangue said that we were going to crack up and crash unless the increase in public expenditure could be halted. He could not permit any increase in the housing programme because he was facing a budget situation in which even a neutral budget would fail to win the confidence of the bankers. So we must all wait until July and then housing must be reviewed along with the other claimants. George Brown spoke next. He replied very well indeed, stressing, as I had also stressed, that the whole increase in the housing programme could be put through by expanding our industrialized building. This would not put a strain on our resources but simply employ unused capital resources in which millions had been invested, and production could now take place.

So it was a straight conflict between the Chancellor and the First Secretary and it was very clear indeed that, despite all the efforts to ensure that D.E.A. was the real planning Ministry, the Chancellor of the Exchequer in Britain today, with all the authority of the Treasury behind him, still holds the power. I suspect Jim Callaghan had done a great deal of quiet lobbying. On my side I had George Brown, the Lord Chancellor, Frank Cousins, Fred Peart, and Jim Griffiths, but very little other support. This was partly because the other Ministers were bound to support the Chancellor. Tony Crosland, for example, was obviously afraid that if housing got more money it would be taken from Education. Tom Fraser at Transport felt the same and so did the Minister of Power. All round the table this was the situation. Only Douglas Houghton was deliberately ambiguous, and Ted Short, the Chief Whip, was a little bit on my side because of the huge industrialized-building programme in the North-East. When I counted the votes I saw there was a heavy majority against me.

But then Harold started to speak, saying that he personally favoured increasing the council-housing programme to 150,000 straight away. So there! I had the Prime Minister, the Deputy Prime Minister and the Lord Chancellor on my side, and James Callaghan had most of the rest of the Cabinet on his. However, the Prime Minister can always decide how to count. He told Cabinet that he had added up the votes and found that there was a tie and then he made a powerful speech in favour of the housing programme. I waited in suspense. In this open conflict between Callaghan and Brown was he really siding with Brown against his own Chancellor? At first it looked as though he was, and then suddenly he switched and began to attack us all for not knowing our figures, and he demanded precise statistics about this and about that—figures we couldn't possibly give. Then he asked whether there shouldn't be licensing of private building, whether we shouldn't cut back office building and luxury houses still further in order to release the labour force and the materials necessary to sustain the council-house programme without inflation. Next he said that I must show how it was possible to get these 12,000 extra houses all built by industrialized methods and built in the right places. He ended by demanding two things. First, an inquiry into the control of private building, so as to cut back office building, and, second, proposals for the control of the production of industrialized houses to ensure that they would be produced and built in the development areas. This was a piece of brilliant stalling: next time it comes before Cabinet we shall get the increase I demanded.

This Cabinet meeting was important for two reasons. Firstly, it showed the depth of the Brown/Callaghan split.* Secondly, it showed that the Prime Minister is siding with Brown, cautiously but decisively. Harold Wilson, I think, is aware that his Chancellor is open to precisely the pressures which a socialist Chancellor must resist. On the other hand, he must also be aware that George Brown is unable to gain the respect of the City of London and that his incomes policy is becoming more and more of a personal hard-sell, a virtuoso performance of exhibitionist politics which no one can take very seriously. By sheer personality, by drive, by imagination, George Brown has in an astonishing way managed to challenge the orthodoxy of the Right and I think Harold by and large supports him against Jim.

And a good thing too—because Callaghan is really representing the Mac-Donaldite attitude to the bankers in 1931. Like MacDonald he is open to moral blackmail by Lord Cromer[1] and the Bank of England, and so are most of my working-class colleagues. One could see at Cabinet how, whether they belong to the Right or the Left of the Party, they can be terrorized, and how weak and pliable they are in the hands of the City and of the Bank of England when a crisis of this kind blows up and they feel they must put the country before their class. In this struggle I can see that Harold Wilson is having a very difficult time indeed.

Thursday, February 18th
Another confused Cabinet meeting, this time on the draft Statement James Callaghan put forward, in which he hoped to explain away the enormous increase in this year's Estimates. The Cabinet meeting took place against a background of news stories in all the papers about the great contest between the Chancellor and the First Secretary on the character of this year's Budget. I must say I have been wondering what is the duty of a Cabinet Minister who doesn't belong to the inner circle and yet must see and hear the sort of stories I had been reading in the papers this week. Should one insist on discussing

---

* A split, by the way, which was reported in most of the main Sunday papers at the end of the week.
[1] The Governor of the Bank.

those stories in Cabinet? Should one put them down on the agenda? The thought came into my mind very strongly when I read Lord Cromer's astonishing speech on Tuesday. Indeed, I was so outraged by it that for the first time in my Ministerial life I wrote a minute to the Prime Minister asking him what steps would be taken to shut up this one-man May Committee.[1] I sent this minute off, after talking to George Wigg and Tommy Balogh so as to make sure it impacted on No. 10. And sure enough on three occasions when we were walking through the division lobby the Prime Minister came up to me and said, 'I've got your minute, and I am dealing with Lord Cromer in my weekend speech.' And on Wednesday I found that there was a longish passage by David Wood[2] in the centre of *The Times* describing how senior Cabinet Ministers were protesting about Lord Cromer and using the actual substance of my minute, which had been obviously shown to him in an off-the-record briefing.

This is typical of Harold's handling of politics. He still thinks he can settle problems just by talking to the press. As for the press reports of the Brown/Callaghan struggle, I suspect they are chiefly supplied by George, who now seems to be relapsing into his old habits. There's no one more talented in the whole Cabinet or nicer or more loyal or more basically constructive. Frank Cousins and I feel ourselves on his side. But he is schizophrenic, and once again the wear and tear is showing in him after the first four months. Leaks and drink will in the end get him down; and we shouldn't reckon on our First Secretary being there overlong unless he mends his ways. Whether Callaghan has talked to the press I rather doubt. He has become a very staid, prim, Bank of England type, almost a parody of the Labour man taken over by his officials—by the Treasury officials in this case. I should say that most of the pro-Callaghan stories are leaked through the Treasury Press Office.

Well, that's the background to today's Cabinet discussion. The Statement was drafted in such a way as to make clear that its main aim was to curb public-sector expenditure. It showed that despite all our efforts the Estimates had gone up by 6 per cent, which of course was substantially less than the 9 per cent the Tories had planned. It also included a firm commitment to permit an increase of only 23 per cent in public expenditure during the next four years, an annual average increase of 4 per cent. This was written into the Statement as a Cabinet objective.

Frank Cousins started the opposition by expressing his dislike of the Statement in rather vague terms. I pointed out that if the Chancellor specified a maximum rate of development for the public sector without displaying an equally iron determination to control the expansion of the

[1] In 1931 the National Government set up the May Committee to propose cuts in public expenditure. A storm followed its recommendations, which included a reduction in unemployment benefit.
[2] Political Editor of *The Times*.

private sector, we should have an economy in which wildly extravagant and unnecessary growth of the private sector went unrestrained and in which, whenever we were in trouble, we only cut back the public sector. In fact, we should be making the same disastrous mistake the Tories have been making for the last ten years. Then Tony Crosland said that we shouldn't commit ourselves to a maximum rate of expenditure in the public sector, and the real criticism started. Round the Cabinet table it went and the Statement was torn to pieces paragraph by paragraph. Even Tom Fraser said it was unfortunate that the principles enshrined by our predecessors in the Tory Estimates were those we socialists were maintaining in office. The truth is that Callaghan just took over the Treasury policy of the Tory Estimates and is trying to hold expenditure down within this Conservative framework. He had fought a stalling battle the previous week on my public-housing programme. I counter-attacked this Thursday, slashing his Statement to smithereens, so that finally he got up sulkily and said, 'Well, since every paragraph has been found fault with, I hardly think it's worth having a Statement.' However, he apparently got down to work later on. When I went to see George Brown about industrialized building he told me that none of the officials were being consulted about the redraft—Callaghan was doing it himself. George went on to tell me that the figures for the Budget had now been agreed. 'God forbid that you should tell me what the figures are, George,' I said before he could pour them all out, but I did get the impression that the crisis between him and Callaghan had been resolved, and this is just possible.

In the afternoon I went into the House to hear Frank Cousins making his maiden speech. I found he was showing, much more than Ernie Bevin ever showed, a sense of the House—a kind of conversationalism and a natural modesty. He seemed to me to be doing extremely well.

Sunday, February 21st

This weekend I have no less than four red boxes to work through; one of them contains the redraft of the Statement the Chancellor is due to make. It still includes the most dangerously firm commitment to cut back the speed of development in the public sector. True, it has had written into it a section about the control of the private sector but the phrases used are very inconsistent. On this I really rather agree with the Accountant-General in my Ministry, Crocker. He is an able Tory and he is right when he says 'Qui s'excuse s'accuse' and tells me that the whole Statement in its latest form will neither impress the bankers nor impress the home front. I am looking forward with keen anticipation to what happens in Cabinet tomorrow. I shall be in a weak situation with George Brown and Douglas Jay away at the EFTA meeting[1] and with the Prime Minister saying that they had agreed the draft before they left the country. However, I shall have a go.

[1] A crisis meeting in Geneva.

Monday, February 22nd

Cabinet went pretty well. It started with an item about the surcharge that we had imposed as one of our first actions on imported goods, which has caused the most appalling trouble with the EFTA countries.[1] Cabinet was now being asked for formal approval to a 5-per-cent reduction in the surcharge at the very moment George Brown and Douglas Jay were announcing it at the EFTA conference! The only exciting part of this item was the lecture the Prime Minister gave us on the leaks which have been coming out of Cabinet recently, one of which anticipated the announcement on the surcharge. I chose my moment and went in to bat. I said I was heartily sick of leaks and I wanted to know how it was that the battle between Callaghan and Brown had been reported round by round in the papers. The reply I got from the P.M. was that there wasn't a word of truth in the story. So far, nothing had been discussed by Ministers. The officials were still at work and he could say quite sincerely, with the support of the Chancellor, that the whole thing was the invention of the journalists.

Then Harold Wilson raised the issue of Anthony Howard. He has just been appointed by the *Sunday Times* to be the first Whitehall correspondent in history, looking into the secrets of the Civil Service rather than leaking the secrets of the politicians. His first article had been an analysis of the relationship between the D.E.A. and the Treasury. The P.M. said this was outrageous and he was going to accept the challenge of the *Sunday Times*. In order to kill Tony Howard's new job he forbade any of us to speak to him.

Then we turned to the Chancellor's Statement. Pretty soon I waded in and threw one copy of my amendments to the Chancellor, whom I had already seen before the meeting, and another to the P.M. While I was talking the P.M. had my draft duplicated and gave each member of the Cabinet a copy. To my amazement it formed the basis of the amended version.

I went back to the office to tell my people what had happened and then walked over to the House for lunch with Harold. I found him walking up and down the corridor outside the Members' dining-room. He started off on leaks and said that they had probably come from George Brown and that in his view the First Secretary had lapsed right back to his old ways, and that quite likely we would have a leak and a Budget inquiry and the end of George Brown. He spoke about this with extraordinary frankness, and he also referred to Douglas Jay's misbehaviour in leaking the story of the surcharge. Then he turned to my affairs and repeated to me a remark that he had made in Cabinet about the need to stop demolition of houses. He asked me to check very carefully whether a house could be demolished without planning authorization. I knew vaguely that whereas you have to have planning permission to put up a building, you don't have to have it in order to pull one down unless it is a listed building. Harold made a tremendous point

[1] The 15 per cent surcharge announced in the Statement on October 26th, 1964, was reduced to 10 per cent on April 27th, 1965, and finally abolished on November 30th, 1966.

of this demolition problem and said that if we were going to obtain the increased housing allocation, we must stop the demolishing of habitable houses and the building of luxury houses. He then turned to legislation and I told him we were on time with the Rent Bill but it might well be that we should find the Tories refusing to vote against us on the Second Reading. Immediately he said, 'Draft a White Paper which forces them to vote against you by describing the iniquities of the Tory Rent Act and the need to repeal it.' That's typical of Harold's tactical ingenuity; and I am immediately taking it up in the Ministry. He also told me that the Steel Bill wouldn't be ready and that I should have to run my Bill separately. Finally, we discussed the general situation and he gave me the very clear impression that he doesn't want to go to the country now and that we must win time—possibly until May of next year. I got a tremendous impression (he was talking very intimately) that he was treating Frank Cousins and me very much as his allies in the line he was taking.

Thursday, February 25th
This was the day of the big Cabinet meeting on my public-housing programme. Harold and I agreed later that it was far the most important and far the best Cabinet of this Labour Government. At long last we did take decisions; and for the first time Harold Wilson came out as a leader—a man who wasn't just content to sit back in the chair and see what happened but was prepared to make sure that things happened the way he wanted.

The meeting had been preceded by a lot of jockeying. My officials and Charlie Pannell's had got together to produce a joint paper on how we could get all the extra 12,000 houses built in development areas by using industrialized building methods. Meanwhile, Pannell himself had got another paper done on physical controls—an insane paper, by the way, simply proving that they were totally impossible; and my Department had done a brief, cautious note on financial controls, saying they were possible but very difficult and if they were introduced it must be in conjunction with differential interest rates, on which I would produce a paper in a few weeks. At Cabinet there wasn't a very good turn-out. Gerald Gardiner and Arthur Bottomley were away in Rhodesia. Fred Peart wasn't there. Barbara Castle wasn't there. Only two-thirds of Cabinet were present when I started the debate. I had been very carefully briefed by the Department and I realized that the main point I must make was that we were now building fewer council houses than were constructed under the last Labour Government. Whereas the private sector had increased output considerably, the public sector had sagged back, despite the desperate need of cheap houses to rent.

So we were talking about a vital social service—the only social service the Tories had ruthlessly cut back. I was asking for a small increase in 1965 to enable the local authorities to make this the first year of their four-year plan. If we denied them any increase this year, I pointed out, we should lose a whole year of house production. I was also able to say that there would be no increased cost to the Chancellor in the budget, and that all the new houses would be put up by industrialized system-building which wouldn't put an undue strain on the construction industry. I was briefly supported by Charlie Pannell. Then the Chancellor made exactly the same speech as before. He disregarded my whole case and said we must have a general review in July and that we couldn't afford to let any Ministry increase its estimates before that review. If the Minister of Housing had his way, how would the Chancellor manage to deal with all the other claims that would be put forward?

I was nervous that Harold would let the debate go on, but at this point he jumped right in and laid down his own line. He said that it was quite impossible for a Labour Government to let public housing continue to run at a lower level than that in 1950. We simply had to jack it up even if it meant cutting back luxury building and using physical controls. And suddenly he said that he had found the solution to the problem in Clause 8 of Charlie Pannell's paper. Poor Charlie did not know whether he was standing on his head or his heels. He wriggled, because he is a passionate opponent of physical controls and here was his paper being taken by the Prime Minister as the text on which to preach a sermon to the effect that by imposing physical controls on the private sector we could permit ourselves a moderate increase of production in the public sector. Harold's speech completely cut away the ground under the opposition. Nobody spoke against us. The First Secretary helped us along, and within an hour the issue had been settled. Afterwards Harold said to me, 'Well, aren't you pleased? That's the best meeting we've had. I enjoyed it.' There was no doubt I had enjoyed it. My whole attitude to life which had been so dejected on the Sunday was improved.

Monday, March 1st
I started reading the Milner Holland Report at Prescote on Sunday.[1] At our first meeting I hadn't thought very highly of Milner Holland. It was therefore an enormous surprise and relief to discover that the report itself is extremely good. And already by today I knew that I could look forward to the publication of something which would bluff the Tories and force them to vote against the Second Reading of my Bill. When I got to the Ministry, full of nothing but Milner Holland, I found them quite pleased but also a bit annoyed. I suspect they are not used to a Minister who reads faster than they do, although it is something that they really quite want.

In the afternoon I had a long briefing meeting in the Ministry in preparation for the crucial Cabinet on the Land Commission. There was a long Cabinet paper prepared not by one of the Ministries but by the Lord President and the Cabinet Office, a completely objective study of Fred

[1] On housing in Greater London. It showed that 190,000 London households were in urgent need of rehousing, and an additional 61,000 single persons lacked proper accommodation.

Willey's proposals and those of our Department. After the meeting the Secretary came in to see me and said, 'Oh my dear Minister, don't let's bother to fight this Land Commission any more. There are more important things in life.' I must say I agreed with her.

Tuesday, March 2nd

But when we came to Cabinet this wasn't so easy. Bowden made a long, perfectly fair statement of the problem. Then Fred Willey explained his position in his usual precise yet vague way. Then I had to defend my position. I started by saying that I didn't pretend to understand the Land Commission fully but I suspected nobody else round the table did and that was half the trouble. We were trying to introduce a very rough-and-ready social instrument into the extraordinarily delicate operation of land purchase. I was nervous whether this wouldn't be a spanner in the works. On this occasion Harold Wilson was wholly against me. Having heard both of us, he said we ought to take 'the more courageous' solution. The moment he said 'more courageous' I knew he was backing Fred. But, to my surprise, it was clear as the meeting went on that I had some supporters. First of all Denis Healey came in—this was almost his first intervention in home affairs—and formulated extremely accurately what he believed me to have been saying. Then Douglas Houghton said he had been embarrassed to hear me disown the position he was so anxious to support. But James Callaghan and the whole Treasury were on my side, and it became clear that more and more people were gradually coming to realize that this was a question not of showing courage or lacking courage but of whether we should commit ourselves to something practical which we could actually put into effect or whether we should go on making a lot of vague and dangerous noises.

It's still anybody's guess who won that Cabinet. On three of the issues things seem to have come my way, and I was aware that the Prime Minister was reluctantly forced into admitting that I had been talking good sense on a subject on which he has always been both vague and extremist. On this whole question of land and planning Harold Wilson is really a complete innocent. And this is all the worse because as an economist, a statistician and an ex-civil servant he tends to think he can understand anything. This segment of life is perhaps the only part of the administrative process of which he is totally ignorant and for which he has no feeling at all.

After Cabinet, talking to the Dame, I mentioned that I found my new Private Secretary extremely unattractive and I didn't want her to take it for granted I was going to keep him. She was very upset. 'He's perfectly all right,' she said. 'You mustn't be so difficult. You do treat our people so badly.' I replied, 'Sorry, Secretary, but it's my Private Office not yours, and I have got to be sure that my Private Secretary is somebody who I feel is on my side. I must warn you that I will keep Moseley if this one is unsatisfactory.' I now know I was too obliging in promising that I wouldn't oppose George

Moseley's move, and I am finding it difficult not to renege on that promise despite the trouble it will cause the Department.[1]

Thursday, March 4th
The second Cabinet meeting this week. There seemed to be nothing on the agenda until George Wigg rang me up and told me that what was at stake was the future of the army museum due to be built in the back of the garden at the Chelsea Royal Hospital. He'd heard that it was to be dropped because the Treasury didn't like it and the First Secretary didn't like it. True enough, it was the first item on the agenda and Harold Wilson had already been got at by George. As for me, I found amongst my Cabinet papers in the red box a single sheet of brief with a note at the bottom from my Department: 'The Treasury passed this on to you and would be grateful if you would use it in debate.' It was in fact an exact description of the Treasury proposal to have the museum outside London and sell the land and ground rent for thirty-four luxury flats.

Many Cabinet members were incredulous when I asserted this but I pegged away and managed to get clear what the First Secretary and the Chancellor really wanted: the alternative to the army museum, which was thirty-four luxury flats. The most interesting feature of this Cabinet was Harold's behaviour. He showed himself once again curiously solicitous to see that we came to a full Cabinet decision. You could see him ticking off the names, counting up the heads on each side and finally coming down himself just, but only just, on our side.

While I was thinking about the army museum at Chelsea, Barbara Castle was once again raising the problem of Vietnam and its repercussions. The subject has been discussed pretty often, but nearly always I have had my mind on something else and have taken no part in the discussion. Indeed, I think I can say that I haven't spoken on foreign affairs since I became a Minister, and I am now beginning to wonder whether one should insulate one's mind as completely as this. Vietnam might become an issue as awkward as the Korean war was for the Attlee government and even more divisive. Certainly there is a growing suspicion in the P.L.P. that we ought to be playing a much more active mediating role, along with the Russians, instead of siding so closely with the Americans. Of course, the Cabinet has the enthusiastic support of the Opposition. But this week we've got open rebellion on the back benches: some forty-five left-wingers are putting their names to a motion insisting on a far more decisive effort to stop the war in Vietnam.

Sunday, March 21st
There have been two episodes in my own semi-private life as Minister which are worth mentioning. The first was the publication of my book *Planning for*

[1] Moseley had completed a two-year tour in the Private Office.

Freedom[1] which took place quietly on Thursday, March 11th. I had assumed that the book would be extensively noticed. Actually, it has been a quite pleasant, harmless flop. Things started off with a jolly well-written review in the *New Statesman* by David Marquand, which was hostile but recognized the book's importance. The only other serious review was in *The Times Literary Supplement*. The full-page anonymous reviewer is obviously Michael Oakeshott,[2] who was so upset by my anonymous review of his book in the *T.L.S.* Apart from the *New Statesman* and the *T.L.S.* nobody has taken the book seriously. It has been glanced at and pushed on one side. It may well be true, as both the *T.L.S.* and the *New Statesman* suggest, that by collecting in one volume my more theoretical essays I have exposed the fact that I am not a serious thinker but a political journalist who takes himself a bit too seriously. Also reviewers may be reluctant to look at a politician in two ways simultaneously—as a writer and as a Minister. Frankly, the feeling is that Ministers should be Ministers and writers should be writers, and Ministers shouldn't write books until they have retired.

Do I mind the flop? In this respect I am a split personality. If I had been offered the chance I would have thrown away practical politics and concentrated on writing. Equally, if Attlee had given me a job fifteen or twenty years ago I'd have been a whole-time professional politician. But then after the fall of the Attlee Government I'd have had twelve years sitting on the Opposition front bench instead of enjoying myself as an active political journalist and back-bencher in the way I have actually done. So I have a lot to be thankful for. Maybe I have got this job a few years too late. But I am at the top of my powers and I think I now have enough experience and maturity to avoid some of the clangers which I'd have made if I'd been promoted earlier in my career. Anyway, I couldn't care less about the fate of the book.

The other personal experience I have to record is the trouble I have had in my Private Office, which culminated in my getting rid of my new Private Secretary and getting in his place, thank God, John Delafons. The more I think about it the greater the loss of George Moseley, that owl-eyed, dark, quizzical character who had been Private Secretary to my two Tory predecessors and who was thoroughly tired and wanted to get home occasionally to dinner. The moment the Dame replaced him I was as isolated in my Private Office as I had been on my first day in the Ministry.

In relaxing the strain on a Minister and enabling him to do his work, the Private Secretary can do an enormous lot of good or no good at all. George Moseley had been invaluable because he knew everybody in the Department and because he would comment intelligently on everything I wrote and tell me if he thought I was going wrong. So he gave me a sense of assurance that I wouldn't ever go very far wrong. And at times he could also be candid and critical of my behaviour. Now all this suddenly disappeared and all I had

[1] Collected essays written between 1938 and 1964 (London: Hamish Hamilton, 1965).
[2] Professor of Political Science at L.S.E. 1951–69.

was an elegant young man who came wafting into my room and stood about the place and never did a damn thing. I suspect his lordly manner, as often happens with civil servants, actually concealed uncertainty and insecurity. But that didn't help me. After a fortnight I went to the Dame and said, 'He just won't do.'

Within a week a young man was hauled out of the Planning Department and delivered to me. Actually, I had spotted him for the first time during a seminar on the West Midlands Review. He has been the Secretary to the Planning Advisory Group (P.A.G.), which is a stunningly able and successful group of town clerks, treasurers and planners who have been working in the last year with the Ministry's planning officials on a drastic revision of all planning procedure. He is tall, almost as owlish as George, but more vital, keen and alert. Within a week he has wholly transformed the Private Office. I brought him down to Prescote yesterday on my way back from an official visit to the Black Country. He clicked with Patrick and Virginia; and he told me that he had never had such a week in his life as his first week running the Private Office. I now know I am all right. I have somebody who can talk to me, somebody I can talk to completely freely, somebody enormously ambitious who also thinks it exciting to work with me, and above all somebody who knows his way about the Department and is prepared to be loyal to me in his relations with other civil servants.

Monday, March 22nd
Apart from two days' electioneering in Saffron Walden and on the Scottish border[1] I spent a whole week almost entirely in preparations for the debate on the Milner Holland Report. But when the weekend came I still hadn't got a speech ready. I had hoped that most of it could have been prepared in the Department, but again they were quite unable to do so. It rained practically throughout the whole weekend so I worked all Saturday evening and for twelve hours on Sunday and produced a complete written speech in time for the debate today.

Poor Anne was due to be in the Commons for the debate but at the last moment she had to stay at home because Patrick and Virginia both went down with a mild virus. So she missed hearing what turned out to be the first effective political oration I have made as Minister. I had thought over my tactics very carefully indeed and I decided to launch an all-out attack on the Tory record and put the whole blame on them for the rent crisis we inherited. For weeks now, George Wigg and I have been discussing our failure to pin the responsibility on the Tories for the troubles we are coping with. Here is a case where we really could do so, and so the speech was a ruthless party

[1] The Saffron Walden by-election followed the resignation of R. A. Butler and his elevation to the Lords and the Mastership of Trinity College, Cambridge. There was a by-election in Roxburgh after the death of the sitting Conservative Member, Commander Donaldson. At the poll on March 23rd Peter Kirk held Saffron Walden for the Tories; David Steel, a Liberal, snatched the Scottish seat from the Conservatives with a majority of 4,607 votes.

political attack on the Conservatives, with my own side roaring enthusiastically behind me. Probably in the long run it was marred by a remark I made about my natural prejudice against landlords. I had put it into the text at the last moment so as to make sure I would carry my own back-benchers with me.

Tuesday, March 23rd
My speech in Monday's debate had a mixed reaction from the press. The *Daily Telegraph* described the speech as the most merciless parliamentary performance. On the other hand, my demagoguery lost me the support of *The Times*, for example, which not unreasonably regarded it as vulgar. However, I had no time to worry because today was the day for my second big Lobby conference within a week—this time explaining in detail the Rent Bill, which I had timed very nicely to come out just a week after the Milner Holland Report.

The Lobby conference took place at four o'clock. I had been asked by Harold Wilson to hold it then because he wanted one as well and Douglas-Home was also having one that day. So I had my forty-five minutes with the Lobby explaining the Bill and the White Paper. I had taken tremendous trouble with the White Paper, writing most of the first half of it myself, and the Dame and I had really slaved away to make the exposition of the Bill in the second half both intelligible and highly political.

Tuesday, March 30th
At ten o'clock we had a short meeting, called by the Prime Minister, to review electoral boundaries before Cabinet at ten thirty. The only people present were the Attorney-General, the Leader of the House, the Home Secretary and myself. Harold was obviously concerned to make quite sure that I was doing my job as a politician on the local boundary decisions, that no adjustment was politically disadvantageous to us. He was equally concerned to make sure that the Home Secretary was doing his job with regard to the warding of the reorganized boroughs. But poor Frank Soskice suffers desperately from arthritis and he's ageing. As soon as he had slipped out the Prime Minister raised his hands to me in horror.

Today we had the long-delayed discussion on foreign policy which Barbara Castle has been asking for. Cabinet meetings have not been very important for me since I got my way about the housing programme and obtained the Prime Minister's backing. I must say I felt that this one was the sheerest waste of time. Long papers had been prepared for us on Vietnam, on the Middle East and on Europe. My only conclusion was that a Cabinet consisting of busy departmental Ministers can't make much impact on how foreign policy is conducted. Proceedings stopped punctually at eleven forty-five to enable us to go to Westminster Abbey for a memorial service to Herbert Morrison.[1]

[1] A former deputy leader of the Labour Party, he had died on March 6th.

Monday, April 5th
The budget Cabinet was a pretty formal proceeding. In fact, it turned out to be a pretty good budget without any of the rows and alarms the press had taught us to expect as a result of the deadlock between George Brown and James Callaghan.

Though I wasn't paying much attention, I did realize that all the tax side had been done by Nicky Kaldor, and that Tommy Balogh's great success was in the decision to limit foreign investment and reimpose investment controls. Of course the decisive role had been played by Harold Wilson. He'd had two long meetings at Chequers and this budget was his real achievement—yet it was also an immense personal success for the Chancellor. Callaghan is a man with great popular appeal. He is so good on television and he is quite competent in the House; and of course he has become the darling of the Treasury. George Brown, on the other hand, has become rather dissolute lately, not his usual self. Also he is no good at running a planning Ministry. So in the battle between the Treasury and the D.E.A., the Treasury is coming out on top in terms of prestige and status. Harold, I suppose, has been content to watch this going on while he makes sure the budget is according to his wishes. After the budget meeting I moved the Second Reading of the Rent Bill.

The budget was introduced on April 6th; and in the same speech the Chancellor announced the dropping of the TSR2. There was still little foreign confidence in sterling although export figures were looking up. It was a deflationary budget, and, as well as the 6d. increase in income tax that had been published in the autumn, there were increased taxes on beer, spirits, tobacco and motor-car licence duties.[1]

Tuesday, April 13th
I had the first meeting of the Standing Committee on my Rent Bill this morning from 11.30 till 1.00. I tried to arrange with the Whips, on George Wigg's advice, to have a big Committee with fifty members in order to give opportunities to our back-benchers, and I got Tam to do all the work of collecting the twenty-six Labour volunteers. We were amazed to discover on Monday when I got back from a day in Coventry launching an improvement grant campaign, that the Committee was only going to total thirty-five. And I was even more amazed when I learned that without a word to me the Lord President and the Chief Whip, acting on the advice of Freddie Warren,[2] had proposed twenty-five on the Committee—the number had only been increased to thirty-five by the demand of the Opposition.

All this is indicative of what's wrong with our parliamentary leadership.

[1] This and subsequent italicized passages cover gaps in the Diary.
[2] Private Secretary to the Chief Whip. The position's permanence provides shrewd and intimate knowledge of the 'usual channels' through which parliamentary business is arranged.

Bowden and Short are run by Freddie Warren just as William Whiteley[1] was run by his predecessor, Charles Harris.[2] They were simply told by Warren that the right number of members for this Committee would be twenty-five and they didn't stop to calculate, as George Wigg and I did, that by having fifty members we would have embarrassed the Tories, who would have found it difficult to man a Committee of fifty, and we would probably have got a better majority than we will with a smaller one. As for the first meeting of the Committee, it was routine Second Reading stuff and it was clear that the Tories were not in an oppositional mood.

Wednesday, April 14th

I had a meeting today with Boyd-Carpenter to discuss the future of the Standing Committee, and suggested to him three meetings a week up to Whitsuntide in order to get the Bill finished. His counter-proposal was two meetings a week, which he said would be convenient to him because he is the chairman of the Public Accounts Committee and if we met on Tuesday it would have to be in the afternoon. I made it clear that I thought we ought to start with three; but I have to admit that after the first meeting I couldn't really complain about any filibustering. Finally Boyd-Carpenter virtually promised to let me have the appallingly complicated Clause 1 of the Bill as well as the first Schedule by the end of the first week after the recess. If he delivers we could hardly move faster by introducing a guillotine. However, I am expecting that when it comes to the point we *shall* have to guillotine the Bill, and indeed the Finance Bill and every other Bill, as soon as we get back from the Easter recess.

Easter Sunday, April 18th

David Butler[3] came over to see me today. This was one of his routine visitations. I suspect he has a diary which says 'See Crossman every four months'. As usual he put his questions to me and put down his answers in his little book. However, his visit did remind me that it was about time that I reflected on these first six months of Labour Government.

Broadly speaking, the analysis I made in the Introduction to Bagehot is being confirmed. Certainly it is true that the Cabinet is now part of the 'dignified' element in the constitution, in the sense that the real decisions are rarely taken there, unless the Prime Minister deliberately chooses to give the appearance of letting Cabinet decide a matter. I was also right to recognize the importance of Cabinet Committees. I am a permanent member of two, the Home Affairs Committee and the Economic Development Committee. In addition, I attend the Immigration Committee and the Broadcasting

---

[1] M.P. for Durham 1922–31 and 1935–56, and a Labour Chief Whip between 1942 and 1951.
[2] Sir Charles Harris was Private Secretary to successive Chief Whips from 1919 to 1961.
[3] Fellow of Nuffield College, Oxford. Psephologist, and author of *Political Change in Britain* (London: Macmillan, 1969) and studies of successive British general elections.

Committee as well as the Legislation Committee. But I am not a member of the Social Services Committee.* Nor, of course, am I a member of the two really important Committees, on Defence and Foreign Affairs. From these I am totally excluded. So I am very much a home-front Cabinet Minister.

The really big thing I completely failed to notice when I wrote that Introduction was that, in addition to the Cabinet Committees which only Ministers normally attend, there is a full network of official committees; and the work of the Ministers is therefore strictly and completely paralleled at the official level. This means that very often the whole job is pre-cooked in the official committee to a point from which it is extremely difficult to reach any other conclusion than that already determined by the officials in advance; and if agreement is reached at the lower level of a Cabinet Committee, only formal approval is needed from the full Cabinet. This is the way in which Whitehall ensures that the Cabinet system is relatively harmless.

Another big surprise was the discovery that Cabinet minutes are a travesty, or to be more accurate, do not pretend to be an account of what actually takes place in the Cabinet. The same applies to the minutes of Cabinet Committees. Normally, what they record is not what was actually said but a summary of the official brief which the Minister brought with him, the official papers on the original policy, and the official conclusions. The minutes never describe the real struggle which took place. That struggle is only abstracted in the form of 'in the course of discussion the following points were made ...'. And in this summary the name of the Minister who made the point is rarely mentioned.

The combination of this kind of Cabinet minute (which provides the main directive for Whitehall) and official committees enormously strengthens the Civil Service against the politicians. Here are three examples of this system working.

1. We have been busy for some time in my Ministry trying to work out the best method, either fiscal or physical, of controlling the total volume of housing, including private-enterprise housing. All this work has been done following discussions at E.D.C. and in Cabinet, and the responsibility has been taken over by the official committee. In fact, this started when Harold Wilson, in Cabinet, backed my increased housing programme but only won his point by saying that we must look at physical controls in order to manage the total. The moment he said this the whole of Whitehall alerted itself, and an official committee began to work on a paper dealing with physical controls. This paper was then presented to the E.D.C. as an 'official' paper. It was a very odd paper, because though it theoretically came down in favour of physical controls the case was never made out; and Charlie Pannell was able to blow it sky-high with the simple observation that we can't anyway have physical controls for eighteen months because they require legislation.

* I was made a member shortly afterwards.

So the whole idea of relying on physical controls before the election was a pipe dream. The lesson of this story is, first, that whatever a Prime Minister says goes in Whitehall, in the sense that if he proclaims himself in favour of something, Whitehall will do its best to make sense of the proposition; and second, that whatever we say as Ministers, or even as Prime Minister, the actual work will be done by the officials.

2. This example relates to local government finance. I think I have recorded already that, much to my regret, I am having Sir Bruce Fraser to replace Dame Evelyn in the autumn, and as a method of appeasing me I was told that he would spend the intervening months in the Treasury doing the initial spade-work on the reform of local taxation, i.e. rates. I had him to dinner along with MacColl the other day, and we had quite a pleasant evening during which he told me his view, which turned out to be wholly negative. He saw no chance of any additional local taxes and he ruled out any prospect of a local income tax as well. 'I'll be putting up a paper,' he said, and I replied, 'Well, for heaven's sake, show it to me first.' But I soon discovered that the paper had been prepared in the Treasury weeks ago and had been seen by the Chancellor and I think by the Prime Minister, but not by me, the Minister most vitally concerned. So the official paper is now in circulation in Whitehall, and unless I am extremely strong-minded it will have pre-judged the whole issue of local government finance to a point where I shall find it impossible to resist.

3. Another very obvious example of how official committees work has been in something I have been watching over the past two months: the development of the Land Commission Bill. Of course, this is an appallingly difficult measure on which poor Fred Willey has been spending nearly all his time. Whenever we have had a disagreement in the Cabinet Committee, the matter has been referred to the official committee. In due course they produce a solution in a six- or seven-page paper which we Ministers then discuss. Naturally, a solution hammered out by the officials is extremely difficult to overturn.

One surprising effect of these official committees is that still greater influence is given to the Treasury. Why? Because the kind of official who sits on these committees is either the Permanent Secretary himself or the Assistant Secretary in charge. When they all get together, though they dispute with each other, they try as far as possible to even out their disputes and then to produce a coherent Whitehall view. And a coherent Whitehall view is nearly always a view dominated by Treasury thinking.

So what this comes to is that there are two ways in which officialdom impresses its views on Ministers. The first pressure comes from inside the Department where the officials try to make one see things in a departmental way. Ministers tend to have *only* a departmental briefing. The second pressure is inter-departmental, coming when the official committee brings its inter-departmental cohesive view to bear on the Ministers in a single official policy paper. I have yet to see a Minister prevail against an inter-departmental official paper without the backing of the Prime Minister, the First Secretary or the Chancellor. And this is where one's relationships with the P.M. are so all-important. If one doesn't have his backing, or at least the Chancellor's or First Secretary's, the chance of winning against the official view is absolutely nil.

But though Cabinet Ministers have this enormous limitation on their power of decision-taking, still their standing is infinitely superior compared with that of the non-Cabinet Minister. The unfortunate Tony Wedgwood Benn as Postmaster-General, Kenneth Robinson as Minister of Health and Peggy Herbison as Minister of Pensions have a far more difficult time than we do. And I am sure they find it much more difficult to impose their views on their civil servants. Because though the discussions of the Cabinet Committees and Cabinet very often don't have much reality and are simply rehearsing departmental points of view, nevertheless we Cabinet Ministers do have status within Whitehall, in Parliament and in the nation at large. A Cabinet Minister counts for something and a leading Cabinet Minister can certainly get his way far more easily than a non-Cabinet Minister, both in his own Department and of course in the Cabinet.[1]

Having looked at the constraints on Cabinet's power, I want to try and reflect upon its function. Of course, it isn't a coherent, effective, policy-making body: it's a collection of departmental Ministers who are in practice divided into groups, and with all of whom Harold Wilson maintains bilateral relations. Most important of all, there is the defence and foreign policy group, from which I and over half the Cabinet are totally excluded. Secondly, there is the economic planning group, which consists of the Prime Minister, Brown and Callaghan and whoever they like to call in—pretty often Douglas Jay, occasionally me, occasionally Frank Cousins. Then there are certain segments of home policy, such as the housing segment which I run as overlord with two Ministers under me, Charlie Pannell at the Ministry of Works and Willey at the Ministry of Land and Natural Resources. Quite separate from us is Douglas Houghton's social security segment and of course, equally separate and quite in a corner, agriculture under Fred Peart. All these segments are given a very free hand provided they run smoothly. For example the P.M. has only called one Cabinet Committee meeting in No. 10 to look at housing since he became P.M.

As for the Cabinet agenda, Harold Wilson is keeping to the rule that we should only discuss things in Cabinet which we can't resolve in a Cabinet Committee or which the Prime Minister thinks so important that we must make our individual decisions upon them. In fact, there is nothing decided at Cabinet unless the P.M. specifically wants to have it discussed there.

It looks to me as though this P.M. very much likes fixing things up privately

---

[1] Crossman discussed these ideas in his Godkin lectures, given at Harvard University in 1970. They are published as *Inside View* (London: Cape, 1972).

with Ministers by bilateral discussions if he possibly can. On the other hand, he is extremely conventional in his desire to make the Cabinet system work in the traditional way. He is equally conventional with regard to legislation. We prepare our Bills in our Departments; then if they are major Bills we submit them to special committees of Ministers with parallel special committees of officials; and then there comes out a White Paper which is discussed line by line by the Cabinet. After that, the Bill is got ready and presented to Legislation Committee, presided over by the Lord President or the Lord Chancellor, and Legislation Committee is supposed to go through the Bill in detail before it goes to the House.

I give that description because my Rent Bill has gone through this process and I have been able to see how effective it is. If the Prime Minister is on your side, you can get your Bill right through with the minimum of bother from your colleagues. No serious effort was made to change my Bill in any important particular at any stage. The same was true of the Steel Bill. We did have a couple of discussions at Cabinet but not of the contents of the Bill; and when the White Paper came up to Cabinet I was one of the few who made suggestions. But they were entirely about the presentation of the Paper, and no policy issue was raised by anyone at all. As far as I can remember there are only two Bills which have been substantially changed in Cabinet—the Land Commission Bill and the ombudsman Bill.[1] In the former case the issue had to come to Cabinet because there was a disagreement between Fred Willey, who is in charge of the Bill, and me, his overlord. As for the ombudsman, this we did discuss at great length only last week in Cabinet. There were two reasons for this. In the first place, Harold Wilson was in bed with flu; and in the second place, the Lord Chancellor, who is sponsoring the Bill, is very weak. He had had great difficulty with his Law Commission Bill, though it was an excellent proposal. Now he is having difficulty with his ombudsman Bill, not because Cabinet didn't like it but because he is so ineffective.

The other big issue brought up to Cabinet was my housing programme. The reason it came to Cabinet was of course because there was a disagreement between the Chancellor and myself. I got the policy through as a result of the firm support of the P.M. and an alliance with George Brown. But even so we had some difficulty, because all the other departmental Ministers resented seeing Housing get more money at the cost of their own budgets. That is why Barbara Castle is against me, for instance.

I think I have listed the main decisions which were the result of genuine collective Cabinet action. Harold Wilson, at the centre of things, has certainly allowed some of us a great deal of Ministerial freedom in forging our own departmental policies. Nevertheless, I would say that he has completely dominated foreign affairs and defence, as well as all the main economic

[1] The measure establishing a Parliamentary Commissioner to examine complaints of maladministration by the Civil Service.

decisions. Here the Cabinet has been excluded and the P.M. has played the formative role by arbitrating the struggle between George Brown and Callaghan.

However, even in the areas in which he runs his Prime Ministerial government a few formal occasions have been interspersed on which he has chosen to have a demonstration of Cabinet government in action. On these occasions he hasn't 'taken the voices'. He has added up the opinions and listed them on a piece of paper. Indeed, I have seen him take pleasure in getting a tie and then forcing us to resolve a closely fought-out decision by a personal vote from each of us.

Let me try to rate the Cabinet Ministers in terms of the power we wield. Well, there's the Prime Minister: not *primus inter pares* – not at all. He is Prime Ministerial in his supreme authority. Below him there is a contest between Jim Callaghan and George Brown. Of course George has emerged as complete king in incomes policy and he has run it on his own, brilliantly successfully. But although he counts for a lot, I should say that in the Whitehall struggle the views of Jim Callaghan have prevailed and the views of George Brown have not. The planning of economic policy, which was supposed to be Brown's essential contribution, has hardly started in the D.E.A. – what planning there is is still basically done in the Treasury. It is the economists and officials there who have had all the influence, not those who were taken out of the Treasury and put on Brown's staff at the D.E.A. So we have the P.M. and the Chancellor counting a great deal.

Who else counts? I suppose the Minister of Defence could count. But it is my impression that at present the only man who has come out on the defence side with a will and a mind of his own is Roy Jenkins at Aviation. I have said that non-Cabinet Ministers don't matter, and certainly they don't elsewhere. But Roy Jenkins is an example of a non-Cabinet Minister who has steadily raised his status. Roy refused the offer of the job of Secretary of State for Education and let Tony Crosland have it – at least he says so. Certainly, he has made his mark at Aviation; so that if George Brown falls he might quite likely become head of the D.E.A. But he has been able to play this role because Denis Healey has not been dominant in Defence but has let it be run for him by the P.M. and George Wigg.

As for foreign affairs, I suspect that under Michael Stewart, even more than under Patrick Gordon Walker, the Prime Minister has been the prevailing, dominant personality.

What about the social services, where Douglas Houghton is the overlord in the Cabinet, with Peggy Herbison and Kenneth Robinson working underneath him as non-Cabinet Ministers? Well, Douglas is certainly respected in Cabinet. He is an eminent trade unionist and an important man and he has been put in charge of the agricultural price review, with Fred Peart below him. So he is a top-ranking Minister in that sense. I don't find him very impressive, and certainly he is a dreadful chairman. Nevertheless, he's made clear to the rest of the Cabinet that he is very much in charge of Peggy and Kenneth, and we have let him implement our social security policy in a way which seems to me to have destroyed the whole of our strategy. But if I were to say so in Cabinet I should come into direct conflict with a personality strong in his own right. Indeed, I suppose in Cabinet he and I are about level in power.

Who else really matters? On the Commonwealth side there are three Ministers, Barbara Castle, Arthur Bottomley and Tony Greenwood; and the last two are mere henchmen of the P.M. Barbara talks a great deal in Cabinet about other things than her own small Department. She doesn't yet cut any ice, but she will. I have talked already about the ineffectiveness of poor Frank Soskice at the Home Office. At Education Tony Crosland is now much more confident than he seemed likely to be a few weeks ago, and is emerging in Cabinet as a man with something important to contribute on the economic side.

Of course, one must not forget the people who have no power, for example Fred Lee and Tom Fraser, the Minister of Transport. Fraser's pretty disastrous. He is the only Minister I have actually seen reversed in a Cabinet Committee. A few weeks ago, on his Department's advice, he came forward at a Committee meeting and said he didn't want the railway workshops given the right to compete for orders outside. Here was a gratuitous violation of a socialist pledge which the Committee couldn't stomach. So the E.D.C. ordered the Minister to change his mind, and change it he did.

I have left Frank Cousins to the last because he's a real mystery man still. He sounds like a terrible old blatherer, talking on every subject and usually saying the obvious thing. But he does say it in a working-class way and that's important, because nobody else talks in that way in this Cabinet and we ought to be reminded of what sensible people think in the Labour movement. This he reflects very faithfully, and he also displays every now and then the kind of expertise which the General Secretary of the T.G.W.U. should show on a subject such as the docks. What kind of a new Ministry he is building in Vickers House on the Embankment I have no idea. All I know is that he is occupying more and more floors and getting tremendous backing from Harold Wilson, who believes passionately that his new Ministry of Technology has got to succeed if he is going to keep his promise to modernize British industry. And of course there is one other thing to say about Frank: he is the only trade-union leader introduced by Harold Wilson into his Cabinet. As such he exerts at minimum a very powerful veto.

Monday, April 26th
My first appointment [on getting back to London after the Easter Recess] was a talk with the Prime Minister about our policy in the home loans debate. I found him, as he always is, very anxious to discuss the general political situation. I finally got round to airing my ideas on differential interest

rates—my main ministerial preoccupation at present. I have got to work out a way of implementing the Party manifesto which promised to give reduced interest rates to the owner-occupier and to the local authority which builds houses. I explained the outline of my idea to the P.M.—a 4 per cent interest rate for house building right across the board, valid for the owner-occupier, valid for the local authority as well. Then he turned to discuss the first censure debate and said that he thought James Callaghan ought to wind up. I said that would be a jolly good idea if Mr Callaghan was really prepared to do it.

Tuesday, April 27th
I should have gone to the Rent Bill Committee, but Jim MacColl is perfectly all right and so I was able to go to Cabinet instead. There the Prime Minister started by saying that he thought I should open the censure debate on home loans for the Government and Callaghan should wind up. Callaghan, as I expected, neatly opted out. He thought he should leave it to me as a pure local government subject. I had to accept that. With an effort I got some kind of authority for telling the House that we would have to have a national plan for integrating housing in the private sector and the public sector. The Cabinet obviously realize that I was in for a bad day on Thursday and when one of us is in for a bad day he doesn't get much sympathy. I was certainly aware that Callaghan was opting out of speaking because at present his image is jolly good, as a result of his budget success, and he doesn't want it tarnished by coming to my help. But it is only a half-day's debate and it has been agreed that Jack Diamond should give what kind of reply is necessary at the end.

Thursday, April 29th
I woke up at six in the morning with an idea for the end of the speech. Why not broach the notion of a national building plan? This is an idea I have aired with the builders and with the building societies and I have had some degree of positive response. I decided to use it for the peroration. All the morning I worked away. Yet when I had made my speech I realized I hadn't pulled it off, mainly because I had failed to attack hard enough. I had made a reasoned, sensible explanation of the situation, followed by a cautious suggestion as to how one might tackle the problem. As a reply to a ferocious vote of censure I am afraid it sounded flat—decent, laborious, but a gimmick thought up at the last moment to get me out of the difficulty. What's more important—in the long run—I had chosen the wrong atmosphere in which to launch my new idea. I hope I haven't kiboshed it altogether.

It doesn't take long in the Commons to realize that a speech hasn't been a success. Today none of my colleagues were there to sit by me and sustain me. When I sat down it was clear enough that I had flopped. Our own people had felt embarrassed and unhappy, precisely because they thought highly of me and were expecting a hard-hitting, confident attack on the Tories. What they got was a diffident, unsure speech, not at all what the situation demanded.

I don't think I have ruined my personal position but it has been a set-back. My friends have felt sorry and said, 'Dick's up against it.' As for my colleagues in Cabinet, their sympathy has been tinged with the malicious thought, 'Well, there's that confident bugger and he has not done all that well.'

Wednesday, May 5th

I went across to the House of Commons to hear the end of the P.L.P. meeting on steel, held as a run-up for tomorrow's debate. I got there in time to hear Desmond Donnelly[1] making a very careful, cagey speech before Harold Wilson wound up. His speech was a combination of (a) a piece about steel, (b) a piece about the second Hundred Days, and (c) a peroration in which he emphasized to the Party the danger of being dictated to by minorities, and said that rather than let that happen, whether it was a steel minority, or a pacifist minority or any other minority, he would tell them to go to blazes. Though I found the rest of the speech, particularly on foreign policy, fairly nauseating—especially the assertion that Britain holds the initiative all over the world—I was relieved to listen to the assurance in the last passage that, whatever happened, the steel minorities, such as Desmond Donnelly and Woodrow Wyatt,[2] would be kept in their place.

Now for my rating debate. I was glad that I had given the opening to Bob Mellish: he made a very characteristic speech, good knock-about stuff, although he had received the same brief as I had. Bob has become a stalwart lieutenant. He is a very rough diamond, a working-class chap from Bermondsey, a T.G.W.U. organizer at one time, an officer in a transport unit during the war, and a real professional politician today. He's a bit crude, a bit slippery, a bit vulgar-minded and very much the supporter of whoever is his boss at the moment. Let me say, however, that, despite hating me before, he has become extremely loyal; and that afternoon he did as well as he possibly could. As for my own winding-up speech at the end, if I won the debate it was because I had to fight for my life, and by means of a conscious rhetorically- and demagogically-forced row with the Opposition I won back both their respect and my popularity among my own Party.

These two censure debates have made me realize that for the first time I really have been up against it, struggling for my political existence. And I recognize for the first time that if the pack gets me down and undermines my self-confidence it could be very difficult to regain that confidence and restore my position.

[1] M.P. for Pembroke 1950–70. He left the Labour Party in 1968 and died in 1974.

[2] According to Wilson, George Brown had 'sweated blood with Donnelly', and he himself had found Wyatt extremely persuasive; see *Wilson*, pp. 100–101. Wyatt lost his seat at Bosworth in the 1970 election and later published a book entitled *What's Left of the Labour Party?* (London: Sidgwick & Jackson, 1977).

Thursday, May 6th

Convinced by Harold's speech to the Party that there wasn't going to be a big Cabinet crisis I allowed myself all day for departmental worries. In the evening I gave dinner to Richard Llewelyn-Davies[1] in order to discuss my research advisory group. After dinner we went in to the House for the end of the steel debate. There wasn't all that much of a crowd in the Chamber. He went up to the gallery to watch and I went down below and was sitting there quietly listening to George Brown's wind-up. I was not apprehensive, having heard Harold Wilson's categoric assurance to the Party meeting. True, I remembered that he had said to me in private conversation that, yes, he had had three or four talks with Woodrow on his idea that a 51 per cent shareholding was a sufficient degree of Government control to exert over the steel industry. But I hadn't taken this too seriously. So when I heard George Brown at the end of his proper speech give himself an extra five minutes in order to address a special message to Woodrow Wyatt and Desmond Donnelly, I was flabbergasted.[2]

Friday, May 7th

At breakfast I rang up George Wigg as I very often do and asked him what the hell was going on. 'Look, George,' I said, 'the P.M. had better know that he and the First Secretary can't get away with this kind of behaviour. It undermines the whole basis of unity in Cabinet.' George Wigg bit my head off. 'Don't be so silly,' he said. 'Harold was consulted by George Brown just afterwards and I have talked to him since. He thinks that good can come out of what happened.' That was characteristic George Wigg. Whenever you take your own line he tries to swamp you.

Monday, May 10th

We set out for the station nine minutes before the train was due and had a terrible rush on an exquisite early summer morning through the back lanes to get there on time. Once safely on the train, I looked at my engagement list and found that by good fortune I had an interview with the Prime Minister at 10.30, half an hour after the train got into Paddington, at which we were due to discuss parliamentary boundaries. Instead of letting him quiz me on boundaries, I had to tell him that at all costs we must have a Cabinet meeting on the steel crisis before the Party meeting on Wednesday. Directly I got to my office I saw Delafons and said, 'Well I shall be seeing the Prime Minister in half an hour.' And he replied, 'It's been cancelled already.' When I heard

[1] Professor of Architecture at University College, London 1960–64. He had been made a life peer in 1963.

[2] At the very end of the debate Wyatt asked the First Secretary, 'If the industry will come forward, [is he] prepared to listen?' George Brown replied, ' "Listen" is the word. Listen, certainly.' The Government survived narrowly with 310 votes to 306. The Prime Minister's view of this was that '[George] appeared to incline more to their views than anyone expected.' See *Wilson*, p. 101.

this I didn't quite know what to do so I sat down at my desk and finally took the phone and rang Frank Cousins. He sits almost opposite me at the Cabinet table and though I don't see much of him I feel we have a good deal of natural sympathy. When he heard I would like to see him, he was obviously glad. So I said I would come round straight away. Then I rang George Wigg and left a message at his office that my meeting with the Prime Minister had been cancelled and I wanted it restored.

I found Frank Cousins full of himself. He told me that he had been thinking of resigning for some time owing to his dissatisfaction with his job. He also revealed that he had spent Sunday evening with Mikardo and a number of other left-wing socialists and that his view, like theirs, was that the whole issue must be settled at the Party meeting. I said I thought this was a great mistake: it was a matter for Cabinet decision and we two ought to requisition a Cabinet on Tuesday morning. Would he support me in that? He said he would. That was about all I could do before George Wigg came through on the phone and began a long explanation to Frank Cousins, assuring him how everything was in order. When Frank told him I was sitting there beside him, George said he had arranged that I should see the Prime Minister after all at 11. So back I sped to Downing Street pretty pleased that my cancelled meeting had been put back on the agenda so quickly.

I found Harold sitting in the Cabinet room. He at once said he had to be careful that officially he was only seeing me about housing; he also explained why he couldn't keep his appointment with me at 10.30—it would have been thought that he was discussing George Brown with me. I said we could certainly discuss housing and I began to talk a little about the Department's new interest-rate policy, but Harold soon switched to George and the steel crisis. I said straight away that the essential thing was to call a Cabinet on Tuesday and then to get the backing of the Party meeting on Wednesday morning. He replied that he intended to hold a Lobby conference that day in which he would explain how George Brown had done it all entirely on his own and how he himself had had nothing to do with it. I said this couldn't be more unfortunate for his own image. The press was already implying that he was backing out of his responsibilities, and an off-the-record conference of this sort might give them an excuse for saying that the Prime Minister was leaving the First Secretary in the lurch. At one point he asked me, 'Do you think I should be left alone to bear the brunt of this?' 'No,' I said, 'I think it is our job in Cabinet to back you up. The moment you bring us together tomorrow, Cabinet will realize that it can't jettison George. We must agree to support what he said and allow him to waste his time listening to the steel magnates. Having given him public support, however, we can trounce him in private about his unfortunate performance.'

We discussed this round and round for some time until a message was brought in that Callaghan and others were waiting to see Harold. At once I went out and mentioned to Callaghan in passing that I had been having a discussion about housing (sure enough in the morning papers next day there was a statement, released presumably from Downing Street, that the Prime Minister had spent a long time discussing the urgent problems of housing loans). I went straight up to George Wigg's room and told him what had happened. George Wigg blew up. 'Who are you to say there is anything wrong with the George Brown line?' he shouted at me. I said it was outrageous that George Brown should take this line with Donnelly and Wyatt just after the Prime Minister had assured us in the Parliamentary Party meeting that he would send all minorities to blazes. 'That's your view, is it?' said Wigg suddenly. 'Well in that case we are fighting each other and that's the end of it.' I began to realize that in this episode George and I were giving opposite advice. Wigg's advice was that George Brown had done nothing very much wrong and that the thing to do was to brazen it out throughout the week and not to have a Cabinet meeting. I was saying that it was essential to have a Cabinet on Tuesday. During the day I was interested to wait and see which of us would win. In the afternoon Barbara Castle came to me about a planning permission for development in central Blackburn. I told her about my talk with Frank Cousins and asked her whether she would support me in requisitioning a Tuesday Cabinet meeting. She said she would. A little later John Delafons came in to tell me that a Cabinet meeting had been called for Tuesday morning at 11.

Tuesday, May 11th
The Cabinet meeting meant that I was only able to look in at the Committee Stage of my Rent Bill; I have been neglecting it a good deal. Harold started with a longish, rambling account, and was followed by a very attractive apologia from George Brown which included the frank admission that he should have informed the Minister, Fred Lee, before he made his Statement. At this, Harold signalled to me and I weighed in, making a full statement with three points. I said first that what we had to decide was whether to jettison George Brown or whether to support him. There couldn't be any half measures. We must either unreservedly accept that we were bound by his offer to listen to the steel magnates or throw him overboard. I personally had no doubt that we must accept what he said as said on our behalf. My second point was that, although I held this view, I also thought that he had done something very unwise because it was in complete contradiction to the Prime Minister's assurances to the Parliamentary Party. It was this, I emphasized, which had undermined the morale of the Party. Finally, I concluded that it seemed to me essential that, when Cabinet had decided its line, the Prime Minister should go to the Party meeting on Wednesday morning and make a statement, but—and here I corrected Harold Wilson—he shouldn't just make a statement; he should subject himself to questioning, because the Party must feel that they have the right to be consulted.

I was pleased when Thomas Balogh rang me up in the evening to congratulate me on a speech which Harold Wilson had described to him in a most enthusiastic way. Apparently he felt the Cabinet meeting had been a success, and I felt so too.

I had a long and hectic afternoon in the Ministry. Then I had to rush off to London University to debate a motion on racial discrimination with Iain Macleod. It is always a bit of a risk speaking off one's subject when one is a Minister, and I had tried to prepare this speech adequately in the intervals of a long series of meetings. I had asked Iain Macleod to pick me up at the Ministry so that I could take him up to Gower Street in the ministerial car because I didn't want to go and dine with the young men at five thirty. So at six o'clock he came in while I was changing into my dinner-jacket. I gave him a drink and I took up my speech notes from the desk. It was only when I was sitting in my place at the debate that I noticed that by mistake I had picked up not only the speech notes and Hansard but some sheets of Cabinet background papers on race relations. The debate itself, a motion of no confidence on the Labour Party's policy on racialism, went pretty well and I managed to win by two to one. Then I took Iain Macleod back to his flat in St James's Street. I had been interested to meet him for the first time since we had come to power, and I told him how much I enjoyed being a Minister. 'Of course you do,' he said. 'Being a Minister is the only thing worth doing in the whole world.' I said I wouldn't go so far as that but it was enjoyable. 'Of course,' said Iain again, 'you and I are politicians. A Minister's life is the only thing in the world worth having.' I realized that he meant it.

I was going to ask Molly to drive me home when I realized I was hungry – I hadn't eaten since lunch-time. Since it was now eleven o'clock and I was in St James's Street, I went to Prunier, where Anne and I always celebrate her birthday. There I found myself sitting next to four people who I thought to be hunting people – silly, stuck-up, well-dressed and slightly bibulous. I felt uneasy sitting beside them and I put my little sheaf of Cabinet papers below my feet and pretended to read my Hansard while I ate my supper slightly sanctimoniously. Then I went out and walked home across the park.

Wednesday, May 12th
This was the morning of the Party meeting, and I went across at eleven to hear Harold Wilson make his speech. He was given his success on a plate by William Warbey,[1] who with a single question turned the ire of the whole Party against *himself* and took the heat off Harold. By the end of the meeting I knew that the tactics I had advised had worked to perfection. The steel crisis was over.

In the afternoon we had the first afternoon session of the Rent Bill Committee. Despite a great deal of Tory fuss I had in the previous week

[1] M.P. for Broxtowe (Nottinghamshire) 1953–5 and Ashfield (Nottinghamshire) from 1955 until his resignation in 1966.

4 With his wife and two
children, Virginia and Patrick,
at Prescote, their home
in Oxfordshire.

5 Inspecting local authority
housing at Romsey.

6 At Cropredy country fête with John Betjeman and Neil Marten, M.P. for Banbury.

7 At Prescote with Patrick and Virginia.

carried the motion extending the number of sessions of the Committee from two to three, the third to be fitted in on Wednesdays at four o'clock. As I sat through this first meeting I was puzzled by a series of messages that I must talk urgently to my Private Secretary. I was in the middle of addressing the Committee on one of the amendments when another message came through that Cabinet papers were missing. Slowly it dawned on me that I had left at Prunier the sheets I had snatched up to take with me to the debate with Iain Macleod.

At six forty-five, when I moved the adjournment of the Committee and went out into the corridor, I was told that I had to go back to my office and wait for an urgent appointment with the Prime Minister, who was then broadcasting a party political—a last-minute appeal before Thursday's municipal elections. However, I said I didn't see why I couldn't go home and see my dear Anne while I was waiting for him. This was the evening when we had decided to accept an invitation to see an American play at the World Theatre season at the Aldwych. We don't often go to the theatre but on this occasion we had been invited by the American Ambassador to a party at the Embassy to meet the cast. When I got home I told Anne about the extraordinary *contretemps* and what I now realized had happened at Prunier. It wasn't long before a message came from George Wigg that I must go and see him immediately. When I arrived, he was all seriousness. He explained to me that nothing could be more inconvenient for the Prime Minister and him than that I should be guilty of a lapse of security. On the previous Monday the Prime Minister had, in order to get a diversion from the steel crisis, announced new security regulations for which George Wigg would be the chief co-ordinator. I then told George exactly what had happened. He looked very grave and said I must wait and see the Prime Minister.

In due course he went down, and I sat on alone in his room. After twenty minutes Derek Mitchell, the Prime Minister's Private Secretary, came and said, 'Come and see him. I don't think it's very serious.' As he went into No. 10 through the back door from George's office I saw the P.M. disappear into the lift. The lift was halted and I just caught it. He laughed when he saw me, saying he had heard from George Wigg what had happened and he would be delighted to answer any questions the Tories liked to put. 'I am in a great state of euphoria,' he said to me. 'I have just given the finest party political broadcast in history. I have really trounced the Tories. As for you, well, thank heavens you weren't dining with Christine Keeler. There's nothing in it, my dear boy, you can go away happy.' So I went to the theatre and on from there to the American Embassy, where there was a vast crowd queueing for food. Anne and I went home to have some there. We had scarcely got to Vincent Square, at about twelve o'clock, when the telephone began to ring. By then the first editions had come out: and Chapman Pincher had a story in the *Express* that had impacted on the rest of Fleet Street. Each of them wanted to write a story of their own for their second editions.

I said nothing to any of them except the man from *The Times*. To him I revealed the key fact that I had been debating with Iain Macleod and that the papers referred to race and had nothing secret in them.

Thursday, May 13th

I woke up this morning to find that Chapman Pincher had written a piece about how someone had informed against me. Apparently this fellow had spotted the papers under my chair, and had taken them home, kept them until twelve o'clock next day and then handed them over to the police. But before doing so he had shown them to the *Daily Express*. Nothing more unpleasant could have happened.

Apart from my own personal Prunier crisis, I had a busy day finalizing my home loans policy for circulation to Cabinet and getting on with my coastline policy. I also had my Rent Bill Committee. Frankly, I hardly had time to register the fact that it was polling day in the municipal elections.

Saturday, May 15th

I wasn't too surprised when I got into my bath on Friday morning to read that we had lost between three hundred and four hundred seats. These times are difficult for a Minister. I had a press conference arranged for eleven that morning and the last thing I wanted to talk about was the municipal election results. Mistakenly, I did find myself talking about them, and, even more mistakenly, I decided to tell people what had really happened at Prunier earlier in the week. I don't know why I did this. Anyway, this morning that story was vying with the municipal election disaster in filling the news columns.

Sunday, May 16th

I have had time to reflect and recover from the shock of the municipal elections. Although I anticipated the total of the losses, somehow when some of the losses happen to you it feels much worse. Birmingham, twelve seats lost; Coventry, four seats lost—this is tremendously serious. No doubt, as seen by the outside world, the effect of municipals will be to knock out a summer election. But that's a fallacy since a summer election was out long before this catastrophe: Harold Wilson clearly prefers spring. No! what this municipal defeat did was to emphasize the precarious situation of the Government. If two of our people die, that could destroy our majority. In the last division we had poor Hayman, the M.P. for Falmouth, ill,[1] and Leslie Spriggs lying in an oxygen tent in an ambulance in Speaker's Yard.[2] We are terribly near the edge of the abyss and it is my impression that if things are at

[1] Frank Hayman, Gaitskell's former P.P.S., had been M.P. for Falmouth since 1950, and was now aged seventy-one. He died in February 1966.

[2] M.P. for St Helens since 1958. He survived the experience.

all favourable we shall seize an opportunity in October, having ended the Session in July.

Tuesday, May 18th
In the afternoon Harold Wilson insisted on taking Questions about my affair at Prunier even though it involved his making a special Statement at the end of Question Time. He really lambasted the Tories and pointed out that an 'officer and a gentleman' really wasn't behaving in a very officerly or gentlemanly way in handing secret papers over to the *Daily Express*. None of the front-bench Tories took any part in the affair. Indeed, some of them were extremely embarrassed and came up to me afterwards to say that this was a case where a personal incident which could have been disastrous was being transformed by Tory mismanagement to their disadvantage. As we walked out of the Chamber Harold said to me, 'Well, I had the pleasure of rehabilitating you and George Wigg simultaneously.' Indeed, George has been in bad odour recently with the press and also with the Parliamentary Party. The Prime Minister had replied by contrasting his treatment of security with that of the 'officer and gentleman' in question.

Monday, May 24th
A meeting of the Cabinet Committee on Broadcasting. Tony Wedgwood Benn put up an elaborate paper in which he proposed to get a firm commitment that the B.B.C. should finance its expanding programme partly by advertising, while on the other hand we should introduce legislation to ban Radio Caroline, the pirate pop-radio station. I was decisively against him on Radio Caroline because I didn't see any point in losing the votes of young people before the B.B.C. had any real alternative to it. As for B.B.C. advertising, I am for it in principle but I am not at all convinced that it is a wise thing to propose just now. If we tried to persuade the Party to commit itself in advance on this issue, we should split it wide open. What we ought to do is have a severe investigation of the B.B.C. without commitment on Government policy.

I like Tony Benn a great deal and I had every hope of him when Harold appointed him Postmaster-General. It's a queer thing but I am not very happy about him now I see him at work. To begin with, on every single occasion when he is about to bring a plan to Cabinet a leak occurs giving the full details in advance. In the second place, there is an odd hardness about him which makes him sometimes unattractive as a colleague. He has certainly got himself detested by the Tories—though that's nothing against him—but even among us in Cabinet he doesn't inspire conviction, partly because, although I doubt whether he is a believer, he has at times a kind of mechanical Nonconformist self-righteousness about him which seems to come out even more strongly in office. I was terribly keen at first that he should be Minister of Transport, but I am not so sure that he will get his promotion when we move into the next stage of this Government. He may have to wait and to learn.

Wednesday, May 26th
I had left lunch-time free but was suddenly told the Prime Minister wanted me to lunch with him in No. 10. I found him sitting in the room down below. We had a glass of sherry with Marcia and then he took me upstairs in the lift to the flat above the official reception-rooms on the first floor. There I found in a little sitting-room a couple of dirty plates with bread and butter on them and a glass half full of milk. Obviously Mary Wilson had had her lunch before rushing out. We had another glass of sherry there before moving into a little dining-room where an Irish maid slammed down in front of me a plate with a piece of steak, two veg and a bit of cold salad. On the table were two tins of Skol beer, which I don't like. Harold saw this and while he took water gave me a glass of claret. After lunch we went along to his little sitting-room and there he offered me a glass of brandy which he likes very much. I refused the brandy and accepted a second glass of claret.

Nothing could be more deeply *petit bourgeois* than the way he lives in those crowded little servants' quarters up there. But the fact that he doesn't, unlike Sir Alec Douglas-Home, use the state rooms for sitting in after dinner is only a proof that he is not corrupted by his new station in life. No. 10 doesn't change him, he changes it so that its rooms look exactly like the rooms in his Hampstead house. Harold's strength is that he has no kind of inferiority complex but lives his own real, natural life. He doesn't respect the upper classes for having superior cultural tastes which he would like to share.

He had got me there to tell me his plans about housing. He has decided that all other social services must be cut back in order to have a magnificent housing drive and bring the annual production of houses up to 500,000 by 1970. 'This is it,' he said. 'We'll make housing the most popular single thing this Government does. We won't build another single mile of road if a cut-back is necessary in order to get that half-million houses a year. That's what I believe in,' he said. 'I have already had the Chancellor here and written him a paper and talked about it. He knows perfectly well now that this is what we have got to persuade Cabinet to accept.' When he had finished I found myself complaining to him about the irrelevance of the Finance Bill. 'Oh no,' he said, 'the Finance Bill is very useful. It fills in time. We have got five weeks ahead of us to deal with the Committee Stage of the Finance Bill and we shall hold out successfully. That's the point. To fill in time and to win.' It struck me as an odd description of the Bill which has been causing alarm and despondency in the City, but of course there is always something in the tactical arguments Harold Wilson puts up. If the Government can survive these five weeks despite a majority of three, and complete the Committee Stage on the Floor of the House, it will be a crushing defeat for the Opposition and a strengthening of our authority.

I found him throughout this meal extremely friendly and forthcoming. So, venturing very greatly, I finally said, 'Well, if housing is going to be all that important I really can't accept Bruce Fraser as a replacement for the Dame.' I summoned up the courage to tell him this because the more I look at the Department, the more I realize, and so does the Dame, that the arrival of Bruce Fraser is going to be a crushing blow—particularly since neither of the Deputies can stand up to a powerful figure. I said all this to Harold and then added, 'If you want the Department really to work you can't give us a Treasury man instead of the Dame. I want the Dame for another year.' This was an idea which came into my head quite suddenly when Charlie Pannell suggested I might have a great farewell dinner for her at Lancaster House and I found she hated the idea. So I had been preparing a little dinner for her with her ex-Ministers and now, thank heavens, there was a chance of her carrying on if only the P.M. would agree.

Thursday, May 27th
The Dame told me that my lunch with the Prime Minister had worked like magic. Helsby had sent for her and told her what the Prime Minister had said I wanted and asked her whether she would stay on and, as he put it, 'share the Ministry with Sir Bruce Fraser'. The Dame told me there had been a great deal of talk in the Treasury along the lines of 'Wait till we get Bruce Fraser into the Ministry of Housing, then we'll bring them to heel'. The Treasury hates the feeling that I have got the backing of the P.M. for this enormous housing programme. Now it looks as though the Dame will stay on and we shall be able to postpone Bruce Fraser for a year. And after all, a lot can happen during the course of a twelve-month postponement.

Thursday, June 3rd
Helsby was due to see me this morning about the future of my Permanent Secretary. He came at 10, having seen the Dame and Bruce Fraser. I had had one long last talk with the Dame on Wednesday. She had urged me to tell Helsby that Bruce Fraser was the wrong man for the Ministry of Housing and that she was staying on to enable me to get someone better, if not Philip Allen from the Home Office, then Dunnett from Labour. I had sense enough to turn her down. I knew that my line should be that I had nothing against Bruce Fraser personally but that since Housing was the absolutely key Department in the Government's strategy this autumn and winter, we needed to keep morale high and it was therefore the wrong time to change the leadership. That was the reason I wanted the Dame to carry on until the spring and that was the argument I used to Helsby, who then said, 'Well, there's only one other Department for him—the Ministry of Land and Natural Resources.' He then asked me whether I knew that Bishop, the Permanent Secretary there, was wanting to leave the Service. Out of this emerged a wonderful new idea—that Bruce Fraser should go to Land and

Natural Resources this autumn and that while he was running that little Ministry he should take on the Leasehold Enfranchisement Bill, which I don't in the least want to do. Then when the Land Commission has been established and leaseholds enfranchised Bruce Fraser should come into Housing bringing Land and Natural Resources with him, as the Permanent Secretary of the new fused Ministry.

'Can we get the Prime Minister to accept this?' asked Helsby. 'Don't for heaven's sake talk about it to him yet,' I replied. 'Oh, we can't deceive him,' he said. 'If we are sending Bruce Fraser to Land and Natural Resources with the idea of his coming back to Housing, that has got to be sold to the Prime Minister.' I persuaded him that we needn't go as far as that in explaining our intentions. So Helsby and Bruce Fraser and the Dame and I are now all in a conspiracy to find the best way and the best time to persuade the Prime Minister to wind up his new Department as soon as possible. It certainly provides an ideal solution for me because it keeps the Dame in charge during this critical winter. As for the future, when Land and Natural Resources comes back to Housing I shan't have to worry about it. It's most unlikely I shall be Minister of Housing at that particular date.

After talking to Helsby I went to Cabinet — the last before the Whit recess. I stayed on throughout because I saw that the last item was future Government business. Sure enough at 12.25 Harold said he wanted to give us a little pep talk. We were all tired, he said, and needed a good week's holiday; and he referred to the rumours in the press that Ministers had been coming to him begging for an October election. Though this wasn't true, he didn't deny that one or two members of the Cabinet had been expressing rather desperate views about the future of the Government. There was no reason for desperation, he said. Once we got into the summer recess and could have two months ahead with no Parliament we should be able to recover. He was working on the assumption that we would carry on at least until next year because by then we would have good things to put into our shop window — the Land Commission, for example, and the incomes guarantee. We would also have a positive programme of reform worked out in detail, which would improve our relations with the public. So we weren't to go away depressed. I then repeated my complaints about the relations between Cabinet and the Party, and pointed out that it was useless to ask somebody to do this job *sub rosa*, alluding of course to George Wigg. What we needed, I claimed, was someone of full Cabinet rank sitting there with us but also in constant contact with the Party. Harold quickly said that he was doing a great deal to remedy this. He couldn't make an announcement now, but there would be a new man talking to the Lobby. I asked who it was and he said it wouldn't be fair to give a name. I said it wasn't good enough just to have another official in the Lobby; what we needed was someone in Cabinet. Harold was resistant and I knew why. In many of his speeches he had gibed at the Tories for spending Government money on a Minister solely devoted to party politics. Once he has committed himself to something publicly there is no one more obstinate than Harold in refusing to go back on it, however necessary it may be to do so.

Friday, June 4th
There's been an appalling anti-climax after yesterday's Cabinet. The appointment which Harold claims will close the gap between the Cabinet and the Party is the return of John Harris to the Lobby.[1] That confirms my view that he has not grown up since he went to Downing Street. Far from adapting himself to his new position he is adapting his new position to himself (No. 10, as I saw the other day, is the spitting image of his little house in Hampstead), and that is why he is not developing into a strong Prime Minister. He lets Jim Callaghan be a Chancellor under Treasury dictation and George Brown go a-whoring after his incomes policy while failing to produce the National Plan which is the real purpose of the D.E.A. Further, although he sees a number of senior Ministers pretty continuously he lacks both an inner Cabinet and a real strategy.

When I look back on him as leader of the Opposition I find I was making exactly the same criticism then. I remember how I said to myself, why can't he have the courage to form an inner group, why can't he have a consistent policy worked out by that inner group? The reason he always gave for not doing these things was that he was going to reorganize the Shadow Cabinet, but actually never did. He just let each member go on within the conventional sphere of his own Shadow office.

Sunday, June 13th
I am now wondering whether I haven't really got to try and use the Cabinet in a way I haven't used it before. Oughtn't I to make one real effort to get some sanity and central strategy into our conduct of affairs? Here we are, drifting along, with our momentum halted and the Civil Service taking over more every day. Policy is now formulated in the various Departments and merely co-ordinated by Harold at the last moment. There is no inner Cabinet with a coherent policy for this Government; and yet that is what we need more than anything else if we are going to regain the initiative this summer. We must have a clear-cut purpose.

This is one of Harold's weaknesses. He sees his job, not as launching a strategy, but as carrying out the manifesto. He is always getting George Wigg and Tommy Balogh to try and convince him that of the seventy-three promises in the manifesto, fifty-two are already being carried out. Yet from the point of view of the electorate this technical promise-keeping is quite unimportant. I have just been reading the draft White Paper on the Land

---

[1] Former research officer for the Labour Party and secretary to Hugh Gaitskell. He was the Party's press officer 1962–4; and after Labour's election victory he became an official adviser to Patrick Gordon Walker, Michael Stewart and Roy Jenkins. Created a life peer 1974.

Commission and if anyone thinks we are going to win votes by that document, they can think again. What we have failed to put over is that we have a purpose and a drive which will get the country on its feet. George Brown's incomes policy, in its present voluntary form, is over-boosted and has obviously come unstuck. The nationalization of iron and steel seems irrelevant, and so does our Finance Bill. Yet we must have a relevant policy which can be seen to be helping to deal with ordinary people's needs. That means incomes guarantee, housing policies and above all a strategy which links all this together in a central, coherent drive. I know all this. In a sense every member of Cabinet knows all this. Yet is it being done? And if it isn't being done, how can I persuade Harold that we need something more?

When I ask that question, I know the answer. If I do try to intervene along these lines, I have to face two things. On the one hand, I shall be accused of splitting the Cabinet and my action will be taken as anti-Wilson. The only way you can avoid being anti-Wilson is by going to him privately and letting him either take your advice or reject it. If I took an open initiative of this kind in open Cabinet, it would mean that I was apparently challenging his leadership. That is the eternal problem of the Labour Party—the problem of Labour leadership. One can't put any views strongly without being accused of factional strife. And that of course is accentuated by the danger that if I staged my initiative in Cabinet our private discussions would be leaked to the press. On the other hand, if I go through this June and July without any effort at all, can I think of myself as a responsible member of this Cabinet? Would I ever be able to forgive myself for my failure? That is a rhetorical question because really and truly I have no strong feeling of guilt and failure, and I don't regard this kind of initiative as my job. Harold hasn't put me in the Cabinet for that purpose. He is perfectly content with me if I do a good departmental job; and he has very carefully excluded me from central consultation and from his Chequers talks. So I can say to myself rather sulkily, why on earth should I make myself unpopular? But I have said that too often in the past. It is about time I made one real effort in Cabinet.

Tuesday, June 15th
Cabinet—and a characteristic one. I went there before going to my Rent Bill Committee despite the fact that there was nothing on the agenda which I cared about. Nevertheless, I was so worried by the Vietnam situation that I thought I had to raise it. It has been getting worse and worse with the Americans becoming more and more deeply committed; and I found myself yesterday looking back to a lunch party at Pam Berry's some weeks ago when Joe Alsop was the main guest.[1] I remember him sitting beside me and solemnly explaining to the assembled company that he was a happy man for the first time in years because in his view the President was now irrevocably

[1] The American syndicated columnist who had been writing about political and foreign affairs since the 1930s. His views on Vietnam were 'hawkish'.

and firmly committed to fighting the Vietnam war to the finish. At the time I was impressed and I believed Joe 75 per cent. Now, alas, I believe him 100 per cent and things look bleaker and bleaker. It is having its effect inside the Parliamentary Party, where the situation is growing very tense and not only left-wingers are beginning to organize letters and stage protests in their constituencies. So the squeeze on Harold is getting tighter. Michael Stewart being 100 per cent Anglo–American in a highly prim and proper way, feels no difficulties. With all this going on, I thought Vietnam must be raised in Cabinet. But it fell flat. This was mainly because, with the Commonwealth Conference just starting, Harold was able to say that a big initiative was now on the way – and he didn't want to say anything more about it for obvious reasons. That seemed to satisfy Cabinet, and I was content since George Wigg has been tipping me off about this initiative each morning on the phone and telling me the enormous success it is going to be.

Thursday, June 17th

George Wigg came across the Members' dining-room and sat with me to urge me once again not to push the Prime Minister too much at this stage. He also told me that the great Statement was due to be made at seven that evening and that I must be there without fail. I told him I was going to Nottingham on an official visit. Then Harold joined us and I told him about the turn-out of my Members in the Rent Bill Committee and he was enormously pleased. But he didn't stay long because he had to take George Wigg off to discuss this important event of which I knew nothing. I guessed by now that it must be a Vietnam peace initiative designed to calm the left-wing of the Party.

In the afternoon I began my negotiations with the building societies about the national housing plan. Representing the Treasury was Jack Diamond, who had written a very cynical paper about the whole idea. He came to the meeting after twenty-two hours on the front bench, so tired that he could scarcely move. Perhaps this was just as well since it enabled the meeting to go very smoothly. The building societies were not merely courteous; they were almost enthusiastic about the plan.

When they left I drove to St Pancras to catch the train to Nottingham. Directly I got there I was asked upstairs in the hotel for a drink by the city architect, who wondered whether I would like to see the television. So I went into another room and was just settling down to Michael Stewart's teach-in on Vietnam at Oxford when it was interrupted for a news bulletin. There was the Prime Minister announcing the Commonwealth mission to Vietnam and Bob Menzies[1] clapping him on the back and saying, 'I give this trip to you,

---

[1] Sir Robert Menzies was Prime Minister of Australia 1939–41 and from 1949 until 1966. He had also been Minister of External Affairs 1960–61. He himself had led such a mission as Wilson's – to Colonel Nasser at the time of the 1956 Suez crisis. In 1965 he was made Lord Warden of the Cinque Ports. He died in 1978.

old boy. Really it was your idea.' The political matiness and gimmickry of the proceedings were in startling contrast with Stewart's performance which preceded and followed it (he was a brilliant television success and put the American case more competently than any American has ever put it). I went to bed not very impressed and thinking, 'Poor old Harold. George Wigg has committed him to yet another of his stunts.'[1]

Friday, June 18th

When I looked at the papers this morning it was clear that my suspicions were justified – this was a last-minute dish, cooked up by George and Harold to get the Prime Minister out of his 'little local difficulties'. I find the whole affair immensely unattractive but I also know that I am being unfair to Harold in having this feeling. After all, he is the kind of man who takes these opportunities; and why, if Harold Macmillan can take them and win applause, should Harold Wilson be despised or criticized for doing so? What really worries me is that the chances of success are so very slim and don't really justify the role he has allotted himself. I gather that it is assumed he will be a month on the job – and it will be the critical month when Cabinet has to take all the decisions about the future of the economy and the priorities between the various Departments. It is on the home front that Harold should be showing his leadership and displaying his courage; but he is going away on a Vietnam stunt.[2]

Sunday, June 20th

Early in the morning I rang up George Wigg because I was still worrying about the Vietnam stunt. So I said to him, 'We must now consider what to do if Wilson is out of action for a month.' He obviously saw the point and replied, 'Don't worry about it now. Let's face it when it comes.' This didn't make me feel any more enthusiastic. Certainly, in the short run it will relieve tension among our back-benchers. But there will be trouble in Cabinet. We were asked our opinion on bank rate before the decision was finally taken; so it really was ridiculous that last Tuesday we were not consulted before the news of the stunt was released. Characteristically, of course, when I read the *Observer* today I found in Nora Beloff's article a round by round description of Harold Wilson's secret preparations for the great coup and a statement that he had to keep it secret because he couldn't trust his Cabinet colleagues not to leak.

Sunday, June 27th

All last week the Commonwealth Conference was going on and also the reactions to Harold's peace initiative. This certainly reverberated through

---

[1] According to Wilson the idea came to him when 'pacing the terrace at Chequers'. *Wilson*, p. 108.

[2] The plan was to visit Moscow, Washington and Peking as well as Hanoi and Saigon.

Whitehall and Westminster but it is now virtually over and the mission is dead.[1]

To be fair to Harold, it had the desired effect in the Parliamentary Party. I was lunching with my Parliamentary Secretaries, as I do each week, when Harold came in and asked me to walk down the corridor with him. I was feeling very critical of him for this political stunt. As we walked together Manny Shinwell came up and praised him in the most exaggerated way; when Manny turned off into the tea-room, I said to the Prime Minister, 'I really was anxious, Harold, that if this stunt had come off you might have been away for a whole month.' 'Oh, I don't think it would have been a month,' he replied. 'At the most it would have been a fortnight.' And he added these significant words: 'Anyway, I think we have got most of the value we can out of it already.' This makes me wonder whether the factor which really persuaded him to take George Wigg's advice was the prospect of the Commonwealth Conference breaking up on the first day as a result of the furious row over Rhodesia. Black Africa is now virtually at war with Rhodesia whereas the white Commonwealth is still trying to keep the peace. In order to postpone that row and create a better atmosphere, Harold needed a personal initiative on the first day and in this sense I have no doubt the stunt was brilliantly successful. He got through the Conference without having to give anything away and he achieved what was a great feat of diplomacy in the circumstances—an agreed communiqué. He requested our permission in Cabinet on Thursday (the only important thing that happened there) to say in the communiqué that Britain would in due course consider the possibility of summoning 'a constitutional conference' on white Rhodesia. I doubt whether such a minor concession to the African viewpoint would have won him that agreed communiqué without the Vietnam initiative on the first day.

In domestic politics he has also gained quite a lot. The tension on the Left of the Labour Party has been eased and the Tories thrown on the defensive. Of course Douglas-Home knows that it was a political stunt, but so was Harold Macmillan's Moscow enterprise. Our Harold has pulled off a diplomatic coup which was popular with public opinion, eased the situation in his own Party and prevented a potential breakdown of the Commonwealth Conference. One can't be surprised if he is rather pleased with himself.

Harold's preoccupations have given me time to reflect and to prepare for the battle ahead. From what I have learnt during the week I have no doubt whatsoever that the period from now to the end of July will be an absolutely critical time in the life of the Government. George Brown has told me in private conversation what the plan is. First, there will be no Statement on housing before the recess—that's definite. Second, we shall recess as punctually as possible at the end of July. Third, the Government will use the recess

---

[1] Hanoi, Moscow and Peking rejected the proposed visit. However, the Prime Minister soon produced another initiative.

to finalize George's National Plan, in which there will be separate chapters on housing and the social services. In preparation for this, a strange new committee has been established consisting of five senior Ministers without departmental problems, who are to make a searching examination of expenditure in the public sector;[1] so much for George Brown's National Plan.

Monday, July 5th

The Sunday meeting at which I appeared before the new PESC in the Cabinet Office was a very strange performance. I was due to arrive at four thirty but my train was ten minutes early at Paddington and I was whirled along the Mall on a beautiful, fine Sunday afternoon so that I had to wait for some thirty-five minutes outside the door of the famous main Cabinet committee room. At last I saw Barbara Castle go away looking rather sad and depressed and then Ray Gunter and George Brown came out to spend a penny. It was my turn. I went in, dropped my papers on the table and sat down on the empty side. This is the committee room where the bust of the Duke of Wellington by Nollekens smiles down on you and you sit round an enormous, heavy, square table. The chairman, who in this case was James Callaghan, was facing the bust. On his left was George Brown. I sat round the corner, facing the Treasury officials on the other side. Beyond me was Frank Cousins, looking rather uncomfortable, and beyond him, facing across to the Chancellor, Douglas Houghton. On his right sat Ray Gunter and John Diamond. They were the five wise men.

To judge from what was said later, I must have given the impression of haughtiness and anger; but the real trouble was that I hadn't very clearly made up my mind what to say. My difficulties arose partly from the unpopularity of the Ministry of Housing and partly from the way the Treasury were presenting their case. The Cabinet had agreed that public expenditure must only go up by 4½ per cent a year to keep it roughly in line with the 4½ per cent increase in national income on which we were planning. To achieve this parallel we had to cut down public expenditure from roughly 6½ per cent to 4½ per cent. So the five wise men have had four-year plans submitted to them by Education, Health, Overseas Development, etc., and in presenting his four-year plan each Minister has tried to state the reasons in favour of his going beyond the basic programme allocated to him. Now this basic programme hasn't been planned by the Labour Government; it is simply the amount which the Conservatives had planned to spend on the various social services in the next four years. In our White Paper last October our basic allocation to each Ministry was the Tory allocation. By tradition the Tories

[1] The Public Expenditure Survey Committee, known as PESC. The first comprehensive survey of the long-term expenditure plans and forecasts of growth had been made in 1961. But 1965, as a result of the PESC deliberations, was the first year in which a Cabinet decision on resources and priorities was made.

believe in owner-occupation and prefer private- to public-sector housing. So they had planned for a considerable expansion in all the public services with one exception—council housing, which they had deliberately kept depressed until the year immediately before the election. All this meant that when the four-year expenditure programmes were compared, my basic line for public-sector housing was far behind the base line of any other social service department. This is the case I argued in two Cabinet meetings when I tried to persuade my colleagues to give me a 20,000 increase in housing starts this year. The five wise men agreed that this figure should be kept steady for some years ahead. They might possibly allow the total housing programme to move forward to 500,000 a year by 1969–70, as Harold and I have proposed. But during the period when money is tight (which may well last till 1966–7) public-sector housing cannot go beyond the figure I had already been given.

So the case was put by the five wise men—the Treasury case. My first argument against it, on which I had been carefully briefed by Thomas Balogh and with which Harold Wilson has a great deal of sympathy, was that the Treasury method of calculating the burden of housing is quite ridiculous. In a normal sense, there aren't any estimates for housing as there are for education or for health because the amount of money I draw from the Treasury is quite negligible. It is needed for subsidies and planning and such things. The real cost of housing is the capital expenditure of the local authorities on the one side and the capital expenditure of the builders and mortgagees on the other. Yet the Treasury separate council housing from private-sector housing, and reckon the council housing as public expenditure comparable with health and education while they don't reckon in the private sector at all. This is an unreal way of considering the matter for two reasons. First, even in the narrow terms of strict Government subsidy it is now admitted that each house built for sale receives more in tax concessions from the Government than the council house receives in subsidies. In fact, it costs the Chancellor more in current expenditure to have a house built for owner-occupation than to have a house built for renting to a council tenant. Second, in terms of the national resources expended it is obvious that private house-building uses up exactly the same amount as public house-building.

When I had put this case we argued for some time; but it soon became quite clear that the five wise men were entirely concerned about a book-keeping transaction. All they had to do was to see that the Cabinet expenditure—by which they meant expenditure defined in the Treasury style—was brought down to an increase of $4\frac{1}{2}$ per cent a year. And that was to be done by the normal method of cutting back the expenditure of each Department. The fact that I started from a base far below all my colleagues simply didn't interest them. After a time I tried another tack. I can understand, I said, that you are afraid that the public sector will suddenly forge ahead next year under my housing drive. But it's also true that the private sector, which is going into a tail-spin at the moment, may be crumpling up next year. And if we are going to have some deflation, you may need public-sector housing to keep the economy going. So I have no objection, I went on, to agreeing that I should have nothing beyond my extra 20,000 next year, provided it is written into the National Plan that we are going to move up first to 400,000 houses a year and then to 500,000 by 1970–71. Provided that half-million is roughly divided into quarter-million private-enterprise and quarter-million council houses I am quite content to give way on the increase I had been planning for next year.

I hoped that this would sound quite reasonable; but it didn't placate my colleagues. Towards the end, when we had been sitting arguing for nearly an hour, Douglas Houghton said, 'I must say I don't like this at all. The others all came in here fearing their programmes will be cut. This fellow saunters into the room giving the impression that we dare not cut him for political reasons.' Of course, what Houghton said was the precise truth. I know I have the Prime Minister behind me. I also know that my housing programme is at the mercy not of any cuts they may wish to make but of economic forces which are threatening and pressuring and bullying this poor Government. The crisis has been hanging over it all this past week.

Saturday, July 17th
I have decided not to go into day-by-day detail about the past week because I find it boring to do it too many weeks on end. So this time I shall deal mainly with the big Cabinet meeting on Thursday. In preparation for it I had a long talk with the Department and decided that the best thing to do was, before Cabinet got to discussing individual estimates, to start the meeting by challenging the whole basis of the work of the committee of five. I got Thomas Balogh to warn Harold Wilson that I was going to do this. Harold started off with a little introduction on the limits of the work of the committee and then let me make my statement. I attacked the whole philosophy of the cuts and then gave my own departmental example. Once again I exposed the absurdity of treating public-sector housing quite separately from private-sector housing and then went on to argue that housing had been put into the wrong category. It had been wrongly put in with the social services, whereas it should be transferred, say, to the category which includes agriculture or the nationalized industries and looked at in that perspective.

When I said this, there was some protest from James Callaghan but not as much as you might expect because I have been working hard behind the scenes and so has Harold. Then George Brown intervened. He said that at first he thought my point was very much exaggerated; now he saw there was more to it. However, in his view the conclusions of the Cabinet paper didn't exclude what I wanted. I intervened and was able to prove that, although I seemed to have got my own way the paper in fact showed that my policy would be frustrated, and I insisted that I couldn't be content with a total figure of half a million houses a year. But if I had to, what was important was that the half-million must be divided, 50/50, between the private and the public sectors. At this point I waited because I really thought I had helped Kenneth Robinson and Barbara and the other spending Ministers a good deal by giving this example and pointing out the case for having the whole thing reconsidered. Not a peep came out of any of them. When I asked Kenneth Robinson afterwards why this was, he replied, 'I wasn't briefed on this.' That was rather illuminating. We come briefed by our Departments to fight for departmental budgets, not as Cabinet Ministers with a Cabinet view. Even Tony Crosland—I suppose because his education estimates were at stake—displayed a completely defeatist departmentalism.

At this point what happened was that, into the silence, Harold Wilson chipped in. 'There is something in what the Minister says. But surely if we are going to have half a million houses, a quarter of a million council houses and a quarter for owner-occupation, there clearly have got to be building controls.' And back we were in the old argument, because the Prime Minister had been slapped down on building controls by the E.D.C. when he urged the need for them a couple of months ago. On that occasion we had agreed that, while we might require building controls, the Minister of Works should go ahead and try to get a voluntary agreement. The Prime Minister now reminded us we must be prepared to institute controls if necessary.

This point having been laid down, we proceeded to a separate discussion of each estimate. I was a bit shocked by Tony Crosland. He pointed out that the cuts required of him would mean that the improvement of the primary schools which had been started under the Tories must be slowed down; he would have to do this because he accepted the view that he couldn't cut back expenditure on university education (as I would have done) and give priority to the schools. I would have liked to hear him protesting much more vigorously. He merely said that if that is the Cabinet decision, well, that's that but it will be very awkward and very unpopular. Next came Kenneth Robinson, who virtually said he was content with what he had got for Health. Frank Soskice was content with what he had got for the Home Office and the police. And then we came to Pensions. Now Pensions, of course, is in exactly the same position as Housing, with a public sector (national insurance) and a private sector, which includes all the private superannuation schemes. The contributions you make to your private pension do not count as taxation but your contributions to national insurance do. In the same way, the tax concessions which the Treasury makes to private superannuation schemes are not treated as a subsidy and so part of state expenditure, whereas the Exchequer contribution to national insurance is so treated. Did Peggy Herbison have the sense to chime in with me on this, or Douglas Houghton? Not at all. Instead, under cross-examination they got into a horrible mess and confirmed my fear that the whole strategy of our pensioneering, worked

out for years before the election, had been jettisoned almost without noticing it by the Minister under the *diktat* of Douglas Houghton. The basic idea
had been that we should switch as early as possible from flat-rate to
earnings-related contributions and in this way pile up enormous sums in the
pension fund which we could use to dynamize the existing flat-rate pension.
That was cardinal. However Douglas and Peggy had turned things upside
down, by first of all conceding an enormously increased flat-rate benefit
financed by increased flat-rate contributions. The net result is the worst of all
worlds as we can't raise the flat-rate contributions any higher without
imposing an intolerable burden on the lower-paid worker. Even worse, the
income guarantee which we had pledged ourselves to introduce would now
be at an absurdly low level as the result of the money we had wasted on the
huge initial increase of the flat-rate pension. After the Cabinet discussion I
became quite sure that it was far too late to go back to the original strategy.
The least damaging thing we could do was probably to abandon the income
guarantee because the pittance we could offer would make a mockery of the
whole concept.

By this time it was twelve o'clock and the Prime Minister had to go to the
funeral of Adlai Stevenson,[1] who had come over to London, fallen down in
the street and died rather dramatically on Wednesday. So we halted the
discussion and will continue it next week.

Tuesday, July 20th

Our second Cabinet on public expenditure. There were only two programmes left to consider, Overseas Development and Housing. Harold
Wilson started by saying, 'Now, let's turn to Housing.' I wasn't prepared and
replied, 'It isn't my turn yet. It's Barbara Castle first.' And so it was. It had
been clear at the previous meeting that both Harold and the Foreign Secretary felt the cut in overseas aid was greater than we could defend as a Party or
as a country. Something had to be restored to Barbara. On the other hand,
the system under which PESC had been working guaranteed that if one
Minister were to get more money another would get that amount less. There
was no play here, just a fantastically rigid adherence to basic programmes we
had inherited from the Tory Government. Tory priorities were prevailing
over our own socialist loyalties, and all that we could hope to do was to
continue a basically Tory spending programme with minor adjustments.

I'd said all this at the beginning of last Thursday's meeting and it had had
its effect. Nevertheless, this Cabinet was in a mood to finish the job off and
had no inclination to give anything away to Barbara. Their attitude was
strengthened when she spoke for thirty-five minutes. The sensible thing
would have been to speak for five minutes and then to ask Michael Stewart,
Arthur Bottomley and Anthony Greenwood to plead her case for her. When

---

[1] The American politician and diplomat, Democratic Presidential candidate in 1952 and
1956. He had become the U.S. Ambassador to the United Nations in 1961.

she had finished Callaghan simply said, 'I'm sorry about this but I can't believe there is any special case here, and anyway, if there is, what other Ministry is to be cut back?'

At this point Harold Wilson intervened. 'We mustn't be absolutely rigid about these programmes,' he said. 'After all, they are not our own – we only inherited them. I suggest we set up a working party to see whether we can't give Barbara at least some increase in areas where the dollar spending is not too severe.' At this point Cabinet suddenly moved into a major row. Callaghan refused to serve on a working party of this kind. 'All these points have been argued out,' he said, 'and at the end of July it is far too late to go back on the basic programmes which we've assumed for the last eight months. You can't challenge them now.' On this he was strongly supported by George Brown, who reminded us that he had to have the final figures by the end of the week for inclusion in his National Plan. After this there came an altercation which took nearly an hour and a half and which most of us sat through looking pretty embarrassed. The First Secretary and the Chancellor, clearly in some sense working together, leapt on Harold like wolfhounds in at the kill.[1] That sounds a bit exalted for Harold, but that's what it was. They tore him from both sides. They insulted him, tried to pull him down in the most violent way, obviously both feeling that Harold was evading his responsibilities as Prime Minister and trying to do an unseemly fix. And of course that is what he was doing. He was trying to help Barbara without openly saying so and planning to get her allocated another £20 million or so and then later to save the money by cutting the road programme of Tom Fraser, who was sitting just beside me. When he was defeated he tried to pretend he hadn't made the proposal and had the whole story removed from Cabinet minutes – historic proof that those minutes never tell you a damn thing of what goes on in Cabinet unless the P.M. and Cabinet Secretariat want to publish it.

After this we turned to Housing and, unlike Barbara, I spoke very briefly. I said that the thing I cared about was getting a firm commitment to a rate of building in 1969–70 of half a million houses a year. Once I got that I would be content to forego any further commitment to increase the public-sector programme in 1966–7 when things were tight. But I added that I wanted the Cabinet to realize how dramatically private-sector housing was sagging (I read aloud the figures for June which showed a decrease for the third month running). Would Cabinet agree that if private-sector housing continued to slump, the deficiency in the grand total could be made up next year by public housing? I then turned to the decision to halve my money for subsidies and said I would accept it provided Cabinet agreed that there should be no question of honouring the mortgage pledge for two years. After this the

[1] There were newspaper rumours that the Chancellor was plotting to overthrow the leadership, and this had come to a head on July 16th while the Prime Minister was in Moscow at the British Trade Fair.

meeting broke up. It was the worst Cabinet we have had, and the worst for Harold Wilson.

Thursday, July 22nd
I discovered in the afternoon that Marcia had allocated me half of Tommy Balogh's time with the P.M. I got to Harold's room at 5.50. At first he seemed curiously complacent and unaffected. He is indeed an unaffectable man, partly because he is so unimaginative. I felt I had to stir him up and I began to walk about the room while I kept on saying, 'Don't have another gimmick. Isn't the best thing to do now to make a virtue of necessity? Since you have to postpone them all anyway, why not announce as a matter of policy the postponement of the incomes guarantee, of help to mortgagors and of overseas development money.' And quite suddenly he spotted the point. He got up from his chair and started walking round the table. We walked round two or three times, he in front, me pursuing him and trying to put ideas into the back of his head. I don't think very much more happened except that I complained to him about having all these cuts discussed behind my back by my own officials in consultation with the Treasury. 'Well anyway,' he replied, 'we shall be discussing all this on Monday at the meeting of Ministers.' That was the first I had heard of it and I said, 'Am I invited as one of the Ministers?' 'Yes,' said Harold. 'Your name is on the list.'

Of course, the main reason why our talk was so empty was because Harold had been thinking throughout about the resignation of Alec Douglas-Home as Tory leader. When I entered the room he told me that he was on the edge of resignation and we must have spent over half our time discussing something which had really taken his mind off the central issue. When I left his room I found that the resignation had taken the House of Commons by surprise and was the only topic of conversation.

Pam Berry rang me yesterday and told me that in her view Harold Wilson had played the most notable part in forcing the resignation because he had gone round saying that Alec Douglas-Home was his greatest asset. One of the people he had told it to was Adlai Stevenson a short while before his death, and Adlai had retailed it to every Conservative he met, including Douglas-Home. There may be truth in what Pam said. Home is a funny man. Perhaps he really *was* doubtful as to whether to hold on for another six months and the determining factor was the story that Adlai was going round London saying this.

Monday, July 26th
When I got to No. 10 this morning I found a great assembly of Ministers outside the door; all the spending Ministers—Health, Housing, Transport, Aviation, Overseas Development—were there. We soon discovered that Harold had set his eye on building licensing. After forbidding cuts in the housing programme he was determined to take the over-heating out of the

construction industry and push the builders and building-material people
away from the construction of inessential shops and garages and central
supermarkets into housing, schools and hospitals.

In a crisis of this kind what a difference the personality of the Minister
makes. I had often heard Nye say this about the Attlee Government but I
had been a bit sceptical. It was literally true today. There is no doubt in my
mind that if we had had a strong Minister of Transport he would have saved
many of his essential roads. But it didn't happen. I had fought hard and saved
my housing. Kenneth Robinson had fought hard and saved his hospitals.
Tony Crosland had fought moderately hard and saved his schools at the cost
of postponing his university and further-education building programme.
And Barbara Castle had fought and fought and fought and got herself pretty
soundly defeated up till now. Cabinet was desultory and disappointing,
chiefly because Harold still felt unable to put us fully in the picture. We were
discussing a Statement with no idea of how it would be timed. Indeed, I was
assuming that it would go to Cabinet on Tuesday and then there would be
negotiations before it was finally made on Thursday. But this actually wasn't
the idea. Another cause of our unhappiness was the feeling of deep uncertainty we all had as to whether there was already a kind of cahoots between
Callaghan and Brown against the P.M., which would produce a repetition of
that terrible row in the last Cabinet.

At 6 p.m. the Dame and I met Charlie and his officials in his room in order
to discuss building controls. It was a rather pathetic meeting. The Dame was
able to tell me that the Whitehall grapevine had it that the Statement would
be made, whatever happened, on Tuesday afternoon because the Prime
Minister, Callaghan and Brown were agreed on forcing it through. As we
talked we began to see the redrafts of the Statement, which was being
distributed in bits to Departments affected by it. Building licensing, for
example, was to be far more drastic than the Ministry of Works had
imagined, since the Prime Minister was insisting that contracts over
£100,000, rather than over £250,000, would be licensed. As we sat there we
heard that the Treasury had brushed aside all Charles Pannell's protests. It
was clear that the careful P E S C review of public expenditure had gone by the
board. Now a Statement was being prepared as a real panic measure to stop a
run on the pound which had started the previous weekend. This made
nonsense of Callaghan's assurance a fortnight before that no further
measures were contemplated. Yes! it was as short-term as that. And it
became clear to me that this would be positively the last Statement before we
went off the pound. The next Statement would announce that the pound was
devalued, or floating.

It was also clear that devaluation was something Harold Wilson could
contemplate as little as George Brown and Callaghan. They were now
united. The division was between, on the one side, these three plus their
political advisers, such as George Wigg, and, on the other, the economic

advisers. All the economists were urging that the pound should float, while the three politicians, strongly backed by George Wigg, were fighting for the pound on the ground that no Labour government could survive devaluation in 1965 after the devaluations of 1931 and 1949.

Tuesday, July 27th

Sure enough, when I got to my office at nine thirty I found a new draft of the Statement which had only been agreed by the Prime Minister, Brown and Callaghan at one o'clock in the morning. What happened then was as near to central dictatorship as one is likely to get in a British Cabinet. At Cabinet we were not given the time either to discuss the underlying strategy or even to consider the document as a whole. We were told to 'take it or leave it as it stands'. The Chancellor revealed that there had been a run on sterling in the previous week and that a huge part of our reserves, including the £200 million we had got from Germany as a result of our negotiations in Bonn, had disappeared. Unless a Statement was made that afternoon devaluation would be upon us. As well as the Chancellor, Harold and George Brown both spoke quite briefly. Each of them repeated that this was a package deal which they had worked out among themselves. I, of course, knew that Callaghan wanted a lot more, including the regulator[1] and a complete moratorium on all building contracts—and that these had been excluded by the efforts of Brown and Wilson. I also knew that building licensing was something which neither Callaghan nor Brown wanted, but on which Harold Wilson was insisting.

So there were rifts between the three of them. Callaghan, in particular, made it clear that if he'd had his way he would have done a lot more but that this had been prevented by the other two. As usual Harold allowed a lengthy Second Reading type of discussion. Frank Cousins was the only person who took up an extreme oppositional position. I said I was doubtful if the package was tough enough. It seemed to me that it would have maximum home disadvantages and would fail to impress the bankers abroad, and I didn't see why the Chancellor hadn't used the regulator. But my main feeling that morning was relief that my main suggestions had been accepted. The central part of the Statement included the announcement that we were abandoning the incomes guarantee for the lower paid, postponing cheap mortgages and cutting back local-authority mortgages. Of course, this would shock our own people to the teeth but it could also have the desired effect on the bankers abroad. Moreover, we would not really be giving up anything but merely making a virtue of necessity. Most of the Cabinet did not agree. They objected with varying degrees of strength to the whole package; and there was a long and rather desperate argument about the relative importance of

---

[1] The Chancellor of the Exchequer was able to increase or decrease certain taxes by up to 10 per cent at short notice, in order to 'regulate' the economy. An increase of 10 per cent would, for example, be anti-inflationary, in theory at least.

sticking to the incomes guarantee as compared to earnings-related short-term benefits. Anthony Crosland, however, was another who, like me, doubted whether the package would be particularly effective, and Roy Jenkins was also unenthusiastic about it for the same reason. The discussion drifted on till nearly twelve thirty, when it became obvious that we wouldn't have time to go through the draft in great detail. It would have to be bull-dozed through. And that's what happened.

By one o'clock something like agreement on the actual text was reached and then came the question of who should make the Statement. Suddenly Harold said that he didn't think he was the right person to make a Statement which included the abandonment of so many promises and pledges. He couldn't possibly do this. I guessed what he was thinking. By this time we knew that the Statement would be made in the House today, when the new Tory leader was to be elected. Moreover, we were having no less than three votes of censure, two during this week and one on the following Monday.[1] It therefore seemed obvious that the Chancellor should make what was basically a Treasury Statement and that Harold should reply to the big vote of censure on Thursday, when the new Tory leader would have been elected. But for some twenty minutes Callaghan wriggled. I at least was quite determined to nail him to our cross—after all he had been mainly responsible for constructing it. Finally, Harold Wilson, who quite obviously wanted him to do the job, took a vote and called our names. There was a two to one majority for making Callaghan do it. And he did it, and the interviews on the wireless and on the telly, extremely well. In fact he got away with murder—very largely because the whole of the Tory Party was entirely distracted from the crisis by its own leadership crisis. I suspect that this was one of the main factors in Harold's mind when he insisted on having the Statement on Tuesday afternoon. If so, the calculation certainly worked.

Wednesday, July 28th

The news of the economic crisis was nicely balanced by the news that Heath had defeated Maudling in the leadership contest.[2] Naturally, I wanted the good man to lose. I knew that Douglas-Home's departure was a real disaster for us (he was *our* asset) and I wanted Maudling instead of Heath because Heath would be the more formidable leader. However, I wasn't unduly surprised when the announcement came that Heath had got a majority on the first ballot, that Powell had come out very badly and that Maudling had at once conceded defeat. As a result we have curiously similar leaders in the Tory and the Labour Parties. Two wholly political politicians, much more tactically than strategically minded. Maudling would have been a far better, wiser political leader. All the disadvantages of Harold Wilson seem to me to

[1] The first two were on the cost of living and on the Government's failure to fulfil its election pledges. The third was a general censure motion on the day before the adjournment and it was the occasion of Heath's first speech as Conservative leader.
[2] By 150 votes to 133, with 15 votes for Enoch Powell.

be incorporated in Heath—and most of the advantages as well—his drive, energy, skill in debate, his dedication to politics. These are all considerable assets; and I dare say it is quite good for the country, in a period when great, high policies are unlikely to be attainable, to have two tactical politicians of this kind in charge. Certainly, it means the electoral battle will be keen and there will be no question of a national government if we are driven into devaluation. Our parliamentary democracy will continue to run along the strictest Party lines.

The Tories were enormously confident. They felt strengthened, and that they had really got us on the run. I asked Tam how things were going and he admitted to me that Tuesday's Statement had been a terrible blow to our back-benchers. I should add that the actual Statement was of course designed for the bankers, emphasizing the negative side and sounding far worse than it actually was. I hadn't correctly estimated the shock to people like Tam of the abandonment of the incomes guarantee and the postponement of the mortgage scheme. That shock was far less for me because I knew that the incomes guarantee had already been abandoned by Douglas Houghton, and I had seen the papers and seen that what they *were* proposing was a disaster which they wouldn't actually dare to put forward. I also knew that the postponement of the private mortgages wasn't an abandonment but was for the time being essential to the expansion of the public-sector housing programme. But these are things known only to very few people in Whitehall. To many of our people it really was the limit. They were feeling, 'We're on the skids, slithering into devaluation. When we come back from the recess we shall find the pound devalued.'

In the evening I dined with Nicky Kaldor and he was able to fill me in on what he knew of events of the past week. He told me that last Friday he, Tommy and Robert Neild had made a joint *démarche* to Harold, urging him not to go in for repressive measures but to accept the floating pound. They had been turned down and on this occasion George Wigg's advice had been preferred.

Thursday, July 29th
I was due to see the P.M. at 9.30 to discuss the national housing plan and local government finance. However, I got a desperate message that I wasn't to go because he was still preparing his big speech for the censure debate. I realized that the speech must be his only concern during the morning. True, it was only Anthony Barber moving the vote of censure, but nevertheless everything depended on how Harold replied.

He didn't have much time, however, because Cabinet met to resume discussion on public expenditure, in particular to deal with the two unresolved subjects—social security and overseas aid. This time Callaghan was on the side of Barbara—which shows how pertinacious Harold can be when he wants. To George Brown's amazement he had brought the Chancellor over and persuaded him to come out with a 'compromise', under which, as far as I could make out, Barbara would get about £10 million more. Callaghan said this was essential because we couldn't renege on firm Government commitments. This produced the expected explosion. Many Ministers pointed out that there were just as firm Government commitments on the home side which had been abandoned in the Statement. Harold fought for Barbara; Barbara talked and talked—weakened her case—and then there came a farcical moment when John Diamond for the Treasury suddenly said, 'But I believe we have got all the calculations wrong. We have been calculating not on 1964 prices but on current prices.' So the issue was postponed again, and we turned to social security.

Douglas Houghton had put in a long memorandum protesting against the abandonment of the incomes guarantee. Having made his fuss he gave way sulkily. It didn't take long. So we came finally to housing. I said I agreed to forgo the increased figures for 1966–7, but only if I could have one clear ruling from Cabinet. Suppose by any chance that the private-enterprise starts should go on sagging, I must be able to fill the vacuum with increased housing in the public sector. Callaghan was, of course, vehemently opposed. I then had a row with him for three or four minutes, won, and got it minuted; so this critical point is Cabinet policy. What really clinched it for me was that the Prime Minister carefully asked me about the national housing plan and the state of play with the building societies. He said this, of course, because I had told him about my success on Wednesday in the renewed negotiations. I was able to give Cabinet a really optimistic picture.

When the others left the room I stayed behind and said to Harold, 'If you say a word about this housing plan in your speech this afternoon you'll kill it stone dead.' He looked very disappointed. Could he not mention the target of half a million? This appalled me. I had heard rumours that he wanted to do it and I said to him, 'For God's sake, don't.' When I got back to the Ministry I found the draft passage in his speech for that afternoon in his own long-hand with the corrections he had made and had photographed and sent over. (John Delafons has got it as a memorial of that morning.) He must have been rewriting right up to delivery that afternoon at 3.30 because I noticed that he delivered it from pencil notes.

I was back in the Commons just in time to hear the end of Anthony Barber's speech—obviously not very effective. Then came Harold and he kept his word. On housing he took just the line I wanted and there was no mention of the half-a-million. So I have still got the announcement reserved for October—which is of crucial importance to me and the Ministry. I sat on to listen to the rest of the speech. He looked very confident leaning against the box, but from where I sat I could see that he was so tired he could scarcely stand up, and he was muttering and reading the speech fast and not doing it very well. Yet it was an astonishing performance because of his wit and agility, and also because he hit the level of the House exactly. 'I wasn't too serious,' he said to me as he sat down. 'I'll leave that for Monday. Let's make fools of them today.' And that, of course, is exactly what he did.

But he did something more. He also remoralized his own Party—gave them back their faith. This is an example of how one speech can really transform a situation. I have seldom seen it happen to the extent it happened today. But then I have seldom had a period in my political life when the Party's morale had reached such a low ebb. By the time he sat down they were all cheering and laughing behind him, and the Tories were totally discomfited. It was a tremendous show.

Monday, August 2nd

I went back to Westminster confident that Harold Wilson's speech had really helped the pound. Well, it hadn't! The fact is that the whole package was not terribly effective. Today the pound is still dithering, Callaghan is still suicidal and Wilson is looking a bit harassed. We all, in both Whitehall and Westminster, have the uneasy feeling that this year's third budget still hasn't had the required effect. As for the Party in the House, it has the rather desperate feeling, underneath the end-of-term atmosphere, that something disastrous could happen while Parliament is in recess. On the other hand, the Tories seem completely confident that Parliament is going to be recalled. I don't think they expect or even want to come to power this October; but they feel the Government is being driven to the wall, battered by its failure to achieve confidence and by having to make concession after concession to reality. One looks back to Harold's immense triumph last Thursday only as an event in the past—yet another desperate remedy already being overtaken and overwhelmed by the events which followed.

This afternoon we had the Statement on immigration and the publication of the White Paper.[1] This has been one of the most difficult and unpleasant jobs the Government has had to do. We have become illiberal and lowered the quotas at a time when we have an acute shortage of labour. No wonder all the weekend liberal papers have been bitterly attacking us. Nevertheless, I am convinced that if we hadn't done all this we would have been faced with certain electoral defeat in the West Midlands and the South-East. Politically, fear of immigration is the most powerful undertow today. Moreover, we had already abandoned the Gaitskell position when we renewed the Immigration Act, and any attempt now to resist demands for reduced quotas would have been fatal. We felt we had to out-trump the Tories by doing what they would have done and so transforming their policy into a bipartisan policy. I fear we were right; and partly I think so because I am an old-fashioned Zionist who believes that anti-Semitism and racialism are endemic, that one has to deal with them by controlling immigration when it gets beyond a certain level. On the other hand, I can't overestimate the shock to the Party. This will confirm the feeling that ours is not a socialist Government, that it is

[1] Entry vouchers were reduced from 208,000 per annum to 8,500.

surrendering to pressure, that it is not in control of its own destiny. If only we had had a Home Secretary who could have done this as a matter of principle and done it strongly and early! But it has been squeezed out of us, just as our economic concessions to reality have been squeezed out of us. I think it will be very difficult to deal with the thoroughly deplorable image we have created when Conference meets. When you add immigration to Vietnam you realize why the rank and file feel that we have abandoned our pledges and are retreating from socialism. The White Paper will probably have a deeper undermining effect on the moral strength of Harold Wilson's leadership than any other thing that we have done.

In the evening I had to accompany the Dame to a dinner with the Hampshire County Council. I rushed back from the dinner to hear the last minutes of Harold Wilson's speech—what *The Times* described as a knock-out blow to Heath slightly below the belt. And that was the effective end of this session of Parliament. Now there is nothing left but bits and pieces before we recess on Thursday.

Tuesday, August 3rd
Cabinet. And the main item was George Brown's National Plan. We had four key chapters in front of us, including the summary at the beginning, and the question was whether, in view of the deflation Callaghan launched in his Statement last week, we should still publish the Plan next September as we had intended. Tony Crosland had this in mind when he asked how we could talk about a plan based on a 4-per-cent average increase of production each year when we now knew perfectly well that for the next eighteen months at least production wasn't going to rise by anything like that—in fact when the Government was actually cutting back production by its deflationary measures. Crosland is the only member of the Cabinet who comes right out with these honest-to-God economic judgments. He then went on, 'We are launched on deflation and I know I shall have to rewrite the whole of my chapter in George Brown's National Plan. It makes no sense any more.'

Thursday, August 5th
Our last Cabinet before the recess took place while the Commons was going through its last stages and winding up its recess adjournment debate. The whole place is completely conked out. But we still had to hold the Cabinet in the Prime Minister's private room because there were Questions at eleven o'clock and he and Tony Crosland and others had to go off to the front bench to answer them. Since both the First Secretary and the Chancellor had to be away at the beginning Harold had put in as a filler a paper proposing to reduce the ban on the publication of state documents from a fifty- to a thirty-year rule. This was a very modest reform, long overdue. Yet only Tony Crosland and I were prepared to support the P.M. and Gerald Gardiner against the civil servants. We had read aloud to us, first by Michael Stewart and then by James Callaghan, the departmental briefs provided for them by

their officials. Here was a Labour Foreign Secretary objecting that a reduction of the ban on publications to a thirty-year rule might damage the reputations of civil servants active during the Munich period while they were still alive. I pointed out that the present ban, quite apart from all its other drawbacks, was rendered intolerable by the permission which a Cabinet Minister, particularly a Prime Minister, can obtain to use official documents denied to academic and objective historians for writing his memoirs. If we are going to go on exercising the right to turn out memoirs which are often nothing but personal *plaidoyers,* there is a powerful case for letting the historians get at the documents as soon as possible. This formed the main discussion but I wasn't surprised to find that not a word of my argument was retained in the Cabinet minutes.

At last we turned to the main item on the agenda, the postponed discussion on the public expenditure cuts in overseas aid. Cabinet was presented with the final result of a lot of haggling behind the scenes. Barbara was to get £10 million extra in the really difficult year, 1966–7. Provided she didn't make another 25-minute speech to us, we were all prepared to accept it. But I did ask rather maliciously where the £10 million was coming from and whose estimates would be cut back. Harold explained that they weren't coming from anywhere. So the proposal went through.

I talked to Tony Crosland afterwards and we agreed that the vital thing is to make Cabinet take the risk of deserting the pound for the sake of the social services. But that is a very difficult thing to do because both James Callaghan and Harold Wilson are personally committed to the defence of the pound to a quite extraordinary degree.

Looking back over this fortnight and putting together the bits and pieces, I now realize that the underlying issue has always been the fight for the pound. I heard about it for the first time at that dinner with Nicky Kaldor when he told me how he and Tommy and Robert Neild had written to the Prime Minister begging that the pound should float. When I reported the conversation to George Wigg he blew up and said I had been talking to Hungarian traitors. George has been one of the men most strongly advising Harold to stand by the pound and dismissing anybody with a different view as a dangerous Hungarian or a tool of the Hungarians. Talking to George Wigg has made me realize that if you commit yourself to the view that devaluation is the end of everything and then fail to defend the pound, then it really is the end and you go down in catastrophe. I agree with the Hungarians. Failing to defend the pound would not mean the end of everything; we have already paid far too high a price in the effort to bolster it up. Indeed, letting the pound float and accepting straight away the measures we should have to take after a devaluation makes sense. Defending the pound by frantic cuts and then in the end finding one has to devalue makes no sense at all.

Tony Crosland is passionate about this, and I agreed that I would write a letter to Harold trying to use my influence with him on the side of letting the pound float when the next pressure comes. Of course, this would mean that Callaghan's personal reputation would be irreparably damaged and that is why he is so desperately concerned. What none of us know is what it would mean for Harold Wilson's personal reputation. I shall have to write to him and tell him that he is the only person flexible enough and strong enough to float the pound and survive. Nevertheless, Harold Wilson and George Wigg will see devaluation as a defeat far more than I do. Indeed, at this Cabinet meeting I was leading those who were saying no more abandonment of socialist policies in order to save the pound. I expect Harold Wilson will reply to me that Tony Crosland's interpretation of the last package is unfair and that it is not really a deflation. But the next package will be; and therefore what happens during this recess is all-important.

Wednesday, September 1st
We had planned our Polzeath holiday on the assumption that I should have to go back on September 8th for the special Cabinet meeting I had demanded. Actually I had to go on the 31st by the night train for a meeting of the Cabinet on the 1st. This had been put forward a week mainly because it was suddenly felt that we needed a new turn in the prices and incomes policy before the T.U.C. General Council met. I at once asked to see Harold Wilson before the meeting in order to discuss my troubles with the building societies, and I got on to Jennie who in turn got on to Marcia and it was arranged that I should have breakfast with him at 8.40 on the Wednesday after getting into Paddington on the night train.

I dutifully clocked in and found him alone, with Mary still in the Scilly Isles. We were rather at cross-purposes. I wanted to talk to him about housing and he wanted to say that he wished the old firm – Benn, Wigg, Crossman and Wilson – to get together again, and that he had decided that I should take charge of Party propaganda policy in the liaison committee. I had known for ages that our propaganda co-ordination was hopeless and had been insisting that he should appoint a Minister in the Cabinet to deal with it. So I wasn't surprised when he said, 'Of course, if it was a Minister, it would be you. However, I don't want to have one now, though I think you have really finished your job in Housing.' This disconcerted me because I had just begun to settle down in the Ministry and thought that in the second year I could do a really good job. He also made it clear that he wanted to transfer control of immigration to my Ministry. This wouldn't suit me – or the Ministry – at all. I said that frankly it wasn't right; the Home Secretary should be in charge of immigration. And added that I didn't like being given the job because we had got an incompetent Home Secretary; he ought to change the Home Secretary. We left it there. He went on to outline to me the legislation required for the new shift in incomes policy. Then we went downstairs at 9.30. Cabinet started at 10.30 so I just had time to go across to the office and see what was on there.

Cabinet began with a longish, rather incoherent, review of the situation by the Prime Minister. He said that the economic situation had greatly improved during August and then launched into a very guarded account of the next phase in the strengthening of sterling, which seemed to include a fresh bout of assistance. I noticed that he told Cabinet a great deal less than he had told me over breakfast. Then he called on Callaghan and Brown to reinforce his account of the economic situation and explain the change in incomes policy. Before they got going on this I intervened to say that I wanted to continue the general discussion of the economic situation. Certainly things were better now but what would happen if there was another threat to the pound? Would there be another package of deflation? When Callaghan said he didn't think this was necessary, I pointed out that though *he* didn't think it necessary there were important people outside that room who did think so. Would we be forced into it? He said this was very insulting. But everybody in the Cabinet knew what I meant—that this new turn in incomes policy was linked with Callaghan's August visit to Washington and his talks with Fowler, the Secretary to the Treasury. It seems that Callaghan must have given Fowler assurances that in return for more dollars there would be an attempt to control wage increases.[1] But nobody else asked a question so we passed on to incomes policy.

It soon became clear that once again there had been a conflict between George Brown and Callaghan, with Callaghan fighting for his wage freeze and George Brown resisting on behalf of the unions. We gathered that they had reached a compromise: there should be statutory power not to regulate wages but only to provide early warning and delay. Here too, as usual with this Cabinet of ours, there was no real opposition.

After Cabinet I had lunch with George Wigg in order to talk to him about the new job of which Harold had spoken. He at once said, 'We ought to share the chairmanship,' and I realized he felt bitterly the fact that I was to take his place. Harold had said to me that, loyal as he was to his friends, he felt George was a bit overwrought and needed a good holiday; anyway he wasn't good on propaganda policy. So he had obviously decided to remove George from this absolutely key position as the only link between the Cabinet and Transport House. Not wanting a quarrel, I agreed with George's proposal for a joint chairmanship and said I would write a minute to Harold about it. But rather characteristically George rushed round to Harold immediately I left him and I found myself summoned to No. 10 at 7 p.m., when the Prime Minister made it clear that it would be impossible to have the chairmanship shared. He wanted me to have a fortnight's holiday and then come back ready to take up new responsibilities as well as a much more intimate relationship with him.

With this at the back of my mind I went out to dinner with Thomas Balogh.

[1] Wilson concedes that it was in the light of discussions with Fowler that 'we began to think in terms of statutory powers'. *Wilson*, pp. 131–2.

I found he had seen Harold after I left and was full of this new job of mine. He also confirmed my impression that in Washington Callaghan had made a series of firm commitments to Fowler in return for strong American backing. It was largely in order to honour these commitments that Cabinet had been brought forward a week, so that G.B. could get authority for the new prices and incomes policy before presenting it the very next day to the General Council of the T.U.C. just before their annual Conference.

After dinner I caught the night train back to Cornwall for the rest of my holiday.

Sunday, September 12th
Today I had to be at Chequers by 9.45 for an all-day Cabinet. No one knows how to find Chequers. Thomas Balogh gave me exact details of how I could get in by the back entrance behind Great Kimble Church. When we got to Great Kimble we found two churches and finally got to the front entrance at 9.58. There must be hundreds of great country houses nicer than this. It is heavily restored and stuffy in atmosphere. After a day there one appreciates why everybody says they detest Chequers.

Before the meeting I just had time for a word with Callaghan. He had made his great statement on the Friday and obviously scored a tremendous success in beating the speculators off the pound.[1] But he had also announced that he had seen the building societies on the previous day and persuaded them not to increase their interest rates. This he had apparently done without consulting my Ministry. I asked him why, and he said, 'For political reasons. I just think the rates must not go up.' I take a very different view. If we want houses built, the building societies must get the cash in, even if the interest rates are rather high.

Today's meeting was due to Barbara's pressure for a whole day's discussion of economic policy. The first speaker was Callaghan, who of course started with his sensational success of Friday. He explained that when Fowler was in London he had listened to a wonderful presentation of our case by George Brown. This had so impressed him that he was ready to provide us with special financial backing. Callaghan also explained the stringent measures he was going to take to catch the speculators. He reckoned that 30 per cent of our losses were the result of speculative betting against the pound. He also said that Heath was not committed against deflation, so that we shouldn't assume that if a Conservative Government came to power it would not deflate. Altogether it was a competent report.

Harold Wilson then made a long speech. His first theme was that he thought that the right thing now was to settle down for another Queen's Speech and another Session; and to have one more year during which we should reach phase two, when we should move from defence of the pound

[1] On September 10th Callaghan had announced that he had secured a further $1,000 million international short-term loan.

into carrying out our positive policies. He said that no poll had been published for five weeks, a sign that things were going our way. Moreover, he himself was having excellent public meetings and so was George Brown. He was convinced in due course we would reap the benefit for our blood, tears and sweat. Churchill wasn't liked for his policy but he was respected for it. He then turned to his second theme—the parliamentary situation after the death of the Speaker.[1] Here again he thought we were coming into easier waters, since there was no prospect of another Bill as tough as the Finance Bill. 'Let's notice in passing,' he said, 'that we carried out a fiscal revolution in that Finance Bill—something we couldn't ever repeat with such a small majority.' Indeed, he seemed to hope for a dull Session in which the Tories would be embarrassed because they would have to commit themselves on a series of difficult issues. They would be having a two-day debate, for example, on the National Plan—should they oppose it? Or how should they react to the Land Commission? To our house-building policy? To rate rebates? These were all subjects which would be favourable to us this Session. Then he turned to the position of the Liberals and gave the assurance that he had had no talks with them about a pact.[2] He *had* seen Grimond on quite a different subject and then Grimond had observed that there could be no question of a Lib–Lab pact. 'Anyway,' Wilson added, 'if I had wanted one I couldn't have persuaded the Party to deliver.' He was convinced that the Liberals understood the need to postpone the election since they would be destroyed if it came early.

He then turned to the Speakership. 'We shouldn't start discussing it this morning,' he said. 'I am not going to meet Heath or Grimond about it. It is a House of Commons matter. If the Tories want to do some political manoeuvring, let them discredit themselves. The Labour Party should leave it to negotiations between the Whips and we should keep our hands clear.'

He ended up with a warning about reflation. 'In our last Cabinet,' he said, 'when we were discussing incomes policy I myself talked of the possibility of reflation if deflation went too far. But we must be careful not to go too fast in this direction. Certainly we should concentrate on growth factors such as housing, and certainly we must turn the easier months which are coming to our advantage. Is this euphoric?' he concluded. 'No, I don't think so.'

George Brown said we were exaggerating the 'browned-offness' of the electorate. 'At my meetings I don't find any signs of it.' Next came Anthony

[1] Sir Harry Hylton-Foster, Conservative M.P. for the Cities of London and Westminster since 1959, had collapsed and died on September 2nd. Labour's majority would be unimpaired if they could secure not only the election as Speaker of Dr Horace King, Labour M.P. for Southampton since 1950, but also the election as deputy Speaker of Roderic Bowen, Liberal M.P. for the County of Cardigan since 1945. The Conservatives threatened to oppose Bowen's candidacy so that the Government would be obliged to lose the deputy Speakership to another of their back-benchers.

[2] The Government's dependence on the ten Liberal M.P.s to provide a deputy Speaker, which would maintain their tiny majority, had nourished speculation about a Lib-Lab pact.

Greenwood, who hardly ever speaks in Cabinet. Like Barbara Castle a little later, he made delicate left-wing hints about apathy in the Party and our failure to get our policy across, and he warned us of Conference difficulties.

At this point Wilson interjected very quickly that if there were faults in public relations—and there certainly were—the first way to deal with them was to see that our Ministers no longer made purely departmental pronouncements but became more political and made more political speeches every weekend. All of us, he said, had been far too Department-conscious. We must turn back into politicians.

Barbara took the Greenwood line. First of all there must be no abdication of socialist principle. If we are going to be thrown out we must be kicked out. Our real trouble is that we do things at the expense of our principles, and she illustrated this with three examples: the squeeze, immigration and Vietnam. She finally warned us of the danger of putting forward the incomes policy as something we had to do to appease the bankers. This was said in reply to something George Brown said in an August meeting. He had remarked that trade-union leaders were unwilling to accept the incomes policy on its merits and had actually asked him to present it as a necessary condition for satisfying the bankers. It would be disastrous, Barbara said, if it were put to the public in this way. Our incomes policy must be presented as a policy looking forward to the new phase, not back to the old crisis.

Callaghan spoke next and made one of the best contributions I have heard from him. He said Barbara was right to point out our dilemma—the conflict between what is popular with our Party workers and what is popular with the electorate. But the most important thing of all is that we must believe our policy ourselves. For instance, the immigration policy, which Barbara had attacked so fiercely, must be sold to the electorate as something the Labour Government really believes in. Our theme at the next general election must be our uncompleted mission. And he added that in his view we had kept our middle-class vote and our losses had all been among the working classes. Finally he said he would like to suggest the five themes we should concentrate on in all our speeches: (1) the National Plan; (2) paying our way; (3) modernization; (4) price stabilization; (5) industrial self-discipline.

Over lunch I talked to Barbara Castle (as fierce as ever about immigration) as well as to Bowden. Harold, alas, is still determined that I should take over immigration policy from the Home Office and he now wants me to make the speech at the annual Conference as well. Somehow I have got to get out of both.

After lunch we started with a formal report to Cabinet on foreign policy. First we were warned that U.D.I. was due at any moment in Rhodesia. We are making all preparations for it, including the possibility of sanctions. But we must face it that if we were to cut off access to the copper mines we might have a large number of unemployed in this country. The second subject on the agenda was Kashmir and the war between India and Pakistan.[1] No discussion took place on either.

So we turned back to our politics, un-minuted. First, we had a report from the Chief Whip, who said that in order to survive at all with our illness record we had to get proxy voting permitted for the sick. Second, we had to deal with the awkward people in the Party. However, the Chief Whip said that given loyalty and a bit of luck we had some chance of getting through, though he didn't feel nearly as optimistic as Wilson. Wilson then turned the debate to the quite different issue of morning sittings. 'If the Tories are bloody-minded,' he said, 'and won't give us proxy voting for the sick, should we not retaliate by having Question Time at eleven o'clock in the morning and starting business of the day immediately after it, running through to the early evening, say to six or seven?' Morning sittings had been ruled out under previous Governments on the ground that Ministers simply couldn't combine them with their work. This produced half an hour of ministerial expressions of opinion. On the whole the feeling was that if we want to modernize anything, the modernization of Parliament is an excellent thing to start with; and we should now begin to decide to work through the day and stop before dinner every night. Sensing the mood of Cabinet, Harold Wilson adroitly shifted his ground. He stopped arguing that we should introduce morning sittings as a retaliation against the Tories and began to recognize that this was something that could be introduced on its own merits.

The next subject he chose to raise was steel. On this, the Chief Whip and the Lord President told us roundly that it is now impossible to get a Bill through Parliament with our small majority. Cousins then said that anyway the nationalization of the docks was far more relevant to the crisis than steel nationalization, which could be postponed. Then came a long discussion on the reasons we should give for its postponement. Should we say quite frankly that we just couldn't get it through this Parliament or should we make a virtue of necessity and say we had come to the conclusion that dock national-ization must be given top priority and steel postponed? Fred Lee, as Minister of Power, said you couldn't just postpone a steel Bill since there had to be a policy for steel in the interim. At this point Wilson talked a great deal about the steel-masters' row with the Tory Party, and began to show only too clearly that he had been discussing with Woodrow Wyatt and other people the various possible deals that could be made with the steel-masters. There was a dangerous moment here. However, it was left that we should have a new Cabinet Committee to study docks and steel. There was no Cabinet decision for postponement, but equally there was no doubt that the Bill will be postponed and that there is no opposition in Cabinet to this happening.

It was quite an interesting day. I felt what a humdrum Cabinet we are—a gang of competent politicians. Once again Harold Wilson showed himself

[1] Despite the negotiations of Arthur Bottomley at the C.R.O. and Harold Wilson's personal intervention, India had invaded the disputed border territory on September 6th.

without a trace of vision—no Kennedy touch, not even the dynamic of Lyndon Johnson. But if the Cabinet lacks spark and originality, that doesn't prove it's a bad Cabinet, it doesn't even prove it won't win an election.

Monday, September 13th
Back to the Ministry after my holidays. The Dame is away on holiday for a whole month and it will be very pleasant running myself in. Considering the instability of the political situation, the Department works for me dutifully.

In the evening I strolled round to the Athenaeum in order to discuss propaganda policy with Wedgwood Benn before going to Tommy Balogh's home to continue to talk on the same subject. I intended this as a quiet beginning to my new life as chairman of the liaison committee. One side of the work is liaison with Transport House on current political issues. On the other is the production of the outline election manifesto, and that is what I was discussing with Benn and Balogh. But it is the last thing we can admit we are discussing because if we do, Len Williams at Transport House will say that we are trespassing on the Party privilege. Each time the manifesto is written its first draft has to be done secretly. Last time it was written by Peter Shore and myself, and then the draft was formally presented to the Executive as though it were entirely the work of the Transport House staff. I found that Balogh and Benn had each produced a good paper on the themes we need. I agreed that, having considered them together, we should now wait until after the decisive event—George Brown's launching of his National Plan on Thursday of this week. How the Plan went over would, I thought, be decisive for our future line. If it was a success with the press and welcomed by our Conference as well, that would fix the central theme for our current propaganda as well as for the election manifesto.

Wednesday, September 15th
My first meeting of the liaison committee at 6 in George Wigg's room. Taking over as chairman was tricky because Transport House was deeply suspicious of me and George himself is a most erratic, difficult, crabby man. I went away after an hour and a half feeling fairly depressed, saying to myself, 'Well, I have either asserted my authority or I have got myself into an unholy row.' I was sure I had got Marcia Williams's support but I wasn't sure of much else.

On September 16th the Government published George Brown's National Plan, which was designed to reinvigorate the economy and stimulate the electorate's faith in Labour's economic policy. It set a target of 25 per cent increase in national output, requiring an annual average growth of 3·8 per cent over six years. The Plan looked for a rise in exports of 5·2 per cent a year and a reduction in the visible trade deficit to £225 million by 1970. Defence spending was to be limited by 1970 to £2,000 million at 1964 prices. The housing programme was to rise to half a million houses a year by 1970. There was to be 40 per cent more invested in the road programme, and education spending was to rise by a third. In the light of the Chancellor's recent forebodings, however, this all seemed very optimistic.

Friday, September 17th

The morning press confirmed that George had done a first-rate job in launching the Plan. Now I had to put the housing section of that Plan across. It had suddenly occurred to me on Wednesday that with the National Plan released we should need on Saturday a statement on housing, however brief. Peter Brown[1] worked away at it on Thursday, and today I held a press conference and put out the statement in which we explained how we were actually going to achieve our half-million target.

In the evening I was due in Coventry for a G.M.C. meeting with council members present. I knew the Coventry Labour Party was longing to grill their Minister so I went down with a copy of the Plan and my housing hand-out and found some forty-five people gathered in the council chamber after tea. I concentrated on the National Plan and the target of half a million houses. Though most of them had come determined to maul me and to get their Member down, by the end of the meeting they were, as often happens in Coventry, half-willingly raped by me into thinking 'Well, dammit, Dick did make a pretty good case and we couldn't really answer it.' Then at last I could go home.

Monday, September 20th

My first job when I got back to the office was to deal with the press leak about my new position as chairman of the liaison committee. The story had been started by Walter Terry in the *Daily Mail*; but all the other papers had picked it up from the first edition, getting more information as they went along. So the damage had been done. I pointed out straight away to George and Harold that I had taken the job on the condition that it was confidential and I couldn't possibly do it now. I further pointed out that the National Executive would be furious; and it was agreed that I would not be able to take the chair on Wednesday. The more I look at it the more relieved I am. It would have been a difficult job and it is a good thing I am out of it.

Wednesday, September 22nd

The fiasco about the liaison committee has certainly brought me closer to Harold Wilson. I am sure now that he wants to have the old firm working together. But he is still showing as much nervousness in asserting his authority as he did when he was leader of the Opposition. He certainly hasn't changed for the worse in his personal relations—he is still as unassuming, as straightforward, as sensitive and also as tough as he ever was. But neither has

[1] Crossman's press officer at M.H.L.G.

he grown into his job in the sense of increasing his dimensions of statesman-ship or at least of losing his reluctance to have a scene or sack anybody. He should have had a scene years ago with Helsby at the Treasury, with Len Williams at Transport House, and he should have sacked Frank Soskice from the Home Office. He should have done a hundred awkward things which need doing, but he prefers to fix if he possibly can.

Today after a talk to Wedgy Benn, Tommy Balogh and Peter Shore, I was deputed to put to him the case for an early election and see how he took it. When I started he replied, 'Don't put it on paper. Why not travel up to Conference with me by sleeper and we will talk on the way?' So I have to prepare myself very carefully for that. We all feel that objectively the right time for an election would be this autumn, with the trade and gold figures good, and with the Opposition ill prepared. We are unlikely to get a better moment during the limited period when we are free to choose. Nevertheless, it is clear that Harold doesn't even envisage this. His image of himself is as a gritty, practical Yorkshireman, a fighter, the Britisher who doesn't give in, who doesn't switch, who hangs on. This is the Harold Wilson he believes in and we shan't deflect him because he is confident he can do it this way. So if we miss a golden opportunity this October it is because of the character of Harold Wilson.

Thursday, September 23rd
The Blackpool Conference for me really started when Tommy, his wife and I went round to No. 10 and up to Harold's room. There were Marcia and Mary (just off to break a champagne bottle on an atomic submarine at Barrow) and we had a really cosy family evening. Most of the things we had discussed behind Harold's back got discussed openly with him that evening. Was he too kind to civil servants? Thomas said he was. Shouldn't he have more outside advisers? Thomas said he should. To which Harold replied that he couldn't afford to have more than one Thomas since he wouldn't be able to read the stuff. No! he is not going to be a president and he is not going to have a presidential staff, and neither is he going to have any fundamental change in the Civil Service. All these things are remote from his mind. As for party politics, he has the greatest contempt for Heath, greater than he has for Alec Douglas-Home. He was also, I remember, very critical of Anthony Green-wood for trying to get a decision to revoke constitutional government in Aden postponed until after the N.E.C. elections were announced next Tuesday.[1] But apart from that he was his friendly, cosy self with us all, and we sat round drinking brandy until we moved up to Euston and got on to the sleeper.

[1] The Speaker of the Aden Legislative Council had been shot by terrorists on September 1st. Meetings had been held at No. 10 to prepare for a military takeover and suspension of the constitution. A State of Emergency was declared on September 25th, two days before the Conference opened.

Friday, September 24th

We were due to be driven to Blackpool after the Prime Minister had been received by the Mayor of Preston on the platform. There he was on the platform at 7.30 punct., shaved, clean, sparkling and saying to me, 'Directly we get to Blackpool, come up to my room and have breakfast.' Unlike Harold I hadn't had either a shave or a wash and I said to Marcia, 'For God's sake give me forty minutes when we get there,' to which Harold said, 'But I always feel so much better after a night train.' Marcia whispered to me, 'He is always like that after a night journey. I can't sleep a wink.' So Harold and George and Sophie and the mayor all poured into one car and behind them Marcia and I travelled alone.

After a quick bath I went down to breakfast with him and soon it was time for the routine N.E.C. meeting which always takes place on the Friday before Conference. As usual we spent endless time discussing resolutions which would obviously never be reached.

Saturday, September 25th

I spent the morning reading the first draft of Harold's Conference speech, which is to be delivered on Tuesday. I found a passage at the end in which he was talking about introducing the new Britain and actually said 'Here we have stepped forward and done it.' I said to Harold, 'But we haven't done it. That's the trouble. And people know we haven't. We haven't even got across the image of a new era. Don't pretend. Let's say instead that we have only built up to the skirting, and ask people to give us a chance to build the whole house.' He said, 'That's a fine idea.' And I replied, 'You know, any idea of our being a Kennedy regime is absurd.' He looked at me and he said, 'I suppose you're right, Dick. You can't really sell a Yorkshire terrier as a borzoi hound.' Fortunately, I was able to reply, 'In Britain we prefer a terrier to a borzoi as our leader. It's a clear electoral asset.' I went upstairs and worked away with Jennie (who travelled up with us on the train) to prepare him a draft.*

Sunday, September 26th

In the afternoon we had the regular N.E.C. meeting to consider for the first time the composites[1] which had been worked out in discussions on Saturday afternoon.

Meanwhile, the Imperial Hotel had been filling up in the usual way with the usual guests. I am pretty used to Conference now, and being hardened I just opt out of the evening entertainments and the endless trade-union dinners.

---

* Of which as far as I can see he used nothing. Indeed, the only thing I managed to do was to knock out a passage on steel which seemed to me evasive and disingenuous.

[1] Motions amalgamating similar resolutions proposed by various trade unions or constituency Labour Parties.

As a Labour Minister at a full-scale Party Conference, one certainly has a very different status from the other members of the N.E.C. Red boxes arrive from London regularly and are brought up to one's hotel room where one struggles to get through them. A Minister has to do all his work in his hotel room and that makes things difficult. I got through by having a little table stuck in the bathroom where Jennie could type. In fact, I insisted on keeping a nucleus of my Private Office functioning up here.

I told all this to Harold on Friday because I knew that he wasn't allowed to bring civil servants to a Party Conference, which meant of course that he had given way to Helsby's pressure again. I told him this was absolute nonsense. If I was to keep control of my Ministry I had to have the civil servants I needed here in Blackpool. Harold was quite impressed when he learned what the Minister of Housing was getting away with and allowed Tommy Balogh to come up on Saturday night.

Tuesday, September 28th
My big moment at Conference was Monday afternoon. Once the housing debate was over I had no more Conference work to do. The awful thing was that at ten o'clock on Sunday night I still had no speech prepared. However, I got something together by two thirty and went down to the Conference hall.

Looking back on the speech I don't think it was very well delivered, and I know it could have been far better if I had had more time and done more work on it. Nevertheless, it really hit the headlines in the morning papers today and the TV headlines too. On Monday evening I did four TV interviews and one radio interview as well as a full-scale Lobby conference. In fact I was busy on these interviews from the moment I left the Conference Hall at five until eleven thirty at night. As a result of this work today's press at least gave the impression that Labour is determined to be building half a million houses a year by 1969.

Today was the day of Harold's big speech and we went down to the Conference Hall at nine thirty to hear it. But first came the results of the elections to the N.E.C. Throughout the weekend Barbara Castle was continually saying, 'Oh dear, Dick, what shall we do? I believe we are going to be knocked off the Executive this time. It's the young ones who are going to win.' I told her that the young ones wouldn't do anything this year; the Ministers would get all the votes. True enough. We did. Barbara of course was at the top of the poll, with Tony Greenwood close behind. I was down one place and James Callaghan was up one place. I was quite content with this. I am unlike Barbara in this respect: the elections for the National Executive don't dominate my life; in her case it is a chronic disease.

Next came Harold's speech, an immensely impressive performance. I knew most of it and was horrified to find that into a speech already far too long had been spatchcocked an enormous new section describing the Conservative Party as the party which sides with management against the workers in a new class war. When Tommy Balogh had finally been allowed to come to Blackpool he had gone straight up to Harold's room and spent a lot of time on the speech. Before he went back to London he had said to me, rubbing his hands, 'My God, this is a masterly speech which Helsby won't approve of. We've really put some teeth into it.' Nevertheless, the Balogh insertion sounded synthetic and made the speech an extra ten minutes too long. That evening Hugh Cudlipp of the *Mirror* told me that he was asked his opinion and said to Harold, 'Well, most people say that your speech was too long.' And Harold had replied, 'How many people?' Hugh: 'Ten people I have spoken to.' Harold: 'Well, now you've spoken to eleven. I think it was too long, too.'

Monday, October 4th

This Monday was very like the beginning of a school term. Our Party Conference was over and here I was, back in the old routine, preparing for the new Session ahead. The chief jobs on hand were: (1) preparing the White Paper on the housing programme; (2) getting ahead with my two local government finance Bills, a short-term Bill (on rate rebates), and a long-term Bill (concerned with the reform of rating); and (3) completing the preparations for bringing the Rent Act into operation at the beginning of December. Yes, it was very much getting down to work again.

Tuesday, October 5th

Callaghan had asked to see me directly I got back from the recess; and when I went along the passage he hummed and hawed and I wondered what he was up to. Quite wrongly I had assumed he wanted to talk to me about staff, since the Prime Minister had told me recently how sick James was of Kaldor and how much Kaldor would like to transfer to the Ministry of Housing. I had liked the idea at first sight and broached it to the Dame but without much success. However, he chatted and chatted and finally said he gathered that I wanted ten thousand extra houses this year. Was that true? I was completely bewildered and frankly told him so, but added that it certainly wasn't true that I had asked for ten thousand more houses. 'I think you are going to do so,' he said rather grimly. And I said, 'Well, that only shows that your Treasury is at its usual practice of spying.' I would go back to the Department immediately and discover the facts.

Back I went and, sure enough, in the afternoon, when I had my meeting on housing allocations, Bob Mellish said that we needed an extra ten thousand approvals if we weren't going to have a first-rate political crisis. This is a very good example of the Whitehall grapevine. Bob had been having strictly private consultations in my Ministry before coming to me with a proposition; and yet the Chancellor of the Exchequer knew about it before I did. I had it out with the Dame. I said to her how deeply I resented people in my Department leaking in this way—because that's what it is—to the

Treasury. Of course, I see that the Department can't in fact approve extra houses without the Treasury discovering what we are up to and that our officials are honour-bound to tell the Treasury of any firm commitments we enter into. But I keenly resent the behaviour of officials who obviously feel that their first obligation is to the Treasury and their second to their own Minister.

I can talk in this way to the Dame but I am not thereby going to alter the structure of Whitehall. All my key officials, the two Deputies for example, know that promotion comes to them not from the Minister—he has virtually nothing to do with it—but from the standing which they have in the eyes of the Treasury and of the head of the Civil Service, Helsby. It is this relationship which makes so many higher civil servants willing to spy for the Treasury and to align themselves with the Treasury view even against their own Minister.

All the Dame could do was to listen to my outburst before we got down to business and decided to write the very letter that the Chancellor knew he was going to get. Actually, I toned it down a bit and said we couldn't possibly get on without seven thousand extra approvals. Before I knew what, the fact of this change from ten to seven thousand was circulating round Whitehall.

Monday, October 11th
I had a working lunch for all the people concerned with Party propaganda. When the transfer of the liaison committee chairmanship to me was leaked after the first meeting I had made a terrible row and told Harold I would have nothing to do with it unless he fixed it with the chairman and the secretary of the Party in Transport House. Well, he hasn't fixed it with them but I have been persuaded to do the job. So there I was, chairing the meeting in my room. All the Transport House people were present, as well as the P.L.P. officials from the House of Commons, Frank Barlow and Harry Mitchell.[1] I managed to persuade them that our job was not to advertise the activities of the Conservative Party Conference or the policy statement Heath had produced by speeches against them but to concentrate on our own National Plan. This was a change for most of them since George Wigg's idea of propaganda was verbal fisticuffs.

Wednesday, October 13th
This afternoon the Tory Conference began and Harold Wilson carefully took all the headlines by flying to Balmoral to talk to the Queen. Everybody immediately jumped to the conclusion that he was asking for a dissolution because this week's Gallup Poll and N.O.P. show Labour eleven points ahead of the Tories. Certainly, the circumstances are perfect: after weeks of awful rain we have had ten days of clear, beautiful, cloudless summer weather—a slight mist in the mornings and warm sunshine afterwards. The

[1] Secretary of the P.L.P. and Deputy Secretary of the P.L.P. respectively.

gold reserves are good and the Gallup Poll is good and I, of course, have been pressing him to have the election now. But in sober truth he had no reason to go to Balmoral except to bitch Heath's opening speech—a typical Harold trick.

Thursday, October 14th

I went to Cabinet this morning at 10.30 for my rate-rebate item much too free-and-easy in my mind. Indeed, I only started making notes on what I was to say while Harold was filling us in about the Rhodesian crisis. This was the first occasion on which I definitely misjudged Cabinet and did very badly. I mistakenly started by bluntly saying that politically we had lost five hundred seats in the municipal elections last May and that we should lose another five hundred if we didn't give some relief to the ratepayer and fulfil our election pledge to shift the balance of the burden from rates on to taxation. To do that on a large scale we shall first have to carry out our major reorganization of the system of central grants to local authorities. For that we need my big rating reform Bill which is due to be introduced in February but which can only be operative from the spring of 1967. It was therefore essential to have an interim rate rebate Bill—like my interim Protection from Eviction Act—to give some immediate assistance now. That was my case.

The moment I finished, James Callaghan weighed in. He said he didn't agree with my political argument; there were no votes to be got out of rate rebates since the people who got the rebates wouldn't be grateful to us.

I was taken aback because he had told me last week that he thought my rate rebates could come this year. Now he had gone back on this assurance, although he knew that it would be a personal defeat for me because I had been going round the country speaking in favour of a short Bill. More important, it would be a defeat for the whole policy of controlled reflation and another victory for the deflationists in the Treasury.

When Callaghan had finished, the Lord Chancellor said that the proposal was unjust, unhappy, unpopular. I realized that by talking about the elections I had upset a number of my colleagues. The Prime Minister came in quickly to put me right. He said that if it was a question merely of votes next May in the municipal elections he wouldn't consider the proposal at all; but what mattered was its social justice. So then I switched quickly into reverse and used the arguments one needs to win the support of Douglas Houghton and Willie Ross. Then Barbara waded in and said, 'Aren't we supposed to be in favour of helping the poor and the weak? Isn't it time we did something solid for them? The rates went up last year by 10 per cent and they will be up another 10 per cent this year. How can we leave the old-age pensioner in a high-rated house to suffer in this way?' Then things began to swing my way. James Callaghan was supported by the Lord Chancellor, by Arthur Bottomley, and by virtually nobody else. Finally, George Brown said, 'Well, if we are all declaring ourselves, I must admit that I came to this meeting thinking the proposal was too complicated and not worth doing. But I fancy I have now been convinced of its social justice.'

This experience was an eye-opener for me. I learnt that you must never go into a Cabinet meeting without carefully preparing your tactics. You must never take for granted that the battle is won merely because the Prime Minister is on your side and the Chancellor has hinted to you—but not sworn to you—that he will support you in the fray. However, after an hour it was through: Cabinet is committed firmly to rate rebates which will start operating next March. I thought it rather significant that the Prime Minister, in his summing-up, pointed out (although he had rebuked me for mentioning politics) that if we were going to have a general election before the municipal elections it might be a good thing to have the rate rebates in operation.

Thursday, October 21st
I had expected Cabinet to deal entirely with the legislative programme. But I was rung up in bed by George Wigg and then Tommy Balogh, who both warned me that the big event would be Rhodesia. A glance at the morning papers showed why. The *Daily Express* had the full story on the front page: Harold Wilson had decided to fly to Rhodesia to try to stop the disaster of U.D.I.

Sure enough, as soon as we started Harold made a longish statement as to why he had to go. He just couldn't let U.D.I. happen without one more effort to stop it. On Tuesday, when I was alone with him, he had told me how enormously aware he was of the internal, domestic problems involved in U.D.I.—particularly the danger of our getting into a state of war with the British white settlers, which would be ruthlessly exploited by Heath. That was one of his preoccupations. Another was the economic fear that if Rhodesia cut off the Kariba Dam we might have our copper supply cut off and all our economic plans brought to frustration. And the third was the sheer risk of world war. If the Russians were to take over the U.N. police force, they might end by trying to march into Rhodesia. Harold repeated to Cabinet all these fears, giving them as the reasons why he felt he ought to go. The discussion lasted some forty minutes. I started it by saying to vague murmurs of approval that I was doubtful. (After all I had talked to Tommy and to George, both of whom were very doubtful indeed.) Why should we allow the P.M. to risk not only his life but also his reputation? Instead, a delegation should be sent out which might well consist of Arthur Bottomley and Alec Douglas-Home, representing the Opposition, plus one other.

Harold resisted this very strongly and it soon became clear that he wasn't discussing the idea with Cabinet before making up his mind—he had not only made up his mind but committed himself. It was also clear that he had nobbled the Lord Chancellor and Frank Cousins, who both saw this as a dramatic piece of statesmanship. The rest of us were uneasy but not really willing to put up much resistance because we felt it was a *fait accompli*.

Tuesday, October 26th

Cabinet, with George Brown in the chair since Harold is still away in Rhodesia. It started with George reporting that things in Salisbury were extremely bleak and Harold on the edge of leaving with nothing achieved. However, there was one more card in his hand which he would play before he left. I am afraid I took all this rather for granted and thought it supported those of us who had been against his going. Nevertheless, the sheer fact that he had gone was in his favour. How important it was was shown by the public's reaction to the Archbishop of Canterbury, who had managed to come out with a statement that if the British Government had to use force they deserved public support. This had caused a storm of indignation which revealed only too clearly that the last thing the British public wants is the use of force or sanctions in Rhodesia. They are prepared to see us standing up for what is right but they wouldn't tolerate a war against fellow white men who are also British subjects. From this point of view Harold is right to be seen doing everything in order to prevent U.D.I. Nevertheless, it looks as though U.D.I. is coming—Smith is making this more and more insultingly clear.

Since Parliament was resuming that afternoon I stayed in the House to see Horace King sworn in as our new Speaker. The atmosphere was pleasant because the tension had been removed by the morning announcement that Roderic Bowen had become the second of the two Deputy Speakers so that we now have one Conservative, one Labour and one Liberal in the Chair. So the Prime Minister has brought off his coup. Our majority of three has not been cut to one! I thought the performance wasn't too bad and what Horace actually said standing on the steps of the Speaker's Chair was quite moving.

In the evening Anne gave a little dinner at Vincent Square for our group—Tony Benn, Marcia, Gerald Kaufman, Peter Shore and Tommy Balogh. We found complete agreement that Harold should not have gone to Rhodesia. We found that we all accepted the decision to postpone steel and had been disconcerted by Harold's attempt to reverse it. In order to keep the Party together, we all agreed that, now steel has been dropped, we must give much more emphasis to the other progressive parts of our policy, especially the modification of investment allowances to favour development areas. The one point on which we were in disagreement was over the decision to drop legislation on immigration. I strongly supported it; but there was a feeling among the others that it would be regarded as too sudden and too violent a switch.

This little group around Marcia is really quite important since she is still the most influential person in Harold's life, far more influential I should say than Tommy Balogh, and infinitely more influential than me. So it is of the greatest importance that she should not feel isolated. She is being gradually ejected from No. 10 by the Civil Service and now does most of her work across in the Commons.[1] This is all part of the battle for the attention of the Prime Minister which the Civil Service has been winning against his political friends. It was Burke Trend, for example, who went with him to Africa; none of his political friends were invited. Marcia has been fighting to get a glimpse of Cabinet papers, but she is still no nearer to achieving it; and she and Tommy cling to their place in Harold's life, well aware that they are always in danger of being thrust out.

Monday, November 1st
Harold presented to Cabinet his report from Salisbury and his recommendation that there should be a Royal Commission. He gave us, however, four choices. Choice one: to accept Smith's view entirely—that is to say on the definition of the terms of reference of the Royal Commission. Choice two: to accept the idea of a Royal Commission but to say we disagree with Smith's terms of reference. Choice three: to accept it and have two bases for a Royal Commission, his and ours. Choice four: to reject the idea of a Royal Commission altogether—which would make U.D.I. automatic and inevitable. From the start it was clear that Frank Cousins and Barbara Castle were the only two of our colleagues who fought for accepting the inevitability of U.D.I. immediately and not doing anything whatever to try to continue to negotiate. The rest of us knew it was right to play for time and it was on this basis that we allowed Harold to make his Statement to the House on the Royal Commission.

Harold's Statement that afternoon on Rhodesia was dramatic and obviously successful.[2] I must say I fell asleep and I realized that I hadn't by any means heard all of it when it came to an end. He read it so quietly, so steadily, so boringly.

Tuesday, November 2nd
A very long day entirely devoted to departmental meetings. In the evening a meeting of the strategy group over supper at No. 10. Present: Peter Shore, Tony Benn, Tommy Balogh, Marcia Williams, Gerald Kaufman, myself (as chairman) and the Prime Minister. When he came in he looked really jaded. The Rhodesia crisis has been telling on him. As soon as he flew in, after a week of activity, he was plunged into Cabinet on Monday morning and the House of Commons on Monday afternoon. Judging by the press, he has had a real success in the Commons and foxed the Tories by his proposal for the

---

[1] See Marcia Williams, *Inside No. 10* (London: Weidenfeld, 1972).
[2] The Prime Minister gave an account of his visit to Salisbury and of his discussions with Mr Smith and other African Prime Ministers. He told the House of the proposal that a Royal Commission should be established, with the Rhodesian Chief Justice as chairman. It would seek to devise new electoral arrangements and amendments to the 1961 Constitution, so that Rhodesia could move towards independence without sacrificing the five principles safeguarding the position of the African population. The Attorney-General and Arthur Bottomley remained in Salisbury to discuss the idea.

Royal Commission, even though it was pretty obvious from the word go that the Commission was a non-starter and we were merely postponing the evil day. Nevertheless, by Tuesday evening he looked tired and found it difficult to talk to us at all. Gradually he got more interested and we had a useful discussion on the line he should take in the Queen's Speech.

Thursday, November 4th
Another Cabinet, with Rhodesia as the first item. But there was very little to report since there was no word from Smith. All we got was an interesting episode illustrating Harold's method of handling a hot potato. On the Wednesday evening David Ennals, who is Barbara's P.P.S., and four other P.P.S.s had issued a statement laying down the conditions which a British Government should insist on for the Royal Commission. They couldn't have been drafted by anyone who had not been briefed by a Cabinet Minister, so it was obvious that David had been talking to Barbara. Tam was another of the signatories and I had a tiff with him over it, but of course he was taking a critical line not about my Department but about Barbara's. It seemed to me outrageous of Barbara to allow David to do as he did, and people said so at Cabinet. Harold Wilson walked round the subject. He was severe about David personally and said he shouldn't have done it, but he let Barbara get away with it. And I thought once again, 'He has been superb in handling Rhodesia but he just doesn't like hurting a colleague and he finds it impossible to sack anybody. So Barbara gets away with gross misbehaviour and Frank Soskice with gross incompetence.'

Wednesday, November 10th
At ten o'clock we resumed the Cabinet discussion of Rhodesia, and at once Harold got into a long and acrid argument with Barbara Castle about the rights and wrongs of making any kind of concession to Smith on the subject of the Royal Commission. It was a bit academic since by then there was only the slimmest chance of preventing U.D.I. and it seemed to be a mere matter of hours before it was announced. However, Harold was permitted to formulate a precise offer along the lines that if we accepted a unanimous decision the Smith Government must be prepared to do the same.

Thursday, November 11th
At 10.45 I went into Cabinet and by 11.18 U.D.I. had been announced. I then listened with some interest to the preparation for the afternoon performance but of course my mind was mostly on housing; however important Rhodesia may be, if you are a departmental Minister you can't help thinking that your debate is the one that really matters. In the afternoon Harold made an extremely good Statement, and then Fred Willey got up to introduce our debate. He did it in a very hesitant speech which he explained by saying that he was ill. So I got him off to bed and had to sit through one of the most

boring debates I have ever heard. It never got going and I was left to wind it
up with nothing to say.

Sunday, November 14th
Since this has been Rhodesia week I want to put down some considered
reflections about the Rhodesia crisis, since it is certainly one of the
Government's turning points—at least if it isn't, Harold has judged it completely wrong. He calls it 'his Cuba'—the test of his strength and statesmanship and power to survive a really difficult situation. Certainly, he has so far
survived personally with ever-growing weight and stature. This week I
noticed for the first time that he seems to have spread in girth and that his
photographs are taking on a more portentous, statesmanlike appearance.
And if anyone should think I am laughing when I say all this, I must add that
the statesmanship is getting across through his TV appearances to the
general public as well as in the House of Commons. Nevertheless, his
growing statesmanship hasn't made him disregard party political considerations. Indeed I think his thought has been largely dominated by the
determination not to leave his flank open to Heath, and to make sure we
can't be blamed for U.D.I. From outside (and even though I am in the
Cabinet I am completely outside the Rhodesian crisis), it has always seemed
to me that U.D.I. was inevitable. But Harold Wilson always felt so appalled
by the prospect that he convinced himself that by his personal intervention
he could prevent it. Only this can explain his astonishing readiness to go to
any lengths in order to delay that final decision.

Looking back, I don't criticize him for this since I am sure he has gained
enormously in terms of public opinion at home. On the other hand, by
concentrating so much on preventing U.D.I. he has succumbed to the
temptation of neglecting to prepare any strategy for facing U.D.I. when it
actually came. It was almost as though he felt it criminal to consider what to
do when it came because it was his duty to prevent it coming. So, whereas
everything he has done to try to stop it has been quite good, I am horribly
afraid he is far less well prepared to deal with it now that it *has* come.

Another strong impression I have had is of the hold that Barbara Castle
has exerted upon his conscience. Barbara, who was his P.P.S. at the Board of
Trade, is the left-winger closest to him, and as Minister of Overseas
Development, even if her influence hasn't prevailed, her conscience has
haunted him and made him uneasy and unsure of himself. All her effort
throughout the crisis has been to avert any concession to the whites and to
see that everything we do satisfies the blacks. Now what pleases the blacks
are sanctions and Barbara objectively has been as anxious to see U.D.I.
announced as the Rhodesians themselves because she felt that any alternative to it would be won at the price of appeasement. I can appreciate her
attitude because it is like mine before Munich: at that time I was positively
afraid that the act of appeasement would succeed in preventing war. True,

she has been overruled in Cabinet—each new stalling device was proposed by Harold, opposed by her and accepted by the rest of us. But he has paid her enormous deference. If you look in Cabinet minutes you will see that every time she protested she was allowed to speak and be listened to at length. On the last day Harold Wilson said that he hadn't slept well the night before because he had been worrying about it. That is most unlike him. What he was thinking about, I am sure, were Barbara's accusations that he was sacrificing the five principles. She got under his skin in a quite extraordinary way.

Thinking about the next moves in Rhodesia, I have the uneasy feeling that not only the Prime Minister but all the Ministers concerned are taking the most appallingly orthodox, narrow-minded view of how we must now behave. I have never forgotten that first occasion when Harold Wilson laid it down as a principle that we would not use military force, and stated it in public. On that occasion I didn't dare press him very hard; but since then I have frequently tried to cross-examine him on what he is organizing, what plans he has for overthrowing the Smith regime by para-military action. I get the impression that he considers the choice for Britain to lie between conventional military action or conventional diplomatic action, and that he denies the possibility of a third course in between. This of course is ludicrous. There are only 250,000 whites in Rhodesia and we have, I presume, an S.I.S., and S.O.E. and the other organizations of para-military war. And yet I am pretty sure that Harold and his military advisers have never considered the use of black propaganda or subversive organization to put pressure on Smith.

It seems to me just as extraordinary that he never considered the possibility of sending out even a battalion to guard the Governor or to give him a bodyguard of British troops. If we had, it would have been infinitely more difficult for Smith to declare U.D.I. A month ago the Lord Chancellor said that the real trouble about U.D.I. was that it would succeed in the short run, that sanctions wouldn't prevail and that these 250,000 people would be able to cock a snook at us and at the United Nations. I thought from the start that this was true, and everything that has happened since last Thursday has confirmed my doubts. True, the Governor has not been forcibly evicted from his home; but I was interested when Mr Pritchett[1] came in this weekend and said, 'If I'd been Prime Minister I would have put a battalion of British troops in Government House and then they couldn't have declared U.D.I.' If he can see it and I can see it, why can't Harold Wilson and George Brown see it as well? Yet I must admit that this view of mine is not accepted by any of my political friends, with the sole exception of George Wigg. Nothing more conventional, prim and proper could be conceived than this Government's reaction to what they describe as rebellion in Rhodesia. It is as though the declaration is what mattered to Harold; and once that had been made, he felt one could do nothing about it.

[1] Crossman's farm manager at Prescote.

Tuesday, November 16th
Right at the end of Cabinet this morning a row suddenly blew up about army pay. I only heard the start of it because I had to leave to prepare for Questions that afternoon. But what I heard convinced me that Denis Healey's case was very strong indeed despite the fact that he was opposing George Brown and Callaghan, who for once were in agreement about a major prices and incomes issue. The issue was the so-called Grigg award, which proposed an 18 per cent increase in pay to the armed services in order to make up for the amount they have fallen behind civilian wage rates in the last two years. The Grigg award was of course the result of the abandonment of conscription. If you are going to build up a voluntary army you can only do so by paying wages comparable to what men will get in civilian life; and so it was decided to have a biennial upgrading of service pay. The only thing wrong was that it worked out this year at 18 per cent, which if it was conceded might be the end of the prices and incomes policy. Simultaneously, we received a report from Oliver Franks[1] on the pay of the higher Civil Service and this, though it isn't as dangerous as the Grigg award, still concedes far more than we should like. And now Kenneth Robinson tells us we are on the edge of a doctors' strike about their lagging earnings.

Wednesday, November 17th
I had agreed to see George Brown late in the evening. When I went into his room in the Commons he was a little flushed and he told me that he had had the most terrible three-hour row with Healey. He and Callaghan had met Denis and offered him as a compromise an unconditional immediate pay increase of $7\frac{1}{2}$ per cent with everything else referred to the P.I.B. Healey had rejected this and claimed that the report by the P.I.B. should only take four weeks and the terms of reference should be far narrower than those that the D.E.A. and the Treasury suggested. He had obviously been deliberately difficult. I didn't at all want a row with George Brown and I agreed that in order to carry the army the immediate award might have to go up to 10 per cent and that the Civil Service and the doctors' claims would have to be referred to the P.I.B. at the same time. I felt gratified by George's anxiety to get me on his side—it shows that I am beginning to count a bit in Cabinet.

Thursday, November 18th
Cabinet started with the first good contribution Michael Stewart has made as Foreign Secretary—a clear, dry summary of the U.N. reaction to the Rhodesia crisis. He had flown in from a brief visit to New York that morning, and he told us how inadequate the United Nations found our action. Reading between the lines you can see the difficulties which will be facing us. There is every reason to believe that the Rhodesians will be holding out

[1] Former Ambassador to Washington who subsequently became chairman of Lloyds Bank and Provost of Worcester College, Oxford.

successfully in six months' time, and that even the oil sanctions the U.N. are talking about will be ineffective with Portugal and South Africa neutral on the side of Rhodesia.

Other members of the Cabinet are beginning to feel my sense of disquiet. After Michael Stewart's report, James Callaghan, for example, said he thought that stronger measures should be used by us and we should try to get a quick kill. Of course this is my view, but in that case the preparations for the quick kill should have taken place *before* U.D.I. If we fail to bring Smith to heel in the next two months, Wilson will soon fall from the height of popularity. Indeed the only counterbalancing factor is the weakness of the Opposition. If, as they seem to be doing this week, the Opposition starts quarrelling fiercely about support or rejection of oil sanctions, we may not suffer too much from the problems we shall face. Anyway, for the moment things look good with the N.O.P. poll today giving Labour an 18 per cent lead.

In the evening I had half an hour's talk over a drink with James Callaghan. This, on his suggestion, is to be a weekly affair. He knows I have now taken George Wigg's place on the liaison committee and that I am providing the link between Transport House and No. 10. So he has asked me to come along and discuss the situation with him. On this occasion the main thing he wanted to say was that there is still far too much inflation in the economy and he proposes to take another £200 million out of it by cuts in public expenditure, and possibly by increasing hire-purchase rates. He asked me whether I could think of other methods of dampening expenditure which weren't too damaging. I suspect that he really meant housing cuts but was too tactful to say so. Was it a pure accident that I was having this drink with him on Thursday when on Wednesday evening I had had a rather similar informal briefing talk with George Brown?

Sunday, November 21st

Arthur J. Schlesinger[1] has been over here from America and I spent an evening comparing the British and American systems. Over there the politician mans the top two echelons of his Department with experts he brings from outside. But an attempt here to have these outsiders in addition to the Private Office simply wouldn't work. The more I see of it the more I realize that the Private Office is the heart of the Ministry, the point where all my instructions and wishes go outwards and where the Department's advice concentrates on me. The Private Secretary's room outside my room is a kind of concourse, a grand vizier's waiting-room. Even the most senior civil servants, such as the Deputies, don't feel it the least undignified to stand about talking to John, asking what mood the Minister is in and discussing how to present something to him. Equally, they don't feel it undignified to

[1] Professor of History at Harvard University from 1954 to 1961, when he went to Washington to serve as Special Assistant to President Kennedy.

listen to John presenting my ideas to them. This central point of contact between the politician and the Department must, I think, be run by a civil servant. John Delafons is superb. Personally we don't know each other much better than we did on the first day. But he is learning a lot from me, and he is dedicated and ambitious and runs the office magnificently; and he really does try to get my ideas across to the Department. Nevertheless, I have got to face it that his main job is to get across to me what the Department wants. The Private Office is the Department's way of keeping a watch on me, of making sure I run along the lines they want me to run on, of dividing my time and getting the Department's policies and attitudes brought to my notice.

Of course, it is also my medium for reaching down into the Ministry. How far down does my influence stretch? Perhaps to an Assistant Secretary level but certainly not below. I reckon I now know the Permanent Secretary, the two Deputies, the four Under-Secretaries and most of the twenty-odd Assistant Secretaries. But the vast mass of civil servants who work beneath that level hardly know me at all. I notice this when I come in in the morning and go up in the lift. Most of the people in it don't recognize me, I suppose, and there's no reason why they should. But this means that my policies are transmitted by the senior civil servants to their subordinates merely by word of mouth and very often in an unsympathetic form. We found this out recently when we had the balls-up on housing allocations; and I am now considering whether we shouldn't call a meeting of the whole housing division, including the executive officers who actually do the allocations to the local authorities. It might be a good idea to get right down to them; and perhaps the next stage in my development as a departmental Minister is precisely to extend my influence below Assistant Secretary level.

In terms of contact with the officials I am probably unusually badly off because my Ministry is run so much as a personal concern by the Dame. By the way, since she returned from holiday in September she somehow seems to have aged and to be feeling a sense of anticlimax. After all, she had all her farewell dinners and was due to retire this autumn. It was deeply gratifying for her to be asked to stay on; but I don't think she is actually enjoying it a great deal. She is certainly not working with anything like the verve with which she started introducing me to the facts of life.

Wednesday, November 24th
At Transport House this morning there was an astonishing scene during the N.E.C. monthly meeting. Suddenly Ian Mikardo said we had to make a decision about votes for the eighteen-year-olds; and he pointed out that if we didn't do it that very morning, the Speaker's Conference on electoral reform might have reached the item without the Labour Members having a view or having put in a paper. He therefore asked for our views. I strongly supported him and so did Tony Wedgwood Benn, and when it came to the point not a single person round the table said anything against it. So it was carried

unanimously and that afternoon the news came out. Ironically enough, Harold Wilson, George Brown, James Callaghan and Michael Stewart weren't there. None of the prominent members of the Government was present, yet the N.E.C. had taken its collective decision. I don't think one can draw any conclusions from this performance except that it occasionally happens and it does the Labour Party a power of good to see the Executive really acting on its own.

Sunday, November 28th

This has been a key week in the Government's life because the Rhodesian crisis has taken a downward turn. Until U.D.I. was declared Harold dominated the scene. There he was, struggling day by day to prevent Smith doing this terrible thing. But now it has taken place there is an awkward hiatus. The drama of the poor old Governor staying on in Government House has worn off and it is only too clear that the British Government has no plans for suppressing the rebellion. We are sitting here in London and the so-called rebels are sitting quite happily there in Salisbury. We have no means of enforcing law and order on the rebels, whereas the rebels obviously have every means of maintaining law and order in defiance of us. This week people began to ask whether this is all the Government had up its sleeve; and the answer seems to be an uncomfortable 'Yes, that's all'.

Monday, November 29th

I was rung up on Sunday night and told that there was a Cabinet meeting next morning and asked if I wanted a car. But I didn't bother, caught the train and arrived about a quarter of an hour late. They were well into the discussion about the proposal to send the R.A.F. to Zambia. I knew about it because it had been the big story in all the Sunday papers. By the time I arrived the only issue was whether we should send ground troops as well. There was some division of opinion. I heard Douglas Houghton pleading against reinforcement and wanting to placate the white settlers, and I heard James Callaghan wanting much stronger measures. He is concerned because the crisis is costing us a lot and might undermine confidence in the pound. The P.M. was very much in the middle. Afterwards, talking to Denis Healey, I learnt that the inner group in Cabinet which 'runs' Rhodesia has been pressing Harold for stronger action, with Healey on Callaghan's side.

Tuesday, November 30th

This was the first easy day I have had in the Ministry for some weeks. I was able to sit back, sign documents, resume an easy relationship with the Secretary and have a long talk to John Delafons. As a result I am beginning to see that one can work too hard in a Department and can overtax the Civil Service as well as the Minister. With the old-fashioned, highly centralized, hierarchical structure focusing on herself on which Dame Evelyn insists, the

Minister can easily impose an appalling strain if he starts too many enter-
prises at the same time. So I am making up a list of commandments and here
are the first three: Commandment One: be careful not to ask for research to
be done and then find that it has imposed a great deal of work for no good
purpose; Commandment Two: make sure that all the instructions I issue are
channelled properly and that the official responsible is warned in advance of
what is coming; Commandment Three: cut back those enormous briefs
which the Department provides for my official visits.

Thursday, December 2nd
Yet another Cabinet with Rhodesia top of the agenda – the result of the row
in the House of Commons when it was announced that we were going to stop
the payment of pensions to retired civil servants in Rhodesia. The P.M.
obviously wanted to smooth things down and pay the pensions after all.
Having an ingenious mind and sometimes also being very naïve, he asked
why we shouldn't pay them in Rhodesian bank notes printed in London. I
thought it funny, but Callaghan got on his hind legs about forgery. I sat there
wondering how the episode would be reported in the Cabinet minutes. I
think I can say now that there will be no reference at all to this proposal of the
Prime Minister's.*

Monday, December 6th
I travelled up to London last night for an early meeting on the Rent Act and
it wasn't until twelve o'clock that I was able to get down to preparing my
speech for the Second Reading of the Rating Bill. Alas, it is still true that I
can't rely on the Ministry, though at least on this occasion I was able to use
the factual description of how rebates work; but the introduction setting the
policy in its context, and the peroration, had to be done over the lunch hour.
Very hurriedly, I decided my main theme: that rate rebates are merely an
interim measure to prop up a bad tax which I wanted to get rid of as soon as
possible. Now, I have used this argument in speech after speech and yet on
this occasion I overreached myself. Because I didn't have quite enough time
to prepare my speech, I said things over-vigorously and too dogmatically. It
really isn't quite the thing for a Minister of Housing and Local Government
to use such language about a tax which, after all, the treasurers have to go on
raising. I realized as I sat down that I was in grave danger of turning the local
authorities against the Minister who was pretty popular with them a few
months ago.

Tuesday, December 7th
Judging by the morning papers I had a very good press for my speech,
perhaps too good. When I got to Cabinet I found some of my colleagues
remarking drily that they were interested to hear that the Government had
decided to abolish rating. One of the interesting facts about the Cabinet
* There wasn't.

system as it is worked by Harold Wilson is the free-wheeling which a department Minister is allowed to do; one gets away with anything until one falters. But one's colleagues' resentments are very real. In this case I paid the price immediately, because that very morning I was due for my tussle with the Chancellor of the Exchequer about housing subsidies.

But before we got to it Cabinet had to suffer yet another of those interminable Rhodesian discussions. On this occasion the trouble was caused by a weekend story in all the papers that Harold was preparing a peace offensive. I have no doubt he is trying to leave as many lines open to the Rhodesian Government as he possibly can; and Barbara and her friends try to cut those lines because they want not an agreement with Smith but military sanctions. So Barbara needled Harold endlessly, trying to make him say that on no account would he ever negotiate with the Smith regime; and Harold time after time wriggled out of repudiating the suggestion. That went on for an hour and a half, and it ended up with such confusion that when two Members of Cabinet, one in the House of Lords and one in the House of Commons, gave their accounts of what was happening in the afternoon they were completely inconsistent with one another.

Finally we got to my housing subsidies. I stated the case for increasing my allocation. Callaghan stated his case against giving me a single extra house, and rallied every spending Minister to his side by asserting that Housing couldn't be given any more concessions without destroying the whole PESC agreement of last July. I reminded Cabinet that it was agreed on that occasion that, if there were any slack to be taken up, the taking up should be done by housing. At once Tony Crosland chipped in, 'Why only housing? Why shouldn't schools have their share of the slack? With building licensing coming in, isn't it essential that we should look at this problem as a whole and not merely in terms of housing, which anyway has got a great deal more than its share and is pushing itself forward time and time again?' I was paying for my prominence, for my success and for Harold's backing behind the scenes. The Prime Minister did his best for me, arguing that in PESC we had created an instrument for controlling our expenditure but that we were now becoming the servants and not the master of our own instrument. But there was no one enthusiastically on my side except the Secretaries of State for Wales and Scotland, who of course have their own housing programmes. Willie Ross said to me afterwards that we had done as well as possible when we got the decision postponed until the end of January. Nevertheless, this was the first really big reverse I have suffered in Cabinet. It was inevitable but it was none the less unpleasant for that.

Tuesday, December 14th
At Cabinet this morning Peggy Herbison put forward the second part of her plan for reforming social security. After more than a year wasted on reflection, Douglas Houghton and she had decided that the incomes guarantee

was wholly impracticable and had to be dropped. What could be put in its place? The scheme she put forward this morning was a cheap substitute, a reformed national assistance which would be sold to the public under the new name of supplementary benefit. I am still sick at the thought of how Douglas Houghton has fragmented our major comprehensive reform and so minimized its political effect. Nevertheless, if you take it for what it is—a cheap substitute—this proposal of Peggy's is brilliantly worked out. Once again Douglas Houghton and James Callaghan got into a sinister combination trying to wreck it. Fortunately, others praised it highly and we got it through without too much delay.

Saturday, December 18th
This was the day of the presentation to mark my twenty years as M.P. for Coventry East. I'd mentioned this to Maurice Edelman and found to my slight embarrassment that it hadn't been arranged for him.

What a book one could write about the influence the constituency exerts on the M.P. The luck of my being chosen in 1937 has kept me in Parliament with a huge cast-iron majority and with a particular kind of Party behind me which has deeply influenced my thinking, keeping me much more on the Left than I would by nature have been. And this has meant that I have not had any of the pressures that are exerted on M.P.s in marginal constituencies: I have never in my political life had to bother about appeasing industrialists or right-wing groups, churches or chapels. Coventry East would simply not have allowed me to be a right-winger, to be an anti-Bevanite, for example. On the other hand, they have given me their loyalty and their permission to be a very egocentric politician with ideas of my own; and though they have often disagreed with me they have given me pretty solid support. Since I have been a Minister I have tended to get depressed about Coventry. It's a difficult place under a Labour Government; and I am also aware of a decline in the Party and a decline in its quality on the council. Mostly it was old people who were there for the presentation; only a handful were young and proud of the part I have played in trying to modernize the Party.

The Prime Minister's handling of the Rhodesian crisis had given him a great deal of publicity but, leaving nothing to chance, he attracted further public attention at the very end of the year by a brief visit to America just before Christmas and, on his return, a Cabinet reshuffle.

Tuesday, December 21st
Cabinet. Harold reported on his talks with Johnson. He claimed that he had managed to get an absolute promise from the President that he would be allowed to work for peace and not send British troops to Vietnam. On the other hand, he got no more than an understanding that if we stood firm on our present position in the Far East the Americans would back the oil

sanctions we were announcing that afternoon. He seems to have adopted a very lieutenant-ish posture, but possibly that is the best we can achieve in the present circumstances. What mainly struck me was his extraordinary physical vitality. On Friday he flies to Washington and from there on to Canada. On Monday he arrives back and makes a Statement in the House, and on Tuesday after Cabinet he is due to open the second day of the foreign affairs debate. All this while he is maintaining a pretty fair control of the other aspects of government.

His speech in the debate had the desired effect: it split the Tory party and it kept the Labour Party relatively united. Indeed, when the vote came the leadership of the Tories abstained and the back benches broke in two with one section voting for oil sanctions and the other section against them.[1]

Wednesday, December 22nd
At last the reshuffle has been announced. Barbara moves to Transport, Tony Greenwood takes her place in Overseas Development and Frank Longford becomes Colonial Secretary. I heard all this for the first time at a Christmas party in Caxton House. It came to me as a tremendous surprise. I had assumed that Frank Soskice would finally be removed and wondered who would take his place. I didn't see how Harold could select Barbara, in view of her violent views on immigration, or Tony Greenwood, because of his proven incompetence. Would he give the job to Douglas Houghton for a short time and move Frank to the Duchy? What he actually decided was to give Roy Jenkins the Home Office, the job he had offered him earlier. I am sure Barbara has paid the price for her pertinacity in taking the black African point of view and in being the one member of the Cabinet prepared to prevent a settlement in Rhodesia. She was moved because he didn't want her formidable, old-fashioned, left-wing conscience there preventing him finding some kind of settlement with the Smith regime. As for her new job at Transport, I have heard from Jennie, whose husband Chris is transferring with Barbara to the new Ministry, that she realizes how much a graveyard of all political reputations Transport has become. But if there is anybody who will get us a fully integrated transport policy it is she and that makes it a good move.

I saw Harold just after the announcement and he wanted to chat with me about it. But I had so much business I had to get through that I ticked off my items for half an hour and made sure I had cleared everything before the Christmas recess.

Thursday, December 23rd
The Christmas feeling has been growing in Cabinet and in Whitehall all through the week. There was a tremendous sense of winding up, and I found

[1] At the end of the debate on the Rhodesia Order the vote was 276 to 48 in favour of imposing sanctions.

my Ministry determined to close down on Thursday, though Christmas Eve came on Friday. I said that was impossible and they finally got me off late on Thursday evening after a solid day's work.

I had thought perhaps I would try a retrospect of 1965, but the trouble is that calendar years mean nothing to me as a Minister. I can't remember what I felt like a year ago and take care not to look at my diary to see what it says. I just can't look back over the whole of 1965. What I can say is that since the summer Harold Wilson has been more and more obsessed with Rhodesia and Vietnam and less and less actively concerned with the home front. But the difficulties of the prices and incomes policy have been steadily mounting and we are getting very near to breaking-point. We can't afford to let the policy fail and yet quite soon we are going to face the 18-per-cent increase of army pay which the P.I.B. will almost certainly award. Then will come a sudden forward surge of salaries and wages which in its turn will produce another round of price increases and then the pound may well be in danger. On the other hand, we are beginning to implement Government policy. Soon we shall have our option-mortgages (the scheme is now pretty well complete), our rating reforms, and Peggy Herbison's reform of national assistance and the beginning of graded benefits for unemployment and sickness.

But the immediate prospect is of course the Hull by-election.[1] From the latest Gallup Poll it looks as though we have a reasonable chance of winning it. But even if we don't we may well carry on with the majority of one which we have got now.

Of course, this means that things are precarious. We have not only got Hayman at Falmouth on the edge of death; I heard over Christmas that Megan Lloyd George is desperately ill with cancer and likely to die at any moment.[2] I suppose Harold calculates that if we are forced to the polls by that kind of thing we may well do better because the public will want to give us a second chance. That brings me to the Opposition. Heath as leader has not really achieved anything yet, no professionalism, no particular competence. He is rather dull and stands no comparison with Harold. But all leaders develop and it won't take long before he improves. Meanwhile the Tories are settling down to the characteristics of an Opposition, beginning to make policy statements against each other. Already a right wing is gathering around Powell, who stands for ultra free-enterprise economics, and a left wing round Iain Macleod and Boyle, who still believe in the incomes policy and national planning. As the ex-Ministers settle down on the Opposition front bench they are beginning to find memories of Government replaced by nostalgia for Government. What they miss are those red dispatch boxes and

[1] Henry Solomons, the Labour M.P. for Kingston upon Hull North, had died the previous month. He had gained the seat for Labour at the 1964 election with a majority of only 1,181.

[2] Younger daughter of Lloyd George. She was Liberal M.P. for Anglesey 1929–51, and Labour M.P. for Carmarthen 1957–66. She died in May 1966.

the secret contact with reality that they give. I remember how mad I got with Hugh Gaitskell when in Opposition he would sometimes say, 'That's an issue no responsible person can decide unless he can see the Cabinet papers.' Now having read Cabinet papers for a year I have more sympathy with Gaitskell and with those Tories on the Opposition front bench. Separated from his sources of information the politician feels unsure of what he knows and starts making assertions which are pure dogma. The Tories are getting these characteristics—a tremendous loss to them which strengthens our position.

1966

Sunday, January 23rd

Alas! this is the end of a long Christmas recess. With Parliament away we Ministers have been able to get down to our Whitehall work and cope with it adequately. Looking back over the weeks, I think I can say that during this time Harold Wilson nearly decided that an early election is inevitable. Last summer he wouldn't even consider my suggestion of a snap election in early November. And when I went back to the idea again before Christmas he was equally hostile, and used the excuse of a Conservative newspaper story to slap down the idea of a pre-budget election. Now in the talks I have had with him since he returned from Lagos[1] he seems to be moving round more and more to the feeling that things are crowding in dangerously upon us, that the prices dam is going to break and that the position he has built up in Rhodesia is strong enough to risk an election. Indeed, one of the strangest things that has happened recently is the transformation in the public attitude to Rhodesia. I still remember with what dread Harold Wilson looked forward to the proclamation of U.D.I. and with what certainty he felt it would lead the Government into a situation where the Tories might win an enormous advantage. Now every newspaper commentator is writing about the benefits accruing to the Government from Rhodesia. We are able to divert attention to Rhodesia, where we are being successful, from the home front, where we are not. Of course, this is all Harold's personal achievement. He now talks about Rhodesia as his Cuba and he has played the crisis with astonishing tactical skill. Although I have felt that he ought to have taken stronger measures, that he ought to have had some advance planning, that he oughtn't have played it by ear, that he ought to have got rid of his Commonwealth Secretary, I can't deny that he has moved step by step always in line with British opinion. First he tried to prevent U.D.I. at all costs; then he put on mild sanctions which wouldn't upset people; now he's moving forward to more serious sanctions. Each time he carries public opinion with him and creates a situation in which an unsure Tory leader has been quite unable to display any qualities of leadership.

One other impression borne in on me during the recess relates to my own position. I am now a relatively popular and successful Minister. The papers say that I am good on television and successful in getting my way in Cabinet, as well as close to the P.M. Nevertheless, I still don't play any central role in the Government. I don't read the F.O. telegrams, and in Cabinet I find myself looking out of the window at Horseguards Parade in excruciating boredom whenever Rhodesia is discussed because I am waiting for my item on local government finance. The other day I was having a drink in Nicky Kaldor's flat in Chelsea when Tommy Balogh said, 'You're getting quite unbearable, Dick. All this evening you have been trying to make out that the really important business of the Government gyrates round the Ministry of

---

[1] The Conference of Commonwealth Prime Ministers had taken place in Lagos, Nigeria from January 11th–13th, 1966.

Housing and Local Government. You think the whole thing depends on that.' In a way he was making a fair criticism because I am now blinkered, narrowed and obsessed compared, for example, with Tony Crosland. He is interested in educational problems only in a secondary way: he remains an economist and his interest is still mainly in general economic issues. That is why he is a real, active Cabinet Minister, whereas I really belong with the inferior members of the Cabinet, the smaller fry.

However, there is one thing that perhaps differentiates me from them: my departmental interests do stretch a very long way. I am not only Minister of Housing. I am Minister of Local Government, and the range there is really remarkable. During this recess I have been dealing throughout with issues like the Meadow road at Oxford, the Ullswater problem and my plan for a blue belt round London, not to mention rating, council rents and local government reorganization. When I see that stretch I think it is fair to say that my Ministry is a very central Department. Indeed, this is Harold Wilson's view and he wants to make it more so. More than once when I have been trying to get a decision from him about a successor to the Dame he has said to me, 'Well, of course, I couldn't possibly promise that Land and Natural Resources should be restored to your Ministry during this Parliament. But in the next Parliament things might be different. I am thinking of a great federal central planning Ministry covering Housing and Works and Land and Natural Resources.' That naturally would interest me a great deal. That's the kind of Ministry I would like to have and that's the idea he is feeding me.

I had arranged to go up by the 7.30 on Sunday for the official meeting with Harold and Callaghan about the rents situation. Harold had asked me to come earlier to have a private talk beforehand. When he rang up I said, 'Oh, for heaven's sake, can't I make it a little later so as not to miss the whole of this weekend?' Back came the tart remark, '*I* haven't had a weekend since I was P.M.' I knew I had blotted my copybook. It is true I have my family down here and he has his family up in No. 10, so I have *some* right to try to get time with my children. But the idea that any colleague takes time off from his work shocks Harold and though when we met he said, 'Of course I understand,' I realized it had put me back in his opinion. My train was an hour late and I only got an hour with him before the meeting with the Chancellor though he had wanted a much longer talk with me.

I briefed him first about the Liverpool rents situation.[1] When I started on the project at the beginning of January it seemed a very long shot. Now it isn't. I had seen Harold about it again last week and he said to me, 'If you are going to do anything, for God's sake make it big enough to make a real electoral difference.' I was able to say that if we really wanted to make a difference, we should ante-date the rent subsidy and pay it for all houses

[1] Liverpool's Housing Revenue Account was in the red and the city's Labour council had urgently requested a government subsidy to help it out.

completed in the year up to November 20th, 1965. Then we would pay out
£6 million this year to the councils and an extra £9 million in successive years
and that would give them a chance of holding down the increases in rent.
After discussing one or two details he told me to work it out and minute him
and Callaghan, with copies to the Scottish and Welsh Secretaries of State.
That minute has now been seen by all the Departments, and the Treasury has
reacted by proposing its own scheme for paying the subsidy a year, or nine
months, or six months in advance, so giving the authorities their cash a little
earlier. But it doesn't give them a penny in the long run and it won't actually
affect the level of rents. A typical Treasury scheme. We got it in time to
organize our answer over the weekend.

He left himself plenty of time to talk about the date of the election and for
the first time he made it clear he was considering March. When I said there
was a case for April, after the budget, he replied, 'But then the rate demands
will already be in people's hands and that will cost us votes.' Also he was
deeply concerned about council rents because 20,000 of his voters in Huyton
and Kirby pay overspill rents to Liverpool City Council.

Then we went downstairs to meet Callaghan in the Cabinet room. I started
by saying that the Treasury proposal meant nothing at all and Jim immediately agreed: 'We want something serious and it is not worth taking up the
Treasury line.' So I put my proposals and then both Harold and Jim said,
'But your proposal involves giving money to everybody all round. Can't we
have a discriminating subsidy?' I was a bit mulish and said, 'Well, we do
discriminate already. The new subsidies are designed to help those people
with the most houses to build and who need to build high-rise on expensive
sites.' But this wouldn't do. 'Isn't there a way of giving a special subsidy for
slum clearance?' Harold asked. I said that I didn't want to do that and I was
even more resistant. Finally I worked out a formula which might possibly
concentrate the cash on big conurbations and the meeting ended.

Monday, January 24th
The Department spent most of the day trying to find a formula agreeable to
the Treasury which made sense on the subject of council rents. As soon as I
got in the Dame told me that my formula was hopeless. Probably it was. She
agreed with Harold that the only way to deal with the problem was in terms
of slum clearance. So we settled down to try to find a way in which the extra
money would go only to the big cities; and finally we got it. We would pay the
subsidy on houses completed in the year up to November 1965 but only to
cities whose slum clearance problem was above a certain level as defined
in an extremely complicated formula. When I finally got the document into
my hands I rang up Marcia and asked if I could come round with it straight
away.

I had a talk with Marcia. She was a bit depressed after long talks with Sara
Barker about Hull, even though the reports from George Wigg were

confident. What alarmed her was the prospect that the national situation would lose us votes there.

By this time Harold had got back from his dinner and I went downstairs to see him. He looked over the paper very quickly and said it was on the right lines and then he added, 'I promise you that while you are up in Hull tomorrow I will try to clear this with James Callaghan.' It couldn't be done during the morning because there was a Cabinet and I was leaving by the 1.21 train. He then obviously wanted to relax and we talked politics for three-quarters of an hour. Once again his mind was moving towards a March election; and I realized from what he said that one of his major problems was George Brown's Bill disciplining the unions, and another that he has now got a complete reshuffle of Permanent Secretaries on his hands and it will have to be followed by a strong Cabinet reconstruction.

Tuesday, January 25th
I caught the 1.21 to Hull and found myself travelling up with George Thomson, the Minister of State at the Foreign Office, who was speaking with me, and a young man called Clark, a member of the Radical Alliance, who was speaking for Richard Gott, the anti-Vietnam war candidate. There were six candidates in all at Hull–Conservative, Liberal, Labour, Radical Alliance (Gott) and two Independents. Hull is a wonderful place to visit since there are five or six hours of physical and geographical isolation in the train. I enjoyed every moment. Transport House had done an excellent job analysing the situation there and I went up with two press releases on which I had worked very strenuously. One demonstrated that in 1965 we had built 9,000 more houses than the Tories had ever built in a single year. The second related to the proposed Humber bridge. I had had to draft this with care because Barbara had duly pledged to build it, and the sentences Harold had used in a letter to the candidate (I had written them in) were in strict accord with the statement I had made at Blackpool. That statement was valuable in Hull because it proved that we had been considering the bridge last September and that Barbara's speech wasn't a last-minute bribe.

When I reached Hull I handed the two press releases to Percy Clark, who processed both of them, and then we had a little supper together. Percy was certain we would get a 2,000 majority. I had a few hours looking round and at the end was convinced he was right: the only disaster we could suffer would be from the impact of the national situation on Hull. When I left to pick up the sleeper in Leeds I was much easier in my mind.

Thursday, January 27th
In the afternoon there was a vote of censure in the House, but the mood was dull because we were all waiting for the Hull result. I was getting telephoned reports from Percy Clark which supported the N.O.P.'s announcement that morning that we would have an 8 per cent lead; I thought we might well win

by 2,500 to 3,000. There was tremendous suspense throughout the day. In the evening our little group met and we went round for a chat with Harold; and there in No. 10 we saw the result on television—so much better than we expected.[1] My immediate reaction was to say to myself, 'Oh dear, will Harold now give up the March election because of this good result? Will it be more difficult to get him to be sensible?' Nevertheless, it was an overwhelming victory and I felt cheered.

Tuesday, February 1st
The papers are full of a Labour split. It has nicely punctured the euphoria we were all feeling as a result of the Hull by-election—which only lasted over the weekend. The trouble was a communiqué the Foreign Office issued on Monday evening announcing the full support of the Labour Government for the resumption of bombing by the Americans in Vietnam after the New Year's truce. I know as a fact that this communiqué had not been approved by Harold and I have my doubts whether it was even approved by Michael Stewart. But last night it produced a tremendous blow-up with twenty-five back-bench M.P.s sending a telegram to L.B.J.[2] So the Tories have held firm under the pressure of defeat at Hull and it is the Labour Party which has split as the result of success—if we had lost the by-election that telegram would never have been sent.

That evening for the very first time the little group was invited to dinner by Harold and I suppose you can say that this was the first occasion on which he allowed himself a kitchen cabinet. Marcia of course was there, Peter Shore, Tommy Balogh, Wedgy Benn, Gerald Kaufman. Mary and Marcia's assistant, Brenda Drew, looked after the food. Then we went down below and sat round the table and at last we felt that Harold was really treating us, his group of friends, as associates with whom he could discuss the future. We all felt it was the beginning of a completely new deal. I expect we were wrong.

In the course of the evening he said at one point, and we all waited on his words because he was obviously talking seriously, 'I have been reading Theodore White's book on the L.B.J./Goldwater Presidential election,[3] and it has made me think of my own role. I am not a father figure, you know, I am a doctor figure. That's what Theodore White tells me, I am a doctor figure.' We moved on to talk about how the election would be won and he said quite openly, 'You, Dick, will have to stay behind in London. You, Tony, I would like to run the television shows but as Postmaster-General you hardly can. As for me, I have got to be at No. 10 most of the time.' At this point I said, 'Well, for God's sake don't rush off to Huyton for the last five days as you did last time.' He agreed this was something that he absolutely mustn't do. We

[1] The Labour majority rose from 1,181 to 5,351, a 4½ per cent swing—the highest pro-government by-election swing for ten years.
[2] According to Wilson, ninety M.P.s sent a telegram to Senator Fulbright, supporting his attack on the President. See *Wilson*, p. 204.
[3] Theodore H. White, *The Making of the President, 1964* (London: Cape, 1965).

went on to discuss what kind of machinery we could have for linking Transport House and No. 10, and there was a lot of talk about Harold's relations with George and James. I told him that on the previous Thursday James had said to me that he didn't want to be Chancellor in the next Government. I had said to him, 'There is one other job you should get if you are not Chancellor and that is Leader of the House. You could be the Herbert Morrison of the Party if we return with a big majority—inspiring the back-benchers, controlling the House of Commons, planning the legislative programme.' Harold was tickled at this: it is something he really would like. But he just listened and then said to me once again, 'I want you to be a federal Minister of Housing, with Land and Natural Resources brought back and the Ministry of Works brought in. I have written a paper about it but I haven't put the part about the Ministry of Works in because otherwise I would have Charlie Pannell hanging around No. 10 every day for the next six weeks.'

It was a delightful evening and it was the first time we felt as a group that we really could do some good because he was trusting us.

Sunday, February 6th

Chequers. This was the joint meeting of the N.E.C. and the Cabinet, which had been long awaited and which we, in the little group, were preparing for so many hours last week. It had been conceded by Harold because the Executive complained it was not being kept in proper rapport with the Government: they wanted a real chance of having it out frankly and fiercely with their political colleagues. Well, from 10.30 a.m. to 6.30 p.m. they had the chance and there wasn't a single moment in the day when anything was had out, when there was any tension, any sense of crisis. What had I expected would happen? I suppose like Harold himself I had thought back to the famous Shanklin Conference before the 1949 election,[1] which Harold had attended though I hadn't. What happened at Chequers this time was very different. We all settled down in the big room upstairs. The officers sat round a small table at one end in the bay window and the rest of us sat on lines of chairs in front of them like a schoolboy class. Physically, therefore, general discussion was difficult and it wasn't rendered any easier by the way the conference was organized. First came Harold Wilson with his general observations; then George Brown ditto; and then James Callaghan giving a long introduction to the first topic—economics. By the time he started the atmosphere was fairly somnolent and few people, I suspect, observed that he was talking in a language not very distinct from that of Lord Cromer. However, at least we were discussing the key problem, prices and incomes, the stop and the crisis. We next had a long speech from Jack Jones, whom I first met when

[1] In February 1949 the Labour Cabinet and the N.E.C. had held a special two-day conference to discuss the draft programme, 'Labour Believes in Britain', for the next election. It was held at the Manor House Hotel at Shanklin on the Isle of Wight.

I was adopted as prospective candidate for Coventry and he had just returned from a time with the International Brigade in Spain. Jack Jones is now a respectable number two to Frank Cousins, but he is still very left-wing and his main concern is to take Frank's place when he retires. He was playing a big role for the first time in our N.E.C. and he made a long, competent, serious speech in which he strongly opposed the statutory sanctions George Brown was demanding for his prices and incomes policy. His speech was followed by another left-wing speech from Ian Mikardo. But that was, if I remember aright, the total of the left-wing opposition on this occasion. Jack and Ian were not followed by any serious questions or threats or pressure from other members of the Executive. In fact this was all that happened before lunch.

After lunch in the somnolence of the afternoon, with the weather growing more and more beautiful outside, all we had was a series of set declarations by Ministers—punctuated by a few mild comments. The net effect of all this was a vote of confidence in the Government; and this will enable Harold Wilson and George Brown, as chairman of the Home Affairs Committee, to say to the Executive, 'You've had it, chums. We've given you your chance to complain—a whole day. You did nothing at all about it.'

When the meeting was over it was clear that writing the election manifesto this time would be child's play. We would describe how we took the job on after thirteen years of Tory rule, and how we now want a mandate to finish the job. And we would insert at a number of points commitments to go a bit further than individual Ministers intend. That's the job we have to do.

I had arranged to go back to London from the conference with Peter Shore, who was there as the Prime Minister's P.P.S. At lunch, however, Marcia came up to me and said she wanted us to stay behind and go up later to dine with the P.M. and discuss what had happened. So at six o'clock when the others were driving away, Peter and I stood aside along with Marcia and Gerald Kaufman. Everybody else went off, including George Brown and James Callaghan. People in the Labour Party are very suspicious and every effort was made to conceal the fact that we were staying on. We succeeded quite well until we went into the little white drawing-room where Mary sits with her family, and there we found Sara Barker and Bert Williams[1] waiting for Len Williams, who was holding the press conference with Harold Wilson. That conference unfortunately lasted one and a quarter hours. We had an awkward period sitting there together because Sara twigged very soon that we had been asked to stay behind and have a private confab with Harold.

However, finally she withdrew and after that down Harold came and said, 'There are still two journalists, old Stacpoole of Exchange Telegraph and someone else, filing their stories. After we and they have both eaten let's have them in for a cup of coffee.' Marcia said, 'If you don't take care they will record who's here tonight and who is not.' And Harold said, 'Oh yes, I must

[1] Number two in the Organization Department of Transport House.

be careful about that,' and the idea fell through. Though he is the most powerful man in the country he is still anxious lest Alice Bacon should be upset to read that Dick Crossman and Peter Shore stayed behind at Chequers to discuss things privately with the Prime Minister at a meeting from which she was excluded. This fear is still very much in his mind. So after we had had our plate of cold turkey and tongue and a glass of not very good, not very cold beer, we moved into the long drawing-room. It was the second meeting of Harold's kitchen cabinet and it soon became clear that he wanted Peter and me to draft the election manifesto and discuss it again in a week's time at Chequers.

Sunday, February 13th

Peter Marriott[1] motored me over to Chequers and when we got there at ten o'clock I found Peter Shore driving up in his car with Tommy Balogh by his side and Brènda, Marcia's number two, coming along in another. So the only people who stayed the night with Mary and Harold must have been Marcia and her brother. We settled down at 10.30 to work through Peter Shore's draft manifesto. He's done the first draft of all our election manifestos, first under Morgan Phillips[2] and then under the new dispensation. But each time I have been brought in to work over them, as I did at Scarborough for the last election, during my holiday. This time the skeleton he provided was pretty complete and pretty handsome. Harold was in pleasant, family form, because when he is getting near an election he suddenly can't rely on his civil servants and has to have recourse to his friends. He has recently got rid of Derek Mitchell, his Private Secretary, who bickered with Marcia[3] and I think he will probably move towards a White House concept of No. 10 if he wins this election.

When Harold left I motored to London with Peter and tried to do a little on the new draft as well as dealing with the rating White Paper, which is to explain our long Bill and which, thank God, my Ministry has at last drafted in a reasonable way.

Monday, February 14th

Cabinet on defence. We spent the whole morning on the Defence White Paper, and there was another two-hour session from six till eight before we approved it.

All the talk in the newspapers was about the threat of resignation by Christopher Mayhew[4] and the First Sea Lord. But this wasn't a subject of

[1] Crossman's gardener at Prescote.
[2] Secretary of the Research Department 1941–4 and then General Secretary of the Labour Party. He retired in 1962 and died in January 1963. His wife Norah was made a life peer in 1964.
[3] See Marcia Williams, *Inside No. 10*.
[4] M.P. for North Norfolk 1945–50 and for Woolwich East 1951–74. He was Minister of Defence for the Royal Navy in 1964–6. He resigned from the Labour Party in 1974 and was unsuccessful Liberal candidate for Bath in the general election of October of that year.

controversy in the Cabinet. The things we really argued about were the
decision to buy the American F-111 and the British role East of Suez. As for
the F-111 it soon became clear that all the details were now cut and dried,
and that the papers for the agreement with the Americans on the purchase of
the plane were awaiting signature when Healey flew off to Washington
tonight. So the whole thing was fixed. All Cabinet could do was express
opinions and influence to some extent the general tone of the White Paper
by drafting amendments. Of course, there were some Ministers like Barbara
Castle who took up postures of protest. But the rest of us felt that there was
nothing we could do and that the procedure under which we had been
excluded was not unreasonable. Fourteen of our twenty-three members of
Cabinet are members of the Defence Committee. To the preparation of this
White Paper these fourteen had devoted nineteen meetings and two
Chequers weekends. After all this, it was natural enough that they should
expect Cabinet to give formal authorization to the recommendations they
had worked out.

The issue which interested me was our role East of Suez. I found myself
along with Barbara and others asking questions and extracting from the P.M.
a very characteristic chain of utterances. First he repeated time after time
that the Americans had never made any connection between the financial
support they gave us and our support for them in Vietnam. Then about ten
minutes later he was saying, 'Nevertheless, don't let's fail to realize that their
financial support is not unrelated to the way we behave in the Far East: any
direct announcement of our withdrawal, for example, could not fail to have a
profound effect on my personal relations with L.B.J. and the way the
Americans treat us.' However, I got the impression that the Defence
Committee want us out of Singapore in 1970 and very much hope the
Australians will turn us down when we ask for a British presence there after
our withdrawal from Singapore. In fact we have to wait for facts to force
withdrawal on us. So, though we are not in any way committed to withdrawal, the Chiefs of Staff have been told to work on the assumption that
Singapore will be untenable long before 1970 and that we shall not transfer
our troops to Australia. Indeed, it is only on this assumption that we can
possibly keep our defence budget within the limit the Cabinet has set—a top
limit of £2,000 million. If we stay in Singapore the budget will go well over
that top limit. All this is concealed from the public by the large under-
spending of our Estimates this year and will go on being concealed next year
when we shall be able to defer expenditure due in the four-year period which
will never take place if we withdraw in time.

Thursday, February 17th
Cabinet started with the Leasehold Enfranchisement Bill. The other item we
discussed was Tony Wedgwood Benn's plan for making the B.B.C. introduce a moderate amount of advertising as a way of helping it out of its

financial difficulties. It was a sound idea but I'd feared he wouldn't get it through. Sure enough, John Fulton, who is the vice-chairman of the governors, had told Harold that they would not accept advertising of any kind on any terms whatsoever. The P.M. reported on his talks with the B.B.C.; but clearly this is something we shall have to put under the mat until after the election just as I have already put under the mat my decision on Ullswater and the Manchester water supply and a good many other awkward items as well.

That evening at five o'clock there was yet another meeting between the Chancellor, the Prime Minister and myself on housing subsidies. Outside the P.M.'s room at the House we found Christopher Mayhew sitting on the sofa waiting to have his resignation talk. After he'd gone the P.M. said to me, 'He's been coming day after day trying to talk to me about his resignation. I wish to God he would finish it quickly and let us forget him.'

Saturday, February 19th
Prescote. All set for the election. That was the mood at Westminster by the end of this week. In the House of Commons there comes a point when election fever is replaced by election acceptance. Whether one likes it or not, at this point the Government has committed itself to the election. I have watched Harold Wilson growing into this decision. There hasn't been a point at which he suddenly decided. He was very near it last Sunday while we were working on the manifesto. But in the course of this week it has been finally decided in the sense that it is now irreversible, and since that is the case let me make some of my hazardous predictions.

First, I predict that the date of the election will be Thursday, March 31st, and that it will be announced by Harold when he comes back from his visit to Moscow.

Secondly, let me say that Harold expects to bring something back from Russia with him, some joint initiative on Vietnam, and he may be able to link with this a Common Market initiative. He has been under tremendous pressure over the E.E.C. from Stewart and George Brown ever since last December. He has been trying to get them out of their purely anti-French position; and it looks to me as though he is right in thinking that there are reasonable chances of a new approach to Europe. As he sees it, the difficulties of staying outside Europe and surviving as an independent power are very great compared with entering on the right conditions.

Now for the Tories. I think they are going into this election beaten before they start. They are appalled by the prospect of it coming in March and they are devastated by our stream of policy statements. Of course, this is the result of their own folly. They started accusing us of breaking our pledges far too soon. We were able to reply that we couldn't do everything in the first months. But now, having held them back, we are putting out statements on practically all our policy. By the time the election gets under way we shall have either (a) actually implemented a proposal, or (b) begun the legislation, or (c) published a White Paper on the policy. There are very few promises in our programme which can't be placed in one of these three categories and that the Tories know.

Are there any snags we face? Yes, of course there are. The main trouble is that we haven't delivered the goods; the builders are not building the houses; the cost of living is still rising; the incomes policy isn't working; we haven't held back inflation; we haven't got production moving. We are going to the country now because we are facing every kind of difficulty and we anticipate that things are bound to get worse and we shall need a bigger majority with which to handle them.

Sunday, February 20th
I had to go to Birmingham for the Labour Party's annual local-government conference; I was to give the winding-up speech in the afternoon before going up to London for an urgent meeting with Harold.

I did my job, made my speech and then went off terribly late to catch the 6.05 to London. I thought I would be late for the P.M. who wanted to see me at 9 a.m. The train got in at 9.15, but when I got to Downing Street there was nothing to fuss about because he was happily back from a day's golf. I found him eating supper in the sitting-room in front of the TV with Mary and Giles, and we went down to his study to talk about mortgages. This is a terribly important election pledge but we still haven't settled the scheme.

Once business was over we sat down for another of those queer conversations I have been having with him almost every week. I pressed him very hard on the need for drastic Cabinet reorganization after the election. I wouldn't say that he took offence but I was aware that I was going a bit far. However, once again I dared to discuss the future of my Ministry. On this occasion he had a new idea. He said that Tony Part, at the Ministry of Works, was a splendid fellow.[1] I wasn't surprised because a few days ago Burke Trend mentioned his name to me, and I began to feel I should have to accept him. We also discussed the future of Frank Cousins. Harold said he thought the best thing was to carry him through the election and afterwards make an issue of his attitude to the national prices and incomes policy. One thing he let out to me almost in passing was that my role for the election had undergone a change. George Wigg, he said, would now be in charge of a business committee whose job would be to link Transport House and No. 10. Tom Driberg would be chairman of the election committee. I asked him what *I* was to do and he said, 'You won't be in Transport House. I want you to be the man who covers Heath all the way through and who acts as my personal adviser.'

[1] Sir Antony Part, Permanent Secretary at the Ministry of Public Building and Works 1965–8. He went to the Board of Trade in 1968.

Monday, February 28th

In the morning Cabinet was summoned and we formally decided the election date. Harold announced it at 6.30 in the House of Commons and he repeated the announcement on television later in the evening.

Cabinet rambled on for more than an hour before we switched over to Callaghan's budget Statement. My main interest of course was option-mortgages, on which there had been yet another discussion between the Treasury officials and mine before Cabinet started. The Chancellor said very unpleasantly that there was no agreement yet and that anyway he wasn't prepared to put these mortgages into his budget package. They should be announced later on by me. I said very sharply this wasn't possible. The whole credit to the Government would be undermined if they were presented as a gimmick of mine. They must be part of the Chancellor's package. 'Well,' said the Chancellor, 'I can't have this forced on me in its present form.' After this bickering Harold called us to order and told us to agree this between ourselves outside before evening. If necessary he would call another Cabinet on Tuesday.

Tuesday, March 1st

We had yet another Cabinet this morning. I didn't see much of it because I was desperately concerned now to get a really good press presentation of my mortgage scheme. Callaghan had finally agreed that the announcement of the mortgage plan should be included in his budget package and that after sitting on the front bench beside him I should then move upstairs straight away to a press conference at which I should explain how the thing really worked. This was all a bit difficult because by bad luck I was first in Questions today and had forty to answer. Nevertheless, everything went O.K. I sat beside Callaghan at 3.15 when I had answered the last of the Questions and listened to a very flat period of Prime Ministerial Questions. Then came the Chancellor's Statement. He did it magnificently with enormous parliamentary skill. He sat down to a tornado of applause from our back-benchers. I knew of course that the whole shape of his speech had been recast by the Prime Minister when he came back from Russia, and again on Monday, and I am sure the link he introduced between paying for the mortgage plan and the new tax on gambling was a typical Prime Ministerial gimmick. But that doesn't reduce Callaghan's credit. On TV in the evening he was equally superb. He is an extremely interesting example of how important image is in modern politics. He has a good public image outside Parliament, his presence in Parliament is exactly right, his personality on TV is just right and he also has a good image inside his own Department in the sense that they like him. The place where he has no reputation at all is in Cabinet where in decision-making with his colleagues he is weak and self-commiserating. But even here he has a very considerable grasp of his subject and a really remarkable power of putting it over.

In the evening we had another of our group drafting dinners at No. 10—this time with Terry Pitt[1] in attendance, since I had insisted that his absence would be disastrous. We had supper and then the eight of us got to work on the manifesto round a table while Harold hovered in the background making sure that it was coming out the way he wanted it.

Thursday, March 3rd

I had allocated this morning for writing my election address but I couldn't resist going to Cabinet, where the agricultural price review was being discussed. The idea that a pre-election review must be favourable to the farmers applies only to a Tory government and this is something my Mr Pritchett can't understand. There was no doubt Cabinet realized that the popular thing for us was to make the farmers attack us. This infuriated me because I think we are giving them an unfair review, and it may damage the British economy by cutting back agriculture's ability to save dollars.

After Cabinet Harold had said to me that he had found me a new Permanent Secretary—Matthew Stevenson from the Ministry of Power. 'He will suit you far better than any of the others,' remarked Harold, and sure enough by the afternoon this had gone round Whitehall. The Dame told me that Helsby had been talking to her. So with a tremendous rush I arranged to have him to supper at Vincent Square since Anne is up in town. Well, he gave me the shock of my life. He looks less like a senior civil servant than anyone you could imagine. No mandarin he. What he looks like is an insurance representative from the Prudential. There is no doubt he is very able. He is obviously a man of what they call first-class organizing ability, but the more he talked to us the more aware I was that in taking Steve instead of the Dame I had substituted for a fellow intellectual an absolute anti-intellectual. One thing that struck me was his characterization of Alf Robens: 70 per cent slyness, alertness and charm and 30 per cent a straight madman—almost as bad as George Brown.

I behaved as difficultly as I could because I wanted him to know the kind of Minister he had to tackle and I am sure the net result was to strengthen his tremendous inner complacency. Why have I accepted him? Because the only alternative was Tony Part, a much younger man whom I liked personally much more but who would be a greater risk for me. I have got plenty of intellectuals in the Ministry—Jones, W. R. Cox, Brain. What we need is sheer organizing ability, and in this respect Steve may serve me very well. I shall tell Harold tomorrow I am prepared to accept him.

Friday, March 4th

My official visit to Nottingham County Council (a Labour county council, but with the normal oligarchic structure and excellent civil servants) was given an unusual twist when they took me up in a helicopter to see the green

[1] Head of the Research Department at Transport House 1965–74.

belt and discuss the relations between themselves and Nottingham town. They were extremely nice and sent me home to Prescote in the helicopter. I arrived on the home pasture at 6 p.m. just before the sun set and found I had a message that I had to see the P.M. again at 9.30 on Sunday.

Monday, March 7th

So again I had to come up on Sunday night and go to No. 10, where our group was waiting to discuss with Harold what we assumed was the final draft of the manifesto. Actually it was the penultimate draft and a copy had already been taken by Terry Pitt and Peter Shore to Transport House last Friday where it had been processed over the weekend. So any changes we made on Sunday evening would have to be amendments that Tony Wedgwood Benn or Harold or I could move at Monday morning's joint meeting with N.E.C. The evening was very pleasant and brought the work of our little group to a close. I think one can say it was pretty useful since it made sure that the manifesto was drafted under the complete personal direction of the P.M.

I had a word with Harold about my new Permanent Secretary, Steve, and found that the announcement was due to be made on Monday afternoon, despite Thomas Balogh's cries of anguish when he heard who I had got, so it wasn't much good my discussing it. He also talked to me about Frank Cousins's future. Apparently he still expects that after the general election Cousins will retire from Parliament and return to his trade union.

At 10.30 this morning we began the mass meeting of the Cabinet and the N.E.C.; we had to sit down together and wade through the enormous 25,000-word manifesto. There had been a big inside story in some of the Sunday papers about a split over the prices and incomes policy, with George Brown insisting that the whole thing should be written into the manifesto and the trade unionists on the Executive demanding its omission. As I rather suspected when I read these stories, they were invented in order to create the split they reported. In sober fact George Brown had had the sense to agree a form of words before the meeting with Jack Jones and when we came to the crucial passage in the manifesto there was no bite in the discussion but a desperate desire to be friendly and helpful on both sides. One has to admit that in this George Brown has come off worst, in the sense that if he really wants to introduce his early warnings, his sanctions and penalties when his Bill becomes law, he will find it difficult to do so; because the Government won't be committed by this election manifesto to a prices and incomes policy with teeth. But even if this is a defeat for George I doubt if it is a victory for Cousins and the T.U.C. That would fit with what happened at the Executive this morning. So we ploughed our way through the home policy sections and at 12.30 it was clear we weren't going to get finished. I finally suggested to the chairman that he should set up a little drafting committee consisting of Tom Driberg and Terry Pitt and me and that we should go outside with the first part and finish it off. That was agreed and we worked away till 2.30, when I went back to my Ministry. As I left Transport House the manifesto was beginning to be stencilled page by page in time for the press conference at 6.

In the afternoon I had a Statement to make in the House on jerry-building. Directly afterwards I went along to Harold's room to make sure of two or three points in the final manifesto—in particular his desire to mention the reorganization of Whitehall. He has insisted on putting this in—the integration of the Commonwealth and Colonial Offices, the creation of a Ministry of Social Security and the absorption into Housing of Land and the relevant sections of Public Works. I was surprised at his insistence until I realized that this would enable him to avoid an awkward scene with the Ministers concerned. After the election he would be able to refer them to the manifesto and justify the changes in this way, instead of telling them himself.

I found him sitting with George Brown waiting for the press conference, and it didn't take long to clear up the vital passages. Then we began to discuss what he should say to the journalists. I suggested the slogan 'Work in Progress' and we all got down to knocking out as quickly as possible the statement he would make.

Thursday, March 10th

I knew that something was up before Cabinet started because Callaghan cancelled an appointment with me at 9.30 in the morning. Anyway, it had been fairly obvious to any newspaper reader for the previous three days that the money market was having a dose of electionitis and heavy selling of the pound was taking place.

Directly we had settled down in our chairs Harold said that the Chancellor wanted to make a proposition. Then, in his usual ponderous way, Callaghan gave us a careful account of how the pound had come under increasing pressure and how he had discussed matters with Lord Cromer and they both now felt it was necessary as a precautionary measure to raise bank rate by 1 per cent. He was very careful after that to add that there was an alternative policy. 'We could go in with all guns blazing to blow the speculators to smithereens—a policy the Bank has adopted until now.' He thought it might work but if it didn't we would have to put up bank rate by 2 per cent instead of 1 per cent.

Even while he spoke it was obvious that there had been a disagreement. On the one side there was Callaghan and the Governor and, on the other, George Brown and Harold Wilson, who very much disliked the Governor's advice. So there followed a longish discussion, or rather, these three argued it out while the rest of us asked questions. The only question I asked was whether the Callaghan policy would mean that the building societies' Council would be entitled to raise their interest rates when they met on Friday. When I asked this there was great anger and Harold Wilson interjected, 'If they do, they must be told that it will be subjected to the Prices and Incomes

Board.' Maybe. But it's not much good saying that to them and I didn't pass on the message though instructed to do so by Cabinet.

As the discussion proceeded it became clear that Callaghan's proposal was fraught with danger. Would it at the beginning of the election campaign be regarded as a sign of weakness not strength? Would it not justify the Tories making the pound sterling an issue in the campaign? When Harold began to wind up there was virtually no support left for the Chancellor apart from Douglas Houghton. The rest of us agreed that Cromer's advice should be disregarded.

Monday, March 14th

Harold rang early to say that he wouldn't be back and that I must arrange at all costs to get Ray Gunter to the press conference that morning in order to handle the Cowley affair. This is the first big event of this election campaign—the revelation of a so-called kangaroo trial by shop stewards at the B.M.C. works.[1] There is something in it, but it has been blown up enormously by the Tory press, and Heath and the rest of his colleagues have leapt upon it so that it has dominated the election for the first week. I always thought it had happened too early to really help the Tories and would conk out, and it really did conk out when Harry Urwin[2] produced an investigatory report, sober and objective, and Ray Gunter handled it at the press conference today.

Tuesday, March 15th

I breakfasted with the P.M. and we decided that the thing to do throughout the first week was to sustain a constant challenge to Heath and Maudling to cost their programme. In fact we are treating the Tories in Opposition just as they treated us in Opposition during the 1959 campaign. Harold observed to me over breakfast that tomorrow would be the anniversary of the day when Gaitskell made his fatal mistake and promised to reduce income tax. We shall smash Heath as Macmillan smashed Gaitskell by constantly asking how much his promises cost. We have costed ours, and, although it is boring, the essence of our campaign tactic is to keep to these comparative costs. Harold, of course, can be entertaining and will be. But the rest of us must be sensible, 'work in progress' politicians, a sharp contrast to a virulent, shrill Opposition. That's what we broadly agreed over breakfast. Harold was tempted to come down out of the stratosphere pretty soon and start mixing in. I begged him not to. 'You've made your decision, Harold,' I said, 'to stay out at least until the week before polling day. Don't go back on it now.'

In the afternoon Steve made his first intervention as Permanent Secretary

[1] Two workers were 'tried' and fined at an unofficial union hearing. A noose was suspended over the 'court'.

[2] Secretary for the Midlands Area of the T.G.W.U. 1963–9, and since March 1969 Assistant General Secretary of the T.G.W.U. He became a member of the T.U.C. General Council in September 1969, replacing Frank Cousins.

at one of my meetings. It had been called on the subject of publications and he said he didn't want a policy meeting on that subject because it hadn't been adequately prepared for. Clearly he has been talking to John Delafons and is busily introducing some paperwork and routine into the Department, which has been run with wonderful informality by the Dame. Personally, I liked her style—it meant I could call a meeting at a few hours' notice. But it is true that she kept no records; and decisions were often taken which were never fulfilled. Steve is going to get the Department's files in order and waste no time on meetings with me when he hasn't made up his mind what is to be decided. I'm not frightened of that.

Thursday, March 17th
When I arrived for breakfast with the P.M. on Wednesday I found the staff didn't expect me and they had to give me my breakfast while he was in his bath after finishing his. He started by saying he wanted to speak about the trade unions that night. I said, 'For God's sake don't do that. Keep out of it for at least two days longer and probably the Cowley business will be dead.' Then he said that we must deal with means-testing and accuse Heath of dismantling the welfare state. There was a chance that day because Hogg had demanded that Harold and I should withdraw our total lie that Heath was going to destroy the welfare state. Harold insisted that I should go on the TV at the press conference that morning and refuse to withdraw it.

That gave me a chance of seeing what the daily conference is really like. It's a pretty boring show. Callaghan started with a longish speech and then there were some rather desultory questions and then I was allowed to make my little statement about Hogg. After that the journalists moved across Smith Square to the Tory headquarters. I suppose these press conferences do provide some material for the evening papers, and I suppose ours are bound to be a bit dull since we are doing the defending. Anyway, it suits the boring style we have decided to assume.

In the evening I was due to speak in London. My first meeting was at Acton where I found an audience of thirty or forty people. What I didn't know at the time was that the B.B.C. ten o'clock News was there as well as a little legman from the P.A. As a result, this morning the *Guardian*, the *Financial Times* and the B.B.C. all reported that I had promised to reduce rates by half. What I had actually said, of course, was that we would reduce by 50 per cent the annual *rate* at which domestic rates are increasing. The fact that quite sensible papers can print such palpable nonsense without a flicker of reaction shows how cynical the press is becoming about politicians during an election. They believe anything of us. When you read *The Times* election page, which consists almost entirely of taunts and counter-taunts, you can see that the press only prints the hustings element in our speeches, which for the most part consist of pretty objective accounts of how we run the housing subsidies, what rent rebates are and suchlike. Then, having given this loaded account of the politicians, the press complains that we are superficial and vulgar. It is one of those vicious circles which we can't break out of.

I turned up late at No. 10 today because I knew the P.M. had been at a monster meeting in Birmingham the night before with 10,000 people booing and jostling in the hall; I had seen it all on the I.T.N. News the night before. I found Harold lying in bed eating kippers, with one kipper skeleton thrown on the carpet for his Siamese cat to finish. Harold sleeps in a tiny little bedroom – I suppose it was the scullery-maid's bedroom in the old days – and there I had my breakfast with him. He looked a bit tired, having got back at three in the morning, but he was enormously elated by the Birmingham meeting and told me with great excitement the story of how Mary had got a scratch on her neck when something had been thrown at her. Should we give that to the press, he pondered, and finally concluded that we should. When I asked him why, he said, 'Well, you see the Tories are deliberately leaving her out of the campaign because Heath has no wife. It's a positive advantage to us that I and Mary appear together and Heath has nothing. So I would like to see her brought back into the campaign.' I said that Mary must hate it. 'Oh no,' he said. 'She liked the meeting last night a great deal.' As I was going downstairs I ran into Mary and said, 'I hear you really enjoyed last night after all?' 'Enjoyed it!' she said, with agony on her face. 'Who told you that? That man?' Her relationship with Harold is fascinating. I am sure they are deeply together but they are now pretty separate in their togetherness. It is one of those marriages which holds despite itself because each side has evolved a self-containedness within the marriage.

Saturday, March 19th
Nomination day at Coventry. We motored over in exquisite weather. Anne was in her best, I was in my best; and the atmosphere was as though Anne and I were getting married again, with the mayor and the town clerk having a drink with us and a great sense of ease and repose. Never have I known an election as easy as this one. Labour voters like to be on the winning side and this will be something like a landslide in which we may well win seventy or eighty seats. If you ask me to make a prediction I would say we are heading for a Presidential victory of extraordinary proportions.

Sunday, March 20th
Prescote. A lovely day here, starting with a thick white fog and coming out into a cloudless blue sky and hot spring air. Steady, perfect electioneering weather. It really is getting uncannily like the autumn of 1959 when Gaitskell was fighting his valiant, hopeless campaign against Macmillan and the country had never had it so good and would have nothing said against him. All this week we have been fighting 1959 in reverse. Now it is we who are on top of the world, we who are the Government being given credit for

the weather, we who are letting wages rise faster than prices. The Tories can't find a way to break through the complacent acceptance by the electorate of super-Harold. At one breakfast I caught him thinking 'You've never had it so good'. And I said, 'Well, for God's sake let's remember to draw the right conclusions and not make the mistake the Tories made. After winning this election we have got to do a drastic reorganization if we are going to hold the country through the difficult period ahead, because we are going to have a devaluation crisis. It will come after this inconceivable tide of success on which we are coasting in.' I should add that this last week has been the easiest since I became a Minister. I have had my breakfast at ease with Harold, strolled across to Transport House at 9.30, and then at 10.30 over to my Ministry for a couple of hours with very little to do. A little work in the afternoon with Jennie at Vincent Square and at most one or two election meetings each evening. What a lovely, easy, floating life it has been.

Sunday, March 27th
Only three effective days left before polling on Thursday. Today the polls agree that Labour still leads by eight points. The press, who treat elections as a sporting event, want to give the Tories a chance of winning so they make what they can of the special regional polls published in the *Guardian* and the *Birmingham Post*, which show a slight reduction in our lead. But the fact remains that Labour are still in the ascendant, the public think that everything is decided and unless something completely unpredictable happens I would still hold to my forecast that we shall have a majority of eighty.

Now for the campaign itself. It was Harold's decision from very early on that he would stay outside and above the conflict and remain the Prime Minister in Downing Street until he intervened actively on the last Saturday of the campaign and then kept on for the next four or five days. I approved of the strategy but it hasn't worked out. Every night he has spoken somewhere and so he has hogged most of the available Labour publicity. He has also been on the radio and TV every night and so the theory that he should descend as the *deus ex machina* at the end of the campaign has been completely contradicted. And the trouble is that when he speaks he puts himself on a level with Heath, neither better nor worse. And so each night we have had a snippety debate between the two of them. Despite a heavy cold, Harold is still on top. But Heath, who began terribly stiff and starchy, is beginning to catch up somewhat, and is getting something of the admiration Gaitskell got for his gallant 1959 campaign. So the Presidential descent from the stratosphere which our strategy said should take place yesterday, Saturday, just didn't happen. It was bad luck that the Grand National and the Boat Race should be held, the one at three and the other at four o'clock, on the day that Harold was doing a big meeting in the Belle Vue Stadium in Manchester. As a result, virtually nothing came through of his speech that night. Indeed, we heard more about George Brown, just back from his nationwide heroic tour (which seems to me even more Pickwickian and old-fashioned this year than ever before). But if our plan for Harold's intervention in the campaign didn't work out this was not important for the simple reason that there hasn't been any campaign. The daily strategy meetings at Transport House have been a fraud because nothing has been happening. We've been sitting round and chatting a little and then Jim Callaghan has been going down to his news conferences, which he has conducted in rather a nice way so that by now the journalists have got to like him. Of course, there were certain routine functions which had to operate, but not a single strategic decision has been taken in Transport House since the campaign started. The only test of generalship is whether you can modify your plans as the situation changes. If you win without a single modification you have hardly had to fight; and that's the case in this campaign. So it has tested neither the relationships between the Government and the Party, nor our abilities to overcome adversity. Instead, we have been coasting along; and in this Harold's personality has played a leading part. He is winning just by being himself and carrying the middle-class vote.

If the Transport House policy meetings have been futile, I have felt that my daily breakfasts with Harold have also been fairly unnecessary. And I was pretty sure that Harold felt it too when he said to me on Thursday, 'My trouble, you know, is that I never have my ideas until just after you have left and I am in my bath.' I think that's true. I have been there each day too early for him, while he was lying in bed and looking at the papers and hadn't really read them through. All he had got from me was some company but I might have been more useful to him if I had gone to see him an hour later when he was downstairs and through with reading the morning papers.

There was, however, one day when I might have changed his mind in quite an important way. It was the morning after the meeting in Slough at which a stink-bomb was flung in his eye, causing a slight injury. Walking across the Park that morning in beautiful weather it suddenly occurred to me that this was a tremendous chance. Why not keep him in bed on Thursday and Friday and make the press report that he was ill? This would create a sag in Labour morale and a sense of suspense in the whole press which would give his Saturday meeting in Manchester enormous psychological importance. When I got upstairs I put this all to him quite impressively; to which he characteristically replied, 'But suppose I don't go to Norwich today, how shall I spend the afternoon?' 'Well,' I said, 'you can govern the country.' He laughed. 'No, there are no boxes coming upstairs now in No. 10. There is no work for me. I should just sit about.' I laughed and said, 'You being you, Harold, that's something you can't do. If you really feel at a loose end this afternoon I can't stop you going to Norwich.' So off he went and made one of his best speeches.

Since the stink-bomb had grazed the white of his eye and he still had an appallingly heavy cold, he had every excuse to take a day off. But he just isn't that kind of man, nor does he calculate in that kind of a way. People think Harold a clever opportunist. But when you put to him the idea of a deliberate 24-hour withdrawal he remembers the people who will be waiting for him at Norwich and feels he can't let them down.

But if these breakfasts haven't influenced the campaign strategy they may possibly have influenced my future. On Wednesday Harold told me he had been discussing with George the possibility of his giving up the D.E.A. and becoming Deputy Prime Minister and First Secretary without Portfolio. Harold explained that George isn't a very good departmental Minister and the planning side of the D.E.A. has not been adequately developed. So it might be a good idea for somebody who isn't so personally inclined to plunge into every industrial dispute to take over direction of the prices and incomes policy. Apparently on the first occasion that this was discussed it was George who told Harold that he would like me to take his place. Now the latest is that he wants to stay where he is, but Harold has warned me that if the change does take place I must move from Housing to the D.E.A. But I have committed myself to reorganizing the Ministry and to building up the enormous central power which I hope the new federal Ministry will get, so it is disconcerting to find that all this may end. It would be promotion for me but to a far more exposed Ministry and it would mean giving up all the projects I have been working on for the past eighteen months.

One other thing that disconcerted me was the discovery that I was the last person in Whitehall to learn about my future. Weeks ago the Dame mentioned the rumour to me and I thought it was too silly to take cognizance of. Now when Harold told me I checked with Steve, who obviously thinks it is an excellent idea for him to settle into the Ministry without my presence.

Friday, April 1st
We got home at 3 a.m. Anne is still upstairs and I have given her breakfast in bed. I am in my study recording my impressions of the victory we have just scored. It has come out as I—and all the polls—anticipated. I predicted a majority of over 80 and that is what we are going to get. We have won Oxford and Cambridge, Sydney Silverman has not been defeated in Nelson and Colne despite the part he played in getting capital punishment abolished, Smethwick has been recaptured from the racialists, Gordon Walker has won at Leyton, and in Coventry we have also done pretty well. In Coventry South, which was marginal, Bill Wilson has more than doubled his majority. Maurice Edelman's majority is up to 8,000, mine up to 18,000, though the swing is concealed by the impact of the Liberal and the Communist candidates. My own campaign in Coventry East was kept down to the usual minimum. I was in the constituency for just over a week, from Thursday, March 24th, until the polls closed.

There was one point in the campaign where I began to get cold feet. That was on Sunday when I suddenly felt that the Tories were winning and people were turning against us. But then next day I went into an owner-occupier estate at Binley and my confidence was restored. I have never seen so many middle-class people in Coventry so anxious to vote for us and I'm sure this is one of the key factors in this election. The middle classes really want us to win—many of the owner-occupiers for the first time. Harold's personality has been a great help—middle class, not professional or upper class. He sees this himself. When I reported the situation on the housing estates, he said, 'Yes, they think they've got a P.M. like them.' They recognize in him a man of their own kind whom they are proud to have at No. 10; they feel they have a competent Government and will vote for it.

That is what we won on: Harold's personality and the feeling that we, a Labour Government, have been active and have helped ordinary people, and that we should be given a fair chance to show what we can do. To some extent the ineffectiveness of the Opposition, and the impression it gave of being divided and not really standing for anything, was a positive assistance to us. I notice all the papers have the usual build-up of the heroic leader so that, just as Gaitskell was the hero of the 1959 election, Heath may well be made the hero this time. My own view is that he fought the election unskilfully—not nearly so well as Gaitskell fought in 1959 under similar circumstances. He started with far too much bang and sprayed his bullets all over the target without any real discrimination. Also, he remained right to the end a curiously synthetic character and I doubt whether he added to his popularity during the campaign. By the way, I don't think Harold did either—though on the other hand his position was already immensely strong. Millions of lower-middle-class people voted Labour because he was someone of their class, someone to their taste, someone they had confidence in, leading the nation and acting like a statesman. Moreover, economically they felt all right. Wages have gone up faster than prices, they are prosperous, they have full employment. There is absolutely no reason why they shouldn't give us a second chance because the disaster which was hanging over us has been fended off.

This was the background issue throughout the campaign—the fight against inflation and devaluation. Heath desperately tried to warn people. He went on saying that we were going bankrupt; but of course this was completely ineffective with an electorate who felt that on this score—the responsibility for our difficulties—honours were pretty even, if not tipped against the Tories. Looking back, I see that timing was everything. If we had carried on without the election in March and gone right forward to the municipals in April and May we would have had a disastrous defeat. With rates going up and rents going up, our candidates would have been swept away. We would have had a thousand losses this year, like last year, and then there would have been no chance of going to the country in May or June. The election would have been pushed off until October and by then we might have had

the most appalling crisis blowing up. So when people regard this as an
inevitable victory, that's a very superficial judgment. It was only inevitable at
this particular time, in this particular month of the year 1966. Suddenly we
have got a majority of 100 and that gives a chance of stability, but heaven
knows it was a very near thing. It was quite possible for Harold to have made
a different decision and lost his chance in March. As it was we have given the
electorate time to get to like our style and see how active we were. But they
haven't had enough time to see our actions put into effect and recognize
them as failures. From now on we shall never again be able to look back at
the Tory thirteen years and contrast them with our eighteen months.

Mr Wilson announced twenty-five changes in the Government. James
Griffiths, Secretary of State for Wales, resigned on grounds of age. Richard
Marsh, a thirty-eight-year-old Under-Secretary, entered the Cabinet as Minis-
ter of Power, replacing Fred Lee, who moved to the Colonial Office. Ten
non-Cabinet Ministers left the Government.
In his reshuffle Mr Wilson indicated the change in Labour's attitude to the
E.E.C. When Harold Macmillan had tried to take Britain into the E.E.C. in
1962, Hugh Gaitskell, then leader of the Opposition, had attacked this as a
'betrayal of a thousand years of history'. But the Government now spoke of
the advantages of membership, and the Prime Minister appointed George
Thomson as Chancellor of the Duchy of Lancaster, with specific responsi-
bility for political relations with Europe. The First Secretary, George Brown,
was given general oversight of Britain's economic relations with the E.E.C.

Tuesday, April 5th
When the full list of changes came out this morning they were even more
depressing than I expected. They were so niggling—and the niggliest is the
one beside me as I sit in Cabinet. I used to have Fred Lee sitting on my left,
an obviously inadequate Minister of Power. Now I still have Fred Lee sitting
on my left, demoted from Power to Colonies. And that's the pattern. Tony
Greenwood is thrown out of Colonies but retained in the Cabinet as Minister
of Overseas Development. Frank Longford is demoted still lower but is still
in the Cabinet as Lord Privy Seal. Jim Callaghan and George Brown are
retained and are still at loggerheads, but all the press tells me, and I believe
it, that the D.E.A. is going down and the Treasury up. That means that
Callaghan's powers will greatly increase. We are going to have George
Brown, along with George Thomson (our new Minister for Europe), concentrating on the Common Market; and as a result Callaghan will be freer to
run his deflation policy, which I suppose is Harold's only alternative to the
devaluation he so absolutely opposes. Deflation combined with a moderate
degree of unemployment will I presume be our economic target. All this will
be done over our heads while the budget is prepared in secret. Callaghan and
Wilson are now in full cahoots, with George Brown in a weak position to

oppose the deflation they both want. Apart from that, Denis Healey is still very much out on a limb—rather like me. Frank Cousins is strengthened in his position, with more powers. Supposedly more powers are coming to me but even here, as I hear on the Whitehall grapevine, nothing is really going to happen—at least not immediately. The liquidation of the Ministry of Land and Natural Resources won't take place straight away and the absorption of the relevant part of the Ministry of Works will be delayed.

In the afternoon I had a routine meeting with Steve and my senior staff. I was able to assure them I was still their Minister. Most of them, I suspect, had rather looked forward to a new Minister; but they settled down bravely to their job and we went through a vast agenda on which Delafons kept full notes. Just at this point Fred Peart came into my Private Office. He wanted to ask whether I would mind if the Ordnance Survey went back to the Ministry of Agriculture. It was something I had rather wanted for myself, since I like the idea of these maps getting done in my Department. But here was my friend Fred saying 'I was a geographer at university' and complaining that Ordnance Survey shouldn't be torn from its traditional position in the Ministry of Agriculture. And as I am an easy-going, good-natured person I said yes.

So that was that and I took the two Parliamentary Secretaries to lunch at the Athenaeum where we began to divide up our jobs. Bob Mellish will remain in charge of London housing and have all responsibility for New Towns, so that we make sure that the corporations take their complement of Londoners from the housing lists and from the London council houses. Then I shall create a new local government division, and make Arthur Skeffington responsible for local government and rates. That leaves Fred Willey and Jim MacColl dealing with planning and Kennet with me on the general side.

Thursday, April 7th
At Cabinet this morning there was a strained atmosphere. Harold started by thanking George Brown for his election tour and Jim Callaghan for his magnificent work at the daily press conferences. Then he said that this being Holy Week, we should perhaps have a little compassion for our opponents. If I had said, 'This being Holy Week, we ought to feel compassion for our enemies,' it would obviously have been a piece of atheistic irony. But when Harold, who claims to be a Methodist, says it, it only increases the puzzle of our Prime Minister.

Next, legislation. The Lord President made it clear that this would be a long session and that we would run right through for eighteen months. Then came a lengthy argument about priorities. Jim Callaghan chipped in straight away to say that we should give leasehold enfranchisement top priority and put the Land Commission second.

He has already tried to do this in the Legislation Committee and been defeated. It is extraordinary how our high-minded Chancellor of the Exchequer becomes just a Cardiff constituency Member when leasehold enfranchisement, which is a vital local problem to him, comes up. I insisted that we must get the Land Commission through first, and had my way though the pressure was extremely strong. I then pointed out that with the accession of Fred Willey and Arthur Skeffington to my Ministry in February I could at once set up a working party to get on with leasehold enfranchisement but we shouldn't expect it before the end of the long session.

It soon became clear that if leasehold enfranchisement was to be in the Queen's Speech something big would have to be omitted. At this point Harold said suddenly, 'Well, should steel be dropped?' There was an awkward silence and then Jim said that he felt steel might be moved back to the second session. Then there was another awkward silence and George Brown said, 'If we are having second thoughts on steel and re-negotiating with the manufacturers, of course it would be a good thing to postpone it.' I then said, 'Well, are we going to have those second thoughts, or is this the best Bill we have got?' To which Fred Lee, who by now was the ex-Minister for steel, observed that the Bill had been run up very quickly and we might now be able to do a better job. It looked as though a well-organized postponement lobby was going to get its way, when Dick Marsh came in with his first intervention as a Cabinet Minister. He clearly intends to be vigorous, young and dynamic. He told the Cabinet bluntly that he was going to push his Steel Bill through in the first session and at once the notion of postponement faded away.

That was another example of Harold Wilson's devious leadership. He raised the issue of postponement himself.[1] He got Jim to commit himself to it and then George Brown to half commit himself. But the moment Marsh intervened and the Cabinet swung the other way Harold closed up like an oyster. I was amused later that morning to pick up the *Daily Mail* and see he had given an exclusive interview in which he stated that the Steel Bill would be fundamentally the same as the White Paper. So he had made up his own mind but was wanting the Cabinet to defeat the postponement lobby.

But there was more to come. The legislative programme was still far too big and a tremendous effort was made to get Douglas Jay to drop one of his Bills. Poor man! Within minutes we were all agreeing that his Companies Bill was a third-rate departmental measure. Then somebody near Douglas Jay said, 'Why not drop the ombudsman Bill this session?' At this point the Prime Minister chipped in quickly. 'That would be very awkward for me. Some people here will appreciate', he said, looking at me, 'that the future of some very high civil servants depends on getting the ombudsman Bill on the Statute Book as soon as possible.' I knew very well what he was talking about. Having failed to get me to accept Bruce Fraser as my Permanent

---

[1] But wrote later: 'I was a little surprised to be met with an attempt by a number of Senior Ministers to draw back and seek a compromise with the industry.' *Wilson*, p. 222.

Secretary, Harold had cooked up the idea that he should become Comptroller-General in place of Compton, who should be made the first Ombudsman. Any delay in the legislation would bitch the idea. Interesting that a Prime Minister in considering our legislative strategy should be mainly preoccupied with the convenience of one of the Permanent Secretaries, or as Harold would put it, the relationships between the Government and the higher Civil Service.

Cabinet drooled on till 12.15. Then we were thrown out because the Defence Committee was there, waiting outside the door with George Wigg. As I walked out I became more and more aware of how fictitious Cabinet government really is. The big issue to be decided concerned, of course, Rhodesia and the action to be taken about the tankers which were breaking the blockade by coming through the Mozambique Channel. So at this point the Cabinet is sent out of the room and the Chiefs of Staff come in. It's the Defence Committee who manage Rhodesia. But at least that consists of half the Cabinet whereas the committee which is secretly preparing the budget consists of only Harold, George and Jim. So the two main decisions to be taken in defence and finance are lifted entirely out of the hands of the Cabinet. The rest of us are totally excluded. I feel a sense of anticlimax, or boredom with the idea of just carrying on as a departmental Minister. I have had enough of it and now I want to be a Cabinet Minister. That may mean trouble for me and also probably trouble for the Cabinet.

Monday, April 18th
The Parliamentary Party met today at twelve o'clock for the purpose of re-electing Harold Wilson and George Brown as leader and deputy leader with seats on the N.E.C. The meeting took place in the rather carbolic atmosphere of Church House. It certainly wasn't the jubilant, thrilling occasion the Beaver Hall meeting in 1945, or even the October 1964 meeting, had been. No, there was a curious air of expectations fulfilled, which was a little disconcerting. What I noticed mainly was the treacly atmosphere of mutual self-praise in the speeches of George and James and Ray Gunter, and also the rather sinister lack of participation by the new Parliamentary Party. When the speakers talked about the new age and the great new Labour Government they were received with acquiescence at best. Indeed I felt—perhaps reading a little of my own mood into the new Members—that they weren't really any more stirred than I was. Why? Why was this election forgotten the moment it was over? Why no sense of a great leap forward? Because this was not a normal general election. All it has meant is that by shrewd timing the Wilson Government has won an increased majority and five more years. And that's why there is no sense of novelty, no excitement. We will produce the same Bills all over again. The only unknown factor is the quality of the new Members and the attitude they will have to a Government which is certainly nothing new.

Wednesday, April 20th
Cabinet. A very important discussion on parliamentary reform. One of the
first things Harold did after the election was to minute the Lord President
that in this Parliament it was essential to make a start with modernizing
parliamentary institutions, and part of that start should be an experiment in
'specialist committees'.[1] Of course, for many years George Wigg and I have
been lobbying for specialist committees on defence and on foreign affairs as
well as on home departments; and fortunately it is one of the things which
our new Members immediately demanded, to give them something to do. I
am convinced it would be jolly good for Departments, which are virtually
free from parliamentary criticism as Question Time is so ineffective. So I was
delighted by the Prime Minister's surprisingly vigorous minute and so was
Roy Jenkins, whose view coincides with mine. However, it was watered
down by the Lord President who presented to the Cabinet Committee last
Monday a disastrously reactionary paper, backed by the Treasury and the
Scottish Department. Bert Bowden proposed that instead of specialist
committees investigating Departments, they should have subjects allocated
to them, such as Sunday observance or drunken driving. It is reckoned that
such committees would be harmless whereas departmental committees, in
the words of Niall MacDermot, who read aloud the Treasury brief at the
Cabinet Committee, 'could well become lobbyists for further expenditure'.
A typical Treasury reaction to a piece of parliamentary reform. In fact the
reformers had a very bad time at the Committee, chaired as usual by Bert
Bowden. But when he put up the majority's recommendations to Cabinet he
was immediately swept aside by the Prime Minister who insisted that
departmental specialist committees should be established as well. What
clinched it was that three departmental Ministers, Roy and I and Tony
Crosland, all individually testified that such committees could provide an
astringent stimulus to our Departments by ventilating issues and exploring
corners which had been covered up in the past. Dick Marsh, our bright new
young Minister, was, however, blankly against it; and so was Fred Peart who
obviously had listened to his powerful Permanent Secretary. However,
Harold's leadership was a tonic. At last he acted strongly, and the moment
he did so he got his way.

Thursday, April 21st
State Opening of Parliament. I went into the Chamber to hear the Prime
Minister, who spoke for an hour and a half. Funnily enough, however, the
longer he went on the better he got, particularly during a long altercation
with Heath. I went out before he had finished to keep an appointment with
my Permanent Secretary. He had already infuriated me that morning when

[1] Small committees of M.P.s taking evidence and examining witnesses on the administration
of a particular department or area of legislation.

Dan Smith[1] came to my office and accepted an invitation to serve on the Royal Commission.[2] After he had left the room Steve said to me, 'That leaves the ninth place unfilled. The one you wanted to reserve for an educationalist. I've got the right man, the chairman of the Education Committee of Wallasey.' As it was a Tory borough I said to him at once, 'Now look, don't be silly, that's impossible.' He replied that it was all fixed and I was forced to say that I could not persuade my five Cabinet colleagues from the North-West that there wasn't a single Labour chairman of an education committee fit to serve on this Commission. But there was worse to come. As I was about to go across to the House he asked me whether I wouldn't just formally sign the Ministry's paper on the legislative programme for the next three years. 'It's an automatic thing, Minister,' he assured me. 'I've just been tidying it up for you.' I replied testily that it couldn't be a mere formality and that I had already told him twice that we must sit down to some serious policy discussion about a three-year programme for housing, local finance, planning and so on. 'It is no good telling me that a three-year legislative programme to which we commit ourselves on paper doesn't matter. I want a really good job done.' 'Sorry,' he said, 'it's got to be in by Friday morning.' This made me see red. 'And you dare to present it to me on Thursday morning?' But then I suddenly realized that he has got used to working like this with his Ministers. When he had Fred Lee at the Ministry of Power he would finalize a whole job with his staff and present the finished package to the Minister. So instead of being angry I reasoned with him. 'It would save you a lot of time, Steve,' I said, 'if you would come to me early on in a project and sit down with me and have half an hour's talk to find out what my ideas are. Then when you've discussed it informally with me, you and your officials can try it out in a draft scheme. But a three-year legislative programme is something which you can't push through without serious Ministerial participation. I am going to call a meeting of all our five politicians and get their views; and after that I will meet the staff again.' He looks pained when I say these things, but how else can I treat him in order to prevent him simply taking over his Minister? He is an obstinate man but I think he is also weak.

Tuesday, April 26th

I was sitting by Harold Wilson on the front bench when he told me that George Brown was ill in hospital and he wanted me to take his place in the last day of the debate on the Queen's Speech. This is regarded as a big occasion—the day when the Opposition moves its vote of censure. On Thursday it was to be moved by Macleod and answered by me. I didn't feel

[1] Chairman of the Northern Economic Planning Council 1965–70. He was charged with conspiracy to corrupt in 1973 and subsequently served a term of imprisonment.
[2] The Redcliffe-Maud Royal Commission on Local Government in England. It reported in 1969.

inclined to play because I would have to talk about steel and the economic situation and I felt very incapable. But there was no choice. Harold said, 'You're one of the people we have to use for general debates, not only for your Department.' So I thought that's that.

Thursday, April 28th

I had to miss Cabinet, where the business was doctors' pay, and worked away at my speech all through the morning. Just when I was going to break off for lunch I had an urgent message that the Chancellor must see me before I made the speech. So along I went and Jim said, 'I've got to tell you what's in the budget because it might make nonsense of what you are going to say today,' and he then began to tell me about S.E.T.[1] Of course, my mind was on my speech which dealt with parliamentary reform and housing figures and I couldn't relate S.E.T. to any of that. And my first reaction to S.E.T. was that in terms of farming at Prescote Manor as well as in terms of building it was absolutely unbearable. I said to him, 'Why treat farmers and the construction industry as though they were service industries when they obviously aren't?' That's about all I could think of at the time.

So I rushed back to my room and got the finished text ready and when I got down to the House all keyed up I found Macleod getting up to speak with sixty or seventy people on his side and some thirty or forty on mine. It certainly wasn't a big occasion and he understood it and made a kind of pleasant, after-dinner speech—absolutely lightweight. I was disconcerted because there was no kind of enthusiasm behind me or tension in front and the speech I had prepared was certainly too serious. However, I managed to get through it, but for me it was a disconcerting hour. Of course I must blame myself in part. As a back-bencher I never dreamed of attending the Queen's Speech debates, regarding them as the most boring occasions. Maybe this was just a normal attendance and I should have known and refused to prepare myself for a great occasion. But I did and I felt thoroughly let down.

Monday, May 2nd

At eleven o'clock we gathered to be told the budget secrets, and S.E.T. was revealed to us. Before I went off to the North on Thursday evening I had had time to see Steve to be educated in the disastrous effect the new tax would have not only on agriculture but on the whole construction industry. Under the Chancellor's plans the building industry would have a new tax piled upon it and also be denied the new investment grants: these had been worked out for the export industries, and were denied explicitly to construction as well as to hotels. Steve emphasized that it was essential at the very least to extract a promise from the Chancellor that if builders had to pay S.E.T. they would at

[1] A payroll tax paid by employers.

least be eligible for investment grants. Over the weekend he got hold of his opposite number in the Ministry of Works and I talked on the telephone to Reg Prentice who, because he is not a Cabinet Minister, was forbidden to attend the meeting on Monday morning. I had to represent him. The only other Cabinet Ministers who had advance knowledge of the secret were the Minister of Labour and the Minister of National Insurance, whose Departments were technically required for collecting the tax but weren't affected by its consequences. So when Callaghan started discussing this tax in Cabinet there was bewilderment and consternation. Nobody could quite follow what he was saying and he had the easiest time in the world. I was the only critic there, having had time to prepare my own position. Over the weekend I had tried to see the tax not merely as it affected housing but as it affected economic policy. It was obvious that Callaghan was bound to have a deflationary budget and I had assumed there would be increases in purchase tax, spirit duty and petrol tax—it was going to be that kind of glóomy budget. So when we heard the news this morning it was a tremendous let-down—a relief combined with a let-down. The whole of the deflation, we heard, was going to be carried out by introducing this single selective tax which would produce the £300 million cut required in consumption. There was virtually no discussion. I made my demand that the construction industry must get its investment grants back and Callaghan hummed and hawed and said he might give some kind of assurance in his speech if it was put to him. Fred Peart from Agriculture was completely flabbergasted because the idea was that the costs to farmers imposed by S.E.T. would be made good in the agricultural price review—a proposal which showed that the Treasury simply doesn't understand how the price review works.*

The more I thought about it the more unrealistic this budget seemed to be. Of course, technically it may help us to deflate; but what it is not going to do is create the confidence in the pound which Callaghan wants to build up. It is not going to ease our situation overseas, while at home it is going to produce an enormous increase in the cost of living. And meanwhile the trade unions are going to have an excuse for putting up wages as fast as possible. In terms of strategy I am sure Callaghan missed his opportunity. People have been waiting masochistically for something to be done to them in this budget; they expect a rise in motor-car duties and petrol and purchase tax and there will be a sense of let-down when it doesn't happen. On the other hand there is no doubt that the budget will be far less damaging in the municipal elections on Thursday week than the budget we expected. But of course by far the most important aspect of this budget is the constitutional issue. It seems to me to make an absolute mockery of Cabinet government and Cabinet responsibility to introduce S.E.T. in this way and tell none of us about it until it is too late to do anything. Barbara Castle and Fred Peart made this point in Cabinet. And I am preparing to write to Harold about it.

* Callaghan had to withdraw this lunatic idea as soon as the N.F.U. heard about it.

Wednesday, May 4th
A real little row in Cabinet this morning about steel. Dick Marsh chose to pick a quarrel by accusing George Brown and Callaghan of deliberately slowing up the work on steel nationalization, because they didn't really want to push it through. He did it very stupidly, because you don't take on Callaghan and Brown at the same time. Marsh should have admitted that the problems of the so-called Hybrid Bill really do produce enormous complexities. True, Callaghan and Brown don't want the Steel Bill much this Session and don't think it is going to help us a great deal. True, even the Prime Minister said that we would need to put the Prices and Incomes Bill on at the same time as the Steel Bill so as to give the foreign bankers something which they really could believe in. The impression I got from this scrappy discussion was of the sheer burden of boring legislation with which they have loaded us this Session.

After Cabinet I went over to listen to Jim Callaghan talking to the Parliamentary Party. I had heard the budget speech in the Commons —brilliantly successful—and I had also watched the Chancellor's superb performance on TV the same evening. He handled the Parliamentary Party with just the same skill. But the oftener I heard his performance the deeper my doubts grew.

By pure coincidence I had been invited to talk to David Butler's seminar at Nuffield College in the afternoon about Cabinet Government in theory and in practice, and it was a strange sensation to try out my thoughts on this subject. I was asked nothing about the budget but David Butler did ask me why we weren't allowed to describe how Cabinet Committees work or even to say that they take place. Now this is a fair question. For instance, when I have to cancel an engagement, as I very often do, I am not allowed to say that it is due to a sudden Cabinet or Cabinet Committee meeting. That would be an intelligible and acceptable excuse. Instead, I have to talk about 'official business' because there is a rule in the Civil Service that Cabinet meetings cannot be referred to at all.

Monday, May 9th
On the way up in the train I noticed to my surprise that I was due to go to the first meeting of the brand new Cabinet Committee on Europe. So I turned up at No. 10. After I had been sitting there for some time the P.M. threw me a little note asking whether I was really supposed to be there. I threw back a note saying, 'Yes, I had received an invitation and the papers.' He threw me back another note saying, 'Your name isn't on the list, it's awkward.' Then there was a long exchange of notes between us in which he explained that Roy Jenkins had already asked to be on the Committee and been refused and that if I were on it it would be unbalanced. However, I stuck out that first meeting and learnt a great deal. It was staggering to hear George Brown taking the bit between his teeth and announcing our collective determina-

tion to go into Europe at the moment when our official committees were advising us that there was no chance whatsoever of doing so as long as General de Gaulle was President of France, and that anyway we couldn't afford to in present circumstances because it would mean a devaluation. But despite these official estimates, Brown and Healey ever since the election have been rushing round Europe to meetings at Oslo and Bergen announcing our determination to enter the Market. It sounds to me just like a repetition of George Brown's handling of the prices and incomes policy. He is a great man at delivering big speeches in order to make big things come true. And I am afraid this technique will have the same effect here as it had on the incomes policy. Everybody is impressed at the beginning but when nothing solid comes of it a reaction sets in.

Thursday, May 12th

Cabinet. When we are dealing with home affairs at least we are confronted with a paper requiring a decision. But on Rhodesia, when the Cabinet gets going, the Prime Minister just sits and chats and we occasionally ask him a question and the meeting disintegrates into amiable discussion, because all the decisions are taken by the P.M. and his little group behind the scenes. I am used to this in dealing with foreign affairs but today it was the same when we turned to the seamen's strike.[1] There was nothing that any of us could say about it. There was nothing Cabinet could do. So the chit-chat went on and I walked out of the room more than ever struck by the ineffectiveness of our Cabinet. It is all right when it handles *ad hoc* problems brought up from the Departments, but when we face a big issue there is no policy discussion.

Sunday, May 15th

This has been an important, sobering week in my life. I have been thinking about the whole theory of budget confidentiality and whether a reformed PESC could play a part in opening it up. I have had no success there. When I sent a note about this to the Cabinet Office I got a formal acknowledgment and Harold hasn't spoken to me about it. As for PESC, Steve has done a little letter to George Brown watering down all my complaints. The truth is that I can't force the pace in Cabinet or in my relations with Harold because the first, gay phase of Ministerial elation is over.

As the seamen's strike built up, the Government assumed powers to control the ports, dock labour and food prices and to regulate shipping, dock and other transport services. A State of Emergency had been declared on May

[1] The employers had granted the seamen a 13-per-cent increase in March 1965 and now offered 5 per cent, with a 4 per cent p.a. increase in 1968 and 1972. The seamen demanded that all work over 40 hours a week should be paid at overtime rates—equivalent to a 17-per-cent increase. On May 13th the Prime Minister met forty-eight seamen's leaders at No. 10 but the efforts of Wilson and Ray Gunter could not avert the strike, which began on Monday, May 16th.

23rd. On June 8th Lord Pearson's Committee of Inquiry made an interim report, proposing a 40-hour week within two years, and as a first stage a reduction from 56 to 48 hours within a year. The report also recommended a percentage rise in earnings slightly higher than the 5 per cent and 4 per cent offered by the employers. It severely criticized the National Union of Seamen, who rejected the report immediately.

Thursday, May 26th

The last Cabinet before the Whitsun recess. We had our usual little address from the Prime Minister about the seamen's strike but this time Dick Marsh intervened. He asked what the devil the strike was about and said how unpopular it was and how much damage we were suffering. James Callaghan replied that maybe it was doing damage but that to stop it now would damage the pound even more. Then everyone else chipped in that we couldn't possibly give way and must fight it out. Of course this is the line Harold Wilson had taken in his TV and wireless Ministerial broadcasts earlier in the week.

Then a curious thing happened. Ray Gunter made a report and then added that though there wasn't any promise of anything happening there was some chance of a contact being established earlier than he had expected. At this point people pricked up their ears and asked what the reasons were. Ray said that there was reason to think that some contact would be made by the seamen. At once Cabinet became suspicious that some kind of deal was contemplated, which upset James Callaghan and also upset George Brown, whose incomes policy is at stake. Gunter, who is a cunning devil, wouldn't have dreamt of saying a word of this if he hadn't been put up to it by Harold. I am still pretty sure that Harold was hoping to get some approval from Cabinet for an approach to the seamen. But he didn't get it. Ray Gunter made it perfectly clear that we could have a settlement at any time, since the owners were ready to put up the cash: it was the Government that was preventing the settlement because of the prices and incomes policy. Ray's intervention produced great unease. The people who were talking about fighting it out and the impossibility of giving way were uneasily aware that standing firm was also going to ruin us. It struck me as a very similar situation to the one we got into over Rhodesia: despite all the high talk about forcing the Rhodesians to give way there seems to be no sign of any weakening in Salisbury. We are given encouraging reports at every Cabinet meeting yet we have drifted into a deadlock which is costing us a tremendous lot in our balance of trade. On both the Rhodesian crisis and the seamen's strike the P.M. has taken personal control and played them by ear from moment to moment. He has never worked out a strategy for winning in Rhodesia and I don't think before the seamen's strike started it had ever occurred to him to plan how he would win it.

I am leaving for my holiday with a pretty gloomy prospect ahead. Not only

is there no likelihood of any solution either to the seamen's strike or to
Rhodesia but, even more serious, the S.E.T. budget, which seemed to those
who thought it out such a brilliant idea, has not worked out. Indeed, it has
gone off at half-cock and done a great deal of damage because it hasn't really
produced a sense of confidence amongst the overseas bankers. I haven't
asked Tommy much about the pound but it hasn't been going too well. I
think we are moving now towards another Government crisis.

Tuesday, June 14th
Cabinet. For the first time Harold Wilson deliberately tried to make each of
us commit ourselves on our attitude to the seamen's strike. We were told that
the T.U.C. had a proposal from the seamen which they would like us to
consider although it went well beyond the terms of the report produced by
the Pearson Court of Inquiry which had just been published. So the issue
was, should the Cabinet stand firm and say 'Not a penny beyond the Pearson
proposals' because these are not the basis for negotiation but a firm offer? Or
should we let the T.U.C. find a solution which made further concessions to
the union? George Brown and James Callaghan immediately said that we
mustn't go an inch beyond Pearson and then each member of the Cabinet
was asked to commit himself to support this tough line. There was obvious
reluctance to do so. Dick Marsh, never exactly enthusiastic for fighting the
strike, said that since Cabinet had committed itself as far as this it had to
carry on. Roy Jenkins took the same line. Only two people stood out really
firmly, Frank Cousins and Barbara Castle. Barbara made the very sensible,
simple point that it would be crazy to find ourselves in open conflict with the
T.U.C. I was one of the last to speak because I had remained silent throughout the long debate. When it came to my turn I said that my major preoccupation was that we must avoid finding ourselves fighting the seamen against
the protests of the T.U.C. This seemed to me an appalling prospect because
we should then quite certainly have more than half the other trade unions on
the seamen's side and we should be fighting a civil war against them.

Maybe we three influenced the Cabinet slightly on its tactics in dealing
with the T.U.C. But the fact is that Harold is out to smash the seamen's
union. It is this which makes us so unhappy as a Cabinet in our relationship
with our back-benchers. We are trying to smash the seamen although we
have just given huge concessions to the doctors, the judges and the higher
civil servants. It is an ironical interpretation of a socialist incomes policy.

*The left wing of the P.L.P. objected, increasingly, to British support for the
United States in the Vietnam war, to the level of defence spending and to the
Government's continued commitment to an East of Suez presence. These
criticisms were voiced on June 15th at a meeting of the P.L.P. to debate a
motion calling for 'a decisive reduction' in East of Suez commitments, to
enable defence expenditure to be cut to £1,750 million (at 1964 prices).*

Wednesday, June 15th
Since we had been instructed to attend by the Chief Whip, I went across to
the Commons in good time to get a seat on the platform. It was a good thing I
did so because otherwise I would have missed an extraordinary incident.
Woodrow Wyatt got up and made a long statement about his having been
hauled before the liaison committee on the ground that he had leaked an
account of the previous Party meeting in his *Daily Mirror* article. He then
proceeded to annihilate the platform by reading aloud the counter-leaks
which had been given out by poor Gerald Kaufman. With all the points
of order which followed, this took so long that Manny Shinwell had a
good excuse for limiting speeches to five minutes and then letting the
Prime Minister wind up. When I saw the thickness of the Prime Minister's
manuscript I knew we were in for fifty minutes and was worried at the
idea that all that Mayhew and Joel Barnett and the other chief speakers
had from the floor was a miserable five minutes each. They could not make
much use of it and there was a good deal of ill-feeling when Harold
replied.

He started by pointing out the strange alliance between Christopher
Mayhew and Woodrow Wyatt on the right[1] with the traditional left-wingers
and then went on to make his usual Bevinite speech. His theme was that
though he was prepared to withdraw and reduce the number of troops East
of Suez he would never deny Britain the role of a world power. He also
asserted once again that there's no kind of understanding between him and
Johnson about Malaya and Vietnam. But most of his audience realized that
there was no understanding because there was no need of one: the President
could reckon on Harold Wilson. While he was talking, Jim came in and sat
beside me on the other side from Fred Peart. Throughout the speech he
whispered to me how totally he disagreed and told me that he thought Denis
Healey holds much the same view as he does and that George Brown wasn't
enthusiastic. East of Suez is solely the P.M.'s line—the P.M. with George
Wigg's backing. Undoubtedly, it's all a fantastic illusion. How can anyone
build up Britain now as a great power East of Suez when we can't even
maintain the sterling area and some of our leaders are having the idea of
creeping inside Europe in order to escape from our independence outside?
Of course, it was done with very great skill, but I was sure when Harold sat
down that if I hadn't been a Minister I wouldn't have held up my hand in the
vote when it was taken.

Sunday, June 19th
The P.M. has intervened in the seamen's strike but has failed to settle it. Now
it is a straight fight and the balance of payments is getting rapidly worse. We
are drifting on to the rocks and another July crisis is almost certain.

[1] Mayhew was upset about defence policy and Wyatt about steel nationalization.

Tuesday, June 21st

Cabinet. The interesting question was how, individually and collectively, we would react to Harold's cool and deliberate Statement to the House yesterday that he knew the names of the active communists who had been responsible for starting the seamen's strike.[1] This had caused consternation on the Labour back benches, but Harold showed no kind of repentance. Instead, he went round the table and forced each of us to define our position. Frank Cousins, Barbara Castle and I were all pretty critical of him, and on this occasion we had rather more support from people like Fred Lee. The Cabinet in fact was fairly balanced and his position is not too strong.

At about twelve o'clock we came to the main issue—prices and incomes. The question was what George Brown would say next day to the Parliamentary Party, where we thought there would be very strong opposition to his reintroducing the Bill (which fell when the general election was announced). He told us that a great deal had been done to make it less offensive and in particular to reduce the risks of imprisonment. Moreover, it might never come into operation; but he demanded complete Cabinet backing for the policy as represented in the Bill.

This started off an excited Cabinet discussion. Frank Cousins, as always, said the whole thing was complete poppycock and this time he would have to make a real stand. Barbara launched the idea of a policy with two different levels of award—a two-norm policy; and Callaghan wanted a complete freeze—a nil-norm—for the next twelve months. Barbara then said we ought to cut our Ministerial salaries and at this point Ministers began to drift away. It was an occasion when Harold's leadership was a bit shaken because we were coming into the open with our anxieties about the whole economic situation. Right at the end I said that a prices and incomes policy was not an adequate substitute for a socialist alternative to the old-fashioned deflation with unemployment into which we were drifting. It was the measures with which he proposed to stop that drift that I wanted to see. I didn't mind them being linked with an incomes policy but what I didn't want was to see us using an incomes policy alone. The P.M. was rather shirty and said he would have a discussion on productivity on July 5th. He had to make the concession when people like Tony Crosland were telling him not to drift into another July crisis like last year. He must also have realized that the reason for all this disturbance was the failure of his S.E.T. budget. We are only just starting on the Finance Bill but already we are having to consider measures to prop up a budget policy which has proved inadequate.

Thursday, June 23rd

Cabinet. We started with the seamen's strike. There was a lot of detailed discussion of the work of the strike emergency committee; but the important

[1] The Prime Minister alleged that hidden forces, 'a tightly knit group of politically motivated men', were working to prolong the seamen's strike.

fact was that the atmosphere is now slightly better and the strike is almost certainly coming to an end since the seamen are prepared for some kind of settlement.

So we resumed Tuesday's discussion of prices and incomes. Right at the beginning Frank Cousins made a melodramatic remark. 'You ought to remember', he said to Harold, 'that the Minister of Technology is first for Questions on the day after the Second Reading of the Prices and Incomes Bill. He ought to be warned of this, you know.' This was Frank's way of telling us that he was going to resign on the day the Bill was debated. James Callaghan pleaded with him and then Harold said that he was impressed by Frank's brilliantly successful ideas and vigorous policies and that he had also received some instructive suggestions about productivity increases. Why couldn't we consider all these? Harold will certainly do everything to keep Frank. He has loaded him with new jobs, expanded his Ministry and given him two first-rate young Parliamentary Secretaries, Peter Shore and Edmund Dell.[1] But can he keep him now? After that, Barbara Castle fired off and really made a very good speech on a socialist prices and incomes policy. She behaved as I should really behave, she was a Cabinet Minister playing that role. Her main theme was the two norms under which we would try to use the incomes policy to improve the lot of the lower-paid worker while holding down the higher salaries. She also urged the introduction of a national minimum wage and the application of the policy on dividends as well as wages.

In the evening, with Peter's help, I started mending my fences with the press, which has been giving me a thoroughly bad time since I got back from Crete. I briefed Anthony Shrimsley of the *Sunday Mirror* and Nora Beloff of the *Observer* as fully as I possibly could on what I am going to say on Friday, including an account of the option-mortgage—Steve and I have virtually worked out the details of what is really a brilliant scheme. I also lunched Jimmy Margach at the Ecu de France, and told him we were going to help the private builders cope with S.E.T., and all about the option-mortgage. So I hope we shall have a relatively friendly press this weekend as a lead-up to the *Panorama* show on Monday, which is really tremendously important for me.

Wednesday, June 29th
I spent the day at Peterborough clearing up another of the New Town entanglements Dame Evelyn left behind.

As we motored back to London I switched on the wireless and heard that the strike had been called off. So Harold Wilson had won yet another of his 'extra' victories. It was good enough to get the strike settled without giving anything away; it was even better to get it called off on the day after having denounced the communists in the union and challenged them to do their worst.

[1] A former history lecturer and I.C.I. executive, elected in 1964 as M.P. for Birkenhead.

In the evening I dined with John Silkin in the House. It was a quiet evening, with the Finance Bill still teetering along in the Chamber. But despite Harold's tremendous victory, Silkin and I found a sense of discomfort in the Members' dining-room. The P.M.'s operation had been too McCarthyite for the taste of our new back-benchers; the naming of names had been gratuitous and unnecessary. Even though it was a great triumph, none of us sitting round the big table that evening really liked it.

Thursday, June 30th
This was the day for my big Cabinet battle on housing. But first we had to discuss compensation for steel owners (much less generous than last time) and then endure a long argument about the Parliamentary situation. Once again the Lord President and the Chief Whip have tried to pack far too much into the Session and we are already being pushed into the second week of August.

I was next on the agenda; and this was one of the few times I spoke in Cabinet from full notes. The moment I had finished speaking Callaghan said that he would talk quite briefly because he had to go out to see the German Ambassador. Poor man, he had been up all night once again, dealing with his bloody S.E.T., and he was exhausted and bad-tempered, and maybe he had calculated that if he left the room he would thereby be able to stop Cabinet taking a decision. He put his case very clearly. Whatever the strength of my arguments for an immediate increase, he asked Cabinet to remember that I was demanding it a fortnight before his own proposals were to be submitted to Cabinet for cutting back public expenditure as a whole. All he asked now was for housing to be considered along with other demands. If this wasn't done, the whole PESC exercise would fall to the ground. He concluded with the threat, 'If you concede this £31 million to the Ministry of Housing I shall take it away from the other spending authorities.' And with that he stalked out of the room.

Before anybody else could weigh in, the Prime Minister backed me to the full. He confirmed that last July Cabinet had cut back the housing programme for 1965 and for 1966 on the express understanding that if there were a sag in the private sector I could compensate in the public sector. Unless this were done, the whole programme would be in jeopardy. At once Tony Crosland and Barbara Castle jumped in to urge that the decision should be postponed until after PESC. I replied that I had been postponing it for seven months, ever since last December when the Chancellor predicted that the private-sector building would go up to 235,000. His predictions had proved wrong and mine had proved right. The figure for 1966 is 210,000, 20,000 short of his own prediction, and I must ask for that number of council houses. At last George Brown came in, more or less on my side. He even admitted there was truth in the complaint I was putting forward, with Tommy Balogh's help, about the intolerable nature of the PESC exercise, and concluded that if I were to get my way, the cost of the extra houses must not be taken from some other social service. And that is how it was finally minuted in the absence of the Chancellor and against the protests of Barbara and Tony. I was to get my extra £31 million but they were not to be taken off anybody else's estimates.

So I got my way—with the help of the P.M. and at the cost of creating a great deal of resentment. The rest of Cabinet complain that the Housing Committee is packed with housing Ministers, and James Callaghan is protesting that no other spending Department is permitted the licence I get. Everybody really feels that we should have waited for the PESC exercise. I know that's how I would have felt if any other Minister has got away with it.

Cabinet wasn't by any means over. We now turned to discuss Concorde. I had to listen to that miserable little Mulley proposing once again that since the Attorney-General could find no loophole we should commit ourselves to it. I said this was absolutely mad and I would rather cancel the whole thing. Others joined in and said that it would be absurd to imagine that General de Gaulle could sue us for £120 million—or, indeed, win his case if he did. It was also pointed out that if only we had held out for ten days longer in October 1964 the French would have given way. This Concorde commitment has been one of our major disasters and I was so disgusted that I walked out.

The P.M. also asked Cabinet to approve the Foreign Office press release issued the day before regretting the American decision to bomb Hanoi. We did so unenthusiastically because few of us, I think, felt it was more than a posture. We knew perfectly well that as soon as he got across the Atlantic and talked to Johnson, Harold would indicate to the President that there was nothing in what he had said or done which made his loyalty to the Vietnam policy less profound. Harold made a Statement of the recorded Cabinet decision to the House in the afternoon. The back-benchers obviously shared our doubts, and a storm broke out. Strange to think that this humiliating rupture with his back-benchers took place less than forty-eight hours after the P.M.'s success over the seamen's strike. The demands for a debate went on for forty-five minutes.

The amended Prices and Incomes Bill was eventually published on July 4th. It gave the Government power to require wage, price or dividend increases to be submitted to the statutory Prices and Incomes Board. It would impose a delay of up to four months on any settlement but, as yet, sanctions were moral rather than penal.

On July 3rd the Minister of Technology, Frank Cousins, resigned. He had argued for voluntary co-operation between both sides of industry instead of an incomes policy.

The Postmaster-General, Anthony Wedgwood Benn, took Frank Cousins's place and the Chief Whip, Edward Short, succeeded Mr Benn. The Deputy Chief Whip, John Silkin, became Chief Whip.

Sunday, July 3rd

The big news in all the papers this weekend is, of course, Frank Cousins's resignation, which has finally been announced. He has managed to do it in the most clumsy way. Having announced his resignation, he rushed round to the T.G.W.U. in Smith Square and spent five hours with them working out what he was to do. After which he made a statement that he had decided to go back to being General Secretary of the union and that his salary had been increased. He added that he might as well stay in Parliament to oppose the Prices and Incomes Bill.

As a matter of fact the Committee Stage won't start till November and the Bill probably won't be on the Statute Book until March of next year so he'll stay quite a long time. Moreover, as all the Sunday papers are saying, he has probably committed a breach of privilege by announcing that he will work for his union while a Member and pay his Parliamentary salary back. He has also got into a bit of a mess with his constituency party. He was foisted on them, but they now like him very much as a good Member and a nice man. Just when they have got used to him, they certainly don't want another by-election! Moreover, being a left-wing Party they support his opposition to the Prices and Incomes Bill, and have unanimously told him that they want him to remain their M.P. even while he is General Secretary of the T.G.W.U. This puts him in a difficult position. If he stays on there will be no sense on the Left of the Parliamentary Party that a great leader has descended from Cabinet on to the back benches. In fact, he is much less dangerous to the Government in the House of Commons than if he goes outside and thrashes about like a great whale in industrial waters.

From what I can see, this Cousins crisis, if it is a crisis, is the kind which Harold is fully capable of overcoming. The resignation could not have come at a less inconvenient time for Harold Wilson. The only danger of it lies in our relations with the Conference where Frank — if he were let loose — could stir up the Left. This is something which Barbara Castle noticed. Directly she heard the news she rang me up (I was down at Slough on an official visit) and asked whether I was still thinking of not standing for the N.E.C. this year. That *had* been my idea, particularly since I had heard that she and Tony Greenwood were thinking of doing the same thing. Barbara said to me straight away on the phone that Frank's resignation made all this impossible. Marcia Williams, as I now hear, takes the same view; so I can assume that when I ask Harold's advice he will be against it. This is a big change for me, since as recently as last Saturday my mind was made up. It was the day of our Cropredy Country Fair and Albert Rose and Betty Healey were over with a lot of Coventry supporters. I discussed the idea very fully with them. They agreed that if I wanted to go this was a good year since nobody could say I was a coward being chased off by fear of defeat. If I resign this year people will know it is because I want to make room on the N.E.C. for younger people. They said that they would put this to the executive of the Coventry

East constituency Party and that when I heard their advice I could make up
my mind. However, I am pretty sure now that the decision must be 'not this
year'.

Tuesday, July 5th
In the afternoon I went and sat on the front bench quite deliberately to give
support to Leo Abse, who was moving his ten-minute Bill on homosexual
reform in order to prove there is a majority in favour of changing the law.[1]
The Lords have now twice passed this particular Private Members' Bill,[2] and
we can only get it through the Commons by showing that the Members want
it so much that any reasonable Government must provide the time. I found
myself sitting between Harold Wilson, who had just been answering Questions, and Roy Jenkins. All our other colleagues stayed away. The vote was
two to one in favour of reform.

Wednesday, July 6th
I was due to spend the day on the Thames Conservators' launch watching
them do their annual inspection and was surprised when the new Chief
Whip, John Silkin, told me that Harold required every Minister to be at the
P.L.P. meeting at one o'clock to vote on the resolution of confidence in him
over the Statement on the U.S. bombing of Hanoi. Since I am allowed to be
absent from the vote of censure this evening, it looks as though a P.L.P.
decision is considered more important than a major debate in the House. I
turned up in plenty of time to get a seat and saw Callaghan come in, pursed
and pensive; he fell asleep beside me. He is in one of his gloomy moods
because of the sterling crisis. The actual show was pretty flat. Sydney
Silverman killed the debate right at the start by moving the motion—it
demanded a new policy in Vietnam—in a very, very long speech. His motion
was really a vote of no confidence. After him the left-wingers were subdued
since they were trying to show that they weren't splitting the Party. They
were really completely answered by Raymond Fletcher, a left-winger from
the Tribune group.[3] He reminded the Party that Harold Wilson was due to
go to Washington to see President Johnson on July 28th. Would it really
strengthen his hand if the Party were at this moment to pass a resolution
demanding total repudiation of American policy in Vietnam? At the end
Harold Wilson read aloud a fairly solid speech which ended with a nasty
phrase about the left wing cheering Heath and a vague threat of a general
election. Then Manny Shinwell got up and asked Sydney Silverman to
withdraw his motion and Sydney Silverman characteristically refused. This
lost him at least half his supporters. He would have done far better to
withdraw; by not doing so he strengthened Harold's hand.

[1] M.P. for Pontypool since 1958. A solicitor, he sponsored several other successful Private
Members' Bills on such subjects as divorce, family planning, legitimacy and widows' damages.
[2] The Earl of Arran had persisted with this measure. See his article in *Encounter*, March 1972.
[3] M.P. for Ilkeston since 1964. A journalist and a member of the T.G.W.U.

Thursday, July 7th

At Cabinet we started with yet another discussion of the parliamentary time-table and were threatened with having to go on till August 10th. The Finance Bill is at last off the Floor, but it is to be followed by the S.E.T. Bill which may well consume ten days in Committee if the Opposition want. I suppose it will have to be guillotined.

Then came my moment on foreign affairs. Michael Stewart said he had nothing to report, whereupon I chipped in, although my Private Office had pleaded with me against doing so. However, though Harold tried to freeze me off, I held on tenaciously and brought into the open the contradiction between the speeches of George Thomson and George Brown and the assurances given to us in private that there is really no prospect of our getting into the Common Market. I got some support from Fred Peart. But Douglas Jay was in Moscow, opening the British Fair, and Barbara Castle was too tactful to join in. (She doesn't want to side with me just now because I am an important rival for money—Housing versus Transport.) Nevertheless, I think I made sure that we shall have a serious discussion of Europe at the end of this month when the official reports are ready.

Then the P.M. had to explain this morning's leak in the *Daily Herald* and the *Morning Star* about his forthcoming visit to the Trade Fair in Moscow; it had completely bitched his plans for winding up in the House that evening with a dramatic announcement. He was very nettled because he foresaw the debate would now end in a complete anticlimax.

That evening there was a big reception in Lancaster House for Monsieur Pompidou. I never even saw him. I found myself talking to Tony Crosland's wife, Susan Barnes, which was very nice indeed. From there I went back to the House and found it difficult to keep awake during Harold Wilson's speech winding up the Vietnam debate. It was (as expected) a flop and the thirty-one left-wingers, whom he had hoped to impress by announcing his Moscow visit, did abstain.

Sunday, July 10th

Reading the morning papers, I see that people are beginning to realize how Cousins's resignation has produced quite an important Cabinet reshuffle. The fact which most of the correspondents missed at first is that Harold has used the opportunity to make John Silkin his Chief Whip. I am told that this has saved me from being moved to the Ministry of Technology, When I ran into George Brown in the Chamber he assured me that this would have happened had not Harold been determined to appoint a new Chief Whip. Since he couldn't possibly make Ted Short Minister of Housing he had to liberate a minor Ministry, and so he moved Tony Wedgwood Benn to Technology in order to make Short Postmaster-General. These stories are never absolutely true but there may be a good deal in this. Certainly, both Tommy and Marcia have wanted to have me put in Technology and the fact that I was quite a vigorous Shadow Minister of Science would have made the move quite sensible. It would also have fulfilled Harold's pledge to give me a big Ministry which is bound to be right at the centre of things.

However, Crossman didn't become MinTech because the Prime Minister realized he very much needed a new Chief Whip. This is something which some of us had been urging for a long time. Bert Bowden and Ted Short were quite capable of managing a majority of three but this new Parliamentary Party with a majority of a hundred is obviously quite beyond them. I welcome the change, but by doing it this way Harold has made sure that all the big changes in the Post Office that Tony was preparing—breaking it up into three nationalized corporations, altering its whole future relationship with the B.B.C. and I.T.V.—will collapse when Ted Short takes charge. We shall watch and see, but I predict all Tony's plans will perish.*

What will Tony be like as MinTech? Up till now he has shown no great administrative grasp and the maximum power of alienating people and so not getting his way. Maybe this is because he was outside the Cabinet. That's what he felt. Now he is going to be a very senior, central Minister, who if he wants can be one of the leading figures in an inner Cabinet.

Tuesday, July 12th
This was the day for the long-announced Cabinet discussion on productivity. All the papers previously circulated were desultory and of no interest. Moreover, at the last moment the Chancellor circulated a sensational Top Secret document. This admitted he had based his budget on the expectation that he could hold consumption until S.E.T. started working in September and that this expectation had been proved wrong; that is why he would need to cut back public-sector expenditure by at least £500 million.

The meeting only really got going when Tony Crosland said that whatever happened he didn't want a repetition of the July 1965 crisis. He didn't want to see us once again combating inflation by cutting public expenditure. I chipped in and said to the Chancellor, 'We came into office as socialists and the essence of a socialist policy is a shift from private to public expenditure. The public sector is not too big now—it's far too small. There can be no question of a cut-back.' At this point the Chancellor woke up and said that he must tell Cabinet frankly that he didn't know how we were going to get out of the mess. We had totally failed to reach our objectives, we were drifting into devaluation in the worst possible conditions and he didn't know how he could retain his position as Chancellor. This set everyone round the table arguing either for or against another July cut in public expenditure. I think everyone who spoke, with the exception of Dick Marsh, was against the Chancellor. And that is about as far as Cabinet got.

In the evening I had to go to Downing Street for a party Harold was giving for the Transport House staff. There I learnt from Douglas Jay that the

* A false prophecy.

reason why Cabinet had been so inconclusive was that the Chancellor and the First Secretary had failed to agree on the cuts. The Chancellor insisted the package should include a £100 million cut in overseas spending whereas the First Secretary said that this was unacceptable if it involved any change of policy.

Thursday, July 14th
As soon as we got to Cabinet Harold made a long statement making it perfectly clear that there had been disagreement between Callaghan and Brown and that a holding Statement would be required in the afternoon. Meanwhile our main job would be to work out our new policy in the fortnight before August 7th. The Statement would come just after the announcement of the increased bank rate and must include the announcement that there would be a £100 million cut in overseas expenditure. Everybody was critical. Roy Jenkins wanted in addition to this cut a specific commitment to a wage and prices freeze. Dick Marsh said that would be fine if anybody knew what a wage and prices freeze really meant and whether it was practical. Barbara wanted the cut in foreign expenditure even though it would include overseas development, whereas Tony Greenwood was fighting against it. But the big confrontation came between the Chancellor and the Foreign Secretary, who obviously hadn't been consulted until the night before. Michael Stewart said he couldn't possibly cut £100 millions without either withdrawing totally from Germany or totally from East of Suez. Clearly this couldn't be done as a sudden emergency plan for helping the balance of payments. On the whole he got his way and it was clear that Harold's Statement would not be specific on the subject of overseas cuts.

During the Statement Jim sat beside me on the front bench. He was back in serene form and turned to me and solemnly said, 'We achieved great things this morning; we prevented the purely deflationary package we are all fighting to avoid.' In fact, of course, the interaction of Callaghan's pure deflation and Brown's pure anti-deflation has produced a disastrous dilemma which the P.M.'s Statement did nothing to resolve.

In the prices and incomes debate in the evening one of my predictions came badly unstuck. Frank Cousins proved himself in parliamentary terms not a blundering fool but a potential left-wing leader. Of course, to read, his speech is impenetrably obscure but he has personality and it came across. The Tories helped him because they wanted him to succeed. But so did a lot of our own side. The question now is whether the new package, when we bring it out, will be able to rally the Left, or whether we shall be in open conflict not only with the Tories but with our own Party.

Sunday, July 17th
When I got home from an official visit to Lancashire I found I was being rung up by almost every Sunday columnist. This is partly because since Thurs-

day's Cabinet the newspapers have been full of startling inside stories. The
Sun has told us how Harold Wilson saved the country from really savage
deflation. The *Guardian* gave us a long statement on Mr Callaghan's views
on cuts in overseas spending. It is clear that these leaks haven't come from
Cabinet because the rest of us had no idea what is going on between the big
three. Nevertheless, the columnists ring us up to ask us our views, all the
more so in my case because I gave a press conference on Friday at which I
said that I knew the private sector of building would suffer even worse as the
result of the crisis but that I was hoping that council house completions
wouldn't be affected this year. This got a lot of publicity on Saturday and the
Daily Telegraph tried to make out that Barbara and I were opposing any
kind of cuts. Harold Wilson had sent me a message via Tommy that I must
stress the unity of the Cabinet in everything I said and this is what I did in fact
do. I saw a lot of Tommy last week and he gave me some useful briefing. It is
now pretty clear that ever since we won the election this could have
happened to the pound. Yet no contingency plan of any kind has been
prepared and our big three were caught completely unawares when the
pound suddenly became unstuck.

This has damaged us in the public eye because it has helped to create the
image of Harold Wilson just opportunizing from expedient to expedient;
and hopping off to Moscow this weekend seems a palpable political gimmick.[1] Tommy tells me the crisis is now so serious that the full Statement will
have to be made on Tuesday of next week if we are to prevent a devaluation.
Personally, I sincerely hope we shall devalue, come what may, because
looking back I am sure the basic mistake Harold made was trying to save the
pound. If he had got off the pound right at the beginning he could really have
given Britain a new start.

Now the question is, can we get that new start twenty months after the
Government came into power? Of course we have a majority of a hundred,
of course the Cabinet has a good deal of experience. But are we doomed to a
bout of deflation such as the Treasury wanted to force through last Tuesday?
Here I think we have to consider how we can persuade Harold to get a policy
group around him to consider the Government's strategy. I have been sitting
outside, as a departmental Minister. So have Tony Wedgwood Benn, now at
Technology, and Barbara at Transport. We all felt last Wednesday that we
must now say to him, 'Look we've let you run things on your own and
they are all coming unstuck. We must now have some strategic long-term
planning.'

I have also got to say the same things about the relationship between the
Government and Transport House. There is no question now of my resigning from the Executive. After Frank Cousins's resignation I have got to stick
by Harold and try to see him through. I was struck that Albert Rose and

---

[1] 'The British press . . . , worked up about the economic crisis, regarded my visit as a purpose-
less and irrelevant interlude.' *Wilson*, p. 255.

Betty Healey, good left-wingers, rang me up and said that Coventry East wouldn't let me stand down in the present crisis, because if I did the wrong person, Sydney Silverman for instance, might take my place. So that's out of the way and instead of resigning I shall now take a far more positive role in the relations between the Government and the Party.

I must add one last word to get things in perspective. I've been talking a great deal about Harold's failures and my disillusionment with his gimmickry. I must say that it was a tremendous shock last night when I saw his face during his interview on TV just before he left London Airport for Moscow and heard the bitter remarks of the B.B.C. correspondent on his arrival. There is no doubt Harold is going through a terrible time, though the N.O.P. poll published on Thursday showed us with a 16½ per cent lead and Harold right up and Heath right down. We must never forget that. But we haven't got too much time before the Gallup Poll shows us collapsing. We had a dramatic by-election this week in which we lost Carmarthen to a Welsh Nationalist.[1] That was due partly to special Welsh conditions but also to the deepseated malaise which set in immediately after the election and which was confirmed by the disastrous S.E.T. budget and, since then, by the fact that Harold Wilson, who showed himself a master of the art of surviving with a majority of three, has shown himself quite unable to use the powers he has obtained by his majority of one hundred. He hasn't yet settled down to a real job of work based on a real strategy, and that is what we have got to see if we can make him do next week.

Monday, July 18th
Since the PESC meeting was starting at 9.30 on Monday I went to London by the Sunday night train and looked in on Tommy Balogh, because I wanted his briefing. At that time I didn't know that the whole weekend had been devoted to a struggle between George Brown and Callaghan—Callaghan wanting cuts and deflation, and George Brown fighting against them and moving more and more into support for the floating pound. I also didn't know that this support had been also forthcoming from nearly all the economic advisers, including Neild, Balogh and Kaldor. Tommy had to be discreet, but he didn't oppose me when I started by telling him that what worried me was the memory of Tony Crosland's remark during the July squeeze last year, that we must never again make sacrifices of public-sector spending for parity. From that I went on to argue that we must go for the floating pound, otherwise we should have another package of cuts in six months' time and another and another, and what was the point of that? The more we talked the more my mind was made up and I went to bed that night with the clear conviction that when Harold came back from Moscow my job

[1] In the by-election caused by the death of Lady Megan Lloyd George, a 9,000 Labour majority was converted to a 2,400 majority for Gwynfor Evans, the Plaid Cymru candidate.

was to put the case in Cabinet in favour of seizing the full possibilities of the floating pound.

This morning before PESC I went into my office and gave John Delafons instructions to make appointments for me that evening with Tony Crosland, Roy Jenkins and Barbara Castle. I would see them separately in their rooms at the House of Commons during the debates on the Selective Employment Payments Bill when we had all got to be present. To my surprise each of them jumped at the chance of a private talk. This was the first time that I have ever tried to organize a cabal in the Cabinet, or, to put it more modestly, to discuss with a group of colleagues in advance the line we should take on a big issue of policy.[1]

The PESC meeting has become our regular July exercise. Its job is to keep the growth of public-sector expenditure in line with the growth of the economy. This year it had been found that although the rate of economic growth had declined, the growth of Government expenditure had jumped from 4½ per cent, the level at which we wanted to keep it, to something like 10 per cent. As part of our regular process of Government, therefore, there had to be something of a cut-back. What was clear to me was that it was useless to attempt this regular annual cut-back until we had seen the crisis measures which were being prepared behind our backs. It took most of my colleagues a full hour before they grasped that official Whitehall was busy quietly working out a precise package of cuts for announcement on Wednesday while we as Ministers were sitting round the table blithely discussing the remote possibility of retrenchment. When they realized, everybody was infuriated. I had remarked right at the beginning of the meeting that it ought to be cancelled, which peeved the Chancellor. By the end there wasn't much doubt that that was the general view of everyone there.

After it was over I went up to George Brown and said that I must talk to him straight away. He said, 'Come round quietly to my office.' On my way I looked into my own Ministry and checked on the situation with Delafons. It didn't take me long to confirm that my Permanent Secretary, without being allowed to talk to me, had been instructed on Sunday to work out the costs he could agree to on behalf of my Ministry. In his case it wasn't too bad because he was told that housing would be omitted and he would have to make cuts only in the rest of local government expenditure. But he had got down to the job and had agreed on my behalf, without consulting me, to a £34 million cut in miscellaneous local government expenditure—town-hall building, town-centre development, bathing-pools, etc. It was already clear that over the weekend the centralized mandarin machine had once again been put to work, working out a desperate programme without Cabinet knowing about it. The total—£500 million—would be achieved partly by cuts in personal consumption, using the regulator, partly by cuts in the public-sector and

[1] But 'there was no plot, no conspiracy, no cabal, no organization. There was a great deal of concern and a lot of loose talk.' *Wilson*, p. 256.

nationalized industries and partly by cuts in overseas expenditure. I was sad that Steve, though he knows me pretty well by now, didn't feel able to ring me up and bring me in.

Armed with this information I went along to George Brown and told him straight away that I was in favour of the floating pound, and that I was going to see Roy Jenkins, Tony Crosland and Barbara Castle that evening to discuss it with each of them separately. He said this was also his view; but he emphasized that he wasn't going to take part in any kind of conspiracy, and indeed the whole tone of what he said that morning was very careful. He had been fighting with Harold while he was in Moscow, using telegrams and messages carried across by Burke Trend. Indeed, Harold had issued a statement saying that Ministers could resign if they liked but they would have to take it or leave it. Yes, he had been tempted to resign and talked a lot about it. But there was no question of that now. He would go all out for persuading Harold, when he got back, to float the pound. Obviously there were strained relations between him and Harold, but equally obviously George Brown at this stage was prepared to have a try in Cabinet on Tuesday. In preparation for the battle he filled me in about the size of the cut the Treasury was demanding and the amount he would be prepared to take. He also told me that, as the result of last week's Cabinet, Harold had decided that the public-sector programme, housing, hospitals and schools, should not be cut. Altogether it was a sensible, coherent talk. When I left I promised that in my talks with Barbara, Roy and Tony I would not mention my talk with him.

Barbara was the first Minister I saw that evening. We had a talk in her room and she told me straight away that she was seeing George Brown later. She expressed herself entirely willing to commit herself to the floating pound. After that I had a quick dinner with Nicholas Davenport. When I asked him what would be the sensible thing for me to advocate, he said, 'The sensible thing would be to have a floating pound, but you can't get that through your Cabinet because it is not a view held seriously by any of the people who matter.' After dinner Roy came to see me. We were going through one of those terrible long summer nights in the Commons—it was the debate on the guillotine on the S.E.T. Bill. Roy immediately said he was in favour of floating the pound and would speak in favour of it, though he made it clear that he would make no offer to resign. He said he had talked it over with Tony Crosland, who shared his view. He had just been dining with George Brown, he observed, who seemed to be in a hysterical, resigning mood. I then asked Roy about the European background to this affair. You know, I said, how Harold is working against you, telling us anti-Europeans that anyone who wants to devalue the pound is trying to do so as a practical way into Europe. 'Tell me, Roy,' I said, 'what have the two things really got to do with each other?' And he said, 'Plenty, of course. I mean we will have to do something about sterling in order to enter Europe. This might mean devaluation; but in my view a floating pound gives a certain freedom of action, either to enter Europe or to do anything else, and what we are trying to regain this week is freedom of action. If we go on as we are, we remain prisoners of the situation and prisoners of our own weakness.'

After this I went back to George Brown, as I had promised. I found him worked up into a passion and plunged into one of his most maudlin, self-commiserating moods. He at once told me there was no chance whatsoever of Harold Wilson agreeing because he was now bound personally and irrevocably to President Johnson and had ceased to be a free agent. That was why he, George Brown, knew he would have to resign. I argued for fighting it out in Cabinet as he had suggested only that morning, and George replied there wasn't any chance whatsoever. Just as I was getting up to go, George Brown said to me, 'Look, would you support me if Harold had to resign?' I said, 'Certainly not.' And he said, 'Well, Barbara said the same thing to me. Of course, you two are bound to Harold, that's why you can't do any good.' I didn't know how seriously to take this, but he certainly implied that there were other people prepared to go with him to the last resort; and Harold had to be replaced in order to float the pound. Maybe it was one of those things George Brown says late at night. But certainly it was something which would get back to Harold on the grape-vine.

I left him very late, knowing that although he had impressed on me the need for absolute security, he had been talking in much the same kind of way to Barbara, Roy and Tony Crosland. The last person I saw was Tony Benn, who also agreed to take the same line. So the numbers had been mounting up that day.[1] We had Roy, Tony Crosland, Tony Benn, Barbara Castle and myself all firmly committed to opposing a new package of cuts except as a preparation for floating off the pound. Moreover during the course of the talks it had become clearer and clearer to me that the scale of the package required to float the pound was not very different from that required to save it. So the issue is not what package of cuts we should have but what should be the strategy behind the cuts, what would make it worth imposing them.

Tuesday, July 19th
Early in the morning I was rung up by George Wigg who said to me, 'There are times when loyalty is all-important. What matters now is that when Harold comes back you support him.' And he added, 'You know, I have good sources. I know what everybody is doing.' I said, 'Thank you very much, that's all right.' That was useful because it showed me what the Wilson line was going to be: a demand for loyalty and toughness—take the package and be damned. Wilson was going to be Napoleonic.

I cleared the whole morning for work with my Permanent Secretary on the

---

[1] 'Seminars were taking place all over the Palace of Westminster: Dick Crossman in the tea-room was instructing the young, and George Brown ... was also involved, principally with junior ministers. But there was no organized movement.' *Wilson*, p. 257.

the Ministry's cuts. We'd expected that the papers would have come round by then. In fact, they didn't arrive until two o'clock in the afternoon and when they were opened they consisted of a rather flaccid set of hypothetical calculations. Excluded from the papers was any statement of the total amount of the package—it was deliberately being hidden from Cabinet members. I just had to try to tot it up with my Permanent Secretary.

When Steve and I had done what we could with our departmental estimates, I rang each of my colleagues to discuss the line we should take. It was agreed that at Cabinet George Brown should hold back. There should be no talk of resignation, and I should start the attack. After this I rang up Bill Nield, an old friend of mine who is now a senior official in the Cabinet Office, and said I must see the P.M. at all costs when he got back. I had begun to realize that, since I had really organized all this, I must in fairness see Harold and warn him of what we were up to. At first I was told that it was impossible. Then Bill Nield said I could see him after Questions. That suited me because I happened to be first for Questions that day and had to spend lunch-time with the Parliamentary Secretaries preparing for a rather awkward bunch on housing which had to be answered before the package was known. Harold came in and sat beside me and then at 3.15 he answered his Questions pretty well and we withdrew to his room. I started off straight away: 'Look here, some of us have been thinking very carefully and we just can't take another package without any kind of assurance that it won't end in another crisis.' I told him that I personally was in favour of floating the pound, but what I had come to discuss was the procedure in Cabinet that day. We wanted a discussion on devaluation before we considered the cuts. Since the packages for floating off the pound and for staying on the pound would not be so very dissimilar, that was all the more reason why we must get the strategy clear first before we came to the cuts.

Harold immediately gave way on this and gave me the assurance I asked for. I then told him that I had been talking to a number of colleagues and we all wanted to argue the case for floating. Harold replied that it was a matter of time-tabling. 'I'm not adamant against devaluation, but we shall have to get the pound stabilized first so that we can float from strength not from weakness.' And he began to outline a plan (of which Tommy had informed me the night before) for strengthening the pound now, getting import controls in the autumn and floating off in the spring.

It was the first time I had led, not a Cabinet revolt, but Cabinet resistance to the personal government he has been conducting. The talk went fairly well. I stayed with him half an hour, listening most of the time and chatting with him a little bit at the end. Then I went back to the Ministry to get my Cabinet papers and looked at the officials' document for twenty minutes and realized how thin it was.

Cabinet started at five o'clock with a very long statement by Harold. As I had agreed with George Brown and the others I came in second. I said that, frankly, the package as Harold had outlined it was the 1965 package, only rather more so. I wanted to consider the possibility of a package based on a properly worked-out strategy and linked to an announcement of a floating pound. I believed that this kind of policy would have much more chance of getting public support and also economic growth. Immediately I had finished, Roy Jenkins came in quietly saying he fully supported me. Tony Crosland said much the same. Up to this point the Chancellor remained silent, and even now the first person to support the P.M.'s package was Douglas Houghton, who represented the lowest common denominator of common sense. Perhaps we should be forced off the pound, he observed, but we mustn't *decide* to float the pound since this would betray our obligations and shock the British people. As the debate went on it became clear that all the people concerned with foreign affairs were for the Prime Minister—the Colonial Secretary, the Commonwealth Secretary, for example—and so were Fred Peart and Willie Ross.

Harold had intended to stop the meeting at seven thirty and start it again at nine next morning. But by seven thirty we'd scarcely finished the stage where each person round the table stated his point of view. So it was decided to go on till nine and start work on the draft statement next day.

This put me in a fix because I had not cancelled the important dinner to discuss the Land Commission that Arnold Goodman had arranged. So I slipped out at eight o'clock just when Barbara was making a dramatic statement about the merits of devaluation. I thought she was making a mistake, because she was playing into the hands of those who say that devaluation isn't a wonderful formula which would save the pound without hurting anybody. And that's true. But the main thing about this Cabinet was that the issue had been put to the P.M. and by nine o'clock he had been forced to make some important concessions. First, he had conceded that there could be no question of just sticking to parity. If we got through this crisis, we would have to work out a strategy; and if the level of unemployment was to rise markedly above 2 per cent (480,000), then he would consider devaluation. This was an assurance he gave across the table to George Brown.[1] And second, he had assured us that the whole issue of the various methods of devaluing the pound, whether by floating or moving to another fixed rate, would be considered by a special Cabinet Committee. This he conceded in answer to Richard Marsh, who was supporting the Chancellor but who also saw the need for a proper, considered Cabinet assessment of a contingency plan.

In the Statement on July 20th the Prime Minister announced the imposition of six months' standstill on all wage, salary and dividend increases, to be followed by a further six months' severe restraint. Price increases were to be frozen for twelve months. The House was told that the Government

[1] 'There was virtually no pressure for devaluation to a fixed, lower parity.' *Wilson*, p. 257.

*planned to strengthen the Prices and Incomes Bill to give the freeze statutory
authority.*

*The White Paper was published on July 29th and the proposals were tabled
as new clauses to be added to the Prices and Incomes Bill. This device caused
anger in Parliament.*

*The voluntary principle was retained in the new Part IV of the Bill but there
was also a compulsory element. In the case of a deliberate breach of the
standstill, an Order in Council could be laid before Parliament, to impose
penalties of up to £500. In Cabinet, the argument over compulsory powers
continued.*

Wednesday, July 20th

As we came into Cabinet George Brown said to me, 'You still think I am
right not to resign?' 'Certainly,' I said, 'there is no question at all.' 'Good,' he
answered, and throughout that meeting he was perfectly all right. He wasn't
very enthusiastic but he took the lead in the detailed discussion of a prices
and incomes freeze. I still regarded this as a theatrical device, an attempt to
make the voluntary system look stronger and I didn't pay much attention
when George Brown spelt it all out in detail. I noticed, however, that he
insisted on going to tell the T.U.C. and the C.B.I. about it at 2.30.

After that we went back to the old problem of the cuts. There were special
papers on such items as building controls and the regulator, and also on
overseas expenditure. The Foreign Secretary had only agreed to a £100
million cut if there was no change of policy. I regard this as the most
dangerous policy of all. By continuing to sustain all our commitments but
cutting our costs, we shall weaken ourselves and make our foreign policy
totally ineffective. There was no concession on East of Suez, no concession
on reducing the troops in Germany and yet there was an agreement to a big
cut. As for the public sector, all we were really doing was slowing up growth
in various areas. Of the £34 million cut Steve had conceded on Sunday I
offered to accept £26 million and got away with it. It meant very little more
than that certain local authorities would take a year longer on various
building projects, particularly town-centre development.

Throughout the whole of this Harold was his dreary, competent self,
tiddling with the figures. George Brown was sulking on the other side of the
table. The Chancellor was talking big about getting tough with Germany.
And Cabinet was a desultory affair. Nothing had been adequately prepared.
Nothing had been thought out properly. We were fixing things once again,
horribly inefficiently, at the last moment.

At one o'clock it was over and Harold got down to drafting the Statement.
Just imagine it. He had had a gruelling Moscow visit with all these crisis
messages coming across while he spent hours sweating round the State Fair.
Then he had flown back on Tuesday straight into this crisis and, as one of his
secretaries said to me, he had had a 21-hour day. Now, on Wednesday, he

had had a 4-hour Cabinet, then 2 hours to get the Statement ready, and then at 3.30 he had to be on the front bench in order to make it. Moreover, he had to make it in the absence of George Brown, and already by then he knew that George was in one of his moods. No wonder he sounded jaded and tired and his replies to supplementaries were verbose. It was a fairly poor Statement and he didn't make the best of it. If it had any virtue, it was that in it he saved our social priorities and avoided deflation across the board. What the Statement gave us was a selective deflation, intensifying controls but saving the key programmes, industrial building, hospitals, schools and houses. So it wasn't a complete Selwyn Lloyd 'stop'. I suppose it was partly in order to impress the bankers that he put it over with a strong emphasis on what was being saved. But it was a sad performance and on this occasion I thought Heath did considerably better.

Later in the afternoon I had a lot of things to do in the Ministry and sweated away there completely unaware of the hoo-ha about George Brown, who had resigned. I had been rung up in the morning to ask whether I would go on television after the P.M.'s broadcast that night and discuss it with Macleod and Grimond. So as well as dealing with departmental worries I had been mugging up the cuts all day and had then gone across to the liaison committee to get myself properly briefed for dealing with all the questions likely to be asked on television. I had also been ringing up Downing Street for bits of briefing, but nobody bothered to tell me about George because they thought I knew that as soon as he walked out of the Cabinet he had shot through the cameras, round the corner to the D.E.A. and announced his refusal to see the T.U.C. and C.B.I. at 2.30. Marcia told me later in the evening that they hadn't taken his letter of resignation too seriously because they had a file of his resignation letters. But apparently on this occasion it was flashed on the news, so all evening George Brown was going to Downing Street, talking to the Chief Whip, being photographed outside.

While all this was going on, Anne and I were dining with Lord Kennet and his charming wife in their lovely house in Bayswater. It was a most enjoyable dinner since they are some of the nicest new people we have met. From there I rushed to the Television Centre; the news about George was being splashed around and I found myself the first Cabinet Minister to react to it. I said quite genuinely that it was a surprise to me, and added that nobody else in Cabinet was thinking of resigning. I then got through the session quite creditably, defending the Government without disaster.

After that I went back to the Kennets and we talked late about the situation.[1] We discussed whether Harold should have accepted the resignation, and my first, instantaneous reaction was to feel that he had muffed it and to think what Attlee would have done in similar circumstances. He would have been short and sharp – 'Goodbye, George. O.K. You must know

[1] After talking to the Prime Minister, the Lord President and George Wigg, that evening, George Brown decided to stay at the D.E.A. and accept full Cabinet responsibility.

your own mind. Out.' Attlee would never have argued for an afternoon and evening with his number two after his resignation and then let him return. But as a leader Harold remains a kind, easy-going man and I think also he must have known that a Brown resignation might have finally pushed us off the pound.

When I got back to Vincent Square very late there was Tam Dalyell to tell me about the mood in the Commons, the catastrophic effect of the Brown resignation and the scenes with Bill Rodgers, his Parliamentary Secretary, rushing about, round-robin in hand, getting M.P.s' signatures praying George Brown to stay, and building up his ego. The more I heard about it the more disastrous I thought it was.

Thursday, July 21st

Cabinet this morning had been called to deal with the Concorde problem and to hear a report from Harold about his discussion of this with Monsieur Pompidou on his visit to London. I got there five minutes early and looked round the anteroom to see George Brown standing in a corner talking to Barbara Castle. The other people standing about looked pretty disgusted and upset. Nobody said anything.

Once round the table we had a long discussion about parliamentary business, which was dragging into August. Then the P.M. made some remarks about our holidays abroad and tourist allowances and then he said, 'Now overseas business.' Throughout the quarter of an hour we had been discussing parliamentary business I had been screwing myself up to be the unpleasant bastard who would raise the problem of George Brown. It was obvious that if I didn't do so, nobody else would, but that once the issue *was* raised, the P.M. and George would have to say something. So I pulled myself together, screwed up my courage and I said, 'Before we move to overseas business I think we would like to hear, Prime Minister, something from you about the events of which we have only read an account in the newspapers this morning.' At this point somebody else muttered the word 'resignation' and at once the P.M. said George hadn't resigned because the Queen hadn't been informed. He had only sent a letter. George Brown indignantly said it was a matter between him and the P.M., and Harold also tried to argue that it was something which Cabinet had no right to discuss. To which I replied that we might have no right but a public resignation, even if withdrawn, undermined the whole Cabinet policy and we did have the right to discuss this. I then repeated my demand that we should have a Cabinet Committee to control economic strategy. The P.M. replied that this was difficult because of secrecy: no Cabinet Committee could, for instance, discuss devaluation. I replied that there was a Defence Committee which worked in secret, and an economic strategy committee could have the same kind of structure. The P.M. reluctantly agreed. Then somebody raised wider objections about the whole issue of secret committees, and even the question of budget secrecy was brought in. Again the P.M. defended himself by counter-charges about leaks. This exasperated Cabinet because 99 per cent of the so-called leaks come from No. 10 or from the D.E.A. or from the Treasury. With the Prime Minister, George and Jim leaking about each other there is no good blaming the rest of us. Yet the Big Three believe that everything they tell the press is 'guidance' and anything ordinary members of the Cabinet say to the press is a 'leak', and this demoralizes all of us.

We went on to discuss Concorde; and Harold admitted that he had got nothing out of the talks with the French Prime Minister. So we would have to go on with the confounded plane.

The morning hadn't been wasted. What we had established as a result of that discussion of George's resignation was: (i) that the Cabinet must now consider the alternative methods of dealing with the pound; and (ii) that we were going to have a discussion on economic strategy and Europe. Both these were conceded under pressure which I had started. I didn't see Harold again on Thursday. All I received was a message from No. 10 that the Committee meeting he had called on housing had been cancelled and the Minister of Housing would have to wait a long time for a decision.

In the evening we were due to have a meeting of our little group. It was cancelled because Tommy Balogh had been forbidden by Harold to attend, and anyway Marcia had not been at the last meetings. With Marcia out, Tommy terrified, me out of favour and Harold retiring into his shell, I guess the group will cease to exist. That's sad.

Sunday, July 24th

Another week behind us and certainly the crisis has deepened. We have had during this week the destruction of the Wilson myth in the public eye and, even more, in my own private eye. It's amazing how his luck ran up to a certain point and suddenly stopped. I could name that point—the day he went down to the House of Commons and listed the nine communists in the seamen's union and pulled off the end of the strike next morning. That was the apex of his luck. But he was never able to cash in on it because of the Vietnam bombing Statement two days later. This also spoilt the effect of the announcement of his Russian visit. What is more, after he had briefed the weekend press that nothing was wrong with the economy, suddenly the crisis hit him and he left for Moscow with the crisis on top of him. Since then catastrophe after catastrophe, culminating in the tragi-comic incident of George Brown's semi-resignation this week.

I suppose it is the most dramatic decline any modern P.M. has suffered. More sudden than Macmillan's, which started with the July massacre of one-third of his Cabinet.[1] The first result is reflected in the N.O.P. poll which

[1] On July 13th, 1962, seven Ministers (the Lord Chancellor, the Chancellor of the Exchequer, the Secretary of State for Scotland, the Ministers of Defence, Education and Housing, and the Minister without Portfolio) were sacked from the Cabinet.

showed a slump from a 16½ per cent lead to a 7½ per cent lead in one week. It's also reflected in the revival of the Tory Party. On the telly even Heath looks much more like a leader these days.

I try and reflect on why all this hit us. Harold, of course, is anxious to say that the seamen's strike was the cause of the trouble, and it is true that the strike was a great blow. But one has to go right back to the S.E.T. budget, which was the first absolutely fatal mistake. Instead of doing what we expected him to do and imposing the austerity budget we are now getting in July, he and Callaghan avoided unpopularity (and helped to win the municipals) by introducing the gimmickry of S.E.T. The fact that the new tax would only operate as a 'deflater' from September left five months of the year in which the price and wage inflation could run wild. That is what has really got out of control.

And together with the Wilson myth, the three-man regime has gone for a burton. Up till now our economic policy has been run by the system of having two Ministries permanently at loggerheads, the Treasury and the D.E.A., with the Treasury gradually gaining mastery over the D.E.A. but sufficient tension remaining between them to cancel out both Departments' policies. Our big economic decisions have been made by Harold's arbitration between the Chancellor and the First Secretary. This system, which looked pretty crazy anyway, came completely unstuck this summer when it was revealed that there is no contingency planning of any kind at all.

What is really wrong—and Tommy has said this all along—is that we have no real instrument of central decision-taking for the home front. In the case of foreign policy and defence, the Defence Committee, on which the Chiefs of Staff at least are present, is a central instrument which has worked for thirty years and gets some coherent decisions taken. When defence problems come up there may be wrong decisions, but at least decisions and contingency plans are made. Nothing of this sort exists to deal with the economy. (Here Harold's proclivity for opportunism completely coincides with Whitehall's desire to prevent a coherent decision-taking body being imposed upon it.) In its absence the P.M. has run the Government Prime Ministerially, arbitrating between George Brown and Callaghan, and in every other field retaining the right of final decision and, in this particular crisis, working direct with the Permanent Secretaries behind the backs of their Ministers. As for his own personal decisions, they've been taken in consultation with a very small inner private circle. In the first place there is the real inner group, the real kitchen Cabinet—that is Marcia Williams, Gerald Kaufman, Peter Shore. And in addition there are three independent personalities—George Wigg, Tommy Balogh and, last but not least, Burke Trend, the one really powerful force in this entourage.

This week we have had the beginnings of a collective Cabinet reaction against this Prime Ministerial method. The odd thing is that I, who wrote the

Introduction to Bagehot, am now busily trying to reassert collective Cabinet authority because I see how disastrous it is to allow Cabinet government to decline into mere Prime Ministerial government. It's better to get back to something much more like Cabinet responsibility; just as it is better to get back to effective Cabinet responsibility to Parliament, and the reassertion of parliamentary control over government—one of those bright ideas Harold announced during the election campaign and at the beginning of the Session but which has got entirely lost since then.

I think it is true after this week nobody in Cabinet will ever again believe that this triumvirate can safely be left in charge. If I achieved anything it was by asserting the right of Cabinet to take part in the making of economic strategy so that Harold conceded that we must be given that right. If we really have achieved an economic strategy committee parallel to the Defence Committee, it could produce a complete change in the relationship between the P.M., the First Secretary and the Chancellor on the one side and the rest of the Cabinet on the other. We shall have to wait and see whether this has been achieved, however, when Harold returns from his two days in Washington at the end of next week.

Sunday, July 31st

I must record a big change in Harold's personal position. Luck was running against him till the end of the week; now it seems suddenly to have turned. I would guess he has had quite a good trip and a real success with President Johnson. But it is also a tremendous help for him that we won the World Cup on Saturday.[1] That may well mean that his luck, which deserted him after he had dealt with the seamen's strike, has really turned now. When I told Anne over lunch today that the World Cup could be a decisive factor in strengthening sterling she couldn't believe it. But I am sure it is. It was a tremendous, gallant fight that England won. Our men showed real guts and the bankers, I suspect, will be influenced by this, and the position of the Government correspondingly strengthened.

I set out for London by the 9 p.m. train. It was five minutes early at Banbury but as it approached London it went slower and slower and finally only got in at 10.40; and I got to No. 10 in pouring rain after 11 p.m. I rushed upstairs and there was Harold in the flat waiting to take me into the little drawing-room. I remembered that I hadn't been there more than once since the election. But here we were, settling down, and I was aware that he was aware that I hadn't come just for a pleasant chat and that his job was to fend me off from saying what I wanted to say. He started straight away with a long story about how the whole devaluation discussion in Cabinet had been a set piece—a trap set by the pro-Europeans. He described how he had told

[1] Harold Wilson had flown to Washington on the 28th, held his talks with the President on the 29th on further dollar support for the pound, and returned—via Ottawa—in time to see the World Cup Final at Wembley. See *Wilson*, pp. 264–6.

Barbara that they had taken her for a ride, and how she had indignantly denied this.

Having discredited the Europeans—he described Roy Jenkins as a dangerous, conspiratorial type—he turned back to James Callaghan and spent the next twenty minutes telling me how inert he was and how he, Harold, had to rescue him time after time, and finally how he had now become a secret European convert, a danger to the cause of all of us who, like Harold, were not prepared to go into Europe except very much on the right terms.

I then said that surely there was not much to be alarmed about in all this after his visit to L.B.J. 'No,' he said, 'that's perfectly true. What I have fixed with L.B.J. is enough to make de Gaulle foam at the mouth. We needn't really worry now about any possibilities of going into Europe.' Harold then began to talk about his Washington mission, which had been pretty fully described in the Sunday press, and the astonishing panegyric L.B.J. had given when toasting him at lunch.[1] I said, 'I suppose L.B.J.'s speech was all written out before.' And Harold said, yes, he thought that most of it was, 'but the passage about Dunkirk did seem to be an impromptu.' He added that it had rather embarrassed him and he thought that Peregrine Worsthorne was a bit unfair in his article to talk as though this had given him any pleasure.

Then I said that what worried me at this week's Cabinet was the fact that this absolutely revolutionary proposal for economic dictatorship was presented to us as a *fait accompli*. It was just as bad as the treatment of the Cabinet over the S.E.T. budget. And Harold replied, 'If you think you were upset and surprised by it, so were we all. You ought to know that George Brown originally intended to push Part IV through without reference to Cabinet at all. It was only I who said it must go to Cabinet. And how right you were, my dear Dick, to insist that it can only be made operative by an Affirmative Resolution. That idea of yours made the whole difference. I entirely agreed with you on that.' So he placated me and I found it very difficult to say what I had intended to say—that he couldn't rely on me not to resign if the attempt was made to lay the Order. I did get as far as saying that the powers were absolutely unworkable, to which he replied, 'Maybe I agree with you, but we may be able to keep the voluntary system and never bring the Order into effect.' To which I said, 'But look, what I am saying to you is that if it were brought into effect I would do everything I could to stop it and get as many other members of Cabinet to work with me as possible.' At this point he said very quietly, 'Never organize a cave in Cabinet, Dick. That's a great mistake.' And then he went on with the conversation. I was aware that now I had made my point things would never be quite the same between us

---

[1] Proposing the Prime Minister's health, the President spoke of '. . . the nation that has given us the tongue of a Shakespeare, the faith of a Milton, and the courage of a Churchill . . .' and now 'a leader whose own enterprise and courage will show the way'. The passage is quoted in *Wilson*, pp. 264–5.

again. But I admired him for the way he just dropped in that remark and then went on with our talk. It gyrated mostly round James Callaghan's ineffectiveness and his monomaniac belief that he could some day replace Harold and possibly be Prime Minister of a national government. All this Harold spelt out to me as well as his problems with George who, though loyal and charming, was so erratic and difficult. Throughout all this talk about colleagues I tried to insist on the need for collective Cabinet responsibility. But of course my insistence sounded at the time as though I was merely asking for a more important position for myself and I was very much aware that to Harold's ear all I was doing was asking a price for my loyalty. I fear I have made a poor account of this conversation which started at 11 and ended at 12.45. Then he took me downstairs and I got into my car in driving rain, went back to Vincent Square and worked at my box for some time.

Thursday, August 4th
In the evening I dined with the Chief Whip at the Écu de France before catching the midnight train to Cornwall for a weekend with my family, who have gone on to Polzeath. In the course of that dinner he made one remark I couldn't help noticing. He told me I mustn't run away back to Cornwall on the following Thursday without a word with him. I caught the train feeling he knew something about my future. Is there a Cabinet reshuffle in the offing?

Tuesday, August 9th
Throughout Tuesday little indications were becoming stronger and stronger that a Cabinet reshuffle was in the offing. I got a tremendous final hint at 3.30. I had answered a Private Notice Question on mortgages and cleared the whole confusion up in a perfectly competent way. When I sat down, Harold turned to me and asked me whether I was still going to stand for the Executive. I said that I was and then I thanked him for putting the Cabinet down for Wednesday, because it meant I could get away to Cornwall early on Thursday morning. 'Oh, don't get off early that morning,' he replied. 'I shall need you here. But don't tell anybody because it might give the wrong impression.' Then he added, 'You could go by the Thursday night train. We'll have finished everything by then.' Out of the Chamber I mentioned this to John Silkin and said, 'This seems to link up with what you were saying to me last Thursday night.' 'I can't tell you,' he replied. 'I'm sworn to secrecy; but it's something that gives me enormous pleasure because it means you and I will be working together.' It was then that I began to ask myself whether Harold could possibly be planning to make me Lord President and Leader of the House, the only job which would involve working closely with John Silkin. With that thought in mind, I went back to the Department and sent for my Permanent Secretary. Not unexpectedly, when I told him what I thought he seemed to be rather pleased, because it is what he has been telling

me. He added that I had probably done my best work in the Ministry and he had had enough yeast in the Department to last him a long time; now he wants as my successor somebody to consolidate the work which I had set in train and which would last them for five or six years.

Wednesday, August 10th

By the time Cabinet met at 11.45 I knew that the appointments would be announced that night, that we had to be at Buckingham Palace on Thursday morning to be sworn in, and that we were also to have our first meeting of the new Economic Strategy Committee.

At 1 p.m. Harold said goodbye to the Cabinet for the summer recess and then I went back and had lunch with Silkin in the Members' dining-room. I was working quietly in my office with Steve when I heard the P.M. wanted to see me at 4.15. I had time to go to the liaison committee, where I couldn't say a damn thing because they weren't supposed to know that I was to be Lord President, and then I talked to Jennie and Marcia and said I was very depressed, disappointed and scared by the new job. I was all the more scared because I had just heard that I would have to make the speech for the Government in the debate on the adjournment for the summer recess.

I hate the idea of giving up the Department where I have just got firm control and where I adore all the various activities, which stretch from planning, through housing, through New Towns, and which enabled me to go all over the country and visit places I want to visit and master techniques which I haven't previously understood. I have got to leave the Department and that knowledge will be wasted. I have got to have a job without any Department at all and be just a member of the Government and a politician. It is deeply depressing.

I saw Harold punctually at 4.15 and he at once made the offer I expected. I admitted to him that I wasn't surprised by it and at once said it was a tremendous loss to me, mainly because it was a loss of power. How often had he told me that a Department is a tremendous source of strength to a Cabinet Minister? He replied, 'Yes, but look. This is a job where I really need you.' I replied, 'Because it means working with you, Harold, I shan't really mind it.' In fact I gave way straight away and didn't resist all the time I was talking to him until I asked him who was my successor. When he told me it was Tony Greenwood I was really shocked and said I would have much preferred Bert Bowden. But he replied that Bert had to be selected as Commonwealth Secretary and when he had told the Queen she had said how delighted she was that that kind of non-political man was in the job. He took tremendous trouble to emphasize the importance of my new job. I was to be a completely different kind of Lord President. The substitution of John Silkin for Ted Short had been the first part of a major change which replaces two bureaucrats with two politicians. We should be in the key positions of Party power and we should form the link with Transport House. That is why, he explained, he had asked me on the front bench whether I was still going to stand for the Executive; he wants to feel that as Lord President I could do the job of linking Transport House and No. 10. He was very much aware of the criticism that Attlee's Government lost contact with the Party and he wants me to do the job of organizing and making sure that the rank and file feel themselves linked with the leadership. In addition, I would lead the House and work as hard as possible for parliamentary reform. And in the House I would be a political Lord President, the C.O. of the Parliamentary army, with John Silkin as my Chief of Staff, leading the Party, taking part in all the major debates, winding-up—indeed, behaving in this 1966 Parliament much as Herbert Morrison behaved when he was Leader of the House between 1945 and 1950.

As for Cabinet, I should be on every Cabinet Committee, including the new Economic Strategy Committee and the Rhodesia Committee and, if I wished, the Defence Committee as well. All this was said, I think, to make me realize that I would be elevated to a completely new level, the top level. And he said that we should be running things a bit differently now, more like an inner Cabinet of which I should be a member.

He asked me to come back at 6, when the time for the announcement would be fixed. This I did and he then told me there would be some delay in the timing of the news release because of George Brown. He added that George was very angry because he, Harold, had forgotten to tell him about my appointment as Lord President and Greenwood's taking my place. I wasn't very clear whether it was my appointment or the fact that he hadn't been consulted which had enraged George. He also made it clear that in all the discussions one of his major preoccupations had been to fox Mr Callaghan. The only person who was not going to get any change, he remarked, is the person who has gone to William Davis of the *Guardian* and got him to write about his wish to be given the Foreign Office.

I couldn't help remembering the time when I had suggested to Harold that Callaghan was the right man to be Leader of the House and he had told me that he couldn't trust him there because he would be a threat to his own future. It looks as though he has selected me for this key job as the only person who *hasn't* got political ambitions against him. I then asked him about the other changes and he told me George Brown was delighted to be at the Foreign Office and Michael Stewart also seemed pleased, though he was sorry to lose it. But mainly it was Harold himself who was enormously exhilarated and openly claiming that he had now got his friends about him. By this time George Wigg, Marcia and John Silkin were there and I was part of the ménage. And Harold said, 'What I have done this time is to surround myself with friends and isolate Callaghan. When people see the result of what I have done they will realize he has been defeated. Only he doesn't realize it yet.'

At this moment Callaghan came in for a further talk, and we retired. I dined quietly in the Members' dining-room and then went upstairs to do my last boxes for the Department. I sat quietly up there until Jennie came in and brought with her Sir Godfrey Agnew from the Privy Council Office.[1] He had rung me up at 5 and I had snubbed him, saying that nothing had been announced. However, along he came at 9 p.m. By this time I was utterly depressed about my loss of a Department and told him I was the last person who one could expect to be given this job with all the mumbo-jumbo of the Privy Council and seeing the Queen.

Tuesday, September 20th
Last night I caught the ten o'clock sleeper to Aberdeen because I was due to have a Privy Council with the Queen at Balmoral this morning. The first thing I noticed was the difference between a trip organized by John Delafons and my Private Office in M.H.L.G. and a trip organized by the Privy Council Office. When we got to Aberdeen at breakfast-time I found no rooms had been booked for us to bath and change in and the hotel was full. I also found that for the return journey we'd been booked on a train without a dining car and we had to change to a later train at 8.30. Though I'm a much more senior Minister now I'm much less well ministered to in my lordly isolation.

We started off from Aberdeen at 10.30 this morning to motor to Balmoral — an absolutely perfect windless autumn day, as we went up the Dee Valley climbing slowly into the mountains. Of course the Grampians are nothing like as beautiful as the west coast. Balmoral was chosen by Prince Albert merely because the weather was drier than in the west. At that time the mountains were almost without trees but now many of them have been beautifully forested. When we arrived we found a typical Scottish baronial house, looking as though it had been built yesterday, with a nice conventional rose garden and by the little church a golf course, which nobody plays on except the staff. As soon as we got there I took a little walk with Michael Adeane[2] by the banks of the Dee and then came back for the Privy Council. As Lord President I had to go and see the Queen first with the papers for the meeting. We chatted for a few moments, then the others came in and lined up beside me and I read aloud the fifty or sixty Titles of the Orders in Council, pausing after every half a dozen for the Queen to say 'Agreed'. When I'd finished, in just two and a half minutes, I concluded with the words, 'So the business of the Council is concluded.' The Privy Council is the best example of pure mumbo-jumbo you can find. It's interesting to reflect that four Ministers, busy men, all had to take a night and a day off and go up there with Godfrey Agnew to stand for two and a half minutes while the list of

[1] Sir Godfrey Agnew had entered the Privy Council Office as Senior Clerk in 1946 and from 1953–74 was Clerk to the Privy Council.
[2] Private Secretary to the Queen and Keeper of Her Majesty's Archives 1953–72. In 1972 he became a life peer and has since then served as chairman of the Royal Commission on Historical Monuments.

Titles was read out. It would be far simpler for the Queen to come down to Buckingham Palace but it's *lèse-majesté* to suggest it.

Thursday, September 22nd
Cabinet. I was asked to go round to No. 10 a few minutes early for a chat with Harold. He had before him a draft directive for the conduct of my investigation of the information services.[1] I pointed out that it covered all services whereas we ought to exclude the Foreign Office and the Commonwealth Relations Office since this had been a clear-cut decision at the last Cabinet. He accepted this and added, 'Even so, we will probably have great difficulty with our colleagues but I'll do my best for you.' So the meeting started and right at the beginning, before anything else came up, he announced the subject and began to prose on about information services. He prosed and prosed and prosed and when it was over Tony Crosland said, 'Well, an investigation is long overdue.' Suddenly a row broke out about the appalling failure of co-ordination of the information services last week when someone forgot to tell the Ministers concerned about an important decision made by S.E.P. It was an utterly ludicrous example of poor co-ordination of information and it certainly was lucky for me that someone remembered it this morning. After the quarrel had gone on some time Harold said, 'Any other comments?' There was a murmur 'Agreed' and there I was with full Cabinet backing for my investigation and my power conceded 'To conduct an inquiry, to recommend what improvements are required in inter-departmental machinery in the field of home information services in order to ensure the most timely and effective and consistent public presentation of the Government's policies without prejudice to the normal responsibility of individual Ministers for the presentation of their own departmental policies and for the co-ordination in appropriate cases of the policies of related departments.'

This afternoon we had a meeting at No. 10 about political Honours. Harold was in the chair and the only other people there were Tony Greenwood as Minister of Local Government, myself and the Chief Whip. Harold again repeated his determination to get rid of political Honours. I had thought this a good idea at first but after I'd talked to Len Williams at Transport House and heard the reaction of our regional officers and Party agents I realized that excluding political Honours really meant excluding Party agents and regional organizers and virtually no one else. When Harold heard this he replied, 'We'll include them all under public Honours.' But of course once you do this your announcement is merely a gimmick because you *haven't* cut out political Honours. The decision only makes sense if you announce that people who serve a political party are excluded from the Honours list and once you discriminate against professional Party agents in

[1] The Prime Minister had asked Crossman as Lord President to conduct a general investigation into the government information services.

this way it causes a terrible depression and lack of morale in the Party. I've talked this over with Doug Garnett[1] and I'm not sure I shall not have to write another minute to Harold saying that we really can't drift into this unless he can find better reasons for the change.

Friday, September 23rd

Morning prayers with the P.M. and Burke Trend was made pretty useless because George Brown turned up. However, I picked up an interesting fact—Julian Melchett[2] has been selected as chairman of the Steel Board, at a salary of £25,000 a year, double the normal salary for the chairman of a nationalized industry. I know Julian fairly well since I've often gone to the parties he and his wife, Sonia, give in Chelsea. He impressed me as an agricultural economist and a really charming man but if he wasn't the son of Lord Melchett no one would dream of this appointment. His own background is banking and agriculture. A strange appointment but I suppose it's the result of not finding anybody in the industry itself.

Wednesday, September 28th

For the first three days of this week I have been pretty solidly engaged on my investigations of the information services. I have still two more Ministers to see, the last being Barbara Castle with whom I shall travel down to Brighton on Thursday evening for the Labour Party Conference.

Burke Trend had done his job: Whitehall had been alerted and Ministers normally turned up along with their chief information officers. The Investigating Committee consisted of myself as chairman along with a man called Pitchforth[3] from the Treasury and Trevor Lloyd-Hughes.[4] Trevelyan[5] acted as secretary. We soon got into a rhythm of examination and it became pretty clear that Harold's decision to wind up what he called the 'Tory Ministry of Propaganda' had destroyed the central co-ordination of information services which was working pretty well in the last years of the Macmillan Government. This meant that under Wilson there has been a great deal of departmental free-wheeling. Each Ministry has evolved its own monitoring system, its own advertising campaigns, its own techniques for handling the B.B.C. and arranging Ministerial interviews. As the investigation goes on it is becoming clear that all the information officers are convinced that the Tory system was superior, that it is obviously right that a Minister supported by a small staff should be in charge of co-ordinating Government propaganda,

[1] Labour Party Regional Organizer for East Anglia.
[2] He succeeded to his father's barony in 1949. From 1967 until his death in June 1973 he was chairman of the British Steel Corporation.
[3] Harold Pitchforth had formerly been Director of Establishments and Organization at the Ministry of Agriculture, Fisheries and Food. From 1965 to 1967 he was Under-Secretary at the Treasury.
[4] Press Secretary to the Prime Minister 1964–9. Chief Information Adviser to the Government 1969–70.
[5] Dennis Trevelyan, Principal Private Secretary in the Lord President's Office 1964–7.

and that without someone in this role there comes a great loss of co-ordination, willpower and drive. Nevertheless, I know very well there can be no question of going back to the bad old days of Toryism. Harold is extremely obstinate. Once he's committed himself to a public decision that Labour will never spend Government money on a Ministry of Propaganda he isn't going to back down on that at all easily.

Another awkward aspect of the investigation has been that about half the Ministers and information officers have complained very bitterly about No. 10. They say that co-ordination is difficult enough between Departments but it is made infinitely more difficult by the fact that nobody knows which information coming out of No. 10 is official and which has been leaked. This is something I don't exactly know about. Of course it's true that Trevor's organization is still the central agency for disseminating information about the activities of the Government. But in addition to Trevor there's Gerald Kaufman in No. 10 who is supposed to provide liaison with the Labour Party but whom Harold uses from time to time for briefings—if you like it, leaks—about which Trevor knows nothing. In the background there's the mysterious George Wigg who, apart from dealing with security and inves-tigating other people's leaks, is also entitled by Harold to brief certain press men, such as Ian Waller of the *Sunday Telegraph*.

By the end of my investigation I couldn't help comparing our Government with the Attlee Government during the Cripps period.[1] At that time there were six or seven home-front Ministers who met every day, knew each other, lunched together, had a common purpose and therefore didn't fight or leak against each other. Owing to the creation of D.E.A. and the permanent rift between Brown and Callaghan, our Government has been riven with dissen-sion and all the other Ministries have become independent and free-wheeling. So the appearance of disorder in Whitehall is a great deal worse than the disorder which exists and which can't be mended without structural alterations in the Cabinet. Nevertheless, most of the people we interrogated have agreed that there should be a Minister who, even if he can't be Minister of Information, is at least able to get hold of his colleagues and suggest that they should get together, issue joint Statements and reduce the amount of chaos in the Government's public relations.

That's the job which the unanimous report of Trevor Lloyd-Hughes, Pitchforth and I will recommend as a task for the Lord President. It's not a real job and involves no real change, but I suppose it's better than nothing. Whether I do it adequately or inadequately will determine very largely whether the P.M. gives me any further responsibility. I'm having to fight for each job whereas I was given the impression that as Lord President every-thing would be at my feet. Well, nothing is at my feet. I'm not even a member

[1] Clement Attlee was Prime Minister from July 26th, 1945, to October 26th, 1951; and from September 29th, 1947, to October 15th, 1950, Sir Stafford Cripps was his Chancellor of the Exchequer.

of the Defence Committee yet, though I asked for it straightaway: I'm simply Leader of the House with a vague responsibility for co-ordinating information as long as I don't upset anybody.

Nevertheless these three days' investigation have been quite an interesting experience. I have enjoyed sitting in that palatial Privy Council Office questioning my colleagues in this particular way.

Thursday, September 29th
At Cabinet we had a report from Bert Bowden and Elwyn Jones,[1] back from Rhodesia. Bert spelt out his mission at great length and was warmly congratulated on what he had done. I couldn't see he'd done anything much — except that he hadn't given anything away. After that we had quite a long discussion on the tactics for the next stage. It seemed to me that Harold and Bert are now thinking again in terms of working up a package which would give Smith yet another last chance. Indeed, I've no doubt that's what they intend to do. In Cabinet I put rather strongly the dilemma as it presented itself to me. We must be clear in our minds whether our main preoccupation in the next stage is to prepare for a break-off or whether to produce a package which Smith can sign. If we think there is any chance of the second, we must be prepared to make some last-minute concessions however alien they may be to African opinion. If, on the other hand, there's no chance of the second, then it isn't worth alienating African opinion. Our whole behaviour from now on must be designed to strengthen our justification when the break occurs at the beginning of December. The evidence of the Bowden mission seemed to me to show that Smith hadn't the remotest intention of permitting any transfer of power from him to another kind of government of which he isn't in full control. All he's prepared to do is to have a formal transfer to the Governor provided he retains all the power in his own hands. And that's exactly what we can't afford. So the Bowden mission seemed to me to prove that deadlock remains absolutely unchanged and there's no real chance of our offering a package he can accept.

In the afternoon I had two important meetings. The first was when John Silkin introduced me to Willie Whitelaw and I found this as exhilarating as I expected. I was completely frank with him and told him all my plans for television; he told me how fiercely he was opposed to morning sittings. I got his tentative agreement to a specialist committee on agriculture in addition to the one on science and technology. After talking to him I really feel there's a hope that we shall get a big advance in parliamentary reform.

After that I had a very big meeting with all the television experts, the B.B.C. and I.T.V. to discuss the Select Committee report on broadcasting

---

[1] Herbert Bowden, the new Commonwealth Secretary, and Sir Elwyn Jones, the Attorney-General, had flown to Rhodesia on September 19th for discussions with the Governor, Sir Humphry Gibbs, and the Chief Justice, Sir Hugh Beadle. They also had several fruitless meetings with Ian Smith before returning to London on September 28th.

the proceedings of the House, and in particular to consider whether their proposal for an eight-week closed-circuit television experiment was practical. The officials were very much against the length because they said it would impose an appalling strain. I then suggested that we should divide the period sensibly with a couple of weeks for the House of Commons and for the House of Lords and some experimental filming of Select Committees and Standing Committees.[1] They seemed to be a bit surprised that the Lord President should have his own ideas and I asked them to report back as soon as possible.

After that I had the last interview of my four-day investigation. The client was Barbara Castle and after it was over we went down by train together to Brighton.

Friday, September 30th
As usual the monthly meeting of the N.E.C. in the week before Conference was transferred from Wednesday to Friday and took place in the Conference hotel. We started it with a farce because we'd only gone to this ghastly Grand Hotel instead of to the excellent Metropole because the Grand Hotel is supposed to have better arrangements for our Conference staffs, and a good room for the Executive to sit and work in. Well, the room we had to work in was impossible. We found after ten minutes that we couldn't hear a word of what anyone said because of the echo so we had to move upstairs to a little balcony where we were able to hear each other but couldn't see each other.

The main business of the morning was to consider the draft statement on economic policy, including prices and incomes, which had been prepared first by Terry Pitt in Transport House and then drastically redrafted by Tommy's Michael Stewart after consultations with Harold and Jim. The main interest was to see what the mood of the Executive would be. Would there be the kind of violent feelings there were in the old Bevanite period? Not at all. There's no kind of deep feeling. Throughout the meeting Government policy had only three opponents—Jack Jones, Tom Driberg and Ian Mikardo. They, like their friend Frank Cousins, were root and branch opponents, but none of the other trade-union members of the Executive made any serious opposition that morning. They were entirely concerned about the problem of redundancy and in particular the impression created by Gunter's public statements that in principle the Government is

[1] Select Committees of the House of Commons (such as the Select Committee on the Nationalized Industries or on Science and Technology, the Public Accounts Committee and the Expenditure Committee) consist of ten to fifteen Members, nominated by a motion in the House, and established either sessionally or by virtue of Standing Order. Their function is either to consider a problem or to hold a watching brief on some matter. Standing Committees have as their principal function the consideration of the Committee Stages of Bills. They consist of between sixteen and fifty Members well versed in the subject at issue, and their size and composition reflects the Party strengths in the House.

opposed to work-sharing in the motor-car industry—the redundancies at
B.M.C. have dominated the news for the last ten days.[1] Quite rightly, Johnny
Boyd of the A.E.U. said, 'Let's be sensible about this', and put a passage into
the document to show that where the staff will be fully employed again in the
spring, firms are entitled to share the work out during the winter. So the
passage was to be carefully written in and everything at the meeting was
sweetness and light. It wasn't long before the document was referred to a
drafting committee with George Brown in the chair and on which I had to
serve.

I spent the afternoon redrafting the document. The meeting was due to
start at 3.15. George Brown drifted in twenty minutes late and said he was
too busy to attend, so I got hold of Johnny Boyd and we went down into the
P.M.'s suite and found a table and secretary. We'd just about finished the job
by five o'clock when the Executive resumed its meeting in order to approve
the foreign policy document.

As a result of this meeting it was clear that both documents would need a
lot more redrafting which I said I would do that evening. After Anne had
arrived, in driving rain, I started work again and at 10 o'clock at night I
finally got George Brown to look them through. To my surprise he turned
out to be a really creative editor. He'd been given a drink by Harold down
below and empowered to clear the draft. I saw that in comparison with
Harold he has a warm and imaginative mind; in any daytime committee
Harold is always a niggler and tries to draft himself. George let me do all the
drafting but told me what he wanted in a way that I could carry it out.

Saturday, October 1st
This morning I had only two concerns. The first was about the decision the
Ministers would take that afternoon about Part IV. On this I had a long talk
with John Silkin and also with Manny Shinwell on the phone. My other
concern was the speech I was due to make at the big Sunday demonstration.
What kind of speech should it be? This morning I went down to Harold and
tried out my idea. I said I thought it should be a definition of the role of the
socialist party under a socialist government. I thought our people were
terribly depressed at the feeling that our Party was of no importance under
our Labour Government. But, as he and I agreed, it could have enormous
importance; it could sustain the electoral machine and provide the Government with eyes and ears—not merely listening to the master's voice and
putting out the master's propaganda but telling the Government how the
public was taking its policies. Thirdly, and most important of all, it was the
Party and the Party alone which had the job of working out long-term policy
for the next election manifesto. I thought the speech should define these
three jobs precisely and set them against the background of our belief as

[1] B.M.C. had now declared 12,500 car workers redundant, and by November 10th another
100,000 were on short time.

democratic socialists in Party democracy and mass participation. Harold immediately thought this was a wonderful idea—just what we needed.

Sunday, October 2nd

I'd worked away at the speech late last night and by 11 o'clock this morning it was ready. I took it down to Harold's room and there I found Marcia, Tommy and Peter Shore sitting about and discussing Harold's speech. I read it and found it not my style of speech at all, but I knew that I couldn't do very much to help him with it. At 12.30 Harold came in, immensely excited because at the Sunday service where he and George Brown had been reading the Lessons he had been interrupted by anti-Vietnam demonstrators. He gave a precise imitation of how they'd interrupted him and how he had stood his ground and repeated the last two verses of the lesson which happened to be apposite.* Poor Tommy was furious with him for not showing a proper interest in the revision of his speech. I'm afraid I got Harold off upstairs and made him go through my speech. After he made two or three tiny suggestions I said that perhaps I ought to show it to Len Williams since it was laying down our view of the relationship between the Party and the Government. 'Oh no,' he said, 'I shouldn't bother to do that.' So that was that. No one else had seen my speech but I'd got the Prime Minister's full backing and I was now entitled to make it on behalf of the N.E.C. committing the whole Executive to this precise interpretation of the relation of Party and Government.

I'd better try to explain why Party organization is so important. When Morgan Phillips retired in 1962 there was a real chance of getting a powerful modern General Secretary from outside Transport House. But Hugh Gaitskell, in order to secure his position as leader of the Party, turned these ideas down flat though Tony Wedgwood Benn and I both pleaded with him. Instead he appointed George Brown to be Chairman of the Org. Sub. and to run Transport House; George Brown proceeded to appoint Len Williams as Morgan Phillips's successor and Sara Barker to Len Williams's old place. Len and Sara are splendid old war horses but their ideas of organization, finance and general structure are incredibly reactionary. In their six years nothing has been done to reorganize Transport House despite quite a volume of complaints from some of the more intelligent members.

At 2.30 the Executive sat down again to the arduous task of going through all the resolutions and the composites. Party organization came right at the end and sure enough there was an outburst. But before it could gather steam, Harold stepped in with a magnificent 10-minute speech saying we had to face the need to modernize the Party. If we are modernizing the trade unions, modernizing Parliament, modernizing industry, we mustn't fail to modernize our own Party too. Naturally, of course, we can't have any suggestion of a

---

* He was right to be excited as next morning he made the headlines again and in good form—'P.M. stands up to demonstrators'.

vote of censure on the present officials or agree to commissioning an outside investigation, but he felt it essential for the Executive to set up a commission to report in twelve months. Harold had spiked the guns of my enemies but there was still a good deal of talk about not being put on the defensive or tolerating any attacks on Len Williams and Sara Barker. 'If attacks are made they must not go unanswered,' said Frank Chapple.[1] In my reply I suggested that the most tactful thing would be for me to be brief and merely to ask for the resolutions to be referred to the Executive. We carried this resolution by 14 to 13. Harold, by the way, voted with the thirteen and said to me afterwards, 'Well, I watched carefully and when I saw you voting one way I thought I ought to vote the other so as to prove there is no collusion.'

The meeting stopped at 6.30 and I had to rush out and get myself ready for the demonstration at the Dome. When I got there it was fairly full — about four or five hundred people. We began with an absolutely unintelligible speech by an Indian socialist. My turn came pretty soon. I spoke from a long written script and I had to deal with a good deal of mild, good-humoured interruption and heckling. I rather shocked some of my colleagues by remarking that Cabinet Ministers couldn't conceivably work out a real socialist manifesto because they were far too busy dealing with short-term current problems to look ahead and show any vision. I came back to the hotel a little depressed and anxious whether tomorrow's press would pick this remark up and get me into trouble.

Monday, October 3rd
I needn't have worried. There was virtually nothing in the press. The *Guardian* had put me bottom of the story and some remarks by the Chairman of the T.U.C. top. Most of them published not a single word though the press release had been issued at six in the evening so that the journalists had hours in which to read it before it was delivered. However there was one report, *The Times*. Before making my speech I had run into David Wood, *The Times*'s political editor and I had asked him to come upstairs and have a chat. In the course of it I explained exactly what the speech was about, how it was linked with my speech to the private session on Thursday, and how I'd concerted with the P.M. that this should be an important declaration on the relationship of the Government to the Party. So today's *Times* had an exclusive story exactly along these lines.

One of the strange things about a Labour Party Conference is that for members of the Executive it's half over before it starts. We had arrived in Brighton on Thursday evening and worked for the whole of Friday, Saturday and Sunday. Today we are nearly half way through and there's only Tuesday, Wednesday and Thursday left, since Friday virtually doesn't count.

[1] Assistant General Secretary of the Electrical, Electronic and Telecommunications Union from 1963 until September 1966, when he became General Secretary. A member of the T.U.C. General Council since 1971.

8 Richard Crossman leaving No. 10 with Harold Wilson, on their way to the
House of Commons, November 1966.

9 With the Soviet Premier, Alexei Kosygin, and Lord Longford, looking round
the Houses of Parliament, February 1967.

10 In office as Lord President, 1967, making a point.

11 At Prescote with his wife and the Labour Party agent for Banbury, John Hodgkin, October 1967.

Nevertheless, when a Conference formally opens on a Monday morning we're always uncertain what the mood is going to be. Moreover, what happens on the first morning is no test. You have the mayor's speech, you have the chairman's address, you have the formalities and you always have a flat debate, as I well know since I've replied twice on social security on a Monday morning. This year it was even more trying than usual because we were housed in the new ice-rink, built by Top Rank Entertainment next door to the Grand Hotel. This must be one of the ugliest buildings in the world and it's planked down on the Brighton front. Inside it's tawdry and tinny, with a huge hall specially designed for conferences but where the ceiling crushes you down and the room's so wide you can't see the walls. Despite the excellent acoustics it's going to be very difficult to keep the attention of the audience and arouse the delegates.

I had to appear on *Panorama* tonight in a 45-minute programme which I'd been assured would be devoted to explaining how a Party Conference works. They were going to follow through the progress of a Nottingham delegate from his selection right up to the Conference—the climax being a four- or five-minute discussion between a member of the N.E.C. and some typical rank-and-file delegates. Of course things didn't turn out that way. Three of the rank-and-filers were ultra-left wingers and my part of the programme developed into a futile shouting match. After that I went over to the I.T.N. studio where I was given a model interview for four and a half minutes which appeared on the news.

I had a certain amount to drink at I.T.V. and when I got back to the hotel I was tired and bad-tempered. Tony Crosland and Susan were just off to the B.B.C., who live in the Metropole, and I decided to join them. We went into Oliver Whitley's[1] suite to find that Michael Stewart and George Wigg were already there. We watched the programme and saw Robin Day making one of his characteristic wind-ups predicting acrimony and hostility among the delegates.[2] I said, 'There you are, there's B.B.C. objectivity for you.' We don't mind personalities attacking us but the news should be fair. While I was describing what happened to me on *Panorama* Robin Day came in. We had a tremendous knockabout even though I knew that in my new job I oughtn't to be behaving in this way and sounding as anti-B.B.C. as the rest of the Party leadership. But there it was—I did it till one or two in the morning.

Tuesday, October 4th

I woke up with a hell of a headache and a hangover and tottered down in order to hear the results of the Executive elections. I was fourth this year

[1] Chief Assistant to the Director-General of the B.B.C. 1964–8, and Managing Director, External Broadcasting, from 1969 until his retirement in 1972.

[2] A television journalist, formerly a newscaster and parliamentary correspondent with Independent Television News (1955–9). He joined the B.B.C. current-affairs programme *Panorama* in 1959 and rapidly made a reputation for incisive interviewing. He introduced the programme from 1967 to 1972.

instead of fifth—I always hover about the middle of the list. Then came Harold's big speech. I found it monumentally dull though of course it had some superb relieving patches. It had been worked and worked over by Peter Shore, Gerald Kaufman and Tommy Balogh until it was a kind of mosaic of Wilsonisms, ideas expressing a curiously anonymous statesmanship. Then right at the end to cheer the delegates up came an astonishing quotation from a prayer by Donald Soper.[1] Considering that Jim Callaghan, Barbara and I who were all sitting beside the P.M. are fervent atheists, it was a little tough to be told by our leader about how the Cabinet was dedicated to God in the Chapel of St Mary-und≈-Croft in Westminster. At lunch he said to me, 'Well, you even let me put a prayer over on them,' and I discovered that he hadn't put the prayer in his press release or shown it to Peter or Tommy or Gerald. He'd spatchcocked it in at the last moment and I'm sure it was his own carefully worked-out idea.

This evening we had a full formal Cabinet meeting. It was timed for 7.15 and I got there a quarter of a hour late because Trevelyan managed to send me to the wrong place. The meeting went perfectly smoothly. Indeed, all I remember of it is that right at the end when we were breaking up Dick Marsh remarked *sotto voce*, 'Well, I hope we shall be able soon to have a disavowal of the Crossman line.' There was a hearty peal of laughter and that was that. Nevertheless, the 'Crossman line' has been talked about a great deal in Conference partly because Paul Johnson has written a remarkable article in the *New Statesman* saying that we blundered into socialism and this theory is now attributed to me. What I said was that we had waited too long and that at last we had done something blunt and crude which gave us time for building a real Socialist prices and incomes policy. Dick Marsh was infuriated because in the Conference it was taken that I'd said we should have to retain an element of compulsion in our incomes policy. I'd been careful *not* to say this but of course the general tone of the speech made it clear that I thought we should have to have more state backing than is implied in part IV of the Prices and Incomes Act. Nevertheless, no one in Cabinet took Dick Marsh's demand seriously. He was asking for the moon in suggesting I should be disowned.

Wednesday, October 5th
This morning came the big debate and Jim Callaghan made a magnificent speech. He raised all the issues which were in the delegates' minds and answered them with magnificent clarity and frankness, making far the best speech of the Conference and pummelling the audience with answers.

Thursday, October 6th
In the afternoon came my appearance at the N.E.C. private session. As a

[1] Methodist minister and Superintendent of the West London Mission at the Kingsway Hall, 1936–78. He was made a life peer in 1965, taking his seat on the Labour benches.

result of a change of plan I was now keyed up for a full half-hour reply to an extended debate and had briefed myself with the greatest difficulty by chatting with everybody in Transport House. It was my intention to reply partly by repeating what I said on Sunday, partly by analysing the nature of the problem which faces us in modernizing a socialist party. It was really quite a tricky job because first of all I had to convince my own trade-union colleagues that I was really defending the Executive, including Len Williams and Sara Barker, and secondly I had to convince the Conference that I was committing the Executive to a genuine inquiry and genuine reform. So I got down there soon after lunch and as I might have expected nothing happened. The meeting drooled on and on. Walter Padley is an amiable, boring chairman;[1] his amiability was to my disadvantage in this private session because he allowed the report on Party activity to be discussed paragraph by paragraph and the hours crept on and on. It was already 4.30 and we only had half an hour to go. It looked as though I wouldn't be given even a minute to speak. Finally, when he had been woken up by Len Williams, Padley told the delegates there was no time for anything more. It was a difficult situation since the delegates too, one from Coventry East and one from South Ayrshire, had prepared their speeches most carefully, expecting a big and important debate. They had to scrap most of what they intended to say and I scrapped the whole of my speech and said what I could in eight minutes. Though I failed to make the speech I intended I said enough to commit the Executive entirely to the inquiry and as a result the newspapers reported that Crossman, now the political boss of the Party, had announced a searching inquiry into party organization.

Friday, October 7th
In the afternoon I found Harold in very relaxed form. I asked him whether he'd received my report on the information services. No, Marcia hadn't shown it to him yet. 'I had my box to read yesterday at four o'clock and I fell asleep—I was very tired.' He certainly has had a tough time. From the beginning of the Commonwealth Conference on he's been working a 20-hour day and he's only going to have two days free next week before Parliament starts.

Monday, October 10th
Though I hope I managed to conceal it, I was really very worried throughout the day. When we motored back from Conference I was already very anxious about what Nora Beloff would be writing in the *Observer* and on Sunday I had noticed that she had a small single article headed something like 'Crossman takes over Transport House'. At the Conference I'd taken the precaution of seeing David Wood of *The Times* and getting a good article out of

[1] Labour M.P. for Ogmore, Glamorganshire, since 1950 and, since 1956, a member of the N.E.C. President of USDAW 1948–64, and Minister of State for Foreign Affairs 1964–7.

him, and at his own request I had briefed James Margach in full for the *Sunday Times*. On Thursday, when I had been about to go upstairs with Tam, Nora Beloff came along and interrupted me and forced me to take her up into my sitting-room. I talked to her extremely carefully with Tam present, telling her what the problem was, reminding her I was not in charge of any commission of investigation, and that everything depended on what the Executive would decide at its first October meeting. She kept on pressing me about getting rid of Len Williams and Sara Barker. Her question, I said, was impossible for me to answer; it was clear they must either go early or have their retirement postponed until after the next election but I added that if she mentioned this in the article as my idea she would ruin me and my job at Transport House. She then asked me whether my speech hadn't implied that I was determined to wind up all the existing publicity. I said this was complete nonsense. Indeed, I contradicted her carefully on each of these points. And on each of these points in her brief article she used my denial as a confirmation of her own view. The article could hardly have been more embarrassing to Harold or to me. This afternoon, when it was raining, I dictated over the phone three letters, one to Len Williams, one to Sara Barker and one to Percy Clark describing the article as ridiculous nonsense and I sent copies of the letters to Marcia Williams. I'm not sure the preventive action will be effective. If it isn't, my whole job at Transport House will be ditched.

Tuesday, October 11th

I was due to see Harold at 3 p.m. about the information services report. But as I expected he at once raised Beloff's news story with me. He was not sympathetic because he'd forbidden any of us to talk to her but he said he hoped that the Transport House people had enough confidence in me to forget the whole thing. If they didn't I mightn't be able to do the job at all.

Our talk about the information services was equally chilly. I had sent a message that I must talk to him and Burke Trend alone before we had a general committee on the draft report with Trevor Lloyd-Hughes and Trevelyan in attendance. But I found that Trevor and Henry James[1] were waiting in the anteroom and so the talk I needed didn't take place and never will take place because Harold doesn't want to discuss No. 10 staff with me and Trend alone. He knew I was going to make some critical observations on it because he found them in the report and he simply avoided this scene. Well! If the P.M. decides not to have a talk he doesn't have it—so we had a perfectly business-like meeting. It was decided that I would need one good man in the Lord President's office and Trevor would need one more assistant in his office. On the surface it was a perfectly satisfactory conversation and we agreed to meet once again with a revised draft to be submitted to Cabinet next week.

[1] Deputy Press Secretary to the Prime Minister 1964–8.

Thursday, October 13th

The first occasion where, as Leader of the House, I had to deal with parliamentary business. I noticed that Quintin Hogg and Sir John Hobson[1] were the Tories selected to open and close the debate on the Second Reading of the Parliamentary Commissioner Bill next Tuesday.[2] When I mentioned this to Cabinet and asked whom they wanted to speak on our side everybody said it was a parliamentary matter and therefore the Lord President's job. I felt it quite a good idea because I shall not often get chances to make speeches and I knew that Harold was trying to get me on my feet in the Chamber. What I didn't know was that poor Douglas Houghton, who's been working on the Bill all the way through, was thinking it would be his big day. I tried to console him afterwards. I've discovered that I shall have to do far more work than I expected.

Monday, October 17th

When I arrived at Paddington this morning I was driven straight to the Privy Council where I had arranged an important meeting between Heath and Whitelaw and John Silkin and myself. By an extraordinary piece of stupidity we had asked Heath to come to the Privy Council Office at the other end of Whitehall instead of my room, which is next door to his, in the House of Commons. He arrived in my palace in a very sulky mood. He has something of Gaitskell's huffiness and much the same cold gleam in his eye. I started him off on specialist committees and said I'd already discussed this with Willie Whitelaw who couldn't have been more helpful.[3] But Heath wasn't going to allow me to appoint a committee on agriculture unless it was expressly stated that it would only be for one experimental year.

Next I got on to television and he at once objected to the whole idea of Standing Committees and Select Committees upstairs being televised. 'If that happened the TV would show the Government supporters writing their letters,' he pointed out, 'and where should we be then?' He was thick and resistant and prickly and difficult and I had to remind myself that he wasn't any more reactionary than Herbert Bowden would have been.

Next I turned to morning sittings and explained what I wanted. 'I know you're opposed to this,' I said, 'but I want you to understand the social reasons why we have to try the experiment. We really must help our people

[1] Conservative M.P. for Warwick and Leamington from 1957 until his death in 1967. He was Attorney-General 1962–4 and Shadow Attorney-General 1964–7.

[2] Hereafter called (as Crossman referred to it) the Ombudsman Bill. New Zealand and Denmark were two of the countries with an Ombudsman, an official who inquired into cases of maladministration on the part of the civil service. The Bill sought to establish the office of a Parliamentary Commissioner for Administration, appointed by the Sovereign on the advice of the Prime Minister, and empowered to consider complaints referred by M.P.s on behalf of their constituents. He would be given the right to send for departmental papers.

[3] Crossman hoped to establish specialist Select Committees of ten to fifteen M.P.s who would examine some aspects of a Department's work, meeting weekly, usually in public, summoning witnesses and producing reports.

to get more early nights at home and I hope you'll collaborate in this.' But he wasn't going to play at all. He didn't believe in morning sittings: he regarded them as absolute nonsense. What he wanted was a really radical reform of Standing Order 9 in order to get the proper number of topical debates.[1] I tried to explain my idea of moving the Standing Order 9 debates on to the next morning sitting. He wouldn't have anything of it and pointed out that the new Speaker[2] was hopeless and the situation was now totally different to when the Tories were in Government and Standing Order 9 debates were a regular occurrence.* Finally I looked at him and said, 'If you want me to help you get really radical revision of Standing Order 9 you ought to help me a bit about my morning sittings.' At this point our Chief Whip chipped in. 'What will you do,' he asked, 'if despite your objections the House accepts the proposal for morning sittings? Won't you help me then?' Heath said, 'No, we shall not help you at all. The proposal ought to fail.' I could see Willie Whitelaw blanching a bit at his behaviour and the psychological hammering he was giving us.

One lesson of this meeting with Heath was that when the House is sitting my headquarters must be not the Palace in Whitehall but the miserable room provided for the Leader of the House in the Palace of Westminster. The House of Commons resumes this week and just when I'm getting used to my palatial room in the Privy Council I have to move across to the Leader's room behind the Speaker's chair in the House of Commons. I've worked quite hard at my Privy Council palace. I've switched the three armchairs and the settee round to give a kind of club atmosphere looking out at the Horseguards Parade. Then behind my own writing table I've put the tables together as a single long table round which we can hold a meeting. Most important of all, I've persuaded Philip Hendy,[3] who runs the National Gallery, to let me choose four pictures from the National Gallery store to hang on my walls and make the room really worth seeing. Now when I've just begun to like it I have to move into those ghastly rooms in St Stephen's.

Tuesday, October 18th
My main job was to move the Second Reading of the Ombudsman Bill. I had worked very hard at it over the weekend, and the more I learned the less

---

* I couldn't correct him at the time but Freddie Warren has provided a list for me to send him which shows that in twenty years since 1945 there have been fifteen Standing Order 9 debates successfully moved so it's no good Mr Heath saying that there's been any change since the change of Speaker.

[1] Under Standing Order No. 9, M.P.s could seek to raise at very short notice debates on matters of urgent public importance, for discussion either on the following day or even at a later hour on the same evening. A wealth of precedent had permitted successive Speakers to restrict this opportunity and it was only when the S.O. was redrafted in 1967 that M.P.s could make full use of its possibilities.

[2] Dr Horace King.

[3] Slade Professor of Fine Arts at the University of Oxford 1936–46 and Director of the National Gallery, London, 1946–67. He was knighted in 1950.

impressed I was by the powers we had given the so-called Parliamentary Commissioner. But I had to make the best of it and found that the Treasury had produced three complete drafts of the speech. Young Mr Couzens was there to help.[1] He was the extremely clever chap who helped me with mortgages last July. Switched to deal with the ombudsman, he only knew what he had mugged up. I managed to reshape one of the drafts to show that the ombudsman will not be taking over the constituency work of M.P.s but would be at their service. I also decided to emphasize something I hadn't realized before—the enormous investigatory powers he will possess. We propose that he should be given access to all the files in Whitehall, permitted to disregard Crown privilege and entitled to cross-examine everyone concerned in the case from the Minister down to the lowest clerk.[2]

When the debate started at 3.30 I got up very nervous and raced through my speech in fifty-five minutes. If I had delivered it properly it would have been quite good, but fortunately I was interrupted enough to keep the interest alive. In the debate Hogg and all the other Tories poured cold water on the whole scheme on the grounds that people with real grievances would be excluded as it wouldn't cover local government, the Health Service or Civil Service grievances. On our own side a number of people showed how little they knew about the Bill by expressing alarm that their constituents would go direct to the ombudsman—something they *won't* be entitled to do. Apparently no effort had been made to sell the Bill either to the House or to the public.

Throughout the debate Sir Edmund Compton himself was sitting under the gallery at the Members' end of the House. I caught him in the act of trying to slip into the officials' gallery at the other end. As I was making a great fuss in my speech of his being not a Government stooge but an independent character I made him move. I took him out for dinner and he said one thing which struck me very much. I had mentioned that on planning appeals, though the ombudsman couldn't deal with the content of a planning decision, the damage caused by delay would be his concern. 'Delay', he said, 'is a major scandal in Whitehall. Given the chance I could deal with cases in every Department, and I intend to do so.'

The debate was far too quiet to get any press publicity. Anyway the Home Secretary had captured the headlines when he announced a free pardon for

[1] Sir Kenneth Couzens joined the Inland Revenue in 1949, moving to the Treasury in 1951, where he remained until 1968. After two years in the Civil Service Department he returned to the Treasury in 1970, and, in 1977, became Second Permanent Secretary.

[2] Not only was the ombudsman to depend upon M.P.s alone to refer complaints to him but his investigatory powers were to be restricted. The Act excluded from his concerns matters affecting the armed forces, the police, hospitals, local authorities and the nationalized industries, as well as matters for which a tribunal or a remedy at law already existed. His authority to make recommendations was to be a narrow one. (In 1973, Sir Edmund Compton's successor, Sir Alan Marre, was empowered to investigate certain complaints against the working of the National Health Service.)

the dead body of Timothy Evans, who had been executed in 1950 for the murder of his daughter sixteen years ago.[1]

Thursday, October 20th

This was my really big day—at 3.30 my first appearance to handle business Questions. I was extremely nervous and I had very little time since I seemed to have a mass of other business to arrange with Harold; I was trotting in and out of his room at the House of Commons and from his to mine and tidying things up with Marcia for the rest of the morning before and after Cabinet.

Cabinet was a curious meeting. It began as usual with parliamentary business and I had to report on the very hostile response which Heath had made to our proposals for parliamentary reform. As I feared, I found myself selected not only to wind up the Party meeting on Monday but also to wind up Tuesday's debate in the Commons.

With parliamentary business behind us we were off on a whole series of characteristic Cabinet items. For a time we discussed import quotas on apples, with one of those bickers between Fred Peart and Douglas Jay which Fred with his charm always wins. The only item which interested me was broadcasting. Harold, who had chaired the Committee, had to report that by a narrow majority Ministers had been in favour of a short-term pop music programme on B.B.C. radio followed by a long-term proposal to set up a sound radio corporation, financed in part by advertising. When I was dining with Hugh Greene, the Director-General of the B.B.C., the other day, I warned him against being too bloody-minded. He sort of dared me to do our worst, and that was one of the things which made me so determined to win in the Cabinet Committee. Now the same debate was repeated in Cabinet and once again Harold asked each member to vote and lost comfortably. One reason for his defeat, I'm afraid, is that the Lord President nipped in after the P.M.G. had put his case and remarked that we really had to face the problem of B.B.C. finance and the impossibility of constantly raising the licence fee. As he'd insisted on taking a vote on the apple quota as well as on the B.B.C. I felt very depressed about his method of handling Cabinet business and arranged to go round and talk to him that evening. But now it was time to rush back to my room, get hold of Freddie Warren and Silkin, get my notes together and go down to the Commons in time to hear Harold conduct a superbly confident and efficient Question Time, scoring off Ted Heath on Rhodesia and on the Scottish economic situation. I watched him in admiration and then there was I on my feet dealing with the business and Anne watching me from the Speaker's Gallery. I think it went fairly well.

This evening, after my first quite successful conference with the Lobby journalists, I went round to No. 10 where Harold had asked me to have a

---

[1] The Brabin inquiry reported, however, that while he probably did not murder his daughter, he may have killed his wife.

chat. I found George Brown and Burke Trend there and George at once burst out about the way Harold had handled Cabinet this morning. I'm afraid I joined in and we both pummelled him on the subject of those votes. At one point George Brown said, 'Of course you can keep a list, but you should know that other people round that table are keeping their lists and taking them away for use in their memoirs. It undermines the whole idea of collective Cabinet responsibility. You ought to take the voices, Prime Minister, and then make up your own mind.' Harold looked down rather sheepish and difficult but he slipped away after the meeting without saying a word. However, he can't feel too badly about me because when I got home that evening I found a little note in my red box which read, 'I was delighted with your maiden effort today—the most enjoyable since the Morrison-Churchill days. On top the whole time, apparently effortlessly so: concilia-tory, servant of the House, yet scoring political points the whole way by being mainly non-political. Above all, a lofty intellectual or mock-intellectual superiority which made their would-be intellectuals look very silly. All our people were delighted. Congratulations.' I had got home to bed and opened my red box, read this note and turned to my other papers when I fell asleep. I woke up at 12.30 a.m. with the telephone ringing and Harold Wilson saying, 'I hope you're still awake. I tried to get you. I was talking to George again last night. You are a member of the inner club—the O.P.D.[1]—I just wanted to ring you up and tell you.' I was slightly bewildered by this as I sank back into sleep after a long and exhausting day.

Saturday, October 22nd
Well, now we come to the great Chequers meeting on Europe—that well-advertised secret conference for which each of us had received a mass of papers provided by the officials, including an introduction by George Brown and Michael Stewart which tried to justify entry as the only way to make sure that Britain kept a place at the top table. There was a curious passage about Little England, suggesting that this would be perfectly all right if we were prepared not to count in the councils of the world. So I was clear before I got to Chequers that George and Michael now wanted full backing from the Cabinet for a new European initiative and it was also clear that ideally they would have liked a declaration of intent to sign the treaty.

The morning was an experimental one. Instead of meeting alone the Cabinet met with a large number of officials taking part in the discussion —officials from the F.O., from the D.E.A., and from the Treasury, plus the economic advisers, including Nicky Kaldor and Tommy Balogh. Of the twenty-three members of the Cabinet seventeen were present. The morning was supposed to be the time when the officials and the experts gave their opinions and subjected themselves to questioning. William Armstrong started in the absence of his Minister, since Callaghan couldn't get there on

[1] Overseas and Defence Policy Committee of the Cabinet.

time.[1] To my great surprise he admitted under questioning that entry in 1968 (which all the papers took as a working assumption) was now a bit too early in view of the time it would take to restore the economy to a state healthy enough for entry. This remarkable confession stimulated a long discussion of the timetable. Some of the officials suggested it would take two years of the slow growth we must now expect before we got the economy right and then another two years to prove that when growth started we wouldn't have an inflation. I could see George Brown getting angrier and angrier at this point. The trouble about the morning session was that the Ministers present were determined to use the officials mainly to supply information confirming their own personal points of view. The questioners, including Tony Crosland, started, 'Now I just want to ask a pure question of information,' and then the question turned out to be an effort to try to get the statement from the official which would push the Minister's point of view. That is the obvious difficulty when you try and have a joint meeting between Ministers and officials. This, I suppose, was a moderately successful one but considering the number of officials massed behind us what we got out of them was very little, either little formal statements which were just repeats of the briefs we'd already read or the wriggling efforts of officials trying to avoid being used in a battle between Ministers.

After lunch Cabinet sat alone and we had a series of statements with very little discussion. George Brown made an initial statement that what he wanted was a declaration of intent. 'The probing', he said, 'really hadn't got anywhere, since nobody in Europe will take it seriously until it is clear that we are determined to join.' Michael Stewart backed him up in all this. They were then cross-examined about the timetable and in particular about the suggestion of waiting four years. George said that four years was far too long. He wanted to start straightaway with a new round of investigations. He wanted to push hard because he was convinced the door was open and we could get in. At this point the P.M. revealed his passionate interest in an article in this week's *Economist*, which I hadn't read but which had apparently charmed him. I read it this evening and found it gimmicky and of no particular significance.

As the afternoon went on it was clear that while George Brown and Michael Stewart were already committed to a new initiative, most of us were agreed that there were at least two points on which it was vital to secure further information before a decision. This was what Harold Wilson had brought out at the beginning of the session. The first of these was whether the abolition of exchange controls when we entered meant that we would have to devalue straightaway. Harold didn't like his colleagues using these words

[1] Sir William Armstrong (K.C.B. 1963) had spent the greater part of his career in the Treasury, becoming its Joint Permanent Secretary in 1962. From 1968 until his retirement he was the official Head of the Home Civil Service and the Permanent Secretary of the Civil Service Department. In 1975 he became Chairman of the Midland Bank and accepted a life peerage, taking the title of Lord Armstrong of Sanderstead.

but the issue couldn't be burked. The second question was whether the Commission in Brussels would really deprive us not only of some of our sovereignty but of some of our power to plan the economy. Would investment grants be allowable or not? Would we still be able to see that new factories are put in Scotland rather than in South-East England? Of course Fred Peart and Douglas Jay pushed their objection to the common agricultural policy. But most of us, I think—and here Tommy is absolutely right—felt that agriculture is really an ancillary argument. If we try to go in when the economy is weak and we have to suffer deflation and unemployment then the increased agricultural prices will be a heavy burden on top of that. But if we go in when our economy is booming and our industry growing then the agricultural prices will be something we can sustain.

The meeting this afternoon, at which there were no officials, was not a formal Cabinet and Harold said we should talk to each other using our Christian names. The result was that the discussion got much rougher than he intended. After Callaghan had made a very judicious and tentative speech supporting George Brown I said there was something I wanted to talk about frankly and that was whether Little England was the alternative to the Common Market. I didn't think so. I regard Little England as the precondition for any successful socialist planning whether inside or outside the Common Market. Whatever happens, we need to cut back our overseas commitments and withdraw our troops from the Far East and the Middle East. 'Again, take devaluation,' I said. 'This is also a pre-condition of our recovery whether we're inside or outside the Market,' and I maintained that what Sir William Armstrong had said confirmed my point of view. This produced a really furious row, with half the Cabinet in disagreement about what Sir William had or had not said in the morning when Callaghan wasn't there. I'm sorry that I deeply upset Harold by talking so openly about devaluation as a pre-condition of our success but it really had to be said. I suppose it was because we weren't an official Cabinet that the discussion got so knock-about. I was on the receiving end for once and Harold, despite finding it acutely embarrassing, had to restrain my colleagues in order to enable me to say my say. So I got back on to Little England and told them they shouldn't go into Europe in order to remain great. On this I got a great deal of support from Dick Marsh, Barbara Castle and Tony Wedgwood Benn. It became clear that there is a pretty even split between the Europeans, who feel we must now try to get in virtually as fast as possible on the best terms we can get, and the rest of us, who are fundamentally uninterested in entry. The Europeans are headed by George Brown and Michael Stewart but they have strong support from the Lord Chancellor and also from James Callaghan, who has reluctantly come off the fence in favour of a new approach to Europe. In addition there is George Thomson at the F.O. supporting them. On our side there is Douglas Jay and Fred Peart one hundred per cent anti-Europe, and there are people like Barbara, Dick

Marsh and myself all saying that the net result of the morning talk with the officials was to show how dubious the economic advantages of going into Europe are. Towards the end Tony Wedgwood Benn made an extremely good speech asking what was European about us and what was American and whether the Anglo–American relationship isn't worth a great deal more than entry into Europe. Some of us tried very hard, including the P.M., to get Tommy Balogh's paper on the North Atlantic Free Trade Area considered seriously.[1] But the trouble was we all know this is a non-starter because the Americans aren't prepared to take it seriously. The real choice is between staying out and seeing what we can do to get in. A very good point was made by Denis Healey, whose point of view I found rather close to mine. He said that at least we must have a proper calculation about what would happen on certain assumptions. For instance, if we have to stay out how will we work our passage outside Europe? He himself is convinced that de Gaulle is going to veto our entry anyway and we shall have to survive outside.

Finally came our Harold. I suppose I was a bit dumb to be surprised by what he said. He started with an elaborate declaration about how he felt more committed than other people there and how everything he said would probably meet with disagreement from everybody else. Then, having screwed himself up in this way, he said that what he proposed was a tour round Europe by George Brown and himself to visit the chief capitals and try to clarify the doubtful issues, their probing centring on the two points we had discussed at such length. He said that if the two of them went it would allay suspicions. His presence would allay the suspicion of the anti-Europeans that their point of view wasn't being fully considered. But his presence would also allay the fears of the pro-Europeans who remember the P.M.'s famous Bristol speech in which he accused Heath of fawning on the Europeans like a spaniel.[2] I admit I was both disconcerted and surprised by this announcement. In order to over-trump George Brown, Harold had in fact conceded him far more than he'd asked for. All George and Michael Stewart came to Chequers asking for was a declaration of intent to sign the Treaty of Rome. But now Harold had conceded a tour round Europe by George and himself which was bound to commit us far further towards entry than any paper declaration of intent. Towards the end of the meeting I begged him to have second thoughts. I said I would trust George Brown to go round on his own but what I didn't want to see was our Prime Minister being committed in this way. Nor did I really see why either of them should go. Why shouldn't the probing on these two main points be conducted through diplomatic channels

[1] The proposal for NAFTA envisaged a free trade area of the EFTA countries, Canada and the United States, possibly embracing Australia and New Zealand as well. It foundered on the rocks of American protectionism and the instinct for self-preservation of Australian manufacturers. Another alternative was GITA: 'Going It Alone'.
[2] During the general election campaign in March 1966, Harold Wilson had said of Edward Heath that at 'one encouraging gesture from the French Government . . . he was on his back like a spaniel'.

and the whole job completed on a professional plane? If one is really probing and investigating it shouldn't be done in the gimmicky way of a tour by the Prime Minister and the Foreign Secretary. But as always Harold had made up his mind. There was no going back. He switched to a discussion about publicity. 'There must be no leaks,' he said. 'It would be fatal to have any suggestion which would commit us either for or against entry. All of us must show absolute discretion about this.'

It was now six o'clock and we'd had three hours of really solid argument after those three hours in the morning with the officials. It was time to break off.

The select few who were to discuss defence stayed to dinner. I begged the P.M. to have the discussion about defence over dinner since we were so tired but George Brown had drunk a little too much and he'd also been cheered up because Sophie's gallstone operation is over and quite suddenly he got drunk. So we had an uproarious dinner and then afterwards, upstairs in the long gallery, we settled down to our discussion. George still wasn't quite fit to take part in it but there we were—the seven of us. Denis Healey started by saying that he had now reconsidered the defence budget and thought it was possible to get it down next year to something below £1,850 million. This would mean cutting between £250 million and £400 million by halving our expenditure East of Suez, cutting our costs in Germany by a third and winding up our Middle East commitment altogether. He said in rather a superior voice that intellectually it might seem to be easier to do this by cutting the East of Suez commitment altogether but our allies would never allow that. All through Denis's exposition George Brown kept on shouting, 'But you just said something different to me last time, Denis. What do you really mean? Is there no cut in commitments? How can you make such an enormous cut without demanding something of me as Foreign Secretary?' Denis replied quietly that no change was required in foreign policy. We would still have the forces to maintain it. What came out of a very long discussion is that the defence policy Healey proposes would mean leaving token forces in the Far East quite unable to fulfil any of the precise obligations we've undertaken in SEATO. And there may well be token forces in the Middle East unable to fulfil the obligations we've undertaken under CENTO. I made this point and said, 'But surely it's far better first to make a major change in foreign policy and follow Ernest Bevin's example? You remember when he totally withdrew from Greece and Turkey and forced the Truman Doctrine on the Americans.[1] Now isn't that the kind of thing we should now do? We should make a proper basic foreign policy change and not merely whittle away our defences while maintaining our commitments.' Again

[1] In March 1947, when Britain found herself unable to meet her obligations to resist Communism in Greece, Ernest Bevin, Foreign Secretary from July 1945 to March 1951, encouraged President Truman to declare that America had the duty to oppose the threat of Communism in any country.

Denis said that intellectually that might be true but practically it was impossible.

Harold tried to stop me and I realized straightaway that I was alone among
the seven. I'm really completely out of sympathy with the whole atmosphere
of this Government's attitude to foreign policy and defence—they want to
maintain our commitments while cutting away the forces with which we
sustain them. What George Wigg and I have argued for years and years is
precisely that the one thing a Labour Government must not do is to assume
huge responsibilities and then deny our troops the weapons necessary to
sustain them. Just think of it. The first Defence Review isn't yet twelve
months old. Already, in July, it's been cut by £100 million. Now Denis is
saying he can cut it in six months' time by another £300 million while we still
retain all our commitments in the Far East, in the Middle East and in
Germany. Both before the meeting and at the end I was reminded in the
presence of the others that I was a new member of the club and must mind
my tongue especially because I couldn't yet fully understand what was
involved. I'm afraid I do understand only too well. But I never suspected that
when I got inside O.P.D. and discovered what was actually being done by
these colleagues it would be so crude, so unskilful—a futile attempt to remain
Great Britain, one of the three world powers, while slicing away our
defences.

While our talks were going on someone rushed in to say that George Blake
had just climbed over the wall of Wormwood Scrubs and made his escape.[1]
George Brown woke up and said we must give instructions to alert all the
ports. The P.M. asked what statement we should give to the press. I asked
why we should make any statement to the press. We've presumably got
capable people running the prison and really we're not much good, as
Ministers, in trying to catch a prisoner who's run away. This was thought to
be in rather poor taste. However George Brown went off to bed and I was
left in the end talking alone with Harold.

This was quite a solemn occasion. 'I brought you into this club—the one
you attended this evening,' he said. 'Do you still want to be a member?
Because if you do, you know, your behaviour has got to be very different.
You mustn't go on talking to Barbara, least of all about the things we discuss
here. You mustn't even let her know what is going on in RX. You've got to
be a member of this club—an insider—along with us. Otherwise it won't
work.' I said I was pretty security-minded after five years at SHAEF. 'No,' he
said, 'it's not only a matter of military security; it's a matter of your relationship with your colleagues. You've got to have a new style of relationship with
the other members of this inner group now that I've brought you right in.' He
said this time after time and I did get the impression that he's trying to tie me
tighter and tighter to himself. Why? He got me in, knowing in advance that

[1] In 1961 George Blake had been convicted of espionage and was serving a sentence of
forty-two years in Wormwood Scrubs.

I'm a Little Englander, knowing in advance my view that we have to change our foreign policy before we cut the defence forces. Then why take the risk of bringing me in as a jarring element? Perhaps he's doing it for the same reason he has Tommy Balogh as his chief economic adviser and George Wigg there in the background. He feels a need to have unconventional people close to him because he knows his own extremely conventional nature.

During our private talk Roy Jenkins rang up in a great stew about George Blake. When Harold put down the receiver he turned to me and said, 'That will do our Home Secretary a great deal of good. He was getting too complacent and he needs taking down a peg.'

Sunday, October 23rd

There's one other very important thing I must add about the Chequers weekend. It was interrupted by more than one big external event. As well as the escape of George Blake from Wormwood Scrubs, on Friday night there was the disaster at Aberfan, the Welsh valley where a huge coal tip broke away and ran over a school killing hundreds of children.[1] Harold Wilson had gone straight down there by helicopter and stayed there and Callaghan has gone over by motor-car. Everybody has been rushing to get into it and I feel the whole thing has been emotionally exploited by the B.B.C. in the most terrible and extravagant way. But I have no doubt whatsoever that Harold Wilson was profoundly moved. The tragedy gave a macabre background to the weekend.

Tuesday, October 25th

This was my big day because I had to wind up the debate on Part IV. I'd been given the job because nobody else wanted it. The debate lagged and sagged and I got more and more jumpy and uneasy. I got the outline of the speech prepared and a last peroration and I planned for the middle an attack on the Opposition showing the discrepancy between Maudling's view and Enoch Powell's view and challenging them to say where they really stood. Looking back now I can see the tactic was right enough but I failed to foresee one misfortune. The debate had dragged on until there wasn't adequate time for Frank Cousins before nine o'clock, when Mrs Thatcher was due to get up.[2] So the Whips did a deal under which she started a quarter of an hour late. She made a good, professional, tough speech and sat down just after 9.45 instead of at 9.30.

I suppose very few people can realize what devastation such a little procedural change can bring about. Everybody comes into the Chamber on a three-line whip expecting to vote promptly at ten and they soon get very

[1] On October 21st, at Aberfan, Glamorgan, a slag-tip slid away, taking a school and houses in its path and killing 116 children and 28 adults.
[2] Conservative M.P. for Finchley since 1959. In 1975 she succeeded Edward Heath as leader of the Conservative Party.

impatient if the speeches go on after that moment. I got up at eleven minutes to ten and I was doing quite well when ten struck. I had got to the central point of Tommy's argument when I looked at the clock and realized that whatever I said the audience would get bored and I wouldn't be able to hold their attention. I should have spoken on till about 10.25 but I lost my nerve and decided to leave out my attack on the Tories and sit down with a very brief peroration. This I did.

As I sat down Harold beside me said, 'Have you finished, Dick? Or are you giving way to Frank Cousins?' I said (perhaps this was the second mistake), 'Giving way,' because the Chief Whip hadn't got up and moved the adjournment. So I had to lumber to my feet again to answer Frank Cousins. Then, of course, Edward Heath joined in and I was caught, getting up, sitting down, trying to get into my speech again until it dragged on into a complete anti-climax. There were no cheers from our side and there were plenty of shouts of 'resign' from the other.

Then we had the division—307 to 239, with 28 abstentions. John Silkin had expected between sixteen and seventeen. I don't think any of them were in the faintest degree influenced by anything I did say or didn't say or by what Frank Cousins had said in the speech before mine.

After the result was announced I went through into the Members' lobby and ran into George Wigg. He looked at me severely and said, 'Well you got through that all right but now we shall have to take action. Unless you enforce discipline I can't guarantee the consequences. I've been trying to hold the boys back but they're thirsting for blood.' I knew very well that he had not been trying to hold the boys back but had been whipping them up and inciting them to a bloodbath and so had Manny Shinwell. It was obvious that John Silkin and Dick Crossman's new deal would soon be put to its first test.

I went home rather shattered.

Wednesday, October 26th

After a haircut at nine in the morning I was at morning prayers with Harold at 9.45. He was cool and collected, and remarked cheerfully, 'That's probably the worst debate we shall have to go through in this Parliament: we survived it fairly well.' He told us we'd been right to hold the Party meeting the day before and get an overwhelming vote in support for the action he'd taken. Of my performance he said, 'Don't be worried about it. It was perfectly all right,' and he soothed me down as only Harold can.

I had to have the liaison committee in my room and I knew we would have a fierce debate with strong proposals to sack the twenty-eight M.P.s who had defied the Party whip and abstained from voting for Part IV. Sure enough Manny Shinwell, Willie Hamilton and Malcolm MacPherson, the three elected members of the liaison committee, all demanded that we should withdraw the whip. But since it wasn't practical to apply this to all twenty-eight defaulters it was suggested that we should pick off the ringleaders. Four was the number first suggested and then came a later suggestion of seven or eight. At this point John Silkin stepped in and said, 'This is not your decision.' He had written down his view very carefully on paper and it was in strict accord with the concordat which Manny had signed. In that concordat it was laid down that while the decision rested of course with the Parliamentary Party the initiative for recommending discipline remained with the Chief Whip.

John's behaviour was absolutely magnificent at this meeting. He had told me beforehand that he was determined to have a special meeting and move the two traditional resolutions,[1] but it was only as the argument went on that I realized how completely we both accepted the liberal philosophy as the only way to run a modern left-wing party. This is based on the assumption that every Member of the Party may well on occasion have to abstain conscientiously; conscientious abstention won't in future be limited to pacifists and teetotallers but will be recognized as a right of every Member. And in particular we would have to realize that when a Government suddenly does things which are not in the Party manifesto and which are profoundly controversial, then Members have the right to challenge that Government and in the last resort to abstain conscientiously. We have got to get all this over to the rank and file next week. What really excited me was the discovery that John and I felt ourselves dedicated liberalizers.

Wednesday, November 2nd
I rushed across to the Party meeting in Westminster where Fred Peart was winding up the first day's debate on prices and incomes. Then the debate on discipline began. John and I were trying to get the Party to accept our new code of discipline. This involved us reintroducing the ban on fraternal feuding which Clem Attlee had introduced, and the ban on the party within a party. This had also been introduced by Clem Attlee in 1952, in an effort to suppress the Bevanites; obviously, Harold Wilson and I were then both against it. I've made some effort to persuade Michael Foot and the other left-wingers to understand what we were doing about the conscience clause and that we were trying to achieve a real breakthrough to a modern liberalized discipline. If I was to have any chance of making the right wing concede on this I had to reimpose these two old disciplinary conditions. Michael was not convinced. Manny Shinwell had agreed that he would open the debate formally and that John should make the speech. But Manny's a crafty, ratty man and of course he didn't like what we were doing because he himself wanted to expel the ringleaders as a penalty for what they did after the Part IV debate. So instead of calling John straightaway he called Konni Zilliacus.[2]

[1] Deploring 'fraternal feuding' and the existence of 'a party within a party'.
[2] M.P. for Gateshead 1945–50 and for Gorton, Manchester, from 1955 until his death in July 1967.

Then he got into a quarrel and began to lay down the law about what the new discipline meant. We had half an hour of very bad-tempered debate between the two before Jim Wellbeloved[1] said, 'What's the good of those two debating before we hear the Chief Whip?'

So at last John was called and he made a deeply moving, simple speech on how conscience couldn't be limited to temperance or pacifism, how it applied to all political issues and must be an individual matter. He emphasized that he wasn't going to allow collective group decisions to be called decisions of conscience and then he made another telling point by defining an organized group as a number of people whose intention to abstain was known to the press before the Whips knew it. There was a sardonic laugh because everyone knew he was referring to the fact that the *Daily Telegraph* had been able to publish the correct number of abstainers when the Whips had got it quite wrong. That showed therefore that the group was in active contact with the press.

After John, Michael Foot got up and made a passionate speech in which he reminded us that Harold and I had led the attack on this motion when it was first moved in 1952. He was not going to give up his principles, he said. He was going to continue fighting just as before. Of course, it was the kind of speech which the right expected and for that reason it was impossible. The debate wasn't too bad. Jim Wellbeloved made the point that he didn't see how there could be any discipline if this new concession were made, and there were then a number of quite sensible questions. Finally, I made a short speech which was not improved by a lot of suggestions on bits of paper which were being pushed to me by Harold throughout my speech. On one of the bits of paper he had written that I should say the Bevanites accepted the decision of 1952. I was a bit doubtful but I said it, whereupon I was immediately asked what had happened. I said it was a damned nuisance because we had to meet informally, and there was a roar of applause—it was thought that I had cast a brick through my own glasshouse. The number of people who bothered to attend this meeting was modest. John and I got 120 votes and those opposed to our new code got 49. There were probably twenty or thirty abstentions. I doubt whether thirty of the hundred members of the Government were there. People stayed away because they hated the idea but knew some discipline was necessary.

Thursday, November 3rd

Most of the papers this morning said that the Silkin–Crossman reforms got a lukewarm reception. That was true enough, but what we were putting over was rather a lukewarm plan. Anyway there was no heart in the attack the Left made upon us since they knew very well we were shielding them from expulsion. Probably the lukewarm mood was what we needed but it didn't make it a cheerful occasion.

[1] M.P. for Erith and Crayford since 1965.

Cabinet started this morning with Harold's delayed announcement about information services. There was virtually no discussion. When one or two questions had been asked the Prime Minister said, 'Well, I'll circulate a notice in Cabinet minutes,' and that was that.

Next we plunged again into the debate on Europe. Today's meeting started with a paper from George Brown specifically giving us the choice of either a formal declaration of intent followed by probing at diplomatic level or a speech at Strasbourg on our intentions followed by the tour of the capitals. He said he slightly preferred the tour of the capitals but he knew that others thought it was too hazardous or difficult. In that case he would accept the declaration of intent. The Prime Minister then at once came in and said that he thought we would have to have the EFTA meeting at the beginning. This put George back a bit but the Prime Minister went on to say that it might be timed simultaneously with the announcement of the tour round the capitals. The choice was then debated. At this meeting Michael Stewart and Callaghan switched their support to the declaration of intent as less dangerous than going round the capitals without any declared policy. This was my view and I'd come to Cabinet to say it, but it was much more effectively said by them. At this point the anti-Marketeers joined in expressing their alarm at the prospect of seeing Harold and George touring Europe as suppliants and trying to clarify the issue before the British Government had really made up its mind.

At the end of a one-and-a-half hour discussion Harold came up with a six-point plan which was very characteristic since it entirely consisted of points of procedure—when exactly to have the first consultation with EFTA, whether there was going to be an address by him in Strasbourg before the round of the capitals, etc. I suggested he'd got the cart before the horse. Before we discussed how to do the tour we had first to consider the policy decisions the Government needed to take in order to brief the Prime Minister and Foreign Secretary for the tour. How far would they be allowed to go? What reservations would they be bound to make? But Harold is still keeping his options open. I shall go to see him this week and say, 'Take your courage in both hands. Have this out with the Cabinet and I'll try and bring the Party round. I'm pretty sure we'd have a clear majority for you if you decided genuinely that you wanted to try to go into Europe and that you wanted to accept the Treaty and get in. If you say that clearly then we as a Government will have a strategic directive which will hold this Party together. At present we're falling apart because we haven't got any central purpose in life.'

Wednesday, November 9th

This was the day of the Cabinet decision about our approach to Europe. We were presented with a very big official paper. It contained a recapitulation of Harold's plan of procedure and attached to it a draft annexe showing the policy to be included in the Statement or alternatively in the brief. This included the key sentences about the Treaty of Rome and our attitude to it.

Cabinet began in the most extraordinary desultory way. George Brown moved his paper, did a little bit and hummed and hawed. Harold did a little bit and hummed and hawed. The Europeans were holding back. Roy Jenkins never says much in Cabinet but he knew that we all regarded him as deeply committed and he didn't see why he should say anything. There was a mild altercation between Tony Crosland and Fred Peart and a little sparring by Barbara Castle, but mostly people were talking about the details of the procedure and the timetable. Even Callaghan, who came in late and said he supported the paper, talked in a rather half-hearted way. I followed Callaghan with a carefully calculated speech. It's the first 'speech' I've ever made in Cabinet in the proper sense of the word. I started by saying that I should make my own position clear. I was not a Common Marketeer. I was one of the minority who believe in Britain's future as an offshore island, cutting down all our overseas commitments, getting ourselves an economic position as favourable as that of Japan in the Far East and living on our own as an independent socialist community. I understood that this was an unpopular view and unlikely to be realized in the near future. Certainly nobody would be prepared to take the decision to accept our position as an offshore island until a genuine effort had been made to enter Europe. And it was no good suggesting there is any real alternative. The so-called Javits plan—the North Atlantic Free Trade Area—is a non-starter because the Americans won't move. The only choice at the moment is between a half-hearted effort to enter Europe and a whole-hearted effort to enter Europe. What we needed today was a Cabinet decision giving a dramatic indication that we are going all-out for entry. If that effort fails I shan't be particularly upset because then we can consider the possibility of the offshore island. But if we try at all, I'm in favour of a whole-hearted approach. We should have the Statement tomorrow in accordance with George Brown's paper and if possible the P.M. should make it his theme at the big Guildhall speech next week. After I'd said all this, Callaghan decided to speak again. 'That's that,' he said, 'and I must add something else in favour of what the Lord President has said. One reason for going into Europe is that it's the only way to give hope to private business and to end the crisis of confidence in industry which is preventing the growth of essential private capital investment which we need to get over the winter slump. Dick's quite right but I must add something else. We are now faced with a commitment in Africa which will almost certainly lead to mandatory sanctions and that will produce grave stresses and strains on sterling. If we are going to face those problems in Rhodesia without any effort to enter Europe I can't give any guarantee about the future of the pound.' That really finished it. Barbara added her own left-wing comment. 'Of course,' she said, 'a strong Rhodesian policy would make it much easier to sell the approach to the Common Market to the Parliamentary Party.' And that was the kind of deal which was struck round the table that morning. It was the knowledge of the appalling dangers which faced us in Rhodesia that prevented any serious opposition to the new approach.

This afternoon in the House I was caught by Gerald Kaufman and asked to go straightaway to Harold's room. There I found Marcia, and the Prime Minister showed me in writing (I was the only person to see it) the draft Statement he was due to make with the key sentence that we meant business. 'That's fine,' I said and ran for my train to Cambridge.

Thursday, November 10th
This was a tidying-up Cabinet after the big decision. The draft Statement was presented to us and the proposed amendments were only part of a defensive move by the anti-Marketeers to try to water down any commitment. I made my own view clear that if we want to give the impression of a serious attempt we shouldn't niggle about the words. But the amending took most of the morning.

Right at the end of Cabinet came an item in which I was vitally interested—my paper on the television experiment. I had hoped that if it came so late in the morning I should have an easy time; I'd already got Callaghan to send me a letter saying that he was keenly in favour of the experiment, though we might have to raise the question of costs, and I'd also got Bert Bowden to agree. Surely the rest of Cabinet would go along? I emphasized, in introducing it, that this was merely a trial run. All seemed to be going very well when Harold was suddenly struck by the problem of television magazine programmes. If the B.B.C. and the programme companies all had full video transcripts of every day's proceedings, would they be able to cut the video-tape up and take a little bit of a speech and introduce it into a magazine programme? 'Certainly,' I said, 'that was the intention.' Harold said that couldn't possibly be allowed. They could only be allowed to do straight direct reporting of what happened in Parliament. I replied that if we insisted on this I.T.N. wouldn't think it worthwhile. And then I tried to soothe him by saying that of course there were a lot of these technical difficulties but surely they were the kind of things we ought to work on in the course of the eight-week experiment. Then suddenly Callaghan said, 'Well anyway, I don't think we ought to have it this spring. It's too expensive and we can't have a supplementary estimate of £150,000 this February.' At this point there was a general clamour, making clear that nobody wanted the television experiment. They didn't want a change of this sort in the Palace of Westminster. Harold saw his chance and took the votes round the table. There were not more than five in favour of having the experiment this spring. So I was left with my whole programme for Parliamentary reform in ruins. What's worse, the Conservatives have already consented to the experiment and I have to go back to Willie Whitelaw and confess to him that Cabinet wants it postponed. It was a terrible blow.

Sunday, November 13th

I woke up this morning feeling a little gloomy and grey about everything because I think there's worse to come this winter. We seem to me to be lurching from a moderate Government-induced deflation into a much worse deflation produced by a crisis of confidence and a failure of industry to expand its investment.

Meanwhile, all I can say is that during this week I have at least helped to resolve the chronic indecision about our attitude to Europe. We've had a magnificent press and Harold has got everything I predicted out of his bold clear Statement. Now we have two years before us when he'll be busy trying to get into Europe and that will give us a clear strategy. The only drawback is that Harold has managed once again to commit us against devaluation. As a result of his last-minute change to the Statement he's now committed not to devalue the pound before entering Europe, yet I'm not sure that we can keep parity throughout the coming winter without so much deflation that we may split the Party. Devaluation is after all the only way to get our exports up quickly and so become economically strong and healthy. Indeed, I believe that a devaluation deliberately planned and timed for next spring or summer would be the best preparation for entering Europe. Yet, characteristically, just before he made his Statement Harold was persuaded by the Bank of England to forbid himself the one economic change which would be necessary to create the conditions for any satisfactory entry into Europe in the foreseeable future.

Thursday, November 17th

Cabinet. The Prime Minister had decided to take my procedure package of parliamentary reform. Actually it took nearly two hours and was a ghastly discussion. How ghastly you certainly wouldn't get an idea from the Cabinet minutes. Discussing how to handle our colleagues, John and I had decided that the order of presentation was extremely important and I would start with morning sittings, then deal with Standing Order No. 9 and finally discuss the Specialist Committees. The Cabinet minutes merely attribute to me the brief which I took with me of which I didn't read a single word because I knew it was unsuitable. The official minutes even change the order of the items on the agenda so that they agree with the brief. According to the minutes Specialist Committees come first and then morning sittings. I record this because it's important to remember how little historians can trust Cabinet minutes to tell what really went on. What they do tell is what went on according to the officials and the official briefs.

I put the case as well as I could knowing it was unpopular. I reminded them that I'd inherited this package from my predecessor and that the Party was deeply committed to it at the general election. The moment I'd finished George Brown said, 'Well, it's asking a terrible lot of us, Prime Minister. We're busy men. What you're asking is that busy Ministers should have morning sittings as well.' I explained that the aim was to get the back-benchers home early two nights a week. I couldn't guarantee that we should achieve this aim and I had put the topical debates in to spice things up in the mornings. Now, however, I realized that a topical debate was something which might take the time of a Foreign Office spokesman and that is the way in which George Brown considered it. He was followed by Minister after Minister round the table simply saying how busy they were, how they were harassed by all these Cabinet Committees, and how they simply couldn't be burdened with any more work by the House of Commons.

Barbara was the only person with any political sense. She said, 'I'm as bothered as anybody about the extra work but frankly, you know, if what's being said here was reported to the Parliamentary Party we would be blown to smithereens.' She was specifically referring to the remarks of the First Secretary. Michael Stewart had said to the Cabinet that these new Members on whose initiative morning sittings had been proposed really must be told that they'd got it all wrong—that a back-bench M.P. has a perfectly satisfactory full-time job to do and there's no reason to create work for him to keep him happy. Indeed, our back-benchers should be thankful that as a socialist government we want to keep the Executive strong, not to strengthen parliamentary control. Michael's remarks had been applauded by many people round the table. When I heard them I remembered that he'd hardly been a back-bencher at any time in his twenty years in the House of Commons. He's always been either a junior Minister or a Shadow Minister on the front bench. I've had nineteen years as a back-bencher and I know what they are talking about so I was tickled when Jim Callaghan joined in and said, 'We've got to be careful of our Lord President now he has transferred his attention from boosting housing to boosting the House of Commons. Just as he knew nothing about housing before he went to the Ministry this fellow was never there when he was a back-bencher. Now he's boosting the Commons with all the strength and power he gave to his housing programme and we've got to resist him in the same way.'

Most of these Ministers were individually as well as collectively committed to parliamentary reform. Yet after two years they've become Whitehall figures who've lost contact with Parliament. And of course what they're saying is pure nonsense. Ministers aren't bothered by Parliament, indeed they're hardly ever there. A departmental Minister has many other major worries what with boxes, Ministerial committees, visits outside London. But the amount of time a Minister spends on the front bench or in his room in St Stephen's is very small. The Executive rides supreme in Britain and has minimum trouble from the legislature. Perhaps it's because Parliament is so entirely subordinate to the Executive that my colleagues were saying, 'We can't allow this Parliamentary Party to bother us.'

In summing up, the P.M. to some extent rebuked Cabinet but he gave way on the crucial point of having Standing Order 9 debates in the morning. On Specialist Committees he helped me a great deal with Fred Peart and it looks as if I got my two Committees through as part of the package.[1] I shall have to submit the draft Statement to Cabinet next week.

Thursday, November 24th

This was the day for debate on televising the House. As usual I didn't have much time for preparation. I felt it was rather a good speech—thoughtful and critical of the Select Committee's report but urging an experiment which was a genuine trial to see whether television would work technically or not. I didn't ask the House to give uncritical or enthusiastic support to the Select Committee's particular recommendation but urged that *experiment* was a good thing. I was followed by Paul Bryan, the Tory front-bench spokesman,[2] who supported it in his own way, but after him I soon discovered, to quote Yeats, 'that the best lacked all conviction and the worst were full of passionate sincerity'. Speech after speech from Charlie Pannell, Quintin Hogg and the rest denounced the whole idea as false to the tradition of the House of Commons and rejected even an experiment. Things got worse and worse and I realized I'd completely misjudged the whole atmosphere in preparing my own speech for the beginning of the debate. I had assumed the motion would be carried comfortably but, as Geoffrey Rhodes, my P.P.S.,[3] warned me, the enthusiasm of the House was turned against the experiment. Right at the end I got up to reply and made a much better, tougher and shorter speech. But it was too late to save the situation. We lost by a single vote.[4] In the lobby I found I was the only Cabinet Minister voting for the proposal.

Afterwards I sat in the smoking-room, which I don't often do these days, drinking gin, which I've now given up, and feeling absolutely sick of life and furiously angry with my colleagues for letting me down.

On December 2nd and 3rd, in an attempt to end the Rhodesian crisis which had now dragged on for a year, the Prime Minister and Ian Smith met in the Mediterranean on the British cruiser Tiger *which had been paying a goodwill*

[1] On Agriculture and on Science and Technology.

[2] Sir Paul Bryan, Conservative M.P. for the Howden Division of Yorkshire since 1955. Assistant Government Whip 1956–8 and Whip 1958–61, he was Minister of State at the Department of Employment 1970–72.

[3] Labour M.P. for East Newcastle from 1964 until his death, at the age of forty-six, in 1974. He was Crossman's P.P.S. for fifteen months, taking the place of Tam Dalyell. After a visit to 'Confrontation against Indonesia' in Borneo Tam Dalyell had criticized the government's East of Suez policy in this area and, in view of Crossman's own controversial background in defence policy, he thought it best to resign as his P.P.S.

[4] The vote was 130 to 131.

visit to Casablanca. At the meeting the British Government understood that the Rhodesian Government had given their Prime Minister plenipotentiary powers, and the hope was that Ian Smith could return to Rhodesia with a signed agreement on a new constitution and a return to a legal relationship with Britain. Though the basis of such an agreement was worked out on board the cruiser, Mr Smith maintained that he would need the approval of his own Cabinet for signing the document, and he undertook to obtain such endorsement by 10.0 a.m. on December 5th. At 4.0 p.m. that day Mr Smith announced that the arrangements which had been devised on board the Tiger *(to be published on December 20th as* Cmnd. 3171) *were after all unacceptable to his Cabinet. He declared that it was the proposals for the restoration of legal government rather than the proposed constitution with its timetable for eventual African majority rule to which his Cabinet objected.*

Tuesday, December 6th
Cabinet was in a difficult and unpleasant mood because we had to consider the consequences of the Rhodesian failure. Of course all the plans for our strategy at the U.N. had been laid down in advance and George Brown was due to leave for New York this evening. The difficulty we were discussing was not what to do but how to present what had happened on the *Tiger*.

Harold Wilson's main concern was the picture of Smith we should give to the British public. Should we name the list of the Cabinet Ministers in Salisbury, who had been named by Smith and Harold as members of his new enlarged government? Should we name the Cabinet Ministers he was going to dismiss and the thirty members of the Rhodesia Front Party he wanted to get rid of? Should we publish all the dirt about him which had come out on the *Tiger* and so try to destroy him, or should we regard him as something worth preserving? I soon discovered that Harold Wilson wasn't really interested in planning psychological warfare because he hadn't made up his mind what he wanted to happen in Salisbury. What he was doing was to work himself up for his swing from his attempt to appease Smith on the *Tiger* to an attempt this coming Thursday to appease his anti-Smith back-benchers in the House of Commons. To this end he was beginning to feel a deep indignation against Smith and to treat him as an absolutely contemptible character, a crook and a waverer. How idiotic it was, he said at one moment, that Smith should be going for this figment, this will-o'-the-wisp of independence. At this point I interjected and said, 'For heaven's sake, let's keep some grip on reality. It's quite probable that what the P.M. calls the will-o'-the-wisp of Rhodesian independence will be a fact long after the Labour Government is thrown out of office.'

Thursday, December 8th
At Cabinet this morning Harold was chiefly concerned with his big speech but we had a not uninteresting discussion on broadcasting in which he scored

a complete triumph over his modernizing adversaries. Ted Short simply reported that the scheme for a public corporation partly dependent on advertising was impracticable and all the modernizers—including Tony Benn, Tony Crosland and myself—gave up. So the idea which Tony Benn rejected when he was Postmaster-General had prevailed and the White Paper will be published tomorrow committing us to a completely impracticable method of financing the B.B.C.[1]

Then came the big Rhodesia debate. It started with a perfectly decent light-weight speech from Douglas-Home. Then Harold began. As I suspected from his attitude on Tuesday morning he had swung right back. Having come to the edge of an agreement with Smith for which he had paid with very heavy concessions, he had now swung back to the other extreme and made an ultra-moralist speech addressed in particular to the forty or fifty left-wingers who'd have refused him their vote if he'd got his agreement with Smith. The central theme was that this was a great moral issue, that anybody who was against Wilson was for Smith, that the Tories were the allies of the rebels in Rhodesia, and he ended with a peroration quoting Abraham Lincoln addressed to the workers of Lancashire[2] and which worked up the Labour Members to such a passion that when he sat down they gave him a standing ovation waving their Order Papers. I found the Chief Whip was standing beside me and I also rose though I couldn't bring myself to wave my Order Paper. But there's no doubt about it, Harold had roused the Party which is a moralistic party and which disliked the idea of any settlement and is delighted to cheer when they are told that no settlement is possible.

That was the high point of the debate but we were all waiting to see what Heath would do. Sure enough when he got up at nine o'clock he made a very powerful speech. 'All this moralism', he said, 'is a piece of hypocrisy. The Prime Minister talks about fighting a moral battle and raises the banner of morality but actually he's been doing everything to avoid a confrontation in Africa, thank heavens, and he will accept a settlement if he possibly can.' Heath was doing fine when he mentioned Aneurin Bevan's remark that the British Tories were lower than vermin. Suddenly there rose a woman in white samite, mystic, wonderful, in the third row back of our benches. It was Jennie Lee denouncing Heath for maligning her dead husband. She so upset Heath that he ran on until 9.38 and left little time for Judith Hart. Judith had been appalled to hear how near we had come to a settlement and she proved again that she's so soaked in the subject that she's able to raise real emotions

[1] The White Paper on Broadcasting Finance (Cmnd. 3169) that was published in December 1966 followed six months of discussion of a proposal floated by Mr Wedgwood Benn, the then Postmaster-General, to establish a new public corporation with one wavelength financed by advertising revenue. Mr Short's White Paper declared that the B.B.C. would continue in its present form, as a public corporation deriving its revenue from the licence fees, paid by the public to the Post Office and voted, as a matching sum, by Parliament.
[2] Asking them to accept privations for their principles.

in the House. She at least had time to give the news from New York for which everyone was waiting—that mandatory sanctions were on.

Then came the vote and we found that we'd won by a comfortable majority since the Liberals were on our side. This was one of the few big occasions in my memory where the events matched the occasion. Both Ted and Harold had made fine speeches, Bowden and Douglas-Home had done very competently and Judith had made her mark. The debate in fact had mattered.

Friday, December 9th
Morning prayers with the P.M. He was wild with fury at the badness of the press. 'The press are contemptible and corrupt. Unbearable! Look at what they have done to my speech.' 'True,' I said, 'but if you lambast the Tory leader you mustn't expect the Tory press to be wildly enthusiastic. And then you have also got to notice that Reg Paget has made the headlines by resigning the Party Whip.[1] I knew it was a mistake to let him resign.' 'What?' he said. 'Yes,' I said. 'I knew Reg Paget wanted to vote against us and John told him he should resign first. I think we shouldn't have let him resign but kept him in, let him vote and then expelled him. Then we wouldn't have had the headlines against you which we've got today.'

O.P.D. this morning was extremely important. We were considering a joint paper from the Foreign Secretary and the Minister of Defence proposing cuts of up to one half in Far Eastern Command and about a third in the Middle East and in Europe. This was the idea which was first broached in the after-dinner talk at Chequers when I was brought into the inner group (I'm not at all sure I'm still there, by the way). In this paper it was worked out in detail—and it was totally and completely unconvincing. It seemed obvious that if you were to make these gigantic cuts in defence costs then they made the previous Defence Review utterly senseless. Alternatively, what you are doing is to make major changes in foreign policy under the veil of cutting defence—and of course the second alternative is nearly true.

Callaghan started straightaway by making this point very clearly indeed. I weighed in on the same side. I added that I noticed there were certain differences. In the case of the Middle East there was an instruction in the paper that a special study should be undertaken on the political assumption of a total withdrawal. But a total withdrawal from the Far East was not even to be made the subject of a study. On the contrary, the whole assumption was that we are there for ever because it is necessary to keep a British military presence in the Far East to sustain our membership of the four-power agreement with Australia, New Zealand and the U.S.A. As a result of my intervention it was agreed that there should be a study of total withdrawal

[1] Labour M.P. for Northampton 1945–74. He became a life peer in 1974.

from Malaya. But the intervention of Callaghan and myself occasioned a considerable speech from Denis Healey. He said, 'One mustn't be afraid of the idea of penny-packages throughout the world. There is a lot to commend them: a penny-package can make an immense difference as we found the other day when a battalion of our troops in Kenya prevented a revolution. A single ship in Hong Kong could make all the difference. One can't dismiss the validity of a strategy based on penny-packages.'

I couldn't help recalling all the lessons I'd received from George Wigg on the fatal effect of the policy of scattering penny-packages round the world during the 1920s and the 1930s since each of these packages involved a large commitment that we might have to honour. And we can't honour the commitment entered into as a result of the penny-package without maintaining a vast strategic reserve. Yet here was George Wigg actually supporting Denis Healey. I realized that the whole weight of the Prime Minister's enormous influence would be on the side of preserving the British military presence in the Far East. I have no doubt, for example, that the Prime Minister has already made a number of personal commitments on the subject to L.B.J. in Washington. At one point, indeed, Callaghan mentioned them by saying, 'I don't want to refer to or argue about any specific commitments, Prime Minister, you have made to L.B.J.' It is the personal commitments in Washington of Harold Wilson, of George Brown and of Michael Stewart which are holding us down in Malaya. They're making it as difficult for us to withdraw there as it is to get out of Aden and there we shall find that our own people will create a situation which will require nothing less than a war in order to achieve a withdrawal.

Sunday, December 11th
This evening I stopped work on my procedure speech for next week for a bit and looked back over the last fortnight of the Rhodesian crisis. I've been watching Harold swinging between extremes. I've seen him at his best and at his worst. First John and I helped him off the launching pad as the man willing to negotiate with Smith and to defy the fifty left-wing back-benchers. I saw him plunging out into the venture on the *Tiger*, cutting loose from the Party and determined to get an agreement even if it meant a couple of resignations from Cabinet. Next I saw him back from the *Tiger* extraordinarily confident that he'd got an agreement in his pocket. (This is something Mary Wilson remarked on at a moment when I spotted her and walked her down the lobby.) Now that I've read the *Tiger* minutes verbatim, I see that optimism as wholly unjustified. Nevertheless, he came back full of this optimism and at the Cabinet meeting on Sunday afternoon persuaded us to give him one hundred per cent support for his plan even though it contains major concessions to Smith. Then on Monday morning he expected Smith's reply at ten a.m. and didn't get it. He busied himself with EFTA to keep his mind off the subject and waited all through the day desperately anxiously.

He was hopelessly cast down when he was gradually forced to the conclusion that no reply is a negative reply and finally, at 8.45, he made a Statement on the failure of the talks. For that he had to use a corrected version of the Statement on the success of the talks because he hadn't, as he promised he would, prepared alternative drafts. All he could do as last-minute preparation was to put some corrections into the Statement he drafted on how the talks succeeded. Next morning we saw him at Cabinet discussing our long-term plans rather vaguely but by then he was wholly concerned with the speech he was going to make and spent a lot of thought in Cabinet drafting Thursday's resolution. Already he'd determined that his main objective was to demolish Heath in that debate and this he did. We had a tremendous scene with Harold, the moralist, rallying his left-wing back-benchers against Heath, the criminal collaborationist, and completely burning his bridges by swinging from a mood of extreme appeasement to a mood of no concession to treason. That's what we saw on Thursday. I had to admit that during those four days Harold didn't consult me and as far as I know he didn't consult anybody outside his No. 10 circle. In that period I had no influence on him. I think the only people he talked to were George Wigg and Marcia Williams. But I saw him again on Friday morning entirely concerned about the effect his speech produced, and planning to demolish the RX Committee, with which he now feels he has had to waste so many weary hours while they tried to run his Rhodesian strategy for him.

After Thursday's Cabinet I walked to the front door of No. 10 with Roy Jenkins, who's a cautious, conspiring kind of man and plays little role in Cabinet. 'Heavens,' I said to him, 'I wish we could have been given a clearer vision of his long-term policy in Rhodesia.' He replied, 'I'd give anything for evidence that we have a long-term plan for any part of this Government's policy, thank you very much, Dick,' and he walked on.

I find I share Roy Jenkins's depression. Because I've watched Harold from close at hand, I've seen him during this crisis as exactly what his enemies accuse him of being—a tough politician who jumps from position to position, always brilliantly energetic and opportunist, always moving in zigzags, darting with no sense of direction but making the best of each position he adopts. But it's far too simple to say he's a simple opportunist: he does have a number of long-term thoughts and he does give a great deal of long-term consideration to certain policies, principles and promises. We've promised to build 500,000 houses by 1970, that's an election promise he takes very seriously indeed and here he is prepared to think long term. He sees the objective and he is determined to take steps to ensure we achieve it.

I expect I could list a number of other long-term convictions. In addition to getting house-building up he's determined to keep our military presence in the Far East, even if it involves keeping penny-packets of British troops scattered over the world. He's also got a long-term conviction that we must keep our special relation with the U.S.A. and that Britain will remain great if we do. But in this Rhodesian affair his main concern is to prove himself right: to prove that he can win this as Kennedy won his Cuba.[1] It's winning that matters here, whether by settlement or by defeating Smith. He can't make up his mind, but he's going to go on hammering, manoeuvring, intruding, evading to prove himself right.

When we turn to the economy we are on much more insecure ground. What are Harold's long-term economic objectives in this country? Does he really want to go into Europe, or doesn't he? I don't think he knows himself. Does he want to devalue? He certainly doesn't want to but is he going to after all? He knew the answer a few months ago; he's not so sure of it now. And what about the long-term future of the Labour Party? Does he see it as a real socialist party or does he, like the Gaitskellites, aim to turn it into an American Democratic Party or a German Social Democratic Party? I see him more than most people and he probably talks to me about these subjects more than he does to anybody else. But he certainly doesn't confide in me any profound thoughts about the future of the Labour Party and I'm prepared to say as of today that I don't think he has them. He has a number of moral convictions: he's a perfectly sincere Sunday Methodist; he's against the legal reforms to deal with homosexuality or abortion. He has a conventional respect for the B.B.C. as a public corporation and won't allow advertising. He likes playing golf with ordinary businessmen; he's devoted to the Queen and is very proud that she likes his visits to her. He's really fond of Burke Trend and sees him as a close personal friend and confidant. In all these ways his moral values are extremely conventional. Yet, on the other hand, he tenaciously keeps hold of Marcia Williams, George Wigg, Tommy Balogh, Dick Crossman—a most extraordinary unconventional collection of personal advisers whom he plays off one against the other and prefers to use individually and not as a group but still retains despite the strenuous advice of most of the people round him. That's the picture of Harold Wilson I've got after this *Tiger* crisis. I'm more convinced than ever that he'll stay as Prime Minister but I'm also more doubtful than ever whether he's going to lead us anywhere, whether he has any real vision of a future for this country which we in the Labour Party can achieve.

His main aim is to stay in office. That's the real thing and for that purpose he will use almost any trick or gimmick if he can only do it. But I haven't completed the picture unless I add something about another side of him. His natural modesty has remained unchanged. So have his modest tastes, his simple liking of high tea, his completely unaffected petit-bourgeois habits, his determination to avoid any unpleasant scene with his friends or, indeed,

---

[1] In October 1962 John F. Kennedy (United States President from 1961 until his assassination in November 1963), officially acting without the overt support of America's allies on the U.N. Security Council, successfully called the bluff of the Soviet Government which had established and were furnishing long-range missile sites in Cuba.

with his enemies. All these are another side to him which exists alongside his opportunism and which help to make him a most disappointing leader for a radical left-wing movement. There are plenty of sensible things he wants to do, plenty of reforms he'll be convinced we should carry out, but radical changes are not in his temperament. He will simply shy away from them because he dislikes them.

Wednesday, December 14th

I woke up early with a sudden realization that the whole of the last section of my procedure speech was quite wrong. I had made it an argument that morning sittings were indeed the thin end of the wedge of a major, modernized reform leading to a brand new House of Commons. Douglas Houghton had warned me that there'd be protests about this and I suddenly realized it was a tremendous bloomer. So early this morning in bed I recast the whole thing. Then I rang up Harold and said I hadn't been able to talk to him last night. I had cold feet about a majority of twenty. 'Well, for God's sake, let's get the Chief Whip to muster the Government troops,' he said. And after that John really got to work and each of the hundred members of the Government got two separate messages—one from his P.P.S. and one from his Private Office telling him to ring back and personally confirm that he would be there to vote for the Cabinet decisions on procedure. Sure enough, this evening we'd never had such a turn out of the political bigwigs—they were all there and our majority was eighty-seven, largely due to Harold's last-minute orders.

I'd hoped to have the morning to finalize the speech and get the new peroration on paper. But this morning Harold kept me from 9.45 to 10.30 with a long fascinating gossip. First of all it's quite clear now that the possibility of devaluation this spring has altogether disappeared as the result of the improvement in the trade and unemployment figures. He's now convinced that the export drive is coming without the devaluation which Tommy had assured him was the only basis for improvement, and this has cheered him up. Then he had a long frank discussion with me about the reshuffle. I said there were two of his old friends who would have to go. He replied, 'It's not so easy. I can't trust the rest of the Cabinet and those two provide me with two important votes.' I said, 'But on really important issues you take the voices and not the votes. You only make us vote on unimportant issues and usually these two are in Fiji or somewhere on the other side of the world.' But then Harold went back to last July and said that when he was away in Moscow he had the Right against him and very nearly the Left as well. I replied, 'If you mean there are occasions when the whole Cabinet tells you not to do something or to do something—last July was an example—you can't avoid that by any Cabinet reshuffle.' It was interesting but we didn't get very far. Anyway my speech still has to be finished.

I left his room when I was summoned suddenly to the Party meeting, where I found Michael Foot in the middle of a great philippic denouncing the Government for signing an unconditional surrender to the Americans about keeping our troops in Germany. I had to sit listening to this for an hour and a half. Afterwards I protested to Manny and found that he had put the item on the agenda without consulting anybody and that when I was away with Harold Manny had got up and abused the Ministers for not being present; when the Chief had tried to protest he had slapped him down as well. This is serious. For some weeks I've been having trouble with Manny. He's suddenly grown old and very difficult. Of course it's true that John and I have been running the Party meetings and John has been running the Party, and Manny hasn't liked it. On this occasion he just took the law into his own hands because he deliberately wanted a good row about Germany. It will get us a terrible press tomorrow about another Labour Party revolt.

It was now one o'clock and I'd missed my two hours' of preparation. I had a desperate time sorting out my speech and getting it typed before I had to go and answer Questions and sit through a Statement on civil defence by Roy Jenkins and a Ten-Minute Rule Bill on Slagheaps. Then I was up and making my big speech. It was carefully calculated. In the long first part I described the utter futility of the modern House, which had lost its main function of controlling the Executive and which must reshape itself and redefine its functions if it ever wanted to be anything again. After that there was a deliberate anti-climax when I put forward my mousy little proposals for Specialist Committees, morning meetings, Standing Order No. 9, etc. Selwyn Lloyd, who followed me, was extremely amusing and didn't do any irreparable harm. Then we had George Strauss and Irvine and Michael English from our side bleating about the great traditions of Parliament and also doing not much harm.[1] I had to go out to the liaison committee where there was a flaming row between Manny, John Silkin and me about the morning's events, particularly about Manny's attack on me for not being there. Then I gave Anne, who'd been listening to the debate, a quick dinner and got back in time for the winding-up speeches. Thank heavens, Douglas Houghton was magnificent. He had to speak for exactly twenty-five minutes because we couldn't have the closure on procedural recommendations and he had to sit down exactly at ten for the Speaker to put our ten resolutions. Everything went well. The majority was eighty-seven and I felt we'd had a thoroughly successful day. But I also had an uneasy feeling that Harold Wilson hadn't liked it. He'd sat beside me while I made my speech and when it was over he had gone out. This feeling was confirmed by Tony Crosland. He leant across and said, 'Well, before anybody else tells you something different, that was a magnificent speech.' I was sure it was one of the best speeches I'd made and I also knew it was a great shock to Harold Wilson.

[1] Sir Arthur Irvine, Labour M.P. for Edgehill since 1947; he was Solicitor-General 1967–70. Michael English, Labour M.P. for Nottingham since 1964.

12 Talking to Stephen Potter at Hinton Manor, the home of Mr and Mrs Nicholas Davenport, 1968.

13 Working at home, April 1968.

14 An official Labour Party rally in Hyde Park in August 1968 expresses condemnation of the Soviet invasion of Czechoslovakia which ended the liberalizing administration of Premier Dubček. In the centre on the platform are George Brown (the deputy leader of the Labour Party), Jennie Lee and Richard Crossman.

15 On October 10, 1968, aboard the British warship *Fearless*, Harold Wilson (left) begins talks with the Rhodesian Prime Minister, Ian Smith (right), aimed at a settlement of the Rhodesian crisis.

Thursday, December 15th

By the time I saw the P.M. at 11.45 the row with Manny was really boiling up. George Wigg was clearly working with Manny and he had talked at length with the Chief Whip and then with the Prime Minister for more than an hour. Manny had sent Harold a long letter. The Chief was standing absolutely firm and refused to have any nonsense from Manny. He made it clear that he wants to get rid of him and he probably will. When I went in, the P.M. looked up and said to me, 'A great many people think you made a very good speech indeed yesterday, Dick.' I knew what this meant. Despite the fact that personally he'd been shocked he recognized that I'd taken a big risk and brought it off. Now my revolutionary reform speech had been accepted by the House so the degree of radical change I thought possible would now be acceptable to Harold. So at once I poured out my ideas and described to the P.M. how I wanted to link House of Commons' reform with Lords' reform. What we wanted was an overall reform of the whole of Parliament. Then we got on to the question of what would be the right Ministerial Committee. Harold suggested the Lord Chancellor, the Lord President, two Chief Whips, Roy Jenkins and Tony Crosland, and I told him we must get the right official committee as well. Then he warmed to it and said, 'Burke Trend must have a unit under Miss Nunn if a proper job is to be done,' and I said that would fit in very well. This was the most constructive meeting I've ever had with Harold. I got it because I'd won the night before.

Back in my office I dictated a memo to Burke Trend recording my discussion with the P.M. and planning a meeting for tomorrow.

Friday, December 16th

In the afternoon Burke Trend came into my office to discuss the note I had sent him about my talk with Harold. He agreed to build up a unit in the Cabinet Office. He likes my idea for planning legislation over the next four years, he also likes the idea of a constitutional reform for the whole of Parliament and he sees that it is going to strengthen the Executive as well as strengthening the Specialist Committees. He's a strange character—a nanny-like, very able, very sweet, very shy man. He strengthens Harold in all his most establishment tentativeness, making him on the whole less abrasive and less radical. On most things he's the opposite extreme to me in his influence on Harold.

Tuesday, December 20th

Cabinet. The most interesting item on the agenda was the future of *The Times*. The Government had already considered the proposal that *The Times* should be bought up by the *Sunday Times* and that one single managing director should control both. Because it gives the Thomson Press astonishing powers this proposal has been submitted to the Monopolies Commission and this morning Douglas Jay was to report to Cabinet. He told us that the Monopolies Commission was going to recommend acceptance.[1] Only Brian Davidson[2] is saying he wants more explicit assurances from the Thomson Press that they would respect the independence of *The Times* and above all that they would not integrate it in any way with the *Sunday Times*. Here was an interesting example of how Cabinet Government works. The future of *The Times* is a major issue of free speech yet we never discussed the issue in principle. It went automatically to the President of the Board of Trade who automatically sent it to the Monopolies Commission and then made his personal report to Cabinet. Government has really played no part whatsoever.

In the Commons this afternoon I expected to have a busy and anxious time since we had put down the motion for the Christmas adjournment of the House to take place at 3.30. What we hadn't foreseen when we did it was that at 3.30 the P.M. would make a momentous announcement on Rhodesia. Since the U.N. had finally approved sanctions we had to implement the Commonwealth Conference communiqué, withdraw all previous offers from Smith—including the *Tiger* offer—and announce that from now on our policy was No Independence before Majority Rule. Harold got up and was in his best form. His declaration was clear-cut and dramatic and it should have produced a storm from the Opposition as well as a prolonged debate on the adjournment. Indeed, Harold was so certain this would happen that in Cabinet this morning he proposed that Bert Bowden should be ready to speak in reply to Heath's attack. I said this was wrong and that if Heath spoke the Lord President should reply to his comments on Rhodesia just as he would have to reply to the comments on Vietnam bombing, German occupation costs and all the other subjects which would be raised on the adjournment. I got my way on this point because I was right on procedure, but Harold didn't like it. When it came to the point nothing happened. There was no blaze-up at Question Time and our Christmas adjournment debate was as much of a formality as ever I remember. I was greatly relieved since it would have been quite a responsibility to wind up that debate if the Tories had made it into a great occasion.

So with that fire unexpectedly extinguished I was able to go to the Christmas party given by the Labour peers. As I walked in I saw, sitting on the left, the ghastly living corpse of Attlee, now virtually stone deaf and almost inarticulate. Patricia Llewelyn-Davies said to me, 'Do go and talk to the old man. He wants company.' I had to say to her, 'I'm sorry, I can't face it. He has always hated me and I now hate him.' I'm afraid I walked the other way. The peers are an interesting lot of people, a much more attractive

[1] Lord Thomson, a seventy-two-year-old Canadian newspaper and television proprietor, who had been made a life peer in 1964, had bought *The Times*, subject to the approval of the Monopolies Commission, on September 30th. The *Sunday Times* now had a circulation of 1⅓ million.

[2] A solicitor (since 1969 with the Gas Council) and a member of the Monopolies Commission 1954–68.

gathering these days than the Labour commoners, and I shan't be the least sorry if I'm made a Labour peer on retirement because the House of Lords is the best club in Europe whereas the House of Commons is one of the worst.[1]

Wednesday, December 21st
The last morning prayers before the recess. This mostly consisted of Harold thanking John and me for what we'd done for him in the Parliamentary Party. I think he's genuinely appreciative of our efforts to change the atmosphere and to destroy the old war between the trade-union praetorian guard and the left-wing rebels. I think he feels that we have transformed the atmosphere and averted what could have been a catastrophic split on prices and incomes policy.

Next, to Buckingham Palace for a Privy Council. In my private audience beforehand I talked to the Queen about her royal television appearances and the proposal which the I.T.V. and B.B.C. have made to the Postmaster-General that they should alternate in future in presenting her Christmas broadcasts and the Opening of Parliament. This was a very good thing to put to her but I'm afraid I rather fluffed it at the beginning by talking about simultaneous cameras. She said she didn't want simultaneous cameras. I then said, 'Well, do you want the B.B.C. and I.T.V. to alternate?' She answered, 'It would be selfish of me not to allow this.' Plucking up my courage, I said, 'It's not a question of selfishness, Ma'am; you must do exactly what you want. That's what we would like you to do.' At this point she revealed that she would much prefer to keep the B.B.C. camera team she had got to know so well. She didn't want to face a new team from I.T.V. Then she mentioned a live broadcast which was said to be being prepared for the States. 'I don't know why I should broadcast live to the States,' she said to me. 'The Prime Minister was telling me the other day how he fluffed something and it was only all right because he was doing it at rehearsal before the live show.' And I said again, 'For heaven's sake, don't do anything you don't want. You must do exactly what you feel like. That's what the B.B.C. and I.T.V. want you to do.' Though I'd not been very clear, I felt for the first time that I might be doing something useful for her. We had a most pleasant time for a minute or two while the Ministers outside were wondering what on earth was going on because the private audience lasted for six minutes. When I came out I told Michael Adeane and drafted a note for Godfrey Agnew and I expect that's the last we shall hear of that proposal from I.T.V.

I had promised Marcia that I would pick up Harold and take him to the Transport House party. When I arrived at No. 10 I was wafted upstairs and taken to the far side of the house where Harold was eating celery and cheese and biscuits and tidying up with Marcia in a frantic last-minute session. I

---

[1] Crossman was offered a peerage by Harold Wilson at their last meeting together on 25 March 1974. The offer was accepted but ten days later, on 5 April 1974, Crossman died.

almost physically pulled him out. We drove round to Smith Square in my car. In the big room where the party was being held we found a few junior officials and their wives but all the seniors seemed to be out—not even Percy Clark or Terry Pitt was there, let alone Len Williams. So we did our duty, spent fifteen minutes drifting round and Harold agreed it was a good thing we'd clocked in. Then I dropped him back at No. 10. He was flustered and hurried and I was flustered and hurried. I suspected he dreaded my coming in and trying to lobby him about the Cabinet shuffle which is bound to come after Christmas. So we said goodbye and that was that.

1967

Sunday, January 1st

Let me reflect on my first five months as Lord President. How have I fared?
1. In relation to the Party outside I was to be the member of the Government who bridged the gulf which separates the Cabinet from Transport House and the rank and file. 2. In relation to the Parliamentary Party I was to work with John Silkin at introducing a new liberalized discipline which would satisfy the new intakes of 1964 and 1966. 3. In Whitehall I was to become the co-ordinator of information services *de facto* while avoiding any appearance of being a Minister of Information. 4. Finally, and in the eyes of the public most important, I must be Leader of the House and as such manage the business and introduce as much parliamentary reform as Members will take.

Well, the first of these jobs has turned out to be a complete flop. I am a member of the Commission of Inquiry into Party Organization but I don't run it and it's going to be utterly futile. As Harold's right-hand man, far from integrating the Government and Transport House, I am resented and suspected by everyone there.

On the other hand my job in the Parliamentary Party has gone fairly well. Of course, I always have to remember that John Silkin as Chief Whip with all his detailed thinking and knowledge of personal relations in the Party is responsible for detailed management and he keeps me pretty severely out of that. The Chief Whip has his own elaborate machinery and his own way of handling the Party and he doesn't expect me to dash in. I'm expected to limit myself to policy matters and leave administration to him, in particular the detailed discipline and reporting to Harold. I think we're working well together because I recognize this distinction between me as the Leader and policy-formulator and him as the administrator and disciplinarian. Together we've achieved the liberalization of Party discipline which we planned without any of the disastrous consequences predicted by the old guard.

There has recently been one very awkward consequence – the breach with Manny Shinwell. As chairman of the Party he was always a difficult cuss and he's never really liked me. We started off well by signing the concordat with him in August and things went smoothly when John and I began to impose the new liberal discipline although he didn't approve of it. But now he is being really difficult. I've described in this diary the last and worst row we had about his mismanagement of the Party meeting on German support costs. George Wigg is now working very closely with him; so far Harold has backed John and me against Manny and George. I can only hope and pray, though I don't expect it, that George Wigg will be out of the Government in the reshuffle next week and that Manny can be levered out of the chairmanship.

The third job – co-ordination of information services – was very nearly totally destroyed right at the beginning by Trevor Lloyd-Hughes's intrigues. Since then I have signed a concordat with Trevor under which he remains complete chief on the official level and my activities are strictly limited to the Ministerial level and this concordat has now been issued to Whitehall as a Cabinet document. It has also been announced in the House that Questions on co-ordination have been transferred from George Wigg to me, an announcement that was received without any murmur of interest in the press. Moreover Freddy Ward has now come into the Office and he's slowly getting his small unit together. I'm pretty sure that on the organizing of official briefs for Ministers' speeches my office will be able to be mildly useful. But I'm also clear that Trevor Lloyd-Hughes will limit my effectiveness as co-ordinator and will also poison my relations with Harold Wilson. Like Manny he really has become an enemy. He sees me as a threat to his position, he sits in on all my press conferences and reports adversely on them to Harold and I think he's going to make sure that I can do relatively little co-ordinating.

As for my fourth job, the management of the business of the House and the introduction of parliamentary reform, I was very slow at the beginning to take it over because I was so mentally and emotionally out of touch. I'm only just beginning to see what can be done in terms of planning the legislative programme but I'm much more hopeful than I ever expected. So that leaves parliamentary reform. Here I have made some real progress, largely thanks to my speech in the procedure debate. The fact that I got away with my demonstration of the ineffectiveness of the present House of Commons is in itself quite remarkable. I got everybody to say that the reforms I suggested were not too drastic but mousy and inadequate and more was needed to give back to the House its proper powers. So there is a reasonable chance of creating a political climate for a major parliamentary reform in 1967/8, including a reform of the House of Lords as well as of the House of Commons and linked with the rebuilding of the Palace of Westminster. I'm now quite hopeful that I may pull this off. I've spent a little time this holiday reading the history of procedure. A. J. Balfour's reforms were the last before mine.[1] I think there's now a real chance because those like Willie Whitelaw and Jo Grimond whose views I take seriously recognize that we must have a complete timetabling of all the legislation so that we can plan the debates for the whole year and create a reasonable framework to give everybody a far better chance of discussing Bills without endless all-night sittings. I can see a big change here and when I link it with the reform of the House of Lords and the transfer to the Lords of a lot of our boring but necessary duties I get a sense that I could leave something behind me when I retire from the Leadership.

I suppose the other thing I should look at in this survey is the amount I've

---

[1] Arthur Balfour was Leader of the Commons and First Lord of the Treasury 1891–2 and 1895–1902; leader of the Conservative Party 1902–11 and Prime Minister 1902–5. Much of the procedural reform at the turn of the nineteenth century was devised to deal with the troublesome group of Irish Members in the House of Commons.

achieved in my role as a senior member of the Cabinet without a Department and therefore with time to read all the Cabinet papers.

I can't say my successes have been very great. So I fear the conclusion is clear. I have been kicked upstairs. Harold found a powerful Minister of Housing using his position to interfere in general Cabinet policy. He nipped that interference in the bud and has given me a new job which is politically terribly vulnerable and gives me far less power and influence than I had five months ago.

Nevertheless what I can do is wait and watch. I can write my diary, I can read the papers much more carefully than before, I can advise him whenever I want. John and I see him more than any other Ministers and are often sitting alone with him while Cabinet Committees fret outside. I suppose most people think that we influence him enormously—I doubt whether we do. We shall see next week when we come to the Cabinet reshuffle.

Most of the changes made in the Government reshuffle of January 6th were at the level of Ministers of State. The size of the Cabinet itself was reduced from twenty-three to twenty-one. Fred Lee's office of Secretary of State for the Colonies was abolished and his duties absorbed by the Secretary of State for Commonwealth Affairs, while Mr Lee became Chancellor of the Duchy of Lancaster with responsibility for concentrating on the wages and prices policy. Arthur Bottomley remained Minister for Overseas Development but left the Cabinet. Patrick Gordon Walker returned to the Cabinet, assuming the place of Douglas Houghton as Minister without Portfolio and taking over the long-term review of the social services. John Stonehouse replaced Fred Mulley as Minister for Aviation, Lord Shackleton became Minister without Portfolio and George Thomson was appointed a Minister of State for Foreign Affairs with special responsibility for relations with Europe and negotiations for entry to the E.E.C. under the overall co-ordination of the Foreign Secretary.

Sunday, January 8th
The Cabinet shuffle at last. Let's see what effect John Silkin and I had by our series of talks with the P.M. We suggested he should replace Longford with Shackleton and drop Bottomley and Lee from the Cabinet. Well, he's gone some way on the first point by bringing Eddie forward to be Deputy Leader to Longford. On the second, Bottomley and Lee are out but they've both been given other jobs: Fred Lee a good one. He's always been an inveterate believer in the wages policy and he's now a Minister of State in the D.E.A. to strengthen the hand of Michael Stewart. That's a good idea. I'm only sorry that in moving Peter Shore also to D.E.A. he hasn't promoted him, but merely put him alongside Harold Lever, another new appointment, as Parliamentary Secretary.

The P.M. has allowed George Brown to shake up the Foreign Office by getting rid of Walter Padley and Eirene White, as I hoped he would. Now we have a new team in there—Fred Mulley and Bill Rodgers. That should do a great deal of good, and even the removal of Harry Walston won't do any harm. George Brown should be allowed to have his own team.

But he's hardly strengthened the Cabinet by substituting Gordon Walker for Douglas Houghton. This seems to me a feeble thing to do. Tommy Balogh tells me that Gordon Walker possesses a promise in writing of a Cabinet job. At least Harold has brought him in at the bottom of the Cabinet as a Minister without Portfolio. Moreover all the papers say that he won't inherit Douglas Houghton's supervision of social security so it looks as though, in response to my request, he's seen to it that that shall be taken over by the Lord President.

I've been doing this diary looking out at our first fall of snow. Prescote is magnificent now the grey skies have blown off. I'm sitting here in comfort and am therefore bound to wonder whether that fierce old Tory, my brother Geoffrey, is reasonable when he says that I can't be a socialist and have a farm which makes good profits. I tell him the two are compatible provided that as a member of the Government I'm ready to vote for a socialist policy to take those profits away and even, in the last resort, to confiscate the property. Nevertheless that isn't a complete answer. Having Prescote deeply affects my life. It's not merely that I'm more detached than my colleagues, able to judge things more dispassionately and to look forward to retirement, it's also more crudely that I'm comfortably off now and have no worries about money. I can eat, drink and buy what I like as well as adding 170 acres to Prescote Manor Farm. Anne and I have a facility of freedom and an amplitude of life here which cuts us off from the vast mass of people and in particular from ordinary people in Coventry. I am remote from Coventry now. I feel it and they feel it too.

But does Prescote reduce my belief in left-wing socialism? Part of the answer to that question is that my radical passions have never been based on a moral or egalitarian philosophy. It's been really an expression of my bump of irreverence, based on my conviction that governments and establishments are fools and that participation by the people will probably improve government in this country. Can I hope that if irreverence is my main socialist quality and not moral indignation, it won't necessarily be blunted by the marvellous kind of life we're able to live here at Prescote?

Wednesday, January 11th

I spent the day at Sandringham. When I got to Liverpool Street for the 8.30 train I found we were quite a party: Cledwyn Hughes, Ted Short, Fred Lee, George Thomson, and myself. There were five Ministers instead of the usual three. The explanation was that poor Godfrey had got three of us to go before he found that the old Chancellor of the Duchy, George Thomson, and the new Chancellor, Fred Lee, could only exchange their seals in the presence of the Queen, so they had been added to the list. I had arranged beforehand that at King's Lynn we would all get out and make a tour of the city as it's one of the five towns I'd chosen for model schemes to preserve the city centre.[1] My colleagues were not enthusiastic. After that we drove out to Sandringham where we found ourselves facing an extremely dull, Edwardian baronial house. We stood about in the main hall, looking at the Queen's jigsaw and a superb photograph of Queen Victoria. After half an hour in go the new and the old Chancellors of the Duchy to exchange their seals. Next I go in for my interview and I tell the Queen that Ted Short has brought along copies of the new stamps which I think she'll like better than the awful Wedgwood Benn series. She said she would be pleased and she was.

Then we had the Council. It lasted thirty seconds. When it was over we'd finished our job. The more I think about this mumbo-jumbo the more intolerable it is, the more I would like to get it changed. Why shouldn't I talk to the Queen myself about the possibility of having it all done by signature?

At lunch she was very relaxed. 'At Sandringham,' she told me, 'I feel a great deal more remote from London than at Balmoral.' They all love this place because it was Edward VII's hideout and has become a family hideout where they feel more like ordinary human beings. It struck me that it would be nice if one could arrange for the Queen to commute from Sandringham in future and to use Buckingham Palace merely as an office. Then she changed the subject and said, 'I see the Labour Party is beginning to admit that civil servants sometimes conceal things from politicians and are difficult to manage. I should have thought they always did what they were told.' (She's been reading the newspaper reports of the Labour Party's evidence to the Fulton Committee.) I said, 'I'm afraid that's not true.' And she then said, 'How do you know?' 'Well, Evelyn Sharp was my Permanent Secretary,' I said.

After our afternoon walk round the huge gardens I found her doing an enormous, incredibly difficult jigsaw. Her lady-in-waiting had told me she was jolly good at jigsaws and sure enough while she was standing there talking to the company at large, her fingers were straying and she was quietly fitting in the pieces while apparently not looking round.

As we left I felt this time it had been a great deal easier. I suppose the truth is that she really likes people she knows and every time you see her she tends to like you better simply because she's got more used to you. I remember once asking Godfrey Agnew whether she preferred the Tories to us because they were our social superiors and he said, 'I don't think so. The Queen doesn't make fine distinctions between politicians of different parties. They all roughly belong to the same social category in her view.' I think that's true.

Sunday, January 15th
Politics is hotting up. All the papers this morning had full stories from Conservative headquarters about the decision to destroy the image of

---

[1] The others were Bath, Chester, Chichester and York.

Harold Wilson and to crucify him as a promise-breaker and a crook. There was also a highly publicized exposure of George Brown in the *Observer* which turned out to be a complete anti-climax. However, it certainly increased George's standing with the general public. By and large we're a Government of pygmies compared not only with the giants of the past but even with the Attlee Government of 1945. That great big straw figure Jim Callaghan, who becomes bigger and hollower and more sanctimonious every week; dynamic George; little eager-beaver, india-rubber Harold—as a troika they are not much. But George Brown has dimensions—though he's illiterate and volatile he has spunk and imagination which make him stand apart from dreary acidulated figures like Michael Stewart. Could I stand up to personal attacks like those to which he's subjected? I shall know more about it in a week's time when the *Sunday Telegraph* publishes my profile. We heard a long time ago in the Private Office that their reporters were roaming round collecting material about me. Then Tam rang up Anne saying that this young chap was going to Scotland to get Tam's inside knowledge of my private life and he'd already been to some twenty people in the Ministry of Housing—from Dame Evelyn right down to the bottom—to talk about my behaviour as a Minister. Finally he turned up in my room when I had Freddy Ward there. He started by saying, 'I'm the man who's due to do a hatchet job on you. It's nearly finished and I thought I'd try some of the stuff out. My job is to show you're no good as Leader of the House and of course we do that by seeing what went wrong when you were Minister of Housing. What do you think of the following comments made upon you by the civil servants who worked under you, including Dame Evelyn?' I can't resist that kind of thing and I talked to him very freely off-the-record and got him to talk to Tam, who also extracted some more information about his assignment. Suddenly it occurred to me—why not write to Michael Berry asking whether it was his usual practice to send a young man off to do a hatchet story on a leading politician? I was careful to say, of course, that the young man may have got it wrong and the directive may never have been given. David Holmes duly took the letter round by hand and back came the reply that the directive had never been given and that the profile would portray me as a rough diamond 'with emphasis both on rough and diamond', whatever that may mean.

Thursday, January 19th
A very short Cabinet meeting at which Harold gave a lecture on leaks and infuriated me by giving as an example the story in last Monday's *Times* about the prices and incomes legislation. When David Wood came to see me I had briefed him carefully and told him that the only new Bill we were likely to have was a Prices and Incomes Bill but Cabinet hadn't decided this yet. Out of this David Wood had deduced a major Cabinet row and of course described it graphically. When the others had left the room I said to Harold,

'For God's sake, don't attack me in Cabinet in that way without telling me first. You must have known that David Wood had been briefed.' 'I didn't know it was you who had done the briefing,' he said. 'I thought David had picked it up from several people.' That shows the difficulty of trying to share press relations between the Leader of the House and the Prime Minister. I'm prepared to tell him everything I do but often he doesn't want to hear it. Yet if I don't tell him and then I do a briefing he draws the oddest conclusions. He is getting more and more leak-obsessed, regarding as a leak what everyone else does and regarding as briefing what he and Trevor Lloyd-Hughes do in No. 10. So he and I are not getting on very well in this particular line of business.

This afternoon in the House was really exciting since Jo Grimond's resignation as Liberal leader had been announced and Jeremy Thorpe was to make his first appearance. The Liberal Party had virtually degenerated into a personality cult of Grimond. Jeremy is charming and young but I doubt if he'll carry the weight to unite the Liberals.

After Jeremy had asked his four Questions, Harold greeted him warmly and then made a little joke at Heath's expense which set the House roaring for a couple of minutes. When it is printed in Hansard nobody will be able to see there's anything funny about it. However it nonplussed Heath, who on that very morning had read in the papers that the rating of the Tory leader had sunk lower than at any time for thirty years.

Then came my business Questions. I've been a bit worried about them for a week or two because there have been one or two comments in the press that I wasn't as well prepared as R. A. Butler and others of my predecessors. So I took special trouble on this occasion. I noticed that the P.M. waited beside me to see how I was doing. He never misses a press comment and he knew that my capacities were in doubt. I had a nasty problem about the galleries upstairs to handle. Apparently owing to shortage of staff we shall have to keep the public galleries closed during Monday morning sittings. However I seemed to get away with it.

Friday, January 20th
We were due to have our business meeting at 9.45. George Brown and I were both punctual and while we stood outside waiting, George told me how badly the Party had reacted to the P.M.'s promotions. He himself had warned him about the unwisdom of the three Minister of State promotions.[1] There ought to have been six and they ought to have been chosen quite differently. At this point we were ushered into the room to discuss the business with Burke as usual.

At the Cabinet Committee on Housing which followed I watched Harold once again trying to sweeten the Chancellor. This time his proposal was that

[1] Dr Dickson Mabon (Minister of State, Scottish Office); Mrs Shirley Williams (Minister of State, D.E.S.); Gerry Reynolds (Minister of Defence for Administration).

the local authorities should be instructed to build houses for sale because a council house for sale doesn't rate as public expenditure as a council house to let does. He seemed to be unaware of the fact that such an instruction would create the most frightful difficulty with the builders.

I stayed behind with Burke to try once again to solve the problem of Trevor Lloyd-Hughes and information co-ordination. We got nowhere. Having announced that I am to do this job the P.M. is fighting shy of the consequences in No. 10 and letting Trevor behave outrageously. As I heard from Gordon Walker today when I ran into him, he hadn't even been told that I was to take over social security. I took the precaution of ensuring that his files are transferred to my office.

By the way, I forgot to mention that just before I left my Privy Council office I was rung up by David Astor[1] who told me cheerfully that he hoped I wouldn't be too upset because they were having a little amusing piece in Pendennis's Diary on the back page of the *Observer* about the fact that I've got a very good contract from Thomson's for my diaries. I said that the diaries weren't going to be published and I'm still under contract to my own publisher, Hamish Hamilton.[2] All that's happened has been that Hamish Hamilton has been taken over by Thomson who would now be able to offer me much more favourable serial rights since they own *The Times* and the *Sunday Times*. Anyway the contract is for two *books* – my memoirs and a book on the British constitution. My diaries, I said, would never be published. 'Ah,' he said, 'that's interesting. By the way, Barbara Castle is having the same treatment as you, and George Wigg and George Brown have also been approached.' It will be interesting to see what will be in the *Observer* on Sunday about the diaries and in the *Sunday Telegraph* when they publish my profile.

Monday, January 23rd

A quiet day until the Committee which deals with party political broadcasts met in the evening. This is a really high-powered show where the Leader of the House and the Chief Whip speak for the Government, with the Leader of the Opposition and his Chief Whip for the Conservatives. There's one official from each party headquarters and the Leader of the Liberal Party and his Chief Whip. We are faced by Hugh Greene and Whitley from the B.B.C. and from commercial television by Bob Fraser[3] and Bernstein. This meeting should have been over quickly because, after long negotiations through the usual channels, the B.B.C. were proposing virtually no change in television and only one minor shift in radio. They only wanted to shift the

[1] The Hon. David Astor, son of the second Viscount Astor, editor of the *Observer* from 1948 until the end of 1975.
[2] Crossman eventually decided that his diaries should be published jointly by Hamish Hamilton and Jonathan Cape.
[3] Sir Robert Fraser, Director-General of I.T.A. 1954–70 and chairman of Independent Television News 1971–4.

party political broadcast from its present position after the evening news at 10.10 to 10.30 when the whole programme was over. Pretty tactlessly Greene said this would reduce the unpopularity politicians incur by being spatch-cocked into the news programme. Ted Heath said huffily that this was quite unacceptable and so did Jeremy Thorpe, who was representing the Liberals for the first time. I saw what an awkward cuss Hugh is. There he was stiffening and rigidifying and I remarked, 'Well, who knows. You may be right about the unpopularity of our party politicals but we can review that question in due course along with other big issues. Meanwhile, Hugh, let's keep things as they are.' Then I really went for him and said, 'You are revealing exactly why we have to have party politicals. It's because the B.B.C. thinks it knows so much better than we do how we should run our own propaganda.' But Hugh was stubborn and finally said, 'All right. As an alternative I'm prepared to substitute several five-minute programmes in the Light Programme for the ten-minute slots you are now getting on the Home.' Heath jumped in straight away and said he would vastly prefer that. Whitley, the B.B.C. administrator, looked embarrassed and rapidly agreed that all this should be considered in the big discussion later on. I think Hugh is a wonderful Director-General but he's certainly no negotiator. On Monday he united the opposition against him.

Wednesday, January 25th
We had N.E.C. in the morning but since nothing much was doing I went across to the Party meeting on German support costs. There weren't many people there and it was going quite quietly. Right at the end a vote was forced by Jack Mendelson[1] and someone challenged the peers' right to vote. At once Manny Shinwell ruled that peers could not vote on this issue. He was clearly wrong since a decision had been taken months ago that in the Party meeting peers were allowed to vote on policies common between the two Houses but not on matters affecting the Commons. I knew perfectly well that within a few hours there'd be a row blowing up. And it's true that during the course of the afternoon we had letters in from peers and from George Strauss. When the liaison committee met, John and I decided that this was the moment when we must counter-attack Manny for what he had done to us before Christmas in his sabotage of the Party meeting. So we got the other members of the liaison committee to tell him unanimously that his ruling was wrong and that this must be announced at the business meeting tomorrow. At first he said he wouldn't do this and he wasn't going to be told to admit a mistake or to apologize. I said there was no need to apologize. We would have a statement drafted and read aloud by Frank Barlow just announcing the decision of the liaison committee. This was the first occasion when Manny and I were openly at loggerheads. He said he wouldn't be treated like this by me. I said I was very sorry. He couldn't make a completely wrong

[1] Labour M.P. for Penistone from 1959 until his death in 1978.

decision to exclude the peers and get away with it as chairman of the liaison committee.

I was just going home when I ran into Barbara Castle, who said to me, 'Have you seen this message from the P.M. on the problem of the publication of Cabinet minutes and books by Cabinet Ministers? Apparently it's going to be raised tomorrow morning.' I went back into my room, opened my red box and there was a note from Burke Trend saying that George Brown was going to raise the issue and another from the Prime Minister to the same effect. I went home that evening somewhat disturbed.

The Prime Minister, Burke Trend and George Brown are all over in Paris for their crucial talks with de Gaulle. Presumably one of them spotted the paragraph in the *Observer* and thought it so important that they telephoned London to insist that it should be discussed on Thursday morning. Strange that Harold didn't give me any notice.

Thursday, January 26th

In my anxiety I woke up too early but the more I reflected the less I could see any chink in my armament. Harold's always known I'm going to write these two books and so have most of my colleagues. I've never concealed from any of them that I keep a diary which covers Cabinet meetings as well, and provided I don't violate the Official Secrets Act I can publish anything I like. The more I thought the less I could see anything wrong.

When we got to Cabinet the subject was raised right away before I could even get down to parliamentary business. Harold Wilson raised his head and said, 'There's something the Foreign Secretary wishes to raise.' Then George Brown in a distinctly modest tone said he wanted to raise something which had been published in the papers. Apparently colleagues were now actually signing contracts for books based on Cabinet secrets which would destroy the sense of collaboration without which effective Cabinet government is impossible. He had felt it was something he had to raise straightaway. George only took about three or four minutes and then the Prime Minister made a speech from a written brief which was thirteen or fourteen minutes long. I have no doubt the brief was prepared in Burke's office. By the end he'd managed to weave a web of hostility and surround me with it. Throughout, of course, he kept repeating that he wasn't discussing individual cases and that no names would be mentioned. But he added that he and George thought the present situation very undesirable and that a Committee to make recommendations should therefore be set up with the Lord Chancellor at its head.

At this point he stopped and Barbara Castle then raised the side issue of whether under Harold's proposals former Cabinet Ministers in opposition would still be entitled to have access to their Cabinet papers, not only for writing books but for an occasional speech. Harold admitted that the present Opposition was exerting its rights and that ex-Cabinet Ministers are publishing more and more Cabinet secrets in their memoirs. The only value of this part of the discussion was that Harold admitted that there could be no objection to Cabinet Ministers keeping diaries or indeed making use of them.[1] What was serious—as Harold put it—was that if a Cabinet Minister signed a contract with a publisher it might mean that the publisher would have an undue hold over him.

Obviously it was Harold's tactic—having got his Committee appointed and woven his web of suspicion—to close this discussion without a single name being mentioned. I thought, 'That won't do. There's nothing for it.' I therefore said 'Before you move on to the next business, Prime Minister,' because he was just going to move on, 'there is something I want to say to you.' Then I made a speech which I wish to God had been taped because it was one of those few speeches which changes things. By the end everybody round the table was roaring with laughter, relaxed, relieved and feeling they were having a really enjoyable time and the atmosphere of hatred and suspicion was dissipated to the winds. I started by saying that for years I'd been determined to write a book which would blow sky high Herbert Morrison's outrageous book *Government and Parliament*.[2] Indeed, when I thought I had no political future under Hugh Gaitskell I had started giving lectures at Nuffield College on this subject. I had signed a contract with Hamish Hamilton for a theoretical book replying to Herbert Morrison and also for my political memoirs in which all the evidence would be found. Then my life changed: in 1963 Hugh died, Harold came in and I knew I would have a chance of being in the Cabinet. When I got into Cabinet I obviously wasn't going to cancel that contract. On the contrary. By sitting there and keeping my diaries in full I was getting invaluable information which would greatly improve my book. In fact what had happened recently had been that Hamish Hamilton, my publisher, had been taken over by Thomson and new contracts had to be negotiated. Since my books were obviously so much more valuable now I was a Cabinet Minister, they were prepared to offer me more. That is why I needed the new contract. However, I saw the danger of

[1] In August 1975 Lord Widgery, the Lord Chief Justice of England, heard in the High Court of Justice an application by Her Majesty's Attorney-General (Samuel Silkin) for an injunction against the publication of Volume One of Crossman's *Diaries of a Cabinet Minister*, and of extracts from the diary, by Times Newspapers Ltd and by the publishers, Jonathan Cape and Hamish Hamilton. After nine days of hearings, during which evidence was heard from the Cabinet Secretary and affidavits read out from Crossman's former colleagues, judgment was deferred until October 1st, 1975. The Lord Chief Justice then declared that he could see no ground in law which would entitle the Court to restrain publication of these matters and that he had not been satisfied that publication would in any way inhibit free and open discussion in Cabinet hereafter ([1975] 3 W.L.R. 606; [1975] 3 All E.R. 484). Volume One was published on December 8th, 1975. A Committee of Privy Councillors, with Lord Radcliffe as chairman, had earlier been established to examine the whole question of Ministerial publications and they produced their report (Cmnd. 6386) in January 1976, proposing that a period of fifteen years should elapse before an author could regard himself free of 'approved rules and procedures governing Confidential Relationships'.

[2] London: O.U.P., 1954.

leaks from a diary and that's why I had kept it on tape and, as a security measure, hadn't let the tapes be transcribed. I also pointed out that the contract I had signed provided me with a large capital sum directly I ceased to be a Minister on which I would be able to draw for five years without publishing a line so I would be able to avoid the disadvantage of having to earn money directly after the Labour Government fell by receiving, say, £1,000 an article for malicious attacks on my colleagues. In all this I'd made no concealment whatsoever and I wondered what had happened suddenly to change the view of the Prime Minister and the Foreign Secretary. I concluded by saying that if the Prime Minister felt that keeping a diary was incompatible with collective Cabinet responsibility I would be the first of many to get out of the Cabinet and I would do so eagerly because it meant I should be able to start work on the books sooner. It was quite all right by me if I had to resign but I just wanted to know where I was.

I must say I managed to make it lively and amusing and Callaghan led the shouts of laughing applause when I stopped. The P.M., rather podgy and puffy, tried to join in the amusement. I could see what was going on in his mind. He had decided to say to George and Burke afterwards, 'I always told you my Dick would have some good reply to you which we hadn't thought of.'

There wasn't very much more after that. The Lord Chancellor's Committee was set up though he himself showed no enthusiasm for it, and said that nothing could come out of it. And of course nothing will.*

This evening I ran into Fred Peart. 'My God,' he said, 'I enjoyed myself listening to you. Of course everybody round that table keeps a diary. I do, and Harold was trying to scare us all. You blew it sky high.' Barbara's attitude was careful. She has kept a full diary for years and intends to base a book upon it. Roy was his usual retiring self. He intervened only when Dick Marsh said that he was bewildered and couldn't imagine how it was possible for a colleague to be sitting there and recording what was on in his private

* I was wrong about one thing—namely that I expected this item would not be recorded in the Cabinet minutes. But it is there including a report of what I said, which is very unusual in Cabinet minutes unless the Minister is introducing a paper. Here is what the Cabinet minutes say about my remarks. 'The Lord President said that in so far as the press reports related to himself they had no other foundation than the fact that before he became a member of the present administration he had signed a contract for the publication after his retirement from political life of a book of personal memoirs together with a study of Government and Parliament. It was intended to be a serious and responsible contribution to informed discussion of these institutions. He had carried the project no further since becoming a Minister apart from negotiating the necessary readjustment of the relevant dates of contract.' The last sentence is quite untrue. It was not the dates of contract but the capital sum of advanced royalties which had been changed and this I had very carefully and candidly explained. I had told the Cabinet that a book by an ex-Cabinet Minister on how the Cabinet works would be worth far more and sell far better than a book by a back-bencher. Yet not one word of all this is put into my mouth. I do not think this is a deliberate falsehood. Cabinet draftsmen are so used to putting in the Cabinet minutes what Ministers ought to say instead of what they actually say that they only half listen to our remarks. On this occasion the Cabinet Secretariat expected me to accept my rebuke in silence. They got the minutes all wrong because I was not silent as they expected.

diary for later publication. Roy added rather dryly, 'It may be better to have publication based on what is remembered and put down next day that on what is put down some thirty years later.' The truth is that most of my colleagues are preparing to write their memoirs because it's their only way of looking after themselves in old age. But I was the only one who actually blew up the P.M.

Of course it isn't a wise thing to blow up the P.M. I'm now in pitched battle with him and even more with Burke who I'm sure organized the whole operation. I hear that Burke sent telegrams back from Paris to the Cabinet Office giving all the instructions and Harold's brief was certainly prepared by him.

After this the report on the discussions with de Gaulle came as a curiously gay and irresponsible anticlimax. However it became clear that George and Harold both thought that they had begun the major job of charming the General. On the other hand, they admitted that he resented the notion of British entry because it would change the whole character of the Community. But it's my impression that whereas George is unchanged Harold comes back from Paris for the first time determined to enter the Market. Something has happened to him to make him get off the fence and most of his terms for entry are disappearing. Agriculture went some weeks ago, movement of capital has probably gone by now. Something seems to have happened during that de Gaulle interview which has made him work unreservedly for entry.

Cabinet then broke up and I talked very breezily to the P.M. who wasn't quite so breezy with me, before going back to my room to get ready for the business Statement this afternoon.

I have to be ridiculously efficient with the business Statement these days, briefed to the last because of all the press criticism that I am not master of my job. I cancelled a lunch with I.T.V., had a quick meal at Vincent Square and then went to the House at 2.30 to master an enormously complicated brief full of summaries of Early Day Motions and answers to all the small questions which might possibly be raised. It all went smoothly and I was in fine fettle when John and I strolled down to the Party meeting. We suspected that Manny might welch on us but we thought he couldn't get away with it. That Party meeting was a colossal blow-up and the political sensation of the week. It started quite quietly. I announced the business and explained that it wasn't really illogical for us to have the first morning sitting on Wednesday and then that night have an all-night sitting on the Consolidated Fund Bill, because that Bill was a back-bencher's paradise which had nothing to do with Government business.[1] Then Manny got up and made his statement about

[1] The Consolidated Fund is the Exchequer's account, kept at the Bank of England, into which all revenue is paid. Consolidated Fund Bills, passed in January, March and July of each year, authorize the grant of 'supply' to the civil and defence Departments. The July Bill also sets out in detail the amount and purpose of the appropriation allocated to each Department. Spring

the Labour peers' rights to vote at our meeting. He added that he didn't agree with it and would like to see the matter discussed in due course. At this point one or two people got up to try to speak, in particular Carol Johnson[1] whom the Chief and I had stopped from going to Brussels because he had been the Secretary of the Party for fourteen years and he could provide the evidence that peers have always been entitled to vote. Manny twice refused to call him whereat I nudged him and said, 'There's Carol Johnson sitting over there.' He was allowed to make his point.

Stanley Orme then raised the issue of an invitation which he had had to attend an Albert Hall meeting on the Common Market at which George Brown was speaking. Stanley asked whether this invitation had gone to all M.P.s and whether they should attend. I haven't had the invitation or heard about it. But Manny knew about it and probably intended Roy Roebuck,[2] a solid right-winger who was sitting on the other side of the room, to start the discussion. If he had been scored off on the issue of the Lords he would get his own back by causing George Brown to blow his top about the Albert Hall meeting. George Brown certainly blew his top and Manny then said the affair should be reported to the P.M. George said he would be reported to the P.M. There was chaos and then shouts of, 'Next business.' Finally I got up beside Manny and said, 'Next business has been called.' This forced him to put next business to the vote and when the vote was taken four-fifths of the Party were against him. Then he shouted at me and I walked out straight through the lobby to the P.M.'s room. 'Harold,' I said, 'this can't be allowed to go on. John Silkin agrees.' Harold said that George Wigg was down in Stoke-on-Trent but would have to be got at in order to control Manny. Meanwhile John Silkin was told to brief the press on what had happened at the Party meeting.

That evening I got a great deal more sympathy than I'd ever had before. For once I was the innocent victim of aggression.

Friday, January 27th

When I looked at the sensation the morning papers have made of our Party meeting I was not so hopeful as I was last night. I thought perhaps I should check with Harold and found that he is due to go to Huddersfield by the nine o'clock train. I rang him at 8.20 but of course George Wigg was on the phone.

Last night I'd been in the Chief's room when he was talking to George Wigg in Stoke-on-Trent and trying to persuade him to give his help in getting Manny out of the chair. I'd listened in to the conversation and wasn't

---

supplementary estimates, for the current year, are laid before the House in February and March, before the end of the financial year in April; the summer supplementary estimates for the new financial year are laid in the following June and July.

[1] Labour M.P. for Lewisham South 1959–74 and Secretary of the P.L.P. 1943–59.

[2] Labour M.P. for Harrow East 1966–70.

convinced that all was well. Yes, he would help, said George, but he was saying it in a crafty way. This morning George occupied the P.M.'s telephone line from 8.20 to 8.45 when the girl rang me back saying he was off the line and the P.M. was now in the bath. I said, 'I must speak to him.' Just after nine he rang back, telling me nothing could be done. I said, 'That won't do. John and I can't take this. Our prestige is at stake. You have either to get rid of Manny or of us.' 'No,' he said, 'we've got to let this thing blow over,' and there was a real altercation between us. Finally I said, 'O.K. Go off to Huddersfield now.' But I couldn't help resenting the fact that he'd had two long talks with George Wigg and not found time to have a chat with John or myself. After talking to the Chief I realized how impotent we were. We couldn't call a meeting of the liaison committee before Monday and we haven't yet persuaded the P.M. to take any action against Manny.

Saturday, January 28th
Down at Prescote I have a moment to reflect on this exciting dangerous week. On Friday there was a great deal of press briefing and other activity and as a result Manny staged a tremendous comeback in popular sympathy. I'm accused of handling Manny tactlessly, of behaving like an arrogant bully and there's a powerful profile in tomorrow's *Sunday Telegraph* providing evidence to show what a bully I really can be. However, to judge by this morning's newspapers, what was a mere fracas in the Parliamentary Party is now being transformed into a Common Market row. When I rang up Harold and finally got a long talk with him, even he had to admit that this was so. He had read the papers, he told me, and had further long talks with George Wigg and Tommy Balogh and they all now feel that it was George Brown who did the wrong thing and was to blame. And the P.M. added, 'I've had a Cabinet Minister threatening to resign if Manny goes.'[1]

Tuesday, January 31st
A special Cabinet was called at 9.30 ostensibly on Malta. But before we got to that the Cabinet spent an hour discussing the Shinwell affair. Officials were present but it was decided that no minute should be taken. Still, we had a long discussion. Harold stated that Shinwell had behaved outrageously and then added that perhaps George Brown had been unwise. George agreed that he shouldn't have accepted the invitation to address the huge Albert Hall meeting and then we discussed whether the eight Ministers whose names were associated with it should have them taken off the list. Quite clearly no one there was prepared even to consider Shinwell's resignation: they wanted the affair patched up and the Party to allow it to blow over. The Chief Whip and I remained completely silent during this wearisome hour. Right at the end I said we would carry on and that was all.
Cabinet then turned to Malta, which we had discussed briefly at O.P.D.

[1] Probably Ross, who was to speak in Shinwell's support at Cabinet on January 31st.

and which I'd thought about very carefully since. We are behaving abominably and Bert Bowden (who was away with 'flu when the decision on the cuts was taken) had agreed on that point. Yet if we concede the Maltese demand that we should maintain employment in the harbour, what answer shall we give in Aden, where I'm told 30,000 people have work related to the British presence, or in Singapore, where there are 40,000? I regret it but we shall have to stand firm and face the fact that we create unemployment when we make our major withdrawals.

Wednesday, February 1st

This was the first day of morning sittings and the Chief and I had made our preparations as carefully as we could. I was in a weak position because I'd been brought in a novice while John has a great reputation. So he didn't have much difficulty in convincing me against some of the Whips' advice that the right thing to do was to take the Consolidated Fund Bill as the business of the House on the first day of morning sittings. After all, this is always a backbencher's occasion and the debates go on through the night until the last victor in the ballot has had his say. John calculated that if he put any Government business on that day he would have to keep one hundred people for the closure if the Tories decided to prolong the proceedings. On the Consolidated Fund Bill, however, all he needed was forty people present to keep the House if a count were called.

I went in to see the beginning of the morning sittings. It was a successful start with sixty people there and a sensible discussion on the Ministry of Aviation Dissolution Order.[1] We knew the Tories would talk it out that morning and we were planning to give it another hour one evening and so get it through. Everything seemed to be going quite well. Our only concern was the fact that the House had been counted out the night before and as a result the Opposition had been denied their full debate on a prayer which they had put down against the Prices and Incomes Order.[2]

Thursday, February 2nd

As soon as I woke up I telephoned and heard that the House had finished at three a.m. That seemed quite all right until, on the radio, I learnt the news that for the second night running the House had been counted out.

Over lunch in my room I prepared for the business statement this afternoon. I knew I was likely to be in real trouble and I briefed myself as far as I

---

[1] The Ministry of Technology was to take over responsibility for the aircraft industry.

[2] Any Member may call for a count of Members present in the Chamber and if there are fewer than the quorum of forty, the House must adjourn. The procedure was abolished on November 16th, 1971, and now if fewer than forty are present, no decision is taken on that item of business and the House moves on to the next business. During a debate any Member may rise and claim to move 'that the question be now put'. If the Speaker believes that representatives of all sides of opinion have been able to put their case he may order the House to vote at once, but there must be a majority of 100 Members in support of the motion for the closure to be given and a debate brought to a sudden end.

could on the rulings about the situation arising from the counting out of the Consolidated Fund Bill. It was going to be a difficult business Statement followed by an even more difficult time when the leader of the Opposition would challenge our decision to put the Bill back on the Order Paper. Looking at the mass of paper I was disconcerted to discover that in fact there was only one precedent which applied to us. In 1952 the Tory Government was counted out on the Second Reading of the Iron and Steel denationaliza- tion Bill. Next day the Speaker advised the Tory Leader of the House that it would not be appropriate to resume debate on that day because it was a contentious measure. The Speaker had agreed that it could be put back but he had advised the Government not to do so. When I looked at this I felt that to call the Consolidated Fund Bill a contentious measure really was unreasonable and I would hope that the Speaker would give us the benefit of the doubt.[1]

The business Questions went quite well though they were long and tedi- ous. I sat down feeling rather surprised that the Tories hadn't touched it, but finally Heath got up on a point of order and raised the issue of the return of the Consolidated Fund Bill to the Order Paper. He made the case that it was a contentious measure and quoted the only precedent. To my complete consternation the Speaker got up and ruled in his favour. I was nonplussed because I had assumed that the Speaker was going to rule for us and I hadn't taken into account the possibility that he would simply back the Opposition. However, I had learnt from my brief that the decision was mine. The Speaker was only advising me. This encouraged me to start reasoning with him but I soon discovered that most of the House thought I was challenging his ruling and soon I was being howled down, not only by the Tories but by some of our own people, who were already moving upstairs for the Vietnam Party meeting.

Looking back there's no doubt I went on arguing too long in my determi- nation even at that late moment to get the facts on record. Of course the record didn't have the faintest effect because nobody cares what really happened. I was now in the dock for unsportingly challenging the rules when I'd lost a round in the parliamentary game.

Friday, February 3rd

I woke up to a terrible press—the worst I've ever had. The news stories about me were long, prominent, detailed and humiliating. I was made to look a fool. And my arrogant refusal to accept the Speaker's ruling was presented

---

[1] On November 26th, 1952, the House was unexpectedly counted out on the Second Reading of the Iron and Steel Bill. The Conservatives wished to take the business again on the following day, even before the customary twenty-four hours had elapsed, and they were at first advised, by a procedural 'fudge', that they could do so. However, the matter was sufficiently contentious for the Speaker to advise the Government not to press the point. It is interesting that in 1967 Crossman seized on the point that the measure was contentious rather than that the procedure was incorrect.

as the climax of a long series of clangers. First there was my ill-tempered row with Manny Shinwell at the Party meeting. Then I'd allowed the House to be counted out on two nights running. And finally I'd argued interminably with the Speaker instead of sportingly accepting my defeat. This was the picture of myself I read in the morning papers. It wouldn't have looked so bad if any of the Tory papers had told the story from the other point of view and treated this as a brilliantly successful Tory manoeuvre for spiking our guns on morning sittings. On reflection I think this is really what it was. I've been trying to bring in morning sittings against the strong conviction of the Opposition, against the wish of the officials, against the Speaker, against even the journalists who have to go and report them. And our own side is divided on the subject. To make matters worse it's a half measure which I would never have dreamt of introducing if I hadn't inherited it as something Herbert Bowden had willed on the Select Committee on Commons' Procedure and the Select Committee had recommended to us in its report. But though I see morning sittings as the cause of my downfall no one else in the country will after this morning's press. I draw the conclusion that I must stop playing the role of the great parliamentary reformer and try to save the situation by just quietly running the business of the House in a wholly uncharacteristic, self-effacing style.

Sunday, February 5th
Looking back over the last fortnight it would be an exaggeration to say that it has destroyed me as President of the Council and Leader of the House. But I shall have quite a job to live down this series of fiascos, particularly if the press goes on with its campaign against me. In today's papers they're still getting at me with the same indictment.

One of the last things I did on Friday was to send for John Mackintosh and give him a dressing down. John is a really brilliant professor of politics who wrote the first book on Prime Ministerial government and who now sits for the Berwick constituency. He's tremendously keen on Specialist Committees and has been one of the most ardent members of our parliamentary reform group. So I was furious when I noticed that he had put down on the Order Paper a motion objecting to the absence of a Scottish member from my new agricultural specialist group. Of course the reason for this is that on Willie Ross's request Scotland is expressly excluded from the terms of reference. I was feeling depressed and rightly or wrongly I gave John Mackintosh hell and told him that if he had any objection to what I was doing the right place to make it was not on the floor of the House but in my room with me. What I hadn't reckoned was that he would go straight upstairs to the journalists and give them a really juicy news story about yet another example of the arrogant bullying behaviour of Labour's Lord President. It is all over the papers this morning.

This evening I was so miserable that I did something I hardly ever do—I rang up Harold Wilson at home because I knew he too would have read it all in the press and I wanted to talk to him about it. Over the telephone he poured out a flood of 'don't worry' talk. 'It's never entered into my mind,' he said, 'to worry about this minor little incident.' And the more he consoled me the more I became aware that there was something to worry about. I think it was that conversation with Harold which alerted me for the first time to the full extent of the damage which has been done.

But most of it is exterior damage. Inside myself, though I wouldn't admit it ever publicly, I am convinced the affair is not my fault. It was Manny who caused the row in the Party meeting. It was John Silkin who was entirely responsible for the House being counted out on Monday and Tuesday. The only fiasco for which I was personally and entirely responsible was my argument with the Speaker on Thursday afternoon, and even there I was at a disadvantage because I hadn't been adequately briefed and warned by Freddie Warren. So I feel no sense of guilt or real blame. On the other hand, I realize that the job of the Leader of the House is to be vulnerable, to be attacked, to take it, to be a St Sebastian. I have been the victim of circumstance during the last fortnight and have got to make the best of it. It was interesting to find that as the P.M. talked to me his only rebuke was for the Mackintosh affair. 'You shouldn't do that kind of thing,' he said. 'You are the chairman of the governors of the school. You should leave the castigation of pupils to the headmaster. Keep yourself completely out of that.' That is sensible advice and I shall certainly do so in future. Secondly, I must regain my imperturbability on the floor of the House and make sure I never even seem to bully anyone. Thirdly, and this is very important, I must be careful in my relations with John Silkin. John is an extremely Jewish Jew, very much the son of his father,[1] and he has an enormous confidence in his own skill at personal relations. That's why he always says to me, 'You're the man who does the policy. I am the man who does the personal relations.' Now that is a very sensible arrangement and I ought to keep to it on my side as he keeps to it on his. This applies even to relations with the P.M. He sees him much more than I do and as Chief Whip he has a more intimate relationship with him. In fact, he's a henchman and one hundred per cent devoted to Harold and politically dependent on him. He's there to run the machine for the P.M. and if I get into trouble on his behalf, as I well may, he will probably survive me. He's much more likely to be still Chief Whip after I cease to be Lord President. I get on with him extremely well though I'm not sure I get on with his wife so well.[2] He is very good at handling me, very flattering, very comfortable, but he's reserved and watches me and is really more of a business associate than a personal friend. I have to retain that relationship while looking after myself since John won't wholly look after me.

[1] Lewis Silkin, who was made a peer in 1950 and, from 1945 to 1950, had been Minister of Town and County Planning.
[2] John Silkin's wife was Rosamund John, the actress.

Wednesday, February 8th

I lunched with Anne and then, at 3.35 when the Consolidated Fund Bill was safely on the Order Paper again and my crisis over, Douglas Jay rose to begin a debate on the Press. The subject had been coming up a good deal in Cabinet as a result of the Thomson takeover of *The Times*. Throughout Harold officially took a strictly non-interventionist view and supported Douglas Jay. But he had also asked Arnold Goodman and me to see if there weren't any practical proposals for preventing, say, the *Guardian* or the *Mail* from folding up. We had looked very hard for some weeks and found nothing practical. That is what Douglas Jay had to report at the beginning of the debate and it is something he could do very well. However Sir William Haley, when he read that there was going to be a debate, thought it was so important that he insisted on coming to lunch yesterday in order to make sure that I was speaking and would say the right thing. I told him I didn't take part in debates which ended in no decision. (See what Bagehot says about that kind of debate.[1]) Then, as our conversation went on it became clear that Haley too favoured a policy of complete non-intervention. When I asked him what the Government should do if it was faced with the certainty of the disappearance of the *Guardian* he replied quite roughly, 'If that happened it would be the *Guardian*'s fault and the Government should do nothing.' I've never met such a smug fellow as Haley. Imagine him urging us to let the *Guardian* disappear because he and *The Times* were safely washed up on the coast of the Thomson press.

After that to the Soviet Embassy with masses of plain Soviet ladies on display. I found myself sitting between the present Soviet Ambassador and the old Soviet Ambassador. Anne was on his right and Michael Stewart on her right. This was an ideal little corner where we really could talk freely and we had some excellent caviar and wonderful blinis before the terrible main course. I found myself testing out Soldatin, the ex-Ambassador, telling him about the trying things in my own life and asking him what was trying in his. When I said, 'Come on, fair exchange, fair play. I've told you mine,' he raised his hands in horror and I realized I had gone just too far for a Soviet Ambassador. Meanwhile there are the usual press leaks about George Brown's drunken behaviour at a Downing Street dinner last night and rumours that he's repeated the performance this evening. Let me add that I'm quite convinced by reading our official papers and by the atmosphere of those two meals that this Soviet visit is a flop.

During Mr Kosygin's official visit to Britain from February 6th to 13th, he and the Prime Minister apparently held lengthy discussions on the Vietnam war. At the very beginning of 1967 the British Foreign Secretary, George Brown, had called upon the Americans and the North Vietnamese to arrange a

[1] W. Bagehot, *The English Constitution* (London: Fontana, 1963), for which Crossman wrote the introduction.

ceasefire, but the initiative had been rejected by Hanoi and China and sca-
thingly received by the Russians. However a four-day Lunar New Year truce
was called on February 8th, and the Americans ceased bombing north of the
seventeenth parallel. President Johnson emphasized that only if the Vietcong
were to end their infiltration into South Vietnam would the American bombing
stop altogether, but as an encouragement to the Wilson–Kosygin discussions,
the truce was briefly extended beyond February 12th. The British Prime
Minister gave the impression that he and the Russian Premier might have been
able to act as intermediaries between the Americans and the North Vietnam-
ese; however their private talks at Chequers and a call that the Prime Minister
and the Foreign Secretary made at Mr Kosygin's hotel at 1 a.m. on February
13th produced nothing more than a communiqué calling for a speedy end to
the war.

Tuesday, February 14th

Cabinet today was extremely interesting. Harold started with a long report
on the Kosygin week, which I think I've described as though it was a mere
series of dinners with nothing really going on. This is quite wrong. There was
something on. They'd obviously used the opportunity for a British attempt
to get in on the peace negotiations in Vietnam.

Harold was in his more elevated form, telling us how he had 'the absolute
confidence of L.B.J.' and now had 'won the absolute confidence' of Kosygin.
Then he told us graphically how on two occasions—first on Friday and then
on Saturday—they'd been on the very edge of success and how it had been
dashed away and how disappointed they were. But, he added, one must be
fair to both sides—we must not be anti-American. On the other hand we
must not be anti-North Vietnam. What we should rejoice at is that the
mechanism for peace negotiations has now been established and in the
coming months they would succeed.

At this point he paused and I popped in two questions. 'Look, if you really
were on the edge of peace on Friday and then again on Saturday didn't the
bombing start again rather rapidly on Monday? Wasn't the explanation that
the Americans thought peace might be breaking out?' He was very sharp in
denying this so I pressed him. 'But look, so *very* soon afterwards?' Then he
began to backpedal a little on 'being so near to peace' and it came out that no
actual contact with Vietnam had been established during the five days. The
only evidence they got that they were near peace was the impression given by
Kosygin. It's worth seeing how the Cabinet minutes report the P.M.: 'We
had taken advantage of the opportunity to try to ascertain whether some
contact could be established between the United States and the North
Vietnamese Governments. There had appeared to be some prospect of
success in this attempt at one stage but in the end it had failed and the United
States' bombing of North Vietnam had now started again.'

What a contrast there is between those words and what Harold actually said in Cabinet. I vividly remember the P.M.'s claiming that he was twice on the edge of peace—by which he meant prolonging the bombing truce. The cautious record smooths out the exaggerations. As we left the room Callaghan said to me, 'You have an irresistible temptation to say what people don't like to hear. You certainly satisfied it by your behaviour at Cabinet.' I suppose I did. It's perfectly true that in putting that kind of question on that kind of occasion one upsets him most of all.

Wednesday, February 15th

After I'd had an official talk with Callaghan about his Department's legislative plans up to 1970 he asked me to go back to his room. When we got inside he said, 'I've decided to stand for Treasurer of the Labour Party and I've got the T & G on my side. What do you think of it? If I do this all my constituency votes will come to you. I've been advised by Len Williams that though I won't be defeated this year, next year I shall be in danger and I thought it was time for a move.'[1] 'Well,' I said, 'I'm thinking of resigning myself this year because there are too many Ministers on the Executive so your votes won't be any help to me.' But what I was really thinking was that this was a pretty suspicious manoeuvre. To think that as the Chancellor of the Exchequer in a Labour Government operating a prices and incomes policy the unions detest he has already got Frank Cousins's vote in his pocket!

We talked about Europe and I said that on the whole I was prepared for the great leap forward and I thought we ought to say we were prepared to sign the Treaty of Rome and negotiate afterwards. What did he think? He said he agreed. 'What about devaluation?' 'Well,' he said, 'Harold and I have discussed this and of course we would accept a 10 to 15 per cent devaluation as a condition of entry. Yes, that's all clear in Whitehall, that's what we face as a precondition for entry.'

We also discussed my position and how it had weakened. He said, 'You ought to be about more, in the tea-room listening to what people say and chatting as I do. Why can't you just be friendly with the chaps?' I said, 'Well, if I go slumming in the tea-room I shall probably talk shop in much the same way as I do in my own room. I have to behave in my own style—I can't change now.' He said how much he thought Harold was upset by what I'd said about the Kosygin meeting and finally he concluded as I got to the door, 'Of course, I know we're all material for your book.'

Wednesday, February 22nd

Morning prayers were cancelled and I had no chance to talk to the P.M. about Emrys Hughes's Abolition of Titles Bill.[2] This is quite amusing. I had

---

[1] Some members of the N.E.C. were elected by the representatives of the trade unions, others by the constituency section.

[2] Emrys Hughes was Labour M.P. for South Ayrshire from 1946 until his death in October 1969.

quietly talked to the Queen about it and received her advice. Yesterday evening I found a note in my red box telling me that Roy Jenkins had written to her and had given her exactly the same recommendations as I had—that Emrys Hughes is regarded only as a jester and that he should be allowed to proceed with his Bill because it would only be misunderstood if we stopped it. However, Michael Adeane had caught on to this and the Court had obviously felt rather differently about it. Adeane had gone to the P.M., the P.M. wanted it stopped, the Lord Chancellor had been apprised, the Chief Whip had been apprised. Ha, ha, there it was. I shall have to arrange it. This is a good example of the P.M. and the Queen hobnobbing together, the kind of stuffiness I don't take seriously. But for all my talk about my bump of irreverence, it doesn't go as far as the Palace. I went off to the Privy Council later this morning and saw the Queen upstairs in a dim, horrible little room with a picture of her corgi over her writing table. She and I had a little chat about stomach upsets but we didn't touch on the matter of Emrys Hughes's Bill because I had agreed not to raise the matter with her.

Thursday, February 23rd

An absolutely key Cabinet, the most important, I think, since the July crisis. We started with a report on Malta and none of us raised a bleat about the incompetence of our disastrous surrender. Thank God we didn't congratulate Patrick Gordon Walker on his success, as the *Guardian* has been doing.

Then we came to prices and incomes. The situation now is that the T.U.C. General Council have unanimously rejected the proposals put forward by Michael Stewart and Ray Gunter after our last Cabinet. They won't have any new legislation and they simply want a return to the voluntary system. Michael Stewart was asking for another meeting with the T.U.C. Executive on March 2nd. Ray Gunter weighed in against taking a firm line and he was backed very strongly by Dick Marsh, a T.U. man, by Fred Peart and George Brown. Unfortunately they were supported by Callaghan as well, the man who as Chancellor had insisted on the freeze but who now—influenced, I am afraid, by his candidature for the Treasurership—is watering it down into a wishy-washy policy. He was saying that the economic situation isn't nearly as bad as some people suggest and there is no reason whatsoever to be afraid of a disaster. My point was that economic *facts* are against us and Barbara Castle, despite all the pressure from Frank Cousins, emphasized that without an effective incomes policy we won't have a basis for a rapid increase in production or for a reduction in unemployment. The only possible alternative to an incomes policy, she said, is perhaps devaluation. Here she got a very cold shoulder from the P.M.

I can't blame Harold for letting us get into this appalling battle between the T.U. proletariat and the socialist intellectuals. He has been away for weeks and has let the initiative slip. And of course he has a traitor within the walls in the shape of Ray Gunter who has been a kind of T.U.C. agent. Well,

Harold didn't get out of it too badly. He's agreed to see the T.U.C. next week and try to come to some terms with them.

This evening we had our weekly meeting with the P.M. on future business. He was obviously rather uneasy about a Question that had come up this afternoon on D-Notices and his remarks suggested that the F.O. had been intervening, through George Brown, and that there might be trouble.[1] Last Tuesday he had referred rather abruptly and savagely to a Question about the *Daily Express* and D-Notices and Chapman Pincher had replied with a denial in the *Express*.[2] The Opposition had weighed in and today Ted Heath had asked for a Committee of three Privy Councillors to go into the matter. Harold had refused this and referred it to a committee from which the Editor of the *Daily Mirror* has now resigned, rather than handle it, and so the P.M. has had to give in and concede the Committee of Privy Councillors. I am wondering what our old pal George Wigg has had to do with this.

Monday, February 27th

This afternoon Denis Healey introduced his defence debate. He had told me last week that he had a strong and immensely powerful speech to deliver which really would convince the back-benchers and I'd made the mistake of suggesting this to the press at my Lobby conference. Well, he certainly hadn't. I dare say what he said would please the students of international affairs and perhaps members of the Institute of Strategic Studies. But it seemed to be addressed to McNamara[3] and it left our back-benchers sitting solemn, listless and bored.

Later that evening I had half a dozen back-benchers in to discuss morning sittings. But I found we were discussing decimals and defence and I got extremely alarmed by their mood. I have been feeling increasingly uneasy during the last ten days but the Chief has been completely resolute and has given an absolute assurance to the P.M. and to George that he knows there are only forty-five people who might abstain. I think it is more like sixty and Tam Dalyell has kept on saying seventy or eighty. Certainly the mood as I went round the lobbies today was not good. People were saying if we don't do it this time how can we ever oppose this bloody defence policy? And on the other side there were loyalists asking why the Leader of the House was allowing the bloody left-wingers to abstain and relying on the right to provide the majority? That was the mood tonight.

[1] The Joint Services, Press and Broadcasting Committee can issue a 'D-Notice' request to journalists not to publish an item affecting national security.

[2] Chapman Pincher, defence correspondent of the *Daily Express*, had reported that the practice of vetting overseas cables had increased under the Labour Government. It was alleged that the *Daily Express* had ignored a D-Notice request not to publish this story. A Committee of Inquiry was established, with Lord Radcliffe at its head.

[3] Robert McNamara, President of the Ford Motor Co., which he joined in 1946, from 1960 to 1961, American Secretary of Defense 1961–8, and since 1968 President of the International Bank for Reconstruction and Development.

Tuesday, February 28th

At Legislation Committee I pushed through the Decimal Currency Bill ready for publication on Thursday. In the afternoon George Brown was due to speak on defence. He made an excellent speech—courageous—and especially good about Germany. But after that the debate was a disaster from our point of view—not that the speeches really mattered. It was the malaise in the Party that was mounting up and I felt in my bones that we were going to get a far bigger abstention than John anticipated. I dined with Joel Barnett and Robert Sheldon—the joint leaders of our back-bench Economic and Financial Group; left-of-centre people, thoroughly sensible and respon- sible. But they are taking the lead and insisting on abstention and I felt angry and told them how outrageous it was.

After dinner I came across to Tom Steele[1] in the lobby—an ultra-right- winger—and he said, 'I'm bloody well going to abstain just to teach you a lesson, just to show you what we think of the new discipline we've got from you.' It was a disconcerting moment.

In his wind-up Denis talked about the split on the Tory side but he was hopelessly out of touch with his own people. Ironically enough the House of Commons' Services Committee had just arranged that the press would be able to get the full division records with all the names within fifteen minutes of the vote being taken. So as chairman of that Committee I'd managed to organize that the extent of our abstention would be advertised more than any previous Government abstention! At ten o'clock it was clear the fat was in the fire. There were sixty-two abstentions by any normal reckoning, and John could only obstinately calculate that his prediction was correct because the others were unofficial pairs.

Wednesday, March 1st

At first the morning wasn't so bad. I had my hair cut as usual at the shop where Ted Heath has his cut too and asked Mr Large, my hairdresser, what he thought. 'We think the M.P.s are better for showing a little indepen- dence,' he said. 'No, we don't think worse of you at all for the news this morning.' I was cheered and that morning I came to the conclusion we hadn't done ourselves any great damage. The Gallup Poll last week has shown that people in the country are very much in favour of defence cuts and I couldn't feel they'd mind their feeling being registered in the Commons. If only the Labour Party had kept calm I think the vote would not have weakened our position in any way.

After my haircut I went straight back to No. 10 for morning prayers. John argued very strongly that his calculations were right and then we all agreed there should be no inquest and no action before the by-elections next Thursday at Pollok and Rhondda. The P.M. didn't seem unduly shaken by

---

[1] Labour M.P. for Lanark 1945–50 and for West Dunbartonshire 1950–70.

the larger figure of sixty-two and it was agreed that we would carry on as quietly as possible in the Party meeting and clamp down the right-wing critics who we knew would be furious. John reported fully on the growing bitterness between Left and Right inside the Party and said it must be relieved if we were to have a reasonable chance in the by-elections.

This afternoon in the House we had a Statement by George Brown on Aden; it was much better than the last one because he didn't quarrel with the Tories. Then we went on to the Navy Estimates. At the usual time John and I went down to the liaison committee where we suggested that at the Party meeting no discussion should be allowed of the vote on the Defence Estimates. The best thing would be for the Prime Minister to make a short statement which would not be debated. When we put this to the meeting Manny Shinwell immediately said that discipline had broken down and asked what we were going to do about it. 'Are you going to take the whip away from the rebels?' he said to me. Reasonably and quietly John said, 'No, I am not.' He was supported by Malcolm MacPherson.[1] At once Manny made it perfectly clear that he would get out of the chair in order to make his view clear that we need a discipline which works. It was this remark which alerted me to a major crisis. John went straight back to the Prime Minister in No. 10 and told him that Manny was out for trouble. No doubt George Wigg alerted him too and made him realize that he would have to intervene himself and make a considered statement at the Party meeting on Thursday.

While John was busy that evening there was another fiasco on the Floor of the House at the end of the Navy Estimates debate. Denis Healey consulted George Lawson, the Deputy Chief Whip, and decided to talk the debate out for fear that a hostile amendment might be called. The result was disastrous, of course, and the management of the Party was accused of being panicked into a cowardly withdrawal. Poor John. George Lawson is fiercely against the new regime and he has been a great pain in the neck to the Chief ever since that occasion at the beginning when he allowed our members to abstain on the count.

Thursday, March 2nd

I had a rapid meeting with the Chief and Freddie Warren to sort out the Navy Estimates muddle and to arrange to have it put straight. When we got into Cabinet we found that the officials had all been ordered out and without telling me or John the Prime Minister said he would now have a discussion of what happened last night. This made me suspicious because it showed that he'd been got at beforehand. Callaghan, Cledwyn Hughes and Willie Ross (to name only three) had all gone to him and said that discipline had completely broken down and that something drastic must be done. Harold started with a long statement accusing us all of being out of touch with the

[1] Labour M.P. for Stirling and Falkirk 1948–70. He was Vice-Chairman of the Parliamentary Labour Party 1964–7.

back-benchers in the tea-room. He also accused Ministers of being disloyal to each other, telling back-benchers things against each other and leaking to the press. It was a long gloomy speech about the causes of the bitterness in the Party. Then he suddenly stopped and asked for views. I noticed he didn't ask either me or the Chief Whip to give a report at this point so Callaghan weighed in as chief complainant. He asked for a re-imposition of discipline since the new liberal system simply wasn't working. There followed a desultory discussion in which only Barbara Castle staunchly came out on our side. None of the other people who believed in liberalization said a word. All the comments came from those who said the situation was impossible and that something really must be done about it. Naturally enough there was no discussion of the P.M.'s rebuke to Ministers for attacking each other; all the speeches were full of discontent against John Silkin and myself. After the discussion had run for more than an hour the P.M. said, 'I think we'll close that now and turn to our proper business.' At once I said, 'But surely before we close it, we should hear an estimate of the situation from the Chief Whip since we've had such a lot of friendly advice from our colleagues?' The P.M. looked annoyed and said, 'Of course.' So John gave a short careful estimate of the situation heard in silence and I then added a few words.'I know that a number of members of the Cabinet are deeply opposed to the liberalization which John and I are trying. It would make it easier if you didn't reveal your opposition but gave us a fair chance by at least tacitly supporting us in public. It's intolerable to have Ministers attacking us in the *Daily Telegraph*.' (I said this because in the *Telegraph* this morning there was a statement 'by a senior Minister' which had clearly been supplied by George Wigg or Callaghan.)

The only thing which emerged from this discussion was a general agreement that the crisis would require a statement by the P.M. to the Party meeting. This was something I very much wanted provided Manny could be got to see that no debate must follow the statement. The Prime Minister should simply read the riot act to the Party.

As we went out I was uneasily aware that the P.M. hadn't warned John and me that he would be raising the issue of discipline – that his mood had clearly changed between Wednesday and Thursday and that he was now under tremendous pressure from the Wigg–Manny lobby. However one could at least say that he was still keeping his options open between the disciplinarians and the liberalizers.

There was nothing particularly interesting in the Prime Minister's Questions and we got on very quickly to the business Statement. It was very soon clear that the real threat was not from the Tories on the Navy Estimates but from my own side on decimals. As a result of the Cabinet decision which had been reinforced that morning, I had no room for manoeuvre at all. I had to refuse a preliminary debate on the White Paper and, as for the proposal for a free vote, I should have said this was something for the Chief Whip to deal with. Looking back now I can see that unfortunately I'd let the two questions seem a single issue and that this suited my critics. There were plenty of nice good people behind me who tried to help by changing the subject and I tried too. But whenever we did so one of the right-wingers dragged us back to decimals and played into the hands of the Tories by attacking me from behind and turning the afternoon into a major demonstration against the Leader of the House. I pleaded with them that this was something which ought to be discussed outside in the Party meeting, not on the Floor, but they wouldn't listen and it went on and on. In retrospect I think it's true that Bert Bowden would have got away with it much better by being negative, narrow and bureaucratic. It's my more expansive personality which makes me say more about a subject and got me into trouble this afternoon.

After this terrible scene I went up to the Lobby conference where I found all the journalists fanatical about decimalization. As the P.M. said to the Party, 'There isn't a vote in decimals in the country.' But there is a genuine interest among Lobby correspondents and M.P.s and for three or four weeks it will be a really fashionable subject. Anyway, the Lobby found it out-rageous that I should assert that decimalization was a subject which the House could not discuss freely with a free vote.

When I'd finished the Lobby I went downstairs and into the P.M.'s room to see what was going on. There I found that he had finished his speech for the Party meeting and it was too late even to show it to me, though there was no sign that he ever wanted to.[1] He was infatuated with its toughness—no-body had ever talked like this to the Party before, he said. He gave me a drink and we had a chat for ten minutes before he went upstairs to deliver his speech.

It was a tough speech and extremely well done in its way. It silenced the critics by smashing them. But no one could say it wasn't a brow-beating speech. And while I sat listening to it I realized that by giving leadership in this sense of the word Harold Wilson was creating a completely new situa-tion which put me in an almost impossible position because it meant the end of the liberal regime. The speech he made was a George Wigg anti-liberal speech and the fact that he made it passionately on my behalf didn't make any real difference to that.

Friday, March 3rd
I woke up to a terrible press. True enough, the P.M.'s action had taken some of the heat off me: if it hadn't been for that I would have been pilloried in every paper. As it was I was only the second lead story—another fiasco for Crossman, more and more indications that his position as Leader of the House is becoming untenable.

I was due at No. 10 at 9.45 for our weekly meeting on business. George

[1] See *Wilson*, pp. 337–8, for his description of his remark, 'very much in a throwaway reference', that every dog is allowed one bite but that, if biting becomes a habit, owners tend to have doubts about renewing the licence.

Brown wasn't there—only Burke Trend. On the way I'd already talked to the Chief and told him that after the P.M.'s speech we would have to fight the decimalization issue through at a P.L.P. meeting. We wouldn't like it but we should have to allow the Chancellor to address the troops, insist on a vote and carry on with a two-line whip. If people chose to have conscientious scruples about decimals rebellion would be the reason for expulsion. It seemed to me that Harold felt that decimalization was an ideal issue on which to discipline the Party. We were just about finishing our discussion when in rushed Mr Callaghan to insist on what we'd already decided, that we must fight on his side. What I hadn't told Harold was my own feeling that my position had become quite impossible as a result of his conducting a more reactionary leadership than anyone had ever previously dared to do.

After that there was a little meeting in No. 10 on the abolition of titles —Emrys Hughes's Bill which I've mentioned before. I had talked to the Queen about this at my last Privy Council but one. At the most recent one I was going to give her our advice formally when I was suddenly told to stop by Harold Wilson and now we were to discuss it together with Roy as Home Secretary who has an official status in the matter. Roy's advice had been exactly the same as mine—namely that we must let it be known that no steps would be taken by the Government to stop this Bill. If he wasn't a court jester, Emrys Hughes was a Commons' jester. Harold Wilson soon made it clear in an elusive sort of way that the Queen didn't agree and that he didn't agree either. However when Roy and I stood firm he suddenly changed and said that on reflection he realized the Bill ought to be debated. So on this he gave way to Roy and me.

I spent the rest of the morning preparing a few paragraphs on the discipline crisis which I would deliver at Warwick University this evening where I was addressing the students. I made sure that it was obvious that the tone of voice I was adopting—cool and reasoned—was at variance with the P.M.'s truculent and vulgar declaration. Then off down the M1 to Coventry where I read the discipline paragraph aloud to quite a nice gathering of Labour students before Anne drove me home.

Saturday, March 4th
I took a long walk over the farm to think things out and I finally decided that I must write a letter to Harold offering him my resignation. What had finally convinced me was the tone of the press on Friday and my own realization of the complete contrast between his attitude to the Party rank and file on Thursday and the Silkin–Crossman liberal regime—that our regime should be saved by a speech of that kind is intolerable. I also became more and more aware as I walked that the position of the Leader of the House is nothing more than a public posture. That's all there is to it and if your public posture is bad and unsuccessful the sooner you get out the better.

Sunday, March 5th

I've just finished drafting a letter to Harold which I will have delivered via Marcia on Monday morning. It runs as follows:

Dear Harold,
I would not be surprised if over this weekend you are beginning to wonder if, or perhaps when, you will require a new Leader of the House. I have been thinking this over carefully. We may get through without the need of a sacrificial victim. But the chances are we shall not. I am sure of two things. (1) If the change is made it should be done in the Easter recess. (2) It should be the result of a resignation, not a shuffle. To have its full tonic effect, the Party must feel that the man responsible for the failure has paid the price.

   Not of course that I'm vain or stupid enough to claim that my actions were a main factor. But my personality was a big factor. On the Friday morning after my row in the Party meeting with Manny I rang up and told you that if he survived the weekend as chairman my position would be gravely undermined. You gave excellent reasons for letting the storm blow itself out. It did, but the confidence the new regime had been building up and its authority were shattered in the critical weeks before the defence budget. The traditionalists were able to reawaken all the old suspicions −especially of me−particularly since it was well known that Manny had been helped in his press relations by George Wigg.

   Of course I may be over-gloomy. I doubt it. In the B.B.C. programme *The Week in Westminster*, Manny was interviewed by a stooge and discussed the breakdown of the new liberal regime. The fact that he and George now feel that they can, with impunity, conduct their vendetta in the open explains why the open counter-protest was launched against me last Thursday afternoon. And of course you realize that the toleration of Manny's original blow-off has enabled him to build up his popularity week by week while my authority has declined.

It's quite an interesting example of the ups and downs of politics that I should be reading this letter into my diary just seven days after the Sunday when I had such a happy, confident sense that we'd turned the corner. What happened of course was a series of catastrophes. It's been a disastrous week for Harold as well as for me though I should add that by Friday some compunction was being felt in the Parliamentary Party and one or two people who had felt outraged by the events of Thursday afternoon expressed some sympathy with me. Having drafted this letter let me try and guess what the result will be. Harold will of course seek to avoid the choice I'm forcing on him. What he's most likely to do is urge me to accept a switch and to make Patrick Gordon Walker Leader of the House while I take over all the Committees of which Patrick is chairman. He would hope that this will patch things up and leave the options open again as well as preserving John Silkin as Chief Whip.

John's position is the other thing I have to consider in this situation. I've been talking to him a lot on the phone this weekend and I think he's disconcerted by what I am trying to do because it's going to be difficult for him to stay as Chief Whip if I resign on the ground of the failure of the liberal regime we tried to introduce. And if he were to resign too that would be a decisive victory for the Right and also a decisive incentive for the Left to sharpen the conflict and split the Party. I'm not surprised that John wants me to stand and fight. But then I look at my own future and I say to myself that resignation on this issue would be an honourable action and it's much better to get out rather than to be reshuffled. If I get out I should be able to see the children, live here, get to work on my books and above all I would be anticipating and resigning before the series of economic disasters which I'm afraid are now coming upon us.

Well, there it is. It's the worst week I've had in politics. Not the worst week in the sense of inner unhappiness—strangely enough I haven't been unhappy this week at all—but I've been reflecting, seeing that we are coming near the real crunch, where the options which were kept open are closing in and where a decision just has to be taken.

Monday, March 6th
Directly I got to London I went to see the Chief and showed him my letter to Harold and promised not to deliver it until I had talked to him again.

Next I went through to No. 10 for S.E.P. where we were discussing the great new idea which has emerged from Nicky Kaldor's fertile mind. He calls it the Regional Employment Premium and it is another development of his S.E.T. The idea is a perfectly simple one. Whereas employers in Coventry or London would only get back 7s. 6d. per worker from the Government, employers in the development areas would get back 30s. 0d. R.E.P. in fact would be a subsidy designed to encourage employers in development areas to take on labour. We all thought the idea first-rate and soon began to discuss how to present it.

After S.E.P. I went out to lunch with Alan Watkins and came back in a furious temper. I turned up at No. 11 and blew my top to John about the impossible situation and how I wanted to get out of politics altogether. Dear old Charlie Grey was present and looked a bit embarrassed and disturbed.[1] I asked John to give me back my letter and told him that anyway I was bound to put it in. John insisted on one change, the addition of four words at the end making it clear that the alternative to my going would be to get rid of Manny. Indeed, after this amendment the theme of the letter was 'You must choose between Manny and me'.

[1] A miner and Independent Methodist minister. Labour M.P. for Durham 1945–70 and a Government Whip 1964–9.

In the House that night the corridors were full of rumours. I heard and the Chief heard too that a full-scale attack was now being prepared by Manny and George behind the scenes. They were putting the heat on the Prime Minister and simultaneously ordering the Chief Whip to repudiate our new discipline. John told me he is absolutely firm and I believe him. Unless Manny has been got rid of by the end of the month I shall resign. That talk with John was very important. He put some spirit into me, made me make that vital addition to my letter to Harold and encouraged me to fight back. I delivered the letter to Marcia and that same evening I briefed Coady of the *New Statesman* on how John and I were going to fight back and win.

Tuesday, March 7th
Anne came to dinner this evening and John brought his Rosamund and the four of us sat together. It's enormously important that we should get along and that his wife should like me and Anne. I'm not sure Rosie does. As for John he's very Jewish and he gives nothing away but he's enormously professional in his personal relations—even with me. I know, even from this week, that he has intimate relations with the P.M. of which he doesn't tell me anything. Indeed, he really tells me nothing of what he does in his room or whom he sees amongst the press—all that he keeps to himself. I'm much more open with John than he is with me. Nevertheless the central fact is that he is committed to fight and win this battle for the liberal regime even more than I am and his faith in it is even simpler and more ingenuous and more direct. All that is fine. The difficulty is that he insists on having his own extremely peculiar personal relationship with Harold and also has a peculiar feeling that he must get on with George Wigg and Manny Shinwell; in these ways he's more of a compromiser than I am. I suspect he finds me abrasive, awkward and impatient and regards himself as wiser, shrewder and more practical. There are times when I can't accept this judgment as absolutely fair.

Wednesday, March 8th
To my annoyance I had found this morning that I was due to speak in a G.L.C. election meeting in Merton and Morden, right down in Surrey.[1] Well, I thought, I'll try once again to get my ideas across because my speech at Warwick on the previous Friday had been printed nowhere and only a couple of lines extracted by the B.B.C. I suppose I was a bit peeved that nobody had thought it worth publishing. Now I knocked off another similar piece and sharpened it by saying that so long as the Chief and I were there, there would be no question of going back on the liberal discipline we had introduced. I made it as sharp as this because of what Manny had said in his interview in *The Week in Westminster* last Saturday where he had directly announced the collapse of the Crossman–Silkin regime.

[1] The G.L.C. elections were to be held on April 13th.

After finishing the draft I had lunch with Peregrine Worsthorne.* After that I had to get back to the front bench to hear another excellent Statement by Barbara Castle. Then back to my office to tidy up the draft of my own speech which had to be issued by Transport House. I had just finished when the Chief looked in. He glanced at the draft and said that it was O.K. I said, 'Right, I must send it straightaway across to the Press Office in Transport House,' and as I discovered later in the evening it was issued at 5.20 having been cleared by the Chief at 4.45 – though I knew that he hadn't had time to read it properly.

After that we went down to the liaison committee. Manny Shinwell said that over the weekend he had consulted with the P.M. and had put to him a form of words which he thought should be put to the whole Party. Then he read aloud, very fast, a form of words which I can't exactly remember but which basically said we should revert to the old conscience clause. This would mean that whenever the Party came to a decision and a three-line whip was imposed Members would have to vote the Party line unless it contradicted pacifist or temperance principles. I'd been forewarned by John about this because George Wigg had rung him up and dictated a similar formula and tried to make him agree it as something the P.M. had already consented to. There wasn't much more to be said and I wanted to get away from the committee and off to my meeting at Merton and Morden.

It was a filthy night and we drove through drenching rain. I sat beside Molly in a thoroughly bad temper and couldn't find my way, knew I was going to be late and was feeling embarrassed at the thought of having to read this damned piece of paper aloud to people who were really concerned with the G.L.C. election. I certainly had no idea as I sat in the car that I was going to achieve a dramatic transformation of the situation.

When I got there there were 120 people in a school hall and I thought I'd better start by reading aloud my press release. I was surprised to find how interested they were in problems of discipline and I then had a perfectly good routine meeting on G.L.C. topics.

When I got back to the House I found that the ticker in the lobby was surrounded by eager M.P.s who were all reading an enormous report of my speech that evening. In addition, apparently, there had been tacked on to it a statement from the P.M.'s office explaining that this speech was not an attack on Harold Wilson but something he fully approved of. Something was certainly up. People who met me in the lobby stopped to talk to me about my wonderful speech. Along came Tom Driberg and took me into the smoking-room and said, 'George Wigg has been here for an hour running you down and attacking you but I think your speech was wonderful.' Then Gerald Kaufman got hold of me and said, 'I've had endless trouble because David Wood of The Times interpreted your speech as an attack on Harold and the P.M. sent me to interpret it to him in the correct way and I got most of the

* The result was, once again, a good article in the Sunday Telegraph.

mistakes removed from David Wood's article. By the way, it's the lead story.' At midnight when I slipped out the Housing Subsidies Bill was over and I knew that what I'd done as a rather routine contribution to the G.L.C. election campaign was likely to hit the headlines next day.

Thursday, March 9th
Right enough, in *The Times* and the *Telegraph* my speech was the lead story and the *Guardian* made it an important back-page story. The fact that the Leader of the House had staked his career on the Crossman–Silkin liberal discipline meant that I had seized the initiative and was fighting for my life. This is what I woke up to this morning.

The attitude of my colleagues at Cabinet showed that they had also been impressed by the news. But we started with parliamentary business and at once plunged into a discussion about decimalization. Callaghan gruffly said it was all nonsense about the Party opposition and we'd better go ahead. Then the Chief gave a warning about the very strong feeling of support in the Party for the ten-shilling against the £ unit. Callaghan replied that it was only because they'd never heard the case against the ten-shilling unit and I said, 'Well, it's really a question of the image you want to present to the country. If you want to give a picture of strength and directness in Government then we push this thing through and I think we could probably get it approved for you next Wednesday at the Party meeting. If we want to popularize ourselves as respecters of Parliament then of course we can insert the offer of a second debate or a free vote.' There's no doubt what the Cabinet wanted. They decisively wished that Callaghan should both speak and wind up in the Second Reading debate and that there should be a straight vote at the Party meeting on the issue, after the Government had stated the reason why it wasn't prepared to concede a free vote.

All through Cabinet, however, I was brooding about the business Statement this afternoon and I concentrated on it once again over lunch. I was determined not to be dragged into any statement on Party discipline: I was determined that decimalization should not be mentioned because it wasn't in the business for this week. The Chief Whip told me he'd arranged to have twenty or thirty on our side getting up to ask about Eric Heffer's Bill to abolish live hare coursing and this should make life easy for me.

Harold's Question Time at 3.15 went quietly enough and then came my critical moment. I got up, Hansard records, to a round of applause. Could it be true? A great warm cheer from behind me? Was it out of a sense of shame? No, these people were cheering the speech I had made the night before. They were cheering the Leader of the House who they'd been booing and jeering last Thursday; they were giving him an ovation for standing up for the rights of the back-benchers and making the right noises compared with Harold Wilson's dog-licence speech. That ovation was about the most surprising thing which has happened to me since my speech on National

Superannuation at the 1957 Labour Party Conference when I received an ovation having expected to be thrown off the Executive that Tuesday morning.

After that the business Statement went perfectly easily. I was neat and concise and precise and none of the Questions on hare coursing materialized because our own people, having heard the ovation, knew the crisis was over and went out. Of course I realized that Shinwell would be infuriated. He went and blew his top to George Wigg and George was busy that evening feeding the press with long stories about my outrageous behaviour at the liaison committee and Manny's threatened resignation. Apparently I should have given him advance notice of my Merton and Morden speech although he hadn't bothered to tell me anything about the interview he gave on Saturday's B.B.C. review.

Late in the evening I went over to the House of Commons to sit in the television room with Tam Dalyell and watch the results of the by-elections at Rhondda West, Pollok and Nuneaton.[1] I knew we would do badly in Nuneaton because a ghastly young man with a beard had been selected to replace Frank Cousins.* The result was about as bad as I thought. Then came Rhondda West and that really was a shock. Twenty-seven per cent of the Labour vote had switched to the Welsh Nationalist. We had to wait till one in the morning for Pollok and at least we were number two which was not too bad.

Friday, March 10th
The press were clearly determined to make the most of the bad by-election results and rubbed the lesson in with huge stories about Manny Shinwell's threatened resignation with every kind of dirt thrown at me. There's no doubt that this press campaign had been organized by George and Manny and I at once rang Harold in a white fury. 'It's no good my coming round before O.P.D.,' I said, 'I want more time than that. I will be with you after O.P.D. is over.' At that meeting I had my first bleeding row with Harold. I told him his behaviour was totally impossible. I had delivered to him an important letter on Monday and he had hardly acknowledged it—merely remarking to me at a committee meeting, 'I got your letter. It's daft.' Then he had gone off to look for Burke. I made my speech mainly because he had completely disregarded me. I felt I had to do it in my own interest because George and Manny were conspiring to destroy me and I knew that throughout Harold had been in contact with them. 'Well,' said Harold, 'I spent hours

* I could not have been wronger. The young man with the beard turned out to be a first-rate constituency Member, Leslie Huckfield.
[1] The Glasgow Pollok by-election was caused by the death of Alexander Garrow in December 1966. Labour lost to Professor Esmond Wright, a Conservative, largely as a result of the intervention of an S.N.P. candidate who polled 10,884 votes out of a total of 38,652. At the Rhondda West by-election, caused by the death of Iowerth Thomas, Labour's majority of nearly 17,000 at the general election was reduced to 2,306. A Plaid Cymru candidate came second. Labour held Nuneaton, but the majority of 11,403 was cut to 4,054.

with George and had him on the phone and he's threatened resignation four or five times this week.' 'Why the hell didn't you accept it?' I said. 'Because of the D-Notice affair,' he said. 'We must keep Manny whatever happens until he has done his job on the D-Notice Committee to which he's been appointed as a Privy Councillor.' I had to admit that Harold couldn't have a row with Manny until that Committee had done its job. But I repeated that the situation was impossible because he had let me down so badly. 'No,' he said. 'What you say about George is always an exaggeration.' 'Shut up,' I said. 'It isn't. As you know perfectly well George has been poisoning the press against me. Look at the *Sunday Telegraph*, for example.' 'No,' Harold said, 'he assures me he didn't write that.' He was pleading with me and rattled and I was for the first time really angry with him. 'I hate this job,' I said. 'It's an abysmal job and I'll get out.' Nevertheless we patched it up and I promised not to do anything over the weekend. In particular I promised not to make any reply to the outrageous attacks upon me which Manny and George had organized in the press.

Sunday, March 12th

It's strange to think that just a week ago I was drafting my resignation letter and feeling absolutely desperate. Today the situation has been completely reversed as a result of my Wednesday speech. I'm now temporarily a hero, at least for the left and left-of-centre back-benchers, and regarded as their patron and protector against Harold. As for Manny's counter-attacks on me on Friday and Saturday they must lead, as far as I can see, to his resignation. It's only now that I can look back a week and see the low level I'd reached last Sunday. My position seemed to be irreparably confused by Harold's dog-licence speech. I'd been made to appear an upholder of orthodoxy and discipline against freedom. I'd been hopelessly compromised by Harold's efforts on my behalf. What happened during this week was first that Callaghan self-assertively came out on Wednesday at Question Time and made it clear that it was he and the Cabinet who had insisted on the decimalization decision, not the Leader of the House. Then on Thursday morning came the account in the newspapers of my own speech which created a completely new atmosphere when I made my business Statement and earned my ovation. All today I've been waiting for the P.M. to ring me up. When I left him on Friday he said he was going to Chequers and would communicate with me on Sunday. He hasn't done so and I haven't communicated with him because I really have nothing to say to him now. To judge from the Sunday papers he has ordered the Shinwell–Wigg attack on me to be stopped. I'm pretty sure he'll want me and John to make friends with George and Manny and work together with them and I suppose we shall be driven to do so. The one good thing is that he hasn't contacted me. I think he knows now that he's got to do something positive for me before he sees me next. Will he stop Manny and George bitching my liberal regime? If he won't I'm out.

Monday, March 13th

At lunch-time I heard that I'm summoned to a special meeting in the P.M.'s room in the House and that everything else must be cancelled. When the Chief and I got there we discovered that George Wigg and Manny were the only others in attendance. Harold Wilson had apparently spent the weekend preparing an ultimatum to us all—a five-page foolscap document laying down the precise behaviours we should adopt to each other. I read it through and as far as I can see it gives one hundred per cent support to John and myself. It excludes George Wigg altogether from any interference with us and it ties Manny Shinwell tightly down and expressly forbids him and George Wigg to brief the press any more against me. The only important concession he makes to the Party is that in future the Chief shall discuss with the liaison committee any discipline he proposes to impose before taking action. Otherwise it's a paper on how to enforce the liberal regime of John Silkin and Dick Crossman through the liaison committee and proposes an enlargement of the committee by two more elected members.

It was read through paragraph by paragraph for any comments and at the end of five pages there were no comments. All accepted it in total silence. Then there was some discussion. Manny said he was going to resign by the end of the month. He is out. George was silent all the way through. Manny and George withdrew, clearly licked, and John and I stayed behind to have drinks with Harold and Marcia as though they'd been solidly backing us all the way through. It was an easy atmosphere and we began to discuss how to get through the next three or four weeks without disaster. Before John and I left, the P.M. took the document back from my hands saying he didn't want anybody to have it. But I suspect that he didn't really want me to have it for my diary and will keep it for his book.

Wednesday, March 15th

In morning prayers the Chief Whip and I were alone with Harold. After Monday's ultimatum had been delivered there was very little to do. We discussed mainly the details of the code of honour the Chief Whip is now preparing in consultation with the P.M. We also had to decide how today's Party Meeting on the decimal problem should be conducted now that Manny has told us he will announce his resignation this morning.

The members of O.P.D. were waiting outside when we'd finished. It was a very important meeting since the paper we were discussing recorded the decision to go ahead with the purchase of fifty F-111 at nearly £2·7 million each. It was clear to me that this should be postponed until our big July discussions on public expenditure when we can consider it in relation to other factors. Taken early in this way it prejudged the whole of our East of Suez policy as well as our home priorities. George Brown mildly supported me. But obviously the P.M. and the Defence Secretary had fixed this between them. I tried to have my disagreement recorded in the minutes but I know very well that this is never done. I then urged that it should go to Cabinet but I was told that technically there is nothing for Cabinet to decide since the policy decision has already been taken. I was glad to see that Gerald Gardiner and Frank Pakenham were pretty upset when they heard the Prime Minister state this. After all, it means that by far the biggest decision on defence expenditure has been taken months before the July Defence Review which shows once again that Denis Healey is a lone wolf who runs very close with Harold Wilson and that Harold and he think they know what they are up to.[1]

We had to get across straightaway to the Party meeting on decimalization which Jim Callaghan had insisted on. He was confident he could carry the Party and he was quite right. Everybody knew you can't pretend that decimalization is an issue of conscience. Moreover, there hasn't been a word of complaint until weeks after the Chancellor had committed himself against the ten-shilling unit. His speech was unanswerable. Then there came fifteen speakers of whom the ten well-informed were all passionately for the ten-shilling unit. So when Jim came to wind up he had to make the practical plea that we are committed already and we can't afford a free vote on our side when there won't be a free vote on the Tory side.

The result of the vote was ninety for the pound and sixty for the ten-shilling unit with some eighty abstentions. it was about the best result we could hope to get and it showed that the liberal discipline was at least making some sense.

After that Manny said he would announce his resignation, and did so. Then Harold Wilson made a charming, skilled little speech praising Manny for his wonderful service while we had a majority of three and very carefully saying nothing about what he had been doing in the new Parliament. With that out of the way I went off to lunch in the press gallery.

Tuesday, March 21st
Cabinet. This was a special meeting at which we were to discuss the Wilson–Brown report on their tour of Europe.

When they'd made their introductions Denis Healey and Barbara at once launched their attack on the account of the meetings with General de Gaulle. Both of them complained that George and Harold had made too much of their success in these talks, in which, they claimed, they had made an immense impression on the General, who hadn't been nearly as adamant as they expected. Denis added that the record they had given us provided no reason to believe there was the remotest chance of getting in. I'm sure Denis was right but I also have a strong feeling that Harold and George want to make an immediate effort to enter and if they do the only way is to get inside first without negotiation and negotiate afterwards. Their idea is to get in by

[1] The order was to be cancelled in the January 1968 cuts in civil defence expenditure, thereby saving some £400 million.

1969. It would certainly be an enormous advantage if we could be there for that crucial agricultural review. But there would certainly have to be one devaluation if not two and we would be in real economic danger since we would be entering with the economy flat on its back, our growth rate low, our capital oozing out into Europe, and our factories being moved there because it's more profitable. On the other hand, would that matter politically? We would have completely outbid the Tories and we would be able to hold an election to confirm our success in 1969 before there was any hard evidence of the hardships we were due to suffer as the result of the devaluation.

This morning Harold was obviously testing Cabinet out. What he learnt was that only Douglas Jay is one hundred per cent against entry. Fred Peart didn't commit himself against trying, nor did Barbara, nor did Denis. I still think he will face only one resignation if he makes a dash to get in before 1969.

Wednesday, March 22nd
I thought it was worth looking in at No. 10 for the O.P.D. which was discussing Aden. But when I put my nose in the Cabinet Room nobody was there and I found Harold Wilson pacing up and down in what was for him real dismay. I've never seen him so rattled before and Michael Halls said to me, 'He really needs your help. I'm glad you're here.' What happened was this. The night before he had gone to see the trade-union group of back-benchers and addressed them in an interminable 45-minute speech which most of the members couldn't understand. This caused an outcry even from the ultra-right wingers who threatened to break away if there was any question of a prices and incomes policy with reserve powers. The whole meeting had been absolutely opposed to statutory prices and incomes. Then, this morning, at N.E.C. there had been an equally violent demonstration against prices and incomes with Jack Jones threatening to disaffiliate the Transport Workers.

For the first time he was realizing what the ruin of statutory prices and incomes meant. Walking up and down, he threw out to me the idea of forming a Labour Party independent of the unions, like the American Democratic Party, but then added, 'But we shan't be like the Americans, we shall be like that miserable French socialist party.' I said I thought we'd missed our chance in October and November of last year. He should never have left the D.E.A. to Michael Stewart and the only way we could have swung the unions would have been if he'd taken over the job and run it himself. No one else could have helped. 'Ah,' he said, 'Barbara Castle could have done it.' That interested me as much as it surprised me. I then told him that I thought the only course he could take would be to prepare for accepting a virtually voluntary system while warning the public in advance that if it doesn't work the Government will have to take other measures. But the one thing he couldn't do was to go back to Part IV and impose a wage freeze over again. 'No,' he said 'that's quite impossible. What we should have to do is to cut public expenditure. If they take too much in real wages we shall have to cut their schools, their hospitals and housing. This is what we've got to tell them.' 'If that's what you want to tell them,' I said, 'the great thing is to get it out in the open now, as soon as possible.'

Thursday, March 23rd
At Cabinet we were expected to talk at length about the Kennedy Round but it's one of those subjects a Labour Cabinet can't discuss—especially when Douglas Jay is in charge.[1] Anyway the P.M. was anxious to talk about the great new subject of the moment—the *Torrey Canyon*—the huge tanker grounded off the Scillies.[2] The moment the news came the P.M. was in action because of the effect on the Scilly beaches but also I think because he adores being in action—acting as the great commander organizing his forces. All the Ministers concerned adored rushing down to Plymouth and taking command of the Navy and issuing orders. This is the kind of politics politicians enjoy. They don't like sweating it out with papers and working out blueprints behind the scenes. They like being ostentatiously in command and being seen taking great decisions. So Cabinet had a fine time discussing the *Torrey Canyon* and setting up an emergency committee which would supervise operations over the Easter recess. I sat there laughing to myself because frankly I don't believe the politicians can do very much. Indeed it's possible, as the *Guardian* says, that what Harold has done by pouring all the detergent into the water on top of the oil has been to destroy the fish. But at least he has taken a big decision and I felt a bit psychologically out of it as I always do on these occasions.

After this I drove down to Windsor for a Privy Council. The Easter crowds were just starting out on the roads in lovely weather. In my usual private audience with the Queen I found myself discussing the future of the Royal African Society, and I'd been forewarned that I should agree that it should be given a charter. Then I said to her something about Emrys Hughes's little Bill for the abolition of titles. The debate had taken place on the previous Friday and Emrys couldn't even sustain it for an hour. I told the Queen there'd been not more than three or four people in the Chamber and it was interesting that a debate which even twenty years ago would have packed the members in was no longer a sensation and nobody took it seriously at all. The Queen said that she'd looked through all the papers on Saturday rather

[1] The final Act of the Kennedy Round, signed on June 30th, 1967, provided for tariff cuts averaging over 30 per cent on industrial trade between some fifty countries and for reductions in agricultural tariffs. The cuts were to be made in stages, beginning in 1968 and ending in January 1972.
[2] On March 18th an oil tanker bearing a Liberian registration ran aground off the Seven Stones rocks near Land's End, spilling a cargo of 100,000 tons of crude oil. The tanker broke up on March 26th and on March 28th the Government authorized the bombing of the wreck until, after two days, it was burnt out.

anxiously and found nothing there. I told her there were actually two reports—one in the *Guardian* and one in *The Times*—which said what a flop it had been. I couldn't resist adding that I was glad Roy and I were correct in our guess that if the Government took no action it would pass without notice. It was a mistake to say this since she didn't reply. Instead we turned to our Privy Council business which consisted of pricking the list of Sheriffs with a bodkin—a bodkin because Queen Elizabeth did it with a bodkin and the tradition has been carried on. Then I had to read aloud all these names and the Queen had to give us a drink. Jeremy Thorpe was there for his first Privy Council looking gallant and romantic. The Queen told me almost straightaway that she wanted to go and see her children and actually she only talked to Anne and myself about a new weedkiller called Paraquat, pointing out of the window to a field where it was being used. Right at the end she asked me how morning sittings were going and I looked at her in surprise. 'Oh, I'm sorry,' she said, 'I wasn't really criticizing.' And I realized how sensitive she is and that my face must have revealed my irritation.

Monday, April 3rd

I was still very gloomy as I travelled up to London but when John Silkin and I looked in on the Prime Minister at midday we found him in full bouncing beaming form, delighted with the *Torrey Canyon* affair, delighted in particular with the prospect of challenging Heath to a vote of censure and if he didn't put one down taunting him with his failure to do so.

On this occasion the P.M. was unusually frank about his luck. 'Yes of course we had luck,' he said. 'If the wind hadn't changed the oil would all have gone on the coast and we'd have been for it.' He was also extremely sharp about the behaviour of Roy Jenkins and John Harris, Roy's public relations officer. This came up when I put forward the suggestion that we should devote next Monday to the *Torrey Canyon* and John had agreed to offer a debate to the Tories—either a full day or a half day. I then said I thought the obvious thing was that Harold shouldn't speak unless Heath spoke and so the speakers would probably be Roy Jenkins and Tony Greenwood on our side. Harold said, 'Yes, Tony should have his chance now. He's done very well: he's impressed me. But Roy? I don't like to give him a big speech after what he did. The moment he took over on that Sunday afternoon he tried to create the impression that he found everything in a shemozzle and that no decisions were taken until he, the decisive Roy Jenkins, took command. That's an impression I resent,' he said, warming to it. 'He's rigged the whole Sunday press as well.'

There was a good deal in that complaint about the Sunday papers. Moreover I must add that having looked at the Cabinet minutes it is clear that no big decisions were taken the moment Roy took over. Indeed, I have a strong suspicion that it didn't make very much difference which of them was in command. Anyway the episode has caused a positive hatred in Harold of

Roy Jenkins and of the readiness of John Harris to put the P.M. in the wrong and his man in the right throughout the episode.

It was only after this that I was able to get on to the main issue which was whether he would back John and me on a full-scale programme of reform of both Houses of Parliament. I began to explain to him how far we had got in reaching agreement on a Bill to limit the power of the House of Lords. When I'd finished he said, 'That would be a very dull Bill. The press will say it's a bore.' 'Of course,' I said. 'But if it was a Bill which modernized the House of Lords as part of the modernization of Parliament and integrated the work of the two chambers, it wouldn't be dull at all. I can see a way of taking a lot of dull stuff off the Floor of the House of Commons, but if we're going to do this we must deal with composition. The simplest way of doing so is with a Bill to make all the existing peers who are active in the House become life peers and introduce a formula providing the Government of the day with a built-in majority. I know Frank Longford has sent you a memo,' I said. 'Yes, that interminable stuff I got from Frank Longford.' 'Well, disregard that memo. Listen to John and me and Malcolm Shepherd, John's opposite number in the Lords. We think we've got a practical plan for a really serviceable and progressive parliamentary reform provided we're allowed to deal with the composition of the Lords.' 'But there's a Cabinet decision against dealing with composition,' said the P.M., 'an absolutely clear and overwhelming Cabinet decision. You'd have to upset that.' 'Yes,' I said. 'But now we've got so far forward in parliamentary reform we can see that this reduction in the power of the Lords is really unnecessary since Lord Carrington himself has stated that the Lords can only use their powers once more without being abolished. The Tories also see the need for a different kind of House of Lords.' At this point, when I was just going to explain more about my plan, he jumped in and said, 'In those five minutes you've persuaded me, Dick. I'll back you if you put it to Cabinet.' 'No,' I said, 'I won't put it to Cabinet unless I'm sure of success and first I want to get the Ministerial Committee established. We've got to have the Lord Chancellor on it and Roy Jenkins and the Chief Whips from both Houses and perhaps the Scottish Secretary as well as me and Gordon Walker. We've got to work out a clear agreed scheme and put that to Cabinet, perhaps orally in the first case, as the big surprise measure for next session.' 'Well,' he said, 'I'll back you if you can do that.' And so we got out of his room, just at one o'clock after a full hour, with a real sense of achievement. It was, this time, my achievement. The Chief Whip demands my support for his discipline and he's willing to support me on this kind of thing although he's not particularly keen on it. I was able to go back to my Private Office and tell Freddy Ward that things were moving.

Thursday, April 6th
At Cabinet we had our second big discussion of the Common Market, this time on the topics of the movement of capital and regional development.

Douglas Jay put the case about regional planning extremely well. Entry to the Market would remove both the carrot and the stick with which we now get our industrialists to put a new factory in Scotland or West Wales rather than in Coventry or London. Hard pressed, Harold came out with a defence which captivated me. He didn't deny the dangers to which Douglas pointed but he said that what regional policy really gave us was a general expansion of capital investment and that's what we must get in the Common Market. Once it's known we are going into the Common Market the industrialists who are holding back now will put in an extra 20 or 30 per cent of investment. That will get the growth rate up. It's the lift we require to restore growth that will help the development areas more than any artificial scheme a British Government could think up. And Harold got so warmed and carried away that he made it absolutely clear that he's now a completely converted Common Marketeer.

Monday, April 10th
I went up to London very worried because of a talk I'd had with Ian Aitken of the *Guardian* on the phone yesterday. He'd rung me up to ask about Harold's attitude to the Common Market. I told him that Harold was enjoying all his elaborate system of Cabinet and Parliamentary Party consultations but in fact knew perfectly well that both the Cabinet and the Party are already converted to the new approach. '*Perhaps*,' I added (and this is where I went wrong), 'this is because he wants to conceal that the real crisis he faces is on prices and incomes, where he's been defeated by the trade-union group and our policy has been largely destroyed.' Instead of treating this as background information, Ian has printed it in full and stated that it came from a senior Minister. It was therefore labelled as a leak and pretty obviously a leak by me. This worried me a great deal and I record it in this diary because in my job I'm now doing a great deal of press briefing and I oughtn't to fall into this kind of failure. No doubt Ian Aitken had let me down badly but in this game it was my fault, not his.

The morning was spent in a crashingly boring Cabinet meeting on the budget. What is one to do at Cabinet when one hears the Chancellor's decisions and it's too late? What's the good of crying over spilt milk? The only comment I made was that I couldn't see why the surtax surcharge imposed in July had been dropped whereas all the other increased taxes had been sustained.[1] Barbara and I tried to get that changed but of course without any success.

Tuesday, April 11th
This afternoon we had the budget statement. I went in well beforehand, sat with the Chief Whip and watched the House filling. Although he had virtually nothing to say, the Chancellor made the appalling mistake of

[1] In July 1966 a surcharge of 10 per cent on surtax had been imposed for one year.

speaking for one hour and forty-five minutes and trying to blow up his minor into major concessions.

My reflections on hearing that budget were that the Chancellor had deliberately used the occasion to promulgate his new doctrine that we should abandon an artificial prices and incomes policy and revert to a higher rate of unemployment and higher cuts in public expenditure. But does Harold hold this view? I'm not so sure and I wouldn't be a bit surprised if he were planning a change at the Treasury fairly soon. He may really have left the Chancellor to kill himself by listening only to city advice and launching a deeply reactionary budget. But all this may be far too clever. I made a point of going to my room and watching the Chancellor do his television interview this evening. It was a superb performance. Nevertheless I had to remember that Jim himself had chosen to have the budget just before the G.L.C. elections in order to give us the maximum aid. Having done this he must take responsibility for the defeat which he has helped to produce and which we shall suffer on Thursday.

This evening a most important dinner-party with Malcolm Shepherd, the Chief Whip in the House of Lords, Eddie Shackleton, the Deputy Leader, and John Silkin. Unfortunately last Friday that idiot George Brown suddenly took it upon himself to order Eddie Shackleton to become temporary resident Minister in Aden during the end of the British presence. This is a disaster because he's a key figure in our reform group and we can't spare him. What was to be done? We knew we are to have the first crucial meeting of the Ministerial Committee next Friday so we decided over dinner to stage a deadlock between the Chief Whips about the methods of curbing the power of the Lords. This should give us time to think out a tactic.

Wednesday, April 12th
The press reaction to Callaghan's budget was dreadful. In a leading article in its new Business Supplement *The Times* pointed out that the Chancellor had now accepted the Paish doctrine[1] that the cure for our ills is a higher level of unemployment and a lower production target of 3 per cent instead of the 4 per cent we so proudly announced.[2]

At morning prayers this morning we discussed at length our preparations for the loss of the G.L.C. majority. We all foresaw defeat on Thursday, and agreed that the Prime Minister should deal with the significance of it either at Fulham on Saturday night or at Huyton on the Friday. The theme should be Nye Bevan's last speech about the test of democracy being whether it can take the unpopular decisions necessary to its survival.

Having settled this the P.M. launched into a discussion of Callaghan. He said that the budget lacked imagination and that Callaghan had never shown

---

[1] Frank Paish was Professor of Economics at L.S.E. 1949–65 and is now Professor Emeritus, University of London.
[2] In the National Plan.

him any draft or asked for any advice until it was too late. He was particularly angry because he was convinced that it was Callaghan who was responsible for the articles in the weekend press about himself as the crown prince and about his future policies for lending. Apparently he thought his great budget would make him even more of a crown prince but he'd come unstuck and Harold was being quite cheerful about it.

We then moved across to the Party meeting on the budget. When we got there there were only twenty people and even by 12.30 when the debate ended there were only sixty or seventy sleepy, tired colleagues at the meeting. Callaghan made a boring speech and Harold beside me kept on whispering *sotto voce* throughout. One of the things he said to me was 'I wonder whether he'll want to resign after this or want to stay on and take credit for the reflation when it comes?' And a little later he said, 'I wouldn't mind seeing him go. I wouldn't mind at all seeing him go this summer.'

Sunday, April 16th
A week ago I certainly wasn't conscious of the impact our cataclysmic defeat in the G.L.C. and the landslide pro-Tory vote in the other local elections would make on the country. In my head I knew that we were heading for a disaster but it just hadn't registered on me as an important event until I watched the results on Thursday. However, as Harold cheerfully remarked to me, it has no immediate importance because we've still got three or four years in which to recover. The results in fact are far more important as a fillip to the Tories and a strengthener for Heath's leadership than as damage for us. If the Tories had not captured London I think it would have been difficult for Heath to retain his leadership. He's now in an assured position and the Tories will go into action against us far more vigorously. That will have its reflection at Westminster as well. The defeat could only affect us if we ourselves made it do so. From what I've seen of Harold since the election he won't allow this to happen. He's remarkably cocker about the whole affair and almost sounds glad that Callaghan got what he deserved from the electorate as vengeance for his empty budget. I'm inclined to agree with him that the utter emptiness of this third Callaghan budget transformed a heavy defeat into a landslide Tory victory.

But I also agree with Tommy that Harold can't blame Callaghan for that. In Callaghan's first two budgets Harold took an enormous interest from January onwards—advising him and pressing him and sometimes ordering him to be more adventurous. This year, so Tommy tells me, there was hardly a budget file at No. 10 throughout January. By the time Jim consulted the P.M. it was too late to make changes and so it's the first genuine Callaghan budget.

Nevertheless, now that they're over, I don't think these elections will make any difference to us except perhaps that the Parliamentary Party may be less difficult to deal with. This week for the first time for months I've been bothering about the Party and not about my own position which has gone on steadily improving. It has also been strengthened by the easy election of Douglas Houghton to replace Manny Shinwell as chairman. He's a liberalizer who, I hope, will stand fairly well with John and myself though I don't underestimate how erratic his temperament can be.

So it's been a good week from my point of view. I've started once again enjoying my life at home without being emotionally agonized by life in the House of Commons.

Friday, April 21st

Instead of our normal business meeting with George Brown and Burke the P.M. said he would like to see me alone. This gave me time to think of the points I wanted to raise. First I asked him when, during the big Common Market weekend, we should discuss devaluation—would it be on Saturday morning with the officials present? 'No,' he said, 'that should bé on Sunday.' And he plunged into a detailed account of how he and the Chancellor had made the most elaborate arrangements to discuss devaluation at the last meeting of S.E.P.—when I didn't raise it. Obviously I was going to get no change so I dropped the subject and asked him about my decision not to stand for the National Executive this year. There are far too many ageing Ministers on the N.E.C. and last year I wanted to set an example for the simple reason that if some of us don't retire we shall be flung off in the kind of landslide which had flung Harold and me on to the Executive in 1952. Harold wouldn't let me because his plan then was to make me the Minister responsible for Transport House and give me the job of chairman of the Organization Sub-Committee. But everything has gone wrong. I'm not chairman of Org. Sub. and with the trade unionists in complete charge I'm completely excluded from any power. Nevertheless, I was surprised when he said that he thought it was really sensible for me to retire because he was going to reappoint a special campaign committee and as Leader of the House I would automatically be one of the officers on it. It was this campaign committee where all the serious work would be done.

Right at the end we just touched on the Common Market. Was he content with progress, I asked him? He said how pleased he was with the role I had played in the discussions and how he felt that the deliberate filibustering was now over. 'But what are our chances of getting in?' I asked. 'Well,' he said, 'perhaps in the last resort I shall have to see General de Gaulle alone and spell out to him the real alternatives. Either we come right in, I must say, or we are hostile members of an American bloc.' Then, as I was going out of the door, he added, 'I shall be seeing de Gaulle on Tuesday.' (He's going to Bonn to the funeral of Adenauer who died this week.)

Harold's illusions of grandeur in foreign policy scare me stiff. If he tries to talk to de Gaulle in this particular way it won't come off any better than his 'straight talks' with L.B.J. when he thought he was speaking on equal terms.

Tuesday, April 25th
For a change we had quite a big issue to decide at the Legislation Committee. Ages ago—in August 1965—Harold Wilson had persuaded the Cabinet to accept in principle the reduction of the fifty-year limitation on the publication of state documents to thirty years. Whitehall didn't like this and has resorted to the usual delaying tactics. Finally, I got a letter this week from the Chancellor himself which I read with interest and compared with the Cabinet minutes of 1965. There was no doubt about it, the Foreign Office had launched a counter-attack and was going to have even more material classified so that after the reduction to thirty years there would be even less material actually available. I sent a stinking minute back to Harold, with copies to Gordon Walker and the Lord Chancellor, arguing that it was no good passing a law reducing the limit to thirty years if there were so many exceptions that the thirty-year rule was really a hypocrisy. I had taken good care to issue this minute in a form which made sure it would be circulated around Whitehall and have maximum effect. The result was quite impressive. The moment I presented the Bill to the Legislation Committee George Thomson for the Foreign Office explained at length how they didn't want to hold back any documents and were only going to have the same reservations as they'd had under the fifty-year rule. The Lord Chancellor spoke in the same way and I managed to see that all these assurances were written into the Bill. I very much doubt if they would have been given if it had not been for the circulation of my minute.

Thursday, April 27th
At Cabinet the P.M. started straightaway by discussing the terrible dangers to confidentiality created by the publication of Nutting's book.[1] He assured the Cabinet that the Lord Chancellor's Committee was working on the problem of diary writers and publishers of books and I was referred to very genially by colleague after colleague but always with a sense of moral horror. Apparently the P.M. was content with this expression of collective feeling because he asked for no action at all.

Then we turned back to the Common Market and the P.M. complained of a terrible leak in the *Guardian.* Ian Aitken had announced the names of eight Ministers who had met together to concert their opposition. I suspect Harold was the only person there who really believed the Aitken story—a ridiculous, ludicrous story. But the P.M. is the greatest reader of the press in the Government and therefore the greatest believer in leaks. In this case he really got a hilarious response from the rest of us because we all knew there had been no meeting. The real trouble about the Wilson Cabinet is that it is a set of absolutely separate individuals who *don't* meet together and co-ordinate their work. Harold is the only conspirator.

[1] *No End of a Lesson* by Anthony Nutting (London: Constable, 1967). Sir Anthony Nutting had been Minister of State at the Foreign Office, resigning at the time of Suez.

Saturday, April 29th

Common Market Cabinet—day one. We were due to have two days on the Common Market—the first session in the morning at No. 10 and the second and third sessions being for a whole day at Chequers. Starting time was 10.30. I had to sit about at Vincent Square and read the papers and a piece from young Michael Stewart on devaluation, which wasn't much good, and be rung up by Nicky Kaldor, who for some extraordinary reason begged me not to raise the issue of devaluation that morning, and by then it was time to go. When I got to No. 10 I found all the officials sitting round the room. As we had agreed, each Minister brought one official with him and permitted him to intervene where he thought necessary. Of course it was a complete flop and made a hypocrisy of the whole morning session—at least until the officials withdrew. Then we started a discussion on the balance of payments with a very short statement by the Chancellor, followed by Michael Stewart. The first important speech came from Douglas Jay, who launched out on his massive unanswerable demonstration that entry to the Market would produce a balance-of-payments crisis in this country. By the time we stopped at one o'clock one thing at least was clear. Whatever the political and long-term economic advantages of the Common Market, entry was going to produce a quantifiable balance-of-payments crisis and one devaluation if not two. I suppose a morning which achieved that was a morning well spent. And with that clear in my head I rushed out and caught the 1.45 train to Banbury.

Sunday, April 30th

At 9.30 Barbara picked me up in her ministerial car and swept me off to Chequers. The morning sitting which started at 10.30 was supposed to be a second reading session. That meant that a lot of people made long policy declarations. Apart from Tony Wedgwood Benn, who is Minister of Technology and who has now been converted for technological reasons into an ardent Common Marketeer, no one seemed to have changed his mind.

I sat next to Harold at lunch and throughout the meal he kept on talking about the press and ribbing me for being too kind a Christian to the journalists and giving them far too much. I felt awkward because in fact I now don't see many journalists. I see Alan Watkins of the *Spectator* regularly but nobody else. Indeed, I doubt if I see more than one journalist a week apart, of course, from my official briefing of the Lobby on Thursdays. But Harold believes that I do and holds me responsible for any number of leaks and in all this George Wigg plays a great role. When he'd finished attacking me he launched a great attack on the journalists themselves and told us all that we should never talk to them or trust them—except the few who were good. I pricked up my ears and said, 'Tell us, who are the good ones?' And he said, 'Well, *The Economist* is quite good now.' 'What about *The Times*?' I said. And he replied that Ian Trethowan and David Wood are utterly hopeless and nobody should talk to anybody from *The Times* at all. 'What about the *Guardian*?' I asked and he answered that Francis Boyd is now wholly hostile and shouldn't be talked to. One I didn't ask about was Jimmy Margach of the *Sunday Times*. In this week's issue there's a really very embittered account, obviously given by an insider, of my ignominious failure to take over as Minister in charge of Transport House and of how I am now generally detested there. It hasn't come directly from Harold but it's certainly come from one of his contact men—either George (with his wonderful anti-leak machine), Gerald Kaufman or No. 10. However, I had the sense to seal my lips and let him go on talking now about a particularly scandalous leak in the *Daily Mail* which has revealed the full details of our decision to withdraw from the mainland in Malaya. 'That was dastardly,' said Harold 'and I know where it came from.' 'So do I,' I said. The main difficulty about it is that he wants to be omnipotent and feels very jealous of anybody else having contacts in Fleet Street, particularly anybody he considers as a rival.

When the afternoon session was over Harold turned to Burke Trend and me and remarked, 'In what other country in the world could the Cabinet sustain a debate for four hours at that level?' I thought the discussion had been pretty good in the relaxed atmosphere of Chequers but that seemed to me a high-flying claim. In fact nobody said anything new except Harold himself, who wound up very briefly by saying that this was an informal discussion and that therefore no vote would be taken and no formal conclusions minuted. Formal decisions would be postponed until next Tuesday when he would present a draft Statement in the same way as he had last November. Having said this he added that there would be a cold collation downstairs and no doubt people would want to get off fairly soon. Obviously his only concern this evening was to see that no decision and nothing approaching a decision was taken which could be reported in Monday morning's newspapers.

Monday, May 1st
Lying in bed this morning I read a characteristic piece by Ian Aitken in the *Guardian*. He claims he knows exactly how the Cabinet is divided. *Yes:* Crosland, Brown, Jenkins, Longford, Cledwyn Hughes, Gunter. *Yes if:* Wilson, Benn, Gordon Walker, Stewart. *Maybe:* Callaghan. *No unless:* Gardiner, Crossman, Marsh, Bowden. *No:* Greenwood, Ross, Castle, Peart, Healey, Jay. I find this a characteristically inaccurate piece of mixed leak and guesswork. The division seems to me to be: *Yes without qualification:* Wilson, Brown, Stewart, Jenkins, Crosland, Gardiner, Jones, Benn, Gunter, Longford. *No without qualification:* Jay, Peart, Healey, Castle, Ross, Marsh, Bowden. *Maybe:* Callaghan, Crossman, Gordon Walker, Greenwood, Silkin, Cledwyn Hughes. That makes ten unqualified supporters. Seven unqualified opponents, and six in the middle. But if one is to be realistic one has to add that this greatly exaggerates Harold's difficulties, since the six of

us who are in the middle are nearly all convinced that if any approach is to be made it should be made quickly with a will. This means that on the issue immediately before him Harold has sixteen on his side and only seven against. Lying in bed and reflecting on this list I felt bound to ring up Harold—a thing I don't often do these days. 'I don't often give you advice,' I said, 'but on this occasion I will. Your danger now is not too much disagreement but too much agreement—that you'll get no resignation on Tuesday morning. I just want to say that you must on no account tone down the draft in any way in order to win anybody over. Your sole concern should be to make a Statement which will have the best possible effect in Europe, not to make a Statement in order to placate any of your colleagues.' Harold replied, 'I think I agree with you.' But he's still not quite sure whether Douglas will resign. 'He's been talking to me as though he would,' he said. 'Well,' I said, 'don't worry about that. It would make quite a difference and you should want him to do it.'

Before I left Vincent Square the Prime Minister had rung me back and asked me to look in and see the draft Statement. 'You and George Brown are the only two who will see it,' he said. I checked that evening and he was right. So I went in to see the draft, which I thought much too long and cumbersome. I got it shortened at various points, but mostly he resisted, and wherever I could I took out any kind of weakening words which implied we were writing conditions into the Statement. He seemed quite pleased and almost grateful for the help.

Tuesday, May 2nd
Cabinet was called solely to approve the draft of the Statement Harold was to make this afternoon. There was no sign of resignation or protest: everybody worked very happily together, trying to improve it by minor amendments but nobody dared to move it an inch away from the form in which it had been drafted. I was tickled by the P.M. who started by apologizing that the draft had not been circulated the night before as expected or even this morning. The reason was that he had been writing it in longhand, he said, late into the night. When I heard this I must admit that I assumed it would look very different from what I had seen on Monday afternoon. But in fact it was the same draft and nothing had been done to it since then except to make the smallest possible changes. When Harold lies he does so with a good conscience. No doubt he had done some minor tinkering in longhand which gave him the excuse for this apology.

The great Statement on the E.E.C. this afternoon went very quietly.[1] What stood out was Shinwell's threat of relentless opposition and Heffer's courageous reply calling him an ancient Briton. All the conflict and tension

[1] 'Her Majesty's Government have today decided to make an application under Article 237 of the Treaty of Rome for membership of the European Economic Community, and parallel applications for membership of the European Coal and Steel Community and Euratom.'

in fact was on our side of the House. But the P.M. didn't put a foot wrong and I was able to say to him afterwards in his room, 'Well, that's a perfectly conducted operation.' But I didn't feel it was in any way a historic moment, mainly because I don't see that anything has changed in France and I'm certain the French will play us along and keep us standing in humiliation on the doorstep. The real question we have to answer is at what point we shall break off this attempt to get in and turn aside to the new policy of de-valuation+ which we shall have to impose and which will include a total withdrawal from East of Suez and a dose of old-fashioned insular socialism. Or will it?

The White Paper (Cmnd. 3269) *announced the Government's intention to apply for entry to the E.E.C., and both Mr Heath and Mr Wilson refused to allow their Parties a free vote on this proposal. Labour and Conservative backbenchers had tabled motions of amendment withholding approval from the decision, but on May 10th the Government's motion was carried by 488 votes to 62. Fifty-one Labour back-benchers abstained and into the No lobby went 34 Labour M.P.s and 2 tellers, 26 Conservatives, 1 Liberal and the Welsh Nationalist. A similar Government motion was approved in the House of Lords on May 9th without a division. On May 19th during the Commons Whitsun Recess (which Crossman spent in Cyprus) the U.N. Secretary General, U Thant, agreed to Colonel Nasser's demand on the previous day for the withdrawal of 3,400 U.N. troops who had patrolled the Gaza strip and the Israel–Egyptian border since the 1956 Suez crisis. On May 24th George Thomson was to fly to Washington for Anglo–American discussions, the U.N. Security Council met, and British ships and those of the U.S. fleet were put on alert.*

In a statement on May 24th the Prime Minister repeated the British Government's policy of regarding the Strait of Tiran, which Egypt had threatened to close, as an international waterway. If necessary the British Government would support international action to ensure free navigation in the area. On May 31st Mr Wilson had talks with Lester Pearson, the Canadian Prime Minister, and on June 2nd he visited Washington with the intention of securing a declaration from all maritime nations to support free passage in the Gulf of Aqaba. On June 5th, however, fighting broke out between Israel and Egypt, and in the ensuing Six-Day War Israel routed Egyptian and Jordanian forces and secured control of the whole of Jerusalem and the land between the east bank of the Suez Canal and the Israeli frontier. On June 5th Britain had declared her own neutrality, and the Foreign Secretary called for an immediate cease fire, but on June 6th President Nasser accused Britain and the U.S.A. of intervention in Israel's support. Iraq and Kuwait were persuaded to cut off oil supplies to Britain and America, and until September Britain suffered from a total Arab oil embargo. Richard Crossman returned from his holiday in the early days of the crisis.

Tuesday, May 30th

Going up in the train for the Cabinet meeting on the Middle East crisis, I had breakfast and throughout digested a short paper from the Foreign Secretary and an enormously long official paper of sixty pages from the Foreign Office. At Cabinet we started with lengthy orations by George and Harold. Harold, just off to Washington, said he was seeking Cabinet authority to go ahead and discuss with L.B.J. full British participation in an Anglo-American initiative. The first thing would be to get the declaration in the United Nations. But if that failed we and the Americans would organize a joint maritime force for action, designed to hold back the Israeli army. Indeed, throughout their speeches George and Harold were constantly urging that we had to do something to stop an Israeli attack. George threw in the news that in talking to the Israeli Ambassador about Israel's possible go-it-alone policy, he had used the most violent language and put the heat on with the strongest force he could. I must say I found this line of talk singularly inane. If you prevent the Israeli soldiers taking the action they think necessary and say that if they go to war we shan't help them, then of course you assume responsibility for action yourself. Harold mentioned that in their talks with Eban[1] the Americans had used the phrase, 'The only danger of your being left alone is if you go it alone.' He seemed quite unaware of the implication which is that the Americans will fully back the Israelis if they seek by military force to maintain the freedom of the Gulf of Aqaba.

The first person to reply to the P.M. and the Foreign Secretary was Denis Healey, who made a speech with every word of which I warmly agreed. He emphasized that everything now depended on our posture. On no account must we seem to be concerting with the Americans an Anglo-American military adventure designed to re-assert Western suzerainty in the Middle East. If we did so we would line up the whole Afro-Asian block in the United Nations against us. Moreover we hadn't got the military force to do it. He added finally that if we went in for such a gamble the Americans would give us titular support and then let us down. There might be one or two mine-sweepers from Denmark and Canada but by and large it would be an exclusively British military effort with nothing better than American backing from a distance. I felt a number of people were waiting to hear what I had to say since I had been away in the previous week and I'm fairly knowledge-able about the Middle East. I started by saying that I thought the talk about an Israeli military attack was exaggerated. 'The immediate military crisis is over. The danger now is that the Israelis will bide their time and the hawks will then find another opportunity in, say, six or eight months to launch a pre-emptive strike and restore the situation.' What we had to fear was an ignominious diplomatic defeat in the sense that we wouldn't achieve very much for the Israelis by our intervention. I then said that we had to face it

[1] Abba Eban, Deputy Prime Minister of Israel 1963–6 and Minister of Foreign Affairs from 1966 to 1974.

that Nasser's action had achieved a considerable victory for the Arabs and the Russians and shifted the balance of power. The only gains they'd been able to retain after the Sinai war were the opening of the Strait of Tiran and of Sharm el Sheikh. With the Russian aid Nasser has torn this back twenty-four hours. I didn't see how we and the Americans could eject the Egyptians and the Russians by military force and we certainly weren't going to negotiate them out of their new positions. I concluded that though I was passionately pro-Israeli I agreed with Denis Healey about the danger of being isolated and classed as a Western imperialist trying vainly to reassert our suzerainty when we hadn't the military force to do so.

My remarks deeply shocked Bowden and Gunter, who turned out to be the two totally committed Zionists in the Cabinet, prepared to take unilateral British action to force the Strait of Tiran. They were the hawks who were trying to push Harold and George into stronger action. I saw Tony Greenwood, just as fanatical a Zionist and a wonderful speech-maker at Zionist gatherings, cave in when it came to the point and he was asked his opinion. He supported me. In the previous Cabinets the opposition had been led by Barbara Castle and Roy Jenkins—on this occasion it was led by Denis Healey and myself. Wedgy Benn was wholly on our side. So were Roy Jenkins and Tony Crosland and, more cautiously, Jim Callaghan and Michael Stewart. This was a case where Prime Ministerial government certainly didn't work. Faced by this resistance the P.M. drew in his horns. He accepted Cabinet's instructions that he should try to extract support from L.B.J. for the declaration by the maritime powers, first in the U.N. and, if not there, outside. Apart from that there should be some contingency probing—some attempt to find out who would contribute to an international force, what the force should consist of and how it would work. It was made clear that until it was certain there was an effective force we would not be committed to any international action and that if it turned out to be merely an Anglo-American force Britain should not take part.

Monday, June 5th
The first thing I saw in London was the early edition of the evening paper announcing that the war in Israel had started. So the statement yesterday by Moshe Dayan that the tension was now relaxed and some of the Israeli reservists had been sent back to work was just a cover. The pre-emptive strike had started after all. I felt a dullish kind of shock.

I spent most of today feeling desperate and distraught because of the war news. In the House George Brown made his first Statement on the situation and it was absolutely first-rate. He declared that Britain must remain completely neutral and it was clear that as the week went on there would be more and more rowing on the back benches. There was, I gather, a foretaste of this on tonight's *Panorama* programme where the viewers were shown Christopher Mayhew interviewing Colonel Nasser in the friendliest possible way and Manny Shinwell staging a ferocious row on behalf of the Israelis. Considering that he, as Minister of War, supported all Ernest Bevin's worst excesses in Palestine it's staggering to listen to speeches he now makes.

Back from the Chamber in my room I was delighted to have a visit from Remez, the Israeli Ambassador, who had asked to see me. He gave me a very full and accurate briefing on how hostilities started. I asked him about Israeli intentions towards Jordan and he replied that they intended to occupy the hills of Samaria.

Tuesday, June 6th

At Cabinet we had a desultory discussion on the Egyptian-Israeli war, where it was already clear who was winning. No one had a word now to say against the neutral line. Indeed, the moment war came it was absolutely clear that neutrality was essential because if we hadn't been neutral our oil would have been stopped and a large part of our sterling balances would have been withdrawn. In fact most of the gains we made by the July measures would have been upset by an unneutral policy. This being so, it was surely unwise last week for George and Harold to barge in and talk about putting warships through the Strait of Tiran. But at Cabinet today that kind of talk had entirely disappeared. Instead we started with Harold's account of his Washington visit, where it was clear that L.B.J. was not in the least inclined to do anything positive to help Israel. George then reported on the war and told us that the Israelis had already blocked the Suez Canal. This made those who had objected to the Wilson–Brown–Bowden–Gunter line feel very self-satisfied. They were able to say how wise it was to leave the Israelis alone, not to bully them but to let them have their one chance.

Thursday, June 8th

At Cabinet the discussion of the war was desultory because it was clear by this morning that Israel was already the victor and that all that mattered was getting the oil embargo lifted and negotiations going. However, the Government's position had been greatly strengthened. George Brown's daily Statements in the House were better and better each day. His line was that whatever our personal sympathies Britain must remain neutral and be seen to make peace between the two sides. By now, of course, the pro-Israel feeling in the country is absolutely overwhelming and there is a great sense of triumph and victory. No one worried about the Israeli pre-emptive strike being an act of aggression. Their army has brought off the biggest military victory in our lifetime against President Nasser. What next? George and Harold made it clear that they doubt the utility of the U.N. Truce Commission and want four-power talks in order to prevent a two-party fix between the Americans and the Russians.

Our routine business was dealt with so fast that the P.M. said we now had plenty of time to discuss what we should do at the Chequers conference on

Sunday. He explained that this had been fixed up in February with the National Executive and that it was entirely designed in order to let the trade-union members blow their tops. It was the job of the Cabinet to sit quiet while they did so. But what does that mean? Who will actually speak? He told us that he would intervene at one point, Michael Stewart—who was not a member of the N.E.C.—at another, and Denis Healey and George Brown as well. It was pretty clear that the rest of us were going to have a deadly boring day and I pleaded that he should provide another cold collation so as to get us back to our homes and into bed early.

But he hadn't finished. Leaning back in his chair and putting his fingers together he began to talk aloud about the economic situation. We'd all got used to the Galbraithian theory of private affluence and public squalor,[1] and under Macmillan and Maudling there had been a switch to public expenditure on a very large scale. Now that had been sustained by us and as we had always expanded public spending—housing, schools, hospitals, roads—we ought to ask ourselves whether we weren't in danger of swinging the pendulum too far over towards public expenditure and cutting back the increase in private consumption to a figure so low that public opinion won't take it. He said he wanted to air this view; it was an interesting and important thought that needed consideration. I immediately pricked up my ears at this because it is exactly the line that Callaghan had been taking. It's my strong suspicion that the P.M. and Callaghan have come to an understanding. It looks as if Harold has decided against devaluation. The only way of getting our growth rate up and our exports up suddenly and dramatically would be devaluation this summer, preparatory to going into the Common Market, and if we don't devalue we have to accept a 3 per cent growth rate, even though the R.E.P. will to some degree mitigate it in the development areas. What we must look forward to is an artificially high rate of unemployment in the south and in the Midlands and an artificially low rate in some of the regions and in order to get the money for these subsidies to the regions we shall have to cut back public expenditure still more if we want to leave more for incomes. If the P.M. repeats this argument at Chequers on Sunday I shall be sure I'm right.

Sunday, June 11th
John and I motored over on a perfect Sunday morning, pretty angry that we had to spend the whole day inside that not very exciting room with all the beautiful weather outside. He's got a very nice fast Triumph and we were there just in time to find the meeting starting with Johnny Boyd of the A.E.U. in the chair and Len Williams, Sara Barker, George Brown and Harold Wilson at the top table. The rest of us sat like a mass meeting in lines on chairs.

[1] Elaborated in *The Affluent Society* (London: Hamish Hamilton, 1958) by John Kenneth Galbraith.

If the aim of the meeting was to permit the trade-union members to blow off steam they certainly blew it all right this morning. In the course of doing so they show that there are as many divisions between the trade-union leaders on the Executive as there are among the Ministers and M.P.s. Jack Jones alone took the extreme position anti prices and incomes. In a very tough speech he said it was endangering the success of the T.U.C.'s voluntary policy. As for the T.U.C., it had been playing the role of stooge for the Government and its position was being undermined. His first suggestion was that the Government should announce a date after which all legislation restricting wage movements would be completely ended. Then he said that the voluntary T.U.C. policy mustn't be restrictive. It must be a strategic co-ordination for trade-union advance to higher living standards. His second constructive point was to discuss the industrial democracy which was the main subject of a N.E.C. report which his committee had just produced. He wanted the modernization of arbitration and then attacked Dick Marsh for his cautious attitude to industrial democracy. This was far the biggest speech of the day.

In the afternoon Ministers replied to the points which had been made. It was clear that whenever any Minister got up there was no answer available from the other side.

In his final summing-up Harold Wilson said there are two sovereign points, the N.E.C. and the Cabinet. Each has its jurisdiction and theoretically of course they're totally independent. But if each insists upon its independence the constitution can't be made to work and this causes total bewilderment outside. Here he was laying down the bi-focal theory as he has often done before and he did it very well. 'As for consultation,' he said, 'we must improve it but it's often impossible,' and he cited the Six-Day War in Israel.

So that was Chequers and now I must have my bath and get off to catch the train to London. I have nothing to add about that meeting with the National Executive except to emphasize the humiliation of its necessity—the inadequacy of Transport House and in particular of Len Williams and Sara Barker. However Harold thought it was a tremendous success since it called the bluff of the trade-union members without causing offence.

Tuesday, June 13th
I started reading the D-Notice documents at 5.30 in the morning. I found the Radcliffe Report[1] a fascinating exposition of Civil Service stoogery and idiocy. Evelyn Waugh at his most fantastic could not have invented it. When I had digested the Report and read through the White Paper I realized two things. First that there was a mass of material in both to show the total lackadaisicalness of the Civil Service and secondly that the White Paper as a

[1] The Report of the Privy Councillors' Committee on the D-Notice affair (Cmnd. 3309). The Committee had consisted of Lord Radcliffe (chairman), Selwyn Lloyd and Emanuel Shinwell.

piece of apologetics is extremely unconvincing and will do Harold untold harm.

When Cabinet got to this item on the agenda Harold started by saying that he had to have a White Paper because he was so profoundly concerned about D-Notices. It was clear that he wanted to get the business through with the minimum of discussion. Neither Denis Healey nor George Brown, the two other Ministers concerned, spoke a word. Harold simply asked us to accept the White Paper.

This was the first occasion when I can remember him taking the strictly presidential line. First of all he'd arranged the timing of that Cabinet so that we should get a vast amount of reading material late the night before. Secondly he'd arranged that the White Paper should be published at four this afternoon so there was no chance of Cabinet amending it. Thirdly he'd arranged that we should discuss Rhodesia and the Middle East, before we came to the D-Notices, for half an hour and that his next engagement should be at 10.45. So we had only half an hour to discuss the D-Notices. In this way he'd made it virtually impossible for the Cabinet to refuse him sanction. Nor had we any inclination to do so since it was entirely the P.M.'s affair and his honour which was at stake. Nevertheless when he'd finished and George and Denis had failed to say anything, Dick Marsh observed the danger that Colonel Lohan[1] would be regarded as a victim, the fall-guy who'd been sacrificed in order to defend the senior civil servants. Harold said he saw the danger of this and I suggested that if he was to take the line in the White Paper it wasn't merely Lohan who should be blamed but the people who had appointed him and kept him at his job. At this point it came out that no one was quite sure whether he'd been positively vetted or not and I observed, 'Well, there are three Permanent Secretaries concerned as well as the Secretary to the Cabinet and they all bear strong collateral responsibility for the mess.' Of course the P.M. was authorized to publish the White Paper but I shouldn't think there was a single person there who thought it was a good thing to publish a White Paper instead of accepting the Radcliffe Report.

As we were walking out I said to Burke Trend, 'You've got a lot to answer for. That quixotic Prime Minister is going out to do battle for your Civil Service against the forces of evil.' He replied, 'I have pleaded with him to accept the Radcliffe Report and I actually drafted a Statement to show how he could do it.'

Wednesday, June 14th
This evening the Chief and I asked Harold Wilson to see us again. He agreed to do so at 9.30. The reason was his failure to ask our advice about the D-Notices; George Wigg has been his chief adviser. We didn't want to

[1] Secretary of the D-Notice Committee (officially the 'Defence, Press and Broadcasting Committee'), who resigned in face of the implicit censure in the Government's White Paper (Cmnd. 3312).

complain but just to make sure that he wasn't suspecting us of turning into enemies. So we consciously went there and sat telling him how we'd begun to collect the back-benchers to speak up for him in the debate and we were glad to tell him that people like Charlie Pannell were spontaneously rallying to fight for the P.M. against the *Daily Express*. I think we succeeded in making him feel that we were solid behind him and not questioning him or querying his decisions. 'You're always at your best in this kind of crisis,' I said to him. He looked at me rather bleakly and replied, 'I'm not sure I shall be on this occasion.' He was full of insecurity and wanted our help.

Thursday, June 22nd
This evening I got Marcia around to see me. When she arrived I found she was utterly miserable about the D-Notice debate which was then going on. She was not being consulted and she felt that George Wigg was in complete control. As for Burke Trend, she was convinced that his concern was not to protect Harold but to cover up the Civil Service. Like me, she was appalled when Harold refused to accept the Radcliffe Report, and wanted to see Harold surrounded by his true friends once again.

All this time the D-Notice debate was going on. It had been started by the Attorney-General because Harold changed his mind at the last moment, with the idea I suppose of deflating the occasion. If that was the idea it certainly succeeded. Elwyn was followed by Anthony Barber[1] who made a vicious but quite effective speech. After that we had speeches from Manny Shinwell and Ray Fletcher,[2] who had obviously been briefed by George Wigg, trying to divert the attack off Harold on to the unfortunate Colonel Lohan, though the one thing we had all agreed in Cabinet when Harold had asked our advice was that Lohan must not be made the fall-guy, and the Government mustn't look as though it were throwing him to the wolves in order to protect the higher civil servants. But this is exactly the impression which Shinwell and Fletcher created by their speeches. And Bill Deedes picked it up and at once began to defend the unfortunate Colonel. I was back on the front bench in time to listen to Heath, who seemed to me never to have got off the launching-pad. Harold, winding up, started very well indeed and gave us the feeling of a Prime Minister really concerned with security. But suddenly, right towards the end, he was stopped by a Question and started making a series of charges against Lohan. It was a fatal mistake, since it almost certainly means that the press campaign will continue and the D-Notice case will not be closed, as I hoped it would be, by this debate.

When I asked Harold afterwards he told me he hadn't intended to mention Lohan and it was only after Bill Deedes's speech that he rewrote his last paragraph and included all these imputations.

[1] Conservative M.P. for Altrincham from 1965 until 1974, when he became a life peer. He was chairman of the Conservative Party Organization 1967–70 and Chancellor of the Exchequer 1970–74.
[2] Labour M.P. for Ilkeston since 1964.

Wednesday, June 28th

At morning prayers Harold was still concerned with the D-Notices and upset by a furious *Daily Mirror* attack on him. He could think of very little else. Soon we went along to the N.E.C. which was quite quiet, obviously as a result of the Chequers conference. It actually finished early and I went back to the House, where the Liberals were having their first quasi-supply day. Despite the protests of some of my colleagues I had given them some Government time because they were an official opposition party without time. They were using it for a discussion of I.T.V.

Just before lunch I had to go to Buckingham Palace for a Privy Council. The Queen was just off to Canada[1] and I said politely that I supposed it would be quite fun though the exhibitions are terrible. She said, 'I'm too small to see them,' and suddenly I saw a picture of the tiny little woman looking upwards and only seeing the soles of the feet of the statues above her as she was traipsed miles and miles around on the red carpet.

Friday, June 30th

The Chief and I walked across to morning prayers at ten o'clock. Harold's mind, of course, was still on the D-Notices and I told him that at a party at Pam Berry's last night I had run into Hugh Cudlipp, who had warned me that the *Mirror* was declaring war on him. Harold replied that this was entirely owing to Cecil King and asked me whether I knew about the cause of their quarrel. When I said 'no' he explained that when he offered Cecil a life peerage, he had insisted that he wanted a real peerage or nothing at all and that is how the rift between them started. This is an interesting story and I've no doubt it is true.

Friday, July 7th

At the P.M.'s business meeting this morning George Brown raised the problem of oil, which is alarming us all and for which no adequate preparations are being made. Dick Marsh was trying to buy up expensive Venezuelan oil and Callaghan was saying we ought to have rationing to save our foreign exchange.[2] What we needed but didn't get, I pointed out, was an Emergency Committee with the power to overlook the whole subject and take decisions. The trouble is that this D-Notice affair has distracted the P.M.'s attention from much more important problems.

Saturday, July 8th

This has been a fairly easy week for me. Now that the Six-Day War is over we're beginning to realize just how expensive it's been to this country in terms of our balance of payments and in terms of our economic stability as a whole. The other day Jim Callaghan observed that it's heartbreaking to see

[1] To visit Expo '67, the World Fair.
[2] The closure of the Suez Canal made it necessary to buy oil elsewhere. On June 30th petrol prices had been increased by 2*d.* a gallon.

all the results of last July's measures being frittered away so that soon we may find ourselves without a balance-of-payments surplus this year. We've also had the threat of oil rationing hanging over us all this week.

Saturday, July 22nd

I had to be at Chequers at four o'clock for Harold's session with his friends. Anne and I had the most delicious drive right through the back of the Chilterns. I hadn't motored up that way from Henley and along through Nettlebed and Christmas Common for many years. It's still absolutely unspoilt, with the odd houses in little openings in the beech woods.

At Chequers the first meeting was for me and the Chief alone. We had asked for it and it lasted from 4.30 till six. We got Harold's agreement for the draft code of discipline and then we spent the rest of the time on parliamentary plans for the autumn. What should we do about morning sittings? I told him of my anxieties and admitted frankly that the Tories had been successful in defeating us. We were winning no advantage for the back-benchers and imposing a great deal of extra work on officials as well as on the Speaker. We must either abandon them or go right forward to a Parliament which really begins its business in the morning and finishes before dinner. Harold at once said we couldn't possibly abandon them and spent the rest of the time discussing the possibility of a four-day Parliament starting at ten in the morning.

By now the others were turning up. They came into the little room where we had found Harold with his wireless, his red box, his cigar and his pipes. The room was crammed and there was a heavy thunderstorm outside. In rushed Marcia. 'Oh,' she said, 'the terrible fug. You can cut it with a knife,' and had all the windows opened by the Wrens. The first session was appallingly scrappy.

After dinner the talk was just as unsatisfactory until suddenly Harold pulled himself together and said, 'Well, we can't let this meeting finish without a discussion of devaluation.' He said this just as he came back through the door, as though he'd gone outside to brace himself. Actually it turned out the best discussion we've ever had. Thomas Balogh was instructed to give the pros and cons, and did so very thoroughly. Then it was discussed in relation to other medium-term measures—import controls, Tony Benn's new enabling Bill, the Regional Employment Premium, etc. At one point he turned to me and said, 'You see, they all agree. Devaluation is too risky.' 'If you don't do it,' I replied, 'the catastrophes are not risks but certainties. Without devaluation how can you get the boost to our exports and the growth we need without creating too much consumer demand at home?' This was a good discussion since I think it enabled him to think more clearly and that, after all, was the purpose of his friends being there. We were able to go away feeling that for at least one hour there had been serious discussion of the problem.

I mention the rain because when we broke off it was clear that Barbara would need transport. She'd been brought by Ted in their car and had no one to take her back to her cottage in the Chilterns. At once Tony and John offered to take her. 'No,' Harold says, 'I'll get my son Giles to take her back.' I couldn't help wondering why on earth poor Giles should be got up in the middle of the night and I asked myself whether a British Prime Minister should really find it so extraordinarily difficult to provide transport for one of his senior Ministers after a long session.

Of course this shows Harold's curious modesty. He adores Chequers but he's still the visiting stranger who is neither accepted nor acceptable. His whole life is still simple and unassuming. As a good middle-class socialist I had my own official car and the driver delivered me to Prescote at 2 a.m.

Tuesday, July 25th
This afternoon I had to sit on the front bench for the summer adjournment debate just twelve months after my appointment as Leader of the House when my first job was to answer this self-same debate. This time it seemed more futile than ever. This is the kind of inferior Oxford Union debating which some Members of the House enjoy. It lasted from 3.45 until 6.30. Strictly speaking, each speaker can only give reasons why the House should postpone its recess or alternatively why the recess should be shorter or prolonged, but they constantly go beyond this and argue the merits of the case. On Tuesday the striking difference from a year ago was that there was no mention of Vietnam. Foreign policy was out. Most people were complaining about the mismanagement of morning sittings or home-front problems. There was no front-bench participation and no tension. It was just not important—which was quite O.K. by me.

This evening the children came up to London for a stay. But when we'd put them to bed I went back to the House for the Consolidated Fund Bill. I wanted to be with the troops and so John and I decided to stay the night. I had two nice periods of sleep—from 12.30 to 2.00 and again from 3.30 to 5.00. Apart from that, I was round the tea-room and the smoking-room and the lobbies and really enjoyed it.

Wednesday, July 26th
To Downing Street for morning prayers. The only subject the P.M. wanted to talk about was theatre censorship. There had just been published a report from a very representative committee which unanimously recommended the abolition of the functions of the Lord Chamberlain as censor of the living drama. This Roy Jenkins had very much wanted to accept but the P.M. told John and me this would be a terrible mistake and he also let us know that he'd sent George Wigg to the Home Affairs Committee to warn them against accepting it. I had had to leave the Committee just when George Wigg was starting to speak and hadn't realized that he was the P.M.'s

emissary: indeed, I thought he'd gone there with a brief from Arnold Goodman, who was a member of the original departmental committee. Harold's explanation was very elaborate, I think because he was a little embarrassed. 'I've received representations from the Palace,' he said. 'They don't want to ban all plays about live persons but they want to make sure that there's somebody who'd stop the kind of play about Prince Philip which would be painful to the Queen. Of course,' he hurriedly added, 'they're not denying that there should be freedom to write satirical plays, take-offs, caricatures: what they want to be able to ban are plays devoted to character assassination and they mention, as an example, "Mrs Wilson's Diary".'

I pricked up my ears. 'Mrs Wilson's Diary' is, of course, one of the most popular features of *Private Eye* and there were ideas about putting it on the stage.[1] When I asked him, Harold told me that he had been shown the text of the play, which made him out a complete mugwump and gave a picture of George Brown's drinking and swearing and using four-letter words. My first reaction was to tell him that he could hardly keep censorship of the live theatre and leave television and radio free. He had a quick reply. 'That'll all be lined up now,' he said, 'because Charlie Hill has already cleaned up I.T.V. and he'll do the same to B.B.C. now I'm appointing him chairman.' It was obvious from the way he talked that he wanted the censorship as much as the Queen. Indeed he wanted it so much that he'd put it on Thursday's Cabinet agenda.

Thursday, July 27th
Cabinet once again. Theatre censorship, as Harold promised, was the first item on the agenda. Despite George Wigg, the Home Affairs Committee had recommended acceptance of the committee's report. One of its main arguments was that one could hardly forbid the portrayal of living persons in the live theatre when it was not prohibited on television. Here Harold had equipped himself with an effective reply, namely an assurance from Charlie Hill that the powers vested in the Governors of the B.B.C. were quite adequate to ensure that character assassination was altogether forbidden.

I had been expecting a great confrontation between Harold and the man he detests and whose influence he really hates in the Cabinet. Faced with the P.M.'s unexpected coup Roy was quite firm, cool and collected. He said of course he would consider this and the matter must certainly go back to Home Affairs for reconsideration. But he added that it would be extremely difficult to evolve any way of controlling the live theatre which didn't mean the reintroduction of censorship and more discrimination against it in comparison with television and radio. The Prime Minister seemed content with this and when I intervened to suggest that we needn't rush the Bill he indicated

[1] The series was to be adapted for the stage by Joan Littlewood. It opened at the Theatre Royal, Stratford East, in September 1967 and was transferred to the Criterion Theatre, where it ran for nine months.

that it should be given high priority and he hoped that Roy would be able to satisfy him on this point. The agreement reached, as recorded in the Cabinet minutes, runs: 'In neither medium would ordinary political satire be forbidden but there should be safeguards against the theatre being used deliberately to discredit or create political hostility towards public political figures.'

Friday, July 28th
I had a Privy Council where we had to deal with the marriage of the Earl of Harewood to Miss Tuckwell, for whom he has left his nice musician wife.[1] Harold brought it up in Cabinet and told us that the Queen expressly wanted to be advised by us. Since he's eighteenth in succession to the throne, the Royal Marriages Act of 1772 requires her to do so. It was my duty, therefore, formally to give her the Cabinet's advice which of course she was duty-bound to take.

Although this was the last day of the Session I didn't bother to go to the House but went straight from No. 10 to an enormously enjoyable lunch at the Gay Hussar given by some of the Lobby to John and me in exchange for the hospitality we've given to the journalists. I rushed home to find Thomas Balogh waiting for a gloomy discussion. He was deeply disheartened by the events of the week. All one can say is that Harold is dead tired and I am dead tired and everybody is dead tired, and we've got to hope that by the end of August we shall have enough energy and ability to pull this Government together.

In the Cabinet reshuffle on August 28th, the Prime Minister announced that he intended to supervise the D.E.A. himself with Peter Shore as Secretary of State, replacing Michael Stewart, who remained in the Cabinet as First Secretary with oversight of the Government's social policy. Douglas Jay, formerly President of the Board of Trade and an implacable anti-marketeer, left the Cabinet to be succeeded by Anthony Crosland, whose place at the D.E.S. was taken by Patrick Gordon Walker. George Thomson moved from the Foreign Office to replace Herbert Bowden (appointed Chairman of the I.T.A.) and Arthur Bottomley resigned from the Cabinet.

Thursday, September 7th
The first meeting of the new Cabinet and I'm struck by the difference from the old one. With power suddenly shifted to Shore and Crosland, the change on the economic side is enormous. But if you want to see a symptom of what has happened you should look at item three of the conclusions. 'The Committee [i.e. S.E.P.] had taken a number of decisions on which the Cabinet would wish to be informed.' And it then lists the decisions of the

[1] It had been announced on January 2nd that the Earl of Harewood was to be sued for divorce on grounds of adultery with Miss Tuckwell. His divorce had been approved on April 6th and on July 31st he married Miss Tuckwell.

S.E.P. This was the first time that I can really say there has been hard evidence that Harold was introducing what I've often described as Prime Ministerial government. Up till then he'd acted in a chairmanly, not a dictatorial, way, co-ordinating everything and leaving all the initiatives to his Ministers. He'd also relied on the creative friction between the Treasury and the D.E.A. Now that phase is over and he is taking the lead himself, laying down the policy in S.E.P. and then telling the full Cabinet of the decisions. I notice also an interesting change in his relationship with Callaghan. It is obviously very intimate. Throughout Cabinet they were chatting to each other, heads together, and there was no sign of anything but prior agreement between the two. Tommy's convinced there's been a sell-out by the P.M. I'm not so sure. I believe he still reserves his position and still thinks that he has the capacity to introduce a new Chancellor and devalue if it were really necessary. Callaghan, of course, thinks the opposite. He believes he has made himself effectively number two on the home front, equal in power with George Brown, the number two on the foreign front.

The only item which concerned me this morning was the House of Lords. The paper the Lord Chancellor had prepared was excellent and everything went perfectly well, as the official minutes record. The only vital fact the Cabinet Secretariat omitted was that both the Foreign Secretary and the Chancellor expressed the gravest doubts about a change of composition. George Brown was unusually powerful, and I felt that people like Fred Peart, Willie Ross and Cledwyn Hughes would naturally join with him if he started a movement against Lords reform. This was confirmed this afternoon when Roy Jenkins looked in to see me about something else and expressed doubt whether, in view of the Cabinet attitude, it was possible to deal with composition. Roy always has a very good nose for changes in public opinion.

I had asked Roy to see me in my office because I wanted to talk to him about the problems of theatre censorship. As Harold's henchman I felt bound to put to him the P.M.'s point of view and say how strongly this was felt not only by him but by all the Royal Family and by the court as well. When I'd finished he said, 'As a matter of fact I don't think anything can be done. I propose to leave the Bill unchanged.' 'You'll be in trouble there, Roy,' I said. 'But I've got a majority of the Parliamentary Party on my side,' he replied. 'Perhaps. But you may not have a majority in the Cabinet and you've certainly got the P.M. opposed.' 'Well,' he said, almost petulantly, 'I'm not prepared as a radical and liberal Home Secretary to have my image ruined by being ordered to impose worse conditions on the live theatre than they are getting now under the Lord Chamberlain.' And he made it quite clear that he was thinking of the threat of resignation in order to get his way.

Tuesday, September 12th
The whole of today I spent at Chequers for the first day of the session on Lords reform, though it was only by the evening that I discovered that

Gerald Gardiner was not only the formal host but had to pay the bill for all the food and drink and everything else. Since there wasn't room for seventeen or eighteen people, including our civil servants, I decided that along with Wheeler-Booth and Freddie Warren I would go out and stay at the King's Head in Aylesbury. When Burke discovered this there was a terrible fuss. 'That's impossible,' he said, 'because if the Lord President is seen in Aylesbury with officials from the House of Lords the journalists will realize you are holding a secret meeting and conclude you're discussing House of Lords reform.' This reveals the way the Trend mind works on security problems. We stayed very comfortably at the old coaching pub and spent quite a time in the bar without anybody suspecting who we were.

From the start Gerald was in his most adamant obstinate mood. 'I've decided,' he said, 'that the best way to deal with this problem is to take the two schemes—the one-tier scheme and the two-tier scheme—and go through each, point by point. I shall record our decisions point by point. We start now with the one-tier scheme and I ask you, Lord President, the first question. What is the total number of peers required in the single House for a one-tier scheme?' My mild protest against the difficulties of operating in this way was pushed aside.

As Jenkins put it to me afterwards, 'This is a typical lawyer's solution.' A lawyer starts with the details of the two plans and having dealt with them *seriatim* he turns to look at the two plans as a whole. A politician, an economist or a philosopher, on the other hand, will deal with the principles or general ideas first and then ask whether he's got the right means to achieve his aim. As the discussion went on somebody remarked in desperation that we really ought to be asking ourselves what the aim and object of the operation was. What were we trying to achieve by Lords reform? I jumped in and said we were trying to achieve co-ordination of the two Chambers and that the principle we must work on is that in future there would be only one source of authority—the Chamber elected by popular vote. Once you abolish the hereditary principle there can be no other authority than the House of Commons, and the Lords must derive its authority from the lower Chamber. That's why I personally wouldn't be afraid of a reformed House of Lords where the balance of power between the Government and the Opposition reflected the results of the last general election.

After lunch Gerald got control of us again and we seemed to spend hours discussing how many bishops and law lords we should have. But at least it was decided that the two-tier scheme should be considered after tea. There we weren't taking any chances. I gave a very brief introduction and then Eddie explained his model at length. At once he was backed by Shepherd, the ex-Chief Whip of the House of Lords, by John Silkin and, to a limited extent, by Gordon Walker. The scheme is based on two principles. First, the immediate abolition of the hereditary principle and, secondly, the creation of a top-tier of voting peers and a lower tier of hereditary peers permitted to speak. From the point of view of the Party managers this is clearly a workable scheme but it is not at all easy to explain and Roy Jenkins, who'd been quiet up till then, launched into a major attack. I've never heard him before either in Cabinet or in Cabinet Committee commit himself so firmly. He accused the two-tier scheme of rigidity and said that it required far more patronage than we could permit. It was this undue reliance on patronage which made it inferior to the one-tier scheme. This brought him into a confrontation with me which lasted for some twenty minutes with the Lord Chancellor an interested spectator.

Suddenly the Lord Chancellor intervened and said, 'Well, we had better come to our decisions. It's clear now we shall have to present a paper to Cabinet propounding the two solutions and asking Cabinet to decide between them.' I replied that this would be fatal. 'Rather than have a divided report from this Committee I would much rather accept the advice of George Brown and Jim Callaghan and postpone the whole issue for a year. Unless we can get an agreement on this Committee I want to see no action recommended.'

This was really the turning point of the conference because suddenly the Lord Chancellor collapsed and said, 'Oh, we can't wait a year: we must have action now in view of what the Tories might do between now and the election. Of course I'll accept the two-tier system under certain conditions rather than face this postponement.' Jenkins quickly added that he too would make concessions rather than face a collapse of the conference.

During dinner a solution suddenly came into my head. I saw a way of getting out of this deadly conflict between two-tier and one-tier. Why shouldn't we announce our decision to legislate on the reform of the Lords in the Queen's Speech but also announce our intention to negotiate with the Conservatives and the Liberals? Then, rather than putting forward the two-tier system as our own plan, we could propound it at the end of the negotiations if we thought there was a chance of it being accepted. This was suggested after dinner and the Committee quickly reached an agreement that we should put a firm commitment into the Queen's Speech to abolish the hereditary element and that we should treat the two-tier scheme not as acceptable on its merits but as a scheme to be accepted only if the opposition parties agree. If they didn't agree we could then be much more radical in a really thorough one-tier scheme. Well, to my amazement, all this was agreed. And Freddie Warren, Freddy Ward, Wheeler-Booth and I went off to the King's Head to celebrate in drinks.

Wednesday, September 13th

This morning we got down to work on a fearful draft presented by one of our officials. We had to work very hard on it but the job was done by twelve o'clock and to the draft was annexed all the appendices on powers, composition, etc. After we'd finished the Chief and I slipped off to drive back to

London in appalling rainstorms that had been drenching down ever since the night before.

That Chequers conference staggered me. I had gone down there extremely gloomy, thinking there was no possible chance of reconciliation between Gardiner and myself and knowing that in the atmosphere created by George Brown and Jim Callaghan I would have no chance of getting agreement to our proposals. Yet now we were able to go back and present a unanimous paper.

I got back late for the meeting of the National Executive at Transport House which was considering the interim report of the Committee of Inquiry into the Labour Party's organization. I think I've mentioned in this diary already how utterly futile this Committee of Inquiry is since it is dominated by Len Williams, the man into whose activities we need to inquire. Anyway I had been excluded from the only important working party on the National Agency Scheme[1] and was not surprised to see that the proposals on political education were just as futile. However, the huge document had come out much better than I expected because at least it concluded a recommendation in favour of earnings-related contributions to the Party following the model of the S.P.D. in Germany, and secondly a completely new concept of the General Secretary's task which would make him a leading political figure. These were the two controversial recommendations my colleagues had been bullied to accept from me. I don't know what people expected when this enormous document was presented to the Executive. It's not in the least surprising that after a long and desultory discussion George Brown proposed that it shouldn't be published at all. Others suggested that it should be published omitting the section on the General Secretary, which would be interpreted as an attack on Len Williams. After they'd finished I pointed out that the Annual Conference would not like to feel the report had been suppressed and that it would be far wiser to publish it in full and have it debated at Conference. On this at least I got my way. Mind you, most of it had already been leaked to the press before we began to discuss it today.

I was curious how members of the Executive would react to my presence now that my decision to retire has been announced in the press and also the reason for it—the fact that there are far too many Ministers on the N.E.C. Of course nobody said a word to me direct, though I was told that most of the trade unionists seemed to think that I'd performed a very clever trick which had made me the most popular member of the N.E.C. Well, I may be popular at the moment but I'm still feeling extremely sore. I've served on this Executive for fifteen years, done as much hard work as any other member and never been made a chairman of anything. Despite Harold's express wishes the Executive refused to make me either the chairman of the inquiry

---

[1] A working party of six were examining a National Agency Scheme whereby the N.E.C. and constituency Parties might jointly pay for a Party agent in every constituency. A scheme was devised but for marginal constituencies only.

or of Org. Sub. That in itself is a good enough reason to withdraw but I also have a growing conviction that it's now too late to reform the Labour Party except by appointing a brand new General Secretary. Once appointed, the right man could reorganize the whole thing. But in that case sitting on the Executive wouldn't be all that important since the key problem during the next election will be the relation of the Party not to Transport House but to No. 10. A party in power can win an election from Whitehall and neglect its organization outside.

Thursday, September 14th
An emergency meeting of O.P.D. on South Africa had been inserted before Cabinet. Here the minutes are worth looking at since they give a totally misleading picture. This is what really happened. The Prime Minister was presented with a formidable official line-up of the three main parties concerned with the problem of selling arms to South Africa. The Foreign Office, the Ministry of Defence and the Commonwealth Office were obviously in agreement that a major shift of policy was essential. George Brown began the attack saying that though he realized it was very painful one couldn't really go on being so unrealistic about the sale of arms. He was then supported by Denis Healey, who said one must surely make a distinction between arms which could be used for suppressing insurrection (such as *Crusader* tanks or *Saracen* cars) and strategic arms—that is to say, the Air Force and the Navy which are needed for our own Commonwealth interests. He said we need the Simonstown base to be kept going by South Africa in our own interest and therefore we should sell South Africa maritime arms but not arms for domestic use. In this sense he felt we should have to repudiate the Prime Minister's Statement of November 1964 when he said that all defence contracts would stop. Both George and Denis emphasized that this was a major switch of policy which couldn't possibly be concealed. When they had finished the Prime Minister intervened to say that this switch was quite impossible. He reckoned that no less than six members of the Government, junior Ministers mostly, would resign; the effect in the Parliamentary Party would be even worse. After the P.M. had finished the First Secretary supported him very strongly, saying that the greatest issue of world politics in the future was race. We were opting out of that great issue if we accepted George's proposal and submitting ourselves to policies of pure expediency and opportunism. Michael Stewart was very strongly supported by Frank Longford. He was followed by Tony Crosland, who made a balanced statement saying he wasn't quite sure that the disasters anticipated were rightly calculated. Then came the last of the spokesmen of the interested Ministries. As might be expected, George Thomson, making his first contribution as Commonwealth Secretary, lined up with the other Departments and read his official brief. I then interrupted to make the point which I'd mentioned to the P.M. on the phone that morning that you

couldn't separate South Africa from Rhodesia. How idiotic we would look appeasing the racialists in South Africa while we were standing pat in Rhodesia! If the South Africans would help us to settle with Smith I would consider a concession on South African arms trade tolerable.

George Brown then dismissed this as totally impracticable, but the P.M. clutched at it. He may possibly be right that what I proposed is really impracticable. The way to do this practically is probably to sell out first in one and then in the other. But you have to start somewhere. My own view is that Rhodesia and South Africa between them are costing us an enormous amount in our balance of payments. We are completely immobilized because of the moral blackmail exerted by the left-wing of the Party and Harold Wilson's personal commitments. It's a miserable situation and this first move by the three Departments was highly significant. I must add, however, that I didn't disclose to the P.M. my private views on the subject. He was so miserable and unhappy and divided in his mind about it that my main concern was to remain close to him and to say nothing without consulting him in advance.

After the Cabinet meeting which immediately followed, the Chancellor, the First Secretary, the Chief Whip and I stayed behind to report to the P.M. about the Chequers conference. We had sent him a copy of our agreed paper to study beforehand. This morning he just looked at us and said, 'Well, that's all right.' He was surprised but I think he'd accepted it and he didn't ask a single question. We'd only spent two minutes with him when he obviously wanted us to go but that wouldn't have been decent. So I then raised the issue of the extension of patronage implied in our proposals and went on to discuss the Queen's prerogative, at which he slightly warmed up. Nevertheless he remained coolly acquiescent, accepting our proposals and telling us he would support them. It was a very curious attitude.

This evening I had a talk with Tam, who agreed to become my P.P.S. again since Geoffrey Rhodes doesn't suit me. We agreed I should make Geoffrey Rhodes the chairman of the Specialist Committee on education – if we get it as we now may from the new Secretary of State. And the Chief agreed to support that proposal. The change will be very important to me since a good P.P.S. makes an astonishing difference even to a Minister without Portfolio.

Friday, September 15th
At morning prayers this morning George Brown was present and we got talking informally about the South African arms dispute in O.P.D. George Brown said that the F.O. had wanted to pretend there was no change of policy. And then he went on, 'You know, Prime Minister, I have come to all kinds of personal understandings about this change of policy, as you agreed I should do some months ago. It will be pretty awkward to go back on those personal understandings just now.' Harold sat silent and embarrassed but

George went on. 'I didn't want to make too much fuss of this at O.P.D. or to emphasize the change of policy. I would have preferred to suggest we were just gradually extending it. It was Denis Healey who insisted that we must accept the important policy shift.' All this came as complete news to me. I strongly suspect what George was saying was basically true.

The discussion then switched to Lords reform. A lot of argument took place and we finally decided not to take it to Cabinet but to have a meeting of the big five—as Harold called it—consisting of himself, George Brown, Michael Stewart, the Lord Chancellor and myself. Actually the Chancellor also had to be included, making it six. 'If the six agree,' said the P.M., 'we needn't have a Cabinet for weeks. And if we don't agree there is no point in having a Cabinet.' So we six shall be meeting next Monday at five o'clock.

Monday, September 18th

I woke up with violent gastric flu, which went on all day and I just managed to hold out till evening. Apparently there's an epidemic now in London. Flu makes one depressed. An extra cause of my depression is returning to work as Lord President when all the other Ministers are back and getting down to their Departments and I am only half employed.

The P.M. started very briefly by expressing his surprise that the Committee had reached unanimity. Then the Lord Chancellor explained the political reasons why we had made our recommendation in the way we had and George Brown and Callaghan were asked their opinions. George was completely unchanged. Any tinkering with Lords reform would be regarded as trying to distract attention from the real issue of unemployment. It would also upset our own socialists and the press would deride us for doing it. Callaghan said he didn't feel quite as strongly as that but he did feel that this was a kind of bread-and-circuses stunt—or at least would be regarded as such. However, if the P.M., the Lord Chancellor, the Lord President and the First Secretary all thought Lords reform important he would go along with it.

We then discussed the two alternative solutions—one-tier and two-tier—and George Brown immediately barged in with a total opposition to the two-tier idea. But I got the impression that his main objection was psychological. He was deeply affronted that the Deputy Prime Minister had not been consulted and that all these consultations had been going on behind his back.

At last the supporters of the plan got their turn and I explained the tactical reasons for going ahead and inserting in the Queen's Speech a pledge to reform the House of Lords with an offer to negotiate with the other Parties. I emphasized that if we did nothing this wouldn't stop the Tories or the Liberals from putting forward proposals for reform of composition. There's no doubt that the strength of argument was on our side. But I went away from that meeting feeling pretty depressed. Having postponed the Cabinet meeting, we would now have it after the Party Conference[1] in very unfavourable circumstances.

By now my cold was almost unbearable and I went home to try to nurse it through the night.

Thursday, September 21st
Cabinet today started with a severe Prime Ministerial rebuke administered to poor Gordon Walker for the mess he'd made in Enfield. He was rebuked for not taking legal advice from the Attorney-General.[2] I talked to him afterwards and found out that his departmental lawyers were certain he would win and that before they entered the court the Solicitor-General expressed the same view. Gordon Walker believes that if the A.-G. had been consulted he would have said the same. However, what he didn't seem to realize was that, quite apart from the lawyers he ought, as the politician in charge, to have seen the political insanity of this behaviour.

Then we came to the Lord Chancellor's report on publications, i.e. on the problem George Brown had raised about my keeping a diary. We had seen the Cabinet paper in advance, which revealed a difference of opinion. The three non-legal members of the Committee (Roy Jenkins, Gordon Walker and Frank Longford) were in favour of Ministers taking the advice of the Secretary of the Cabinet. The two lawyer members of the Committee (Gerald Gardiner and the Attorney-General) wanted Ministers to be made to sign in advance a document promising to abide by the decision of the Secretary of the Cabinet on whatever books they wanted to publish. When Gerald and Elwyn had briefly introduced the paper, Roy Jenkins spoke up. He accepted that they should try to work together but he couldn't swallow the recommendation that the last word should belong to a civil servant. He also made the very sensible point that even if Ministers did sign this promise they would make a secret reservation in their minds between theory and actual practice, particularly since the person who would make the decision might be an unknown civil servant twenty years later on. Quite unexpectedly the Prime Minister turned to me. I was unprepared but I remarked that it's absolutely astonishing to propose that in the book I intended to write on the relationship between the politicians and the Civil Service a civil servant should be made a complete censor of my work. What was even more outrageous, I went on, was that if this report was accepted there would be censorship of all books written by Ministers about their political experiences but not about newspaper articles, which could be far more damaging and malicious. One advantage of a long-term contract for a book is that a Minister would not be tempted by an acute shortage of money just after a lost election to earn £10,000 from the *News of the World* or the *Sunday*

[1] To be held at Scarborough from October 2nd to 6th.
[2] Patrick Gordon Walker had the previous week been overruled by the High Court in a case involving the transformation of Enfield Grammar School into a Comprehensive.

Express for spicy anecdotes. That's what the papers really want to print and that is what destroys collective responsibility. The P.M. then rapidly intervened to say that there could be no question of Burke Trend or his successor having the final word on anything except defence security. Shouldn't we as reasonable men agree that where the Secretary of the Cabinet told us that a passage had to be omitted for reasons of national security we were bound to omit it? But Roy Jenkins and Frank Longford even objected to this, saying that we ought naturally to take his advice but there was no reason to tie ourselves in advance.

Having had no luck here the P.M. then said that he thought the real issue is 'collective responsibility to each other and to the Party', and he evolved the theory out of his head that the leader of the Party (he might be leader of the Opposition then) should informally read all manuscripts written by members of his ex-Cabinet before publication. I'm afraid he was made to look a complete jackass, not only by Roy Jenkins and Tony Crosland, but also by Gordon Walker. One of them asked him whether he would really have been willing to accept Hugh Gaitskell's censorship of his own autobiography. And another question was whether it would be wise to compel the unfortunate leader of the Opposition to make himself unpopular with his colleagues by vetting their manuscripts. If he didn't remove an offensive passage it would have been said to have been printed with his approval and if he did remove it there would be a terrible row.

This whole discussion lasted for a full two hours. It was one of the most futile I've ever heard. But I should recall that the opponents didn't have it all their own way. Dick Marsh supported the Lord Chancellor, saying how appalling it was that these professional writers should be preparing their diaries in order to do him down. He didn't mind an odd dirty newspaper article by an ordinary colleague; what he minded was the prospect of serious weighty attacks by professional writers equipped with all the advantages of a detailed diary. How could he reply to that? Tony Greenwood also made one of his rare interventions, saying he was deeply disturbed about the security of these diaries—what would happen if the diarist's home was broken into?

Having been chivvied all round the place Harold finally said that he would draft a new memorandum, at which I burst out quite spontaneously with the remark, 'Oh heavens, don't let's have this again. We've had this discussion twice already. All this talk about the books we shall write after the Government has fallen is ghoulish and makes me feel that the Government is falling.' What I remembered was that it was the day of the by-elections and we were faced with an imminent political débâcle and all we could talk about was leaks and publications.

This evening I had Tony Crosland and Tommy Balogh to dinner and when we'd discussed the January prospects I said I was going home to see the by-election results on my own filthy little television with Tam Dalyell. Tommy said he would ring up Marcia and as a result I found myself watching the results with Marcia and the P.M. 'I hate the television taking one inside so that one is present at the count,' he said, and it was clear that he was very jumpy. In came Gerald Kaufman to tell us there was a recount at Walthamstow so we knew the worst—we were in for another Leyton over again. So when the final result came it wasn't really such a blow.[1] We just talked and chatted trivialities while we waited for Cambridge.[2] Of course, that result was an enormous help because in Cambridge the swing was 9 per cent whereas it was 18 per cent in Walthamstow. That steadied the P.M., whose mind was fixed on the failure of Heath and who kept on assuring himself that this was merely a Labour protest against the prices and incomes and that there was no swing to the Tories.

Friday, September 22nd
How should the P.M. be handled on the morrow of defeat? I had long talks that morning with John Silkin and Tommy Balogh on that subject. Out of the Leyton catastrophe we had got from him the small committee which linked Transport House and the Government. Out of this catastrophe we all agreed that we should try to get an inner group which would guide propaganda policy.

At ten o'clock I popped off to my weekly meeting where—Burke Trend being in Canada on holiday—Bill Nield was in charge and we found there was very little work for Cabinet on Thursday. When the business was over I asked the P.M. to see me alone and put the proposal to him. His first reaction was that I was inventing a device which would enable me to push devaluation and such things. 'No,' I said. 'It's not that. I want to use this, with Peter Shore and Tony Crosland, for getting the prices and incomes policy sold in a way you have never done so far. That will be the first job. Maybe we shall have other suggestions about action to take, for instance referring rents to the Prices and Incomes Board, for the Alcan project for smelting aluminium and saving imports of so many million a year. Maybe we shall have ideas about regionalism.' Then he began to say, 'Yes, but let's think about what I ought to put into my Conference speech.' And I knew I had to stop.

I then went back to my office and there I had a talk to Agnew which is well worth retelling in full. Ever since I came back from the Dordogne I've been told by him that we would have to have a Privy Council with not less than four Ministers present before October 11th: otherwise the Legislature of the Seychelles Islands would automatically lapse. After some beating about I suggested that we could manage the last Friday of the Labour Party Conference. I could catch the sleeper to Aberdeen on the Thursday night with Eddie Shackleton and one or two others and we would all go up together, have the Council on the Friday morning, lunch there with the Queen, have a

[1] Labour's majority of 8,725 at the general election was turned into a majority of 62 for Frederick Silvester who kept the seat for the Conservatives until 1970.

[2] At Cambridge, Labour's majority of 991 was turned into a 5,978 majority for the Conservative also, David Lane, who held the seat from 1974 until he resigned in 1976.

walk in the afternoon and come back by the night train on Friday. This had then been checked with Michael Adeane at the Palace and had been found suitable, though there had been a great difficulty in collecting my four Ministers. Suddenly, however, last Wednesday Agnew told me that it had been put to the Queen and the Queen had said, 'I'm so sorry I have a private engagement—it just can't be done.' I was annoyed that when an arrangement had been found suitable and convenient by her own palace staff, by the Privy Council and by the four Ministers, she should simply say that she had a private arrangement. We set to trying to find another date and Agnew began to insist that we must have it on the Monday after the Conference—that is, on the 9th if the Seychelles Legislature were to be safe. I said that would be almost impossible. All the Ministers would have been ten days away from their offices in London and would certainly not like to go up on the Sunday night and come back on the Monday. Despite Agnew's protest I insisted that we should have it on Tuesday. When I got into the office this morning he told me he'd received another note from the Palace that the Queen had consented to it happening on Tuesday, though she has another private engagement and wouldn't be able to give the Ministers lunch that day. I felt pretty angry. 'All right,' I said, 'if we don't have lunch with her I don't really mind. We can have it in the servants' quarters. There will be plenty of her staff having their lunch and she can have her private entertainment in another part of the house. But I do insist that we should be given a meal after the Council and before we leave.' Poor Godfrey Agnew got to work again and this evening, just before I left, he came up to me and said, 'It has all been fixed up. She's going to be able to entertain you to lunch on Tuesday.'

It's an interesting story because it illustrates the relationship between the Queen and her Ministers. First of all it's striking that when the Government is at work in London and the Privy Council is called, she doesn't come down from Balmoral to the Palace but the Ministers have to go to her private home in the north of Scotland. If this is necessary to the magic of monarchy, I accept it as fair enough. But surely there must be a limit to which busy Ministers are compelled to sacrifice their time to suit royal private engagements. This I think is unchivalrous. It's only fair to add, however, that I am pretty certain that the Queen herself knows nothing about all this and it's all a matter between endless courtiers.

Sunday, October 1st

Although the Conference demonstration takes place tonight and I should have been at the N.E.C. meetings on Friday and Saturday I'm still at Prescote. The reason of course is the flu. I came back with the family on Friday and I've been upstairs sweating it out in bed ever since—listening to the wireless half asleep, watching the television we've got in our bedroom and having a very pleasant time reading Pepys. Do I really mind? No, I don't at all. After all I'm resigning from the Executive this year and so it doesn't make all that much difference whether I miss the agitations of this year's Conference or not.

Monday, October 2nd
After I had taken yesterday off to convalesce today we motored quietly up to Scarborough, first pausing to see the marvellous minster at Beverley and arriving at five o'clock when the first day's session was just concluding.

As soon as we'd got ourselves unpacked in our room at the Royal Hotel I went downstairs to have tea and meet people. It was clear at once that on this first day when one takes the temperature of the delegates things had gone well from the N.E.C. point of view. I also learnt from Wedgy and John Silkin that at the weekend, when the Executive prepares for the Conference, nothing very much happened. Last year we took nearly five hours on the Sunday afternoon to deal with all the composite resolutions. This year it was finished in just over an hour and the draft Executive statement on the Common Market was passed without discussion and with mere formal opposition by Jack Jones, Ian Mikardo and Driberg.

Whatever the delegates were feeling in the other hotels we in the Royal, where the Executive is all together, felt rather complacent at tea-time today, all the more so because of the gigantic press build-up about the revolt of the delegates which would take place. Fleet Street had apparently concluded that what happened at the T.U.C. Conference at Brighton must be repeated in the Labour Party Conference. There had been a large majority against any support for the Government's prices and incomes policy. They'd snubbed the Government decisively. Now that much the same people were meeting a few weeks later at Scarborough, weren't they bound to do the same thing? And wouldn't there also be a great left-wing revolt on Vietnam? I'd always thought these expectations a mistake and I'd rightly guessed that Walthamstow and Cambridge would put the delegates from the constituencies up against the difficulty that to attack the Government would be suicidal. I thought it would be an uneasy, unhappy Conference, but not impossible, and that we would get away with most of the votes, though perhaps not on prices and incomes. Everything that happened this first day confirmed it.

Hearing that the new draft of the Prime Minister's speech was nearly ready I went downstairs to his room. Just as I was being greeted by Marcia he came in in his shirtsleeves—rather podgy in his grey flannels and white shirt—and told me that this speech would be the best that he'd ever delivered. He would like me to come back and see the finished draft. Actually I went to bed early and though I got my copy of the draft from Marcia I didn't read it until next morning.

Tuesday, October 3rd
We started with the N.E.C. election results and, as I usually do, I found myself sitting next to Barbara on the platform and she was certainly

expecting to come out top. But no, this time Ian Mikardo and Tom Driberg were made number one and number two, clearly as a minor anti-Ministerial demonstration. Barbara came number three, Tony Benn number four, then Frank Allaun[1]—one of the newly elected people—and after Tony Greenwood the second newly elected, Joan Lestor.[2] James Callaghan had transferred to the Treasurership where he was not in danger. The retirement of James Callaghan and myself had probably saved the life of Tony Greenwood and had brought on to the Executive two new people, neither of whom will be a tremendous force.

Then we got down to an appallingly dreary debate. While it went on and on and on I began to work on Harold's speech. The draft that had been brought to me was far too long and Marcia had said Harold should cut out a fifth of it. During the debate I did some hard work subbing and editing.

After lunch I talked to Harold about his speech. When I left after more than an hour I felt it had been enormously successful. He seemed to have adopted so many of my suggestions. At one point Michael Halls came in to say that George Brown was very upset because he believed that what he'd read about himself in the morning papers had come from the P.M.'s camp. Harold looked up and said sharply, 'There aren't any camps, Michael, and George ought to know it.' Apparently what had happened was that yesterday George had seen a passage in the E.E.C. Commission report in which our financial situation is extremely damagingly analysed by a Frenchman. George had taken tremendous umbrage and ordered all his Foreign Office experts to fly up to Scarborough at once. The press had reported this, along with an account of his behaviour at the agents' dance last night. Harold tried to brush it all aside and told me that George was being more crazy than usual.

This afternoon Callaghan replied to the economic debate and made the speech of the Conference. From the first moment he displayed an extraordinary assuredness as though he was completely at home with this couple of thousand people. He was able to jibe at the chairman of the National Farmers' Union for negotiating the wrong way—and to get away with it. He was able to make the Conference laugh at itself. He knew exactly how to combine good-humoured raillery, emotion and an appearance of serious statesmanship while carefully avoiding the main issues. He never discussed devaluation, he never mentioned the permanent pool of unemployment, he didn't put over a very powerful case for a prices and incomes policy but described instead a voluntary incomes policy exercised by the trade unions with some mild Government action. Conference was wanting to believe in the Labour Government and here was Callaghan giving them an excuse for believing and for getting back their faith after the inhibitions of Walthamstow. Some people say that when there's a Labour Government Conference is a hopeless sounding board. This was not true today. The confrontation of

[1] Labour M.P. for Salford East since 1955.
[2] Labour M.P. for Eton and Slough since 1966.

the Government with the rank and file was real but so was the delegates' desire to support us. Probably the vote would have been almost the same—the miners' vote was very largely obtained beforehand by the pit closure concessions—and the Government got just the majority they wanted and a bit more. But Jim's importance was that he asked for a vote of confidence and got it by showing himself to be completely *en rapport* with the rank and file.

Wednesday, October 4th

The P.M.'s speech came as the first big event after the fraternal greetings from the T.U.C. As I sat there listening I was spellbound to hear a speech on which I'd worked so hard actually delivered. What struck me was the sheer punch of the delivery. Harold looked young and cheerful and vigorous and, my God, he put it across. As he went along he added many additional little touches and there was a great use of hand and expression. I would say he added 30 per cent at least to the quality of the speech we had worked at. I think he deserved more than the minute's ovation he got. After all, Jim Callaghan had been replying to a debate and that is what Conference likes and that is what it's relatively easy for an N.E.C. member to do. But Harold had to make an oration cold without any previous debate and that was an astonishing achievement. There was no doubt that these two speeches have absolutely transformed the Government's relations with the Party. Whether they've had the same impact on the country outside is slightly more doubtful but I shall be surprised if they haven't.

Friday, October 6th

We had intended to get up fairly early and drive straight down to Prescote, where the Chief and his wife were to stay the night with us. It was a filthy morning and very early I was rung up to ask whether I would do a radio programme at 2.30 for the main B.B.C. Conference programme that night. I said I couldn't be bothered because I was off. Then I ran into Harold in the hall and he said that he very much wanted me to do this programme because it's a new idea, an informal discussion for reflections on the Conference. I was suitably impressed and so we changed our plans. This was quite a good thing because as an outgoing member I went down to the last debate and took part in singing the 'Red Flag' and 'Auld Lang Syne' and then had a quick lunch with Tam Dalyell before I started the recording. They treated it very much as my swan-song and kept on asking me why I was resigning, and it was a long time before we got on to the questions I wanted to raise about the morale of the Party and why it was losing its soul.

Monday, October 9th

I had insisted on Tuesday for my Balmoral trip because I'd assumed that the Monday after Conference would be crammed full of Cabinet business.

Actually today was the day when the Prime Minister was taking the chair at N.E.D.C. as part of his new job of running D.E.A. The Committees were all postponed till Tuesday. I decided to get hold of Burke Trend, back from his holiday in Montreal, and establish the new Ministerial Committee on publicity. I saw him just before lunch and he told me everything was in order as he had checked with the Prime Minister and the official notice appointing the Committee would go out later this week. Chairman—Lord President. Members—First Secretary, Economic Secretary, Chief Whip and attached to it the normal official committee. All in charge of the co-ordination of home publicity. Now that I've got this after more than a year's struggle against Harold and Trevor Lloyd-Hughes, what can be achieved by it? Certainly we can co-ordinate the advertising campaigns of the Departments, we can look at the provision for a monitoring survey of television, we can prepare a campaign to put over the prices and incomes policy as Peter Shore is demanding. Whether we can go beyond this and I can use my position as I did during the war in order to influence policy is very doubtful. The membership of the Committee is favourable but everything really depends on the Prime Minister's attitude.

After this the Chief and I went to make an official call on the Speaker who's filled his vacation with official tours in Rome and other places. He seemed much younger, less flyblown than he was before, no doubt as a result of his marriage. We went carefully through our reform package with him. He was obviously delighted that in future the Deputy Speaker would have the power to give the closure on Report Stage of Bills. He was obviously reluctant to see the Clerks get rid of their wigs. He liked our idea for the new type of morning sitting as really helping him and the officials of the House. He did raise one or two difficulties about having the Finance Bill upstairs, which John Silkin promised to look at.

Tuesday, October 10th

One arrives at Aberdeen at the comfortable hour of seven o'clock and I had a long bath at the hotel before going down to breakfast. Then Elwyn Jones and Eddie Shackleton came in from a later train. It was a morning as lovely as on my last visit to Balmoral a year ago. This time, forewarned, I'd taken tremendous trouble with Martin Charteris, the Queen's Assistant Secretary, who has promised to spend the afternoon walking me round the estate. And we'd real luck for that walk, because it had been a drenching day yesterday and now there was a pale blue sky with clouds moving across constantly, seeming to thicken and then spreading out again. A perfect autumn day.

The driver of our car was a young Welshman with whom Elwyn Jones conversed a bit in their native language. When we got near to Balmoral we all said we wanted to write postcards to our children whereupon Leigh[1] told us we couldn't do that because we had to get there by 11.15. Under pressure

[1] Neville Leigh. Deputy Clerk of the Privy Council 1965–74 and, since 1974, Clerk.

however he admitted that the Council was at 12.30. Since the Lord President wasn't just going to sit in the equerries' quarters and wait we got out and picked our cards, wrote them and sent them off before proceeding further.

Martin Charteris was at the front of the house waiting to take us round to the equerries' entrance at the side and there he and I had an extremely pleasant talk about Palestine, where he was Chief of Army Intelligence to General Macmillan when I was a member of the Anglo-American Commission, in 1946.[1] Then he told us what he'd laid on for the afternoon and showed us the geography of the house before taking us out for a little walk in the garden to see the autumn flowers. We learnt that there are twelve London policemen up there as well as a whole section of the London Post Office.

This week the Queen is alone, since the children are at school and the Duke is away on business. Apparently she enjoys this since what she really likes is riding. Indeed she was out riding when we arrived and we saw her return by the back entrance.

Yesterday I'd checked with No. 10 and learnt that on his recent visit Harold had discussed the Lords reform with her so I was entitled to mention that Cabinet was discussing it on Thursday. This I did in our normal talk before the Privy Council. I said I didn't quite know which way the Cabinet would react. She wanted to know why. And I said that some members of the Cabinet, like George Brown, think that socialists shouldn't handle this type of thing but I believed we could do it by agreement with the other Parties. 'Agreement,' she said. 'That will be a great feather in your cap, won't it?' And I said, 'Yes, it would be an extremely good thing.' Then she pressed the button and that was the end of my talk. In came the rest of the Privy Council and four busy men stood there for a couple of minutes while I read aloud the usual collection of bits and pieces, including the prolongation of the Seychelles Legislature. Then we moved into the next room for drinks and here she explained (she didn't of course apologize) why she was twelve minutes late for the Council. When she was farthest from the house her horse had got a stone in its foot. 'One always carries one of those penknives, doesn't one, as an instrument for taking out stones, but today was the one day I didn't have it.' Then she mentioned that the horse she was riding was a Russian horse which Bulganin gave her on his visit. 'These Russian horses,' she said, 'are very obstinate. Some weeks ago Margaret took this horse out and had gone over six bridges and at the seventh bridge it had refused, although it was exactly like the others. It just wouldn't budge.' Hours later the rest of the family had gone out and found Margaret and the horse standing by the bridge with the horse still mutinous.

Over lunch I started to discuss the Philby story, which had dominated all

[1] Crossman, appointed to the Palestine Commission by the Foreign Secretary, Ernest Bevin, had been largely instrumental in getting a unanimous report that favoured the foundation of the state of Israel.

the Sunday papers, and asked whether she has read it. She said, 'No, she didn't read that kind of thing.' I was suddenly aware that this was not a subject which we ought to discuss.[1]

When we finished lunch she shook my hand, she was off and that was that, and we were left to have our afternoon tea with the equerries.

The afternoon was absolutely lovely. Martin Charteris had planned a magnificent ride around the estate in the Queen's great big estate car. We climbed up through the deer forest at the back to a waterfall with a little bridge built over it by Queen Victoria. The paths there, we were told, had been kept up by three whole-time gardeners, but they were getting a bit decrepit now. How we climbed towards the River Dee! I observed the usual problem. It's difficult to combine a deer forest for stalking with serious tree planting since the deer eat all the young trees unless they're enclosed with enormously expensive fences. And of course the erection of the fences takes all the profit out of the trees.

After a quick tea we were off on the afternoon flight from Aberdeen airport since I had changed my mind that morning and decided to go back to London early by air. I had to have a talk with Frank Longford and Eddie about the preparations for Thursday's Cabinet meeting. The plane took off at 6.35 and we were in La Rève—a little restaurant in the King's Road, Chelsea, which Frank likes—by 8.45, which is pretty good going. It was really an excellent evening. Eddie was being driven frantic by his working party, which is far too full of officials who want nothing to be done. He also has to contend with his Chief Whip, Frank Beswick, who, as I had suspected, was proving a man with a chip on his shoulder, all the time worrying about his new status and being thoroughly difficult about reform.

We decided that the first thing to do was to get the Prime Minister to agree to the size and composition of the delegation to negotiate with the other Parties and work out our plan. It should consist of three from the House of Lords (Gerald Gardiner, Frank Longford and Eddie Shackleton) and two from the House of Commons (myself and Roy Jenkins, or alternatively Michael Stewart, if Harold insisted on that). Alas, we should have to keep John Silkin out in order to keep Frank Beswick out. As soon as this delegation had been set up Harold should give instructions to wind up the Ministerial Committee and the official committee so that we could start again and get the work done by a selected team of politicians and officials. When all this had been agreed Frank said that he thought that I should lead the delegation. I must say this was very good of him because as Leader of the House he would naturally like to lead it himself. Considering how passionate he is about this and how much he knows and how little I know, he has shown an

[1] Kim Philby, a former Foreign Office man who had warned the two agents Guy Burgess and Donald Maclean that they were about to be arrested in 1951, had himself fled to Moscow in 1963. This had been the subject of two articles which revealed that for many years he had himself been a Soviet agent, recruited before the war.

astonishing power to put his personal feelings behind him and a real care for the cause we all have at heart.

Thursday, October 12th

This was the great Cabinet day for me. We started at 9.30, in time for Harold to go to Attlee's funeral. I don't think I mentioned that Attlee died on the Saturday after Conference and Harold insisted that he must go to the actual funeral while the rest of us would attend the memorial service in Westminster Abbey next week.[1]

The first thing to say about this Cabinet is that very few people attended. There were quite a number away—not only Tony Crosland and Roy Jenkins but also Tony Greenwood, Dick Marsh and Cledwyn Hughes. Four people, including Barbara, came in late. Gerald Gardiner and I put the case pretty concisely and immediately George Brown and Jim Callaghan joined battle with us. Both of them struck me as extremely excited, incoherent and surprisingly ill-informed.

George made a long speech saying that our scheme was ill thought-out, and that for instance the thing that would happen would be that all these life peers would come and vote at P.L.P. meetings, and as they had no discipline we would have undisciplined voting. He didn't seem to know that there was a Whip in the House of Lords.

Jim was equally incoherent and complained that our proposals would give the peers control of Statutory Instruments. He was apparently unaware that this is a power they now have but that we would remove.

Listening to their speeches, strong and emphatic as usual, I suddenly realized that this was the first time I had ever heard George Brown or Jim Callaghan speaking without a departmental brief. For once they were floundering in an area where they had no knowledge.

The key speeches on our side were from Peter Shore and Barbara. I had mentioned that the younger generation of Labour M.P.s were strong supporters of Lords reform and Peter underlined the point. Barbara took much the same line but was a good deal shrewder and got on to the question whether the two-tier system we were proposing was in our eyes an interim solution before we got to a wholly nominated House without any speaking peers at all or whether we regarded it as permanent, with a great extension of patronage. She'd spotted that. We had Ray Gunter and Fred Peart sharply but firmly supporting reform as inevitable, so I was quite wrong to anticipate that the proletarians would line up behind George. Indeed, it was striking that only George Thomson, though he supported us in principle but made a number of objections, lined up behind George. Tony Wedgwood Benn helped us a very great deal though he was unhappy about it and, knowing all about the Lords himself, wanted to limit our scheme. What Dick Marsh would have done I don't know but he would probably have been against it. So there it was. We

[1] He died on October 8th at the age of 84.

had won. It was an overwhelming victory and afterwards the P.M. said to me that he was relieved we didn't win with seven or eight votes against us.

Why were George Brown and Jim Callaghan so excited? I should say their predominant motive was resentment at not being consulted. This is the only major Cabinet decision since 1964 from which they have been excluded until the last moment. We'd been working on this for six months and they hadn't known anything whatsoever. Indeed this has been one of the few Cabinet secrets which has been successfully kept. I think it might have been much wiser of Harold to bring in George Brown much earlier on.

Friday, October 13th

I had to act quickly in order to get Lords reform moving after the Cabinet decisions. What I needed was a memorandum circulated in Whitehall. Burke, who can be very helpful when he wants, rang me up to give me the three essential points. One, that the five people who do the negotiating for the Government must also prepare the Bill; two, that the staff required, whether they are of the Home Office or of the House of Lords, must be selected by him; and three, that in any case the officials we should ask for should be Wheeler-Booth from the House of Lords and Moriarty from the Home Office. I went through this with Gerald and the memorandum was prepared in his office. This is an interesting sample of how Whitehall works when the officials want to make it work.

Thursday, October 19th

No Cabinet because Harold has to go to Scotland on one of his D.E.A. expeditions. It was a crucial day when the Cabinet should have met. The dock strike was coming to a most ferocious hopeless climax and there seemed to be very little chance of a settlement. Simultaneously the railway strike was getting hotter.

However, there was one item of great interest at Home Affairs—the problem of the Kenya Asians.[1] Soon after we got back from the recess Roy Jenkins had come to see me in my Privy Council Office to tell me that he might urgently need a slot for legislation to deal with the problem of Kenya Asians with British passports. There are some 200,000 of them who are now threatened as a result of the black-Africa policy. This morning he put this problem to the Home Affairs Committee in a very indecisive way. I couldn't blame him for that. It's quite clear we couldn't allow some 50,000 Asians from Kenya to pour into Britain each year. On the other hand it's doubtful whether we have any legal or constitutional right to deny entry to these people from Kenya since they have British passports. This is the kind of problem which Labour Ministers discuss rationally and well. We finally agreed that Roy must of course face the possibility of this threat developing

[1] Some 500 Asians a week had been leaving Kenya for Britain after the introduction in August of new legislation making it more difficult for them to obtain work permits at home.

into reality and that he must work out appropriate policies and consider the practicability of legislation.

I then went across the river to lunch with the Archbishop[1] and the Church Commissioners at Lambeth Palace. I found a great roomful of people but fortunately I found myself sitting near to the Archbishop and he gave us an excellent lunch—good white wine, good red wine and pâté. Yes, the Church does itself well when it lunches with its Commissioners. Finally, afterwards, I had a quiet talk with him about Lords reform. 'Supposing we were to reform the Lords, Archbishop, how would you like to see it?' I asked him. We talked round it for some time and then I popped a direct question. 'I want to know about the future of the Bishops in the Lords.' 'Well, the kind of cleric in a future House of Lords would be Donald Soper, the Methodist minister, selected on his merits as a life peer. That's the way I'd like to see clerics chosen in the future.' 'So you don't want a block reserved for the Church of England Bishops?' I said, to which he replied that their pastoral duties make it impossible for them to attend regularly and if they do so it may not be desirable. (I believe by this remark he meant the Bishop of Southwark, who attends regularly and is too political.)[2] I was interested by this since I hadn't thought of the line we would take.

Tuesday, October 24th
This morning came the virtual French veto on our entry to the Common Market. They declared that we couldn't be considered for membership until the pound had ceased to be the second international currency and we had got the problem of parity under control.

I had arranged to brief the Opposition leaders about our intention to reform the House of Lords. But now I discovered that Heath and Whitelaw refused to meet us before the Queen's Speech. The reason was simple and I should have foreseen it. They'd obviously been informed of every detail by Carrington and Jellicoe[3] because Frank Longford can't resist talking to them out of office hours. I don't blame them for their decision. But today, without saying anything to me, Longford proceeded to talk in even greater detail to Carrington and Jellicoe and the news began to percolate down the corridors into the House of Commons.

By far the most interesting episode of this day however was my meeting with Michael Adeane—at the Palace to discuss my attendance at the State Opening of Parliament. Let me explain. Weeks ago I received a programme from the College of Heraldry telling me of a rehearsal which as Lord

[1] The Most Rev. and Rt. Hon. Michael Ramsey, Archbishop of Canterbury 1962–74. He became a life peer on his retirement.
[2] Mervyn Stockwood, Bishop of Southwark since 1959.
[3] Lord Carrington was Leader of the House of Lords 1963–4, and Leader of the Opposition in the Lords 1964–70. Lord Jellicoe was deputy leader of the Opposition in the House of Lords 1967–70 and Leader of the House from 1970 until his resignation in 1973.

President I had to attend. Without very much thought I wrote back saying that I didn't want to attend the State Opening so I would just like to have a diplomatic illness. For a fortnight or so we heard nothing. Then Harold told me that he had received a letter from the Duke of Norfolk[1] saying that he heard I objected to attending the State Opening owing to my anti-monarchical sentiments. This letter was actually shown to me by Michael Halls and it certainly indicates some amount of malice among the court officials. I was delighted when Michael Halls drafted a reply from the Prime Minister saying that he was amazed to receive this extraordinary epistle from the Duke. 'The truth is the Lord President is keenly distressed because he suffers from a phobia about public occasions of this sort which make him unable to attend.' I thought this letter would be the end of the business and I heaved a sigh of relief because I really was dreading the idea of having to go to Moss Bros and hire morning dress, which I've never in my life worn before, and parade up and down in the Royal Gallery. I was looking forward to doing a quiet morning's work during the State Opening of Parliament as I did during the Attlee memorial service. However I underestimated the court. Last Tuesday I received a letter at Vincent Square from the Duke of Norfolk stating that he was deeply alarmed and disturbed by what I had said about not going to the State Opening and that only the Queen could relieve me of the obligation to go. Harold by now was a bit flustered by the affair and I rang up Michael Adeane and he asked to see me at 7.45 tonight before I went off to dinner at the German Embassy. When we had driven in to Buckingham Palace it was pitch dark and I found some difficulty in discovering the door into his little office. He told me that Harold Wilson had just come in to discuss the Queen's Speech with the Queen and said that I'd mucked things up terribly by writing to the Heralds and the Duke of Norfolk. 'Why didn't you come to me?' he said straightaway. 'I could have cleared it with the Queen and I can clear it now if you really want not to go. Indeed, all you need to do is to write a letter to her asking to be excused without stating any reason why.' He then went on to add, 'Of course, the Queen has as strong a feeling of dislike of public ceremonies as you do. I don't disguise from you the fact that it will certainly occur to her to ask herself why you should be excused when she has to go, since you're both officials.' I sat down this evening and wrote a letter to Michael Adeane saying that I would attend. His handling of the affair had been as masterly as that of the Duke of Norfolk had been clumsy.

Wednesday, October 25th

I had to go over to Downing Street to tell the P.M. that as a result of Frank Longford's talks with Jellicoe and Carrington it had been revealed that Carrington was deeply upset by the text of the Queen's Speech because it

---

[1] Bernard Marmaduke Fitzalan-Howard, 16th Duke of Norfolk, Earl Marshal and Hereditary Marshal and Chief Butler of England. He died in 1975.

didn't specifically refer to all-party consultation. So we added the necessary words and by 10.30 the draft was corrected and ready. After this I suggested to Harold that he or I should have a Lobby conference on Thursday as usual and then Frank could have his on Friday. But he was adamant. He wanted to announce nothing because he was proud that security has been so well kept.

This afternoon we had another meeting of the Broadcasting Committee. The Chief and I represented the Government and Ted Heath arrived with his Chief Whip and Jeremy Thorpe with his.[1] We had the usual senior officials from I.T.N. and the B.B.C. It was quite lively because Heath had decided to stage a great demonstration. He proposed in a very rapidly delivered speech that we should first of all depart from the rule that party broadcasts should be simultaneous on all channels so losing the captive audience, and secondly, in exchange, that we should allow the broadcasting time available to each Party to be divided up into as many five-minute intervals as we could get in. He thinks this would endear us to the public and he also thinks we could then pay much more attention to regional interests. These proposals were slapped down immediately by Hugh Greene and the other officials as technically impossible. The Chief and I were pretty wholly on the side of the B.B.C. I want to keep the captive audience, keep simultaneity and though I want shorter programmes I don't want us to degrade ourselves with endless short snappy advertising captions.

Ted has come back the hero of his Party Conference but this afternoon he seemed nervy and almost violent. At one point he said, 'I've just spent five years going round England and I can tell you how they all hate central government. Regionalism is the great thing. We've got to concede this to people if we want to endear ourselves to them.' Willie Whitelaw looked rather embarrassed.

Thursday, October 26th
As I feared the leaks about Lords reform are beginning to appear. There's one in the *Guardian* and another in the *Express*. If we're going to keep our intentions secret till next week we must give the Lobby some more news about the Commons and since I can't have my own Lobby conference I'm going to see a number of individual journalists—for example, from the *Financial Times*, the *Guardian* and the B.B.C.—and brief them about our plans for morning sittings.

At Cabinet I slipped in my amendment to the paragraph of the Queen's Speech about House of Lords reform and got it through without comment.

Friday, October 27th
All the press had the news about the abolition of morning sittings, which is a relief. At O.P.D. George Brown started a discussion on Aden by apologizing

---

[1] The Liberal Chief Whip was Eric Lubbock, M.P. for Orpington 1962–70 when he lost the seat. He succeeded to the Barony of Avebury later that year.

for having to tell us that we'll be out in November instead of January.[1] The rest of the Committee couldn't be more pleased. Really we've been miraculously lucky in Aden—cancelling all our obligations and getting out without a British soldier being killed. But George feels desperate because it's different from what he promised. We spent an hour trying to encourage him and we shall have to go through the same process in Cabinet on Monday.

Then the P.M. and I went across to the House for the Prorogation ceremony. I've never seen this before. First we sit in our House and then we march into the Lords and the Lord Chancellor reads out at dreary length all the Bills that have been passed. Then there is a Prorogation Speech repeating the whole thing, then we march back to the House of Commons where the Speaker is found sitting below his chair at the Committee Table and he reads the whole damn thing all over again. Then I was off after wasting a whole hour.

Monday, October 30th

The special Cabinet to authorize George Brown's decision to withdraw from Aden a month earlier than planned went according to form. Once again he spent his time apologizing for what all his colleagues considered a wonderfully lucky and fortunate result. That the regime he backed should have been overthrown by terrorists and has forced our speedy withdrawal is nothing but good fortune. It now looks as though we shall get out of Aden without losing a British soldier, chaos will rule soon after we've gone, and there'll be one major commitment cut—thank God.

This afternoon came the rehearsal for the State Opening of Parliament. I wandered down the corridor towards the House of Lords and in the Royal Gallery I found a woman with a bogus train wandering about surrounded by a lot of men. One of them I recognized as the Duke of Norfolk and in due course we were marshalled by our Earl Marshal and made to walk up and down. It was one of those wonderfully incompetent English performances where no one is really in charge. There were Monty and Eddie Shackleton standing together because one will hold the Sword of State and the other the Cap of Maintenance tomorrow and march in front of us. Then comes the Lord President and the Lord Privy Seal (the only two civilians in civilian costume), then the Lord Chancellor, then all those Heralds Pursuivant, and that's about the size of the procession before you come to the soldiers—the dragoons and the horseguards. This rehearsal was only for officials and dignitaries. I was anxiously thanked by the Earl Marshal for coming and Frank Longford seemed surprised at my being there.

After this I did a little party political broadcast on pensions which made me late for the Prime Minister's annual eve-of-session party at No. 10 where the Queen's Speech is revealed to all the members of the Government. I

---

[1] Aden became independent on November 29th.

missed his speech including his defence of Chalfont and I also missed the murmur of applause which greeted the announcement of the only thing they really liked—the reform of the House of Lords. I saw Chalfont and tried for a moment to give him a cheerful look. He's in appalling trouble because of the way he talked to journalists after the E.F.T.A. Conference at Lausanne last week.[1] Then I went across to the Privy Council office and I knocked out a draft of my Balfour anniversary speech.

Tuesday, October 31st

Although this was the day for the State Opening of Parliament I put on my ordinary suit and went along to my room in the House of Commons. From there I found my way to Eddie Shackleton's room where champagne was already being served. In the Lords there was a great sense of party—almost like Derby Day. The State Opening is a festive occasion. Eddie got into his uniform and his robes and I sheepishly got into my morning suit and actually found it perfectly comfortable. I could wear my ordinary white shirt and didn't have the separate hard collar for which I'd carefully gone out and bought the collar studs for 1s. 3d.

In due course Frank Longford and I stroll through the anteroom of the Lords and there we are suddenly in the Royal Gallery—usually a huge empty corridor with the vast picture of the battle of Waterloo on the one side and that of the battle of Trafalgar on the other. Now there are boxes on each side, packed with people who've been standing there for hours. They've done this just to see the Queen emerge from the Robing Room and walk with her procession behind her into the House of Lords. Then they won't see anything more until she has read the Queen's Speech and walked back down the Royal Gallery again. That's all that this distinguished crowd of waiting people will see. Gradually the boxes begin to fill up and the space where we are standing fills up with chaps wearing swords. Frank and I are told we should be stationed behind the Lord Chancellor on the stairs leading down to the Norman Porch, where the Queen enters. These stairs are also packed with troops on both sides and when we stand there it is very difficult not to get knocked by the trooper behind you when he presents swords, which he seems to be doing on and off for twenty minutes or so. Above us in the Royal Gallery are Field-Marshal Montgomery and Eddie getting ready for their function, surrounded by Air Marshals and Generals. But I am down on one of the lower stairs and suddenly looking up I see a bloated caricature, whose eyes you can hardly see because he is covered by a helmet with white plumes flying at the edge. It is Frank Bowles, walking very gingerly down the stairs

[1] On May 23rd Lord Chalfont had been appointed Chief British Negotiator for Britain's application for entry to the E.E.C. His words in Lausanne had been interpreted as a threat that Britain would be obliged to reassess her European policy, especially where defence was concerned, if General de Gaulle should block her application. Lord Chalfont, who had supposed his remarks to be off the record, offered the Prime Minister his resignation but it was refused.

so as not to trip over his golden spurs because if he did he could never get up.[1] And then I see Frank Beswick[2] looking almost as idiotic in his costume of Captain of the Gentlemen-at-Arms. In all this fancy dress Frank Longford and I stand out because we're the only people in ordinary civilian clothes— yes, my morning coat felt quite ordinary in that assembly. We are able to stroll about and talk to our friends and quite to enjoy ourselves.

What do I think? I think it's like the *Prisoner of Zenda* but not nearly as smart or well done as it would be at Hollywood. It's more what a real Ruritania would look like—far more comic, more untidy, more homely, less grand. The only grand things I saw were the Crown dazzling with jewels on its cushion and the Queen herself, with the royal princes and princesses. However, even there one could see that Snowdon's top hat had fallen off before he could get out of his car. The older royals are the best—particularly the Dowager Duchess of Kent, but not the goofy Duke of Gloucester, looking terrible with his very dull wife. Well, they come piling in one after another, the Cap of Maintenance comes, the Sword comes, the Crown comes and then down comes the Lord Chancellor in his magnificent robes and stands just in front of Frank and me—I on the right and Frank on the left. And suddenly I notice that the lace under his chin is trembling. The whole Lord Chancellor—though he adores these ceremonies, he tells me, because he always wanted to be a great actor—is trembling. Is it emotion or fear or tension? I don't know, but for more than half an hour he stands there trembling before the Queen arrives. And, of course, we never get more than a glimpse of her because as she arrives we have to turn and march smartly ahead of her up the stairs whereupon she turns left into the Robing Room while we form up and wait inside the Royal Gallery and then in due course process in front of her into the House of Lords.

On this state occasion the House of Lords is really magnificent—all the Law Lords, the Bishops, then the diplomats and their ladies with all their jewels, and behind them lines and lines of peers and peeresses, and above all of them the gallery and enormous arc lights for the televising of the Queen.

I come in at the right-hand door and stand just by the throne next to the Lord Chancellor and the Duke of Norfolk. And I have to watch her reading the appalling Speech for which I am responsible. It is certainly not designed for reading aloud in the House of Lords. Next time I must take some trouble to get a speech that sounds good when it's read aloud because this one sounds difficult and Harold Wilson's sentences about inflation are imposs- ible to enunciate. But I did notice that when she read the sentence about curbing the power of the Lords she made a little pause and read it with just a *frisson* and the whole House had just a *frisson* too. The moment she has

[1] Labour M.P. for Nuneaton from 1942 to 1964, when he made way for Frank Cousins. He became a life peer in 1964 and from 1965 until 1970 served as Captain of the Yeomen of the Guard (which accounts for his appearance on this occasion). He died in December 1970.

[2] Labour M.P. for Uxbridge 1945–59. Created a life peer in 1964, and Captain Hon. Corps of Gentlemen-at-Arms (Government Chief Whip in Lords) 1967–70.

withdrawn I have to dart out behind her with Frank Longford and we process back along the Royal Gallery and she disappears into the Robing Room. And then the Earl Marshal comes up to me and says, 'I suppose you're anxious to be off as soon as possible? If you go back the way you came you'll get out straight away.' So I walk slowly back through the Royal Gallery chatting to Frank as we go with everyone looking at us and within seconds we're back in his room drinking a glass of champagne.

Afterwards I took a quick lunch because I felt I ought to be on the front bench at 2.30 for the opening Speeches on the Address. I've never attended this kind of ceremonial and I thought the House would be packed and even the front bench full. But when I got there the House was only half full at most and there were four people on our front bench. I understood why when I had to listen to the long series of ridiculous announcements by the Speaker about the Amnesty Act and so on. It was twenty minutes or so before Hugh Delargy got up to move the Loyal Address in an excellent constituency speech full of humour, with Jack Ashley seconding—not quite as good but a very good pair taken together.[1] And then we were ready for the first combat of the Session between Wilson and Heath.

I went straight up to my Lobby conference. The P.M. had forbidden me to hold one last week and I did today's jointly with Frank Longford and Eddie Shackleton. I had thought out my initial statement and my answers pretty carefully. The only difficulty was that Frank Longford kept on making additions all the way through about his own personal two-tier reform scheme for the Lords. We have told him time after time that Cabinet is not committed to a two-tier scheme or indeed to any scheme at all, and that we want to negotiate with the other Parties on equal terms. Whenever I was asked about details of the scheme and reserved my position, Frank would rush in and say, 'I personally feel ...' and give another long answer. However, I don't think it really did much harm. What was clear by now was that the anticipations of Callaghan and Brown were completely falsified. In the House of Commons the only loud cheer on our side had come when the P.M. mentioned the reform of the Lords. Provided we make it a good reform they are going to like it.

Wednesday, November 1st
Lying in bed and thumbing through the morning papers I knew that our press conference had been a great success. But then I switched on the eight o'clock news and after it heard the recording of George Brown's astonishing scene at the Savoy, where he really misbehaved himself in public.[2]

This is intolerable, I felt, and I took up the phone and rang up Harold and

[1] Hugh Delargy, Labour M.P. for Platting (Manchester) 1945–50 and for Thurrock from 1950 until his death in 1976, and Jack Ashley, Labour M.P. for Stoke-on-Trent since 1966.

[2] George Brown had clashed with Lord Thomson, proprietor of the *Sunday Times* newspaper, in which one of the articles about Kim Philby, the Foreign Office official and Russian spy, had appeared.

told him what had happened. He'd read something in the press but he hadn't heard the radio and he said quickly, 'Don't say any more. I'll act on this. This is it but don't say a damn thing to anybody.' And he rang off.

At the Party meeting this morning I made a full-length statement on the reforms we were introducing in the Commons. It went quite well. When I had first told the P.M. that John and I had decided to drop morning sittings because the Opposition had succeeded in frustrating us, he had said we couldn't possibly do it because we would never live down the defeat. Well, on this occasion I frankly told the Party that morning sittings had failed and the Tories had done what they intend to do to them and we therefore wouldn't go on with them. The statement was received in silence with obvious relief. Indeed, when I sat down after explaining the whole package I got the nearest thing to an ovation which I've had since I became Leader of the House—a continuous round of applause for what they obviously thought was highly satisfactory, including of course the reference at the beginning to the Lords reform.

Thursday, November 2nd

This afternoon at Question Time the House was seething with excitement about George Brown. Would Alec Douglas-Home as Opposition spokesman take the occasion to attack and destroy him? I sat next to the P.M., who said he thought that Alec would launch the attack. I replied, 'I'm certain he won't. First of all he's a gentleman and second he's too clever a politician to get you off the hook. To attack George would be to make him safe from dismissal.' 'You're probably right,' said the P.M.

Friday, November 3rd

The bashing, crashing news of defeats dominated the morning papers. What a week. The Chalfont scandal, the Brown scandal, the by-election defeats[1] —all one after the other. I rang up Harold and said, 'Look, I was going off today but I'd like to see you. Can I look in this morning?' 'No, but I'm there all the afternoon.' 'I've got to go to Dulwich, may I come in afterwards?' 'Yes.'

I went out to Dulwich College to talk to the sixth form and got back at five in time for my appointment, which I assumed would enable me to catch the 6.10 to Banbury. But though the P.M. was punctual he kept me there longer than I thought possible and I had one of the most interesting talks I've ever had. I told him I'd come there simply to talk as a friend about the by-election results. 'In Transport House,' I pointed out, 'there wasn't a single person capable of considering the strategy of our propaganda, the effects of the by-elections and drawing conclusions from them. This kind of work simply isn't going on either in Transport House or in Whitehall.' 'You want an inner

[1] The Government had just lost two seats—Leicester South-West to the Conservatives and Hamilton to the Scottish Nationalists.

Cabinet,' he said at once. 'Yourself, Michael Stewart, Jim Callaghan, Roy Jenkins—yes, I'd have him in now but notice I don't bring in George Brown.' I said I'd noticed that and he added, 'Well, he's got to go, but not straight-away.' 'Nobody realizes', he went on, 'what an awful time I've had with him.' And he told me a number of stories of George's behaviour and how Harold had had to cut the phone off because of what George was shouting down the line. Suddenly he said, 'I want you to do something—see Jimmy Margach today and tell him that Cabinet is against George.' 'Have you got that information from Cabinet?' I asked and he looked at me with those great grey eyes and said, 'Well, they told Burke Trend.'

In addition, he asked me to talk to the press about Chalfont having not got a glimmer of information from No. 10. 'I don't like asking you to do these things often,' he said, 'but in this case do it quickly. Some action must be taken.' Then he began to talk about his reshuffle. He said there were many choices and I pointed out that he couldn't move Jim Callaghan to the F.O. unless as Chancellor Jim had already carried out the devaluation. That was a bold thing to say to the P.M. in his present mood. 'Of course my mind is open on that,' he replied. 'It's Jim who has a closed mind on devaluation.' 'It may be closed,' I said, 'but you and I have got to make him do it. And he's got to have done the job before he can get the Foreign Office as his reward.' 'But the issue,' he replied, 'is the floating pound. I agree with Thomas, I'm for the floating pound but the fixed pound is what the other side want.' I said I thought he would find Tony Crosland on his side about this and he said, 'Mind you, my mind is open, we shall have to discuss all this at S.E.P. on Wednesday.' And then he came back to his idea of an inner Cabinet. 'I'm not sure you need an inner Cabinet,' I said, 'but you certainly need political staff and civil servants here in No. 10 to help you to work out a policy.' 'Then we must use Marcia,' he said. 'We must have our meetings once a week.' 'That's what I suspected,' I said. 'It's an enlarged kitchen Cabinet you want, not a new inner Cabinet. Well, let's try to get it done and to have John Silkin in as well.'

The new fact to emerge from this conversation was his reference to Roy. He's now determined to bring Roy into the inner circle and to have George out. He now thinks highly of Tony Crosland and regards him as wholly reliable. Tony looks to me like the man booked for the Treasury. Just when we were finishing Harold suddenly looked at me and said, 'Is it time for you to go back to a Department?' 'Yes,' I said. 'Provided I've got through these reforms in the Commons and the House of Lords reform's well launched I'd like to go back to a Department, but it rather depends what Department it is.' And I'm still wondering what it might be.

Monday, November 6th
This afternoon in the House I had to answer Questions on behalf of the Services Committee. When a session ends all the Select Committees end too

and have to be reappointed so this week there is no chairman of catering, etc., and only the Lord President can answer for all the sub-committees. I had one very delicate question about tipping. The Office bluntly committed me to replying that there was a 7½ per cent surcharge but actually 5 per cent of this goes to increased wages and 2½ per cent to a pool of tips. I dare say this may be common practice in hotels but it seems to me something which we can't possibly tolerate as Honourable Members of the House of Commons. If we have only 2½ per cent deducted for tips we should tell the Members so. One of the troubles, I gathered, is that only about forty of the total catering staff get any tips, mostly those in the Strangers' dining-room. The men and the girls in the other room never see a tip and never reckon on them. So if you have a tips pool and divide it equally among the whole staff those in the Strangers' dining-room lose enormously and everybody else gains slightly. That, I gather, is the real grievance which has got to be dealt with. However I was careful this afternoon, and told the House that the new Committee was in the middle of its negotiations and I couldn't make a Statement until they were completed. I didn't let out a single word of what I had learnt about the actual division of the surcharge.

The rest of the day until 1 a.m. was taken up with preparing my speech.[1] I was determined not to repeat the fiasco which I'd suffered in trying to reply to part IV of the Prices and Incomes Bill. During the morning I'd been glancing through the Treasury brief and noticed seven points which Iain Macleod had given to the Brighton Tory Conference. It suddenly occurred to me that I could make the House laugh by taking his seven points and showing the hollowness of the Tory alternative. A wind-up speech is always a difficult thing to prepare because you start at exactly half an hour before the vote is taken and you've to sit down a few seconds before it strikes ten. You've got to look at the clock all the time and have your speech carefully divided up into sections with a final two-minute section which you begin at exactly two minutes to the hour. I knew that my two-minute section and, indeed, my last seven or eight minutes must be about the record of the Labour Government, but I was going to make my demolition of Macleod the centre of the speech. In preparing it I had to remember that I was winding up an eight-day debate which was mostly about economic problems. That's a real difficulty for a Lord President who isn't an economist. If you try to ape the Chancellor or the President of the Board of Trade you're howled down. If you talk ordinary Party propaganda the Opposition in its post-prandial mood tries to drown you with quiet conversation. The man who knew how to behave on those occasions was Harry Crookshank and he was the model which I had to imitate.[2] It must be the kind of clever near-Oxford Union speech, hard-hitting, light, humorous and yet with a bite. This is what we

[1] Crossman was due to wind up the Debate on the Address.
[2] Conservative M.P. for Gainsborough 1924–55, and Leader of the House of Commons 1951–5. He became a viscount in 1956 and died in October 1961.

worked on this evening until finally Molly, who was waiting, motored my secretary home to her place in Dulwich and then took Freddie on to his place at Leatherhead while I walked home.

Tuesday, November 7th

At Legislation Committee I had to play my traditional role as controller of the legislative timetable and haul the Ministers over the coals. Each of them had promised me six months ago that if I gave their Bill a place in the programme it would be ready to go to Second Reading before Christmas yet now we come to the end of the Queen's Speech and there are fewer Bills ready than ever before. All the big Bills are teetering over and it looks as though they won't start till after the Christmas recess. I told the Committee that their Bills would be lost if they weren't ready by the end of the Session.

The debate this afternoon was delayed by a long series of points of order. At last Iain Macleod got up. He didn't make the expected thundering attack on the Government. Instead he delivered a very careful, thoughtful oration discussing with great learning the unemployment figures, and expounding their real significance. I suspect he didn't attack the Government's policy because basically he knew that if he were Chancellor of the Exchequer he would be doing much the same as Jim. But I didn't care about the details of his speech. What caught my attention was an odd remark he made at the end of this long and detailed analysis of the movement of unemployment figures during the last ten years. At this point he remarked, 'We can all make our points on by-election platforms and I am as good at selective quotation as anybody else. But nobody can seriously argue that when the performance of both Governments ...' The moment I heard this I knew I had got him because he had frankly admitted the difference between the kind of non-sense one talks outside and the serious speech one makes in the House of Commons.

Then we came to poor old Jim Callaghan. He was tired and overwrought and he made the mistake of being offensive to our back-benchers. 'Now I come to the question', he remarked, 'of the Governor of the Bank of England, who made the speech—which I very much doubt many honourable Members have read ...'[1] Callaghan then made things worse by quoting the Governor of the Bank. 'He said: "It is impossible to manage a large industrial economy with the very small margin of unused manpower resources that characterized the British economy in the 1940s and 1950s." That is true ... We must have a somewhat larger margin of unused capacity than we used

[1] In a speech in Argentina on October 5th, the Governor of the Bank of England, Sir Leslie O'Brien, had said that the Government's economic policy was based on retaining a margin of unused capacity in the economy. It seemed that the Governor's remarks were made with official approval and Labour M.P.s attacked this suggestion that there was a deliberate pool of unemployment. The Chancellor had refused to repudiate the speech and some seventy Labour M.P.s put down a motion of censure.

to try to keep. That is the truth of the matter.' If you read it in Hansard[1] you realize how terrible it was for a Labour Chancellor to say such a thing, particularly if he profoundly believed it, and was suspected of believing it by his back-benchers. Immediately Callaghan sat down Michael Foot and Mendelson rose and made fighting speeches against the Labour Chancellor who was insisting that we needed a higher level of unemployment.

The Tory wind-up was provided by Reg Maudling. I'd had a cup of coffee with him and Quintin Hogg after lunch and he'd told me that this kind of rough and tumble on the last day didn't suit him. I said it didn't suit me either. He got through his speech perfectly respectably and then came my turn. I knew I had won the House over when I looked across the table and said to Macleod, 'You've told us you have one style of serious discussion for us here and something very different for the boobs in Brighton.' This brought the House down and then I was able to take him through his Brighton programme point by point and tear it to farcical smithereens. The Tories laughed themselves out of their discomfort and the back-benchers behind me roared. At two minutes to ten I began my little carefully rehearsed wind-up and as Big Ben started striking I sat down to a deluge of applause. That hadn't happened to me for a very long time—everybody coming up to me in the lobby and wanting to shake my hand. Everybody was voting for the Government with a good conscience. Of course they'd have voted for the Government anyway that evening but they'd have gone into the lobby surlily regretting they were not abstaining whereas on this occasion they went with gaiety in their hearts. I'm afraid that many of them were talking about the contrast between poor Jim and me and next day a vote of censure was put down not on the Lord President as it was a few months ago but on the Chancellor of the Exchequer.

After the division I asked Jim whether he had planned to make those remarks about unemployment. 'No, no,' he said. 'It was that fellow Mendelson with his awful *sotto voce* interjections in my speech. They made me so angry that I lashed out and attacked them much more than I intended. I should have put it the other way round—the way Harold puts it.' That often happens in life. What you don't intend to say is what you really mean. What he'd said that afternoon were the true sentiments he shared with the Governor of the Bank of England about the pool of unemployment.

Wednesday, November 8th

Of course, I got no press at all for my very successful speech. It was just mentioned in a line or two in one of the quality papers but everybody else virtually ignored it because the big parliamentary story for them was under the headline 'Callaghan rows with his back-benchers'. They had got their story conveniently early and they weren't going to change it merely because of what I said at 9.30 p.m.

[1] *House of Commons Debates*, Vol. 753, cols. 874–5.

This morning we had a meeting of the Cabinet Social Services Committee to reconsider next April's package for increased family allowances with supplementary allowances and children's tax allowances, the price of school meals, the price of welfare milk all considered together.

I then moved on to the long-awaited S.E.P. meeting on imports and devaluation. It started with a speech by Tony Crosland, very skilful and cautious, and strictly along the lines he had discussed with me. His main aim was to show that import quotas were no substitute for devaluation—a subject he skirted around until the Prime Minister himself brought it right out in the open and said we must discuss the pros and cons. At once the Chancellor made it clear that he was still against devaluation and believed we must soldier on. Floating of the pound was, he said, a delusion. If we were forced off, that was that: it would be a disaster but there could be no question of freely deciding to go off. The P.M. was keeping his options open. 'I am politically open on this subject. I am prepared to think there could be some merit in a free decision, and in that case we must of course decide whether we float or devalue by a certain amount. My mind isn't closed,' he said. Long before this it had become clear in the general discussion that no one objected in principle to devaluation except the Chancellor. Jim was absolutely isolated, with the possible exception of Ray Gunter, and Harold had got what he once told me he wanted. He had smoked the Chancellor out, and proved he was alone in his objection, while at least three of us—Tony Crosland, Michael Stewart and I—were convinced we should do it as soon as was practically possible. Each of us begged Harold not to wait until he was forced off.

Out of this came a second statement by Callaghan. He was just not prepared to reconsider the issue for several months. But, he added, there was a serious chance of our being forced off in the immediate future—in a matter of days, the next ten days or so. This he said more than once and Cabinet decided to leave that to him and the Prime Minister to handle. Up till now Crosland had made all the running but at this point I interjected that I felt we couldn't possibly leave things as they were and urged that we must have another meeting because most of us were convinced we must now devalue as soon as possible. To this Jim replied that we must not underestimate the catastrophe of devaluation. It would be a political catastrophe as well as an economic one. I couldn't resist telling him that he mustn't underestimate the catastrophe of our present policy. 'We are in the middle of a political catastrophe now,' I said, 'and there's no prospect of getting out of it until there's a new breakthrough which we can only get by devaluation.' But it was also true, I concluded, that we could only get it if the Prime Minister and the Chancellor of the Exchequer carried it out themselves. These two are essential to the credibility of a Labour Government which devalues. I simply want them to do it as soon as they can. Harold insisted there should be no minutes of this part of Cabinet and assured us that he and Jim would hold on and see what possibilities there were of rallying support from our allies in the Six, in Basle and in New York.

I was told later in the day that the Prime Minister was pleased by what he had achieved at the meeting. I was pretty worried because I could see that he and Callaghan are determined not to devalue until they're forced off and I wouldn't be a bit surprised if they borrowed another £300 or £400 million and led us into debt over the £2,000 million point in order to avoid making a decision.

Thursday, November 9th

Bank rate went up by another half per cent[1] and very obviously there is another sterling crisis. But of course it was not mentioned in cabinet today.

At lunch-time I first heard the rumours that George Wigg was to go to the Lords and become the head of the Horse-race Betting Levy Board. Later I got the facts from Harold.

The Party meeting this evening lasted a full forty minutes and the P.M., John and I had the job of keeping our colleagues quiet. They were full of indignation, wanting to get at Callaghan and attack George and we had to expend a lot of our fund of goodwill to soothe them.

I left John at No. 12 and went through to my business meeting with the P.M. I found him alone with Burke; George came in later. The three of them then had a long and fascinating discussion about Vietnam. They felt that the Government must now move from its present position of close association with L.B.J. but not too far away. This, they all agreed, was a delicate operation and it must be reflected in the paper they were preparing for Cabinet. I listened quietly and learnt a great deal about the delusions of grandeur which are the fatal defects of George and Harold and which are constantly stimulated by Burke Trend. They believe that as acknowledged actors on the world political stage they can perform these manoeuvres, moving a little bit away from L.B.J., and influencing him from a distance. They all seem unaware that they are figures of fun as long as Britain is on the edge of economic ruin. They should accept their lot, concentrate on home affairs and stop trying to obtain opportunities for appearances on the world stage. This is my basic disagreement with them.

After they'd gone I had a word with the P.M. about George Wigg. He explained to me that Antony Head had been offered and had refused the job.[1] This gave George his chance and if he didn't take it now he would miss it for ever. 'Anyway, I think it's the right time for him to move on.' This confirmed the impression I'd got that afternoon from Trevor Lloyd-Hughes that George didn't really want to go and had to be pushed, but in a nice

[1] From 6 to 6½ per cent.
[2] Conservative M.P. for Carshalton 1945–60. He was Secretary of State for War 1951–56 and Minister of Defence 1956–January 1957. In 1960 he became a viscount and first High Commissioner to the Federation of Nigeria. From 1963–66 he was High Commissioner to the new Federation of Malaysia.

favourable way. The Prime Minister confirmed that this would require a by-election at Dudley and when I said, 'Oh hell,' he replied, 'Well, we could hold it over until next June when it ought to be all right. George's going will be a great relief, you know,' he added. 'He was becoming a great early morning pressure on my telephone, as you very well know.'

Physically as well as mentally Harold's beginning to show some strain in conversation. I don't like the fact but he now sits at the Cabinet table sipping whisky instead of water. Callaghan hasn't got much nerve left and George Brown is on the way out. There's a real danger that our people at the centre of things are cracking from sheer exhaustion.

Saturday, November 11th
I spent the night with the Baloghs and next morning walked across the Parks—an exquisitely beautiful day, lovely beech trees and copper beeches beaming in the sun. I was going to see my sister Mary and her husband, Charles Woodhouse, who told me they would motor me out to Prescote. But directly I got inside their house I was told that No. 10 wanted me on the phone. They'd rung Prescote and found I wasn't there and now they were ringing me here. It was Harold. 'I'd like to have a good long talk to you. Can't talk on the phone, come up tomorrow any time.' I said I would come on the last train from Banbury so that during the day he could write his speech for the Guildhall while I wrote my speech on parliamentary reform. I would be there at 10.30 p.m. He told me to make sure that everyone knew I was only coming to see him about parliamentary reform. I said I would take care that this was rumoured. So now I'm due to see him alone tomorrow evening when the whole world is aware that we're going to devalue, and when Jim and he are palpitating, resistant, uncertain, unable to cope.

Sunday, November 12th
I went up to London on the last train and clocked in at No. 10. Harold is there waiting in the big room downstairs and we settle down for two hours from 10.45 to 12.45. And it's fencing all the time. He chooses to keep the argument on the technical problem of devaluation and I keep on saying, 'I'm not an economist,' to which he replies, 'What about those thousands of hours you spend with Thomas? Of course you're a trained economist.' And then I say, 'But you can always defeat me in argument on economics,' and he tells me I'm misguided and that devaluation will be a disaster. I wonder what on earth the point of it all is and finally I say to him, 'I think you have the choice, Harold, between doing it freely and being driven to it miserably. What matters here is the posture you adopt.' I then rub in a second point which I've agreed beforehand with Thomas. 'We must have this inner Cabinet,' I say, and at once we turn to a longish discussion about the membership. He says he's ready for it this time and he's talked to George and he's talked to Jim, and they quite like the idea. Michael Stewart? They thought it wasn't worth

having him because he didn't count. He would have liked to have Gunter but he leaks too much. I asked about Roy, but there's no enthusiasm for Roy. He's off Roy for the time being.

So there we are. He's going to have his inner Cabinet. But I finally remind him that though he has cancelled the S.E.P. meeting tomorrow there must be consultation. We can't permit another of those packages slip-slapped on the Cabinet table at no notice. The inner group must have a reasonable discussion of the social policies to be pursued. He says 'Yes' — and I have a feeling he doesn't really mean it.

I slipped off to Vincent Square thoroughly frustrated because I know I've achieved nothing at all by all that talk.

Monday, November 13th

I ran into Jim on his way to the Chief from No. 10 and he took me into his room. 'Well, we are for it,' he said, 'unless we get the right answers this morning. This time the bankers' terms will be unacceptable.' He then gave me a great deal of detailed information about the American and German attitudes and finally, in utter dejection, added 'The only point of devaluing would be the package we could lay down.' I said, 'What do you mean? Why should we lay down a package?' and he replied, 'Because it'll be a chance to teach the people of this country what a fools' paradise they've been living in.' Poor Jim, he's Treasury-minded now and the only pleasure left him is to anticipate what people in this country will suffer before they learn what bloody fools they've been.

This talk so shocked me that I went straight back to my office and composed a careful letter to Harold Wilson in which I again told him that he can argue rings round me about devaluation but what really matters now is his posture when it comes. That, I told him, is the only thing on which he now has to decide. It's like the outbreak of war in 1939 when Chamberlain said, 'My life is all in ruins.' But Churchill felt all the better and relieved that it had started. 'I want you to be Churchillian, to feel better for the devaluation when it occurs while Jim is feeling his life is in ruins. Jim must be the Chamberlain of our time and you the Churchill.' It was a goodish letter and I put it in an envelope marked 'Personal' to be opened only by him and sent it across at lunch-time to Marcia.

Tuesday, November 14th

I found, reading the papers, that Harold had been at the Guildhall the night before and made a great speech about the European technical revolution — a cover-up of course of the utterly disastrous trade figures which are to appear tomorrow.[1] He'd obviously done the job well and hadn't mentioned the pound except indirectly.

[1] There was a trade gap of £107 million.

At Cabinet this morning Roy asked quite briefly when there would be a Statement.* He was told by the Chancellor that it would come in a few days.

When he'd said this, Callaghan, who sits by me, muttered to me in a loud whisper, 'I hope this isn't regarded as too disingenuous. Is it too disingenuous, Dick?' He was almost telling me that we were going to devalue in a few days. I hadn't known it before but I knew it after that.

Wednesday, November 15th

When we went into O.P.D. and I passed his chair the P.M. said *sotto voce*, 'I've got your letter and want to reply to it,' and I said, 'Don't worry.'

Late this evening I was sitting quietly in my room when in comes David Marquand[1] with a group of followers saying, 'My God, Dick, it's on the tape that we're negotiating a loan with the French.' I was completely flabbergasted but, my God, they were right.[2] My first feeling was that this was just what I had feared—Harold had double-crossed me and was negotiating behind my back. But it was too late to ring him that evening.

Thursday, November 16th

I rang Harold up at breakfast time. He was still in bed and had had nine hours' sleep for the first time for days and he hadn't seen the papers. When I told him my news he was baffled.[3] After half an hour he rang me back and said, 'Come round here at once.' When I got there I discovered that he had no idea how this story had broken but he didn't deny that it was true. What he added was the information that devaluation is going to take place this week so I was then able to discuss how the business of the House would have to be rearranged before Jim Callaghan arrived to see him.

As soon as Cabinet assembled this morning the Chancellor started reading aloud the details of his package—so much on hire purchase, bank rate, etc., £75 million cuts in public expenditure, abolition of domestic rate-payers' de-rating with a saving of £30 million and the postponement of the raising of the school-leaving age. There was no Cabinet paper. Everything was announced verbally and so fast that there was only just time to write it down. When he'd finished I blew up. I said I'd never seen business done in such a deplorable incompetent way. Roy Jenkins backed me up. 'Why do we have to pre-announce a winter budget?' he asked. 'This will give us the worst of both worlds. And anyway, why do it on education? We can't have these

---

* This, by the way, is recorded in the Cabinet minutes, which is extremely unusual.
[1] Labour M.P. for Ashfield 1966–77.
[2] On November 11th the Governor of the Bank of England had discussed the state of the pound with the central bankers in Basle. On November 13th it was reported that Britain was seeking a £90 million loan from the central bankers, meeting in Paris, and, on November 15th, that the Government was making arrangements to borrow $1,000 million from the I.M.F.
[3] See *Wilson*, pp. 455–6. 'I was wakened ... with a telephone call from Dick Crossman, in a great state and demanding to know what was going on. He was told that all would be revealed when Cabinet met ... but this did not satisfy him ... I opened my morning papers and realized why he had been so upset.'

decisions taken in a split second.' This interjection held things up. Until this point no one in Cabinet seemed to object either to devaluation or to the Chancellor's package. Tony Crosland had obviously been nobbled in advance. He said that the size of the package was roughly right and so did Peter Shore for the same reason. Barbara didn't take much part because her mind was still on her transport plans which were to come later on the agenda.

But the great problem facing us was Robert Sheldon's Private Notice Question which had been put down for the Chancellor this afternoon about the $1,000 million loan. There was a long discussion about how we could prevent it being answered. At last John Silkin was sent across to ask the Speaker not to allow it to be called and at least not to permit an emergency debate under Standing Order 9. This, I knew at the time, was a great mistake. The Speaker is a man who considers his status and undoubtedly if we wanted to please him they should have sent the Lord President across, not the Chief Whip. However, John left the room and I turned to Callaghan and said, 'Well, if necessary, will you be able to deny that devaluation is taking place?' 'Yes, if necessary,' he replied, 'I certainly should have to.' I thought that was firm enough. I was utterly appalled by this meeting. Instead of having an inner Cabinet working things out carefully, the Treasury have been allowed to throw together a collection of items which made no political sense. They and the Governor of the Bank seem to have been dictating the whole policy.

I didn't have much time to feel depressed. I had to get out of No. 10 and back to my office to work out the business Statement and then to go down to the House before the Private Notice Question. Instead of the blank denial required of him, Callaghan merely said he knew nothing about it and made confusion worse confounded.[1] Soon afterwards when I went into the P.M.'s room I said, 'What the hell was Jim up to? He promised to deny devaluation and stop the rumours.' 'You could hardly blame him for that,' he said. 'He could hardly have been asked to make a blank denial. That would be too much to ask him.' The interesting thing is that though Callaghan had promised Cabinet that he would make the denial, clearly after Cabinet Harold had agreed that this was too much to ask and had let him off. This kind of softness is pretty expensive. I must say that if you ask soldiers to die in battle the politicians should be prepared to die politically in battle. Harold's softness probably lost us £200 million that day. It certainly precipitated the appalling sterling crisis. I could say absolutely nothing either to the Questions after my business Statement or to the journalists in my press conference upstairs. But meanwhile the sense of crisis was working itself up in the lobbies. Upstairs in the Party meeting this evening we sat on the platform listening to shouts of 'We mustn't surrender' from all and sundry. Afterwards I ran into Joel Barnett and Sheldon and was so angry that I said, 'What

---

[1] 'I did not start the rumours and I do not propose to comment on them.' *House of Commons Debates,* Vol. 754, cols. 632–5.

the hell do you think? Do you think you can't trust any of us for one moment?' little knowing that this would provoke a major story in every newspaper next morning that there was a split in Cabinet and some members were standing out against the conditions of the loan.

Friday, November 17th

First I rang up Harold and told him I must have a proper talk after our weekly meeting since I couldn't take this any more. Next I rang up Thomas and blew my top to him and then I rang Roy and told him I found all this utterly chaotic. We had to have an inner group and we had to have a package with a social philosophy. I would try to raise these issues with Harold that morning. After this there was one more person to call—Peter Shore. He, of course, was one of the people who *had* been consulted and I tried to get a little sense into him.

Then off to my haircut, which did me a power of good. After that I strolled down from Duke Street, St James's, and across the park to No. 10. I found Harold with George and Burke—Burke utterly exhausted—and said straightaway, 'We're going to lose a lot of money through Jim's answer yesterday—the whole operation is going as badly as it could.' It was obvious from the newspapers that Callaghan had utterly destroyed any confidence left in the pound. We finally arranged that George and I should come in this evening to discuss the draft press statement produced by the Treasury with the P.M. What I didn't fully realize yesterday was that, though we discussed the winter budget in some detail, the timetable and the method of carrying out the devaluation had not been mentioned at all. That is another reason why George and I now insisted that we must see the Treasury statement and approve it before it was issued. I also got Harold to agree that Callaghan's Statement on Monday must be submitted to a meeting of S.E.P. that morning and there must then be a Cabinet on Tuesday, which of course would be a formality because it would come after the event.

Outside it was a lovely autumn day and Harold suddenly announced he was popping off to Liverpool, whereat I said, 'Right, I will pop off to Prescote for our annual shoot.' Gosh, what a splendid idea—all our farming neighbours were there and they managed to get thirty-five birds and a goodly number of wild duck and hares. Back at ten I found Harold with his inner family. Marcia and Gerald were sitting about, and he was drinking whisky. We had a long discussion on whether he should make his broadcast to the people on Saturday or Sunday.[1] I favoured Sunday but he said that if the devaluation could be announced at three on Saturday and he could make his Statement at ten, it would give an interval before the press could start attacking him. This discussion went on until George Brown arrived.

George had had dinner at Prunier but was in good form. Like me he

[1] It was to be Sunday.

realized we must have lost most of our reserves in the course of that disastrous day. We got down to discussing the dry hopeless text provided by the Treasury. George and I are expansionists and wanted to give some feeling that devaluation, though a defeat, can be used as a springboard. We wondered why in the first Statement about devaluation the Chancellor intended to announce increases in fuel tax and corporation tax. (The Chancellor, by the way, was in Cardiff. He is due back on Saturday and will redraft the Statement all over again—as far as George and I know. This is the way the Prime Minister still works.) George finally left by the front door through a battery of photographers—which he loves. I was left behind with Harold and the No. 10 family for an hour and a half to talk about his speech and Harold read aloud to us the notes he had made in the train on the way back from Liverpool. I found them ghastly—all about the wicked speculators who have been disloyal and made life intolerable and have driven us off the pound. I said we must get rid of the apologies and the excuses. 'Put it like this,' I went on, '"I fought for three years as you wanted me to. We fought a gallant fight but we had too heavy a price to pay and I've decided we can't go on paying it and we can't be held enthralled. I don't deny we've been defeated but there are certain possibilities now." Take that line,' I said, 'admit the defeat.' 'Ah,' he said, 'Dick, you like admitting defeats. You admitted you'd failed with morning sittings but I never do that kind of thing.' I could feel him twisting and turning and trying to wriggle out of it. On the whole I had Peter on my side but at 1.15 when we two went home, I felt profoundly depressed because, though I've done my best, I doubt if I've changed him.

Saturday, November 18th
Before I caught the train back to Banbury I talked to Harold once again on the phone and tried to drive home the lesson that he must admit the defeat and then look forward to the chances of success when the country really gets together. Be Churchillian, not Chamberlainite was the slogan I again used.

Then I was off to Warwick to address the annual meeting of the Warwickshire Parish Councils Association. I found them gathered together in the splendid but modern shire hall and they gave me an excellent lunch and reminded me of old times when I was Minister of Housing. I gave them a rousing talk about local-government reform and democracy and answered questions at length. In the middle of the questions Anne came in; she was wearing trousers and a thick leather coat, and looked lovely and fresh. We motored home for another exquisite day with the children. And then I had a lovely moonlight walk over the farm and came home to play gramophone records and prepare myself for the devaluation Statement.[1]

[1] The Statement was made by the Chancellor on Saturday, November 18th at 9.30 p.m. He announced that sterling had been devalued by 14·3 per cent, from $2·80 to $2·40 to the pound.

Sunday, November 19th

Devaluation Sunday. I've been arranging my transport by phone with Freddy Ward. First I motor over to Hinton, where I lunch with Nicholas Davenport to meet a Jewish textile millionaire. From there I motor on to Windsor, where I have to be well before six o'clock when the Privy Council will be held and the Queen will approve the Orders in Council. From there I motor on to Hampstead to talk to Thomas.

By the way, the Prime Minister will also be doing his broadcast exactly at six o'clock and I've just been talking to him on the phone. He's in tremendous form, thank God. Though I thought today's papers pretty hot, he finds them fairly good and he especially enjoyed Nora Beloff's detailed story in the *Observer* of a Cabinet split, including the names of the people who were for and against. Of course, as I've recorded, there was no split and Cabinet was unanimous. Harold told me that his broadcast is now a great deal better than when I saw him last Friday evening and he has now adopted my central advice that the theme should be 'Yes we fought this for three years and failed but now we have certain advantages.' He was also full of optimism because of the wonderful response he'd had from all over the world to his courageous decision. The $1,000 million standby, he told me, is now available and we must now try to be nice to the central banks who have proved such loyal friends. We've also been fortunate that the right people have devalued with us—Denmark, Ireland, New Zealand and probably Australia. He was in a mood of real euphoria.

I was able with a good conscience to add my own and John's assessment that in Party terms devaluation will, in the short run, be a considerable advantage. It will diminish opposition and rally support provided we can get the package with the right social mix and prove that unemployment will go down and that we are not going to impose further prices and incomes legislation.

So far I could join in Harold's optimism but I also have to consider the events of last week in terms of central Government control and here the picture is pitiable and almost unbelievable. Having summoned me to London specially last Sunday and agreed enthusiastically about the need for an inner Cabinet, he slapped the package on the table four days later in the worst presidential style after consulting, quite separately, Callaghan, Crosland, Peter Shore and one or two others. Thomas and Peter, for example, were both briefed by him on Monday but with the express condition that they mustn't talk to each other, and I suspect George and Jim were given the same instruction. The handling of this crisis has been just as bad as the handling of the 1966 crisis and we haven't advanced one inch towards any central strategic control. So we've got the devaluation I've been wanting for three years but we've got it under very bad conditions with an empty till and with a disastrous public display of incompetence by the Chancellor which has cost us hundreds of millions of pounds from the reserves.

We went over to Hinton to lunch with the Davenports. There I met a great Jewish businessman called Joe Hyman.[1] Apparently he's the boss of Viyella and within minutes he'd told me how he employed 40,000 people and what a driving forceful man he was. I couldn't get much out of it but I think I ought to see him again. Anne drove me on from there to Windsor and got me there in just nice time for the Privy Council. The Lord Chancellor, Patrick Gordon Walker and Peter Shore were waiting for me and we had arranged that we would hold the Council a little early so as to be able to see Harold's television broadcast, which began at six o'clock. This, the Court told us, would be agreeable to the Queen. We got our business done in record time and she immediately said to me, 'Well, we must get along the passage to the television room,' and we practically ran along that great long corridor which I think George III constructed and which the royal children bicycle up and down. Then suddenly she turned sharp left into a little sitting-room and there by a great big coal-fire and a great big television set we watched Harold performing on the screen. He'd already got started about two minutes before. She sat us on her sofa and summoned me to sit beside her while the others got down into comfortable chairs and it wasn't until some minutes after we had started watching that I realized that she and I were in some difficulty. What on earth were we to say to each other when the broadcast finished? I saw her wrapping her fingers round each other and I too felt more and more uncomfortable because I realized that any comment she made would be political and indeed any non-political comment might itself be a political criticism. Sure enough when it stopped there was a long, long silence and then she said *sotto voce*, 'Of course it's extraordinarily difficult to make that kind of speech.' I made some sort of polite noise but before I had replied Patrick Gordon Walker had boomed in—he's the most tactless man in the world—'Oh a wonderful performance.' She couldn't say 'yes'; then I got her on to foot-and-mouth disease.[2] But though we talked about foot-and-mouth disease both of us felt that this was an uneasy evening and after I'd had a quick drink I slipped out quickly and went up to Hampstead, where I'd arranged to see Tommy.

Monday, November 20th
First S.E.P., where we spent hours working over Callaghan's Statement for this afternoon. I suppose we got about a fifth out of it and enormously improved it because in the first draft there was a clearly masochistic tinge of laboured apologia. As usual he sat next to me and we had our odd spasms of mutual confidences. Today he told me *sotto voce* about how he had come to make that terrible answer in the House last Thursday. 'Well, you know,' he said, 'if it hadn't been for the back-benchers I would have brazened it out and

[1] Chairman of Viyella International 1962–9 and of the John Crowther Group since 1971.
[2] A bad outbreak of foot-and-mouth disease was affecting the U.K. at this time—leading even to the temporary cancellation of horse racing.

said negotiations *were* going on. But I didn't want a second row with the back-benchers after that vote of censure.' That reveals Jim's special weakness. When he got up to give his answer he was concerned not about the pound but about the back-benchers. His failure to keep his promise and say the negotiations were going on and to deny devaluation cost us £1,000 million that day, I gather, and perhaps after a few days a net £200 million out of the reserves.

Now I come to the Statement itself. It was a brilliant success. Callaghan put on one of the best parliamentary performances I've ever heard. The only new twist which he put in just at the end was less than a whole sentence suggesting he wouldn't be Chancellor for ever.

Tuesday, November 21st
The papers clearly showed that Jim had been successful with his hint of resignation.[1] It had indeed scored headlines. Cabinet had to start early because of the Party meeting at eleven and, of course, it was a mere formality since S.E.P. had already approved Jim's Statement.

We started with a word of congratulation by Harold on 'a perfectly managed operation'. I was so horrified that I still haven't asked myself whether he was congratulating Cabinet, the Civil Service or himself. By that morning Tommy had been able to confirm to me that the Friday loss was something like £1,000 million and the net loss between £150 million and £200 million from our foreign reserves due to the incompetence of Callaghan last Thursday. I suppose Harold must have been congratulating the experts. None of us said anything in reply and then Fred Peart made a statement on foot-and-mouth disease and asked for an immediate ban on meat imports from all countries with foot-and-mouth and Argentina in particular. It is very striking that Australia, New Zealand, the U.S.A. and Ireland, which ban all imports from countries with foot-and-mouth, don't have the disease whereas we do. But nobody thought we could do it. Cabinet didn't feel capable of making any great decisions.

At last we came to the devaluation package and the more we looked at it the thinner and more inadequate it seemed. The defence cuts were mere postponements and even the decision to drop Aldabra wasn't a genuine cut because anyway no money was going to be spent this year. And most important, all the heaviest cuts have been levelled on industry and exports by dropping the export rebate and cutting the S.E.T. premium. The only good feature of the package was that Callaghan had dropped the increases in fuel tax—yet another imposition on industry.

In the course of the discussion John Silkin had come round the table and

[1] On November 18th the Chancellor had offered his resignation to the Prime Minister but the announcement was delayed until November 29th in order, it was said, to permit the Chancellor to deal with the immediate consequences of devaluation and for the Prime Minister to persuade him to stay in the Government in some other office.

whispered in my ear to ask me whether I could persuade Callaghan not to apologize for the past but to make a forward-looking speech. I put this to Callaghan, who was sitting next to me, and he then said, 'Do you think it would be a good thing for me to apologize for my Statement about unemployment a fortnight ago?' 'Well,' I said, 'if you really want to sweeten relations with the Party that kind of apology would do a lot of good.' But I didn't believe that he would do it. However, when we went across to the Party meeting at 11 o'clock and he opened proceedings he made a most ingratiating speech and apologized for what he had said. He got a tremendous ovation and then immediately Michael Foot rose to make a great speech saying he suspended his censure motion and that the Left would not now vote against the Government because there was a possibility of getting it on to the right lines.

It was an amazingly pro-Government meeting and completely contradicted all the press predictions. For instance, in the *Sunday Times* Jimmy Margach (who perhaps for the first time hadn't been briefed by an insider as no one had time) had written a piece saying that the P.M. would have his biggest crisis inside the Party. Well, there was no crisis at all. Heath has been working up a certain amount of anxiety about devaluation and maybe his people won't like it, but in the Labour Party we have no difficulty at all. It was obvious from this morning on that Harold is going to have a swelling atmosphere of goodwill.

The debate this afternoon in the House was just as good for us. Tony Crosland made an extremely able speech and was followed by Macleod, who took what is obviously the official Tory line — attacking the P.M.'s personal honour and making the sharpest distinction between that little twister Wilson and poor honest Jim. I had to go out to the P.M.'s room, where he had the miners protesting about the Fuel White Paper. He had, of course, conceded that the debate should be postponed and told me to make the arrangements. I said to them that I hoped this time they wouldn't leak it all to the press and would let me announce my decision on Thursday. But I had no expectation that they would keep quiet and of course by this evening the Lobby knew that the miners had had their way and that the Government had climbed down and would have to revise their policy. Well, it may reach that point but I hope it doesn't.

After that I went back to hear Keith Joseph give quite a good wind-up for the Tories, saying that devaluation was all right provided you make sure of it, and then Peter Shore made his second wind-up, once again totally ineffectively. He carries no guns, partly because he just hasn't got the feel of the House, but mainly because he's regarded as the P.M.'s henchman at the D.E.A. and not as a full Cabinet Minister.

I went back from there to the P.M.'s room to discuss his speech for the second day of the debate tomorrow. I had a tremendous go with him, once again saying that he must make a personal Statement on how he had struggled and why he didn't adopt devaluation in 1964 and why he had decided to devalue last week. He said what I was doing was superb, but I didn't have any great confidence that it would make very much difference. I had had this confidence when we talked over the broadcast but very little had got through! So, when I came away from No. 10 at 11.30 leaving Harold with his gang—Marcia, Gerald Kaufman, Tommy Balogh and Peter Shore—I wasn't very hopeful.

Wednesday, November 22nd
The morning papers were all dominated by Lord Cromer's speech attacking the Government's economic policies.[1] Outrageous behaviour for a civil servant but why any of us expected any better from Cromer I never understood.

I was in the Chamber for the debate on the economic situation and what we hoped would be the big clash between Heath and Harold. (By the way, Harold was extremely dull in the Party meeting, where he made a short wind-up speech which lasted twenty-five minutes and greatly contrasted with Callaghan's contribution.) Neither Heath nor Harold were much good. Both made long thoroughly partisan attacking speeches and Harold never got near to admitting the defeat he had suffered until right towards the end.

After dinner I went in to hear the wind-up—Barber versus Callaghan. Barber made the Harry Crookshank kind of wind-up—clever, brilliant and dynamic. Callaghan had been supplied with an enormous brief on how to annihilate the case Heath had mounted this afternoon. He scrapped it and I noticed he had a few odd bits of paper on the dispatch box. Instead he gave an informal chat followed by a kind of appeal from a retiring Cincinnatus. It was a deliberate consensus speech, modelled very much on the style of Anthony Eden, and he managed to make everyone in the House feel he was being appealed to individually. Up till then it had been a slap-bang party political debate. Jim put party aside and spoke as though he was above the dust of battle. He showed himself superior to the rough-and-tumble of the party knockabout of the previous two days. I had wanted Harold to do this but in his speech he had remained the party politician. Jim had then seized his opportunity.

When I came back from the division I found Jim sitting on the front bench and said to him, 'That was a marvellous speech, Jim, but it won't do much good in the Cabinet.' 'I know,' he said, 'but it won't be for long.' And I took him to mean that he was going to resign fairly quickly. Knowing how Harold would be feeling I slipped along to his room and found him there with Gerald and Marcia and then, along with Tommy who came a little later, for a very long time we discussed the meaning of Jim's speech. They all thought Jim

[1] Lord Cromer, who had succeeded to his father's earldom in 1953, had been the Governor of the Bank of England from 1961 to 1966. He was British Ambassador in Washington 1971–4.

was intriguing with the Tories and the City. I told them he was planning to retire to the back benches and sit there for four or five months and come back with restored vitality. I've never been in one of these discussions with Harold and his kitchen Cabinet and I felt that his suspicions of conspiracy were unduly strengthened by it.

Thursday, November 23rd

In the morning papers Callaghan had certainly come out on top and Harold had staged no real recovery. His only chance of achieving that was to be in the I.T.N. programme *This Week* which he had to do himself this evening.

As far as Callaghan's speech is concerned, *The Times* has an astonishing article in which Peter Jay (Douglas Jay's son, who was up till quite recently a Treasury official)[1] gives a completely detailed and, as far as I know, truthful inside story of all the previous occasions on which the Treasury and Harold's advisers had pressed devaluation and he had turned them down. The point of the article is perfectly clear—to show that it was Jim who was flexible and Harold who was adamant—and it's all the more sinister because I'm told there's a very similar article by Sam Brittan in the *Financial Times*. It's clear that in the briefing of the press Jim has come out number one and Harold number two. This was clear enough when Harold spoke to me on the telephone and asked me to do a certain amount of briefing about the Jay article, something I tried to do throughout the day.

This evening, in a private room in the Café Royal, Frank Longford was giving a dinner for Carrington, Jellicoe, Shackleton and myself. As an exercise in personal relations this was very successful indeed. I found Carrington able and I think I convinced him that I really want functional reform and to make an effective second Chamber. Indeed, when the evening had ended I was certain I could settle with Carrington and Jellicoe. Next Tuesday we have the second meeting of the inter-party consultations and there's an agreed paper coming up from Eddie Shackleton's working party.

Indeed there are only two snags. Carrington told me that Ted Heath, Macleod and Maudling don't so far show the slightest interest in Lords reform. It's all right, Carrington says, if they really will leave it all to him, but he's not quite sure about the Tory back-benchers. The second snag is that this isn't the time for consensus politics. This crisis has a kind of Suez atmosphere and he thinks it's the wrong climate in which to get Tory Party agreement to proposals which are only possible if fully supported by the usual channels on both sides. He hoped that I wouldn't try and rush them through until the crisis had eased off. I said I didn't want to rush negotiations and we'd wait till well after Christmas before moving. After all, we have to sell it to our party as well.

---

[1] Economics Editor of *The Times* 1966–77 and before that a civil servant in the Treasury. In 1977 he was appointed British Ambassador in Washington.

Friday, November 24th

The morning papers were full of the Wilson I.T.N. interview. Apparently he has at last talked about a set-back, a defeat and mistakes. But the bloody fool should have done this on Sunday and captured the initiative from Callaghan. He has said it nearly a week too late.

I was over with him for my weekly meeting at ten this morning and found that he was not in a hurrying mood. I asked when S.E.P. would be taking our strategy decisions before submitting them to Cabinet and he replied that officials were preparing papers for a fortnight's time and that meanwhile the Treasury was consolidating our position. So it looks as though this Labour Government is settling down to a routine which will dissipate our chances for a breakthrough.

At Home Affairs theatre censorship came up again. Roy had been asked by Cabinet to look into the practical problems and he returned to Home Affairs to say that Harold's suggestions were quite impossible and that though Arnold Goodman had been given five months to find a solution he had offered nothing that could appease the Palace. Roy pushed this right through Home Affairs and there wasn't any serious statement, partly because I had to get on to the front bench to move that the Committee on Privilege should deal with some Welsh nationalist who's been threatening to blow us up.

Sunday, November 26th

So this is the end of the second devaluation week and we're still completely without any central control or central decision-taking in this Labour Government. And the chances of getting this as a result of the devaluation are very small indeed. It's a fortnight now since I went up to London to plead with Harold for an inner Cabinet of six and he agreed entirely. Yet when devaluation came he carried it out not with an inner team but by playing each of us off separately one against another. And now the Whitehall routine is being put into operation. The officials are preparing a huge paper under the direction of the Chancellor and the President of the Board of Trade for presentation in a fortnight's time, and the tremendous possibilities of this crisis and of the fine morale in the Parliamentary Labour Party are being totally wasted.

I've seen a great deal of Harold during this fortnight and I've watched him gradually settling down after the shock and feeling that everything is O.K. and he's on top of the world. His resilience, his bounce, his india-rubber quality which are a tremendous strength but also a drawback! But his worst drawback is that he apparently can't trust more than one person at a time. This is why he has difficulty in accepting an inner Cabinet. If it is to have four or five people in it who shall they be? When I first talked to him Roy Jenkins was to be in, now Roy Jenkins is out. On the second occasion George Brown was to be excluded, now George Brown must be included as long as he's

Foreign Secretary. On both the first two occasions Jim was an essential pillar of the inner Cabinet, now he's regarded as a menace and a threat. This is why Harold never has a solid group of collaborators round him. He's always distrusting somebody and manoeuvring the rest of us against him. I dare say this is the most pessimistic assessment of his leadership that I've made since I started writing this diary, but it's my considered view now and I feel very depressed indeed.

I feel it all the more because the lower the Government plummets the stronger my position grows in my own little corner. Suppose the impossible happened and as a result of the crisis Jim replaced Harold. That's not inconceivable when you remember Macmillan replacing Eden after Suez. But it's something I wouldn't tolerate because I know the qualities of Mr Callaghan. He's not an adventurous bold forward-looking Macmillan who would rejuvenate the Party. Right inside he's a coward with a wonderful outside image and a very likeable personality. And that's why at present he's the only alternative to Harold. But if Callaghan were to be promoted there would be a strong anti-Callaghan movement and the question comes: who would be the anti-Callaghan candidate? At the moment, curiously enough, the answer might well be me. I think I'm the only person who could keep Callaghan out. Eighteen months ago this would have been utterly impossible nonsense. But now inside Cabinet, where these decisions are taken, it isn't. In certain ways I am the Macmillan who could take over from Harold having been very close to him, but the chances of my doing so, thank God, are utterly remote. For one thing I wouldn't last long physically. And yet I'm the only Cabinet Minister who has consistently stood up to Harold and argued my policy of England the offshore island against his futile attempts to keep Great Britain great. Having said this, however, I don't see the remotest chance of Harold going. It's much more likely that he will drag us further down until, in two or three years' time, there is a landslide of 1931 dimensions.

Monday, November 27th
I got a message that the P.M. wanted to see me straightaway in his room. I found John Silkin there and guessed we were to discuss the Chancellorship. The P.M. filled us in as rapidly as possible. On the day of devaluation Jim had handed him a letter resigning not from Cabinet but from being Chancellor. Secondly, on Thursday of last week Jim had been to see George and told him he didn't want to be Foreign Secretary and he therefore got George's strong support for his getting whatever he wanted. He began to talk to George about going on the back benches, though he also mentioned the Ministry of Education. By the way, he made it clear he didn't want to be Leader of the House. Harold explained that at last he now had to make a quick decision because either Jim went to the I.M.F. conference this week or his successor went. Should we bring matters to a head and get a new Chancellor or should

we let Jim go to the I.M.F. first and resign afterwards? Above all, who should we have? At this point Harold looked at me and said 'What's your idea?' I said I'd no doubt in my mind that I wanted Roy Jenkins. The Chief said the same thing and I think Marcia and Gerald, who were also there, were impressed. I said that a straight swap had obvious advantages and that Jim was the right man in the sense that in Opposition he'd earned his living as the parliamentary spokesman for the Police Federation. The Home Secretary is a senior job, he is the senior Secretary of State but there was just the question of whether he would take it. I concluded that I rather thought he wouldn't but I felt it was essential to offer him the job as soon as possible to find out.

Tuesday, November 28th
I went along to the new *Economist* building in St James's Street for lunch. I found them all full of rumours about Callaghan's successor and as there wasn't a word I could say I tried to divert the conversation to foot-and-mouth disease.

From there I had to go straight to a Privy Council at Buckingham Palace for the approval of the final wind-up orders in Aden while George Brown was simultaneously making a Statement in the House. Of course all the papers today have been dominated by yesterday's statement that General de Gaulle had finally vetoed our entry to the Common Market. The P.M.'s Questions dealt entirely with this subject, and he handled it extremely adroitly. However I missed it, and when I got back from the Privy Council I was at once called away from Question Time to the P.M.'s room. He told me he had an urgent decision to make because Callaghan was coming at 4.15 that afternoon and the P.M. had to be clear in his mind what he wanted. He certainly didn't want Callaghan at the Foreign Office. He certainly wanted to offer Callaghan the Home Office but if Jim refused it he would have put himself in a thoroughly bad position because he'd turned down an office for which he was well qualified and would go on to the back benches in a sulk. 'But he may well refuse,' I said. 'Who should have it then?' 'Who do you think?' asked the P.M. 'Well,' I said, 'there's always Michael Stewart.' 'But I've only got one Home Secretary,' he replied. 'That is you, like Chuter Ede[1] and Butler you should combine it with being the Leader of the House. I know it would be a strain but you've been complaining about not having a big Department. Here's your chance.' 'That's the last thing I want,' I said. 'The Chief and I have important things to do. For instance, the House of Lords consultations. Still, if you insist I'll think about it,' and that afternoon for four or five hours I had the unpleasant burden of thinking I might be Home Secretary *and* Leader of the House if Callaghan turned it down. I had to leave him and go down the corridor to the inter-party consultations on the

[1] M.P. for Mitcham March–November 1923 and for South Shields 1929–31 and 1935–64. He was Home Secretary 1945–51 and Leader of the House in 1951. He died in 1964.

House of Lords, where Roy would be sitting beside me. Harold said that if Callaghan accepted he would summon Roy out of the consultations.

On November 30th James Callaghan was appointed Home Secretary and Roy Jenkins Chancellor of the Exchequer, in a straight exchange of the two offices. On December 8th the issue of the Government's ban on the sale of arms to South Africa, put into effect on November 17th, 1964, had been raised at a meeting of O.P.D. and some members of the Committee had suggested that the time had come to review the matter. Crossman proposed that discussion be deferred until there had been a complete review of Government expenditure and economic policy. According to Harold Wilson's own account (Wilson, pp. 470–76), while the Prime Minister was himself opposed to the sale of arms to South Africa, other embargoes had to be considered as well. At a meeting of younger Labour M.P.s, James Callaghan, apparently unaware of the O.P.D. discussions and perhaps lightly, questioned the policy of the South African arms embargo, and, alarmed by leaks, some 140 Labour M.P.s signed a motion, published on December 12th, demanding the retention of the embargo. The Chief Whip, it appears, approved of the motion as being in accordance with Government policy and, so the diaries suggest, encouraged back-benchers to sign it.

Cabinet considered the subject on December 14th but, in the absence of the Foreign Secretary, delayed by fog, the item was postponed. In the House that afternoon, the Prime Minister answered a Question put down by Dingle Foot and affirmed that the embargo policy still continued but that a fuller Statement would be made in the following week. When Cabinet met again, on the morning of Friday the 15th, the decision taken at O.P.D. was confirmed. Matters relating to defence and economic policy would be considered in the forthcoming review of defence expenditure. There were many accounts in the press at the time, some of which held that the Prime Minister faced defeat from his Cabinet on this issue and had sought to make a delaying Statement to the House until the matter was fought through Cabinet.[1] An emergency Cabinet was called on Monday, December 18th, and in Parliament that afternoon a Statement was issued repudiating the stories in the press. The policy of an embargo was to continue. The Prime Minister's own lengthy account shows that there was undoubtedly a group of 'possibly like-minded colleagues' in the Government who did not entirely agree with the policy of embargo (Wilson, pp. 596–603).

Wednesday, December 13th
Next week is the last before the Christmas recess and this means that the business of the House is terribly difficult to fit together. We have to find one or two days for the Report Stage of the Transport Bill, we've got to find room

---

[1] There are no transcripts of the passages recording these discussions. It appears that they were accidentally erased from Crossman's original tape-recordings.

for the debate on the adjournment for the recess, we have to get a full day on foreign affairs to please the Opposition, and we're buggered on Monday because Private Members have got the time from 3.30 to 7 p.m. John and his Whips wanted to solve the problem by giving only one day for the Transport Bill and letting the Tories roar themselves silly in protest. I said, 'That's all very well for you but it means that next Thursday at business questions I shall be massacred and with good reason.' We had a thoroughly bad-tempered meeting before John and I went down to the liaison committee where there was another exhibition. Last week when I had been on the front bench dealing with the procedure debate both Willie Hamilton and Douglas Houghton had exploded about the rebellion of the eighteen who voted against the terms of the Letter of Intent to the I.M.F. The row began again.[1] Both Douglas and Willie insisted that there must be sanctions against the rebels and that we must introduce the Party's new Standing Orders at once and set an example by disciplining them. Just to make a perfect evening, Willie Hamilton added that this should be the first step to throwing these eighteen out of the Party.

Of course the row in the liaison committee is a reflection of the row which is now tearing the Party to pieces. I left John to stick it out and went up to the Small Committee where I found the Transport House people in a mood of absolute hopelessness. How, I was asked, can we arrange any effective publicity for this Government when this kind of row is going on about South African arms? In a sense I don't blame them because they are sitting on the outside looking at the ghastly spectacle. Nevertheless their sheer inertia drove me frantic and I said, 'Of course there are lots of things you can do. For example, you could launch a "Can I Help You" campaign. Throughout this winter Party members could go out and canvass the general public saying "Do you have the rent rebate to which you are entitled? Do you have your rate rebate? Is yours a house entitled to leasehold enfranchisement?" There are at least a dozen things this Government has done to help ordinary people which ordinary people need to know about.' Everybody else thought this a lousy idea. I still like it.

From there I went up to the Lobby journalists' Christmas party and found the Prime Minister. The whole South African arms crisis was steaming up around him. I persuaded him to come back to No. 10 and sit there quietly. He gave me a long briefing on his intentions: how he would go to the Queen if necessary and hand in his resignation and how he had made arrangements that if he had to resign the Queen wouldn't send for anybody else. There'd be

[1] On November 23rd the Chancellor had sent the I.M.F. a Letter of Intent outlining the Government's proposals to restore a healthy balance of payments. The new Chancellor, Roy Jenkins, published this on November 30th, and to left-wing Labour M.P.s it offered support for the suspicion that the Government had accepted stringent conditions set out by the foreign bankers who had given Britain credit. The Chancellor defended his predecessor in a debate on December 5th in which eighteen Labour M.P.s voted against the Government and sixteen abstained.

a day or two to organize the election of a new leader and he would get himself re-elected by the Party. He told me he was letting this all be known through the *Guardian* and said, 'I'm taking on the briefing of the press myself. This time I'm damn well going to get the result I want.' I was a bit taken aback and I thought, 'I suppose he will get what he wants at Cabinet but he's piling it on a bit thick.' And, by God, he was!

Thursday, December 14th

The morning papers looked terrible. A £158 million record deficit on the balance of trade in November and the worst N.O.P. poll we have ever had. But all the attention was on South African arms and all the stories made it clear that there was a major parliamentary revolt in progress, that the Prime Minister strongly supported the back-benchers and that he was going to get his way in the Cabinet that morning.

I went round to the Chief Whip's office to see what had finally been agreed about business for next week. John was with the Prime Minister preparing for the Cabinet row. But Freddie Warren told me that I would have to take the debate on the Christmas adjournment next Thursday afternoon and that there would only be one day's debate on transport. At first I blew up and said I refused to have this imposed upon me. But I knew very well I would have to accept it and actually I did rather an ingenious job. I accepted the one day before Christmas and then decided to bring Parliament back a week early with a two-day debate on foreign affairs and a second day on transport.*

As soon as we got into Cabinet I cleared the business of next week and then a general attack was launched on Harold about press briefing, partly against John Silkin for his work with the Party and partly against me, since it was assumed that I had done all last week's briefing. Denis Healey explained how terribly upset he had been when a journalist had come to him to say that the Lord President was briefing people against the F-111. I immediately intervened to say I was grateful to hear this because he could now give me the name of the pressman. (Of course I didn't get it, and he didn't know it.) At Cabinet the atmosphere got more and more unpleasant and the air was loaded with charges and countercharges. At first we waited for George Brown, who was late in getting back from Brussels, but when it finally became clear that he was fog-bound for the day it was obvious that Cabinet couldn't come to any decisions. So we proceeded to the only other item on the agenda apart from South African arms, which was whether B.E.A. should buy the Trident or the 211. We decided on the Trident because it cost less.

In the House this afternoon Harold was answering Questions and had told the Speaker he wanted to deal with No. 18 on the export of arms to South Africa. When the P.M. did so he said formally that Cabinet was waiting for the Foreign Secretary but in all kinds of ways Harold implied that he's

---

* As we shall see, the trick worked.

standing firm by his decision of November 1964. Then came my business Statement. I was prepared for a tremendous row about the one day on transport, but there was no row at all. Just before going in I'd run into Peter Walker in the lobby and told him that I had arranged to give him two days but it wouldn't be in the Statement. 'You get one before Christmas and if you press me I'll arrange to come back a week early and give you the second then,' I said. It was a clever tactic but I hadn't really appreciated its cleverness. The offer scared him stiff—everybody in the House really wants the full month's holiday at Christmas. So I never had to make him the offer and one day on transport sufficed.

At my Lobby conference I gave a very full and careful briefing on the background to the South African arms controversy as well as on the Industrial Expansion Bill. Quite deliberately and carefully I treated the journalists very well.

Then the Party meeting, which was absolutely formal because nobody was worried any more. They think the thing is fixed and not a single question was asked.

There was the same feeling over in No. 10, where I went for my business meeting. Burke is still away, Bill Nield is standing in for him and the Prime Minister wanted the meeting over as soon as possible because he was completely confident he's going to get his way tomorrow.

Friday, December 15th
Cabinet. What happened this morning must have come as a shock to Harold. Yesterday he'd been completely confident that he'd worked it all out and was going to get his way. I don't know where he got this confidence from and I didn't share it. We started with an hour and a half of mutual abuse which was nothing more than a repetition of yesterday's meeting. George Brown, back from Brussels, complained that he'd been presented as the villain of the piece and said he has never been so victimized and vilified in all his life. Then there was a great moral outburst from Healey and another from Crosland —all of them complaining about the rigging of the press, virtually accusing the Lord President of doing it, and of the rigging of the Party, which they openly attributed to the Chief Whip. Finally we got down to the issue and Harold made his statement. It was clearly intended to split his opponents and if possible to isolate Healey and Brown, whom he was quite determined to get rid of. He had reckoned that they would be devastated by the exposure to which they had been submitted by the press and by the clear evidence that the Party was fully organized against them. But not at all. They came back at him one after the other. George Brown, Denis Healey, Tony Crosland. The three of them stood together and it was clear that an alliance had been formed in the last twenty-four hours—an alliance of Ministers infuriated by the Prime Minister's campaign against them in the Party and in the press and also, I think, really scared because they realized that they might be for the

high-jump if Harold had his way. I'm sure the fact that they stood together saved them and saved us from a real Cabinet split. They hit back extremely effectively and in concert. They made their points as a united front. At one point Crosland observed, 'If we have to tolerate this South African arms policy I must insist on the postponement of the Industrial Expansion Bill,' and that in itself was a sinister revelation of how carefully their operation had been planned.

After some time it became clear that Harold Wilson's attack had failed to split them and that the Cabinet line-up was almost the same as last week. On the Prime Minister's side was first Michael Stewart, the clearest and most logical of his supporters throughout the crisis, and Gerald Gardiner plus Barbara Castle, Tony Greenwood, Peter Shore and Wedgy Benn who were really satellites. In addition there was Cledwyn Hughes, who finally rallied to the Prime Minister and should perhaps be reckoned as his eighth unqualified supporter. Against them were ranged the seven implacables—George Brown, James Callaghan, Denis Healey, Gordon Walker, George Thomson, Ray Gunter, Tony Crosland. In the middle were the moderates—Roy Jenkins, Dick Crossman, Fred Peart, Dick Marsh, Frank Longford. We wanted the compromise we had suggested at O.P.D. It was a terrible meeting for me because as it went on it became clearer and clearer that the P.M. had miscalculated and that instead of splitting the opposition he was uniting it into a phalanx. Instead of isolating Brown and Healey so that he could get rid of them and keep the rest the Prime Minister had consolidated the opposition. So right towards the end I put forward my mediating proposal. I proposed that instead of deciding today the decision should be postponed and South African arms considered along with all the other items in the post-devaluation package. 'Why pick this one item out and make the policy decision in isolation?' I asked. 'Denis Healey has been complaining that people were campaigning against the F-111. But there's been no decision on it yet. George Brown has been complaining that people had been campaigning for postponing the raising of the school-leaving age. But the decision has still to be taken, like the decision on prescription charges. I propose that everything, including South African arms, should be decided in one single package decision.' That, I said, was the line the P.M. should take because it would keep the Cabinet together. As soon as I put this forward Harold's unqualified supporters burst into shouts of fury and said it would be fatal. At this point James Callaghan observed, 'That's far worse than anything.' But, apart from Callaghan, George's supporters came out in favour and so did Frank Longford. At this point Harold also accepted it, adding, 'If that is really wanted by Cabinet I'll accept it, but is it really wanted?' I said, 'Please, Prime Minister, don't count the votes again, make up your own mind, decide for yourself.' He said, 'Well, as for what I want personally I would rather not accept your mediating proposal.' 'Very well,' I said, 'don't accept it,' and he replied, 'No, if it's the wish of Cabinet I will.' So he got himself into this curious situation of forcing Cabinet to decide for him. But I wouldn't take it and said, 'No, I can't accept that. This mediating proposal will be useless unless the Prime Minister really believes in it himself.' So he was forced to say that he did but that it would all depend on the closest possible secrecy. The original O.P.D. decision, he reminded us, had depended on secrecy and there had been no leaks. So, this time, there must be no leak from Cabinet before Monday, when he would make a Statement on the lines of the mediating proposal.

Just when I was packing up Michael Halls, the Prime Minister's Private Secretary, came in to tell me about the inner Cabinet on the Wednesday after Christmas and added that there would be a full Cabinet on January 4th and January 11th when the whole post-devaluation package has got to be signed, sealed and delivered. Would I, Michael Stewart and Judith get on with the social security aspects of it as fast as possible? And with those words ringing in my ears I caught the train to Banbury to have my birthday dinner with Anne. We dined together and cut my cake. What a day, what a day!

Saturday, December 16th
I was wooding on my island all the morning until the Prime Minister rang me up in fury about the morning newspapers. The front pages were all full of stories which had obviously been provided by George Brown and Bill Grieg, his Press Officer.[1] I had thought things over and was aware that this fury was partly synthetic. Harold had allowed the opposition the weekend in which to destroy themselves. His plan was that we should say nothing and they should be allowed to fight back and tell the story of their brave resistance. Since I knew they were delivering themselves into our hands by doing this I wasn't shocked though I doubt whether there's any precedent for a Cabinet opposition publishing their dissent in the press so flagrantly and openly as has happened on this occasion.

Sunday, December 17th
Well, I read the papers and the accounts were at about the same level as before and I reflected on this. Soon I was rung by Wedgy Benn, still white with anger at my mediating proposal. 'No,' he said, 'we must force these buggers to eat dirt, make them accept unconditional surrender. The P.M. must reassert himself and this is the only way he can do it.' 'If you ask them to do that after the last two days,' I said, 'some of them are bound to resign and there'll be a crisis. I don't recommend it.' So I rang Roy, who agreed that on balance we must continue with the mediating proposal and that it would be extremely dangerous to have a Cabinet tomorrow. Then Peter Shore was on the phone to ask me what I would do if the Prime Minister recalls Cabinet. I thought for a moment and said, 'If he recalls the Cabinet tomorrow Roy and I won't have changed our minds; he shouldn't have changed his mind and we

[1] Former political correspondent of the *Daily Mirror*.

shouldn't have changed ours. I talked to Roy and we're going to stand by the mediating proposal.' I knew that Peter would talk to the P.M. straightaway and I'm sure he did. Within two hours Harold had asked me to come up to London and added that in the meanwhile he must call a Cabinet for tomorrow. I said that was his decision and O.K. by me and arranged to go up by the 8.58 p.m. Just before I left Roy called me and I told him what had happened. He too had been down in the country and had been sitting in his Berkshire home waiting all day for the call from No. 10. But the P.M. hadn't spoken to him at all. I had spoken to Roy, I had spoken to the P.M. but the P.M. hadn't bothered to consult his Chancellor and had simply had a message sent telling him to attend at ten o'clock tomorrow morning.

So in the evening I came up to London and went into that little, horrid, stuffy room and there were Tommy, Gerald and Peter Shore – the same gang all busy on his Statement. The P.M. took me into his room. He had kept his word, he hadn't gone back on the mediating position, he was drafting his Statement on that basis and he was going to put it to Cabinet tomorrow.

I had assumed that his anger about the press leaks was a bit synthetic but I was wrong. He raged on and on and he was mostly concerned about the separate resolution he was drafting, which was due to be given to the press, in which Cabinet would repudiate the lies of George Brown. Once again he was insistent that he would never work with George Brown or Denis Healey. I remarked that he should be careful since Denis could surely be given another job. Harold replied that at least he would never work with George Brown after such an act of deliberate treachery. George had put his assistant, Bill Grieg, to work in the press and he, Harold, had hard evidence of it. No one knew the burden he had borne and this was the final bloody limit.

But I'd heard all that so often from Harold that I still didn't take it seriously. I was more struck by his bitterness against Denis for his ruthlessness, for his behaviour as the stooge of McNamara. He wasn't so harsh about Crosland or Gunter or the rest but he was sure he had them on the run. Finally he remarked that he was now certain that he would get the big defence cuts he'd always wanted. Then we went back into the other room and I stayed there for another hour and in the atmosphere of the clique I felt very depressed. Why hadn't he called Roy? Why hadn't he spoken a word to George Brown? Why did he sit there with his coterie? He certainly doesn't make things easy for himself.

Monday, December 18th

I rang up Roy from my bed, told him about my meeting with the P.M. and about Harold's mood. Roy was due to go in from ten till eleven with the P.M. before Cabinet. I spent most of my time on the phone since all the Haroldites were ringing me once again – Wedgy Benn, Peter Shore, both furious with me, and Barbara as well. I didn't think I was doing very much good by talking to them.

At Cabinet the P.M. kept his word to me. He didn't abandon the mediating proposal—on the contrary he demanded unanimous support for it from Cabinet and was overridden by Cabinet itself. It was a tactical manoeuvre which worked out extremely well. As was only to be expected, the discussion began with a tremendous personal attack delivered from the chair against all the people who had leaked to the press over the weekend. I had had a word with Tony Crosland while we were waiting to go in and realized that it was no good appealing to his conscience since he felt that George was perfectly entitled to hit back after the treatment he'd received. Nevertheless, I can't help feeling that George was abashed by the castigation he received. I've never heard anybody publicly scourged as George Brown was scourged by Harold this morning. The P.M. didn't mention his name—he just looked across the table and said everything that could be said and when he had finished there was total silence. George Brown never said a word in reply, nor did any of the others. The whole issue of the weekend leaks dropped dead at that moment.

After about half an hour it was clear that Cabinet had swung in favour of the P.M. and was prepared to make no change in our policy of November 1964. I passed a message to Roy saying that if George Brown was instructed by Cabinet to announce that we'd made up our minds against selling arms to South Africa it would be a first-rate result and we shouldn't oppose it. Roy seemed to agree. Nevertheless we both continued to support the mediating proposal which of course now found a great deal of favour with Brown, Healey and Crosland, all of whom said this is the only thing which could possibly be done. But they were clearly in a small minority. The Cabinet switched, led by James Callaghan (who, to do him justice, was merely repeating what he'd said on the previous occasion) and now by Patrick Gordon Walker. We soon reached agreement that Harold's draft Statement should be modified to include a Statement that we had completed our consideration of the sale of arms to South Africa and that none would be sold. At this point I said that, as the proposer of the mediating plan, I recognized that as a result of the weekend events my suggestion was no longer valid. The P.M. ought to decide whether it should be dropped, to which he again replied that he wasn't going to decide anything and he would leave it to Cabinet, otherwise he would be accused of dictating to it. And so he got exactly the conclusion he wanted. Cabinet conscripted the Prime Minister to write into his draft Statement the sentences he had always intended should be there. It was a complete and total victory.

This afternoon at 3.30 Harold made his Statement—and made it extremely well. It was greatly improved by the work he'd done on it over lunch. All the Tories were certain that he was going to offer the mediating proposal as all the papers had predicted. So in the early part of his Statement they were laughing and jeering and even when he said there would be no change of policy they couldn't believe it. Heath rose to challenge him and said that the Statement was like a piece of wet blancmange, thereby putting off the whole House. In his supplementaries Harold made his unexpected decision more and more explicit and the complete transformation of the atmosphere he achieved was one of the most remarkable parliamentary *bouleversements* I've ever seen. The Opposition were completely flabbergasted by the Prime Minister, who like Houdini had escaped from his bonds. The scene was all the more dramatic because George Brown was sitting on one side of him scowling and gloomy and the Chief and I on the other happy and confident.

Tuesday, December 19th

The press is so passionately anti-Wilson that instead of reporting straight his sensational and unexpected triumph in the House they announced that there had been a compromise between the Prime Minister and his critics by which, in exchange for announcing that no arms would be sold to South Africa, he had been compelled to commit himself to cuts on the home front. This of course is utterly untrue. On the economic package Harold and Roy are working closely together and no pressure was needed from their critics to make them impose cuts on Cabinet. Yet there were columns of well-informed accounts of a powerful opposition which Wilson still faces inside his Cabinet.

I lunched at the Epicure with Alan Watkins. He had come in last night to talk to John and me and we had given him a very detailed account of our side of the crisis. John and I have had a tremendously bad press and we've been presented as the villainous henchmen doing Harold Wilson's filthy work. Poor John, he looks tired and puffy and has a spot on his lip. He doesn't like unpopularity and he now faces a complete transformation of the situation at Westminster. Suddenly a whole segment of the Parliamentary Party has turned against him and accused him of being a creature of the Left. We did our best with Alan Watkins.*

At 3.30 this afternoon we had the postponed S.O.9 debate on South African arms. I didn't hear much of it at the beginning because I had to go to the consultations on Lords reform. The discussions had reached one of the most delicate points—how long the Lords' period of delay should last and from what precise point should it start. To our amazement, Carrington gave us almost everything we asked for. There would, in his view, be a formal period of delay after which legislation would automatically be enacted. Let's take an example. The Lords veto a Commons' Bill in June. But if Carrington is right, we shall automatically have it on the statute book by December. That's an enormous concession by the Opposition and it makes me rather fancy we shall reach an agreed solution.

We broke off the consultations in time for Maudling and me to get back to the House to hear the wind-up. Ted Heath was in quite good form and raised

* Actually, his article was as near the truth as I saw it as anything can be.

the level of the debate. But then came Michael Stewart, the hero of the hour. He made an enormously impressive speech based on moral principle and after he had spoken the Tories must have seen that this was not merely a matter of Party manoeuvre and in-fighting. Thank God I got him to speak, but it was only because neither George Brown nor George Thomson wanted to do it.

I was so busy during the afternoon that I've forgotten to mention one quite important thing. Suddenly the news came through that Harold Holt, the Prime Minister of Australia, had been drowned and that someone from London would have to represent us at the funeral. It was assumed that George Thomson would go. But suddenly it occurred to us all, should not Harold himself go? The Chief Whip was against it because he said the P.M. was too tired. I said, 'Nonsense. This is a big chance. Get him away, for God's sake. Let him be a Prime Minister outside the country. Let him have his talk with L.B.J. and display a bit of confidence.' I'm glad to say that Burke Trend thoroughly agreed and so in the course of the evening it was announced that the Prime Minister was going to Canberra to be present at the funeral.

Wednesday, December 20th
I woke to a fairly good press. The Tories in Fleet Street had been flabbergasted because they had assumed Cabinet was split and Harold Wilson couldn't get his way. Now they must admit that he had extricated himself from this particular locked safe and is still quite a man. There's also no doubt that Michael Stewart's speech at the end of the three-hour debate has done us a power of good. He's given some dignity and sincerity to what has otherwise been a fairly tawdry affair of party politics. Another thing I noticed was that the decision of the E.E.C. to accept the French veto on our exclusion took second place in today's papers to South African arms. It hadn't been made to look so depressingly important as I had expected.

Our black marks this morning were that six Labour M.P.s had abstained because they were in favour of arms to South Africa and there was one sinister little piece saying that now there would have to be a reimposition of old-fashioned discipline. This of course had been put in by Douglas Houghton who, after being so tremendously pro-Silkin, has now as a result of the events of the last day or two turned against the Chief Whip and is demanding the reimposition of the P.L.P.'s Standing Orders. This will make things much more difficult.

I spent the morning at the Special Committee the P.M. had set up to decide how we should protect the poorest in the country against the effects of devaluation. I had hoped that we should be able to use my new rate rebates but this was not possible. On the other hand it seemed that more and more Cabinet members were being driven to accept some form of claw-back such as Peter Townsend and Brian Abel-Smith are proposing. Right at the end of the meeting Cledwyn Hughes suddenly said, 'We ought to abolish family allowances altogether.' I didn't take this seriously but it sounded odd when he said it.

Then it was time for Harold's last Cabinet before he left for Australia. The first item was the paper marked 'Top Secret' which Jenkins sent round to us ten days ago, revealing the fact that so far devaluation has been completely unsuccessful since none of the money we'd lost in those terrible days has come back and we are losing even more day by day. Even at its new reduced level the pound is having to be sustained. Jenkins used this as his justification for demanding that we now need public sector cuts of some £800 million. The paper also revealed that next year's estimates are 12 per cent above this year's estimates. Why is that? Nobody seemed to know and it's obvious that when such estimates are published in February there will be another parity crisis unless we announce a real austerity budget. As we obviously couldn't discuss this for very long because there were no detailed proposals for the cuts, the Prime Minister explained his timetable. There is to be an inner Cabinet meeting on the Wednesday after Christmas, though he admitted to me afterwards that this so-called inner Cabinet now consists of half the Cabinet. And then at the next full Cabinet we shall try to reach a big decision on the package.

Sunday, December 24th

The Sunday papers are pretty good. Apparently Harold had his forty minutes with L.B.J. in Australia but unfortunately L.B.J.'s main concern was to talk to the Pope about mediation in Vietnam. This completely confirms my view that there will never be a role for Harold and George as mediators in that dispute. At this point I might as well read into this diary something which Tam Dalyell told me about the meeting of the Foreign Affairs Group on Vietnam last week. Jack Mendelson had made a speech asking why we didn't back U Thant and the United Nations instead of backing the U.S.A. In the reply, which Tam took down virtually verbatim, George Brown said, 'I have an understanding in Moscow so that at any moment when we can get a breakthrough I can act as intermediary. The only basis on which I can stay in play is if the communists in Peking and Hanoi believe that I can deliver the Americans. The U.S. trusts me not to deliver them unless they can get something suitable in return. I could deliver Johnson in two minutes flat from here if I could get something from Hanoi. I am the one chap who has influence with the Americans. The communists do not ask me to cut myself off from the Americans: the Russians ask me to keep in contact with the United States and keep our association. It is only nice chaps like you who want us to dissociate.' I had always imagined that George Brown spread it on pretty thick when he was speaking safely off the record. But I never imagined that he would talk quite such tripe as that.

Wednesday, December 27th

And so the famous inner Cabinet has come and gone. It wasn't much of an inner Cabinet because as I expected there were ten of us there apart from the P.M. — Roy Jenkins, myself, John Silkin, Peter Shore, Fred Peart, Tony Crosland, Denis Healey, George Brown, Michael Stewart, Jim Callaghan. The proceedings were pretty futile because in the end all we had was an informal pow-wow about the Chancellor's package of cuts. We all suspected it would be a fair waste of time as we stood about outside the Cabinet door. Tony Crosland came in his sports clothes and took off his waistcoat and said it was very stuffy and it was a cursed nuisance coming back from his cottage. Next came Roy back from his cottage in the Hendreds and we all stood apart from each other, eyeing each other rather suspiciously. And then out of the room came the Chiefs of Staff and I knew the P.M. and Roy had been having a meeting of the defence chiefs first to which his own Defence Committee had not been invited.

Roy gave us nothing on paper but said that £850 million had to be taken out of the economy and then began to go through the major areas and show what cuts the Treasury required. 'Before we go through this package in detail,' I said, 'let's get a picture of how the home cuts relate to the defence cuts.' Roy replied that he had reached the conclusion that whatever economies we made on paper there could be no economies in the 1967–8 budget and only £100 million in the 1968–9 budget. But that didn't mean that he failed to see their importance. Indeed it made it all the more important to have strategic decisions taken firmly and decisively now and this is what he hoped to get. I said that I found this intolerable because we were being asked today to agree to specific cuts on the home side while there was nothing specific or hard on the foreign side. To this George Brown replied that the defence chiefs were doing all they possibly could but that we had to consider the security of our allies and the needs of our soldiers and he added the words, 'We simply can't guarantee anything firm by January 15th.' I replied that in that case no announcement could be made on January 15th, because it would be impossible to announce home cuts without an equally fair announcement on foreign cuts. Denis Healey said, 'If we're going to have our policies decided by the number of people who vote for us in the House that's a poor way to consider the national future.' I couldn't help replying that if one could not achieve the credibility of the pound without a return to prescription charges and the postponement of the school-leaving age, it's equally true that one can't achieve the survival of this Government without firm corresponding defence cuts abroad. Roy passed me a note telling me that the defence people had only had one meeting and had agreed nothing and urging me to go on being as tough as I could in my demands about commitments on defence abroad.

After a time we did turn to the home side but with an understanding that no firm decisions could be taken. I insisted on this although it made the

meeting completely futile. Indeed, somebody asked what the point was of
our coming to London today if this group was to take no kind of group
decision. There was no answer because of course this group was to be the
inner Cabinet but the inner Cabinet idea once again has been shattered. It's
profoundly depressing because this is the third time all this has happened.

Sunday, December 31st
New Year's Eve. Today's papers are fairly gloomy but Jimmy Margach has
written the kind of story I hoped he would write and I think it will help
Harold Wilson a bit. One can't deny that the South African crisis has left a
great deal of ill will and distrust of Harold among over half the Cabinet. This
Government has failed more abysmally than any Government since 1931. In
Macmillan's case, after all, it was after six years of fantastic success as
Supermac. But in Harold's case the failure consists in tearing away the magic
and revealing that he's really been failing ever since he entered No. 10. We
have simply not succeeded and this feeling has been getting into my bones.

1968

Monday, January 1st

The day of the New Year's Honours list and my first job was to ring up Pam Berry and congratulate her on her husband, Michael's, becoming a newspaper peer.[1] That won't make the P.M. any more loved at the *Daily Mirror*, where the first of three great anti-Wilson articles appeared today. It looks as though someone made a last-minute change of policy because instead of attacking Wilson they now chiefly build up Jenkins. In terms of psychological warfare this is far more damaging since it will at once raise Harold's suspicions that Roy and his press agent, John Harris, have been at work.

I did my telephoning from Prescote because I had taken the day off. When I rang up Roy I found that he was going to spend it at his cottage in the Hendreds and so I only went up that evening to see him at 10.30 p.m. I had forgotten the number of his London house and it was a slushy evening with a lot of wet snow. I traipsed around Ladbroke Square from No. 9, where I tried first, until at last I found him at No. 34. He duly gave me a tot of whisky and we sat down to discuss the central strategy that we both know we require. When I said to him that the Statement must not be merely a package of cuts but a new start based on a new strategy he straightaway agreed and said that he felt it was essential for him to make it in the House. I said he was certainly the dominant person who should be responsible for the new thinking and that I would do all I could to see that Burke Trend and Harold both took the same view.

Wednesday, January 3rd

I strode across to No. 10 to see how the Prime Minister would react to the idea that Roy should make the great Statement. I first tried it out on Burke and he was fiercely against it. Then I went in to the P.M. and he was just as strong. I'm pretty sure his resistance was partly due to the build-up of Roy in the *Daily Mirror*. Harold had rung me earlier this morning to say that he had heard that Jenkins had persuaded Cudlipp to build up the Chancellor instead of attacking the P.M. Harold had said, 'With this build-up of Roy I can't possibly afford not to make the Statement myself. I don't see why Roy shouldn't make the Ministerial broadcast.' I rang Roy back and told him that it was a good idea provided that he opened the debate with a longer Statement. He said, 'Well, would the P.M. take that?' I then tried *that* out on the P.M. and he said that Roy would of course do the Ministerial broadcast and then open the debate on Wednesday.

Thursday, January 4th

The inner Cabinet started at ten and went on most of the afternoon. It achieved nothing except to reveal how the balance of power lay. We started with foreign policy and defence and never got away from it because such a welter of papers had been put in from the F.O., from Defence and from the

[1] As Lord Hartwell.

Commonwealth Office, all arguing that it was utterly impractical to complete the Far Eastern withdrawal from the Persian Gulf.

The opponents were all lined up on the other side of the table, this time with Michael Stewart added to the old gang. There they were, Brown, Healey, Callaghan, Stewart, the four who for three months with their Departments behind them had advised that any withdrawal would produce insurrection in Singapore and in the Persian Gulf. Now they were arguing with the same ferocity that our presence must continue to 1972 in order to avoid these disasters. When we turned to the F-111 the line-up was very much the same. What we were asking for in fact was a vote of no confidence in the four pygmies on the other side of the table—Michael Stewart, George Brown, James Callaghan and Denis Healey—who had been running our foreign policy for the last three years. To my amazement we got it with a large majority. Apart from Willie Ross and Fred Peart every other member of Cabinet voted with Harold and Roy.

There was a far stronger case for the F-111. The Exchequer will pay $80 million in compensation, there are no savings in year one and there will be a lot of cancellations of contracts for offset purchases. Healey also strengthened his case by saying there could be no question of cutting down the numbers in the order. There must be either outright cancellation or we must purchase the lot. Once again Harold put this carefully to the vote and the result was a tie, with the P.M. giving his casting vote against the F-111. Not unnaturally Healey pleaded for a second chance and was given it. If he can find another way of saving £400 million he will be entitled to present it to Cabinet. That was all Cabinet achieved before we broke off at seven.

Friday, January 5th
In the morning we had a Home Affairs meeting where Callaghan presented a paper on certain aspects of the Race Relations Bill which he's inherited from Roy. Once again he was his new breezy irresponsible self. In yesterday's Cabinet he had opposed with all his old-fashioned Great Britain jingoism the cuts he had been trying to impose as Chancellor. Now as he sat down beside me at the Committee he said *sotto voce*, 'I haven't got a liberal image to maintain like my predecessor; I'm going to be a simple Home Secretary.' He was so breezy that he made it a good-tempered meeting and we got through it fairly well.

We re-started Cabinet by considering the £35 million Roy wants to save on social security. I managed to make it clear that he shouldn't say exactly where he's going to manage to impose cuts and that he shouldn't altogether exclude either the principle of a claw-back or the abolition of universal family allowances and personal tax allowances. Cabinet had no objection to this so we have plenty of time to work out a solution.

Next came education and George Brown, who'd obviously hotted himself up a bit at lunch-time, came out with an attack before the feeble Gordon

Walker could say anything. It was an unpleasantly class-conscious speech, strongly implying that no one except the middle-class socialist who had never felt the pinch or never had a child at a state school could dare to suggest postponement of the raising of the school-leaving age. Ray Gunter and Jim Callaghan followed much the same working-class line while Tony Crosland and Gerald Gardiner spoke as socialist ideologists. Fred Peart and George Thomson provided the professional trade-union case as represented by the N.U.T. Gordon Walker sat through this debate speechless and obviously trembling. He had been off the day before to a great meeting in Newcastle where he had talked about heartbreak decisions. Damn him! What an idiotic thing to say—heartbreak decisions! Either you take the decision and don't resign or you resign with heartbreak, but you don't stay put with heartbreak. Roy Jenkins put our case very moderately. He pointed out that no one had suggested another way of getting £40 million out of education without irreparable damage. Then he quietly added that there were really quite a number of teachers and parents of children at comprehensive schools who would welcome postponement. Denis Healey then bashed in saying that if he was going to have cuts of far more than £40 million he wanted to see adequate cuts in home policy. Dick Marsh, the youngest member of the Cabinet and also a trade unionist, clearly didn't feel a crisis of conscience any more than Peter Shore. They both sided with Roy. Barbara, of course, was in a difficulty. Her left-wingism would make her naturally opposed to postponement but on the other hand she wanted to preserve her road programme and to support Harold. It was obvious that we were getting terribly close in numbers and that if there was a majority on Roy's side it was very small. At this point Harold said that Gordon Walker should tell Cabinet what his view was. 'It's an agonizing decision,' he replied, 'but in the last resort I must accept two years' postponement.' I don't know which I disliked more—the pathetic weakness of Gordon Walker or the outrageous cynicism of Callaghan, who as Chancellor of the Exchequer had urged the postponement and was now joining the working-class battle against it.

I was ready for a tremendous fight on prescription charges but Harold very neatly avoided it by announcing, as soon as Roy had made his statement, that he had offered Kenneth Robinson and Judith Hart £15 million of the £40 million to be saved for exemptions to people over sixty-five, nursing mothers and children and possibly for the chronic sick. He informed us that a reply had come from Kenneth Robinson that no formal exemption was administratively possible. Of course I recognized at once that this was a political tactic which probably Michael Stewart had advised the two to adopt in order to prevent any increase of prescription charges. Presumably they hoped that Jennie Lee's passionate plea in this week's *Tribune* would scare Roy into surrender. What it has done is to persuade him to accept a compromise which Peter Shore and I were trying to work out last night. We proposed that 6*d.* of the total cost of exemption should be paid for out of the National

Insurance contribution and that there should be absolute exemption for the old and for children. Kenneth replied that he would like to pay for the whole thing by a ninepenny increase in the N.I. contribution but Roy said he couldn't accept this because the issue had become a matter of confidence with the bankers—just as the F-111 was to be an issue of confidence with the parliamentary parties. So Cabinet agreed that prescription charges and the F-111 should be brought back to Cabinet next week and only three people, I think, including Barbara Castle, voted against any kind of prescription charge at all.

The last item I heard discussed was housing with Denis Healey, Tony Crosland and Barbara Castle complaining that Roy's proposal to cut the annual approval rate by 15,000 a year was far too small. At this point I had to catch my train to Coventry.[1]

After I left I gather that Concorde was discussed and it was decided that we could not abandon it. Economically, of course, the saving would be enormously worthwhile but I don't think this Labour Government can in the same package cut the F-111, withdraw from East of Suez and scrap the Concorde without demoralizing people absolutely. If we virtually abolish military aircraft we still have to believe in civil aircraft, particularly if we're concerned about jobs in the aircraft industry.

Sunday, January 7th
Looking back on the week the first thing I must record is an astonishing improvement in public opinion. This is the result of something none of us expected—an excitement among ordinary people of seeing the Government in almost daily session and of reading endless stories in the press about the struggle we are having in Cabinet to work out a fair and just policy. People in the country seem to have had a sense that they were participating in our discussion and even influencing our decisions. Traditionally in our parliamentary system the Government decides first and afterwards expounds its decision to the people. This time, almost by accident—because of the complete disaster of devaluation and the collapse of the old Chancellor, we are doing things in series and in full sight of the public. First we had the actual devaluation plus its immediate measures. Then time has to be given for the new Chancellor to settle in and plan his expenditure cuts, which will be announced in January, and then in April will come his budget and a new prices and incomes policy. Three quite separate stages. We thought it was a tremendous disadvantage but at least in terms of public opinion it has some real advantages. I'm told that even the pound has responded well since the New Year despite the awful December trade figures that were published last week.[2]

---

[1] The programme was eventually reduced by 165,000 houses a year.
[2] There was a £65 million deficit in December 1967. In January 1968 it was to be £35 million rising to £70 million in February.

Another political windfall has come from five ladies of Surbiton who decided to help Britain by working harder and who thereby launched the 'Backing Britain' campaign, which is now expanding vigorously. It's something we should have nothing to do with but it's certainly been a useful antidote to such black spots as Jennie Lee's threatened resignation this week.

Inside Cabinet, as I've reported, our discussions have confirmed the impression that there is now a powerful right-wing junta of George Brown, Denis Healey and Michael Stewart reinforced by Jim Callaghan. I've listed the four members of the junta who for three years refused either to devalue the pound or to withdraw from our untenable positions in the Far East. But of course the fifth member was formerly Harold Wilson, who stood for precisely the same policy and is now working with Roy and me and insisting on the new policy. Roy's attitude is not resented because everyone in Cabinet knows that he was a critic of the Great Britain addicts and that like me he was in favour of devaluation and of breaking through the status barrier. The status barrier is as difficult to break through as the sound barrier: it splits your ears and it's terribly painful when it happens. And so it's really not surprising that when this sudden about-turn takes place the four are resentful that Harold is siding so quietly with the Little Englanders. Since Harold has scrapped Prime Ministerial government for the time being and is operating Cabinet government the battle has been to shift round the tiddlers in the Cabinet. The top seven or eight members in a Cabinet tend to have serious views and seldom change their minds—they're permanently lined up against each other—but the tiddlers are always sensitive to changes in the wind. When I asked Harold the other day why he is now regularly counting votes he said that if he didn't insist on doing so his position would be challenged by the junta. That is perfectly true. Six months ago he could take the voices and interpret the voices as he liked. But if he had interpreted the 11–10 majority he got to axe the F-111 the other side would have said that he had falsified the vote and insisted on a recount. It's interesting to see how the tiddlers gave Harold his majority of one on education. Against him were ranged Michael Stewart, George Brown, Wedgy Benn, Tony Crosland, Lord Longford, Ray Gunter, Jim Callaghan, Fred Peart and George Thomson. On our side apart from Harold, Roy, myself and Gerald Gardiner and Barbara Castle we had to rely on Tony Greenwood, Cledwyn Hughes, Willie Ross and Patrick Gordon Walker.

Friday, January 12th
This afternoon we had our last Cabinet meeting on the package—the general discussion of the economic situation which Tony Crosland had asked for and which should really have begun the whole proceeding. He made a very able speech, as he always does, suggesting that not more than £400 million should be cut back on the public sector. Roy's reply was fairly devastating. Even

with £800 million cuts, he said, he would have to impose more than half the necessary cut in demand by increasing taxation in the coming budget. And it was at this point that he revealed that the trade deficits in the last three months of 1967 had come to over £300 million,[1] the same as in the autumn of 1964 when Maudling was having his election spending spree. So we were not merely back to square one but back to square zero. We had lost everything we had won during these three years. I could not help recalling how in October and November Harold talked to me week by week about recovery being in the air and persuaded himself that no drastic measures were really necessary. For those of us who knew about the autumn behaviour of Harold and Jim this was a deadly rehearsal of the facts and Roy brought it out with deadly effect. Cabinet just had to accept the size of his public-sector cuts.

By now George Brown had bustled into the room and we decided he should give us a special report on his interview with Dean Rusk and on the message from L.B.J. which had arrived at the F.O. this morning. Now in considering his behaviour one must realize that he'd travelled round the world in a week and was obviously psychologically and physically upset by this jolting of the passage of time. So, not unexpectedly, he sat down and gave us in his most dramatic and most incoherent way a half-hour description of the appalling onslaught to which he had been submitted, first by Dean Rusk and then by a State Department official whose theme had been, 'Be British, George, be British—how can you betray us?' He told us that he had faithfully reported the decision to leave Singapore by 1970–71 and to scrap the F-111 as unalterable Cabinet decisions. They had expressed nothing but horror and consternation. 'I put the Cabinet case—the case for the new strategy—as well as possible. I put it as well as the Lord President of the Council himself could put it and one can't ask more than that,' he remarked at one point sarcastically. Despite all his rhetoric and confusion one point stood out from his report. The main American complaint was not about the withdrawal from the Far East but about the decision to leave the Persian Gulf. When the Americans made this clear George Brown had explained that it didn't cost us much more to hold the Gulf if we were in Singapore and Malaya but that as we had to abandon Singapore and Malaya we couldn't hold the Gulf without incurring colossal expense. His contention was that irreparable damage had been done by his having to make this statement at all and having to tell the Americans of our decisions. And yet something could be done by going back on the decision and giving ourselves an extra year to get out, and by abandoning the decision to cancel the F-111.

So far Roy Jenkins had remained silent. Now in his usual terse way he summed up in a very few sentences. I can't quote him verbally but what he said came to this. Just because there can't be genuine savings in the next two years on defence there has to be a major change of foreign and defence

[1] In October £111 million, in November £158 million and in December £65 million.

policy from that of the last three years. He said it in a way which destroyed the credibility not only of George but of all the other people who have been running the Great Britain policy since 1964. It was the challenge to the authority of the old Government which he managed to bring out and that was about as far as we got by lunch-time.

After lunch came Healey's last-ditch effort to save the F-111. I had gathered before the meeting that he was now pretty confident that he could win the extra vote required to defeat us. After all there had been a tie before and Harold had given his casting vote. Now Denis knew he had got Longford secretly over to his side and he reckoned he had a safe 11–9 decision. He also hoped that the impact of George's catastrophic news from Washington would switch some timid votes to his side. Denis is not a very successful speaker either in Cabinet or in the House. He plays the role of the young McNamara—the man who is briefed on all the top-level secrets and who can mock and deride any ideas put forward by his amateur colleagues. The supercilious sneering expert is always in danger in a British Cabinet but Denis has a further difficulty. After all, he had already presented us with no less than four successive defence reviews and he had defended each as it came out with new facts, new figures, new statistical demonstrations. Moreover I remembered that he had sold the F-111 to us as an aeroplane essential for defence East of Suez which would in fact be based East of Suez and not used in Europe. Now he was defending it as essential to European defence. I got the impression that he could defend it just as brilliantly as essential to southern Irish defence. When he'd finished the P.M. asked him four questions very unsuccessfully, since he was scored off by Denis in a fairly rude and devastating way. But when Roy began his interrogation things went very differently. He did far better than the Prime Minister in fencing with Denis, undermining him first on the economic side and above all on the political side, showing the essential need to match the cut in commitment by a cut in hardware, and challenging him as to what hardware should be cut, challenging him on *Polaris* as well. Denis was no match for Roy. Indeed, his only convincing case was for *Polaris*, which I had wanted to see scrapped or given away. He was able to demonstrate that it now costs only £20 million a year and that all the enormous capital costs are paid already. If we're to have an enormously expensive top-level weapon system we should keep *Polaris*, he argued. To this I was able to reply, 'Yes, I'm prepared to agree that *Polaris* at £20 million a year maintenance is worth keeping provided we scrap the F-111.' At this point Longford suddenly interjected and revealed the great secret of his switch, which most of us knew already. As soon as he'd done it Cledwyn Hughes intervened to switch his vote our way. Finally Patrick Gordon Walker hummed and hawed and said that in view of the remarks on education he felt he must now vote for dropping the F-111. And so we were 11–9 without the Prime Minister—safely home. Healey looked really shattered, and as he got up George Brown said, 'Well, I shall be resigning.' But he was obviously too tired for anyone to take him seriously.

Monday, January 15th
I had to go up to London last night to be in time for the final Cabinet this morning. I knew that yesterday Tommy had been working away drafting the Prime Minister's Statement and that it was all being put together out of bits and pieces. I also knew that this morning George Thomson would have got back from the Far East to report on his visits to Malaya, Singapore, New Zealand and Australia. And then there was also a report in all the papers today on what had taken place in that five-hour meeting between Harry Lee, the Prime Minister of Singapore, and Harold Wilson, Roy Jenkins and George Brown.

Cabinet started with George Thomson's report and then with the P.M.'s account of his five hours and his dinner with Harry Lee. After that there was a tremendous effort to get Cabinet to reverse the decision on East of Suez withdrawal we had taken by such a large majority only ten days ago. It was clear after an hour that the weaker brethren of the Cabinet were swinging back. L.B.J. had certainly stepped up his threats to George, particularly in the economic sphere, which will be a terrible blow to British foreign trade in the U.S.A. It was Gunter, I think, who swung first, then Cledwyn Hughes, then Dick Marsh, and then Gordon Walker. They were all swinging towards the position of the old junta and when the score was about 8–6 I knew that the P.M. would have to act. What he did was to nip in very neatly and offer as a compromise that the terminal date for withdrawal from Malaya should be the end of the calendar year 1971. What he conceded was nine months' further occupation and instead of withdrawing by March 1971 we were now to withdraw by December 1971. That was something for Harry Lee to take back with him to his Cabinet and that was something to satisfy my anxious colleagues. Afterwards Roy said to me, 'I always had that compromise up my sleeve.' Harold delivered it in the nick of time this morning.

In his Statement to the Commons on January 16th the Prime Minister announced reductions of some £716 million in Government expenditure. The road-building programme was to be cut and 165,000 fewer houses built each year. The raising of the school-leaving age from fifteen to sixteen was deferred from 1971 to 1973. Free milk for secondary-school pupils would no longer be available. National Health Service prescriptions were to carry a charge of 2s. 6d. per item, with exemptions for children, pensioners, expectant mothers and the chronic sick, and dental charges were to rise from £1 to £1 10s. Weekly national insurance contributions were increased by a shilling for employees and sixpence for employers. The proposed family allowance increases would remain, but taxpayers would carry the cost, and the civil defence service was to be drastically reduced.

As far as defence spending was concerned savings of some £110 million for 1969–70 and £210 million to £260 million by 1972–3 were envisaged. All British forces in the Far East save for Hong Kong and the Persian Gulf would be withdrawn by the end of 1971, and the previously announced withdrawals of service personnel and civilians accelerated. By 1971 aircraft carriers were to be phased out of the Royal Navy, and another £400 million was to be saved by cancelling the order for 50 F-111 strike aircraft from America.

Tuesday, January 16th

I had to make a business Statement this afternoon and everything went quietly with the minimum of protest. I'm living now in a quiet world. Throughout this week I haven't been mentioned and nobody has attacked me in Cabinet or outside it. Moreover I'm not treated as though I was anything to do with Party discipline. So no wonder I have it easy.

After the business statement we started a highly contentious little Transport Holding Company Bill which we want to get through with the minimum of attention. Barbara is now away with pneumonia and the competent, efficient Stephen Swingler does her job admirably for her. So I was able to go off to the Prime Minister's Lobby at 5.30 and found it only half full partly because Frank Longford was staging his resignation Lobby at the same time. I hear, by the way, from the P.M. that Harold has seen Jennie Lee and because there has been no cut in the Arts Council programme nor in the Open University funds we have kept Jennie safely in the Government. She says she has conscientiously read the package and doesn't feel any need to resign in view of the major importance of the defence cuts. So that leaves Frank as the only resigning Minister. He made his attitude clear some days ago and I think he's quite sincere, but it's also true that he knew some time ago that Harold wanted to replace him as Leader in the Lords by Eddie Shackleton. Nor has he been very enthusiastic about taking part in the Lords reform consultations; I suppose because I have taken them over and he feels pushed aside.

Tuesday, February 6th

This evening I had a long-delayed talk with Roy. I went over to see him installed in his residence at No. 11—it seemed exactly the same as it was under Callaghan, heavily furnished over-brocaded rooms which Chancellors inherit from one another. How ghastly it must be to live there. However, there he was and he gave me a gin and bitter lemon and himself a whisky and we settled down. He had an agenda but I started by asking how he was getting on with the P.M. He replied that yesterday Harold's mood had changed and he'd become quite cordial and co-operative. 'What happened before that?' I asked. And Roy admitted that he'd hardly seen the P.M. in the previous ten days. One would think that was impossible. In the critical days when the P.M. and the Chancellor were supposed to be preparing for the Government's greatest test they just weren't on speaking terms. He then told me that recently Denis Healey has been very difficult and bloody-minded, 'Because he hasn't got my job,' he added, and yet Denis doesn't want to be thrown out of Defence. So he's throwing his weight about in an erratic way. Then Roy asked me about John Silkin's position and said that he thought the sacking of Will Howie[1] had done the Chief a great deal of damage. Roy is obviously staunchly right-wing in his views on discipline and dislikes John Silkin, seeing him as somebody who should be shifted. I then asked him about the inner Cabinet and he said, 'We won't get it yet because there isn't the right kind of confidence between the P.M. and his colleagues. For instance, Harold can't make up his mind about Callaghan,' he remarked, 'he doesn't know whether he wants him in or out.' 'Which would you want?' I asked, adding, 'I would rather have Denis in and Callaghan out.' I think Roy would like the same but he doesn't think Harold is ready to act and he wanted to talk to me more about Callaghan. 'I should tell you,' he said, 'that the Home Office regards him as the most reactionary Home Secretary they've had for some time. He's certainly making his mark. He made it quite clearly at the Legislation Committee the other day on the kerb-crawling Bill and the liberal image is going by the board. It's true that he's had to carry on with my Gaming Bill but that has nothing to do with the liberal image. He'll also have to do my Race Relations Bill, but he'll do most of it with a heavy heart. What'll make him really happy is if he has to introduce the Bill to ban Kenya Asians with British citizenship from entering this country.'[2] (On this, by the way, I myself would be nearer Callaghan than Jenkins.) There's certainly tension enough between the ex-Home Secretary (now Chancellor) and the new Home Secretary (an ex-Chancellor).

Sunday, February 11th

This has been another week of Government indecision. The latest instance is in the Home Office. Months ago we decided that if the situation got urgent and there was a threat of a mass expulsion of Asians with British citizenship from Kenya and therefore of a mass entry of these same citizens into this country we would have to clap on a quick special Immigration Bill. But then we changed Home Secretaries and we waited and waited and now we've missed the right moment because Duncan Sandys is up in arms and Enoch Powell too is demanding urgent action.[3] If the Government makes its

[1] Labour M.P. for Luton 1963–70. He was an Assistant Whip 1964–6, a Whip 1967–8 but had failed to get on with John Silkin. He became a vice-chairman of the P.L.P. after leaving the Whip's office.

[2] Under the 1963 Kenyan Independence Agreement, non-citizens of Kenya had been allowed to choose either Kenyan citizenship or to retain their citizenship of the United Kingdom and Colonies, so that while the entry of citizens of the Colonies and of other independent Commonwealth countries was controlled, the Kenya Asians were unhampered by immigration restrictions. Some 7,000 came to Britain in 1966; by 1968 about 2,300 a month were coming.

[3] In forthcoming months, Enoch Powell was to warn that Britons were being made 'strangers in their own country' by increasing waves of immigrants.

decision now it will seem to be surrendering to the most reactionary forces in the country.

But does Callaghan want to look as though his hand is being forced? I'm not sure: anyway it's another issue where drift is creating the very impression we want to destroy—that nothing has really changed since devaluation.

Monday, February 12th
Coming into S.E.P. I noticed there were some Ministers there already with the Prime Minister—Tony Crosland and Roy Jenkins, for example—and I knew they'd been having some pre-budget talks. But I also guessed that they'd been talking about the front-page story in the *Financial Times* this morning. This was a piece by John Bourne referring to the new law and to Jenkins and Gunter, obviously based on knowledge of the paper we were due to discuss this morning. It wasn't a very full leak, not nearly as well informed as usual and it didn't seem to me to have the characteristics of a Gunter leak from the Ministry of Labour. Indeed, it was rather anti-Ministry of Labour and pro Roy Jenkins, and I had a suspicion that it was a John Harris leak, but the extraordinary thing was the P.M.'s behaviour. He said, 'We shan't discuss this paper at all now. Take if off the agenda while we make inquiries about this leak.' So this vital question of prices and incomes legislation disappeared! If it was known that no decision was being taken it would be dreadful for Jenkins, since his budget must be prepared on firm assumptions about our prices and incomes policy. And the whole point of this meeting had been to give Roy a firm basis for his budget. If he could be sure that Cabinet would introduce an intensified prices and incomes policy and make a real effort to hold increases to 5 or 6 per cent at the cost of further legislation—then he could afford a less heavy budget. If there is to be no effective prices and incomes policy then all the burden must be imposed by heavier taxes. Of course Harold knows this and I'm sure he decided to take the item off the agenda because he wanted to fix it quietly with Roy behind the scenes.

In the afternoon we had a meeting of the prices and incomes Committee—this time about railway wages. As usual the Chancellor was in the chair and I sat beside him with beyond me the two key men concerned—D.E.A.'s Peter Shore and Ray Gunter. Of all Cabinet Committees this is the one I hate most because I know perfectly well that the statutory prices and incomes policy is one of the few things which makes the difference between a socialist and a Tory Government and I can see that without it we shall have to rely on a rising level of unemployment. And yet whenever I sit at this Committee I come to the conclusion that a statutory policy is unworkable. When I listen to the mumbo-jumbo of nil norms and the rest of it, and criteria, I feel they're infuriatingly bogus and I'm inspired by an Enoch Powellite desire to tear the whole thing to pieces. Yet in the end I have to vote for one of these legalistic formulae.

After that I went up to my room where Callaghan and his whole staff of officials came in to discuss with Freddie Warren and the Chief and me how we could deal with the matter of the Kenya Asians. Now we weren't dealing with the substance of the issue but with what was to happen if the need for a Bill was actually agreed. We decided that if such a Bill was agreed we should try to get it in the shortest possible time. But what was the shortest possible time? After some discussion we agreed that we would conceivably put to the Opposition through the usual channels the proposal to get the Bill through in one day and one night, sitting right through twenty-four hours. The justification for this would simply be that once such legislation had been announced there would be a rush of immigrants coming in on charter flights, with thousands of Indians sitting on the doorstep.

Well, I thought about this and about my own role, and I did give the warning that this would be a Bill that would be infringing the freedom of British nationals, and that we must have a certain decency in dealing with it in the House of Commons. Would it be respectable to take the whole thing through in one day? I felt that Willie Whitelaw and Ted Heath would agree to our doing it in this particular way but should the Leader of the House misuse the Government's big majority and the usual channels to make life easy for the Executive in a matter which would be dismissed as unconstitutional in any country with a written constitution? By the evening I came to the conclusion that I'd been too easy this afternoon. I was surprised to find the Chief going along with me in the quick solution because he has tremendously strong feelings about Black Africa. But perhaps he too was enraptured by the skills of party management.

Tuesday, February 13th
The big news in the morning press was Duncan Sandys's call for action against the Kenya Asians. This of course is despite the fact that it was Duncan Sandys who signed the Kenya Independence Treaty in 1964 and gave special assurances to the Kenya Indians that they would remain British nationals. Our first Cabinet Committee was that on Commonwealth Immigration with our friend Jim Callaghan in the chair. Here's an interesting point about Prime Ministerial government. In normal circumstances the line we should take on Commonwealth immigration would be considered by the Home Affairs Committee but this Kenya Asian problem had been sent to a special committee appointed for the purpose with Jim Callaghan—not Michael Stewart—in the chair. As a matter of fact if it had been considered under the chairmanship of Michael Stewart, things would have been much better. Jim arrived with the air of a man whose mind was made up. He wasn't going to tolerate this bloody liberalism. He was going to stop this nonsense, as the public was demanding and as the Party was demanding. He would do it come what may and anybody who opposed him was a sentimental jackass. This was the tone in which he conducted this Cabinet Committee and it was

extremely interesting to see the attitude of the members round the table. Whitehall had lined up the D.E.A., the Ministry of Labour, the Ministry of Education, all the Departments concerned, including even the Foreign Office, behind the Home Office demand that the law must be changed. Only the Commonwealth Department stood out against this pressure and George Thomas, the Minister of State, made a most passionate objection to the Bill in strictly rational form, saying this was being railroaded through and Jim was getting backing from all the Departments. A few years ago everyone there would have regarded the denial of entry to British nationals with British passports as the most appalling violation of our deepest principles. Now they were quite happily reading aloud their departmental briefs in favour of doing just that. Mainly because I'm an M.P. for a constituency in the Midlands, where racialism is a powerful force, I was on the side of Jim Callaghan and said that we had a sharp choice. We had either to take the risk of announcing in advance that there would be no ban on immigration in the hope that this would stem a panic rush, or we had to announce the Bill. The one thing not to do was to hesitate and be indecisive. Between these two courses I felt that a country such as France might possibly choose in favour of the first but the British people wouldn't. There was virtually no opposition to this view except from George Thomas and Elwyn Jones.

Thursday, February 15th
At Cabinet this morning the main issue was the Commonwealth Immigrants Bill. The Home Secretary wanted sanction for an immediate Bill. We turned him down because we considered it was ill thought out. Michael Stewart explained that though it might be necessary to impose a quota on Kenya Asians with British passports the controls on their entry to Britain must be quite different from the controls for people who are not British nationals. At the very least there must be a separate quota. 'Moreover,' said Michael, 'before we're driven to this we must make every kind of effort to reach an agreement with Kenyatta.' So the week's delay which we proposed was a pretty good achievement. It was an interesting debate. Barbara was away because she is busy and, like the Lord Chancellor, had been against any Bill on principle. But the key thing to notice was that Roy Jenkins switched at the critical moment. After all, he had come to me last September to warn me that we might have to have this Bill early in the New Year and he had wanted me to slot it into the list and I had slotted it in. Yet on this occasion he showed himself, to put it mildly, unenthusiastic. He didn't give his support to Callaghan, partly because he hates him and partly because Roy was convinced that if we plunged into this in the kind of spirit Callaghan showed we would have offended every decent instinct. Roy pleaded for delay whereas Harold was ready to impose the quota that very day.

I was able to use the Lobby conference that day for an off-the-record explanation of the Kenya problem. I tried to follow Harold's technique of adult education and explained all the difficult problems involved and how careful we must always be to make it clear that the Kenya Asians are British nationals unlike other restricted immigrants. I think the Lobby regards me as a well-informed Minister who can really help them and when a story becomes topical, as this did today, the Lobby can provide invaluable inspired news next morning. On the other hand, I know perfectly well that my colleagues are extremely jealous of me. In particular they dislike the feeling that I handle most of the Sunday press each week. This they hate and detest and Harold also detests and distrusts me, even though he's instructed me to brief these journalists. He's always looking out for leaks from Dick, taking the place of briefs from Dick. My position comes very badly out of this.*

Friday, February 16th
I was so worried about the exemption plan for prescription charges that I had asked Kenneth Robinson to look in this morning. There was no reason why the Lord President or the Leader of the House should summon him. Nevertheless he was glad to come and I found that he hadn't talked to a single Cabinet Minister since the last Cabinet on the subject. So far he had had one meeting with the doctors immediately after January 23rd and he had set his next meeting for February 16th, nearly a month later. In between his Permanent Secretary had been negotiating with the other interested parties. He told me that at the very first meeting the doctors had put forward an ingenious and superficially attractive scheme for a kind of Barclaycard—an embossed stamped card—which people would take to the chemist as evidence that they were genuinely exempted. I said, 'That sounds good,' and he said that the Ministry didn't like it. It seems to me strange that the Ministry should turn down a proposal put forward by the B.M.A. and I get the impression that there are some officials who still hope that the prescription charges will not be imposed. I finally told him that he must make his alternatives clear in a short paper and present it on Monday morning at 10.30, when we shall be grappling with the problem under Michael Stewart's chairmanship in the Cabinet Committee. Kenneth was friendly and easy and added, 'We'll get the exemptions in the end,' as though there was no hurry at all. He then explained to me how his constituency G.M.C. had voted by thirteen to five against prescription charges and ordered him to oppose them. Apparently the whole affair had been organized by a girl who works in the Research Department at Transport House. I hope I sent him away a little

---

* My record in the diary was more prescient than I knew at the time. In his personal record Harold Wilson devotes a whole paragraph to the disastrous results of my press briefing on Thursday 15th and describes how next morning the whole press headlined a split in Cabinet over Kenya immigrants (see *Wilson,* p. 505). Fortunately I preserved the press cuttings which were supplied to Harold Wilson and which I also obtained as Lord President. On Friday 16th they show no news story of this kind at all. Indeed there was absolutely no evidence of any Cabinet division on this issue. I suspect that Mr Wilson got his impression from the fertile imagination of Sir Trevor Lloyd-Hughes.

happier. I felt a good deal clearer myself and was able to report to the Chancellor through John Harris on how the exemption plan was going. Harris had come with a message from Roy about the Kenya Asians. He told me that though Roy didn't feel as strongly as he did a few days ago, he felt there would be a major crisis in the Party unless this problem was handled carefully by the Home Secretary. I thoroughly agreed.[1]

Sunday, February 18th

Last week's Gallup Poll showed a $22\frac{1}{2}$ per cent Tory lead—an absolute record—and that is sustained by the monthly analysis which the N.O.P. does and which we also got today. It too rubs in the sensational decline in the Government's standing. The sad thing is that devaluation didn't do it. We had a real chance afterwards and our stock rallied a bit but in January came the announcement of the public expenditure cuts which sharply reduced Harold Wilson's prestige and the confidence in the Government. What I think is even more important is another figure revealed in the monthly analysis. 'Question: Do you think the Conservative leaders would have done any better or the same or worse?' The replies are, among Labour voters, 3 per cent think better, 61 per cent they would have done the same, 36 per cent think they would have done worse. This is the point on which we have to concentrate, that for an ever-increasing number of Labour voters there is no difference between our Government and a Tory Government and the effect of the reimposition of prescription charges has greatly increased this feeling.

Though Ted Heath is still not popular, the decline in Harold's prestige is a blow to us. For the first couple of years he was such a brilliant personality that his personality carried the public even when the Government was doing unpopular things. Now there's a deep distrust of Harold by the public even when the Government is doing something of which it approves. What used to be our biggest positive asset has now become a negative quantity. It's also going to be a big task to rebuild the party's reputation as long as Harold Wilson is leader. Yet I'm absolutely certain he'll remain leader unless there's a second devaluation and a national government, from which he is thrown out. All this means is that at the end of this week we're still slithering down-hill. We're faced with a catastrophic series of six by-elections[2] ahead of us and the knowledge that whether we have them in March or in May or in the autumn Meriden is bound to be lost, Dudley with a 10,000 majority is very unsafe, and even if Coventry East were fought today it would be unsafe, while the other two parts of Coventry would be certain losers.

[1] On February 22nd the Home Secretary announced that emergency legislation would be introduced to restrict the entry of Kenya Asians to Britain, just as other Commonwealth citizens were restricted. The Bill was introduced on February 27th and all its stages were so swiftly pushed through the Commons and Lords that it received the Royal Assent on March 1st.

[2] Dudley, Meriden, Acton, Oldham West, Sheffield Brightside, and Nelson and Colne.

Monday, March 4th

This evening Roy had asked me to look in and I knew he wanted to talk to me again about the budget. He could hardly have been gloomier. He repeated that very few of the ghastly losses of the reserves we had suffered in devaluation week have come back to London since then and if they are ever to come back it will be in the two months after the budget. If confidence in the pound is not restored there could be a second devaluation within three months and in that case the Government won't survive. I replied that this was nonsense and that the Government could survive though maybe the Prime Minister could not. And I told Roy pretty clearly that if Harold had to go the Chancellor of the Exchequer was the only person who could take his place. 'After all,' I reminded him, 'Churchill was First Lord of the Admiralty when he took Chamberlain's place in 1940.' So he brushed this aside and repeated that the Government couldn't survive a second devaluation and that is why we had to have a tremendously effective budget.

Tuesday, March 5th

Cabinet, and we began with a great attack against Harold and Roy for their prices and incomes policy by George Brown and James Callaghan. George Brown had 'resigned' in 1966 on the issue of statutory sanctions and he repeated once again that the trade unions wouldn't take this and it really wouldn't work. Callaghan went very much further. He said he thought that it would be difficult to get any legislation[1] through Parliament and anyway would new legislative sanctions in fact keep wage levels down? Wasn't it true, he asked, that despite our prices and incomes policy wages had probably gone up by roughly the same amount as if we'd had no prices and incomes policy at all? So the battle went on and on and a decision was postponed till next Tuesday.

Wednesday, March 6th

This was the day of the execution of three African resistance leaders in Rhodesia sentenced over three years ago.[2] It was announced on the B.B.C. in the morning and I knew we would be in for trouble from our backbenchers.

[1] The 1967 Prices and Incomes Act was due to expire on August 11th, 1968, and the Government were considering new powers to replace the old legislation, with the hope, once again, that both employers and unions would exercise voluntary restraint so that compulsory powers need only be used as a last resort. In the White Paper (Cmnd. 3590) provisions of a new Bill were set out. There was to be a 3½ per cent ceiling on wage increases except in cases of genuine productivity deals. The Government were to be empowered to delay price and wage increases for a further twelve months, to limit increases in rents and dividends and to order price reductions on the recommendation of the P.I.B. These powers would continue until December 3rd, 1969.

[2] The Rhodesian regime ignored the Royal Prerogative of Mercy, by which the Queen, acting on the advice of the Commonwealth Secretary, had on March 2nd commuted the sentence to life imprisonment. On March 4th the Rhodesian Appeal Court ruled that the British Government had no right to give the monarch such advice.

Thursday, March 7th

As a result of the Rhodesian executions we were bound to have a speech from Barbara Castle in Cabinet demanding that we should think again about military sanctions. But nobody else was prepared to listen. George Brown, Denis Healey, George Thomson, Tony Crosland and Roy Jenkins all want to damp this down because they see the danger of committing ourselves any further. If only Harold Wilson shared Barbara's mood of excitement. His new idea was an all-party resolution to be drafted by the Lord Chancellor. We discussed this and agreed it.

Then we turned back to prices and incomes, which was on the agenda because of the powerful resistance to Peter Shore's plan that had been registered at last week's Cabinet. The counter-attack was delivered by the Chancellor of the Exchequer and was so terrifying that it was not recorded in Cabinet minutes. What he said was roughly what he had said to me on Monday evening. He described the terrible dangers we were now in and the pressure on the pound in the markets and also the pressure of the I.M.F. He put it to the Cabinet even more strongly than he put it to me that a second devaluation would occur within the next three months if the budget didn't restore confidence in sterling. This is exactly what Cecil King had said to me in January. At that time it had been indignantly repudiated by everyone. But he had been proved right and Roy was now drawing the conclusion that in such a case the Government couldn't survive. This was the big stick with which he decided to beat Cabinet into accepting a tremendous budget and also accepting the prices and incomes policy.

At his Question Time this afternoon the P.M. was in fine form. In an answer on Rhodesia he made it practically impossible to resume talks with Smith by describing him and his government as wicked and evil men, thereby pretty well scuppering the proposals Alec Douglas-Home has just brought back from Salisbury.[1] I doubt if Alec feels sore about it because he knows how very remote they were. It's already clear that the Tories feel that a final burning of the bridges would be a terrible thing and they don't want to see us delivered to the United Nations, who will only hoist us on a wave of further sanctions which might roll us nearer and nearer to the confrontation with South Africa which we must avoid at almost all costs. But the P.M. is on his Rhodesian high horse and nothing can stop him talking in this style.

Friday, March 8th

We started with a big O.P.D. meeting on Rhodesia. I've described in this diary how I have been fighting the battle between activism, which means

[1] Sir Alec Douglas-Home had been in South Africa to discuss whether a future Conservative Government could resume the supply of arms, and on his return journey he had seen Ian Smith in Salisbury and emphasized the need to agree to the five principles before legal independence could be granted. Sir Alec and Mr Smith had detailed talks on two principles (those dealing with unimpeded progress towards African majority rule) but the mathematics of the voting arrangements Mr Smith suggested turned out to be to the Africans' electoral disadvantage.

intensifying sanctions, and quietism, which I describe as working to rule. This morning Harold started by saying that in the new situation the paper we drafted describing these two alternatives is out of date. No one can now say that after the executions we ought to consider quietism. We have got to think how we can handle the situation vigorously and suddenly Harold was plunging in on ideas about further sanctions, cutting off television programmes, jamming radio broadcasts. Thank heavens Denis Healey held firm and told the P.M. that we ought to have a look at the situation. 'Do you want to intensify sanctions and expose the European nations who are letting their goods go through, Prime Minister?' he asked. 'Haven't we got to bear in mind the cost to our European policy of another plunge forward in Rhodesia?' George Brown supported him, Tony Crosland supported him and I said, 'I think we ought to look at this again, Harold. It's no good saying the long-term strategy is outdated by the new situation, it's made more relevant.' And then came a long discussion in which it was clear that he had the full support of the Lord Chancellor and the Attorney-General. Against him were ranged the Defence Secretary, the Foreign Secretary, the Commonwealth Secretary, Tony Crosland and me. Nevertheless I predict that in the end Harold will get his way because we can't stop him. We shall go on plunging ever deeper into the morass.

On March 8th sterling fell to its lowest point since devaluation as some hundred tons of gold were sold in London. Simultaneously the U.S. Treasury announced that since the beginning of the year America's gold reserves had fallen by $100 millions. On March 9th the Governors of the Central Banks of Britain, the U.S.A. and five Western European countries met in Basle and announced their determination to maintain the price of gold at $35 an ounce. But the speculators were not to be reassured. On March 13th a hundred tons of gold were sold in London, and on March 14th two hundred tons. The price of silver soared. The British Government was asked to close the London gold market and on March 14th at midnight, to a hastily summoned meeting of Privy Councillors at Buckingham Palace, the Queen declared March 15th a Bank Holiday. The financial outcome was to give the governors of the central banks a breathing space, and at a meeting in Washington on March 17th they and the British Government agreed to close the London gold market until April 1st, while, in the meantime, stand-by credits to the U.K. to safeguard sterling against speculation were increased to $4,000 million.

There was however a more immediate political result. The Foreign Secretary and Deputy Prime Minister, George Brown, offered his resignation to the Prime Minister, ostensibly because he had not been consulted on March 14th or summoned to the meeting of the Privy Council.

Thursday, March 14th
It was at 11 p.m. in the Commons that I got the first message from Michael Halls saying that the P.M. wanted to talk to me. I went up to my room and

over the phone he told me there was a major international crisis: the whole liquidity system was in suspense and the Americans had asked us to close the gold market. He had decided that we must have a Bank Holiday and for that we needed a Privy Council. Would I want to go to the Palace? I said straightaway that I didn't want to go. I'd prefer to stay on the front bench and see the guillotine debate through.[1] I'd be delighted if the Prime Minister would represent me and take anybody else he liked. Strictly speaking, of course, the Lord President, if he's in the House, should automatically go to the Palace for an emergency Privy Council but there was no reason on this occasion to keep to tradition.

It was a typical post-prandial guillotine debate. The Tories were making long and amusing speeches to each other and celebrating the Kensington by-election result[2] which had just been announced. As there is never anything new to be said such a debate is always wholly artificial and it usually degenerates into violent personal abuse of the Leader of the House and the Minister in charge of the Bill. Somewhere near midnight George Brown came wandering in, sat down on the front bench and leant across to me and said, 'What's all this I hear?' And I said, 'I've known for some time that something is up because I am Lord President.' He got very angry at this and when we got to the first division on the first amendment there he was getting Ministers—like Tony Wedgwood Benn—and saying he must go over to No. 10 and raise hell with the P.M. for not consulting us. There was obviously trouble in the offing. But I was determined to get that guillotine motion through and at last we got on to the second amendment. This was due to take another couple of hours and in the course of it the Tories tried to move progress, i.e. to abandon the debate. It was actually while one of them was moving progress that the news appeared on the tape of the Privy Council meeting at Buckingham Palace. At this Parliament began to get out of control. The Tories all jumped to the conclusion that this meant that the pound had been devalued and most of our people feared the same thing and began to feel that it was no good sitting all through the night on a guillotine motion when a crisis of this sort was occurring outside. Why should we waste time on this motion, they felt? Why not stop and abandon the debate? During the vote on the second motion Heath and Willie Whitelaw got hold of me and said, 'We can't control our people here unless you get Roy Jenkins over tonight.' I had previously announced that he would speak at eleven tomorrow morning and this had only aggravated the trouble. I had to think quickly and immediately I rang up the Prime Minister, who was sitting in No. 10 with his semi-Cabinet, to tell him the House of Commons was collapsing into complete disorder and that I was going to announce that in forty-five minutes he and Roy Jenkins would be in their places ready to make a

[1] On Barbara Castle's Transport Bill.
[2] A by-election at Kensington South took place on March 14th. The Conservative candidate, Sir Brandon Rhys-Williams, won easily.

Statement. Somewhat to my surprise he agreed at once over the phone and I
went back into the House, which immediately became quiet once I made this
announcement. In due course Harold and Roy arrived and the Statement
was made and Harold answered Questions admirably. The House was quiet.
Then they left and the difficulty was to get the guillotine debate started
again. Even John Silkin was saying to me that he didn't think we could really
carry the motion through that night. I replied, 'Balls. We'll get it through.
We've got nothing so far and I'm going to see that we get something.' I had
been in the tea-room and heard one of our Scottish M.P.s complaining that it
was intolerable for our people to be kept there full of alarm and despondency. Nevertheless we did keep them there, we did rally them and, though I
say it myself, I had to do most of the job because there was nobody else to do
it. I had no Parliamentary Secretary. Barbara's two assistants had disappeared and she was all the time rushing out to smoke cigarettes. We faced
three Tory amendments, then three specialist amendments and then the vote
on the Third Reading. We got the second amendment with quite a good
majority and then I had to steer the three specialist ones through. I'd done
the first and Barbara had done the second rather badly and when we came to
the third I had a good idea and gave it away. That did the trick. Suddenly the
whole Opposition packed in and the debate was finished by 6.15 in the
morning. There I was walking home with Tam and the job finished. I had my
bath, got into bed and read the morning papers, and I was back in Downing
Street for a meeting before Cabinet.

Friday, March 15th
After we'd finished our business meeting at 9.30 Burke remarked that we
can't possibly afford to have George out of the Government now and in fact
Harold and John didn't want him sacked and nor did I. I hadn't had time to
discuss George with anyone except Tam Dalyell, who had said to me that I
ought to make a bid for the Foreign Secretaryship. But I knew that wasn't
serious and I didn't play any great part in that discussion with Burke or for
that matter in the morning Cabinet. I'd been up all night and I slept most of
the time.

Sunday, March 17th
At last I've had time over this lovely weekend first to think things out and to
reflect on the events of this remarkable week. As I've mentioned in this
diary, I slept through most of Cabinet just as Barbara Castle did a week or
two ago when the Immigration Bill was being discussed on the morning after
her all-night sitting on the Transport Bill. So I missed hearing Roy's exposition of the crisis which nearly brought us into catastrophe. Since then I've
been filled in by Tommy Balogh. It looks as though the threat of another
devaluation within four months had suddenly become a threat of devaluation within four days—just before the post-devaluation budget. We could

have lost £500 million or £600 million a day of reserves and we haven't got them to lose because we've already pledged them against the stand-by loan from the I.M.F. So on this occasion we'd have been really busted and the pound would have floated down and down and down. I gather all this was pretty frankly admitted by Roy Jenkins on Friday morning and it wasn't a tremendous shock because he'd already given us his earlier warning a week ago.

One of the things I asked myself is whether we mightn't have been better able to resist the strain of this crisis if last January Roy Jenkins had overruled the Treasury and taken the advice of most of the economic experts to clap on hire-purchase controls at the same time as his cuts in government expenditure. It looks to me as though the way the post-devaluation package has been divided into three parts—though it may have had its domestic political conveniences—has been thoroughly bad for the presentation of the policy to which we are now committed. I know that when Jenkins got to the Treasury he was told that it was impossible to get a budget ready in time to publish a single package. But once again if he'd been strong-minded he could have overruled his advisers. If he'd been strong-minded. But that's something I certainly failed to do on a critical issue at the Ministry of Housing.

Now the whole internal crisis was of course aggravated by George Brown's resignation on Friday night.[1] I've had a word with Bill Rodgers about it and he confirms my impression that George resigned reluctantly. If there had come a word from No. 10 George would have withdrawn it, but all through Friday he'd hung on in his flat waiting for the word. When the word didn't come he was compelled to write his resignation letter. It was immediately accepted and Michael Stewart was slipped in straightaway. Harold had made up his mind that this time he wasn't going to have George back. And the very next day George Brown hammered a nail into his own coffin by succumbing to the temptation to write an article for the *Sunday Times* for £5,000. This letter of George Brown's reads strangely because it says that he couldn't stay in Cabinet owing to the way things are being run. This has been interpreted as a mere expression of petty opposition. But it isn't. There's a

[1] In the first week of March there had been heavy sales of sterling and increasing speculation that there would be a rise in the price of gold. Although currency revaluations were expected, the Prime Minister hoped to keep the parity of the pound with the dollar, and on March 14th he and the Chancellor of the Exchequer met to discuss the rapidly worsening situation. To this, and subsequent emergency meetings that evening, George Brown was invited, but he could not be found. The Chancellor and the Prime Minister, with the advice of the Governor of the Bank of England, decided to follow the American proposal to close the gold pool, which meant that the London foreign exchange must be closed and a Bank Holiday declared, by Order in Council. As well as the Prime Minister and the Chancellor, the Lord President of the Council was told of the immediate need for a Privy Council, and so was Peter Shore, who had telephoned the Prime Minister for news, and who was summoned to the Privy Council, at 12.15 a.m., to make up a quorum. At 1 a.m. George Brown telephoned the Prime Minister, incensed that he had been excluded, and Peter Shore included, from the proceedings. On March 16th he resigned from the Foreign Office, complaining of 'dictatorial' methods of government. See *Wilson*, op. cit., pp. 505–15.

great deal in it. If I was ever to resign it would be precisely because I can't stand the way Cabinet is run. It's because of Harold's inability to create a firm inner group with whom to work consistently and his determination to keep bilateral relationships with each one of us and arbitrarily to leave us out of absolutely vital conversations just because we don't happen to be in No. 10 or because we're out of favour that afternoon.

There was no earthly reason why on Thursday evening Harold shouldn't have quietly permitted Burke Trend to organize a meeting of all available members of S.E.P. or of Cabinet, including the Deputy Leader.

I found George the most attractive member of Cabinet, certainly the most gifted, certainly the most imaginative, possessing a mind which has a sense for the evidence buried in the documents or in a speech and which can smell it out. For years George detested me because I was an intellectual from the universities. He openly detested such people. He sloshed them, he smashed them, he sneered at them and he grew famous as the Party's hatchet man to deal with left-wing intellectuals.

When Gaitskell died George failed to become Leader because the Parliamentary Party had seen him very close for years on end and knew about his feet of clay. So he had to serve as number two to Harold and there was a complete incompatibility of temperament. Harold can be tender-hearted but he's also cool, careful, prim, nonconformist, intellectual, book-ish: George is none of these things. He's tough and crude and yet brilliant and imaginative. There's something of Palmerston in George and of Lord John Russell in Harold (I've been reading my Greville of that year over Christmas). Long before the 1964 election Harold Wilson had told me that he was bound to make George his deputy and to create D.E.A. as his new vital Ministry. But in those days Harold used to add, 'He won't last long. He'll trip over himself sooner or later and destroy himself.' The only thing wrong with this judgment was that the final trip came so much later than anyone thought possible. George must have survived nearly seventeen or eighteen resignations and so many appalling misbehaviours, in nearly all of which he'd been tenderly spared by the press. So it has taken over three years before he finally got rid of himself. I believe Harold would never have got rid of him. Harold feared him partly because of his immense strength inside the Parliamentary Party. When he threatened to resign in the 1966 crisis a hundred names went down the same night below a motion asking him to come back. However, his position is not nearly as strong today. He certainly horrified many of our back-benchers as well as Cabinet by his exhibition last Thursday night, which only confirmed the suspicion and fears that have been growing for a good many months. The rumours about his increasing drunkenness and rudeness to his officials, and his gross misbehaviours at important banquets have piled up to a point where Members found him pretty unbearable.

One always found George pretty unbearable as long as one merely heard about these misbehaviours. But next time one sat opposite him in Cabinet he was so sensible and practical that one forgot all about it. In fact during the last seven weeks I've found him easier to work with than ever before and the press was beginning to wonder what the hell George Brown was up to. He's been so quiet and good, they commented, that there must be something new blowing up. But will his resignation make him a great menace either in the Parliamentary Party or in the Party outside? Our people don't easily forgive Ministers who in a moment of international crisis suddenly pull out in a pet. He will find it difficult to restore his position either inside or outside Parliament and I shall be interested to see whether there's any serious support for the idea he is now promoting that he should remain deputy leader of the Party concerned with restoring Party morale in the constituencies. I don't yet see how a man outside the Cabinet can do this job effectively.

Now let's turn from George Brown to Michael Stewart—Minister of Education, then Foreign Secretary when Gordon Walker went, then at D.E.A. when George went and now back to the Foreign Office when George went again. To be the man who's always put in when somebody resigns is not very attractive and the press practically disregard Michael's appointment today. It will be deeply disappointing to the Parliamentary Party because of his doctrinaire support for the Americans in Vietnam and his opposition to our withdrawal from the Far East and indeed to all the main radical decisions this Cabinet has taken. Harold Wilson told me yesterday that he's a little less doctrinaire about Vietnam now and I hope this is true, but in Cabinet and in the Foreign Office Michael Stewart will be a force for consolidation—a strengthener of the establishment without any of the liveliness and imaginativeness of George. Was there any alternative to him? The newspapers say that Denis was the alternative but to move Denis from Defence would have caused a reshuffle. Certainly I would have staked a very strong claim to replace Denis not because I particularly want Defence but because with Denis in the Foreign Office I would have been determined to get a position where I too could influence foreign and defence policy, which frankly has been left almost unchanged for three years. But the Chiefs of Staff know me far too well and Harold would have had a hell of a job to get me made Minister of Defence in one Friday afternoon in the middle of a world liquidity crisis. But could I have succeeded George Brown? Frankly I'd have liked to and I think I would have been an imaginative Foreign Secretary and a pretty confident administrator in the office as well. Nevertheless, I have to admit to myself that Harold Wilson never even conceived the possibility of making me Foreign Secretary and nobody round him suggested it—neither Burke Trend on the one side nor Gerald Kaufman and Marcia on the other. Partly this is because I'm doing a useful job, as my record on Thursday night in the House showed, but it's also because in foreign affairs from their point of view I'm not trustworthy since I'm a fanatical Little Englander who wants to see us settling down as an offshore island and dropping our special relationship with the U.S.A. So for quite different reasons both Denis Healey and Dick Crossman were excluded from serious consideration and Michael Stewart went in. It's a dumpy dull substitute which gets us through the short-term crisis but intensifies the need for a drastic Cabinet reshuffle as soon as possible.

Finally, just a word about this famous world crisis into which we've been plunged. I've never felt a greater sense of this Government's impotence than I do now. The question whether we devalue again or not is entirely determined by whether the Americans will let us have the cash to sustain the policy they want without forcing devaluation on us. That's our situation two days ahead of a budget in which Roy will ask for immense sacrifices in order that this Labour Government can at last get a firm control of the economy. The truth is that we shan't get control of the economy.

I had to come up to London tonight because I got a message from Downing Street that every member of Cabinet must sleep near enough to attend an emergency Cabinet if it is called. However, only the Chief and I were compelled not only to sleep in or near London but to clock in. The Chief, by the way, duly clocked in at No. 12 and sat there for two and a half hours before they remembered and brought him round. I insisted on coming into the building and I was once again warned to enter through the Cabinet office and not through the door of No. 10 so that the press wouldn't think there was anything going on. I got all those doors unlocked and came down the passages and down the stairs into the anteroom and finally opened the door into the Cabinet Office, and found Harold sitting in his chair at the middle of the big table with the Chancellor and a number of other Ministers round him. One peep and I went round the back into the little room where the old gang always sits. There were Marcia and Gerald Kaufman and Tommy and myself and, a little later, John Silkin. So I was back in the Wilson coterie and we settled down and Thomas started briefing me a bit. Then Harold looked in and said that he'd have got rid of them all in a minute and that the crisis is over. The details, he told me, were now being worked out in New York by the British delegation headed by Harold Lever and Leslie O'Brien, the Governor of the Bank of England.[1] When the Ministers had finally gone off Harold came right into the room and said, 'What about some supper and sandwiches?' and Marcia said, 'Why shouldn't we all go upstairs?' and she rang up Mary and asked her to give supper to the family, so to speak. So I found myself at an old-style supper in No. 10 with Mary looking after us. I hadn't talked to her for some time and she said to me rather awkwardly, 'I remember the only time you came to see us at our home in Hampstead, I offered you Nescafé and you said you'd rather not and we went out to a restaurant and there you got some ordinary coffee. So I

[1] He was Deputy Governor 1964–6 and Governor 1966–73. He became a life peer in 1973.

suppose you don't like tinned salmon but that's all we've got tonight apart from a bit of cold ham.' We were sitting in that miserable little dining-room and there on the table-cloth was a bit of mutton wrapped up in Cellophane, a bit of butter on a plate, a couple of tomatoes and some lettuce, and beside them a very large tin of salmon which had by now been emptied out into a potato dish. 'But I like tinned salmon,' I said to Mary, 'especially in fish cakes.' 'Oh, you do like it in fish cakes?' she replied. 'So do I.' And somehow a part of a terrible barrier had been broken down between us. I'd been made to realize how snobbish the Wilsons regard the Crossmans' attitude to Nescafé and tinned salmon and a thousand other things. So we settled down to supper, and I ate my tinned salmon and my slices of bread and butter and Gerald Kaufman was served with his fried Jewish eggs,[1] and then we all had hot buttered toast, which came in late, and Marcia provided us with some apricot jam.

After supper Harold disappeared downstairs and Tommy disappeared too, wandering round in attendance on his boss waiting to be useful. I stayed with the rest in the living-room helping to take things out to the kitchen next door and pretending to help to wash up, and in the course of this Mary explained to me that they had intended to spend that evening at Chequers giving dinner to John Fulton and two other guests. But they'd had to cancel the dinner and come back to London for the meetings. They had meant to bring the dinner back with them but they hadn't been allowed to because Government hospitality said they would be charged for the dinner if it was taken from Chequers to No. 10 and not given to the guests for whom it was arranged. I said, 'What? Does Government hospitality treat you in that way?' I was thinking how Winston Churchill would have reacted to officials who tried to order him about. But this is the position Harold and Mary are in at Chequers and No. 10. They are very modest people and tremendously correct; they adore being at No. 10 and even more they adore being at Chequers so Chequers is being used exactly as it ought to be used by a Prime Minister who hasn't got a country house and needs an escape in the country. They love every moment there and just because they love it in a very nice way they are bullied and chivvied by Government hospitality and closed and hemmed in by the Ministry of Works and made to feel they are interlopers in a way quite different from what would happen to Alec Douglas-Home, I'm pretty sure.

I had got there at 8.30 and left just after midnight with Tommy just as the Chief arrived, looking very ill, and stayed chatting alone with Harold until 1.30. Nothing happened up there except gossip. There was one moment when the P.M. went down to see Denis Healey, who had looked in. When Harold came back he said, 'Well, he is a cool customer. He asked me about my intentions. I said Michael is there for keeps and he said he didn't believe

---

[1] A figment of Crossman's culinary imagination: no such dish exists.

it.' Denis had replied, 'Michael is only there temporarily, and you will be having me in the F.O. next autumn and I want you to make GeorgeThomson Minister of Defence in my place.' Of course this is only Harold's account of the conversation, but it is an example of Denis's bloody-mindedness and uncooperativeness, refusing to help himself. To behave like that with the Prime Minister means that in the next reshuffle the P.M. will keep him where he is and give him hell.

After this Harold sat down and at extraordinary length rehearsed his version of exactly what happened on Thursday night. He told me that the moment when George's letter had finally come on Friday afternoon he had sent for Michael and he said, 'Actually I warned him just after devaluation that if George were to resign again, he would get the job. Well, that made it easier for me.' I had had those vague feelings about the kind of job I could do as Foreign Secretary and I wondered whether it was possible to bring such a dull man as Michael Stewart in instead of me. But in fact it is clear that Harold never conceived any other possibility. Michael is the man he can trust and the fact that he was a disastrous First Secretary and Minister of D.E.A. makes no difference to that. By the way, Harold was very careful this evening to remind me that though as the result of Michael going to the Foreign Office I was to take over the chairmanship of the Social Services Committee and run Michael's conference next Saturday on the social services, this was all purely temporary and would just be a holding operation while he was making his ultimate decisions.

Monday, March 18th

Budget Cabinet, and really the only point of interest was how complacently the Chancellor's paper was taken once it was clear that there was going to be a dividend ceiling of $3\frac{1}{2}$ per cent corresponding to the wages ceiling of $3\frac{1}{2}$ per cent. That closed one area of complaint. Roy was very skilful in the presentation of his main proposal—a new tax on investment income of over £3,000 a year. This was his new tax and it impressed us. After he'd finished we had a little discussion and the only thing on which there was any pressure at all was on the subject of hotels, where Roy announced the increase of 50 per cent in S.E.T. for which Nicky Kaldor had been pressing. I took the lead in urging that as well as the special grants for building hotel rooms in the development areas he should have investment grants for hotels in general and no S.E.T. for those in development areas. I kicked Willie Ross, my neighbour, into action and kicked Cledwyn Hughes, and as there was a feebleness in Cabinet this morning I got into the budget speech a reference to the possibility that there might be concessions to hotels in the rural parts of development areas, and that was the best we got. Otherwise there were no changes and we turned to prices and incomes. As the discussion went on it became clearer and clearer that since the cost of living was going to be put up by 6 per cent, the $3\frac{1}{2}$ per cent wages ceiling would be unrealistic. Tony Crosland wanted it raised to 4 per cent, which was neither here nor there, but when somebody else said 4½ per cent Roy said that was an increase he simply couldn't take. Then once again he repeated his story of the second devaluation, this time reminding us that it might have occurred last Friday night if it hadn't been that the President of the United States had rung up and asked to have the gold market stopped and given us an excuse for a Bank Holiday. Without that Bank Holiday we could have had a catastrophic run on the pound leading to a second devaluation. 'That,' he said, 'is how near we were.' But having lost so much in the first devaluation and got very little back since then we now had to have a budget speech which at all costs will bring back the reserves to London—and that means it has to include a prices and incomes policy. It's always been a puzzle why bankers in Zürich and New York should insist that the British economy is subjected to a degree of Government intervention in the area of wages that they wouldn't tolerate in their own countries. This, I think, is something we have to thank Mr Callaghan for, because it was he who sold the prices and incomes policy to Mr Fowler, the American Secretary of the Treasury. Certainly Roy now feels that for the next three months he has to have a tough incomes policy. So I put the precise question to him. 'I can see that if you have a tough policy it will help you with the bankers for these critical next three months, but it may make the economy unworkable later on and it may precipitate a strike which ruins the Labour Government. Which is the greater risk to you—the break-down of the incomes policy in the next twelve months or a run on the pound in the next three?' 'No question,' he said. 'A run on the pound in the next three.' 'In that case,' I said, 'go ahead because we can modify the policy later.' I found Roy's admission important because it's clear that personally he doesn't believe in a prices and incomes policy and he'd rather have a free-for-all, like the strongish group in the Cabinet headed by Dick Marsh who've been rooting against a statutory policy week in and week out. But so grave is the immediate threat to sterling that he has to have a strong prices and incomes policy even if it causes catastrophe in a year's time.

Tuesday, March 19th
I strolled across St James's Park to get my hair cut and when I got back to the office with very little to do I was suddenly told the P.M. wanted to talk to me. At once I felt that this was a talk about the future and, sure enough, when I got down there it was the most relaxed conversation I've had with Harold for a very long time. I've been very rough to him and completely aloof and now suddenly he wants to make me an offer in a major reshuffle. He started by saying he was talking in the closest personal confidence and I wasn't to tell anybody what he said. What he intended was to make me First Secretary and Minister of Social Services, which would mean combining in a single Ministry the Ministries of Social Security and Health. I paused and said I would like to think it over but my first reaction was that I ought to be Minister of

Defence. 'No future there,' he said abruptly. 'Maybe two years ago you could have gone there when the decisions still had to be taken. It's too late now. You would find that a dead end. You won't leave anything memorable if you go to Defence, but you could be as memorable as Beveridge[1] if you go to the other job and make a go of the two years of reorganization there. You can have something for your memoirs,' he said, looking at me, and I was clearly aware that these are the last two years of my political life, and he was offering me a really big chance to be right at the top with a key job and a genuine promotion.

By now I'd had time to gather my thoughts and I said a good deal would depend on who succeeded me as Leader of the House and what happened to John Silkin. 'John Silkin is not a healthy man now,' he said. 'I'll have to move him and I've got ideas about that. Have you any ideas for your successor?' And before I could answer he said 'I have an idea. Fred Peart.' Since then I've thought of Fred Peart and it's quite a good idea. He's a very different type from me – working-class, a non-intellectual, and so on. Moreover, I've started all the big parliamentary reforms and he may do extremely well in getting people to settle down with them.

'There's one thing,' I added, 'you will have to face, Prime Minister. It is quite impossible to have Peter Shore as head of D.E.A. with you purporting to run it. He's despised by his fellow members of Cabinet, he's hopeless in the House of Commons and he can't put your policy to the T.U.C. and the C.B.I.' 'I know all that,' he said, 'and I see my way through but I agree he has to go.' Then I asked him cautiously about Michael Stewart and he made it clear once more that Michael is a permanency until the election: there's no chance of George Thomson taking his place. As for Denis Healey, Denis is so bloody-minded he will have to stay at the Ministry of Defence. Harold had been talking to him about Technology and Power and he'd shown the same snooty disdain.

I returned to the problems of my own job and he said, 'If you don't take it, Dick, I'll give it to Barbara.' 'If I take it,' I said, 'why not make Barbara head of D.E.A. as you nearly did last summer? She's due for promotion too.' He concluded by saying that he was determined to get the final Cabinet for the run-up to the election – one good enough to last two years. It must be a really new Cabinet with a new look and he added, 'For the first time I can get rid of the people I took over in the Shadow Cabinet. When I became Leader I only had one person in the Parliamentary Committee who had voted for me and when I formed my first Cabinet in 1964 it contained only two or three of you who were my supporters. The rest were opponents. Now I shall be strong and need not worry about any debt I owe to my enemies.' This fierce vindictive tone alarmed me a bit but at least it's interesting that he wants to make some

[1] In February 1943 the Commons gave blessing to Sir William Beveridge's Report setting out a plan for universal social security. It was substantially enacted after the war.

16 The official Cabinet photograph, October 1968. Left to right (standing): Judith
Hart, George Thomas, Cledwyn Hughes, Richard Marsh, Edward Short,
William Ross, George Thomson, Anthony Wedgwood Benn, Anthony
Greenwood, Lord Shackleton, Roy Mason, John Diamond and Sir Burke
Trend. Left to right (seated): Peter Shore, Denis Healey, Barbara Castle, Lord
Gardiner, Michael Stewart, Harold Wilson, Roy Jenkins, Richard Crossman,
James Callaghan, Fred Peart and Anthony Crosland.

17 In February 1969, just three months after his election as President of the
United States, Richard Nixon visits Prime Minister Wilson at No. 10
Downing Street. Britain's Foreign Secretary, Michael Stewart, is on the left
and the American Secretary of State, William Rogers, is on the right.

18 Richard Crossman listens to nurses putting their grievances to him on the steps of the Ministry in April 1969.

19 & 20 Arriving to address the Labour Society at the London School of Economics in May 1969, Crossman finds the front of the building heavily picketed by protesting students but eventually enters by a door at the rear.

drastic changes. Then we discussed George Brown's future and I suggested that he should become head of Transport House. 'I wouldn't object to that,' said Harold. 'Let me try that out.'

Thursday, March 21st
In the House this afternoon the P.M. and I were both in good competent form. After us came Tony Benn's Statement on computers and I went out to talk to the P.M. 'I've been thinking it over,' I said, 'and I certainly shouldn't look a gift horse in the mouth. I accept the offer. I would like to be First Secretary with these responsibilities. But I thought that since I wouldn't have a Ministry to sit in I'd have to stay somewhere in the Cabinet Office. So I might as well stay in my present Lord President's Office for the time being.' He seemed a little puzzled that I was interested in this and couldn't conceive that I really cared about it. But quite honestly the only thing I do mind about is moving from the office where I've collected my pictures and where at last the silver is properly presented and the chairs are properly placed. I want to stay there for as long as I can and let Fred Peart go to Michael Stewart's rooms in the Cabinet Office. Ideally I'd like to be First Secretary and Lord President simultaneously, but I doubt if that is possible.

I then discussed the whole issue of George Brown retaining the deputy leadership: Harold said he wouldn't touch the idea with a barge-pole. Already on Sunday at supper he had suggested that Douglas Houghton should take George Brown's place as deputy leader but that of course is entirely for the liaison committee and the Party to decide. What George Brown should do is to resign from the deputy leadership and accept the general secretaryship or something like it at Transport House. After all the deputy leadership is quite a modern invention. It was created to give Herbert Morrison a place on the N.E.C. when I knocked him off. He had been Deputy Prime Minister but that hadn't given him a place on the N.E.C. and so the constitution was changed and he was elected to the N.E.C. as deputy leader and as a second representative of the parliamentary leadership. But no one expected that the Deputy Prime Minister would walk out of the Government and on his resignation make an attack on the Prime Minister and then try to stay on as deputy leader. If George tries to fight this issue there'll be a big struggle because I think Jim Callaghan will go for the deputy leadership and so will Barbara and Michael Stewart and almost certainly Roy. Nevertheless, there is quite a problem on the N.E.C. As a result of a series of accidents the Foreign Secretary won't be at the meeting, the Chancellor won't be there and I won't be there because I've resigned, so if Harold isn't there the parliamentary leadership is extremely weak.

This evening Peter Shore made another of his languid disastrous speeches and I got a message that Roy wanted to see me. I went in and before he could speak I said that I wanted to fill him in. 'I've seen the Prime Minister and told him that Peter will have to go,' and went on to say that Harold had told me he knew that already and had made up his own mind. I got all that out quick and Roy said, 'Well, I really sent for you to say the same thing to you. It's a relief we all agree.' Then I went on, 'I'd better tell you now that Harold has talked to me about the future and offered me a new job,' and I described roughly what the job was. He at once said that I was right to accept and that it was far better than Defence.

Tuesday, March 26th

I had to be at the House of Lords at 10 a.m. because we were resuming our conversations after a fortnight's interval. We had chosen 10 a.m. in order to get a solid day's work in which to discuss Mr Macleod. From the start he had said that even if we agreed a scheme of reform its implementation must be postponed until the next Parliament. Last Monday we'd had a long talk with Eddie Shackleton, who provided an excellent paper showing what a fatal thing this three-year delay would be. Of course we all knew that if the momentum of the agreement were dropped and if for example a Tory Government were elected, reform in this form would simply never take place. But there was a further powerful argument, the effect of delay on the composition of the House. If we delay reform until the next Parliament we will have to create a hundred new peers. Instead of starting with people who know the tradition and are able to evolve a new House out of the old we will have a complete break. After all, that is something no Tory will accept. Under our scheme we intend to introduce a retiring age first of seventy-five and then, fairly soon, to reduce it to seventy-two, but the old boys are needed to initiate the new House and cushion it for the change.

Eddie's excellent paper provided me with the unexpected arguments I needed to rebut Macleod. So I got to the committee room and settled myself in at 9.55, at 10.05 Frank Byers[1] from the Liberals slouched in and at 10.10 Jellicoe and Maudling came along and said that Carrington was ill again. Our people line up punctually but the slackness and informality of the Tories is remarkable. And at 10.15 (I had to go to the P and I Committee at 11) Macleod was still not there and we had a message that he had forgotten the meeting was in the morning and thought it was in the afternoon. So once again we agreed to drop consideration of his objection. But as a result we got one advantage because we clipped our way through a whole series of secondary points—the problem of the bishops, the problems of affirmative orders, and the law lords—three of the most important and difficult secondary issues were settled.

When we deal with this kind of detail Jellicoe clearly understands because he's on Shackleton's working party, but Maudling is completely out of his depth. The contrast between the enthusiasm of the Tory peers and the lack of interest of the Tories from the lower House is striking and alarming. As

---

[1] Lord Byers, Liberal M.P. for North Dorset 1945–50. He became a life peer in 1964 and, since 1967, had been Liberal Leader in the House of Lords.

for Macleod, he shows no interest except a mild desire to sabotage, while Maudling is amiable, conscientious and willing to go along with almost anything we propose. I haven't ever been able to decide why the Tories have taken this acquiescent co-operative line in these talks. I suspect the reason is that they regard House of Lords reform as very much their own subject and the kind of thing they would do as a Government on the basis of official papers provided from Whitehall. Since we have all the Whitehall official papers they by and large accept our proposals.

Wednesday, March 27th
The big news in the papers was George Brown's decision to stay on as deputy leader.[1] I had missed the liaison committee last week when they had discussed the idea that Douglas Houghton might take his place. But it had become clear that there would be a contested election and that is something we have to avoid even if it means leaving him in the office. There's also a considerable advantage in his staying deputy leader as it prevents him from attacking the Government in any way whatsoever, either in his newspaper articles or in speeches.

Thursday, March 28th
At the Party meeting this evening something remarkable happened. George Brown came in a few minutes late and nobody stirred. The meeting went on absolutely quietly. Indeed, it was too quiet for my taste. The members accepted Michael Stewart's Vietnam discussion without a vote and then accepted my explanation about the three-waiting-day period for sickness benefit which was the main thing for which they had come. And so George slips out again disappointed.

I may as well deal with the three-waiting-days now. There was a point in the January discussions on public expenditure when Judith wanted to get the extra three-shillings increase of family allowance and she wasn't going to get it unless she paid for it out of her estimates. So she tried to do a deal with the Chancellor. She found that the cost of the three-waiting-days that occur at the beginning of sickness is £15 million. This sickness insurance provides that if you are sick for ten days or more you are paid at the end of the tenth day and the three-waiting-days at the beginning are included, whereas they don't count if you haven't had ten days' sickness. She told Cabinet she would abolish this benefit, save £15 million and so finance the £3 million extra for family allowances. I doubt whether Roy knew anything more about the waiting days than Judith Hart. The swap was approved twice in Cabinet and the Chancellor thought it was very clever and was well satisfied. Only much later did Judith discover that this was causing her appalling trouble with the trade unions. Apparently when Jim Griffiths,[2] as Minister of National Insur-

[1] George Brown retained the deputy leadership of the Labour Party until 1970.
[2] Labour M.P. for Llanelli 1936–70. He was Minister of National Insurance 1945–50, Secretary of State for the Colonies 1950–51 and Secretary of State for Wales 1964–6.

ance, tried to abolish the three-waiting-days in the 1945 Government he had to withdraw under pressure and there's a tremendous history of rank-and-file opposition to this economy. It was obvious from the way she was treated in the Party meeting today that she's in for very serious trouble when she meets the Social Services Group on Monday.

I'd eaten a bit too much at dinner and got indigestion so I didn't stay downstairs and watch television but went up to bed and put the radio on by the bedside. Already the Dudley result had been declared and there was an 18 per cent swing against the Government. So we knew what we were in for at Meriden and Acton. I heard the rejoicing over the disasters in a kind of doze.[1]

Friday, March 29th

I woke up quite suddenly at five in the morning and thought that I must make a big speech at Basildon in which I would call for a Mark II Wilson Government. Since we can't change the measures, we've got to change the men. And I thought out this speech: we can't have a general election now—it's unconstitutional and it's also our duty to carry on and do our unpopular job. We can't have a national government. Right, what can we have? Wilson Mark II. There's a speech there, I realized, and I worked on it till breakfast time.

It so happened that I had my weekly business meeting with Harold. When I got there Burke and Michael were already in attendance, as well as the Chief Whip. We planned the meetings for next week and then I said to Harold, 'I must talk to you about the speech I'm making this evening.' 'All right,' he said. 'We shan't have time at the end of this. Stay on after O.P.D. and I'll get it through quickly.' This was cutting it a bit thin since there was only half an hour for O.P.D. before Harold had to leave for Euston to catch a train to his constituency. Even though the business meeting had finished twelve minutes early, nobody dared to talk about the by-elections. Harold puffed his pipe, Michael Stewart and John were discreet, I'd got my time booked. We just filled in until O.P.D., which we got through in a quarter of an hour; it was merely about the treaties in the Persian Gulf.

So I had a full eighteen minutes to tell him the shape of the speech. 'No,' he says, 'I don't like men not measures. You mustn't separate it as sharply as that. You must deal with the measures as well. But I like Mark I and Mark II. Wilson Government Mark I and Mark II. Yes, I like that and it will be a great help to Harold Wilson.' I saw what he meant because, of course, in the reporting on the election catastrophes the Wilson-must-go campaign had been very prominent. A speech which diverted attention from Wilson Must Go to Wilson's New Team would do the public good and also put the fear of God into Cabinet.

[1] In the by-elections on March 28th there was an average swing of 18 per cent against the Government. At Dudley a 10,000 majority was turned into an 11,000 majority for the Conservatives, at Meriden a 4,581 Labour majority was turned into a 15,263 majority for the Conservatives, and at Acton 4,941 was turned into 3,720.

Then he revealed to me what the Mark II Cabinet was. There was going to be an inner Cabinet of six or seven—Harold Wilson, Michael Stewart, Roy Jenkins, Dick Crossman, Barbara Castle, and Fred Peart, the new Leader of the House. Should Denis be in or out? I said, 'Out, he must earn his passage home.' I said that it's important to get much better connections with the Trade Union Group and he mentioned two names so incredibly dismal that I've forgotten them and then he added four names of the most boring back-benchers whose promotion he thought would enliven our constituency parties. But it's clear that Patrick Gordon Walker at least is to go and that Barbara is to be the economic boss while I'm to be the Social Services boss and have Education and part of the Home Office as well. Then there's Michael Stewart, who's the foreign boss, uniting the Foreign Office with Defence and Commonwealth, and Fred Peart as chairman of all the special Cabinet Committees. 'Barbara,' he said, 'is to be the new inspiration: she'll spark the new model. Tell her that today when you see her at lunch but don't tell her any more. She's to make the whole difference by taking over relations with the trade unions.'

This was the closest meeting I've had with Harold and I don't think anybody else—including Michael Stewart, Burke or the Chief Whip—had been told as much about his intentions.

I struggled away and got my speech done and then cancelled a lunch with Independent Television to be able to have lunch with Barbara and I told her Harold's news. She was thrilled and excited. Could she tell her husband? I said she could tell Ted she has a big job coming and perhaps I told her more than I should have done, but she is very discreet. We went through my speech and she said the end was too flat—'You must put in a piece about partnership with the Party.' She absolutely made the speech and it is now first-rate, all five pages of it.

I had warned the B.B.C. and the I.T.V. that I was going to say something important that evening and I had also told David Wood of *The Times*. The press releases were got out just in the nick of time as I set off to Fenchurch Street. I found a decent little meeting of a hundred or so people in a church hall. So I got up and of course my speech was hearty and bright and they even listened to the piece I had to read aloud with very close attention. There were lots of journalists there and I knew it had got across to them.

Saturday, March 30th
It was certainly the sensation of the morning papers, though David Wood chose to assume that I made the speech without consulting the Prime Minister and called it tactless. This is pretty silly since I tipped him off. On the other hand the *Financial Times* and the *Guardian* have seen its impor-tance. Jimmy Margach rang up this morning and I said that I had nothing to add and I gave the same reply to the B.B.C. and the I.T.V. I didn't want to give any interviews on the speech because I knew that many of my colleagues

were either shaking in their shoes or green with envy. They knew very well that when I announced the Mark II Government their days were numbered and that they'd better behave properly if they want to stay in the new Cabinet.

At lunch-time I had an urgent message from the office that the B.B.C. wanted me to go on the air and I said no. Then I had a message from Tommy saying the P.M. was very pleased with the effect of the speech. Now this was interesting because everybody including Callaghan and Gordon Walker was anxious about the meaning of the speech. I said that I had of course done it with Harold's approval and that it may well mean that many of us have to face resignation. 'Does that mean', says Patrick Gordon Walker, 'that you and Michael want to resign?' and I said, 'Well, we've got to face the possibility.' Poor Patrick, he's for it and he knows I'm not for it. Callaghan also felt the situation ominous, that I was much too like an executioner polishing the axe. Certainly the speech was having the effect inside the Cabinet which we had intended.

Monday, April 1st

On the wireless this morning I heard the news of President Johnson's astonishing broadcast announcing that he isn't going to stand for re-election and is going to dedicate his time to trying to get peace in Vietnam.[1] It sounded momentous but I must say my own assumption is that he's planning a tremendous comeback and this is a typical Johnson trick.[2]

Tuesday, April 2nd

In the House we had the P.M.'s Questions and then the admission of new Members. The P.M. was really quite angry with me because I'd arranged for lots of Statements on Monday and no Statements today so that he would have to sit there, he said, and watch the Tory victors of Meriden, Dudley and Warwick and Leamington all come past him with storms of cheering. Actually it was quite a good thing he did sit there beside me because it was most curiously formal and the cheering wasn't all that loud. Certainly these victories haven't given them all the confidence they needed, and instead of depressing Harold it cheered him up.

Afterwards we went out and had a talk when he told me about the difficulties of Mark II. He had planned that Barbara should go to D.E.A. while Peter might move to Mintech and Wedgy to Education. But when that plan was put to Roy he had turned it down flat and said he wouldn't have it because he didn't want Barbara in a key position in the economic sector reproducing the tension which had caused such appalling damage when

---

[1] The President also declared a partial end to the bombing and, on April 3rd, the North Vietnamese announced their conditional agreement to negotiate for an end to the war.

[2] Crossman's suspicions, though not fulfilled, were not entirely unfounded: see Theodore White, *The Making of the President 1968* p. 279 (London: Cape, 1969).

George Brown was head of D.E.A. and Callaghan head of the Treasury. Roy made it clear that he was going to jolly well run the show on the economic side without a rival. Certainly he liked Barbara but he wasn't going to have her at D.E.A.

What then was to be done? The P.M. told me that he was now thinking of making Barbara Minister of Labour and also Leader of the House to raise her status. I said I found this difficult to believe but when Barbara came to see me this afternoon with the same story that she was being pressured by the P.M. to take Ray Gunter's place and add to it the Leader of the House I said to her, 'God forbid, Barbara. How could you be Leader of the House and Minister of Labour? Supposing you're busy with a gas workers' strike and there's turmoil in the House of Commons and they complain the Leader isn't there because she's dealing with the gas workers! No, you can't run those two jobs together and anyway if I was the most unsuitable person to be Leader of the House, you're the second most unsuitable. You don't care about procedure and if you take this it's just for status, which is a thoroughly bad reason.'

Later this evening I at last went across to No. 11 and found Roy and John Harris. Roy has had three long talks with the P.M. and is quite content with the reconstruction. 'Is it true that you won't take Barbara?' I said, and he said, 'Yes. I don't want to recreate D.E.A. as a centre of power and therefore she can't be there. . . .' But it was hopeless to have her simply as Leader of the House unless we got rid of Callaghan and popped her into the Home Office too. But he wasn't so sure about her being Home Secretary and rather fancied her as Minister of Labour. Then we began to discuss the need to cut the dead wood out of the rest of the Government. He agreed the excision should be drastic and I then said, 'Well, who in your view should replace them? If all this is done while you're away, it will greatly reduce your influence. Shouldn't you, if it's humanly possible, have at least the second part of the shuffle delayed for five days?' He then agreed to let me have a list of the twelve to fourteen young people he thought due for promotion and promised he would try to have the appointments delayed.

Thursday, April 4th
I was still lying in bed looking at the papers when Barbara rang up from Windsor and asked how things were going. I said, 'I think there is a chance and I've got an idea for you.' Then I put it to her direct. 'What about your being First Secretary instead of me? Why don't you become First Secretary while I stay Lord President and keep my lovely room in the Privy Council? I don't really mind. It's only stuff and titles to me.' She leapt at it with tremendous energy as though it made all the difference to her.

I'd arranged to see Barbara at one o'clock before she went to No. 10. She had to come to my room in the Privy Council because the press are watching No. 10 so carefully. When she strolled in I was talking at the time to my

Private Office about my very last business Statement and my very last Lobby conference. She listened for two or three minutes and then she went down the corridor into No. 10 and after two or three minutes, as Harold had carefully arranged with me, I followed after her. I found them both looking extremely happy. She had confirmed to Harold that I'd made the whole difference to her by yielding to her the First Secretaryship and Harold was delighted that she is as happy as she is. Barbara Castle is going to be First Secretary and Minister of the Economy and of Production. But then comes the question of whom she should have as number two. Harold of course wants her to take the terrible Tom Urwin but I said that she ought to keep Roy Hattersley. 'That's impossible,' said Marcia, who had just come in. 'Roy belongs to the other side. He's a Gaitskellite, a conspirator.' 'Look here, Marcia,' I said, 'I've seen a lot of that boy. He's not a Gaitskellite or any other kind of ite. He's a very ambitious young politician. And the only thing Barbara will find embarrassing is that he may become too fond of her and too closely tied to her coat-strings.'

I shall be interested to hear what Harold finally decides. Meanwhile he turned to me and said, 'You don't have much self-interest, Dick, in this affair, do you? I think it's very generous what you've done.' And I replied, 'Well, it's much more important to get Barbara in a good humour as First Secretary and Minister of Labour or Labour and Production or whatever she'll be called. That makes sense. We can build her up in that particular way and I don't need the title anyway.' As we sat there talking and drinking it was clear that Harold had backpedalled a long way from the idea of the Mark II Government. The only major change in this reshuffle will be Barbara's promotion, with mine coming a very poor second. Roy will be upset that by keeping Barbara out of D.E.A. he hasn't kept her out of power. Harold likes this as well and he is doing it in Roy's absence. This may be the saving of the prices and incomes policy because Barbara has already told me that she intends to look at this positively, to go to the trade unions and offer them an 8 per cent increase if they give her some production. If what Barbara said is correct we're going to have a return to the philosophy of George Brown's prices and incomes policy far back in 1964 when it was an expression of expansionism. This shouldn't upset Roy too much because he isn't really a restrictionist and he wants productivity and an export drive.

So we sat and chatted, Barbara and I and the boss and Marcia until I had to go down to the House for my business Statement after Harold's Questions. Once again it went swimmingly, tossing the balls in the air and catching them—there is nothing in this job of Leader of the House except procedure, posture, performance. I can do it easily, effortlessly and successfully, and I have got the House in the hollow of my hand.

But this Thursday evening I begin to get a sense of let-down. I saw a news flash on the tape saying that the one certainty is a really big promotion for me, and I began to wonder whether I haven't given my future away and been too generous. I've given the First Secretaryship to Barbara and for myself I've got the hire of a beautiful office. So I got hold of Tam and talked to him sadly.

Friday, April 5th
All the papers were speculating about the reconstruction but Walter Terry in the *Mail* had an inside story, which though it was not complete was correct in every detail it printed. I was still feeling so unhappy that I rang up Harold and said that I just wanted to make sure what my own position was after the shuffle. He said, 'Well, you certainly haven't been looking after yourself, Dick, these days.' But he gave me the kind of assurance of his goodwill that I needed. I couldn't be really demoted after all this so I slouched over to my last weekly meeting. I think I'm really the only Minister who has been consulted by Harold throughout all this. Probably this is the last time I shall be really close to Harold because there are sharp choices in this world. You can either have a job like the Leader of the House with no effective work to do but a lot of intimate contact with Harold and the Chief Whip or you can have a real departmental job which cuts you off from internal leadership politics. I've taken my choice to go out of the centre into a huge Department. In the short run I may find that I've fallen between two stools because there are going to be six months in which I neither have the Leadership of the House nor any Ministry of my own at all. I shan't really be able to run the Ministry of Social Security and the Ministry of Health through Judith Hart and Kenneth Robinson. This has been made very clear to me at a meeting I had with Odgers[1] and Burke Trend when they came in to discuss my accommodation. For the present I'm staying in my Privy Council room because there's no room for anybody else, but in the end Fred Peart will have to take it over and I suspect that he will take over Freddy Ward at the same time while I keep my two Secretaries.

On April 6th the Prime Minister announced a major Cabinet reshuffle. Barbara Castle became First Secretary of State and head of the new Department of Employment and Productivity. Ray Gunter, hitherto Minister of Labour, became Minister of Power. Richard Crossman was given overall responsibility for the Department of Health and Social Security, with Kenneth Robinson and Judith Hart as Ministers for the two respective wings of the Department. Patrick Gordon Walker resigned from his office as Secretary of State for Education and Science, and George Darling from being Minister of State at the Board of Trade. Richard Crossman remained Lord President of the Council but Fred Peart became Leader of the House of Commons and Cledwyn Hughes took his place as Minister of Agriculture.

[1] Paul Odgers, who had previously worked as an under-secretary at the Dept. of Education and Science, had joined Crossman's staff in the Lord President's office the previous month. He moved with him to the D.H.S.S.

Sunday, April 7th

I suppose I can say that this was the first Cabinet reshuffle in which I was a Minister who worked right on the inside, and I finally persuaded Harold to accept Barbara as Minister of Labour and showed him how to make that job attractive enough. On the other hand there's a great deal which I failed to get through. None of the dead wood has been cut away except poor old Patrick Gordon Walker. Even Gunter has shuffled into Power. So the Sunday papers are already beginning to say this is a characteristic Wilson shuffle. Once again he started off with really big ideas but in the end he just shuffled the pack. I think this is roughly true and from Roy's point of view it's a good thing that it is true since he was away in America during the crucial days and had to rely on Barbara and myself. As for my new job, it's no good talking about that yet.

Monday, April 8th

This afternoon Fred Peart had to be blooded in the House. He was answering a few Questions and replying to the Easter debate. I was still in my old room in the Commons, No. 4, trying to clear up before he took over. As I walked along the lobby I realized I was no longer Leader, no longer a person people wanted to talk to about the future of the House, no longer a person the P.M. wanted to talk to about prices and incomes or whatever may be. I am clean out of all that consultative work with No. 10 and out of those relationships with John Silkin and the Whips, with the back-benchers and with the Tory Party. I've forfeited it all and chucked it away and now I am just the Lord President with a collection of unknown jobs in Whitehall which count for nothing outside. I've lost them all and no one really minds. I got one or two little laments—a note from the Lord Chancellor saying it was a disaster that there'd be no more reform in the Commons, and a note, strangely enough, from our Clerk, Barnett Cocks, but nothing in the press except a couple of bare paragraphs saying I'd been a good Leader. I'm afraid I felt sad this evening because I was beginning to see the emptiness of the desert into which I was entering in my new job.

I gave Judith Hart dinner with Tam Dalyell and as time passed it became clearer and clearer that the so-called clear understanding the P.M. had given me that I was to take over control of these two Departments was something Judith and Kenneth Robinson had not been told themselves. She had the impression that I had accepted the position of a Michael Stewart co-ordinator with the creation of the new Department a very long way ahead, probably in March of next year. As I went to bed I realized that I'd opted myself out of a job in which I was succeeding and jumped myself into another where its very basis is insecure and unestablished.

Tuesday, April 9th

At Cabinet Harold started with a harangue about the new organization.

More and more work must be devolved on the Cabinet Committees and Cabinet itself should meet less frequently than before. In addition to O.P.D. and S.E.P. there will now be a Parliamentary Committee dealing with political questions. He halted at this point and Tony Crosland, who always asks the awkward question, said, 'May we take it that the names of the Parliamentary Committee are those we find in the press?' It looks to me that with ten people on it it will still be far too big for an effective inner Cabinet.

As soon as Cabinet was over I had to get Harold and nail him down about my powers as Minister. 'I'll have a letter drafted,' he said. 'I must have it', I replied, 'in the hands of Judith Hart by five o'clock because I'm seeing her then with her Permanent Secretary and they must both know exactly what the position is.' Harold said that was perfectly all right but I'm only too aware that I'm going to have some very awkward trouble with Judith and with Kenneth, who certainly have not been informed of the fate which is hanging over them.

The time had now come for my confrontation with Judith Hart. I took Paul Odgers with me and went round to her Ministry—a nice cosy little office in the Adelphi. I started by suggesting that we should base our discussion on the Prime Minister's paper. She pulled herself together (I saw that she was nearly in tears) and she whispered, 'I'd rather discuss that with you alone.' This nonplussed me for the moment but to fill in time I explained what I want to do in the next three months, both in getting to know the Ministry and also in hurrying up the work on the pension plan. Directly I broke off the meeting and was alone with Judith over a drink, she said, 'I only got that minute from the P.M. five minutes before you arrived. It was the greatest blow in the world to me. I went to see him personally and he assured me that you would just be co-ordinating until the new Ministry was formed and that it couldn't take place before January at the earliest. I feel terribly let down since you will be taking all the credit from me and it's the third time this has happened. At the Scottish Office I got no chance to shine. Then I went to Commonwealth and there I had some achievements but only in obscure areas like Mauritius and Gibraltar. Third, I took over a really unpopular job when I replaced Peggy Herbison and just at the point when I'm winning a little popularity and a bit of position in my career you barge in and take all the credit from me.' I think I managed to make her see that I wasn't going to behave in this way and that if she had new ideas she would get full credit for them. I told her she would of course answer all Questions in the House of Commons but it was an impossible meeting and I crawled out of that building thinking, 'My God, Harold's kindly indecision certainly creates problems.' First he gives me an absolutely clear-cut guarantee that I would take effective control of these two Ministries in the period before amalgamation, and at the same time gives fair assurances to the two Ministers that there will be no effective change in their standing before amalgamation. That's not an easy position for me.

Wednesday, April 10th

I had planned to go across to Kenneth Robinson's Ministry and do the same for him as I'd done for Judith Hart. I'd known that Judith would be much easier to deal with because she's ambitious, a close friend of the Prime Minister, and knows she will work herself out of her Ministry into a job in the Cabinet. Moreover, she also knows that I am the expert on pensions and she can't get on without me. So in her case it was only a psychological affront that I had to deal with. It was a very different situation with Robinson. He's a dry little man with a dry little moustache and neatly brushed hair in whom I first got interested when I heard that he, as a Labour candidate, had published a book on Wilkie Collins[1] and I then came across him again when we met once or twice at Covent Garden. There aren't so many Labour M.P.s who go to the opera. The real difference between Kenneth and Judith is that Kenneth is a genuine expert. He's worked for years inside the hospital service and he's proved himself a skilled and competent Minister, dedicated to his Ministry, knowing it from A to Z and handling the doctors with conspicuous success. What he's hated is being outside the Cabinet with people like Patrick Gordon Walker and Michael Stewart and myself stuck on top of him when he thinks he ought to be at the Cabinet table. All this being so I knew that I'd have far more bloody-mindedness from Robinson than I would from Judith Hart and he'd make things as difficult for me as possible. So I wasn't surprised to hear that instead of going down to Elephant and Castle I was to see the Prime Minister at No. 10. I looked in at 4.30 and he told me he'd had Kenneth there already, cold, furious and threatening resignation. The P.M. had told him that'd he'd make a pretty good fool of himself if, having failed to resign on prescription charges, he resigned now about some personal affront. 'Nevertheless,' Harold added, 'I think he might do it in his present mood and we don't want that at all in view of the problems we shall soon be facing with the doctors. Are you prepared, Dick, to work out a letter to him which clarifies his situation?' I said of course I was and there was nothing I wanted less than to interfere in Kenneth Robinson's affairs during these next six months. All I need are the reserve powers and an ultimate veto if he were to do something I didn't want—on exemption charges, for example. So Harold and I sat down at the big table and began to draft out in longhand the kind of letter which one should leave civil servants to write. I finally persuaded him to let me take it across to my Mr Odgers.

I had asked Brian Abel-Smith[2] and Richard Titmuss[3] to dinner at the Garrick to meet Paul Odgers. Brian had written me a formal letter of congratulations on my new job but it was soon clear that he and Titmuss are

---

[1] *Wilkie Collins, a Biography* (London: Davis-Poynter, 1951).

[2] Professor of Social Administration, University of London at L.S.E., since 1965. He was to serve as Crossman's Senior Adviser at the D.H.S.S. 1968–70.

[3] Professor of Social Administration, University of London at L.S.E., since 1950. Appointed deputy chairman of the Supplementary Benefits Commission in 1968, he served until his death in 1973.

both ardent supporters of the Ministry of Health and considerable sceptics about the whole idea of integrating the two Departments. As the meal went on the reason was revealed. They were nervous of a merger working right the way through from the top to the bottom of both Ministries with transferability from section to section and from job to job. They dislike this whole notion because they believe that the jobs in the Ministry of Social Security—the special work of the Supplementary Benefits Commission, for example—are totally different from the work of the Ministry of Health, and the kind of person who is being trained in the old bureaucratic tradition of the National Assistance Board and the National Insurance Office would not be suitable for work with the doctors in most sections of the Ministry of Health. Of course, as I pointed out to them, what they were revealing was a very strong social feeling—that the officials of the Ministry of Health feel superior in every way to the officials of the Ministry of Social Security. Richard Titmuss did not deny this but he tried to prove his point by emphasizing the terribly low standards of the Ministry of Social Security. Apparently they're testing the accuracy of assessments now and they found that a quarter of the claimants are getting less than their entitlement because of the incompetence of the staff. There is a huge turnover of this unskilled lowpaid staff and Titmuss himself is deeply dissatisfied with the section he's responsible for. So, very tactfully, both he and Brian led me to see that whatever I do I mustn't ruin their splendid Ministry of Health by just mixing it up with the vulgar Ministry of Social Security.

Thursday, April 11th
I had made careful arrangements to be the first member of the Cabinet who saw Roy on his return from the States so I had arranged to give him lunch immediately after Cabinet. He had left on Wednesday of last week, had his talks in Washington, made a speech to the Pilgrim Society in New York and stayed in Boston and then stayed on a day for the funeral of Martin Luther King in Atlanta, Georgia. So he'd only returned last night and he sat through Cabinet looking rather sleepy. I took him off to the Garrick, and there in the back room I found the Chief sitting with Brian O'Malley at a table very close to the one reserved for me, which was slightly awkward, and it must have been obvious because another member noticed it and said, 'Ah, ha, awkward to discuss Mark III in that company!' I thought it illuminating and interesting that he sensed we belonged to different parts of the Cabinet.

I reported on all that had happened and filled Roy in on the minor appointments. I was anxious lest he would feel I had failed in my trust to him and allowed Barbara to be built up in opposition to him. No, he was quite cool and said, 'I don't want her as another economic Minister with her own economic advisers arguing against me: but I have no objection to her being Minister of Labour up-graded and made First Secretary.' That was something of a relief.

He was also interested in the failure of the Mark II Government, particularly the failure to sack anybody except Patrick, and the appointment of Cledwyn Hughes as Minister of Agriculture. He told me he was due to see the P.M. that afternoon and that one of the points he would have to make was Harold's failure to fulfil his promise to find Jack Diamond a place in Cabinet. Roy had asked Harold about this already on the phone and found the explanation unintelligible. He told me he was also worried about the rumours that Tony Crosland was being excluded from the Parliamentary Committee and would raise this as well. He was worried, he said, about 'the little deviousnesses' of the Prime Minister and the lack of a sense of candour in what he said. 'I can feel a sense of candour in my conversations with Barbara which I never feel when I'm talking to the Prime Minister.' Then he spent a long time talking about John Silkin, telling me how unsatisfactory he was and protesting his bewilderment at John's appointment as Deputy Leader of the House.

Just as I was settling down to give an interview to a Mrs Lapping—a representative of *New Society*, who'd been waiting for ages—an urgent message came that the P.M. wanted to see me. When I got there he said that Kenneth Robinson had rejected the redraft of the terms of my appointment and submitted another which was utterly fantastic. He had demanded that a new statement be prepared and issued to the press saying that he was in absolutely full charge of his Department and that the only matter I was entitled to interest myself in was amalgamation. 'That's impossible,' I said and Harold replied, 'I leave it to you. I give you full power and I will support any draft you get him to sign. Let me know if you fail to reach agreement.' I knew I was in for it. He came at 3.30 and from 3.30 to 6.30 he sat in my room and argued. After an hour I thought it was hopeless. 'Did you ever imagine', he said to me, 'how I would react? The least I can demand is a public statement that I am in complete control and that you have nothing to do with it.' I told him that would be very difficult because I had agreed a draft with Judith and I couldn't give him specially favoured treatment which I hadn't given her. However, I could give him personal assurances. He said he had not the faintest interest in personal assurances. What he required was a press statement to repair the terrible damage done by the Prime Minister's minute. Finally, I said it was a waste of time to go on and rang through to Michael Halls to tell him that I must come over and report to Harold that I couldn't reach agreement. 'You can't come at the moment,' he said, 'because Roy is in the room. Come after he's finished.' Maybe it was fortunate that Roy stayed for a full hour because during that hour I got what I wanted. Robinson had typed out his draft himself and after half an hour I took hold of it, knocked out one or two words, threw it across to him and said, 'Will these sentences do?' With the word 'full' omitted, the sentence said that while the Minister was in control of the Department he would submit all major decisions to the Secretary of State. This negotiation came off, I suppose,

because we started so rough and finally settled down into reasonableness as
we became more and more tired. Finally he agreed on a form of words which
would be kept secret, not issued to the press and with no question of any
further press comment. Only he and I and the Prime Minister and his
Permanent Secretary would see the document. It would not go to the
Ministry of Social Security. On these conditions I agreed that this *aide-
mémoire* should clarify the Prime Minister's minute, but not, as Robinson
wanted, be a substitute for it.

Harold seemed to think I had done all right. It would have been a great
mistake to let Robinson resign because the whole problem of doctors is
hanging over us and anyway it's most unlikely I shall want to intervene in his
Ministry in the next six months. I shall be busy inside the Ministry of Social
Security, where I must get on with the pensions plan and also on the planning
of the superstructure which will unite the two Ministries into one
Department.

Monday, April 22nd
I made my first visit to the collection of huge modern glass blocks that was
custom-built for the Ministry of Health at the Elephant and Castle. It is on a
ghastly site and Kenneth Robinson told me they chose it for its cheapness. It
cost only half as much as normal sites for government buildings but a great
deal of the money they saved is now being spent on air-conditioning and
double-glazing because the building stands right on top of an underground
railway which makes the most dreadful din. It's also appallingly inconvenient because, though it's only three-quarters of a mile from Westminster
and though from his room at the top of the twelve-storey block the Minister
can see the House of Commons, he may take anything from three to twenty
minutes to get there through the traffic. It was hoped that one effect of
plonking the building down there would be to improve the area and attract
other government buildings. It hasn't happened and the Ministry stands
isolated and terrible.

I had a quiet talk with Kenneth, Sir Clifford Jarrett, his Permanent
Secretary, and one or two other officials. Whatever they think of the merger,
the civil servants were not unfriendly and I had little to complain of in this
first contact.

Tuesday, April 23rd
I spent the first part of the morning with Burke Trend, preparing my work as
co-ordinating Minister, and listing all the Cabinet Committees I have to
chair or to serve on. Burke said he'd never known Harold more difficult,
uncommunicative and wrapped up in himself than he is now; or more
suspicious of his colleagues, I added. I went on to tell Burke very frankly my
ideas for an inner group and the hopelessness of getting Harold to allow it,
and if Harold wouldn't do it, I said, we must do it ourselves so I am arranging

an evening with Roy and Barbara this week. I was aware that this would be passed on to Harold and I thought that would be a good thing.

Back in my office I spent the rest of the morning discussing our new co-ordinating staff with dear Paul Odgers. All round me now there's the sense of a new office growing up. Odgers is a very professional civil servant, who's tremendously skilled at swelling the size of our staff, and he's also busily acquiring office accommodation all around the Privy Council. I've already referred in this diary to the trouble it takes to go the 120 yards from my office through the back passages into No. 10. First my Secretary has to provide the key which unlocks the back door of the Privy Council and lets me in to the Cabinet Office. Then a senior official of the Cabinet Office has to be fetched with the key to open the next door at the head of the staircase down to No. 10. I have constantly complained to Burke that this double barrier is an infernal waste of quite important people's time and asked him how many thousand pounds a week it costs to have this endless dislocation every time a Minister passes through. Civil servants are allowed keys; I'm not. It shows you how Whitehall is run for the convenience of civil servants and not for the Ministers who are supposed to be in command, but Paul Odgers has now pierced through the barred doors.

I went into the House to listen to the Prime Minister's Questions, where the Tories were prising out of him the admission that he had abandoned his control of D.E.A.[1] Harold had announced this by means of a Written Answer, and when Peyton[2] nudged him he repeated testily that he didn't advertise that kind of thing. He loses a lot of credit by this kind of deviousness. It would have been far wiser to announce the change candidly rather than have it extracted from him.

After that we came to the big debate on the Second Reading of the Race Relations Bill.[3] The first part of Jim's speech, where he outlined his

[1] On August 29th, 1967, Peter Shore had succeeded Michael Stewart at the D.E.A., with the Prime Minister assuming overall responsibility for the Department, but in April 1968 Peter Shore was given sole charge of the portfolio. The Department was henceforth to concentrate on the general allocation of real resources, investment, export policy and import replacement, and on co-ordinating the work of the industrial departments.

[2] John Peyton, Conservative M.P. for Yeovil since 1951.

[3] The Bill made it unlawful to discriminate, on grounds of colour, race, ethnic or national origin, in the provision of goods, facilities, housing accommodation or land, or to publish discriminatory advertisements. Breaches would constitute civil offences with the right of action in special county courts for damages where loss could be proved. The legislation was to be administered by a Race Relations Board which would establish local conciliation committees.

The number of Commonwealth immigrants, largely coloured, who had been granted work permits had fallen from 30,000 in 1963 to less than 5,000 in 1967 although, in the same period, there had been a rise from 26,000 to 52,800 in the number of dependants entering Britain.

On April 20th, in Birmingham, Enoch Powell made a speech in which he charged that the Bill would 'risk throwing a match into gunpowder', encouraging immigrant communities who were already making Britons into 'strangers in their own country'. He added that he was filled with foreboding: 'Like the Roman, I seem to see the River Tiber foaming with much blood.' On April 21st Mr Powell was dismissed from his Shadow Cabinet post of

philosophy, was done in a decent, unassuming way, which was very successful precisely because it was straightforward and completely bipartisan. Then
up rose Quintin Hogg and made one of the most statesmanlike speeches I've
ever heard, transforming the whole party situation. If he hadn't made this
speech and we'd just been left with the attitude adopted towards Enoch
Powell by Heath and Maudling, bipartisanship might well have broken down
and the Tory Party lurched nearer to Enoch.

Wednesday, April 24th

The morning papers show it's Hogg's day. He's got a tremendous press for
his speech and his is the only name which stands up against Enoch's. It's clear
that Powell now has enormous public support behind him and for the first
time, I'd say, he's appealing to mass opinion right over Parliament and his
party leadership. The movement he is arousing has no respect for Parliament
and for our institutions and it detests the bloody things that so-called
educated people in the Establishment are doing to ordinary, decent mortals.
That's the feeling Enoch has let loose and that's what Hogg's speech has, to
some extent, stemmed.

This was the evening that I had arranged to have Roy and Barbara to
dinner. Roy and I sat waiting for Barbara and he told me how jittery and
unstable is the state of the economy and how little we have achieved so far.
He is a very worried man. The unemployment figures remain very bad and
the import figures not much better.[1] 'We aren't making much headway,' he
said, 'and the money which should have been sucked back to London still
isn't coming in.' I remembered that he had told me that everything depended
on getting the money back after the budget, so this was an admission that so
far he's failed in the budget's major objective and we are still teetering on the
edge, in a position where we could be knocked off by any twist of the gold
crisis. On the other hand, as Roy also pointed out, the immediate threat to
the pound has vanished. Our friends seem to have given us a chance to make
good and I suppose that is the first stage of getting money back into the
reserve. The Americans have accepted our new reduced status, shorn of our
overseas commitments and with our new home policy. We have been given a
chance and the heat is now off but we've only achieved half of what we need
since we're not getting the money back.

Finally Barbara came along and we found ourselves entirely concerned
with the speech she was to make to the A.E.U. tomorrow.[2] Roy and I

---

spokesman on defence policy, on the grounds that his speech had been racialist in tone and
liable to exacerbate racial tensions.

[1] In the first quarter of 1968, unemployment stood at 510,000 (2·2 per cent of the total
number of employees) and imports at £1,793 million. There was a deficit of £83 million on the
balance of payments.

[2] The A.E.U. National Committee, led by Hugh Scanlon, were discussing their tactics for a
major wage claim. Mrs Castle had succeeded in inducing the Committee to invite her to their
meeting at Brighton.

contributed a great many good ideas towards it and that was the only real discussion we had. On prices and incomes it's clear that Barbara's prepared to be as good as her word, to stand loyally by Roy and get the Bill through in its present form by stressing the need for higher productivity, exactly as she said she would. They must get the Bill through before the old legislation slackens off because the policy is required to maintain the credibility of the pound.

Thursday, April 25th

Harold had called a special Cabinet Committee at 11 a.m., which turned out to be the famous Parliamentary Committee.[1] There are eight members: the Prime Minister, the Foreign Secretary, the Lord Chancellor, the Secretary of State for Defence, the Chancellor of the Exchequer, the Lord President of the Council, the Lord Privy Seal and the First Secretary. Also present at the first meeting were Peter Shore and Tony Crosland for the first three items, Willie Ross and George Thomas, the Secretaries of State for Scotland and Wales, in a waiting capacity, and the Minister of Housing for items four and five. There was also the Deputy Leader of the House of Commons, as John Silkin is now called, David Ennals from the Home Office and the full Cabinet Secretariat.

We started by discussing next week's Parliamentary business until we realized that the poor Cabinet Ministers who weren't present would have to hear it all over again. We went on to discuss next Sunday's big meeting between Cabinet and the National Executive Committee and finally we got on to race relations. This was a perfectly sensible and extremely useful discussion which did justify the existence of the Committee. It was the kind of discussion we would never normally have in Cabinet and which we ought to have regularly.

Friday, April 26th

I have tried to keep the details of Lords' reform away from Harold but this morning I had to go across and discuss one vitally important question with him and Eddie Shackleton. This is how in future the life peers shall be selected and, in particular, whether the role of the Prime Minister should remain the same. If all the effective power in the Lords is taken out of the hands of hereditary peers and put into the hands of life peers in effect the whole patronage of the House of Lords will be in the Prime Minister's hands. This is only theoretical, of course, because, to take our own example, Harold nominates the Labour life peers, but he nominates Conservative life peers on the advice of the Conservative Leader and Liberals on the advice of the Liberal Leader.[2] In our reformed House perhaps the most important issue

[1] The small 'inner Cabinet' that the Prime Minister had promised at the time of the Cabinet reshuffle on April 5th.
[2] The Crown creates life peers, on the nomination of the Prime Minister. He asks the

will be the composition of the cross-bench peers for they may well exert an absolutely decisive balancing role.[1] Should the Prime Minister appoint the cross-bench peers or should he only act on the advice of a committee, and if so, who should be on it? I told him there were those who wanted to reduce the P.M.'s patronage by creating a committee to advise him and, as I had guessed, Harold was extremely opposed to this idea. He said he wouldn't mind a committee which discussed the party balance of the Lords after each of his batch of appointments but they weren't to advise him on the appointments themselves. From his point of view he's right because his position would be undermined. He certainly showed himself extraordinarily alert to the problems of patronage, taking it all very seriously. What's so staggering about it is that nevertheless he does select such extraordinarily conservative and reactionary people.

Sunday, April 28th

We spent the whole of today on the meeting between the Cabinet and the N.E.C. in Downing Street. There was only one word to describe it, flat. There was flatness on the part of the Prime Minister and flatness on the part of the critics, the latter largely resulting from the absence of Jack Jones, who is now on the T.U.C. General Council and has been replaced by Harry Nicholas, a complete time-server.[2] The morning was mostly devoted to an uncompromising but muted trade union attack on our new prices and incomes policy.

The after-lunch session was on social services and the difference was remarkable. In the morning there had been a sense of deadlock, exasperated but quiet and resigned. Now we were discussing problems where we are completely agreed on our basic long-term aim and where, if mistakes have been made, we all want to see them cleared up. There was a short speech by our new Education Secretary, Ted Short, who has replaced Gordon Walker and who seems to know what he wants. He is a handsome, decisive schoolmaster, whose main point was that there must be a stop to all this nonsense that education should be child-directed and community-directed. He was going to see that the child was made to feel its place in the community. His speech impressed everybody. Even more surprising was the ease with which I was able to deal with prescription charges. Here the real complaint of the

leaders of the other major parties for their lists of names but decides himself how many nominees each party will have. The final list is also submitted to a Political Honours Scrutiny Committee of three peers, one from each of the major parties, but their approval is usually formal.

[1] Cross-bench peers are those who take no party whip. They sit on benches placed across the Chamber, facing the Throne, overflowing only if there is a shortage of places on to the benches occupied by the Conservative, Labour and Liberal peers.

[2] Assistant General Secretary of the T.G.W.U. 1956–68 (Acting General Secretary October 1964–July 1966), a member of the T.U.C. General Council 1964–7, of the N.E.C. 1956–64 and 1967–8: he was in July to become General Secretary of the Labour Party, an office he held until 1972. He was knighted in 1970.

N.E.C. was that we should never have promised to abolish them and we were urged not to make such precise promises again. The final session was supposed to discuss the relationship between Party and Government. Harold should have given a speech about the role of the new General Secretary but the N.E.C., having wrongly decided that even for the rest of this Parliament the new man won't be allowed to remain in the Commons, has knocked out either Merlyn Rees, Jim Callaghan's candidate, or Tony Greenwood, whom Harold is said to want, and no one can really talk about the relationship of Party and Government unless Len Williams is replaced by someone of real political importance. We know this isn't going to happen so the last session was a complete flop.

Monday, April 29th
This afternoon I had the delicate task of meeting for the first time the Party Health sub-group. I knew there might be difficulties because the merger had been proposed by a number of back benchers but not by this group, which is run by Laurie Pavitt, an old Ministry of Health employee, and Shirley Summerskill, daughter of the famous Dr Edith. Sure enough, the group turned out to be a lobby for the Ministry of Health, just as the Social Security Group is a lobby for its Ministry. I think I managed to placate them but it was a dicey job and showed that we don't have much support in the Parliamentary Party for the new Department we propose to create.

Tuesday, April 30th
At the Lords' consultations today we broached the ticklish item of the powers to be given to speaking peers. The issue is between Eddie Shackleton and Jellicoe on the one side and me on the other. They think the new House won't function unless the speaking peers have the right to vote in committee whereas I am obsessed by the need to stick to the single principle that a voting peer must vote and a speaking peer must only speak. Eddie said, 'You won't get it through. It will be a breaking point for the other side,' but to my great surprise Maudling supported me on this and Jellicoe was slapped down. We established that we would have speaking peers only to speak but that we would look favourably on the possibility of their being allowed to move motions and amendments and so on.

The last thing I did this evening was to look in on the radio broadcasting experiment in the House of Commons.[1] A little box has been built in at the back where the officials sit and here we have a man from the B.B.C. and one of our door keepers to tell him the names of the people who are up. The B.B.C. are now experimenting with half-hour and quarter-hour programmes using the actual words of the M.P.s. I find it doesn't add very much but you

[1] Just before Easter, the House had agreed to a recommendation of the Services Committee that the B.B.C. should experiment in making a radio recording, for internal broadcasting only, of its proceedings.

do get the noise and the atmosphere of the House. I think the fact that it is being taped for radio is bound to influence Members and a lot of the silly noise and interruptions during Question Time will be discouraged, and a good thing too. Indeed, I am greatly encouraged. Of all the reforms I've introduced this is the one I'd like to see pushed through, since it would change the House more than anything else if people outside could hear the misbehaviour which now goes on.

Monday, May 6th
My first job in London was to see Burke Trend, Eddie Shackleton and the Lord Chancellor about the draft White Paper on Lords' reform. The Chancellor wanted to put down a skeleton outline of our proposals in the shortest and simplest language possible. At first I thought this a good idea but it was pointed out to me that if we just plonked before the public, especially before the Parliamentary Party, detailed proposals for a two-tier chamber of voting and speaking peers, they might well be greeted with derision. In six months' committee work we have developed a scheme which really is the next stage in the evolution of the Second Chamber. It fits today's circumstances exactly and it's designed to secure the abolition of the hereditary principle with the minimum of trouble. But the scheme is so closely fitting and so expertly made and it depends on such inside knowledge that to the outside world it will look fussy and unimportant.

Tuesday, May 7th
At the Lords' reform consultations this afternoon we at last dealt with the Macleod objection that though we could put our scheme into law this session we couldn't set up the new House of Lords until the next Parliament. I replied that this was quite all right and that we would write it into the White Paper. Macleod then began to argue that this was impossible because his objection was so basic that he couldn't sign an agreed White Paper if at the same time there was to be disagreement about the timing of the implementation of our scheme. By saying this he infuriated Carrington and Jellicoe, who want to have a reformed House as soon as possible. But Macleod had got the decision of the Shadow Cabinet behind him and he was now pushing it a good deal further. Maudling protested vigorously and said that of course we could publish an agreed White Paper while disagreeing about the timing. I managed to keep my temper and said on behalf of our people that we'd get on with drafting the White Paper and ask the Conservatives to state their disagreement in a paragraph at the end. I also suggested we should put, finally, to a free vote of both Houses, the question of the date of implementation. Macleod grunted a lot of opposition on the ground that a free vote wouldn't be fair.

I am aware that if we seem to be rushing and skedaddling we might lose everything and the White Paper might go off at half-cock. So we turned to the timing of our programme and decided after a lot of to-ing and fro-ing to get the White Paper through Cabinet before we break off for the Whitsun recess and then to let it go to the Shadow Cabinet first thing after the recess, with the debate soon after that. I was quite pleased when at the end of the meeting Jim Callaghan said to me, 'You will have nothing to blame yourself for if you don't get this reform. I think you have conducted the negotiations, if I may say so, perfectly.' One of the things that has annoyed me about Harold, the great negotiator, is that I have been excluded from all negotiations whether domestic or international but on the House of Lords we haven't done too badly.

Friday, May 10th
I woke up early and went downstairs to hear the local election results on the radio.[1] Listening to the national results I assumed we were done for in Coventry. However I rang up Albert[2] and found that, whereas in Birmingham every ward had been lost, in Coventry we had lost two, won one and had no change in the others. It's astonishing how one's local results influence one's general political views. The London defeat, losing control of Islington and Hackney, for example, was really devastating. So was the loss of the Labour majority at Sheffield. But the draw we had achieved at Coventry was what really interested me.

When the *Coventry Evening Telegraph* rang up, I said at once that I hadn't seen the detailed election results and the voice replied, 'We don't want to talk to you about that but about Mr Cecil King.' That was the first I heard of the demand in the *Mirror* that Harold Wilson should go, the revelation of a grave financial crisis concealed by the Treasury and the Bank of England and, finally, the resignation of Cecil King himself as a director of the Bank. I told the *Coventry Evening Telegraph* I had nothing to say and sat down in my study to draft the Lords' White Paper.

Heavens, it was hard work. I hate redrafting from somebody's old half-done manuscript. I slogged, slithered and wasted the morning and then I said to myself, 'I'd better do a press release for my speech tonight.' I'd been asked to address a new dining club organized jointly by the Northampton, North Oxon., South Oxon. and Banbury consituency parties. Just as I was starting this I was rung up by Roy, who told me he was in some trouble because Barbara was insisting that he should repudiate Cecil King and assert his belief in Harold Wilson's leadership. 'If I do this', said Roy, 'there are great difficulties. I can't afford to get into an argument about the financial situation because there's a run on the pound today and, as for reasserting my faith in Harold, I shall be accused of doing it precisely because I am conspiring against him.' I thought for a moment and then said, 'I tell you what. I'll ring

---

[1] The Conservatives made a net gain of 535 seats to Labour's net loss of 596 and won 27 out of 32 London boroughs.
[2] Albert Rose was Secretary of the Coventry East Labour Party 1955–71.

up Barbara and tell her I'm the man to make the speech.' Barbara appreciated that I could speak as an ex-*Daily Mirror* journalist as well as a member of the Government. I went back to my study and wrote a short, sharp press release reminding the country that Cecil King was the nephew of Lord Rothermere and Lord Northcliffe, the two megalomaniac press lords who tried to dictate to Prime Ministers. I made sure that Transport House would put it out for 8.30 p.m.

I slogged away at the White Paper all afternoon and at the evening meeting I was able to deliver my piece on Cecil King before turning to the problems of the party. I particularly discussed with them the thing which worries me most, that what is turning the electorate and the party against us is not the things we've done wrong but the things we've done right. Our own people are turning away from us because we won't go along with Enoch Powell, because we insist on using family allowances to protect the lowest-paid workers against the effects of devaluation, and because we must have a prices and incomes policy if we're not going to have mass unemployment. These are essential policies for any socialist government and are the very things our staunchest Labour supporters are blaming us for.

Saturday, May 11th
I woke up to find my speech was the main B.B.C. news story and it was apparently a lead story in many of the papers, even the *Telegraph*. Harold rang through delightedly and told me what an effect the speech was having. He asked me about other Ministers. I explained Roy's difficulties and Harold finally agreed that Roy was right not to make a speech.

Let me sum up my reflections at the end of this astonishing week. The vote in the local elections is not the most depressing feature. It's the financial and economic situation which is really depressing, the appalling impact on the P.L.P. of our intentions for prices and incomes and the lack of success of the interventionist policies of Peter Shore and Tony Wedgwood Benn, young men who with carefree arrogance think they can enter the business world and help it to be more efficient. It's the amateurishness of Harold and his bright young men which gets me down.

Could Roy take his place? Well, quite certainly Michael Stewart and I could not and Barbara could not because she's a woman. So Roy is really the only possibility. But is he a serious possibility? Can this elegant, patrician, easy-going, tennis-playing, aloof, detached dilettante be a Labour Prime Minister who could get a grip on the situation and restore public confidence? I have my doubts. But it may well be true that within six months any change will be better than no change. And if so a change will take place. My job this week has not been to prevent change taking place but to tell the press to keep their bloody nose out of our affairs so that we can make our own decisions about our leadership.

I don't dispute for a moment that Cecil King's attack has temporarily strengthened Harold's position a great deal. Nevertheless I have no doubt that this week has seen another move in the direction of a new leadership. I think the party will sooner or later insist that whether it's going to win the next election or at least lose it honourably (which is the least we can hope) it will have to have a new Leader, unless Harold can show a power of retiring into the background and letting leadership headed by Roy and Barbara give the inspiration which he can't give. I think all that will happen but it can't happen just when our press lords start ordering the party about.

Monday, May 13th

I went into the House to hear Roy Jenkins reply to a Private Notice Question from James Dickens about Cecil King.[1] It was a superb performance. He withered him up, dealing with King with an Olympian detachment. As a result the miners whom Alf Robens had invited to the annual party of the National Coal Board walked out when they saw Cecil King on the other side of the room and more than 150 Labour M.P.s have now signed an Early Day Motion saying that King must be sacked from the N.C.B. It's gone far enough, as Harold remarked to me.

What a stroke of luck Cecil King has been to Harold. As one Tory put it, he was the only flaw in a perfect day of Tory victory news last Friday. At once he provided the positive factor required for rebuilding Harold's reputation. This was confirmed to me when Alma Birk rang me up in the greatest distress to tell me how terrible life had been,[2] that the directors were now all working together to try to get rid of Cecil King, that her husband, Ellis, who had been in Paris was now considering whether he should resign from the *Mirror* board and that she had persuaded him to stay on and fight the King influence. She also told me that 98 per cent of the letters which the *Daily Mirror* and the *Sun* had received were pro-Harold and only 2 per cent pro-King. She was terribly shocked that Sydney Jacobson and Hugh Cudlipp had both accepted the Cecil King line and failed to foresee and warn him of the consequences. Indeed, they'd all celebrated with King at a great dinner on Friday night. Despite this, she added, I must understand that there were no enemies of the party at the *Daily Mirror*. Alma's terrified female social agony about the clanger King had dropped was a tremendous revelation. The one thing the *Mirror* doesn't like is failure or being made to look silly and this is what King had done for them over the weekend.

This afternoon I had rather an interesting meeting with Kenneth Robinson. Our Minister of Health has cooled down a bit since his threats of resignation when I took over and is really rather pally with me. He came along with a very stuffy-looking, dapper little man to discuss the publicity for

[1] James Dickens was Labour M.P. for West Lewisham 1966–70 and since 1970 has been Assistant Director of Manpower at the National Freight Corporation.
[2] Alma Birk was a former Labour Parliamentary candidate and in 1967 became a life peer. Her husband is lawyer to the *Mirror* Group.

explaining the prescription charges exemption scheme. The official said, 'We are going to spend £60,000 on advertising and here is the text of the advert.' He pushed across three pages of foolscap. I said, 'But you're not going to print all that, are you? What you had better do, surely, is to have an advertising campaign in the first week saying "Are you entitled to exemption? Are you an old age pensioner, chronically sick, a nursing mother?" and hadn't you better have another simple advertisement telling them to go to the post office?' 'Oh, you can't just tell them to go to the post office,' said the official. 'On the other hand,' I replied, 'they can't read an advert that length.' 'But their reading it is not the important thing,' he replied. 'If my Minister puts everything in, my Minister is not to blame for their not having read it.' So I said, 'But that is £60,000 down the drain.' They then pointed out that the Ministry of Health never gets its fair share, that the Ministry of Transport has just got £1 million for a breathalyser campaign, and that £3 million a year is spent on advertising for recruitment to the armed forces. I said, 'Well, you won't get your fair share if you and your press officer behave in this ridiculous way.'

This is not the first time I've noticed this ghastly small type-kind of Government advertising. The truth is that a great deal of it is printed not to induce people to take up their claims or to explain Government policy, but simply to ensure that the civil servants won't be criticized for not having informed the public of the details.

Thursday, May 16th
Cabinet. The big thing was votes at eighteen. When the Parliamentary Committee's report was submitted I'm glad to say that Richard Marsh raised the whole issue and said it was a zany thing to give young people the vote. Quite an interesting discussion followed. Peter Shore gave the obvious reply that the modern Labour Party has for years been committed to votes at eighteen and we had put the case for this to the Speaker's Conference. It would look very strange for us, having approved the Latey Report, to deny the vote to eighteen-year-olds. Michael Stewart repeated his admirable argument that people aren't granted rights, they grow into them, and the group rights of youth have changed in the last ten years just as the group rights of women changed in the 1920s. Wedgy Benn made it clear he wouldn't stay a member of the Cabinet unless the eighteen-year-olds got justice.

Marsh was supported by an odd collection, including Cledwyn Hughes, whose grounds were that in Wales and Scotland the Nats would gain since young people tend to vote nationalist. Gunter was worried that schoolboys and schoolgirls voting at the age of eighteen would be unduly influenced by their teachers. Barbara Castle, in her new position as a woman of power, wondered if it was really wise to do this, while Roy sat there careful, canny and saying nothing. We have left it open and it will be considered again.

Monday, May 20th

This afternoon Fred Peart held a meeting of his Future Legislation Committee. All my efforts to reorganize the planning of future legislation have been blown to the winds. Once again we simply had a fight between various Ministers, who all want their Bills as soon as possible. Here was Dick Marsh saying he must have Nationalization of the Docks in the next session even though the Bill isn't ready. Here was Kenneth Robinson with his Bill for banning coupons in cigarette packets, a Bill which he had already touted unsuccessfully round the Private Members.

The big unknown quantity is the Trade Union Bill which we are pledged to base on the Report of the Donovan Commission. There seems to be hopeless dissension on the kind of Bill it should be but it is clear that the next session we shall have three major constitutional measures – the Trade Union Bill, a Representation of the People Bill to give votes at eighteen and Lords' reform.

Wednesday, May 22nd

I had one enormously important meeting, as I imagined, where we were to present our draft White Paper on Lords' reform to the Cabinet Committee. It showed how things are going that Fred Peart, the Leader of the House, turned up without having read the draft and Jim Callaghan, whom I met just outside the door, wasn't even bothering to attend though his Department is responsible for the Bill. From their point of view Lords' reform is a lost cause. They won't knife it, kill it; they'll let it go on until it dies or collapses ignominiously.

This evening the Home Policy Committee of the Party gave a dinner at the St Ermin's Hotel. While we were sitting on the front bench together Harold had mentioned that he had forgotten to invite me and that he wanted me to take Jim Callaghan's place. When I arrived George Brown had just bashed in and insulted Roy and when Roy said he would have to be going on to another dinner George added 'Oh, we can't spare you. We want the Chancellor here to knock him about.' It was all a bit testy and uneasy until Harold came in and sat down at the other end of the table. I wondered what on earth the dinner was for until George Brown got up and said, 'We all want one Cabinet Minister to liaise with the N.E.C. about all home policy affairs and I think it should be Dick Crossman.' Good old George Brown. One day he hates my guts and wants to throw me out, the next he wants to put me in sole charge – but only now I have finally resigned from the Executive.

I think the explanation of the meeting is that the Home Policy Committee is overawed by the catastrophe that the party has suffered and is anxious to rebuild bridges with Westminster. But what odd views you hear expressed at Labour dinners. Sara Barker, who had scarcely said a word, looked across the table at me very severely and said, 'I'll tell you what really matters now, all those scroungers getting more social benefits than they deserve.' It made me realize the difficulties I shall find as Secretary of State for the Social Services. The Labour Party wants to be the great liberal party which expands the social services but it also wants at all costs to avoid the unpopularity of being accused of giving money to scroungers.

Monday, May 27th
This afternoon I answered my first two Parliamentary Questions as co-ordinator of the Social Services. They were quite simple and took a matter of seconds. It reminds me that if you look in Hansard I've said nothing in the last six weeks. I'm neither a departmental Minister nor Leader of the House. I sit about on the front bench quite a lot but I don't do anything there and I won't do it until I get control of my new Ministry.

Tuesday, May 28th
Up to the P.M.'s room to discuss the B.B.C. licence fee, which we've already been discussing for two weary years. Wedgy Benn, Ted Short and I have all been convinced that the B.B.C. must go over to advertising, at least in part.[1] This has always been opposed by Harold, the Methodist, and by Michael Stewart, the atheist, on the grounds that it's immoral to permit a virtuous organization such as the B.B.C. to be in any way related to commercial profit.

This time we had an even more ridiculous proposal than ever from the Postmaster-General.[2] Instead of raising the licence fee by £1, as the B.B.C. have been insisting for the last eighteen months, to prevent them running into the red, he proposed that we should raise each £1 by getting 15s. from the increased licence fee and 5s. from permitting advertising on Radio One. Everyone in Cabinet thought this pretty futile. The whole subject could have been settled in five minutes because after we'd turned down that proposal there was really no doubt that we had to give the B.B.C. their £1 rise. But no! The P.M. chose to indulge in one of his tirades. He'd been listening to Radio One and noticed how some of the disc-jockeys bring in news items with an anti-Labour slant. He insisted that a special study must be made with the Lord President in charge. He supported this decision with an extraordinary outburst about the wicked political bias of the B.B.C. contrasted with the honesty of commercial television under Charles Hill in the old days, and now under the virtuous Bert Bowden. Every now and again someone would

[1] In 1966 Mr Wedgwood Benn, then Postmaster-General, floated a proposal to establish a new public broadcasting corporation with one wavelength financed by advertising revenue. After six months' discussion, Mr Short, Mr Benn's successor, published in December 1966 a White Paper on Broadcasting Finance, Cmnd 3169, declaring that the B.B.C. would continue in its present form, as a public corporation deriving its revenue from the licence fees, paid by the public to the Post Office. Crossman had originally been strongly in favour of the B.B.C. deriving at least part of its revenue from advertising, though he had always been sceptical of the chances of getting such a proposal through a Labour Cabinet.

[2] Roy Mason.

quietly say, 'But Prime Minister, look, fine, but shouldn't we have the £1 licence increase?' And finally, of course, we got it.

This afternoon I went along to the Lords to finish redrafting the Reform White Paper. We worked for two hours and got final agreement but at the end I said to Peter Carrington, 'You know, the chances of getting it through now are zero.' He agreed and said, 'We've missed the quiet time.[1] Now I'm having to make noises about the House of Lords standing up to the Commons in order to appease my back-benchers who are anyway pretty uncontrollable. What's the chance of your back-benchers doing what you want?' he said, turning to me. 'None,' I said, 'they're going to be infuriated by the proposals. If we put the baby into the bathwater at this temperature it will die. I'd better see Harold and tell him that the best thing to do is for him to find some excuse for delay. We need to go into purdah for a couple of months.' It was a depressing conversation but it's pleasant that we could talk about it with such complete freedom. Eddie and I, Peter and George have really become quite a band of brothers.

Wednesday, May 29th

Some notes on a characteristic O.P.D. meeting. The first item was Hong Kong. As a result of withdrawing from Singapore we are putting two more battalions into Hong Kong as well as fighters and frigates and minelayers, a bloody fleet, because Hong Kong must now have its own defences. 'That may be a justifiable short-term policy,' I said, 'but what about our long-term policy for withdrawal?' Michael Stewart replied, 'There's a special Hong Kong Committee at work on this.' Once again something really important is being discussed not at O.P.D. but in a special committee which I know nothing about.

The second subject was minor dependencies. What on earth are we to do about Ascension Island, Easter Island, the Falkland Islands, the Seychelles, Gibraltar, etc.? The paper submitted went right through the list, providing us with excellent reasons for staying in each one and increasing the amounts of troops available. Not a single recommendation to wind up.

The next paper was on the need to maintain forces for the evacuation of British personnel. At present we still accept the commitment to have forces available for evacuating any largish group of British citizens living abroad. The paper noted that most of the countries of Europe had no forces for this purpose and that, if they need to evacuate, they pay someone else to do the job. We, however, as the third world power, have always maintained this commitment. I said, 'Look, we've just ceased to be a world power and are becoming part of Europe. Wouldn't it be possible to find out what they do?'

---

[1] Major and contentious measures, like the Transport Bill, were now going to the Upper House for their Lords' stages. Moreover, Conservative peers felt that in the second half of the five-year Parliament they could justifiably oppose the Government's programme more vigorously.

A withering look from Harold. 'But they wouldn't tell you.' 'I didn't mean to *ask* them, I thought you had other means of obtaining information.' Michael Stewart primly replied, 'One can hardly waste money on finding out that kind of thing.' I accepted the point and then asked whether we couldn't ask a couple of reliable journalists to give us a report. This was very bad form but Denis Healey did agree that it really would be sensible if we gave up this kind of contingency planning and that I was on to something. It's great fun behaving in this way but it's not much good. All I contribute to O.P.D. is a macabre joke.

I stayed behind to discuss with the P.M. Mr Callaghan's notorious speech to the Firemen's Union. This had been causing a tremendous sensation. He had apparently told them without any qualification that there would be no more legislation on incomes and prices. Harold said, 'That fellow's getting above himself. We must teach him a lesson. I will do so after Cabinet tomorrow.' 'Fine, Prime Minister,' I said, 'and we'll all support you,' and we had a nice drink together.

The Party meeting this morning gave me a chance to assess back-bench morale. It is clear that the House has settled down to the appalling routine imposed upon it this week. Despite all the talk of chaos the Bills are churning their way through and what pleases me most is the marvellous success of the device we invented to allow us to stop business at 11.30 p.m. and start it again at 10.0 o'clock next morning. This is working like clockwork.

After the Party meeting I went into the smoking room where I spotted Mr Callaghan and after a minute or two he came across and we had a drink together. 'I think I'd better tell you frankly,' I said, 'that there's a bit of trouble between you and the P.M. He's taking a bit rough what you said to the Firemen's Union and especially that you treated Barbara in that way. After all, she's the Minister in charge.' I added, rather maliciously, 'This is the electioneering season, of course, for the seats on the National Executive. Last year in order to get the trade union vote you knifed Michael Stewart in the back when he was trying to do the prices and incomes policy at D.E.A. Now you seem to be knifing Barbara in the back.' Jim was quite cool and collected. He said, 'But I don't want their votes this year,' and I replied, 'Quite right. It's not trade union votes you want, it's their money. As Party Treasurer you've got to collect the funds for the next General Election campaign and you're going round the trade unions telling them that if they give us a good donation you can give them the assurance that there won't be any more prices and incomes legislation.[1] It's been very clever of you, Jim, and you've forced the P.M.'s hand. But you mustn't expect to be loved by him. Anyway, he'll talk to you about it himself.'

At this point his temper began to rise: 'How often did you or Barbara knife me in the back in those three years when I was Chancellor? I've never

[1] Mr Callaghan, previously a member of the N.E.C.'s constituency section, had been elected Treasurer of the Labour Party (and thus an *ex officio* member of the N.E.C.) in 1967.

forgotten how time after time you went behind my back to the Prime Minister and tried to destroy me. You got your own way against me. Why shouldn't I get my own way now?' We had a nice drink together for forty minutes or so and eventually Jim said, 'You're one of the few people I can talk to frankly, Dick. All I care about is the Party.' And I said, 'Well, that's fine, Jim. I feel you're right back on top of your form and playing for the highest stakes again. You're obviously feeling the better for the change to the Home Office.'

Then I went in for a quiet lunch with Michael Foot and told him what Jim had said.

This evening I was to dine with the Chancellor, who had been saying to me for some days that he had to talk to me alone, and would take me out to Brooks's. So we drove off in his great big Daimler, unloaded ourselves halfway up St James's Street and went into the club. Upstairs is the gaming table with the slice cut out to give room for Charles James Fox's tummy. At the bar down below were Mark Bonham Carter[1] and other willowy young men. It's a classy club, not at all like the Garrick, and after we'd had a drink we went into the dining-room and had claret and gulls' eggs and were gentlemen together. We had a good talk about Callaghan and Barbara Castle. Roy and I are both worried about her health as well as about the line she's taking on prices, which really looks as though it can't be sustained.

Then we got on to Harold's future. What are the alternatives? Roy thinks Michael Stewart is hopeless. Barbara? Splendid but a girl. Callaghan? We would fight to the death to stop him. 'Well,' I said, 'there's no alternative,' and Roy said, 'There is you, Dick. I would support you as successor to Harold without hesitation.' I was taken by surprise and replied, 'Well, it's lucky for Harold that it's me.' Roy passed on to the next part of the conversation but I'm sure this was the point of the meeting.

At 9.0 p.m. we retired from Brooks's to the House of Commons, where I found a deadly hush because everyone was watching the European Cup match on T.V. Harold was at Wembley and when he came back later in the evening he asked me what I thought of it. 'What match?' I said. 'I think it's such a waste of time and I stopped poor Tam from using my T.V. upstairs because I was working.' Harold clearly felt this attitude makes me incapable of being a great political leader because the mark of a leader is to be a man who sees football or at least watches it on television.

Thursday, May 30th
I briefed Barbara on Callaghan before we went into the Parliamentary Committee. We all waited for the great moment when we were to have the

[1] Liberal M.P. for Torrington March 1958–9, first Chairman of the Race Relations Board 1966–70 and Chairman of the Community Relations Commission 1971–6. Since 1976 he has been Chairman of the Outer Circle Policy Unit and since 1975 Vice-Chairman and a Governor of the B.B.C.

P.M. on Callaghan and nothing happened. We had a little bit about the B.B.C. and party political broadcasts and then at 10.30 Cabinet was called in.

Finally the P.M. got himself together and said, 'There is, of course, Home Secretary, your speech.' The Home Secretary said, 'I've got absolutely nothing to apologize for at all. There's nothing inconsistent there.' But the P.M. said, 'I think there was something a little bit inconsistent, wasn't there really?' and Jim brazened it out and then there was a mild interjection from Barbara and a much stronger one from Michael Stewart. 'Well,' the P.M. said, 'I think we can move on now.' I said, 'But we can't move on, Prime Minister. Has the Cabinet disowned Mr Callaghan or not?' Callaghan said, 'Not at all, nothing to disown.' From that point we spent twenty minutes fencing round this business, all done on the issue of what we should tell Fred Peart to say at his weekly press conference this afternoon. I insisted that Cabinet should disown Callaghan and indeed the whole Cabinet insisted.*

The only other item on the agenda was votes at eighteen. I had to manage this because Callaghan had now disappeared to a Committee upstairs. At the Cabinet Committee we had unanimously held the view that Cabinet would be wise to accept the Speaker's Conference decision to reduce the age from twenty-one not to eighteen, but to twenty since this would make the danger of the young Scottish and Welsh nationalist vote less grave.

We had just been on the point of reporting this to Cabinet when Gerald Gardiner, in one of his liberal moods, insisted on making an announcement that we had accepted all the Latey Commission's recommendations on the age of majority being reduced to eighteen. It was obvious that if you reduced the age for everything else it was impossible to keep voting at twenty so our Committee had to come back to Cabinet and say that despite our previous view, owing to the Lord Chancellor's precipitate announcement, we now had to recommend votes at eighteen.

A fortnight ago Cabinet had said it wanted more information on this, Gallup polls and so on. There wasn't very much material but we got it all together for them. This morning was one of the occasions when Harold Wilson asked for individual votes. Michael Stewart, who's often very good on this sort of thing, looked across at Harold and said, 'You can't *give* votes to young people. They're taken from you. The young are insisting on their rights and you'd be mad to resist now. Of course you must give way.' The fanatical supporters were Wedgy Benn, Peter Shore, Michael Stewart, Gerald Gardiner, and the fanatical opponents the Welsh Secretary and Dick Marsh, our youngest Cabinet Minister, as well as Eddie Shackleton who is always cautious and corky. I think Barbara would have been against if she'd been there. The unenthusiastic supporters, by the way, were headed by Tony

---

* But in the next day's press there wasn't a single newspaper reference to Callaghan. He had in fact called the P.M.'s bluff and clearly Harold had carefully given instructions that the Home Secretary was not to be disowned.

Crosland and myself. However, we are now, by this peculiar form of argument, committed to votes at eighteen.

I dropped in on the front bench to hear Harold Wilson conducting a quiet and good-humoured Question Time and Fred Peart handling what could have been a very awkward incident when he was furiously attacked by Ted Heath about the chaos of the timetable. His reply was innocent but artful: 'I hope the Rt Honourable Gentleman ... will not exaggerate. He should approach these matters in a more relaxed fashion.' If I had said this it would have been regarded as insulting and arrogant but Fred can say it with charm and sincerity.

This evening we had the debate on prescription charges at a time when Fred hoped most people would have already left for the recess. Kenneth Robinson ought either to have resigned on this issue or fought, but he did neither and just sat about being feeble. Three Tories were present on the other side. At the end there were 52 votes against the charges to about 129 for and there was a terrible sense of dreariness in the House but also of relief that soon we would be safely out of the place.

Friday, May 31st

I rang up Harold to say goodbye and he told me that things had been looking up for the last fortnight and he smelt success in the air. I thought, 'Holy God, I hope it isn't the kind of success which hit us last November.'[1] I believe we face another disastrous batch of by-elections. However, it's nice that Harold is optimistic.

The big news of the day was the sacking of Cecil King by the *Mirror* Board of Directors. Alma Birk had told me weeks ago they were planning to do this but I hadn't believed a word of it. What was really cheering was that this could actually happen in Fleet Street. Here is the Chairman of the I.P.C. overthrown successfully by a *coup d'état* in the same way as he overthrew Guy Bartholomew and made himself king.[2] I rang up Hugh Cudlipp, his successor, and without thinking said over the phone, 'It's marvellous to think it possible.' I heard a great laugh at the other end of the phone and I said, 'You must draw no conclusions from that, Hugh.'

Talking to Anne last night, I reflected once again on that strange conversation with Roy and his quite consciously expressed willingness to serve under me. No doubt if I were physically capable and had the mental energy to do it I could make a better job of it than Harold for the remaining life of this Government. I certainly don't have any desire to do it, I really genuinely don't. Is that a good reason for doing it? Possibly it is, as Plato said about philosopher kings.

[1] When the pound was devalued. The by-elections were at Oldham West, Sheffield Brightside, and Nelson and Colne.

[2] Guy Bartholomew was Editorial Director of *Daily Mirror* Newspapers Ltd from 1934 to 1944, when he became Chairman. In 1951 he resigned and was replaced by Cecil King. He died in 1962.

21 A grim Harold Wilson sits between Acting General Secretary of the Trades
Union Congress, Vic Feather, and the Secretary of State for Employment and
Productivity, Barbara Castle, at the press conference in June 1969 at which
they announce the eleventh-hour deal between the unions and the government
that resulted in withdrawal of the controversial Industrial Relations Bill.

22 August 27, 1969. The Home Secretary, James Callaghan, visits Belfast to
talk to the people and get a first-hand view of the violence that is dividing
the Catholic and Protestant communities in Northern Ireland.

23 Harold Wilson with his Political Secretary, Marcia Williams, and Joe Haines, who became his Press Secretary in January 1969.

24 Towards the end of 1969 Richard Crossman and Barbara Castle go to the Prime Minister to implore him to confide with his friends in the Cabinet rather than with his personal staff in what became known as the 'Kitchen Cabinet'.

Sunday, June 16th

We got back from our fortnight's family holiday in Cyprus today. As soon as we arrived we found big political news. Apparently Roy Jenkins made a big speech in Birmingham yesterday, threatening that the all-party talks on Lords' reform might break up if the Tories voted against the Rhodesia Sanctions Order. This was given tremendous prominence and I was a bit surprised at Roy because his speech was unlikely to help the all-party talks to survive.

Monday, June 17th

When I got to the station this morning I read in the papers that a firm decision had been taken by the Tory Shadow Cabinet that the Tory peers would be whipped and would vote against the Rhodesia Order when it is taken tomorrow. Apparently there's to be a one-day debate in the Commons today with a Commons decision this evening and a two-day debate in the Lords with a vote at 5 p.m. tomorrow.

My main job this morning was to chair the meeting of the Social Services Committee. I'd been warned about this when I was on holiday and told that together the Chancellor and the Prime Minister were proposing cuts in the social services. When I got back to Prescote I found the usual secret document which I have been studying over the weekend to see what Harold and Roy had been up to. Paul told me there was a great deal of waiting about last Friday because the Chancellor had suddenly changed his plans and persuaded the Prime Minister not to make one single big cut of £113 million but a series of cuts, spread over all Departments so that they could be brought in imperceptibly. It was a nice idea, but directly I heard it I realized it would be difficult to fulfil.

Immediately after this I went across to No. 10 for a drink and within a minute Harold had plunged in on the subject of Roy's speech. 'Now there can be no question of any more talks. We must break them off and force through a Bill taking away the powers of the Lords.' I said, 'For God's sake, Harold, are you mad?' and he replied, 'That speech of Roy's in Birmingham was deliberately intended to put me in my place. I must show that I am stronger than him.' We were in the middle of a party, with the butler standing beside me. Harold was excited, suffused with a jealousy which shocked me. Somehow I began to get just as emotional, probably because I was angry and personally injured that behind my back he had thrown away, as I always suspected he might, our negotiated settlement on Lords' reform. Now he was careering along on his old-fashioned, radical high horse, determined to outbid Roy in capturing the radical Left.

I had to go back for the 10 o'clock vote on the Rhodesia Order and ran into Roy who asked me back into his room.[1] I described the meeting of the

---

[1] The Order was approved by 319 votes to 246.

Social Services Sub. 'If you present my Committee', I said, 'with this *fait accompli* and try to make them take it as it stands there'll be a rebellion.' When I said, 'I can't persuade them to do it,' he replied, 'I must have the £113 million. Don't talk to me like that.' He twice tried to get out of his own room saying, 'I'll resign if I can't get it.' I said, 'Look, two can play the resignation game, Roy. I'm as good a resigner as you,' and I dragged him back into the room and made him discuss it all over again. I finally said that the best thing would be a week's postponement to give me time to reason with the Ministers. Meanwhile he should send round a further paper giving the second-year programme as well as the first so we could judge the two together.

I smoothed him down but then he had another major complaint. While I was away Harold had apparently circulated a paper recommending that we immediately accept the main recommendations of the Fulton Committee.[1] This included making a considerable section of the Treasury into an independent Department to deal with the civil service, something which obviously affected the Chancellor, but Harold had come to his decision without saying a word to Roy. 'That's very tough,' I replied. 'But tell me, Roy, did you discuss your Birmingham speech with Harold before you delivered it?' When he said he hadn't, I told him that Harold was furious and convinced that Roy is competing for the radical vote. Roy said, 'But on the way up to Birmingham I was making some notes and I took the line of the No. 10 briefing in the press. I can't be blamed for taking the Prime Minister's own briefing.' Clearly a thoroughly bad mood has grown up between these men and while I was in Cyprus it has got a great deal worse. I was just leaving the room when Roy said, 'Now, Dick, let's be practical. If I agree with you about postponing the decision on Social Service cuts for a week will you give me your full support on Fulton?' 'Yes,' I said, 'if you will support me on Lords' reform as well.' And that, roughly speaking, was the deal we came to.

Tuesday, June 18th
In the Commons this afternoon we had another Question to the Prime Minister on the Home Secretary's speech to the Firemen's Union. Harold mildly disowned Jim and that was that. Meanwhile the Lords were finishing their debate on the Rhodesia Order and, to everybody's amazement, the Government was only defeated by nine votes.[2] I am told that 166 of the 300

---

[1] Lord Fulton, Vice-Chancellor of the University of Wales 1952–4 and 1958–9 and of the University of Sussex, 1959–67 was Chairman of the Arts Council 1968–71. The Committee on the Civil Service, which he chaired, was to publish its Report, Cmnd 3638, on June 26th, 1968. Its recommendations included the establishment of a Civil Service Department and of a Civil Service College and the abolition of 'grading' between administrative, executive and clerical appointments.

[2] The Order was defeated by 193 votes to 184. It was reintroduced and passed on July 18th.

odd Tories on the Tory whip turned up to vote against the Order, along with a few cross-benchers. The Government supporters consisted of 90 per cent of the Labour peers, all the Liberals, 18 bishops and some 30 cross-benchers. The built-in Tory majority had nearly been defeated by the new House of Lords which has been gradually growing up since life peerages were introduced.[1]

I went along the corridor to celebrate in champagne with Eddie and Michael Wheeler-Booth and then Alma Birk came in and I brought them all back to the Strangers' dining-room. Sitting at the next table was the Chief Whip with his Whips and Gerald Kaufman. I strongly suspected they were up to no good but they were very discreet until Freddie Warren came over. 'How's life?' I said, and I discussed our triumph in the House of Lords. 'What do you think is going to happen?' 'One alternative,' he said, 'is a Bill to end the powers of the Lords.' 'That's absurd,' I said, 'they couldn't possibly do it.' 'Couldn't?' he said. 'It's all fixed. We've prepared the Bill already.' Now whether the Bill was really prepared and printed I didn't know but Freddie Warren had alerted me about what the Chief, Fred Peart and Harold were up to. No doubt it had finally been clinched in Harold's mind by his furious reaction to Roy Jenkins's speech and indeed he had hinted this to me yesterday. All round me was rising a tide of popular indignation against the House of Lords which had now finally proved itself a reactionary body, worthy only of total abolition. Not a very bright prospect for our reform.

Wednesday, June 19th

I had received a message that Peter Carrington wanted to meet me on secret ground in Michael Wheeler-Booth's room in the House of Lords. It was a puzzling talk. I said I had heard from Harold Wilson this morning that in the Prime Minister's view Heath had deliberately seized this opportunity, confident that he could force a General Election by inflicting a humiliating defeat on the Government. 'That is quite untrue,' said Peter Carrington. 'In fact I made up my own mind.' He said he had a meeting with the Lords and offered them two alternatives, a vote of censure without a vote on the Order and, when they turned that down, a vote at once on the Order, strictly in conformity with the proposed reform, where the reformed House would retain the right to vote down any Order so that the Government could think again but with the limitation that the Government could reinsert it into the following day's business. 'I made it very clear that they could only do it on this one occasion.'

When he'd finished I said, 'But if you appease your back-benchers in that way we have to appease ours and the Commons will get out of control.' He replied, 'I had to decide either to ride the storm or be thrown out of the Leadership and Heath rather reluctantly allowed me to ride the storm.' On

---

[1] Peerages for life had been introduced in 1958. Simultaneously the hereditary peerage was being steadily depleted.

the whole I believe this story but I had to reply that he'd set off something tremendous because there is now overwhelming pressure not only from the Labour back benchers in the Commons but from inside the Cabinet for an immediate Bill to remove the Lords' powers. 'It's going to Cabinet tomorrow,' I said, 'and I can't be sure what they will decide. As far as I can see, Roy is still on my side but there will be tremendous pressure from all the abolitionists. But whatever happens in Cabinet, my dear Carrington, I don't now see our agreement being ratified by either side. The talks are bound to be suspended for the time being and I'm not sure they can ever be resumed again.'

That concluded our conversation. We were both perfectly friendly and I believe I was wise to be completely candid. Several times he said, 'I may have been wrong in the position I took and if so I'm sorry.' He certainly saw he had put me in a difficulty by doing what his back benchers wanted and then relying on me to stop any back-bench reaction from our side.

Thursday, June 20th
Practically every newspaper confidently anticipated that the Prime Minister would announce in the House this afternoon a Bill to limit the Lords' powers. At Cabinet the House of Lords came up as item one and Harold was quite fair and put to the Cabinet exactly what we had agreed. He pointed out that we should denounce Heath strongly for an outrageous action which failed to correspond with the spirit of the inter-party talks. The talks clearly cannot be continued and Harold would, as Prime Minister, retain freedom of action to carry out a comprehensive and radical reform of the Lords.

Barbara Castle keenly welcomed this initial statement and nothing was said by Gerald Gardiner, Eddie or me. Barbara then made it clear that she wanted to go back on the agreed solution and simply abolish the House of Lords as such so I then had to go all over again into the arguments about the importance of composition rather than powers. Surprisingly, the traditional opponents, Ted Short, Gunter and Greenwood, didn't speak. Michael Stewart was the one man who said we ought to resume the talks straightaway since we need the agreed solution more than the Tories but no one else supported him. Roy Jenkins was discreet but on our side, Healey pretty well on our side and Tony Benn against us because he had his own idea of how to end titles. Certainly there was no kind of a majority for continuing the talks. Though we won the argument, my God, we didn't win the battle because from the beginning of the meeting it was clear that Harold had jettisoned the talks and during last weekend committed himself to a radical reform. The fact that I made him back-pedal at the last moment hadn't won me any liking.

We still had what was for the Prime Minister the main item on the agenda, the Fulton Committee report. I haven't asked him but I'm pretty sure that the reason he has committed himself to this report so early and so personally is partly because he has a strong liking for Fulton and even more for Norman Hunt and partly because he thinks this way he can improve his image as a great modernizer.[1] He put his case for immediately accepting the main recommendations of the report, including the creation of a Civil Service Department. Then the Chancellor put his case against what he described as precipitate action. Denis Healey, Michael Stewart and I supported Roy and all the support Harold got was from Wedgy Benn and Peter Shore, his two hirelings. He was so upset that at this point he stopped the meeting and asked that it should be resumed later.

In the afternoon I went down to hear Harold. I had denied him the triumph he really wanted but he was able to reassert his authority over the House and over our own Party and to the exterior world there was nothing wrong at all. He got cheers from our side. If they are uneasily aware of the, from their point of view, disappointing ambiguity in the Statement they don't care.[2] As Carrington said, no one else on the Tory side but him and no one in the Lower House but me cares a fig about Lords' reform or knows anything about it.

As I was leaving the House tonight the *Daily Telegraph* number two lobby man met me in the street and said they'd got a story that there had been a Cabinet split and that Eddie Shackleton and I had managed to stop the Prime Minister from legislating to remove the Lords' powers. 'Well, I don't know where they got that from,' I replied, hiding how disconcerted I was.

Friday, June 21st

I was much more disconcerted when I read the papers. There wasn't much in *The Times* or the *Guardian* but David Watt, whom I'd briefed at lunch last Monday, had an extremely good article in the *Financial Times* and the story was in the *Telegraph* and the *Express*. I don't believe this was a leak from our side and indeed the only explanation I can give is that after I filled Carrington in he must have told the Shadow Cabinet some of what I had said about Peart and Silkin's attitude and one of the Tories, probably Willie Whitelaw, had gone to the press. This shows that the intimate relations and mutual confidence we've had for months must stop. Even though Carrington had talked to me with such freedom about exactly what had happened and who

[1] A Fellow and Lecturer in Politics at Exeter College, Oxford, since 1952, Norman Hunt was a member of the Fulton Committee and, later, of the Royal Commission on the Constitution. He was Constitutional Adviser to the Government March–October 1974 and Minister of State at the D.E.S. 1974–6 and the Privy Council Office 1976. He became a life peer in 1973, taking the title of Lord Crowther-Hunt.
[2] The Statement ended: '. . . there can be no question of these all-party talks in these new circumstances continuing. Although the time has not been wasted, and valuable proposals have been put forward about the powers and composition of another place, I must tell the House that it is the intention of Her Majesty's Government, at an early date of the Government's choosing, to introduce comprehensive and radical legislation . . .' (*House of Commons Debates*, Vol. 766, cols 1314–6.)

had taken the decisions on his side I shouldn't have talked to him so freely about our goings-on. I think there'll be a good row about this and I shall have to tell my colleagues what I think happened.

Tuesday, June 25th
A special Cabinet had been called to come to a decision about the Fulton Report but it started with a statement from Harold about the leak. He complained that, unlike the disagreement about the Fulton Commission where the confidence he specially asked for had been kept, in the case of Lords' reform there'd been an appalling and deliberate breach of loyalty. Five of Friday's papers had come out with a detailed and accurate account of a Cabinet split. He then indicated in the smallest detail the Ministers who could have known about various parts of the leak. There was no question, he said, that this was an example of a systematic briefing of five newspapers by one or two of the people sitting round the Cabinet table. He knew that it was one of a very small number because there was at least one thing in the leak which only he and one other person knew. Then he glared at us and stopped.

There was no discussion and Harold started on the Fulton Report, where we gave him a very easy time. It's a second-rate Report written in a very poor style by Norman Hunt. He and Harold are tremendous buddies who live in the same world of uninspired commonsense. The Report is perfectly sensible but, oh dear, it lacks distinction. However it's been a success with the press and the public. Harold needed a success for himself and Cabinet consented to his getting it with a Statement tomorrow.

This afternoon Harold had summoned me to No. 10 so I knew the fight was on. I said to Harold, 'Why have you infuriated Roy by virtually accusing him of the Friday leaks? In your speech you said this was like the South African arms struggle and that there was no doubt that there are people in the Cabinet who are trying to throw you out of your job. You added that they could have your job because it doesn't provide much pleasure to anybody. That's all outrageous,' I said. 'There is absolutely no conspiracy in Cabinet. There is no attempt to get rid of you and I happen to know it because on this occasion I know how the story got into the press.' I then told him in detail. 'You mean you talked to Carrington?' he said. 'I wouldn't have thought it possible.' 'Well, you haven't got a very wide knowledge of human nature, Harold,' I replied. 'My relations with Peter Carrington have been extremely intimate for four or five months and we have been talking completely freely to each other.'

I explained how Carrington had given me every detail of what went on at the Shadow Cabinet meetings, the role Heath and Quintin, Macleod and Maudling each played, and how Carrington had always utterly disparaged the futility of them all. I also told him it was completely untrue that Heath ordered Carrington to whip the Lords into the Division Lobby on the

Sanctions Order. It was Carrington's own decision on an issue about which he desperately cared and where he felt he might possibly have been wrong. When I'd finished, I said to Harold, 'I haven't said a word in Cabinet about these talks with Carrington because it was all in confidence but now my confidence has been let down by this leak so I'm telling you the truth.' 'If you talk to the enemy,' said Harold, 'if you have that kind of bedwetting mania for compulsive communication you get what you deserve.' 'If you have such loathsome thoughts about me the less we see of each other the better,' I replied. 'Anyway, what you've got to realize is that at Cabinet this morning you made a false accusation because you jumped to the wrong conclusion. This is the first time I've been able to catch you out and give you positive facts to prove how ridiculous you are to expect a conspiracy.' 'I'm not wrong to expect a conspiracy,' he said, 'I've had them in the past. It just happens not to be so in this case but it's given me the opportunity to dress the Cabinet down.' 'No it hasn't, Harold,' I said. 'It's given you the opportunity to reveal once again to Cabinet your persecution mania and how obsessed you are by these suspicions of an inner conspiracy. Instead of assuming that it came from the Opposition you always assume it came from your closest friends.' 'Of course,' he said. 'Who else could it have come from? What you've told me is utterly incredible. I still can't understand it.'

He then said that Roy had stayed behind after Cabinet for a long talk, in which Roy had insisted on a full explanation. 'Don't do that,' I said, 'because the only other person who's been talking freely to the other side about Lords' reform is Freddie Warren.' I told Harold the whole story of Freddie's behaviour last week at dinner and how he'd revealed the existence of the Prime Minister's secret Bill. 'Now,' I said, 'that's a piece of information which almost certainly went to Willie Whitelaw from Warren. Anyway the whole House of Commons expected you and Silkin to announce a Bill on powers and every newspaper predicted it on Thursday morning.' 'It didn't come from me,' he said and I replied, 'Of course not. It came from John Silkin and Fred Peart, doing their job and feeding the press. I'm not blaming anybody, Harold, but trying to make you see facts.' We had a fairly rough row.

Wednesday, June 26th
On the front bench this afternoon Harold sat down beside me and at once started telling me of a wonderful talk he'd had with Roy in which the two men had completely restored their trust in each other and now understood each other completely. 'This row has cleared the air,' he said. 'Has it?' I replied, and he said, 'Come and see me after the Party meeting.' I went to his room and he repeated all the wonderful things which had happened and all the assurances Roy had given him that John Harris would be kept to his last. He then was kind enough to add that he accepted my story and would just report the affair to Cabinet, explaining that he was satisfied that a Minister

had been indiscreet, making it clear that the Minister wasn't Eddie Shackleton and assuring me that he wouldn't of course point a finger at anyone else.

Thursday, June 27th

In Cabinet Harold made his statement about the Lords leak and carefully avoided saying anything indiscreet or referring to me at all. He just said he was completely satisfied that the information had gone to the Opposition through the actions of one member of the Cabinet who was perfectly sincere and who had discussed it with an Opposition peer. Fred Peart tried to discuss the principle of this but he was smacked down and we turned to our big discussion of public expenditure. After what Roy had told me there were no surprises when I listened to his account. Having tried and failed to win ministerial co-operation for spreading the cuts equally across the board Roy realized that he had to decide on one or two big victims, investment allowances and the I.R.C. on the one side and house-building on the other side.[1]

As usual there were endless protests about the PESC method of accounting. What depressed us all was that we should be having another of these ridiculous affairs only six months after the January package. But there is one serious financial crisis which Judith and I have discovered. There's a real danger of the national insurance fund running into the red because of the unexpectedly heavy expenditures on unemployment benefit following on the very heavy sickness payments last winter and spring. It may be necessary to rely on the £1,000 million reserve fund but, to do that, the Minister has to get an affirmative order out of the House of Commons and the Government's equity holdings have to be sold. The public would therefore see that we are selling £260 million government stock in order to get £200 million of available capital. An appalling situation.

Monday, July 1st

The morning papers show that Harold had been quick and decisive in handling the Gunter crisis.[2] Roy Mason has taken his place at Power, the fourth change in a key Ministry.[3] I gather there were three possibilities, Reg Prentice, Roy Mason and Bob Mellish. Personally I would have preferred Mellish as I have never thought very highly of Mason but I've no doubt that the decisive factor was that Harold wanted to put in a miner to placate the miners.

[1] In October 1967 the Royal Assent was given to the Act establishing the Industrial Reorganization Corporation, empowered to borrow up to £150 million from the Treasury to enable it to set up new companies, and buy, hold shares in and advise existing ones. The first Managing Director was Ronald Grierson and its Chairman Sir Frank (later, Lord) Kearton.

[2] Ray Gunter's resignation as Minister of Power had been announced on Sunday 30 June.

[3] From October 1964 to April 1966 the Minister was Fred Lee and from April 1966 to April 1968 Richard Marsh, whom Ray Gunter had succeeded. Roy Mason's place as Postmaster-General was taken by John Stonehouse, formerly Minister of State in charge of the Aviation industry at MinTech.

Tuesday, July 2nd

In *The Times* there is an extraordinarily inane proposal that, to test his popularity, Harold Wilson should stand for re-election as Leader of the Party. I was much more disturbed by another story that Tony Greenwood had said that he would be prepared to stand for the secretaryship of the Party. For weeks there have been rumours that Harold is determined to fix this key appointment and this has provided the evidence everybody wanted.[1]

Wednesday, July 3rd

I had lunch at the Savoy with nine American correspondents who were solely concerned with the Gunter affair, the leadership crisis and the rumours of who was to replace Harold. I tried very hard to make them realize how futile it is for us in the Government even to consider the possibility of a change of leadership this summer. The credibility of the Government and of the pound is undermined. How can we now suggest that we should undermine credibility still further by a *coup d'état* against the leader? I needn't go through it all over again in this diary but I went through it with the correspondents as clearly and as candidly as is possible in a purely off-the-record briefing.

Thursday, July 4th

As Chairman of the Cabinet Housing Committee, I'd had a bad conscience about Tony Greenwood and had asked him to set up a meeting and to provide a paper. He had got massacred in the last PESC cuts by having no friends and going along alone. I asked him to give us full details of his situation and he had circulated a most miserable paper, though this was no worse than his behaviour under cross-examination. Poor Tony. He's a weak stick, accomplished in certain ways but cowardly. At present he's suffering under an odious press campaign. There was a horrible story in yesterday's *Times* about his refusing to become General Secretary unless the salary was raised to £6,000 a year. As we were going out of the room he said to me, 'I couldn't put my mind to this meeting, I was so upset by all that's happening about the General Secretaryship. I never wanted it, I never asked for it. I was asked a question at a press conference and I didn't know how to avoid saying what I did and then suddenly it blew up into a front page story.' I am sure this is the precise truth.

I met Harold hanging about in the division lobby and he took me into his room. He had told me yesterday at Cabinet that he'd been trying to get me for an informal chat on life in general, nothing in particular. 'I just want to talk to you,' he said.

I asked him about a minute on devolution I had sent over ten days ago but apparently he hadn't read it yet so I tried to switch him over to discuss the

---

[1] Len Williams was about to become Governor-General of Mauritius and there had been rumours that Anthony Greenwood would succeed him at Transport House as General Secretary of the Labour Party.

merger and the need to get Judith another job before the autumn. 'Oh,' he
said, 'I can't guarantee that. We may have to wait some months to find her
something else.' The merger is one of the least of his concerns. I mustn't push
him too hard but on the other hand I must make sure it takes place in the
autumn, at the same time as the Commonwealth Relations Office/Foreign
Office merger.[1] I must be in charge by then because I didn't give up being
Leader of the House in order to be totally unemployed.

His next topic was Anthony Greenwood and he gave me his version of the
facts. The National Executive saw the short-list and thought none of the
candidates good enough. So it set up a committee of eight, including the P.M.
and George Brown, to look at two possible candidates, Alf Allen and Tony
Greenwood, and they were both approached to see whether either of them
would do it.[2] This elicited the fact that Allen is most unlikely to do it so the
issue now seems to be whether, despite the vile press campaign and all the
nauseating things Gunter has said, Greenwood can become General Secretary. I think it's true that Harold wants Tony for the job but it's not true that
Greenwood wants the job or was formally approached or did anything about
it. Indeed, from his point of view, it's a miserable affair and the sooner ended
the better.

This long conversation took place in a very friendly atmosphere over
brandy. Harold was obviously mending his fences with me. Though I got
nothing out of him about the merger, I did get a great deal about the House
of Lords, where he's back on the lines laid down for him before he
skedaddled.

Wednesday, July 10th

On his own initiative Burke came to see me this afternoon and we had the
most interesting talk we've ever had. He said straightaway, 'As for your
merger, we must have it by October or November. That's already decided in
Whitehall, even if it means formally carrying on with Kenneth Robinson and
Judith Hart as Ministers.' I said I was delighted to hear this and then Burke
got down to his main point. 'Apart from the merger,' he said, 'can you give
me an assurance that once you've got your huge new Ministry, you will keep
your co-ordinating job?' I said I would try and he said, 'Well, at least you
must keep your room here in the Cabinet Office. You can't co-ordinate the
social services from across the river at Elephant and Castle or from that cosy
little Ministry in the Adelphi. You can only co-ordinate from the central
point of power where people come to be co-ordinated, the Cabinet Office.[3]

[1] The merger took place on October 17th, 1968.
[2] Alfred Allen, General Secretary of USDAW since 1962, is a member of the T.U.C. General
Council (Chairman 1973–4). He has been a Crown Estates Commissioner since 1965 and
became a life peer in 1974.
[3] During the two years that he had served as Lord President of the Council and Leader of
the House of Commons, Crossman had become very attached to the beautiful room which
he had furnished. When Mr Peart became Leader of the House on April 6th, 1968, Cross-

You see the point, Dick, of your keeping an authority here which otherwise you'll lose when you go out there to Elephant and Castle? Why not keep the title of Lord President and your co-ordinating staff under Paul Odgers? You can run them here in addition to running your merged Ministry. What none of you politicians realize,' he said, 'is that being promoted from departmental Minister to co-ordinating minister is a promotion to real and more effective power. Of course you're doing a job when you're Minister of Housing or Minister of Health but you're doing an even more important job when you're getting the basis of block budgeting for the social services worked out. I want you to go on with that job. It could make more difference to the Government than anything you achieve inside a merged Ministry of Health and Social Security where you'll get immersed in the details of negotiations with the doctors.' I said I would think it over and that I'd have a talk to Harold about it.

But Burke was really thinking of his own peculiar co-ordinating powers. It's ludicrous to say that I have more power in my present job than I did at Housing.

Right at the end I asked him about the paper on devolution I sent to Harold weeks ago. I said I was disappointed that the P.M. hadn't read the follow-up letter I sent over a fortnight ago in which I'd commented on the comments from Willie Ross and George Thomas. Burke replied, 'When his box is piled up now he doesn't read through it.' He made it very clear that he thought Harold wasn't working as hard as he had before. I said, 'Yes, that's right and of course the truth is that he is becoming a wee bit of an Asquith and he's in nothing like the physical condition to go through his boxes late at night that he was eighteen months ago.' Heaven knows, no one can blame him for that in view of the strain to which he has been subjected. But I never expected to find myself discussing it with Burke.

Wednesday, July 17th

This evening Harold was having another of his No. 10 parties (I think it was for an organization for the blind) and I wouldn't have bothered to go if I hadn't heard at 6.30 that the Seebohm Report[1] is on the Cabinet agenda and that he has made four Ministers prepare their proposals about it and is hoping to bring the matter to a head tomorrow. In due course I got him to the end of the room. He was floppy, airy, pleased with himself, with perhaps a little bit of drink in him, and when he had shuffled all the people out of the way he said in his own Harold fashion, 'Well, you ought to get what you want

man remained Lord President and was able to retain this room in the Privy Council Office. He was obliged to relinquish it on October 18th, 1968, when Mr Peart assumed the office of Lord President of the Council.

[1] The Report of the Committee on Local Authority and Allied Personal Services (Cmnd 3703). It recommended that major local authorities should each create a single, unified social service department with a central Government Department assuming responsibility for overall planning.

but we can't push it too hard and maybe I shall have to do the job for you myself. But I'm not sure whether you're in the right.' 'Well, if unifying the social services isn't in the right what on earth am I at a merged Ministry for?' I replied very indignantly. 'Of course you're in the right in that sense,' he replied, 'but you don't know what pressure Callaghan is putting on me. He sees enormous Home Office prestige at stake and feels that he's fighting for his life.' I got nothing out of him except a vague sloppy support and I was fairly unhappy.

Friday, July 19th

The Caerphilly majority has slumped from 21,000 to under 2,000 and though the Tories lost their deposit their vote hasn't gone down quite as badly as ours.[1] This was a disaster, yet it was a relief that we had won. Indeed, just imagine if we'd lost? Then all Harold's troubles would have been back and the divisions in Cabinet would have started again.

There was another item in today's *Times* which caught my attention. It occurred in *The Times* Diary and ran:

> James Callaghan is still fighting inside the Cabinet to keep his Home Office empire intact, in spite of all the arguments of Mr Wilson and Mr Crossman that a chunk of it should be detached and built into the merged Social Security and Health Departments in the autumn.
>
> When he constructed his Mark Two Cabinet in April, with Mr Crossman designated as the overlord for all the social services, Mr Wilson planned to wrench responsibility for children's welfare out of the Home Office. The first Mr Callaghan heard of the proposal was when he read it in the papers.
>
> His initial spasm of annoyance has been succeeded by a shrewd rationalization of the case for leaving child welfare with the Home Office. He insists that it is important for the morale of the Home Office that they should not be stripped of creative social responsibilities and left simply with the regulatory responsibilities which now and then are bound to bring them into a harsh glare of controversy.
>
> It makes a very respectable argument and a portent that it may prove to be the winning argument will come next week in the Commons when Mr Callaghan, not the Minister for Housing and Local Government, will make the Statement on the help the Government are going to give the urban authorities whose social and financial problems have been bedevilled by a high density of immigrants. In other words, the Home Office has become the co-ordinator of Ministers and Departments who are involved in helping local authorities to improve community relationships, the kind of overlordship the Home Secretary wants.
>
> Mr Callaghan may have lost his place on the Cabinet economic

---

[1] Alfred Evans held the seat for Labour; the majority fell from 21,148 to 1,874.

committee since he ceased to be Chancellor, but the signs are unmistakable that he is quickly re-establishing his influence in the Cabinet and the Labour Party. The elder-statesman role of the Chancellor who has lived through it all before suits him, and now that he is fully recovered from the two or three months of exhaustion which followed his three years at the Treasury, he is putting a lot of energy into consolidating Cabinet and Party unity.

Long before the next General Election comes he is likely again to be a force to be reckoned with.

That had obviously been inserted into *The Times* by Jim's excellent Public Relations Officer.[1] It came as a shock and a warning to me because it's very sensible and because the threat is a very serious one. Jim does regard me as his rival and he has begun the battle of the Departments. Moreover he backs winning causes whereas I back losing causes like devolution.

This morning there was the usual meeting of the Home Affairs Committee, a vast affair attended almost exclusively by number twos and Ministers interested in a particular item. Sure enough, round the great table in the great ministerial committee room about twenty Departments were represented. The only item which interested me was Kenneth Robinson's old proposal to forbid cigarette advertisers to use coupons. At an earlier meeting I'd been a lone voice saying it was a mistake to give him permission to make a statement vaguely announcing legislation. At Legislation Committee I'd made sure the Bill was not included in next year's programme and this was ratified by Cabinet, which instructed us to reconsider the matter at Home Affairs. I had only two or three people on my side. However I'm still just powerful enough to hold the thing up and finally I suggested that instead of forbidding coupons we should ration the amount of money to be spent on advertising and leave it to the cigarette manufacturers to decide how they should spend their money. I found this infinitely preferable. Harmony achieved. Kenneth Robinson is submitting another draft Bill and meanwhile I'm pretty sure it will be too late for the election.

I went back to my room to find the indefatigable Callaghan had sent me a letter saying he thought it unfair for me to preside at the press conference Seebohm would give on his Report. I rang the P.M. who had seen *The Times* piece and understood the battle that is going on. He was friendly but pretty detached and in this case he clearly wasn't prepared to defend me. Indeed, he made it quite clear that he thought I was, in his language, 'doing a fast one' and should not take the chair. So I had lost this round and had to write and admit it to Callaghan. I was surprised at the reaction of my Private Office. Janet Newman, my beautiful secretary,[2] was appalled when I dictated the

[1] Tom McCaffrey who in April 1976 became Mr Callaghan's Press Secretary at No. 10.
[2] Janet Newman had joined Crossman's Private Office at the Ministry of Housing and Local Government in August 1966 and remained his secretary both in the Lord President's Office and at the D.H.S.S. In 1970 she moved with him to the *New Statesman*.

draft and said that she'd never known me surrender in a letter such as this. Well, she hasn't known me defeated before and I have a deep sense of having been driven into a corner this week. Callaghan has been able to demonstrate the power and authority of the Home Secretary against me, a mere co-ordinating shadow. I resigned the Leadership of the House in order to regain the power of a big departmental Minister but here I am an impotent co-ordinator licked by a cool and calculating Home Secretary. Of course I need my new merged Ministry but will a new merged Ministry be able to stand up to the Home Office? Will I from that little Ministry in John Adam Street and that horrible place in Elephant and Castle be able to challenge the revered power of the Home Secretary, second only to the Chancellor in Whitehall prestige? Well, it's an open question, but if I have the energy and heart for departmental battles I had two years ago I can do it. I'm not sure I have it still.

Sunday, July 21st
The Sunday papers carried a number of stories about the departmental battle which is proceeding in Whitehall between Callaghan and me. Since I have not seen a journalist all the briefing's been provided from the Home Office side and the stories all commit me to making a bid to capture the children's service from Jim as soon as I take over in the autumn. This clash has come as a complete surprise to me. It happens in my life. I drift along for weeks and everything seems fine and then suddenly I see a danger I haven't seen before and the clash is on me before I know it. This time it has left me full of doubts, largely because of a talk with Burke. He says that running a huge merged Department, even if Kenneth Robinson and Judith stay as Ministers under me, is going to be a cumbersome and burdensome job which will stop me doing the co-ordinating work which I do so well and which is so desperately important to the Government. He says that if I'm to be a fair-minded chairman I shouldn't simultaneously be the Minister fighting for the new merged Department and he wants the merger postponed at least until after the crucial decisions on the Seebohm Report have been taken.

But what future have I got as a pure co-ordinator? Is it right to say that in the next six months this co-ordinating work is more important than getting myself back the power of a departmental Minister? If I stay a co-ordinator I shan't be able to appear more than very seldom in Parliament or to be effective on the public platform and Callaghan will take over more and more of the big shows which get publicity. On that *The Times* Diary was quite right.

What complicates matters is the character of Jim Callaghan. He's not merely a schemer, he's also got a very nice side to him and I like him because he can't resist talking to me. His feelings about me are very much divided. He's attracted by my ability and probably knows that ultimately I'm not nearly as thrusting and ambitious as he is and that unlike him I am intellectually honest. So he talks to me in the friendliest way possible and fights me ruthlessly behind my back. It's not an attractive combination but in politics it's sometimes inevitable.

Wednesday, July 24th
I spent most of the morning in Downing Street at a meeting of the Supplementary Benefits Commission, which has taken the place of the National Assistance Board and is an independent commission loosely connected with the Ministry of Social Security. We started by discussing a lengthy report on immigration collected by their managers, which showed that immigrants are law-abiding, decent people unless and until they are corrupted by the Irish, to put it crudely. Next they dealt with the problem of supplementary benefit paid out during strikes and for this item they had in three of their managers, one each from Oxford, Liverpool and London. I had assumed that the families of lower-paid workers would all apply for supplementary benefit but I couldn't have been more wrong. Even at the time of the Liverpool dock strike in the autumn of 1967 only some 35 per cent of the strikers applied, although the strike lasted six weeks. How did they avoid it? Partly because of the income tax rebates for strikers but, even more important I suspect, they take odd jobs. It's certainly true that when a strike is on in Coventry everybody's windows get cleaned and for three or four weeks there are 10,000 jobbing gardeners about. I found the whole thing fascinating and took them back to the Privy Council Office for a quick lunch before they returned to their work.

Meanwhile at Transport House the famous N.E.C. meeting had been going on, when against all expectation Harry Nicholas was selected as the new General Secretary by 14 votes to 12 instead of Tony Greenwood. Poor Tony, from the beginning he hadn't been in the least keen to stand but had been persuaded to seek the post and, having finally warmed himself up to it, was now publicly repudiated. I was sitting beside Callaghan on the front bench this afternoon while he was making another of his great Statements, this time about electoral reform, votes at eighteen and party labels.[1] He gave me his version of what happened and on the whole I must say I thought Harry Nicholas a far better choice. To take a failed politician and shove him into Transport House is an insult both to the unions and to the party workers. Harry will be quite an efficient administrator though he can't be the second focus of power which we recommended in the Advisory Commission's Report last year. The fact is that Tony would have been the P.M.'s stooge and that's why he lost. It's my considered view that Callaghan, Brown and

[1] In a White Paper (Cmnd 3717) published that afternoon, the Government accepted all but four of the conclusions of the Speaker's Conference on Electoral Reform. They recommended, however, that the voting age be reduced to eighteen, not twenty, that polling hours be extended to 10 p.m. and that party labels should be allowed on nomination and ballot papers. A ban on public opinion polls and betting odds on the outcome of an election, 72 hours before polling, was considered impracticable.

Alice Bacon,[1] who organized the anti-Greenwood coup, may say what they like about the P.M.'s supporting Tony but he would probably have preferred the old trade unionist, Alf Allen. Tony was the P.M.'s number two choice but, alas, Harold played his hand very unskilfully and has subjected himself to a gratuitous defeat.

Back in my office Peter Carrington came to see me. The conversation didn't add very much to my knowledge and was clearly a mere introduction. Just as we were saying goodbye I told him what had happened about the Lords' reform leak. He apologized and admitted straightaway that he had talked to Heath.

Thursday, July 25th
The papers were terrible. The big news was how the P.M.'s nominee had been defeated at Transport House and there was an account of the Callaghan/Brown/Bacon plot, and of how Eirene White[2] changed sides. Everything was in full detail with tremendous headlines.

I suddenly had a message to see the P.M. at 11 a.m. He led me in and said he was very surprised by my minute [about Callaghan]; had I lost heart? It seemed a resigned, sad minute. Did I not want to be a Minister? 'God, no,' I said. 'I merely wanted to give you the choice in an increasingly awkward situation. I would prefer you to bulldoze it through but it will take some bulldozing.' He said, 'I do want to bulldoze it.' And suddenly I realized that the Callaghan plot yesterday had completely changed Harold's mind. This morning he was now willing to back me 100 per cent against Jim in a way that he certainly wasn't twelve hours ago. The evidence is quite clear. I had, as I've mentioned already, got an acknowledgment of my memo with an unenthusiastic statement that he would see me next week. Now he sees me today although he is due to make a farewell holiday speech at the P.L.P. meeting.

I found it very difficult to get my words in. 'If you want me to be the new Secretary of State,' I said, 'I'll take the job on, but you've got to support me and that means not giving Callaghan any more responsibilities like the urban programme.' Harold knew what I was talking about. I then said we'd got to deal with William Armstrong and Burke, both of whom are very strongly against the merger. 'Oh, Burke,' he said, 'he's always wrong,' and the fact that Burke opposed the Ministry was actually in my favour. 'What about Armstrong?' I said. 'I know he's against it,' Harold replied. 'But how will you get rid of the obstruction?' I asked. 'Will you set a timetable and will you give an instruction that my merger will be completed at the same time as the Commonwealth/Foreign Office merger in October? At present Whitehall is

[1] Labour M.P. for North-East Leeds 1945–55 and for South-East Leeds 1955–70, Minister of State at the Home Office 1964–7 and at the D.E.S. 1967–70. A member of the N.E.C. 1941–70, she became a life peer in 1970.
[2] Labour M.P. for East Flint 1945–70. Minister of State at the Welsh Office 1967–70. A member of the N.E.C. 1947–53 and 1958–72. She became a life peer in 1970.

full of uncertainty about my future. You must clarify it now and give me full backing.'

On such occasions Prime Ministerial decisions really do count. I've now no doubt that before he goes away to the Scillies he will have given all the necessary instructions, everybody will know the timetable and be prepared to do what they're told.

Wednesday, July 31st
Rather thoughtlessly the Prime Minister had set up a new Cabinet Committee on the finances of the B.B.C. and it had its first meeting this afternoon. I asked straightaway whether anyone there thought we still had a chance to go for advertising. John Stonehouse who's the new P.M.G. and Roy Mason, the old one, both said they were against it. But I told them that if nobody wanted advertising what this Committee had better do would be to try to improve the system of licensing. That's what we agreed and so under my chairmanship a major Cabinet controversy finally spluttered out.

Later this afternoon Paul Odgers had set up in my office a very solemn meeting about the merger. William Armstrong was there with the two new Permanent Secretaries, Jarrett and Marre, the old Permanent Secretary of Health, Arnold France, and Miss Nunn from the Cabinet Office. Paul had prepared exactly the kind of paper they like. Burke at once raised the problem of whether I should be allowed a small co-ordinating unit in the Cabinet Office or whether my whole headquarters, including my outside advisers, should be moved to John Adam Street. Should I have two lots of civil servants, one lot as co-ordinating Minister and one as super-Minister? Everyone except Burke was against separating the co-ordinator's office. As I also thought it was quite unrealistic, I said I would as co-ordinator only retain the Lord Privy Seal's present suite of rooms for myself when Fred Peart moves into my Privy Council palace. What will be the name of the Ministry? It was agreed that in the first instance it should be called the Department of Health and Social Security, so as not to claim control over the other social services too imperiously. We agreed that I should sit in John Adam Street and that this should be the headquarters of the merged Ministry for the meantime, until we could get a decent new building for the merged Department. The only staff to be merged are the press relations people and I immediately said I'd try to get Peter Brown back from Housing.[1]

Towards the end of the meeting my mind began to wander because I was looking forward to entertaining Alfred Gollin,[2] the political historian who wrote an excellent book on Garvin and the *Observer* as well as a biography of

[1] Peter Brown, for whom Crossman had a very high regard, had been his press officer at the M.H.L.G. 1964–6.
[2] Professor of History at the University of Santa Barbara since 1967. He is the author of *The Observer and J. L. Garvin 1908–14* (London: Oxford University Press, 1960); *Proconsul in Politics: a Study of Lord Milner* (London: Blond, 1964) and *Balfour's Burden* (London: Blond, 1965).

Milner. He's now writing on Baldwin and he came to see me the other day so that I could show him the House of Commons. He's a shy young man with a treble voice that is hardly broken and that day he was suffering from a terrible cold. I had also offered to show him No. 10 and he was duly thrilled. However, just as we were leaving today who should walk into the hall of No. 10 but the P.M. and John Freeman.[1] John used to be a rather willowy, elegant young man with wonderful wavy hair but he's thickened out and his actual complexion has roughened so that he looks like an extremely tough colonel of a polo-playing regiment just back from India—big and bluff. Beside him was little Harold, relaxed and gay, having undoubtedly been drinking with John. Harold was full of interest when he heard who Gollin was and immediately offered to show him the busts in the passage from the front door, the photographs of his predecessors on the stairs and all the rest of the Prime Minister's standard display. This he did with stories about everybody since Pitt, genial, well-balanced and humorous. When Gollin's tour was over Harold suddenly turned to me and said, 'How dangerous it is to be a Christian. Look what happened to me with Callaghan. I showed a perfectly Christian mood. I did nothing whatsoever. I didn't react at all when they appointed Harry Nicholas but, by God, the time will come when I'll dig Jim's entrails out for what he did to me. By the way,' he said, turning to me, 'you've been a bit of a Christian this week too, haven't you? You had a moment when your courage failed and you were just going to give up.' 'I didn't know how much backing I was going to get from you, Harold,' I replied, 'and I shall be very glad if it's really all right. But I'm not yet sure.' I suppose the whole incident lasted twenty minutes. It was Harold at his most relaxed and happy and I felt relaxed too because I'm not so close to him any more. Instead of me he's got Fred Peart, an excellent boon companion who, though he hardly has a policy-making mind, fortunately knows it.

On the night of August 20th Czechoslovakia was invaded by Warsaw Pact forces, at the request, it was alleged, of unnamed Czechoslovak officials, and several prominent members of the Czechoslovak Praesidium and Secretariat, including Smrkovsky and Dubček, were arrested by the Russians. Riots, strikes and demonstrations broke out against the invading troops, over 500,000 soldiers, with 500 tanks in Prague alone, and protests were broadcast from secret radio and television transmitters. President Svoboda flew to Moscow on August 23rd and secured the release of his colleagues, and a communiqué issued on his return on August 27th announced that the troops would not interfere with internal affairs and would be withdrawn as soon as the situation became 'normal'. The invasion was condemned by Yugoslavia and Roumania and by nearly all the West European communist parties.

[1] British High Commissioner in India 1965–8 and British Ambassador in Washington 1969–71, and then Chairman and Chief Executive of London Weekend Television from 1971 until 1976, when he became President of the organization.

In Britain the Prime Minister and Foreign Secretary had immediately returned to London on August 21st and in a statement issued from No. 10 Downing Street the British Government condemned 'a flagrant violation of the United Nations Charter and of all accepted standards of international behaviour'. Britain had joined six other Western countries in tabling the resolution at the U.N. Security Council, calling for a withdrawal of all the Warsaw Pact forces from Czechoslovakia and for a declaration that the sovereignty and independence of Czechoslovakia would be respected. Parliament was recalled for a two-day emergency sitting on August 26th.

Monday, August 26th

House recalled. I had lunch on the train and went straight to the Commons where the carpets hadn't even been laid and everything was being spring-cleaned. I went in through Speaker's Yard and wandered round before coming back to Harold's room while Prayers were still on in the Chamber. He was just getting his speech ready. Then it was time for us to go in and there was horrible nasty pushing and shoving because there was no Question Time during which Members could slowly drift in to take their places. If anybody wanted a decent place he had to do some fighting with his arms and shoulders. I saw just ahead of me Roy going round the corner into the Division Lobby, determined to get the place he wanted. I nipped in and just got the last seat on the gangway, the Chief Whip's seat. Fred Peart wasn't yet there but there was a fight when John Silkin arrived, back from Montreux, and he just got his big bottom on to the edge beside me. Fred Peart then squeezed in beside him and the P.M., Michael Stewart and Roy Jenkins, all tight as sardines on that front bench but trying to sit back and look important. The P.M. made a perfectly decent speech but one thing tickled me. I had started my speech at Hyde Park by saying that anyone who compared the crisis in Czechoslovakia today with the Munich crisis in 1938 wanted his head examined. Harold started his speech by saying history repeats itself. He then took the superficial F.O. line about the situation. There was even the passage about the Czechs' love of democracy whereas our concern is that the Czech Communists should be allowed to liberalize a regime which is in no sense democratic. Harold doesn't take to philosophy. Indeed he has one of the most un-philosophical minds in the world and when he claims that he never got past page one of *Das Kapital* it's probably true. Still, the speech was perfectly decent and Heath followed him with an equally pedestrian oration. Later on George Brown was on his feet for an excellent little speech, very much on my line, urging us not to abandon our cultural contacts.*

It was certainly a big occasion. The floor and galleries were packed, some 300 M.P.s had come back from their holidays and for these two days they had nothing else to do except crowd into the Chamber. It was obviously right

* He was rebuked by *The Times* the next day for making a weak speech!

to recall Parliament but these historic occasions are anyway a bit depressing, and this one was more so than usual because everyone now knows that Britain can do nothing to help the Czechs. I suppose that with President Johnson and de Gaulle both opting out Britain had a chance to count for something if Harold could have spoken for the uncommitted nations and said something really striking. But he couldn't and so he didn't. And perhaps that's the feeling which made us specially depressed.

Tuesday, August 27th

This afternoon my most important job was to talk to my new Permanent Secretary, Jarrett, about the siting of the headquarters of the merged Ministry. I had assumed that we would have the Ministers and the senior staff in John Adam Street, which is just off the Strand and which you can reach in three or four minutes, and that we'd let the mass of the officials live at Elephant and Castle. But Jarrett had discovered that John Adam Street isn't big enough to handle five Ministers and their offices and in addition all the Permanent Secretaries, Deputy Secretaries and Under-Secretaries. The choice before us was either to have a tiny headquarters staff in John Adam Street or, after all, to settle in the Elephant and Castle. I made Molly spend a couple of days measuring how long it takes at various times of the day to get from Vincent Square and from No. 10 to each of the two buildings. As I rather feared, the difference is only two or three minutes so I can't use the excuse of the time it takes to get from Elephant and Castle to a Cabinet meeting to defend having John Adam Street as our headquarters. It looks as though it's got to be Elephant and Castle.

Wednesday, September 4th

I heard the P.M. was back from his holidays so I sent a message asking whether he would like to see me after lunch. Sure enough, he was there waiting for me at 3 o'clock when I went through to No. 10, after a long chat with Odgers. I was taken not into the Cabinet Room but into Harold's brand-new study. I didn't much like the bare boards or the panelling but I admired his Lowry painting very much as well as his new chair and table and above all I liked the sense of his having a study where he could think alone. 'This is good,' I said. 'Yes,' he said, 'I can work here.' 'Well, why didn't you have it before? It was Churchill's room, wasn't it?' Harold said that as soon as he came into No. 10 in 1964 he gave up this study because he thought he could do all his work and his writing down in the Cabinet Room. As a result he hadn't done any writing and it's taken him four years to learn this lesson.

He asked me what I'd been doing and I said I'd been writing the revised chapters of my textbook and was really happy. He looked quizzically and said, 'You like writing, don't you, Dick?' I knew he was thinking that I wouldn't mind retiring and that my attention is not wholly on my job. Then we switched to the T.U.C. All this week at their Conference they've been bashing the Government,[1] defeating the prices and incomes policy by an overwhelming 7:1. 'Do you think we have to worry about Congress this year?' he asked. 'You can take a detached view.' When I didn't answer straightaway, he went on, 'I think we can safely disregard them. The Government's standing with the public won't be affected by T.U.C. hostility, will it, Dick?' He wanted my support and on the whole I felt it was better to give it. But I realized for the first time that he doesn't feel himself representing the Labour movement, really caring about the trade union leaders or feeling great loyalty to the party. He cares about being P.M., about politics, about power. He has become de-partied to a great extent, an occupant of Downing Street who adores running things well, an occupant who has had his leftist loyalties battered by the roughness of relations within the party.

Very soon he got round to the subject of Callaghan. Harold's now building me up consciously as the big Minister of the Social Services who will teach Callaghan a lesson at the Home Office. Once again he told me that Callaghan was intriguing against him and trying to create a position favourable to his succession to the leadership. 'He's inordinately ambitious and inordinately weak,' said Harold. 'So weak that as Chancellor he used to weep on my shoulder and then go away and intrigue against me. That's a pretty fair analysis.' Then he turned to Tony Crosland, about whom he expressed a great deal of disappointment. 'In Cabinet,' he said, 'he very often contributes an idea but never a policy or a decision.' I found that a shrewd judgment and remarked, 'What a contrast with Roy.' 'Yes,' he said, 'but neither runs his own Department. Tony is run by the Department and if Roy isn't too it's because he has a cabal to run it for him. But at least when Roy's made a decision he sticks to it and that's why I'm thankful we've had him since devaluation. Right at the beginning,' he went on, 'I had decided in favour of Roy.' It's obvious that Harold's imagination is now rewriting history to show that he made the decision alone and no one else had any influence on him.

Finally we turned to my own Ministry and I said I would like the merger to coincide with that of the Foreign and Commonwealth Office on October 17th. 'That would be O.K.,' he said, 'if Roy for some reason doesn't oppose this timing and insist on January 1st.' 'Well,' I said, 'it's much better to put the big change before Parliament when it is in session.' He liked that idea and then we went on to the name. He would like it to be called the Ministry of Social Services because Burke Trend and William Armstrong have obviously sold to him the importance of my co-ordinating function in the Cabinet Office. 'You must have your co-ordinating brains trust over here,' he said, 'and spend a lot of time with it. I must arrange with Burke and Armstrong that you have a real team, including Tommy.'

It was a pretty solid discussion and it meant his relations with me were established and sensible. Not terribly intimate but on the level. He was liking

[1] The Trades Union Congress met at Blackpool from September 2nd to September 6th.

having me there. He kept on saying, 'Can't you stay to tea?' and I had to say that I had to catch a train to Bristol to look at a health centre and a supplementary benefit office.

Tuesday, September 10th
I had a visit late in the afternoon from William Armstrong about the progress on the merger. He had of course heard about my talk with the P.M. and told me that Harold had said no instructions should be issued until I had talked to Armstrong. They had both agreed that my title should be Secretary of State for the Social Services. The Ministry is to be called the Department of Health and Social Security, so I shall have one title as Secretary and another as departmental Minister. The merger will take place on October 16th or 17th and the debate on the Affirmative Order creating the new Department on the 22nd. But the P.M. had once again emphasized that he wouldn't make the announcement on the 16th or 17th and William Armstrong is pretty sure he'll make it during the Tory Party Conference week. So we are moving ahead under the careful control of the P.M. who has also agreed that we must have the headquarters at Elephant and Castle, but that I must also have a suite of offices in the Cabinet Office for co-ordination purposes and a brains trust. There's no doubt that the Government and Whitehall are deeply committed to the merger and after this talk with William today I knew I could sit back for an easy life of relaxation before the strain of the enormous new job I shall be doing.

Thursday, September 26th
Burke, unfortunately, came back from a three weeks' holiday and immediately retired with a bad throat. This means that until he recovers the exact placing of my co-ordination unit will remain in doubt but it's clear from what Armstrong and the P.M. have said to me that I shan't be able to keep the Lord Presidency and I shall therefore have to let Fred take my offices and move into his Lord Privy Seal's office, which is a pleasant suite at the corner of Downing Street.

Friday, September 27th
This morning we had a meeting of the Home Affairs Committee and once again cigarette legislation came up. Last Friday I was told that a paper was going before the Cabinet this week recommending once again Kenneth Robinson's Bill outlawing gift schemes for cigarettes. This was an outrage because Kenneth should have submitted the paper to me before sending it in to the Cabinet Secretariat. But when I rang him up this morning he said that he thought the whole thing was perfectly in order and had no idea that I wanted to see it beforehand. There was nothing I could do but to ring up the Lord Chancellor and he agreed that the item must be removed from the agenda, which it duly was. When I told the story to Harold he said that

Robinson might be trying to get a cause for resignation but I don't think this is true. No, it's the bloody-mindedn ss of a man isolated out there at Elephant and Castle and sore at being thrown out of his Ministry in order to give place to me. I am more and more aware that if he is left out of the Government when I take over it will be very bad for me since he has built up a very high reputation in his four years as Minister of Health. If I seem to chuck him out in order to take his job it won't do me any good in the National Health Service. On the other hand, everything he is doing now is making it very difficult to avoid just that.

This evening was the big dinner for Erlander.[1] The P.M. normally goes to Conference on Thursday with the rest of the Executive, to be at the N.E.C. meetings on Friday and Saturday. But this year, making an excuse of Erlander, Harold is only arriving early on Sunday morning. I happen to know that he only asked Erlander a week ago. The dinner took place in No. 10 at the horseshoe table with too many people and in terrible heat. (Macmillan spent over £2 million restoring No. 10 and left it without air conditioning or adequate ventilation.) At the dinner I sat next to Mrs George Thomson and started talking to her about the ghastly position of politicians' wives who have to attend these ceremonial occasions, telling her how Anne and I had never gone to anything at the Palace and how we managed to get out of most of the formalities. She told me she loved all these things and even adored living in Government accommodation in one of the flats in Admiralty House. She finds the Foreign Office life perfect. 'Doesn't George want a change?' I asked her. 'No,' she said, 'neither George nor I would like to move.' Mr and Mrs Thomson are the perfect, professional External Affairs Minister and wife, because they are absolutely inoffensive. I have never heard him take a personal line at Cabinet or O.P.D. He has an excellent presence in Parliament and I am sure that when he goes abroad he is excellent at negotiations, just carrying out his instructions. Since Michael Stewart is also totally ineffective this pretty well explains what's happened to Labour's foreign policy. After the Erlander dinner Anne motored me straight down to Prescote where we prepared for what must surely be the last weekend of summer.

Tuesday, October 1st
All the papers are full of the crushing 5:1 defeat which Barbara suffered at Blackpool on her prices and incomes policy.[2] The first two days of the Conference—on Sunday a split in the Executive and yesterday this major defeat—have been as bad as we expected. On the other hand this probably means, as Harold calculates, that the worst will be over before he arrives.

---

[1] Social Democratic Prime Minister of Sweden for 22 years. He retired in 1969.

[2] At their meeting on Sunday the N.E.C. had agreed to support the Government's prices and incomes policy only by a casting vote, and on Monday a motion moved by Frank Cousins demanding repeal of the policy was carried by 5,098,000 votes to 1,124,000.

This morning I found myself invited, as Lord President, to the Lord Chancellor's annual reception. This is a very curious occasion on which the Lord Chancellor receives in the Royal Gallery behind the House of Lords all the judges down to the rank of recorder, all the Q.C.s and a select number of junior counsel. I walked in from the Lords and saw a queue hundreds of yards long winding up the stairs to shake hands with the Chancellor, so I got the servants of the House to take me round the back and push me through the catering tables to an open space. There I found the judges standing about in full fig, their regalia of black, gold or red, and white ermine. They vary enormously in looks. There is a small thin-looking drunken minority but most of them are judges cherubic and all of them are marked with the judicial glare. It struck me once again how separate we keep ourselves in Britain. There is the legal world, the doctors' world, the artistic world, the dramatic world, the political world. We are tremendously separate and here was one world having its annual get-together on beer and sausages.

Wednesday, October 2nd

I lay in bed, read the papers and heard the wireless and delighted in Harold's triumphant speech yesterday morning. Even the Tory papers couldn't refrain from slightly spiteful cheering. By first refusing to come until Sunday and then by making this kind of speech he has shown his disdain for the Executive's intrigues and I think this has probably been good for his public image and his T.V. persona. Now he is in a position to sack any Minister he wants and the only thing I am doubtful about is whether once again he will fail to use his power.

Tuesday, October 8th

Cabinet, and of course the T.V. cameras were outside No. 10 with all the usual excitement you get when the Prime Minister announces he's off to secret talks with Smith. I went from my own office along the passage, staying inside the building to avoid the cameras, and as I came down the steps into the ante-room in came Harold, plump, round and bouncing as ever. Before I could say a word, he started 'No, I didn't do it in order to spike the Tories' guns at their Conference.[1] Why, I wanted them to have all the press they possibly could to advertise their split. I decided on this date months ago.' He was perfectly friendly and merely anxious to disabuse me of the obvious idea that for the third year running he was making news in Tory Conference week. The real truth, as William Armstrong remarked to me, was that this was the one week when the P.M. could go away without there being a major hiatus. There won't be another chance until August and it just happens to be the week of the Tory Conference as well.

Directly we sat down in Cabinet Harold began his lengthy and laboured

[1] The Conservatives met at Blackpool from October 9th to October 12th.

explanation of why he had decided on the Gibraltar talks without consulting Cabinet or O.P.D. He explained that it was best to have a working party composed of those most keenly interested and so during Conference week he had consulted Gerald Gardiner, Elwyn Jones, Fred Peart, Eddie Shackleton, Michael Stewart, George Thomson, Denis Healey and Tony Crosland. He had also got Jenkins's consent before Roy flew off to Washington. That's an interesting list of names, since every one of them was committed in advance to Harold's going if he wanted to go. It's worth noticing that at the time when this meeting was taking place there were available at Blackpool Barbara Castle, Tony Greenwood, Wedgy Benn and Jim Callaghan but none of them was asked or even briefed about the idea because all of them would have been against the journey.

This is a good example of how a Prime Minister can get his way against the clear wishes of the Cabinet and O.P.D. It is worth noticing, as William Armstrong pointed out to me, that it wouldn't have been so easy if Harold hadn't had a completely compliant Commonwealth Secretary. For instance, when Douglas Jay was President of the Board of Trade, a vital Ministry in all Common Market matters, Harold was terribly inhibited by the need to consult him throughout. George Thomson, in contrast, provided no difficulty as he's a perfectly pliable person. However Cabinet made a fair amount of fuss and Harold took a tremendous amount of trouble to ascertain our views. Every single person had to express his point of view in turn round the table. This went quite well until the P.M. asked Jim Callaghan his opinion and Jim said, 'I get a bit sick of being asked for my view when the T.V. cameras are outside and everybody knows you're going. I will wish you good luck and say no more.' I was the next to speak and said I would rather Harold didn't go because I didn't like the feeling that a British Prime Minister was having an annual stunt meeting with Smith at which I saw not the remotest chance of success. Denis Healey, I went on, had said there was a 15 per cent chance. I thought that much too high an estimate. I added that if we were to have negotiations with Smith Harold should send somebody dispensable and not somebody indispensable. Why not send George Thomson or even me, people who could be got rid of without any effect on the strength of the Cabinet? Harold took this up very quickly and said he wouldn't dream of sending anybody else. This was a Prime Ministerial problem he'd inherited and if he didn't tackle it himself he would be failing to give the necessary leadership. So he gave us a good long lecture on how Smith needed a solution much more than we did, however economic sanctions had reached their maximum, how the South Africans wanted a settlement and how there was every reason why Smith should finally come to heel.

It's my impression that this lecture didn't convince a single member of Cabinet. In fact the only result was that Harold got a practically unanimous warning that he couldn't diverge one iota beyond the *Tiger* agreement.

Thursday, October 10th

Harold is in Gibraltar and the talks are obviously bogging down, as they were bound to do. Meanwhile the Tories are settling down to a very successful Conference. I never shared Harold's view that this Conference was going to be terribly embarrassing for Heath. On the contrary Enoch Powell is a positive advantage to him and clearly the Powell threat has, as threats often do, strengthened the Leader's position and developed his personality.

Tuesday, October 15th

At Cabinet the Prime Minister reported back from Gibraltar. He had flown in yesterday and got quite a good press this morning, though I still doubted whether he had achieved very much.[1] But by this morning I was pretty clear that I had been wrong to oppose his going. By staying till Smith got sick of it and walked out he had created a situation where nobody could say that the British had not tried to make peace.

Harold was bouncy and full of energy; he had enormously enjoyed it but the new factor was his attitude to Smith. He admitted to me that their thirty hours' debate was the most exhausting experience of his life. Harold said Smith was the quickest-witted debater he had ever been up against and it was amazing that this former flight-lieutenant, with no real political background, had such ability and drive. I said to him, 'Yes, and isn't there something else amazing, Harold?' and I pointed out the article by Colin Legum in Sunday's *Observer*,[2] which asked why, after all, if Smith was a crook, the Rhodesians didn't at any rate sign on the dotted line, get their independence and then double-cross us.

'No,' Harold said. 'Quite right, Smith wouldn't do that. He wouldn't like to sign if he didn't mean to carry it out. In that sense he is basically an honest man.' It's clear that Harold has come back not despising Smith as he used to but admiring his qualities and this has made a very big difference.

Then we turned to the Queen's Speech and here you will find an interesting point in the Cabinet Minutes. Old Fred Peart said, 'This time we are trying to make the speech more readable for the Queen.' There was a hearty laugh all round, as though Fred Peart had really scored off that literary Crossman. As a matter of fact it was I who had first put this up and who had had the whole thing looked at because after last year's Queen's Speech I had learnt this from the Queen herself and had passed it on to Fred Peart. I hope it will mean that for the first time the Queen's Speech will be more than a mere rigmarole of Civil Service phraseology.

Afterwards Harold asked me to stay behind and we had a very short talk

[1] Before leaving for the talks on board H.M.S. *Fearless*, the Prime Minister had said that any agreement must include guarantees of unimpeded progress to majority rule and of a veto on any subsequent retroactive amendments to the Constitution. When the talks ended Mr Smith announced that his Cabinet in Salisbury would consider the British proposals but that 'disagreement on fundamental issues' remained.

[2] The *Observer*'s Correspondent on African Affairs.

about the situation. He simply said, 'Look, this may be a very great disappointment to you but I am afraid you are not going to be able to keep Judith. I shall want her in the Cabinet.' I said immediately, 'I've always told Judith that if she is to get into the Cabinet she will have to leave me. That's absolutely clear but it's a great loss.' 'Yes,' he said, 'but doesn't that mean that you will need to keep Kenneth Robinson?' 'I'm afraid I can't,' I said, 'because I don't think he'll stay under me but I will have a try. The important thing, Harold, is to see that he gets another job and, as I told you before, he ought to take Niall MacDermot's place.'[1] 'Yes,' said Harold, 'but I don't want these changes to be a Cabinet reshuffle. I want to close them off and just deal with the two mergers, with no other changes until I have had time to reflect. I haven't had time because of the Rhodesian talks.' 'Well,' I said, 'shall I go back to Kenneth straightaway and ask him to consider whether if Judith goes he will now stay or whether he will go and, if so, would he take Niall MacDermot's place?' I was given the authority to do it that way.

I rushed back to my room and immediately assumed that the decision must have been taken to sack Willie Ross and put Judith in for Scotland, because there didn't seem to be any other possible place. So I got hold of Kenneth Robinson and he came rattling round. He is a curious man. Once again he had been desperately hoping for a place in Cabinet. He had been told there was no chance but that makes no difference to Kenneth. He said to me, 'I'm a fighter, you know.' But he is not a fighter, he hangs on in the hope of something turning up. I said, 'It's not for you,' and I made it worse by saying, 'Judith is going to the Cabinet so you will be the only person here. Will you stay and work with me?' Fortunately we had the sense to say to each other that it wouldn't work because the doctors would be coming to him behind my back, which wouldn't be fair on either of us. 'In that case,' I said, 'why not take Niall MacDermot's job?' 'That's a step down, a mere Minister of State,' he said. 'On the contrary, Niall has been virtually running the Ministry of Housing. Poor old Tony can't do without him unless he gets a substitute. You would be infinitely better, my dear Kenneth, than anyone I could possibly imagine,' and then, warming to it, I said, 'and also you would get the responsibility for the Maud Commission and we could increase the salary and make it a special responsibility.' 'Ah,' he said, 'with a different title?'[2] 'Yes, a different title,' I said. 'Now please go away and think about it and talk to the P.M. Please do, because you will make all the difference.'

At 3.30 Harold made his Statement on Rhodesia. It was a triumph. I think this is the first time since devaluation that the P.M. has carried both sides of the Commons with him. This afternoon he convinced the Tories that he had

---

[1] Labour M.P. for Lewisham North February 1957–9 and for Derby 1962–70. He was Financial Secretary to the Treasury 1964–7 and Minister of State at M.H.L.G. 1967–8, and since 1970 has been Secretary-General of the International Commission of Jurists.
[2] He became Minister of Planning and Land.

been prime ministerial, that he had done an honest job and had genuinely tried to do what they asked him, while on our side there was the sense that there had not been a sell-out. The sense was still strong because people hadn't had time to study the terms and because they were themselves moved by the mood of the House.

Then I had to give the news to Judith. She swallowed a bit, because she had become unpopular in Scotland when she replaced Peggy Herbison at Social Security and now she realized that she would be unpopular because she is English. Yet of course she wanted to be in the Cabinet and here was the offer. Poor girl, she didn't sleep all night because with the best of faith I had given her the wrong information.

Wednesday, October 16th

This afternoon Judith came up and said, 'You were wrong. I can't tell you what it is.' She had just heard from Harold what she had been offered. In the evening Anne came up for dinner. We had to stay in the House as it was a three-line whip on the Lords' amendments to the Transport Bill and we were dining together at one table and Judith and her Tony at another near by. She was happy and gay because she had got her Cabinet job and Tony was delighted. Afterwards we had drinks with them. Everybody was curious about Judith's job. I racked my brains, I couldn't see what it could be and didn't guess that Harold was going to make her a female George Wigg and put her into his old room at No. 10 as Paymaster-General.

Thursday, October 17th

The announcement of the mergers had an excellent press. Michael Stewart and I received a great deal of attention and it had been a good day for the Government.

At Cabinet we got Lords' reform through in eight minutes, the tactic and the whole White Paper. It was curious, a whole elaborate piece of reform agreed when they have never really read it. It's something that happens in our Labour Cabinet. I had been reflecting on how to handle all this and when I talked at length to Eddie Shackleton we agreed that Callaghan must be brought in to take over the Bill. At the meeting of the Cabinet Committee on Lords' reform where the White Paper was presented, Jim had been in a dangerous mood, saying it wasn't popular enough and that we must now angle it towards our own supporters and not go on praising the House of Lords. So we had deleted a great many passages mentioning qualities the House of Lords possesses. I have been fascinated by the absolute arrogance of our Commons Members, led by Jim, who say about the Lords, 'They've got no more distinction than the House of Commons.' The fact is that the Commons is an absurd place. But no one ever goes up from the Commons to the Lords to see what is going on there and M.P.s feel it is a place they have to retire to and are insulted when someone suggests that it has any merits. On this I really am a minority in Cabinet. Carrington said ages ago and Gardiner said again today, 'You are the only member of the House of Commons, Dick, who has seen enough of us to appreciate us.' And I think they are right.

Thursday, October 24th

At Cabinet we had Gerald Gardiner making a great protest on Biafra. As usual he was completely ineffective and was quietly demolished by the Foreign Secretary and George Thomson, the old Commonwealth Secretary, who said, 'Look, every African State is with us. They are supporting Nigeria against Biafra.[1] Don't be so ridiculous.' Then we had the P.M. on Vietnam,[2] which had been raised, I think, by Barbara, with pleas that we should change our policy. The Prime Minister and George Brown had decided long ago to play their role as mediators for peace and standing close to the Americans is the price. I am convinced that this is the central issue. The P.M. passionately thinks we have been effective and can still be important. Denis Healey and I feel we really can't play any part in peace-making precisely because we have not been able to denounce the Americans. Denis put it very clearly. He would like to see us behaving more like Europeans, more like the Germans, and we should dispense with postures of this sort. This is the opposite of what people like Barbara, Peter Shore and Tony Benn want. They all believe that this country still can be great, and they don't see that if we are going to cease to be a great power and withdraw from East of Suez and go into Europe then the peculiar Anglo-Saxon lecturing will have to go.

Back to my room for a quick plate of meat, and then I had to rush round to the House of Commons to see Ted Heath. There I found Reggie Maudling, who had just come from the Escargot, where he had eaten a great many snails and said he smelt of garlic. What he smelt of was having had too much to drink for lunch. He was unable to follow what we were saying, but Ted Heath was very dignified and statesmanlike. I delivered the message, gave him a copy of the White Paper and left.

After P.M.'s Questions I had to make my little speech on the Merger Order and then sit through two hours of debate. It seemed interminable. I wound up with a pleasant little reply and my new Private Secretary, Ron Matthews, an extremely efficient young man, who was watching me with great care, turned and said to Paul Odgers who was in the box with him, 'By jove, he is surprisingly relaxed, your fellow.' It's true that compared with the

---

[1] As the Nigerian civil war continued the eastern state of Biafra sought diplomatic recognition. Only four states, Gabon, Ivory Coast, Tanzania and Zambia, were prepared to grant this.

[2] On March 31st President Johnson had announced that the bombing of North Vietnam would be limited and in May the Americans and the North Vietnamese had their first talks in Paris. It seemed that some understanding was reached and from November 1st the bombing of North Vietnam was completely halted, although the war between North and South continued.

tightly buttoned attitude of Kenneth Robinson my general method of informality and candour is quite different.

Friday, October 25th

I was up at 8.0 to breakfast in the House of Lords with Eddie and Michael Wheeler-Booth. They had the draft letter to Heath confirming our conversation yesterday and at 10.30 I had to go into the Prorogation with the P.M. to talk to him about it. I found him in his room with Fred Peart. In the Commons Fred and I, the two atheists, stood for prayers on the Government side and then the House filled up a bit while we waited for the Lords to finish. We had the usual performance, the march across to the Lords, standing, hearing the interminable list of all the Acts which have been passed. Second came the Transport Act. I said 'Hear, hear,' and the P.M. looked round, shocked because for him it was the middle of divine service. He looked the most respectable man, standing there with his head in the air, in his black coat with his grey hair. He was due to go to Princess Marina's memorial service and enjoy that as well. Oh, dear, I really am an irreverent, independent old boy compared with our Establishment Prime Minister.

Tuesday, October 29th

Cabinet. The first thing was to congratulate Jim Callaghan on what had happened on Sunday.[1] There had been weeks of build-up for the great revolutionary demonstration, the march through Trafalgar Square and along the Embankment, with the Trotskyists and revolutionaries intending to break off and rush to Grosvenor Square for a confrontation. Five thousand or so turned up and the police held successfully. Callaghan was there to congratulate them afterwards. Jim's real strength was that he wasn't rattled and that he took police advice not to have troops in readiness. There were American Marines inside the Embassy but no troops of ours. He deserved our congratulations because he would have got all the curses if after all the demonstration had turned violent. No doubt it has added even more to his strength, building him up as the only alternative to Harold Wilson.

After this we had a sudden announcement by the Prime Minister that the Chancellor had a surprise statement to make. He wanted to add just a touch of the whip and impose higher hire-purchase terms on cars and certain other things. We had a long discussion. One or two of us, I particularly, made the point that it does seem very puzzling that if before the Budget we can only do one thing it should be this minor thing. What are we to do if it doesn't work? Roy immediately replied, 'No, I must make it clear. It is not one thing only. If this doesn't work more will be in store.' That, from my point of view, settled it for me.

[1] Some 30,000 people took part in what was largely an unprovocative march, ending with a rally in Hyde Park. The 5,000 who filled Grosvenor Square spent five hours trying to storm the American Embassy but they were firmly and calmly restrained by the police.

This afternoon I got an urgent message that Eddie Shackleton and I were to see Heath after the Shadow Cabinet had met and discussed Lords' reform. Eddie came over to talk to me beforehand. We were both very gloomy and felt sure the Tories would now take the opportunity of using the constitutional commission[1] to postpone House of Lords' reform. We went along to the Leader of the Opposition's room and stood outside his little office where we used to stand waiting for Gaitskell and subsequently, and even more, waiting for Harold Wilson, chatted with the girls and thought how crowded and mean it was. Then we were in with Peter Carrington and Ted Heath. Heath gave me a very reasonable letter which went much further than I expected. He said the Tories agree in principle that they would like to have talks about the conventions for the new House. It looked therefore as though he was clearly saying to us that if we could get the Bill through the Tories would operate it. That seemed to me encouraging and I went away quite excited. I rushed across to No. 10 where Harold was having the annual party for all the Ministers who had come to hear the contents of the Queen's Speech. I got in first and told him what had happened. He said, 'We must publish the Lords' White Paper on Friday and you must get the whole thing done in time. There will be a leak if we don't and there have been enough leaks in Nora Beloff's *Observer* column already.' We had hoped to have three days to deal with the amendments which Ted Heath and the Liberals wanted but Harold said no, so now I am busy on this.

Wednesday, October 30th

Queen's Speech day was wet and spongy with pools of water. I remembered all the fuss and bother I had last year as Lord President. Now I am free of all this so I spent the morning with Michael Wheeler-Booth tidying up the White Paper. I also had to write a little party political broadcast on the Queen's Speech for radio this evening. This took me most of the morning until I drove off to lunch with the B.M.A. at their magnificent place in Russell Square.

Molly,[2] by the way, is leaving me. I have had her for four years and we get each other down. I now have a new kind of Austin which she hates. However I am getting a new driver now, a man, who will be at Paddington when I arrive on Monday morning. A driver is important to a Minister because he is the person with whom you are together more than anyone, except perhaps your Private Secretary. Somebody once said in a very biting leading article that Harold Wilson can't nominate peers because the only person he knows intimately is his driver. There is something in this. You do get to know him or her extremely well and you chat together. Well, Molly couldn't love me, compared with Keith Joseph whom she could mother. I was rough and I

---

[1] On devolution.
[2] Molly Crawford had been Crossman's official driver since he was appointed Minister of Housing and Local Government in October 1964.

shocked her in almost every way because of my attitude to royalty, to the
Privy Council, and so on. I am only relieved that the change has taken place
with the change of office, although for all I know the young man may actually
be unbearable.*

This evening the phone rang and the Prime Minister said, 'This is really
urgent. Would you come over straightaway?' I trotted round to find him
sitting in his study with Roy Jenkins. Mr Short had resigned. He had sent a
letter saying that the Prime Minister must make some sense of the education
cuts that he had been asked to accept. If the Chancellor insisted on the £10
million increase in further education fees Mr Short would go. The P.M. said,
'This is really serious. It could be disastrous for the Government.' It was true.
Ted Short, an ex-Chief Whip from the centre-right of the Party—if he
resigned and spilt the beans on the educational cuts it could create a kind of
Bevanite revolt. I saw this immediately. The Chancellor on the other hand
wasn't willing to give an inch, so I said to the P.M., 'Look, it's quite simple.
The first thing to do is play it off. Thank your lucky stars for what we did
about the rate support grant. We needn't have all these announcements of
cuts and we can postpone the issue. Play it out, Roy. You can still get your
cuts but at least let us stop him resigning this week. The reason he has given
for resigning now is that he is compelled to make a Statement announcing
the £10 million increase on Thursday evening, the day before he goes off two
days in the North. You defuse this by merely saying, "You needn't make a
Statement".' 'Is that really true?' asked the Prime Minister and Roy was very
dubious. Finally we agreed to meet at 10 p.m. and that I should bring
Matthew Stevenson with me for a proper discussion. Roy couldn't possibly
be there so we would have Fred Peart instead.

I went back again with Matthew Stevenson. Ted Short was there and we
spent till 12.30 a.m. convincing him, not with drink because he is a tee-
totaller. What did I give him in exchange? I first got Steve to say, as head of
the negotiators for the rate support grant, that they didn't need the
announcement and indeed it would be slightly convenient for them not to
have it. Steve loyally supported everything I said because I had had a long
discussion with him beforehand, cleared it up and got it in writing. He
couldn't have been better on this occasion. He was in on high politics and
excited that he was doing it well. We gave this to Ted Short, who swallowed it
hook, line and sinker. Fred Peart said to me later, 'He wasn't going to resign,
it was all bluff.' Bluff or not, it took two and a half hours of the Prime
Minister, Fred and I, steadily drinking whisky, as Mr Short sat silent but got
more and more human. That was Wednesday evening and I think the job was
done decently and well.

* As a last request, by the way, I asked Molly to buy a bottle of the bay rum lotion for my
hair. This lotion is nice and cheap and old-fashioned and I can only get it from a shop in St
James's Street. She gave it to the Private Office to put in the box, though I didn't want it
down here at Prescote but up in London. It smashed, rather as if it was a farewell time-
bomb.

Thursday, October 31st

This was the day I took over my new office, the day Kenneth Robinson went to Housing and Judith to the Paymaster's Office and I became Minister in charge at the Elephant and Castle.

Saturday, November 2nd

Here I am, Secretary of State for Social Services, and the terrible problem has been what to call me. S.S.S.S.? Impossible! So in Cabinet they are now saying Social Secretary, which has a slightly comic ring and was invented by old Jim Callaghan. This use of titles still goes on in Cabinet and, though it has its convenience, with so many Secretaries of State and so many odd titles it is getting more and more difficult. I noticed another small thing when the boxes came down this morning. True, the hair lotion had smashed in one of them and had covered all the Cabinet papers with a wonderful scent of bay rum, but the boxes were very fine. The civil servants had been determined that on the first day as the new S.S. for S.S. I should have brand new boxes with a beautiful new gold name across them. This is what they adore. To do them justice, all this weekend they are working away on the transfer of my files from the Privy Council to the Elephant and Castle. The danger is that out there in exile I might become detached unless I very consciously try to make good the deficiency. I have lost my nearness to Burke Trend, being able to ring him up at a moment's notice and go round, and the nearness to the P.M. I must struggle and the civil servants have been struggling. In Ron Matthews I have obviously got a really conscientious nice, efficient man, who will establish continuity and is obviously going to be a first-rate Private Secretary. My staff are dividing up but Janet Newman is heroically coming with me into exile. I am leaving Paul Odgers behind in my co-ordinating office in Fred Peart's old rooms, quite a decent office where I shall have to go after the Cabinet and where I shall have to be a great deal. One of my difficulties will be to spend sufficient time over at Elephant and Castle.

Monday, November 4th

Today we took over Alexander Fleming House, the great skyscraper at the Elephant and Castle. I have a long room in a suite of offices on the seventh floor with magnificent but not very pretty views of modern skyscrapers. Still, it is exhilarating up there and when the door from my Private Office is shut and I sit alone I am totally insulated. That's the first thing I notice. I'm not in an ivory tower but a steel tower miles away from Westminster and Whitehall, with double glazing to give a sense of absolute silence, so far up above the world that nothing seems to be relating to me. I got there this morning at the right time, 9.30. I was photographed coming in with David Ennals and Stephen Swingler,[1] and the B.B.C. interviewed me for 'The World At One'. Then I had to get across to the other side of the river for a big

[1] Crossman's two Ministers of State at the D.H.S.S.

S.E.P. meeting to ratify last week's decisions on the rate support grant. Ted Short is to be permitted to submit a paper to Cabinet on the crisis in education and it will come to our Social Services Committee in a fortnight or so. I am very doubtful whether we can do anything about it and whether by playing for time we can prevent his resignation.

Wednesday, November 13th
This morning at 11.30 we had the big debate at the Party Meeting to discuss the White Paper on Lords' reform. We had agreed in Cabinet that Callaghan should start and I should wind up and we should reverse the order when we debated the White Paper on the Floor of the House. We published the White Paper twelve days ago and it was striking how little had happened.[1] Eddie and I had worked hard with the press but there had been no flurry of excitement or any real stirring of indignation from our own back benchers. The whole thing had fallen flat, thank God, in the sense that people had remarkably felt resigned acquiescence.

The White Paper recommended a two-tier system of voting peers, with a right to speak and vote, and non-voting peers with a right to speak. Succession to a hereditary peerage should no longer carry the right to a seat in the House of Lords but existing peers by succession should have the right to sit as non-voting peers for their lifetime. Voting peers would be exclusively created peers but some peers by succession would be created life peers. The voting House would initially consist of about 230 peers, distributed between the parties in a way which would give the Government a small majority (of some 10 per cent) over the Opposition parties but not a majority of the House as a whole when those without party allegiance were included. All serving Law Lords, the Archbishops of Canterbury and York and the Bishops of London, Durham and Winchester would continue as ex-officio *voting peers: the remaining 21 bishops would be re-appointed members of the House on the basis of one new bishop to every two retirements until the number was reduced to 16. Voting peers would be required to attend at least one-third of the sittings of the House, they would be paid some remuneration and would be subject to an age of retirement (of seventy-five during the transitional period until the new Parliament, thereafter of seventy-two). A committee with a chairman of 'national standing' would be established to review periodically the composition of the reformed House.*

The reformed House should be able to impose a six-month delay, which should be capable of running into a new session or a new Parliament, on the passage of an ordinary public Bill sent up from the Commons and it should then be possible to submit the Bill for Royal Assent, provided that a Resolution to that effect had been passed in the Commons. The reformed House should be able to require the Commons to reconsider an Affirmative Order or

[1] *House of Lords Reform*, Cmnd 3799.

to consider a Negative Order but the power of final rejection should be removed. All peers should in future be qualified to vote in Parliamentary elections.

What was to happen when the Party got together? When we started about thirty-five people were there, over half of them members of the Lords. It had grown to about eighty by the time I got up to speak at 12.30. First of all Jim made a very careful, friendly, deliberately muffled speech, saying, 'I'm not an expert on this at all. Dick must take all the credit for it.' He was followed by Manny Shinwell at his most wild, saying it was dreary rubbish and that the least we must go for is abolishing all peerages by succession and then Michael Foot whipped himself up. The striking thing was that the opponents, and nearly all of them were opponents, were oldish people, Charlie Pannell, Michael Foot, Manny Shinwell, Willie Hamilton. After nine speeches I had to reply. I managed to explain how the Party had given us our instructions to go in and get the terms, the advantage of getting an agreed solution passed in this Parliament if we could, and the importance of Macleod's denial of our right to bring in the reformed House in this Parliament. It went pretty well, but Douglas Houghton showed that he has now got into a very nasty mood. As Fred Peart said, 'He's a maverick, you know. He's gone wild now and is against us on everything.' So we've got the Chairman of the P.L.P. agin the Government.

Monday, November 18th
This afternoon I settled down to prepare my speech on Lords' reform. It was a great problem to know how to introduce the White Paper. I know it is going to be difficult with our own side but I can't anticipate how difficult it will be with the Tories. I worked away with Janet and Ron Matthews and the invaluable Michael Wheeler-Booth and David Faulkner, who rallied round, as they have done with all the other speeches. We sweated away again after supper in 70 Whitehall until 11.30 or so, when I sent them all home.

Tuesday, November 19th
In the morning we tidied up the speech ready for 3.30. First there were P.M.'s Questions, then a Statement by Willie Ross about a warehouse in Glasgow which caught fire yesterday and caused twenty-two deaths, a ghastly thing. The Scots wallowed in it and it was also bad for me because all the Scots then left and I began in an empty Chamber.* After this awkwardness I got going. I had cut out about a fifth of our final draft and, looking

* The Commons' debate on the White Paper took place over two whole days, November 19th and 20th, with three whole days in the Lords, and during that period Tam and I counted pretty carefully. There were never more than 70 people in the House. I had 70 when I sat down and after that there were usually 30 or 40. Of our back benchers about 40 attended some part of the first debate, so I reckoned that we were lucky if 150 M.P.s out of the 630 heard anything of the debate before coming in and voting.

back, I delivered it too fast and too self-confidently. My greatest mistake was that when I was interrupted, which was a great deal, I replied cleverly, intellectually, superiorly, and the more I was questioned from behind the more clearly I showed what fools they were to put things to me in that way. So, though the back benchers didn't dislike me, by the end I had done nothing whatsoever to persuade them. What I hadn't realized was the inferiority complex, the deep suspicion that if at the other end of the passage on those red carpets we set up a nominated House of Lords with a real, nice, tidy, neat job at £2,000 a year, it would be far more attractive to be a peer than to be a commoner, sitting on the green benches.[1] M.P.s cannot tolerate the idea of giving the Lords a sensible job in the best club in the world. There really is something in this.

I felt this very strongly when I went along to the Lords and sat on the steps of the Throne and had a drink with Eddie in their bar, a magnificent room, a club room. It was frankly a far more civilized, clubby atmosphere. I must admit that though people laugh and say 'Lord Crossman of Banbury' there is a great deal of truth in it because I would be wholly at home in the reformed House of Lords I have been creating, and I think back benchers have a point when they feel that we on the front bench are creating a better hole for ourselves.

Wednesday, November 20th
The debate continued and Elwyn Jones, who had exactly the same brief, couldn't have been more different from me, in the canoodling, soft, diffident way he pressed things, just as Macleod, who came after him, couldn't have been more different from Maudling, who had followed me with a kind of bumbling. Maudling wasn't actually letting us down yesterday or failing to admit his own and the Tories' support for the scheme, but he didn't really commit his party in any clear way. Macleod, on the other hand, today committed himself fully and resolutely to the scheme, differing only about the timing. Then the back benchers resumed their emotional, ribald attack on the front-bench mafia, as they called us, who were putting over this iniquitous extension of prime ministerial power.

There were two other reasons why we had peculiar difficulties in this debate. First was the astonishing fact that, though the two front benches had agreed to have a two-day debate, 'taking note of the White Paper', i.e. without a division, at the last minute the Speaker permitted Willie Hamilton to move an amendment to reject the White Paper. It suddenly meant that instead of my introducing a general discussion on the reform the debate became quite a different thing, a defence of the reform against back benchers who would organize all their effort to get an adverse vote. This

[1] At the junction of the corridors of the House of Commons and the House of Lords the colour of the carpets changes from green to red. The benches in the Commons Chamber are of green plush and in the Lords red.

meant that the speeches were much more ferocious and violent, and as Bagehot says in *The English Constitution*, debates are a waste of time unless they end in a decision. My God, this debate became different, full of edge and passion, precisely because suddenly and unexpectedly we were to have a vote. As it turned out we managed to win by a substantial majority, with only 47 of our people against us and 40 abstentions. We had most of the Tories against us in the lobbies. Nevertheless, the Speaker's obvious prejudice against the scheme (I believe that is true) did have a deep effect on the debate. The other factor, of course, was the international economic situation. People were saying, 'What the hell are we doing discussing the House of Lords when the whole international monetary system is breaking up, with the Chancellor of the Exchequer flying to Bonn to try and patch up the pieces?' That told against us a good deal.

Speculation against the franc and £ continued and on November 19th Western Finance Ministers were asked to attend a hastily convened meeting in Bonn on the following day. Although the Prime Minister and the Chancellor felt that to call such a meeting was unwise and would lead to further loss of confidence they agreed that the Chancellor should attend. Meanwhile the German Ambassador was asked to come to Downing Street, where the Prime Minister, the Chancellor and the Foreign Secretary explained the British Government's distress at the creation of further uncertainty and the hope that the Germans would now revalue the Mark, an episode that considerably upset the German government. The Chancellor of the Exchequer returned to London from Bonn on November 22nd, in time to see the P.M. and show him the draft of a Statement to be made to the Commons before the Friday adjournment at 4.30 p.m. Mr Jenkins's emergency Statement was intended both to reinforce sterling against speculation and to dampen internal demand. The measures were designed to raise an additional £250 million a year in taxation. Indirect taxes were raised by 5d. on a gallon of petrol, 5d. on a packet of twenty cigarettes and 4s. on a bottle of spirits. All rates of purchase tax were increased by 10 per cent, bank credits were to be severely restricted and a new scheme of import deposits was introduced, requiring traders to deposit for six months 50 per cent of the value of a large number of imports before the goods were released by Customs.

Thursday, November 21st
The whole House of Lords issue, has been submerged by the economic crisis and by the usual press rumours of a new Jenkins squeeze. We had been expecting a Cabinet but instead a Parliamentary Committee was called, as Harold had told me yesterday, to deal with the squeeze proposals in a smaller, more leak-proof group than full Cabinet.

Roy was in Bonn and the P.M. explained that we were going to have import deposits. That was all right, nobody contradicted. Then there was to be a credit squeeze, bank credit tightening, all that. Then there came—yes—the full 10 per cent of the regulator, including purchase tax on cars and consumer durables. Discussion centred almost entirely on this last point, because Wedgy Benn and I heard it for the first time and Barbara was against the whole thing. It was too restrictionist, too anti-expansionist, and, after all, it is only three weeks since we announced hire-purchase restrictions to hit the car industry. I said that what bewildered me was that three weeks ago we had asked if it was really wise just to have hire-purchase increases. Why, I asked, should we suddenly do this now? The answer was that we had to make a presentational case to the world. It was clear that the aim was to use this opportunity to make our necessary changes on the home front and cover them up with the international crisis. Jenkins had in fact been thinking of these measures before the Bonn meeting.

Friday, November 22nd

At 9.0 o'clock we met again in the P.M.'s room at the House of Commons, not in No. 10 because that creates so much notice. Cabinets in the P.M.'s room in the House are nearly always failures. It's a bad shape, there's not enough room round the table and somehow it inhibits, cramps. We crouch there not as Cabinet Ministers but more like American Cabinets, more hopeless and impotent. We had an interminable four-hour meeting, from 9.0 till 1.0 since we met in Parliamentary Committee first and then in Cabinet. This morning there was still no communiqué and when at last a telegram came from Roy describing what was happening, this was the first intimation Cabinet had received since he left for Bonn yesterday. He had been carrying on on his own without any briefing or any consultation, trying to force the hand of his colleagues.

When Cabinet joined us at 9.45 we went on with a great attack about briefing. We knew nothing except what was in the newspapers but they contained everything about the international conference. We heard that Roy had been bitterly complaining about the Germans. 'Well,' said Jim, 'the briefer outbriefed.' He said it *sotto voce* but the whole Cabinet laughed grimly, because we also suspected that all last week Roy had been briefing the British press in order to bounce the Cabinet.

Perhaps the most remarkable thing was that when we asked about the details and machinery of the import deposits scheme no one knew. Tony Crosland was in Vienna, the P.M. didn't know, neither did Jack Diamond nor Barbara. The inner group of six who had prepared the package didn't know what goods were covered by the scheme. Three-quarters of an hour later a note was brought into the room and we learnt that the list of goods would be the same for the import deposits as it was for the import surcharge,[1]

[1] An import surcharge of 15 per cent had been announced on October 26th, 1964. It was reduced to 10 per cent on April 27th and finally abolished on November 30th, 1966. The exceptions to the import deposit scheme were to be on basic foods, feeding stuffs, fuel and raw

with two or three minor exceptions. I threw a note across the table to Jim saying that if they are going to have these crises (this is the seventh time, I think, we've sat around impotently discussing a plan with the three or four people who have known of it beforehand but couldn't answer our criticisms effectively because they knew none of the facts), if they are going to consult Cabinet at the last moment like this, the only possible way to make sense of it is for us to bring along our senior civil servants so that we have some departmental expertise, and to have people from the Treasury and the Inland Revenue too, so that politicians don't discuss these things and make last-minute decisions in almost total ignorance. It is fantastic that in this particular case there was no bit of paper giving the package or the reasons for it. It was all told us verbally and we have serious doubts whether a clear-cut plan had ever been worked out. The most depressing fact about the whole of yesterday's and today's meetings was that there has been no change from the original 1965 July meeting, the 1966 meeting or the 1967 devaluation meeting. All the way through we have had the same phenomenon of a small group suddenly saying to Cabinet, 'This is it. Take it or leave it. It's too late to do anything else.' If a Cabinet meeting is based on adequate paper preparation the absence of the Departmental civil servants may be defended but where Cabinet works without papers the absence of officials is devastating because it leads to the most appalling mistakes.

Thursday, December 5th
We had two subjects of excitement at Cabinet, first Biafra and then the House of Lords. I have been reluctantly supporting the Government in its policy of support for the Federal Government of Nigeria. We did not cancel the supply of arms to the Federal Government but we have unsuccessfully tried to make peace between them and Biafra. Now we are being blamed because there is a danger of mass starvation in what is left of Biafra, which the French are supplying with arms. It is clear that we have utterly failed in our attempt to put over to the British public the fact that the Russians are supplying arms to the Federal Government and the French to the Biafrans. The Gallup Poll shows that 70–80 per cent of the public are in favour of our sending help to Biafra, an emotional but intelligible view. However Cabinet did revolt on this. A lot of people felt that we can't go on like this. We've got 150 people filing a resolution and if we have a debate in the House we will be defeated. As I said, we may have to face it that unless Harold can get what he hoped for, ourselves, the French and the Russians all working together to stop the supply of arms, it is probably impossible to stop the war. We ourselves might have to take the initiative in giving up the sale of arms.

_____

materials and some categories of goods, largely imported from developing countries. The scheme would therefore apply to about a third of Britain's total imports, worth some £3,000 million a year.

Frankly, I said, this is something we have to do for public opinion, though in a sense there is no justification for it.

Then we turned to the House of Lords. I was aware that there was no enthusiasm in Cabinet for this and I wasn't expecting an easy time. I was also aware that Harold Wilson had been nearly persuaded by the Chief Whip not merely to defer consideration of the Bill but to drop it. On the other hand, I was confident that Harold would be very reluctant to drop a Bill which was in his election manifesto and to which he had committed himself anew last June, in a statement that he was going to push the Bill through. How did it go? The Lord Chancellor was asked to begin and he did it very badly. He started by taking two dreary secondary issues, of Scottish peers and their rights under the Act of Union of 1707, and then remuneration. I knew how dicey this second one was and I thought the best thing was to say we would set up Committees to consider the remuneration of both Houses in the next Parliament. Harold and the Chancellor would have none of this, the increase of M.P.'s salaries could not be mentioned, so very reluctantly I agreed that the only thing to do was to maintain for the time being the present system of $4\frac{1}{2}$ guineas expenses.[1] Then we found, ironically, that the people most against Lords' reform, Willie Ross, Jim Callaghan, Tony Crosland, said that they wouldn't take this, it was very unjust. However we got it through but Cabinet was already in a thoroughly bad mood for the third point, the timing of the Second Reading. The Lord Chancellor said he wanted it before Christmas and then Callaghan said, 'Before we do anything about this, I think we ought to abandon the Bill altogether.' He then launched into a fantastic, wild, flailing attack on the whole concept of Lords' reform and of the two-tier House. He said it was nonsense, that we should break down with attacks from the right and the left, that it was a hopeless, silly, futile reform which he had gone along with but, as he had made clear all the way through, this was what he really felt. I have never heard such an outburst. Callaghan was hysterical once or twice before, as Chancellor, when he was overpowered, and Harold has always told me how he does break down and his whole funkiness comes out. I am sure he is overwrought by the tremendously heavy burden of legislation in the last five or six weeks when three or four of his Bills have been going through the House. Actually he gave it to us. We would never have got the firm decision to go ahead with the Bill if it hadn't been for this embarrassing outburst. Fred Peart came in and though, as I know very well, he doesn't like this Bill and has never liked it, he is a man of honour and as Leader of the House he stood by it. He roundly turned on Callaghan and said it was quite untrue, the Home Secretary had never disclosed this kind of attitude before. However as we went round Cabinet it was clear that there

[1] Payment of travelling expenses depended on frequency of attendance, but after 1957 peers were entitled to claim, in addition, for every day that they attended the House, reimbursement of up to 3 guineas a day, untaxed. In November 1964 this sum was raised to $4\frac{1}{2}$ guineas a day and in December 1969 to £6 10s.

was no support for this measure. Tony Crosland didn't want the Bill and I can't think of anybody there who did, except for Peter Shore, the P.M., the Lord Chancellor, Shackleton, myself, Peart now and of course Tony Wedgwood Benn, who also said we couldn't go back on it. Michael Stewart was away. Most of the others reluctantly said that they detested the Bill as a difficult nuisance but they didn't see how we could go back on it. Fred Peart and I made the most of the point that a Government which abandoned a Bill of this sort when there were only 47 left-wingers against it, fewer than were against Prices and Incomes, would find it very difficult to rally the Party to other things. So we decided to publish the Bill before Christmas, and have a Second Reading in January.[1] The fight has been won for the time being.

Tuesday, December 17th
At Cabinet a most illuminating little altercation occurred between the Prime Minister and Michael Stewart. The P.M. said across the table, 'I hope you won't forbid me to send a Christmas card to the Russian Ambassador,' and Michael Stewart said, 'It's a personal decision. I should send one but I have decided not to this year.' This is fascinating because here is a man with a clear, rational mind who can see as clearly as anybody I know the issues involved and, in particular, the principles involved in a course of action, yet, when it comes to the point, the action Michael Stewart takes never seems to match up to the principles he enunciated before he took it. The Prime Minister obviously felt peeved because he hadn't been told about Michael's decision and felt himself half bound by it. The rest of the Cabinet exploded and there was raucous laughter from Dick Marsh at the other end of the table. 'Quite right,' everybody said. 'If you were deciding to send Christmas cards for the first time that's one thing but if you are going to make it a decision not to send them this year as a mark of your disapproval it's absolutely ridiculous.'

Wednesday, December 18th
O.P.D. I couldn't help remembering yesterday's little scene about the Christmas card when an infinitely more important issue came up, what we should do about the strategic embargo on Soviet goods in the light of the invasion of Czechoslovakia last August. There has been every kind of pressure from the Prime Minister and Tony Wedgwood Benn that though we should register our disapproval of the invasion of Czechoslovakia it should not be allowed to affect our economic connections or our trade. For Tony Wedgwood Benn trade, in this instance, means selling computers to Eastern Europe. For months there has been an argument about this behind the scenes between us and the Americans. There has also been tension between MinTech and the Ministry of Defence. After the invasion of Prague the one

---

[1] In fact the Second Reading did not take place until February 3rd, 1969.

thing we can't do is to loosen the embargo and Denis Healey has been against our pressing to relax it.

I went to the meeting today determined to raise all this but in fact we heard an agreed statement from the Foreign Secretary announcing that MinTech has surrendered. It all seemed to me characteristic of our Cabinet and, probably, of all British Governments. We sedulously avoid drawing any conclusions about the Russian invasion of Prague. Why do we not face the consequences for our future foreign policy? Partly for the reason I have given, partly because we desperately want trade, partly because Harold still feels himself to be an essential link between Washington and Moscow. For four years he pretended to himself that he was an important mediator in the Vietnam discussions and now he feels the same about this. He says all the time that we mustn't lead the way in making anti-Russian noises and he wants a special position both in the White House and in the Kremlin. Here lies the whole idiocy of the Christmas card episode. If Harold is working for that special position it is quite illogical and irrational to use such pin-pricking tactics as refusing to send Christmas cards. If on the other hand he feels so strongly that he must withdraw his card, he really can't be in a minority of one in the West trying to urge what would be virtually the end of the British strategic embargo against the U.S.S.R. I record all this in some detail because it seems to me an extremely interesting example of the total ineffectiveness of Michael Stewart as Foreign Secretary and of the extent to which Harold Wilson's so-called foreign policy is based on his image of himself as a maker of world policy.

Monday, December 23rd

The children went off to the pantomime and I did my Christmas shopping, looking after presents for Peter Smithson, my new driver, Janet and Anne. At 4.30 I went along to Downing Street and found Harold in his study, comfortable and easy, a little careful with me. I filled him in on the difficulties of reorganizing my Ministry. I said I was rather remote now, something that had been brought home to me on Thursday when Gerald Gardiner had said that he had to go off to No. 10 for talks about the Donovan Report and assumed that I was coming too.[1] I must say I had expected to be on the inner group which decided that, but I'm not. Harold told me a little, rather reluctantly, about Barbara's White Paper and how it had been decided, in one meeting, to put it on the Cabinet agenda a fortnight before mine.[2]

I got a little bit of talk about the Cabinet and the future of George Thomson, who, poor man, has been chucked out because Michael Stewart

---

[1] The Donovan Report was published on June 13th.

[2] The First Secretary's proposals for the reform of industrial relations were to be set out in the White Paper *In Place of Strife* (Cmnd 3888), published on January 17th, 1969. Crossman's White Paper, *National Superannuation and Social Insurance, Proposals for Earnings-Related Social Security* (Cmnd 3883), was published on January 28th, 1969.

insisted on it.[1] Diplomacy was the one area where he was first-rate, he was the perfect Commonwealth Secretary and now there he is sitting in Cabinet at £8,500 a year with absolutely nothing to do. Harold said, 'He might be given something in a reshuffle but would he be any good on the home front?' 'Why not make him Home Secretary?' I said, and Harold looked at me and said, 'That's a job I can't take away from Mr Callaghan at the moment.' I was assured that there would not be a shuffle until after the Commonwealth Prime Ministers' Conference, which is absorbing all the P.M.'s thoughts. He was perfectly easy with me but there was a certain distance. He was watching me, realizing I was accepting my position outside the charmed circle. For instance, I suddenly realized that I have hardly seen or talked to Marcia for six months. I got a printed Christmas card from her. I hardly ever see Gerald Kaufman. Fred Peart has fully taken my place and Harold is delighted to have him there because although Fred hasn't any great intelligence he has a kind of shrewdness. Harold praised him highly. I said, 'Yes, Fred Peart is in our Labour Cabinet what the Duke of Omnium is in a Trollope Cabinet, a man of natural breeding, nobility and decency who speaks with a kind of commonsensical wisdom.' We talked rather guardedly about Roy and the difficulties of the Treasury. No, Harold wasn't giving much away to me and I wasn't giving him anything, but I think my going along was useful. In due course, after forty-five minutes, in came Michael Halls and Trevor Lloyd-Hughes, off I went and Harold left for Chequers to have Christmas laid on for him by the Wrens.

Tuesday, December 31st
I gradually got back to work and my first job was to deal with the popular version of my White Paper. Hugh Cudlipp had sent John Beavan[2] and Alan Fairclough, the *Mirror* leader-writer, down to Brighton and locked them in an hotel with some stenographers and it was clear when we sat down together this morning that they had turned out a first-rate version. We hardly had to change a word before it went to press.

This afternoon I had to see the Chancellor and clear with him and the Treasury the cost and the giving of top priority to this popular version. I also had to meet a major crisis in my own life which is still hanging over me. It concerns Barbara Castle's White Paper on trade union reform and the timing of its release. As I have already reported in this diary, I had discovered from Harold that Cabinet was to meet on January 3rd to discuss Barbara's White Paper, which is to be published on January 9th. Harold had let the cat out of the bag. He realized it would upset the trade unions and the Labour Party but felt that didn't really matter because this was going to be a

[1] When the Department of Commonwealth Affairs was merged with the Foreign Office on October 17th, 1968, George Thomson ceased to be Minister of Commonwealth Affairs and became Minister without Portfolio.
[2] John Beavan was Editor, *Daily Herald* 1960–2 and Political Adviser to the *Daily Mirror* Group from 1962 to 1976. He became a life peer in 1970, taking the title of Lord Ardwick.

great popular success. This had shaken me quite a lot and I brooded over it during Christmas. I realized that as Secretary of State for the Social Services I should have been consulted so last Friday I finally gave instructions that at all costs I must see the Chancellor today and Barbara tomorrow to discuss the situation. I didn't want to break with her or have a row about it in Cabinet without prior discussion, but I was alarmed at this effort to railroad Cabinet.

When I went to see the Chancellor today I cleared the whole future of my White Paper with him relatively easily and then I turned to the other subject. He said, 'Yes, it's true. I have been supporting Barbara on this but we only had one meeting of this Miscellaneous Committee just before Christmas and after Christmas another brief meeting.' This was the meeting which I've mentioned in this diary, to which the Lord Chancellor went, the Law Officers, the Chancellor of the Exchequer and the Leader of the House. But that was about all, because Peter Shore, who was supposed to be there from D.E.A., was ill with bronchitis and suspected embolism of the heart. 'Frankly,' said Roy, 'I just went along at the last moment and I don't know very much about it. I had given Barbara my approval.' I warned Roy, saying, 'Won't she be in some trouble in Cabinet?' and we went through the people who are liable to react. I said, 'Dick Marsh is a friend of yours, Roy, shouldn't you get hold of him quietly? In the same way I will try to quieten other people and I will talk to Barbara about it.' I was aware that if you suddenly summon Ministers and say, 'Here's a draft White Paper for publication next week,' and it's revealed that there's been no meeting of Ministers to go over the policy and no preliminary work, even our tame Cabinet might blow up. Roy seemed to understand this and I left feeling I had at least done something.

1969

Wednesday, January 1st

The first thing I did today was to visit the Harperbury sub-normal hospital and when I got back I saw Barbara for an hour and a half, with one of her personal advisers, a highly political young man. It took me some time to make her realize what I was saying. 'I haven't come', I said, 'to see you about the content of the White Paper as I'm not an expert on that and I can't judge. I have come about the row you are going to have because even this Cabinet isn't going to have this railroaded through in one afternoon.'

'Oh,' she said, 'there will be plenty of room for Cabinet to change its mind on Friday. It will be open to reverse me on any point; I have made arrangements for the White Paper to be published on Thursday, 9th, even if we only get the corrected version on Monday, 6th. Even if we give it in that late I've got top priority at the Stationery Office.' However, as she said, things would get rather more complicated because she had agreed to see the T.U.C. General Council again on Tuesday, 7th, and perhaps it would look a bit odd to publish within two days of that and might seem to be an insult to the Council. She explained what had happened. 'It seemed to me,' she said, 'that we had to do this because of Jim Callaghan. We planned to have a Ministerial Committee reporting to S.E.P., and S.E.P. or even the Parliamentary Committee reporting to Cabinet in the normal way. But when I went to see Harold he suddenly said, "Let's foreshorten all this. You bring it to a special small meeting of Ministers. That's the only safe way to do it and we will clear it there."' 'Barbara,' I said, 'that was a pretty reckless thing to do.' 'It was the least dangerous thing to do,' she said. 'Remember that on all previous prices and incomes policies we've always done it.' 'Nonsense,' I said, 'we haven't. You can't give me a single instance where Cabinet hasn't authorized you or your predecessor to negotiate with the T.U.C. and the C.B.I., but you have always had to come to Cabinet first to get the broad line of policy agreed. Then you have to negotiate on that basis and then come back to us. We've permitted you to make changes in between but this is something absolutely unprecedented.' Well, she admitted all this but she said it was something she had to do.

I then spent the rest of a very, very long hour with her, saying, 'Has anybody spoken to Michael Stewart?' 'No.' 'Well, shouldn't Harold speak to him? He is a prickly, difficult man. You really have to persuade him that this is a reasonable course of action.' I said that meanwhile I would talk to Judith and see that she was cleared. I hope that Roy will square Crosland and Denis Healey. Denis will be O.K., I think, but Tony might be a bit difficult.

I presume that Tony Wedgwood Benn and Peter Shore have been pretty well squared by the P.M. The more we talked round it, the more aware I became of how determined she was. 'Frankly, Dick,' she said, 'you don't know much about this, any more than I know about pensions. If I back you on pensions, you back me on this. It will be popular, there will be no real opposition in the Party and, though I am having difficulties with the T.U.C,

George Woodcock says he isn't really basically opposed to me.'[1] She and Harold have got themselves into the mood of saying that if they can get this through Cabinet on Friday there will be no difficulty in handling it but I have the gravest doubts, I must admit, and they are only somewhat allayed by what she said to me today.

Thursday, January 2nd

I have been struggling at my own merged Ministry and becoming more and more convinced of the appalling difficulties caused by the physical division of the two Departments, the Elephant and Castle south of the river and John Adam Street north of it. This may well determine our Ministry's failure. Though I have two excellent and technically quite competent Ministers in Stephen and David I am not very cheerful about the future or my success in getting on top of the Department.

Meanwhile I did what briefing I could for tomorrow's Cabinet. I had a word with Fred Peart, who was loyal but not enthusiastic and I found that John Silkin was unbriefed. I saw Judith, who was very unsympathetic indeed, and, as a result of talking to her at lunch, another thing struck me. We can't possibly have both prices and incomes legislation and anti-trade union legislation next autumn, so at the very least Roy will have to give up his prices and incomes legislation in order to get Barbara's Bill through.

Friday, January 3rd

A six-hour Cabinet, from 10.0 to 1.0 and again from 3.0 to 6.0. Barbara and Harold started on their explanation, which was taken relatively well, and then, to my surprise Jim Callaghan said he had no objection to what she had done and the order in which she had briefed people. It was clear that when she saw him yesterday at least she had succeeded in squaring him too. (However, as we saw later on, it didn't give her much advantage.) I tried to support Barbara by remaining totally silent. It was also noteworthy that, just as we expected, Barbara got tacit support from Roy, fanatical support from Harold Wilson and strong support from Roy Mason, our trade unionist Minister of Power. There was scepticism and considerable opposition from Marsh but Cabinet was pretty well silent, most of them doubtful but the middle ready to be swung into support. Tony Crosland led the middle-of-the-road group but not really standing by it and I bided my time. That was the morning. We accepted the explanation she and the Prime Minister gave and then we allowed her to present her case.

Barbara made her first mistake by speaking for forty-five minutes, after she had said she would simply give a shortish Second Reading account, and as it got on towards midday it became clearer and clearer that she wasn't all that conversant with the details of her scheme. She is able and driving but

[1] George Woodcock was Assistant General Secretary of the T.U.C. 1947–60, General Secretary 1960–9 and Chairman of the Industrial Relations Commission 1969–71.

like all the rest of us she is an amateur, quite new to trade union law and legislation, a tremendously complex subject. Here she was trying to give us her explanation of the relationship between trade unions and the law and her proposals for a package to deal with it.[1] It all seemed perfectly sensible. She wanted the setting up of a statutory Commission, with all sorts of positive things to help the unions, and two negative things: powers to enforce a ballot before an official strike and powers, backed by the threat of a fine, to order unofficial strikers back to work whenever she felt inclined. These were the two key controversial themes.

Callaghan then led for the other side. He didn't deny, he said, that he had been talking to members of the T.U.C. General Council. 'They're all old friends of mine,' he said. 'I'm Treasurer of the Party, we are bound to discuss it. Frankly I think it is absolutely wrong and unnecessary to do this. I think what you ought to do is to set up the Commission, put the trade unions on their honour and do what you can.' Harold and Barbara then made it clear that there would be a horse-laugh from the general public and that the Government must take action to control strikes. Dick Marsh opposed. He was extremely dubious about these proposals and as upset as I was by the unconstitutional nature of trying to do it all in one go. Tony Crosland, who had broken his elbow just before Christmas and is going away to convalesce on a tour of D.E.A. installations, very sensibly said he had read the Donovan Report and, though he was an amateur, he thought there was an alternative to the sanctions which were implied by the powers it proposed for the Government. That was to rely on the Shonfield proposal for strengthening the Commission itself and this ought to be looked at.[2]

By the time we broke off it was clear that Barbara had failed to get Cabinet to agree. We came back at 2.45 and finished at 5.45. I weighed in, mostly emphasizing the procedural problems and insisting that there must be a further meeting, with the Ministerial Committee in between, and that the Prime Minister couldn't rush us like this. He needed a Cabinet consensus. Adopting the Shonfield alternative of strengthening the Commission and

[1] The Secretary of State proposed the establishment of a permanent Industrial Relations Commission to advise both sides of industry on ways to improve industrial relations and negotiating machinery, and that a register of collective agreements reached by firms of more than 5,000 employees should be kept by the D.E.P., though the White Paper rejected the principle of making collective agreements enforceable. There were to be a number of reforms to strengthen the bargaining position of trade unions, to establish the legal right of a worker to join a union and to give statutory protection against unfair dismissal. Financial assistance was to be given to smaller unions that wished to merge, and to help the unions to become more efficient. The White Paper proposed that the Minister should have discretionary powers to order trade unions to hold a ballot of their members before calling an official strike and to impose a 28-day delay, the 'conciliation pause', on workers threatening an unofficial strike. An Industrial Board would be empowered to impose penalties for failure to follow the Minister's orders.

[2] Andrew Shonfield was Director of Studies at the Royal Institute of International Affairs 1961–8, a Research Fellow at the Institute 1969–71, and its Director 1972–7. He had been a member of the Donovan Commission, writing a minority Report.

dropping the penal clauses would meet the objections of the trade unions and the Party. 'We haven't had time to look at this and we must before Cabinet sees it again.' Harold said, 'All right, but Cabinet shall meet next Wednesday morning, after Barbara has had a report from the General Council, and we will see where we are.' So that is the proposal. Harold intends to railroad it through Cabinet. It's clear that at present he has got only one serious opponent in Jim Callaghan, with a number of doubters, including Tony Crosland (who won't be there next week), myself and Judith Hart. I am entirely doubtful. I made it clear to Barbara, to Roy Jenkins and also to John Harris that if we could railroad the Bill through, get the penal sanctions this year and then enter 1970 with the difficulties behind us, I could tolerate it but I find it difficult to see how we can go into an election year, 1969/70, with the legislative burden of a White Paper launched this month, followed by legislation next November. It sounds to me tactically disastrous because it leaves almost a whole year for gnawing at the bone, with possible defeat in the autumn at the Trade Union Congress and at Party Conference. Then to try in November to order the Parliamentary Party to carry a Bill after such a defeat seems an intolerable burden for us to impose on ourselves. I am not so much objecting to the Bill itself. Probably it would be quite popular with the public and I daresay the powers wouldn't actually be used but I am extremely doubtful about our taking, once again, symbolic powers giving the state ultimate sanctions and the right of discretionary intervention to the Minister, even though she promises not to use it. We have tried it in prices and incomes and it hasn't really worked. I am afraid the same thing will happen here. Either we will have to use these powers against unofficial strikers and fine them tremendously or in fact the whole system won't work at all.

That wouldn't matter so much if it wasn't for the crisis of our relations with the Party and the unions and I just think that if we are to have any chance of avoiding absolute disaster in the election we must spend time between now and then recovering their confidence. We can't do it if we have a Bill of this sort ahead of us in the autumn and spring.

I made this point very strongly and got Roy to do so too. We must either have the Bill immediately as Barbara wants or have a much weaker version next autumn. Towards the end there was a great speech by the Prime Minister, saying that on no account must Barbara be embarrassed by any press leaks. Callaghan said, 'We can't prevent leaks but we'll all do our best.' I said, 'When Barbara goes back to the General Council on Tuesday, it's her scheme she is taking. Let's be perfectly clear that Cabinet has not approved it.'

Saturday, January 4th
But this morning all the newspapers said Barbara's scheme had been approved by Cabinet. I rang up Harold at Chequers and said it was imposs-

ible. I suspect he had already been rung up by Callaghan. Of course he denied doing any briefing himself from No. 10. Probably he thought Barbara hadn't done it either and that it had been some rather ebullient junior person. I pointed out that the stories even said the White Paper would be published in January, something which Cabinet explicitly said was impossible if there was to be genuine consideration of the Shonfield alternative. All the newspapers were saying Barbara had won. 'I quite agree it's impossible,' said Harold. 'Can you do a counter-briefing,' I asked, 'through Trevor Lloyd-Hughes, for the Sunday papers?' Harold said yes and rang back an hour later to tell me he had given these instructions. It shows what a bad conscience he had.* I also rang Roy and said, 'You are aware of the fact, are you, that to have both prices and incomes and this Bill together is impossible? Are you prepared to have a package agreement and drop your prices and incomes?' 'Oh, no,' he said. 'We can't possibly drop it now. Perhaps we won't have legislation next autumn but we couldn't announce that now.' 'Well,' I said, 'you may be faced with the necessity of announcing it because I don't think you are going to get Barbara's Bill through except by conceding on prices and incomes.' He said, 'I shan't be present next Wednesday,' and I replied, 'You had better make sure you are.'

I must say I am more depressed than ever before by this whole episode because it is absolutely characteristic of Harold and, to a lesser extent, of Barbara to try to carry their colleagues without any proper Ministerial Committee, without an official Committee, without either the Ministers or the officials getting together and pooling their knowledge. It seems utterly ludicrous after the experience of the last four years, reckless too, and it's impossible for us to do anything about it without wrecking Cabinet. It's so characteristic of Wilson to say that they would short-circuit everything and rush it through Cabinet and then, when he is in difficulties in the Cabinet, to back-pedal, put himself into another jam and then try to have the press briefed to give the victory to Barbara. I have no doubt that next Wednesday he will make every effort to get this half-boiled thing through by fair means or foul and I also have a feeling I shall be the only person who will be independent enough to say no and delay him. I can't ask my Coventry people to approve another anti-labour measure, another beating of the trade unions with no beating of the employers. We haven't the authority to do so and I shall fight very strongly against it. But I don't know—I've got no alternative to propose. There is no time to think of one. I may well be forced to toe the line and see us tearing ourselves to pieces all over again.

Wednesday, January 8th
Cabinet began at 6.30, an interesting meeting that went fairly well for the opposition. Callaghan opted out for the first hour or two, remaining silent. Dick Marsh tried a bit, and then I took the lead in asking about procedure,

* But the Sunday papers had very little about it.

really to get the meeting on to the subjects I wanted. First, timing. How were we going to fill in the year? Had we faced the full results of having a Bill after we had been defeated at Congress and Party Conference? What was to be the effect on the local parties and on the P.L.P. of airing all this, especially the impracticability of the conciliation pause, for a whole year? I concentrated the discussion on that one section.

It became clear that on our side were Judith, myself, Dick Marsh, Tony Crosland, who was away but who had sent a little letter, Roy Mason, surprisingly, who had come out strongly in favour of strike ballots and equally strongly talked of the impracticality of the 28-day cooling-off period, and we had Tony Greenwood, rather courageously, and Callaghan. We seven were pretty resolutely opposed, on the grounds that the broad tactic of slapping this on the table and rushing ahead, getting into a point-blank conflict with the T.U.C. and the party in this particular year, was crazy and doomed to defeat. We had a long, arduous, free discussion which mostly consisted of us critics making our point at length, with very short statements of support for Harold from the other side. I think (as Jim Callaghan has now said on two occasions) I was pretty effective because I was dealing with the political and not the practical issue, talking not as an expert on trade unions but as an experienced member of the Party and also as someone who is able to read and discuss a White Paper. By the time we finished at 9.15 it was clear that Barbara wasn't going to get what she wanted today because we were holding out successfully, and it was also clear that Harold would have to put me on the Industrial Committee. He can't have me conducting all the opposition in full Cabinet if he is to get anything like an agreed document.

Thursday, January 9th
Harold's plan had been, I suppose, to finish the White Paper and get it out before the Commonwealth Conference began but I had entirely defeated this ludicrously optimistic idea. The Conference is now in full swing and Harold is having to deal with this in the middle of it all, so today we began Cabinet at 9.0 a.m. The discussion was chiefly about procedure. All last night and early this morning I was thinking of an idea and, right at the beginning of the meeting, I said, 'The key thing is, why should the cooling-off period be something to which we are irrevocably committed? Why can't it be drafted in such a way that we put it to the unions and clinch it that we want them to consult their members?' It had suddenly become clear to me that the real difference is one of our attitude during this coming year. If we have to have a whole year on this, through Conference right up to the Commons' discussion of the Bill, we must spend it negotiating not quarrelling with the T.U.C. To achieve this, we should draft the White Paper in such a way that, willy-nilly, whether they want it or not, they should be induced into negotiations to keep them quiet. This was the tactic I wanted to evolve. It was pretty hostilely received by Harold, who didn't at all like the idea of climbing down

or of giving the impression that there was no clear-cut smack of firm government. Barbara didn't like it either but most of the others did. It was on this
that I worked, the idea of making the White Paper as Green as possible as it
relates to these particular critical problems.

After Cabinet those of us on the Industrial Committee stayed behind. I
have now been put on this by Harold, who has realized he had made a great
mistake in taking me off it.[1] We agreed to meet twice on Friday and once
next Monday before Cabinet on Tuesday, in a frantic effort by Barbara to get
her White Paper passed and approved, printed and published next week. I
am still not clear what the desperate hurry is but I said, 'All right, we'll have a
try.' In fact I am pretty sure this will actually happen.

At 4.45 I was to see Roy to learn whether on the first indications of the
trade figures we should be able to launch the superannuation White Paper on
Tuesday, January 21st, as we were planning. I went in with a pretty sure
feeling and he took me aside almost like a doctor giving bad news, saying,
'I'm awfully sorry, old boy, I'm afraid I shan't be able to tell you. I've had a
good look at the figures and though they're not very bad they are bad. We
have a £55 million deficit for December. It's largely owing to vast unnecessary expenditure on some foreign ship but there it is, it's very dicey now and
we must look carefully.' 'How long must we postpone it?' I asked. 'Until the
28th?' 'Yes,' he said, 'but you might want to postpone it until March.' I said,
'No, I think we'd better have the 28th because, after all, if we can't get it
then, when can we do it?' He was obviously apologetic and unhappy at the
idea that the position was so unstable that he was scared at launching even a
pensions plan, which is in a sense a savings plan, just because of one month's
unsatisfactory trade figures. On the other hand, he also knew very well that
Barbara's White Paper was coming out and he argued, not unreasonably,
that I might want to separate mine from hers by a certain distance. She hopes
hers will come out on the 15th. Would there be anyone at all listening to
mine on the 21st after the row there will be about hers? I think this may be
true but nevertheless I told him that I would go back quickly and advise my
people. I went out feeling thoroughly depressed, not so much about the
week's delay till the 28th but at the instability of the Government which it
revealed.

Friday, January 10th
Back at Barbara's Committee, we started on the policy, beginning with my
corner of it, supplementary benefits for strikers, and then we got on to the
main issue, the presentation and drafting of proposals for consultation rather
than for an already decided Bill. Barbara stressed once again that this was a
purely jurisdictional matter. The conciliation pause would only be ordered
when there was an unconstitutional, i.e. unofficial strike. That was about the
end of the morning.

[1] When Crossman had become Secretary of State for Social Services.

We resumed at 2 p.m., having just got a huge bunch of amendments, to find that over lunchtime Barbara herself had completely redrafted the section on the conciliation pause. It was now quite different. The new section described the cases where she would be able to order people back to work not only when a strike was unconstitutional, but even in official strikes when there were no clear-cut procedures for conciliation she would order them back and produce her own procedures. We had a long wrangle and I said, 'In that case you have misled Cabinet because you told us that official strikes are perfectly O.K., and that what is really wicked is neglecting official proce-dures. Now you are saying that you want to intervene even in the very many cases where there is no clear-cut procedure because you have large numbers of unorganized workers or badly run managements. You can't call this an unconstitutional strike. You must say, "all strikes except those which are run by strictly official procedures". I can't see that the men are to blame if there is no constitutional procedure for them to be breaking.'

We had a long and arduous struggle and she thought I was just sabotaging and filibustering. To some extent I think it's fair to say I was. (Judith told me that when she got into the room she overheard Barbara saying to the others, 'My God, a colleague rewriting a White Paper for another colleague. By jove, when he has another White Paper, what won't I do to him.' What Barbara forgets is that in the case of my White Paper every word of the policy has been approved after long consultations with Roy Hattersley, her own Parliamentary Secretary, whom she sent to represent her. There is no aspect of the policy which hasn't received his approval.)

Barbara got pretty hysterical in the course of the afternoon and the Committee got more and more angry with me, saying I was unreasonable, until slowly it at last began to dawn on them that they had been misled. I challenged the Solicitor General,[1] saying, 'Wasn't it your view that it was only when the strike is unconstitutional that she has the right to intervene?' 'Certainly,' he said. 'That was my impression but she has made it very clear now that there are these other cases.' 'But,' I said, 'it makes a great deal of difference to the argument, and I think there is going to be quite a row when this is disclosed to Cabinet on Tuesday.' We went on until 5 o'clock when we agreed to break off and that we would all work on our drafts over the weekend and come back on Monday morning at 10.15.

Saturday, January 11th
I have been studying Barbara's proposals all weekend and very late tonight, as I was just going to bed, there came a ring at the bell and there was a dispatch rider from the Ministry of Works bringing the revised text of the White Paper. It was sent to press at the same time so that if it is approved next Tuesday evening in Cabinet Barbara can go ahead and publish. She is

[1] Sir Arthur Irvine, Labour M.P. for Liverpool Edge Hill, 1947–79. He was Solicitor-General 1967–70.

determined on this rush, which also struck Stephen Swingler as odd, and then, apparently, after it has been rushed out she will wait till next November for the Second Reading of the Bill. This time-tabling also disturbs me.

Monday, January 13th
I found a big banner headline in the *Guardian*, where Ian Aitken had a very accurate story that Barbara and I are at loggerheads and that I am pleading for green edges to her White Paper.

I wondered uneasily whether this would have upset Barbara and certainly she was very cross this morning when we settled down at 10.15 to continue the Committee work on her White Paper. In Cabinet I had said, half-jokingly, that if she didn't have a Ministerial Committee before the White Paper she should jolly well have one after it and this was what she was getting. It was our third meeting and she was still ferociously angry at the idea that any Cabinet colleague should submit her to this indignity. However here we were. The copy which had come down to me at Prescote had already gone to the printers but she bustled in and took out of her bag yet another whole mass of redrafts which she had been preparing herself during the weekend. It soon became pretty clear that there was still one major issue, and only one, worth fighting. This was for green edges, that is, to get a White Paper framed in consultative form, which didn't close our options but if necessary permitted us without loss of face to drop either the strike ballot or the conciliation pause. This was what I wanted and I wanted to see how she took it. When I had gone through the White Paper at the weekend I had noticed that all the amendments I had proposed, including those she had ferociously opposed, had been wisely accepted by her officials in their redrafts and this had tickled me a good deal.

However, all that really mattered was Clause 18 (I think it was) on the conciliation pause and there she drew out a new draft and said, 'I have a much better draft to propose.' She had toughened up sentences in the redraft of the White Paper, having decided, I expect with Harold's backing, to move the other way. She had removed any suggestion of conciliation altogether and now it said that if the trade unions were to propose positive recommendations it would reduce the need to use her powers to intervene. It is clear that she is determined to take these powers, and she is going to tell the unions without qualification, 'Right, I'll take them and then I won't have to use them.' She had obviously decided this over the weekend. At this point I cut the Committee short, saying 'Look, this must go to Cabinet,' and after a bit of discussion she said, 'I'll report it to Cabinet.' 'No,' I said, 'I think the Paymaster and I would prefer to put it in a paper.' Barbara obviously didn't like this but when Judith and I left the meeting we immediately got on to Sandy Isserlis,[1] a very good man who was with me at Housing and who is now

[1] Assistant Secretary at the M.H.L.G. 1963–9, Under-Secretary at the Cabinet Office 1969 and at the M.H.L.G. 1969–70, Principal Private Secretary to the Prime Minister 1970

at the Cabinet Office, but working full time for Judith. Over lunch and this afternoon he produced a very decent draft, which I changed once again in time for it to be circulated in this evening's boxes so that Ministers will get our paper and Barbara's simultaneously.

Tuesday, January 14th

As the morning had been taken up by the Commonwealth Conference, Cabinet took place at 6.30 p.m. The Prime Minister proposed to take Barbara's White Paper clause by clause. 'Surely not,' I said. 'We should take the main issue first because it colours the whole attitude to the White Paper. Whether the White Paper should have green edges or not will determine the consequential amendments.' Harold gave way and we then had something like a two-hour debate on my amendment and Barbara's reply. I needn't rehash all the arguments here. They are not unfairly expressed in the Cabinet minutes, except of course for the really powerful argúment on my side, the argument about politics. As I wound up, I made this point even more strongly, simply saying that whatever the desirability and popularity of what she was doing and the rather doubtful fact as to whether it would work there was the other question of its impact on the Labour Party and the Labour Movement. If, instead of going through in a rush now, the Bill is to be fought over throughout the spring and summer, voted upon at Congress and the Labour Party Conference and only put into Parliament in November, maybe finishing next March or May, we could just imagine what a preface to an election campaign that would be.

Right at the end I said there was something else I wanted to add. At the previous Cabinet I hadn't had clear answers about the relationship between this Bill and the Prices and Incomes Bill. Surely it was clear to everybody that we couldn't have both of them in the new session next autumn? That had been the case for rushing this Bill through this session and having the Prices and Incomes Bill next session but since it had been decided not to rush this Bill through presumably there would be no Prices and Incomes legislation. When knowledge of this got about it might produce a grave crisis in the autumn. Supposing the Chancellor needed stronger prices and incomes measures to save the pound and was inhibited from introducing them? It might force an autumn election. One or two people had strongly advised me against saying this but I dropped it in. Roy immediately intervened. He couldn't accept any of this and at this point he cut the discussion on his Prices and Incomes Bill. I had noticed that on the Cabinet agenda there was a second item after Barbara's, the timing of legislation, and my suspicions had been aroused. Roy was clearly siding with Barbara, but I could do nothing apart from making my initial speech.

It was rather a formal Cabinet. Harold wasn't there at the beginning, and

and Assistant Under-Secretary at the Home Office from 1970 to 1972, when he became Director of the Centre for Studies in Social Policy.

the Foreign Secretary had started it from the Chair but now the P.M. was back he took the greatest trouble to commit everybody on this. Four people were away, paired, on our side Tony Crosland and Tony Greenwood and I have forgotten who the two were on the other side. Each person was asked for an opinion and it was fairly predictable, 6:6. We had all known that George Thomas would be for Barbara and George Thomson for the Prime Minister, the Establishment side, but then there were the critical votes. The surprising ones were Ted Short, who came out for Barbara in a short speech, and Wedgy Benn, who had ended the previous Cabinet by saying how important it was to have consultation but who had obviously now been brought into line behind the scenes. Our only surprising convert was Peter Shore and on this hangs a comic story. He had been away with a suspected coronary embolism so this was his first Cabinet on this issue. He has a lackadaisical voice and, so Roy Jenkins told me afterwards, directly he began, the Prime Minister, who was making a list, put him down firmly for Barbara. After talking for three or four minutes in a very ambiguous way Peter suddenly said, 'I agree wholeheartedly with Barbara about her policy but if the only issue is consultation and whether we should give an impression of willingness to consult between now and the Bill, well, of course, I favour consultation.' The P.M. was chatting with Roy so he didn't hear what Peter was saying and later on he had to be told to correct his list because he hadn't heard his Secretary of State for Economic Affairs. Willie Ross came down on our side for the same sort of reasons as mine. We therefore had as solid allies the three trade union members, Callaghan, Mason and Marsh, all against Barbara, as every other trade unionist would have been too, I think, if they had been there to hear the argument. She had got what you might call the normal Establishment characters, Michael Stewart, Gerald Gardiner, Eddie Shackleton, Fred Peart (despite all his worries) but, as everybody had really known would happen, the result was a predictable 10:6 and Harold Wilson would have been the eleventh if he had been asked to cast his vote.

I had known that however reasonable I was and however obviously I was right, it would be impossible to win as Barbara had Roy and Harold on her side. The whole drama of the meeting, therefore, came after this. Barbara wasn't allowed to wind up. I did and I think everybody felt it was a pretty devastating repetition of all the political difficulties involved and of the reasonableness of consultation. I said, 'You have got six major issues in the White Paper on which you promise consultation. Why not talk about it on the other two issues as well?' Roy Jenkins leant across and said, 'By jove, that winding-up has nearly persuaded me that you are right.'

The Prime Minister came in immediately for fear Barbara would upset people, and she wasn't allowed to reply. He called on Roy to introduce the second item on the agenda, the timing. To my astonishment, Roy said that there really was grave danger next autumn and he now said himself all the things I had referred to in my speech which he had refused to accept before, the possible need for a severe Prices and Incomes Bill and the impossibility of dropping that. He *said* all these things and it was obvious that people were shaken by what seemed to be a carefully contrived conspiracy between Roy, the Prime Minister and Barbara. Having given her the White Paper, Roy was now going to say, 'Yes, but you must give me the precautions I need to get a Prices and Incomes Bill as well. My Bill came before this demand for her early legislation. Her package ought to go through this session.' But technically, both in terms of parliamentary drafting and parliamentary time, and in terms of Barbara's own machine, it is quite impossible to rush her Bill through. She still has only the vaguest statements of policy. Pages and pages of half-baked White Paper had been redrafted, stiffened and improved but she is nowhere near the preparation of a Bill and endless consultations have to take place before her policy is developed. She couldn't give Roy his point but we were all uneasily aware in this case we might well be faced with a major crisis next autumn. It might well turn out that the whole prices and incomes policy and the future of the pound have been jeopardized by railroading Barbara's Bill through Cabinet. Once Barbara has got her Bill approved in Cabinet, who will say in the autumn that it should be postponed in favour of a severe Prices and Incomes Bill? Indeed, it is quite clear that both Barbara and the Prime Minister are gambling on being able to avoid new prices and incomes legislation altogether. This was the drama at the end of the meeting and, as Eddie Shackleton said on the telephone later on, 'You know, if Roy had spoken before the decision was taken I would have voted for you. Most of us were only very marginally in favour of Barbara on that issue you put and many of us thought you made a very strong case. Roy has made a very bad impression on his colleagues by doing this.' By jove, that was certainly true.

Wednesday, January 15th

I lunched at the Athenaeum with Nicholas Davenport and in came Callaghan with his Parliamentary Secretary, Victor Stonham. I went across later and asked Jim, 'What did you think of Cabinet yesterday?' and he said, 'The plot thickens. Roy has been thinking of an autumn election.' Jim had come to the same conclusion as me as a result of Roy's intervention. I said, 'I don't think it would be fair to say they have made up their minds but it does look as though Roy and Harold must be saying to themselves that in the last resort we can have an election this October.' Certainly on three or four occasions in our discussions Harold had said that we might not have to implement Barbara's Bill. Maybe he really is thinking of using it as a White Paper to win popularity and then never implementing it at all, and this would explain his willingness to face the possibility of forging ahead at the autumn Conferences.

My suspicion was confirmed by a conversation I had with Roy later today. I had to see him again about the timing of my own White Paper and in the course of this I took the liberty of saying that I thought he had made a great mistake yesterday evening and done himself no good, and I quoted what Eddie Shackleton had said. 'Well,' Roy replied, 'I may well have been wrong. The truth is, I was convinced completely by your arguments but I promised my support to Barbara and I couldn't let her down. That's why I did it.' I said, 'How did that happen?' 'I think it was on December 10th or 12th,' he said, 'when the Prime Minister, Barbara and I discussed the tactic of pushing her Bill through. I didn't know anything about it and I still don't know much but, whether it was right or wrong I gave her my support.' 'Surely,' I said, 'you realized that by doing that you were possibly prejudicing the survival of the prices and incomes policy, certainly prejudicing your new legislation and finally knocking it on the head?' 'I realize it now,' he said, 'and that's why I am so insistent on early legislation for her Bill.' 'You won't get it,' I said. 'I'm not beaten,' he said. 'In a month's time we shall see the situation more clearly, when we know what the impact of her Bill is. Perhaps it's not as controversial as we think. I shall have to come back to Cabinet if the situation is serious and say I can't survive without a Prices and Incomes Bill. I may have to say that Cabinet can face the choice, either to rush a short Industrial Relations Bill through this session after all or to postpone it for a Prices and Incomes Bill which must be rushed through before Christmas.' This conversation confirmed that, at least in Roy's mind, there is now a possibility of an autumn election.

I discussed with Judith my talk with Roy and I went to see Fred Peart to explain that we have the prospect of being forced to go to the country as a result of a secret deal, if it is true, between these three people, Harold, Barbara and Roy. I told Fred, who was extremely worried, what Roy had said and that we must talk to the Prime Minister about it, because a really serious and dangerous situation is developing behind the scenes.

Thursday, January 16th
A second Cabinet where Harold prosed on for nearly two hours on the Commonwealth Conference. An enormous, absolutely unreadable, pompous communiqué has been published. There is no doubt, though, that he has handled it quite skilfully and got through far better than he anticipated. The people who came to curse had gone away blessing. Trudeau had been a flop but Harold was a success.[1] It is clear that he is at his best chairing a Commonwealth Conference, where nothing much is happening and all that is required is skill, tenacity, agility, subtlety at keeping the thing going and no great imagination or strategy. He had surpassed himself on this occasion and wanted some commendation from Cabinet. I am afraid everybody sat around, rather bored, and didn't give it because their minds were either on Barbara's policy or on the following item on the agenda, immigration.

[1] Pierre Elliott Trudeau, Prime Minister and Leader of the Liberal Party of Canada since April 1968.

Callaghan was to report on this. Now though Harold has been pretty good at chairing the Conference the man whose personality has dominated the British press has been Mr Callaghan. There he was standing up for Britain against the Africans, saying, 'No more bloody immigrants whatever happens. We won't increase the immigration quota, and if the Kenyan Asians have to come it will be at the cost of other voucher-holders from Pakistan and India.' He has had tremendous coverage for his presentation of the British line and Harold was very much aware of it.

Here came Callaghan, asking in a modest, quiet way for Cabinet approval. No, he didn't ask for it. Barbara raised the question and Jim gave an answer. Barbara said, 'We must have the papers first and the decision afterwards.' I had completely forgotten this. I had thought that we had already given a decision but we hadn't. Jim had taken the liberty of announcing a policy firmly and clearly and coming to Cabinet afterwards. He is now doing this more frequently and more successfully and there is no doubt he is building up his position in the public eye. He did it as the only person who stood up against Barbara's Industrial Relations Bill, apart from Dick Marsh. On immigration, on everything you see, there is Jim Callaghan, sensible, constructive, sturdy, thoroughly English, doing his job, a big man who could keep the movement going even when it is defeated and gets rid of Harold Wilson. That is what he achieved even at the Commonwealth Conference, to Harold's great annoyance.

The other little episode today was a meeting of the Lords' Reform Committee to tidy up the legislation. My God, it's going to be awful to get this Bill because it's going to be so unpopular, and it will be even worse now with the I.R. Bill and the Superannuation Bill in the offing. Gerald Gardiner had taken the precaution of seeing Harold to ask whether he still wanted to speak in the Second Reading debate and the P.M. had replied, 'I will if the Committee wants me to.' Gerald put this to us, and immediately Fred Peart said, 'Oh, no. I don't think we would want to engage the Prime Minister in this.' That was the general view of several other people there, a dangerous view that we had to stop very quickly. 'Look,' I said, 'if the Prime Minister is prepared to speak, who on this Committee says that it wouldn't help the Bill through the Commons and who will say that his absence wouldn't be noted as further proof of our half-heartedness?' So we got it.

Wednesday, January 22nd
The P.L.P. had insisted on a second meeting on Lords' reform directly we came back, so here we were at 5.30. Callaghan had said he probably wouldn't be able to come, and I had said that I would only have a watching brief. But I got in there and found myself sitting at the end of the row next to Callaghan, who had Harold beyond him. On the far side of Douglas Houghton were Eddie and Gerald Gardiner, and down on the floor some thirty or forty people. I saw Michael Foot, Denis Coe and Eric Heffer, the usual gang.

When I arrived Douglas was saying, 'Come along now, who is going to speak?' and nobody spoke. This fantastic situation went on for about ten minutes, until some middle-of-the-road M.P. made a speech against the scheme and Denis Coe a speech for the scheme. The others sat tight. They wouldn't take part in the debate they themselves had demanded. Harold and I left the meeting at 6.45 and Harold said, 'Well, that's that.' 'We will get a very bad press,' I said, 'because Douglas Houghton will make the worst of it.' 'That's all right,' said Harold, 'we shall have no difficulty with them. They don't really care either way.' It's also true that they are all waiting for next week's P.L.P. meeting, when we shall be discussing Barbara's White Paper, which is the one the Left really wants to fight. They didn't want to speak this time and risk not being called next week. I also feel that Lords' reform is different. Though they don't like it it is in the party manifesto. They haven't got a passionate objection to it, unlike their attitude to the trade union legislation.

Thursday, February 6th
The morning was spent on the so-called Parliamentary Committee and then at Cabinet. This Parliamentary Committee was started when Harold produced his Mark II Cabinet, and it's not too bad, but its membership is very arbitrary. We have a little less than half the Cabinet, just as at S.E.P. and O.P.D. I am sure Harold has dozens of these miscellaneous committees because he is more and more inclined to solve a problem by setting up a new committee where he can select who deals with what. This morning we considered the issue of party political broadcasting during elections. While I was in Sweden the Parliamentary Committee had almost decided that we should accept a B.B.C./I.T.V. proposal for a reduction of at least a quarter of our party political broadcasts. When this was put forward Harold Wilson, thank heaven, had shown a little doubt, and said that at least we should postpone it until the B.B.C.'s new Director-General had taken up his post. I pointed out that I hoped there would be no question of getting rid of party politicals. We were going to face a totally different situation from the last General Election. In 1966 we were bound to win and it didn't matter what propaganda we did, good, bad or indifferent. Next time we shall want above all to communicate with our old rank and file, to raise and hold their morale, and for this our party politicals are absolutely indispensable. People may be said to resent being a captive audience but we know our own people listen to them in very large numbers. How can we dispense with them? The very fact that the Conservatives say they can should make us suspicious because they reckon to have the press on their side and they can afford to dispense with a captive audience in a way which we can't. It was an effective intervention and I can claim I changed their minds. Callaghan said later that was clearly what had happened. We held the item up for further consideration and I think that on this kind of thing my view really does count for something.

We went straight on to Cabinet and perhaps the most important thing came up when we discussed Parliamentary business. I learnt that I had no hope of a debate on my pensions White Paper this week. They were planning my debate for me on March 21st, nearly seven weeks ahead, and a debate on Barbara's White Paper in the same week.[1] They had pushed me right back. I pleaded that this was futile. Here we had something to sell. Until I had authorization from the Commons I couldn't get into full swing on my campaign of public education and discussion, and I would have a disastrous hiatus between the launching and the follow-up. I said this very briefly and there was a silence. 'Well,' said Peart, 'everybody wants their own White Paper and the Minister of Social Services must be patient.' It came out that the Tories had been saying 'Why debate Dick's White Paper before Barbara's, when Barbara's was published first?' The Tories know that Barbara's is embarrassing and mine isn't. I looked around the room and realized that there was no collective feeling to back me. Judith was the only person who spoke up for me and she is head of publicity. She did her duty and so did the Prime Minister and I think I may get forward a bit on this. But Cabinets are selfish things and, though they all know that this is one of the few things we have that has gone down well, they won't actually help a fellow Minister to get his own White Paper a bit of publicity.

Wednesday, February 19th
When I came in for a meeting in my office at lunchtime, I was told that Stephen Swingler died quite suddenly last night.[2] I had given Anne Swingler lunch yesterday and she seemed definitely more cheerful. In the evening she and Judith had dinner together, so we looked after her all day, and she said the viral pneumonia seemed to have cleared up, and the only area of danger was his bronchial tubes. At the hospital in the evening they sent her away saying it was all right and she could relax but when her back was turned his heart failed and he died. It has been a great shock. He was not a wonderful administrator but he had other superb qualities.

This morning from 10.0 to 1.0 we had the postponed session of yesterday's Committee Stage of the Parliament Bill, and Mr Callaghan, who had been away the whole of the first day and practically the whole of the second, put in an appearance, made a ferocious speech attacking the Opposition front bench for breaking their part of the compact and threatened to use the guillotine. This afternoon he took me into a near-by room and said, 'I made a great speech this morning. I have shown our line. I think the tactic is to just plough the Bill through in eighteen days. Either we plough it through or drop

---

[1] The Debate on the National Superannuation White Paper was eventually held on March 6th and that on *In Place of Strife* on March 3rd.
[2] Stephen Swingler, Labour M.P. for Newcastle-under-Lyme from 1945, had been Minister of State at the D.H.S.S., with special responsibility for social security, only since the previous October.

it altogether, or we can try making a deal with the Opposition, but the one thing we mustn't have is a defeat. Both you and I have got to be tough and we must have no truck with them. I am the leader and this afternoon I am going to show them how I will lead.' I thought this was fine. However, I was sitting in my room upstairs when suddenly the telephone rang. It was Jim's Private Office saying he had to be away at 7.0 for dinner and asking if I could take over, a request that went to Fred Peart's office as well. The fact is that Jim is absolutely split-minded. He doesn't want the Bill, he has predicted it will fail, he wants it to fail and to be destroyed by the House of Commons, and yet he doesn't want himself to be injured in the process. He wants it to be known that he was gallantly trying to get the Bill through and that it wasn't his fault if it didn't, so he is being both very tough and yet is prepared for tactics which are bound to provoke the maximum irritation. It's obvious that people on our side can stand seeing me and Fred pushing the Bill through because we genuinely want it but they can't stand the dishonesty of Callaghan and nor can the other side.

This evening began the political story of finding Stephen Swingler's successor. Harold rang me up to say that he thought that the right man was Reg Freeson. Reg Freeson, that little wet Jew from Willesden who should never have been promoted to Parliamentary Secretary in the Ministry of Power and who has been a deeply unpopular flop there.[1] I blew up, and when I was asked whom I wanted I said, 'Roy Hattersley, of course.' Harold said, 'You can't have him, partly because Barbara can't do without him and partly because he is disloyal and belongs to the wrong side. I must have the political balance kept. We must have another left-winger, and Reg Freeson is on the Left.' 'Well,' I said, 'I must consider competence and Roy Hattersley and Dick Taverne, both of whom I know are C.D.S., are the only two.'[2] Harold said, 'Oh, do be serious, that's impossible. I think Freeson is the man for you.' 'We'd better think it over,' I said, 'and I will ring you tomorrow morning.'

At the end of another evening of the Parliament Bill I was sick to death and I started to walk back through the heavy deluge of snow that fell today. As I was wading through the slush a little Mini stopped in front of me and there was Marcia Williams, whom I hadn't seen for weeks and weeks. She said, 'Get in. I'll be your chauffeur.' As she drove me to Vincent Square, I said, 'Heavens, Marcia, save me from Reg Freeson.' She said, 'What?' I must say, to Marcia's credit, after she tipped me out in Vincent Square she drove straight back to talk to Harold about it.

[1] Labour M.P. for Willesden East 1964–74 and for Brent East since 1974. He was Parliamentary Secretary, at the Ministry of Power 1967–9 and at the M.H.L.G. 1969–70; he has been Minister for Housing and Construction at the D.O.E. since 1974.

[2] The Campaign for Democratic Socialism was born after the Labour Party's 1960 Scarborough conference decided in favour of unilateral nuclear disarmament. It organized in the unions and constituencies with a view to reversing that decision. It dissolved itself on the return of a Labour Government in 1964.

Thursday, February 20th

When I rang Harold this morning there was no more talk of Freeson. That had been knocked out and I was told I could meet him with new ideas just before Parliamentary Committee at 10.15. I went in at 10.10 and this time he did say, 'We'll see if we can fix Hattersley with Barbara.' He called Barbara in and alluded to it and then we moved to Parliamentary Committee and on to Cabinet.

The main incident at Cabinet was the de Gaulle explosion. I had vaguely noticed in our telegrams an account by the Ambassador, Christopher Soames, of an interview he had had before a luncheon with de Gaulle. This morning, in the course of a report by Harold Wilson on his visit to Bonn and by Michael Stewart on his visit to the Western European Union and the manoeuvres there, they both referred to this conversation. It became clear that Harold had felt compelled to tell Kiesinger in Bonn of the astonishing proposals de Gaulle had made to Soames. It would prove Harold a good boy and a loyal NATO and E.E.C. man if he passed on what de Gaulle had suggested about the breakup of the E.E.C. and NATO and the need to formulate new ideas.

Since the breakdown of the negotiations for British entry to the E.E.C. President de Gaulle had made no contact with Sir Christopher Soames, the United Kingdom's Ambassador in Paris, but on February 4th he had invited him to luncheon, and outlined his views on the future of Europe. The General's plan included the virtual end of the existing Common Market and of the European commitment to NATO, and its replacement by an enlarged European Association, led by a small inner council of Britain, France, West Germany and Italy. Mr Wilson was to visit Bonn from February 12th to 14th and President Nixon was coming to Europe in late February so the British Government suspected the the General's remarks might be a device to compromise Britain in the eyes of her European allies and of the United States. Accordingly, the Prime Minister told Dr Kiesinger, the West German Chancellor, of the conversation and then disclosed the General's remarks to the press. On February 24th the French Government made a formal protest to Britain, alleging that the President's remarks had been distorted and diplomatic channels and the press improperly used.

I must admit that I hardly listened to this item. As Michael Stewart had not suggested that the de Gaulle subject was particularly important and had preceded it with four other items, with his boringly dull voice drilling through your head, on and on for half an hour, I didn't really notice. Harold Wilson did of course discuss it more and then Fred Peart made some observations on whether it was really important for us to make ourselves examine this proposition for something beyond the Common Market but he was hardly listened to.

Later this evening Harold rang me up again. There were great difficulties about my Minister of State. He had had further reports. Roy Hattersley had made three disloyal remarks recently and we couldn't really promote him. What about other people? 'Well,' I said, 'do a few remarks matter?' We cast round and I suggested Dick Taverne. He said, 'Have you lost all your political antennae that you fail to remember what our loyalties are? Dick Taverne, he is a silken, treacherous member of the C.D.S. group, he is most unpopular in the Parliamentary Party. If you have him it will be a betrayal of all we stand for. I am amazed at your forgetting.' I said, 'It's not I who have forgotten, Harold. I think these young men have forgotten their past. I know Roy Hattersley is no more loyal to Roy Jenkins than he is to you. He is just an able young man on the way up and I think Dick Taverne has rather more loyalty and decency about him. He is a loyal Jenkins supporter but he is not going to be disloyal to you in his job for me.' Then Harold said, 'It's out of the question.' 'Look,' I said, 'can I perhaps move David Ennals from Health?' 'Yes,' said Harold, 'you can, and put somebody else into the Health side in his place. What about Shirley Williams?' I said, 'Shirley Williams is much more C.D.S. than Roy Hattersley or Dick Taverne.' 'But she is a woman, it would suit you. Shirley Williams, that's a good idea.' I don't know what to think.

Friday, February 21st
I rang Harold again because I didn't want to discuss this at Stephen's funeral, and said, 'Shirley won't do.' 'Yes,' he said, 'I agree with you. What about Bea Serota?' 'She won't do for Social Security,' I said, 'she's in the Lords, but she might do for Health.' Yes, this was a possibility. Bea Serota, ex-Chairman of the Children's Committee of the L.C.C., a very powerful woman, now one of the Whips in the House of Lords. I tried this out on Clifford Jarrett and Marre later on during the day and asked them to try it out this afternoon.

At lunchtime I went to Stephen's funeral at Golders Green crematorium. When I rang up yesterday his brother Humphrey had said he would fix the funeral for Saturday afternoon. I got that changed, saying, 'Look, it will cost each Labour M.P. £10 to stay in London on Friday and Saturday night. Do have it on Friday if you possibly can.' So there we were at 12.30. A big snowfall was melting away and there was snow mist all around us, green grass with yellow crocuses growing through and pale sunlight, all desperately forlorn. Nearly all our civil servants from Social Security turned up and there were our two Permanent Secretaries. They had been fond of him in the Ministry. There was a good round-up of left-wing M.P.s, and Barbara Castle, in the front row Harold and Mary Wilson and up in the chancel Harold and Mrs Davies and Michael Foot. There wasn't a service, just the coffin waiting to slide down into the fire and a chap playing the organ. Michael got up and said a quiet obituary, then Harold Davies, more florid but curiously touching. I thought, 'My God, I'd rather have a bit of ritual at a funeral. It's too desperately heartbreaking for the wife and the kids when it's all addressed to them as human being to human being and though God may not exist there is something to be said for him to stop everybody from mopping their eyes as we are all doing.' We walked out through the back of the chancel into the sunshine and saw the flowers and each other and couldn't say much.

Sunday, February 23rd

I rang up Harold this morning and told him Bea Serota was O.K. I also took the opportunity of asking Harold about the Soames affair and he said, 'Well, when we got back into London at about 1.30 from Stephen's funeral, just before I went off to Ipswich I got a proposal from the Foreign Office that in view of the French leaks we should publish. Of course I didn't want to lay a trap for de Gaulle but maybe I was wrong.' I said, 'My God, do you mean that is how it was fixed?' 'Yes,' he said. 'I gave my consent then. I am not so sure it was wise.' 'What will Christopher Soames do about it? He's coming back today.' Harold said, 'He will be in a terrible fury because he will think his honour has been impugned.' Then Harold explained how he had told Kiesinger before Soames had got permission from the French Foreign Office, although the plan had been for Soames to go to the Quai d'Orsay the evening before Harold talked to Kiesinger. It didn't work that way because Soames's meeting was postponed until the next morning and so technically we had put ourselves in the wrong by telling the Germans before we had got the leave of the French. This had been followed up by the Foreign Office announcement of the content of the conversations. No wonder the French talk about a crisis. I suddenly became interested in foreign affairs again. For ages I have been saying to Tommy that I wasn't really interested in anything but my own Department but here I am aroused once more and aware that I was slack in Cabinet on Thursday morning. I rang up Roy and tested him and he said that he knew all about this episode as he had been in Paris, but he was as surprised as I had been about the publication of the General's remarks and he suspected that it was that infantile Foreign Office again.

I rang up Barbara too. When I asked her about the de Gaulle episode she admitted that, like me, she had found Michael very boring on Thursday morning and as she had been busy waiting for her items on the two big strikes, she hadn't paid adequate attention. As she said, Michael has the power of making everything equally unimportant and boring. She saw enormous dangers to us in this overture of de Gaulle's, the danger of being trapped, particularly when de Gaulle said that Harold, not de Gaulle himself, should take the initiative and, unlike me, she thought that Harold shouldn't have said anything to Kiesinger. We both agreed, however, that this was a terrible thing. She emphasized, of course, the futility of our trying to get into the Common Market with £600 million shortfall on our balance of payments and the humiliation of trying to get in and failing, so she said that if this episode stopped that, it would be a good thing. We both agreed that the real trouble was the infantilism of Harold and Michael Stewart, priggish children who showed moral disapproval of the de Gaulle overture. They threw up their hands and averted themselves from it in horror. They didn't see it as possibly permitting a breakthrough in Anglo-French relations, but instead they created a situation in which we have managed to come out as villains of the piece. It's an extraordinary story, another proof of Harold's ineptitude in foreign and external affairs, the area where he prides himself so much.

Monday, February 24th
Bea Serota saw the Prime Minister this morning and I have got her as my new Minister of State. At 10.30 David Ennals went round to hear the news that he had been transferred. He rang me up last night very sad and of course it is sad. He had been doing extremely well on the Health side, which suited him and gave him plenty of publicity and T.V. appearances. Now he has to go to a very different, tight little group of people, a rather monastic collection of inward-looking experts working on the incredibly complicated subject of social security.

The de Gaulle affair has gone on just about as I expected. This afternoon Michael Stewart answered questions and he put up the best possible defence of his and the Foreign Office's rather prissy, self-righteous line. He didn't give a very convincing account of the thinnest point in his argument, that Harold had been sent off to talk to Kiesinger before de Gaulle was informed and why all this had been given out to the press on Friday, but he is always extremely good in Parliament and he did it well and with conviction. But surprisingly the Speaker permitted a discussion for tomorrow under Standing Order No. 9 and the effect will be to postpone the starting of our next two days on the Parliament Bill.

Tuesday, February 25th
I went across to the House at 7 o'clock. No progress had been made on the Parliament Bill, we were struggling with Clause 2 and there, as we sat on the front bench, we realized the utter futility of the filibuster that is now going on. Michael Foot on the one side, in his most brilliant, demagogic, amusing form, and Enoch Powell on the other, in his most brilliant historical form, were supported by a whole series of people like John Boyd-Carpenter and Robin Turton[1] on their side and on our side Bob Sheldon, and a lot of absolute rag, tag and bobtail. Every single amendment was being discussed and the chair was getting more and more scared. There is the alliance between twenty to thirty distinguished, reactionary fundamentalists on both sides and the fundamentalists who want total revolution of the Second Chamber, and they are enjoying themselves with no whips on. It was a

[1] Sir Robin Turton was Conservative M.P. for Thirsk and Malton 1929–February 1974. In 1974 he became a life peer, taking the title of Lord Tranmire.

terribly depressing performance which I watched until 7.30 when I popped off in my little dinner jacket to the Guildhall. There was the Builders' Association in full regalia. I moved a toast to the Builders, which I did competently but not outrageously well. I had to rush away because before I could get back to the House of Commons I had been instructed to go into No. 10 for Nixon.[1]

He is due to leave tomorrow morning and this evening there was a dinner party for him at No. 10, to which a select number of the Cabinet had been invited, Barbara, the Lord Chancellor and the Chancellor of the Exchequer. Fred Peart, Jim Callaghan and I were excluded. Interesting to see who was there and who was not. Those of us who had not been invited had been told to get back to No. 10 at 9.45 so that Nixon could have a sort of short Cabinet Meeting with us. I needn't have rushed back from the Guildhall because it was 10.15 before they got out of the dinner, which had obviously been very boring. After a bit of standing about in the drawing-room upstairs we went down for Harold's pseudo-Cabinet and there Burke Trend sat himself away from the table and Nixon beside the Prime Minister, with Roy, myself and all the others in their usual seats around the table. It was a sort of ghastly parody of a Cabinet. We started with Nixon being asked to talk, as Harold said, about the problems of youth and race and he gave us a perfectly competent address on the need for a new religion and idealism.

There was absolutely nothing extra or new in it (why should there be?), but already I saw that he was different from his television image, fresher, more vigorous, in contrast to Hubert Humphrey who, when I last saw him at dinner, had given me a long, ideological, Democratic lecture for forty-five minutes about the need to support L.B.J. in Vietnam. Nixon was altogether nicer than he used to be, with a certain charm, a man, as Harold had said to me earlier this afternoon, without the doctrinaire ideology of the anti-communist crusading democrats, Dean Acheson, Walt Rostow, Hubert Humphrey or L.B.J. There was clearly a great change in Harold's attitude and he was finding Nixon's pragmatism and lack of doctrinaireness a positive relief. This struck me too.

Harold then called on us, starting with the Home Secretary and going on to Ted Short. Messages were passed round; each of us was made to do our little piece. I noticed that those like Barbara who had been at the dinner were a bit left out and the others brought in. We put on quite a decent show and finally I got a message that after the youngest member of the Cabinet had spoken the senior member would make a philosophical wind-up, so I found myself having to finish off these proceedings. I started by describing how everybody talked about youth and revolution and how we had to find a philosophy to satisfy youth, but that I very much doubted this because the

[1] Richard Nixon visited London from February 24th to 26th. He had been elected President of the United States in November 1968 and was re-elected in November 1972 but resigned, rather than face impeachment, in August 1974.

numbers of youth in revolt were a tiny minority of university students, with
no philosophy, just an anti-philosophy. The significant fact is that they are
sentimentalists with no understanding of power and this is how they differ
from all their predecessors, who at least understood Marx and that politics is
about power. These don't. They think it is about protest and it makes them
so hopeless. I made my observation about 1968 being like 1848, the year of
unsuccessful revolutions, when the tottering Establishments hit back. I said,
'It was the crushing of Czechoslovakian modern liberal communism which
was the really characteristic event of 1968 and, equally, de Gaulle's crushing
of liberalism in France while in America the Establishment rose up and you
took over.' I had got up enough momentum to carry me along without this
being thought rude and it was not too bad. I went on to say that even in our
countries, America and England, the great problem of the day was the
difficulty of combining the general growth of liberty with the authority and
efficiency of the executive, how we were trying to do this ourselves in
Parliament and how our specialist committees were all turning against us.
There were great cries of protest and excitement and laughter and we ended
in a bit of a chaos. Nixon said, 'I'll swap our Professor Marcuse any day if you
will give me your Professor Crossman', so that was all right.[1] I suppose I had
put on a turn to serve the Prime Minister and given a certain intellectual
cachet to some fairly dreary proceedings. Then it was over and there were all
the dispatch riders outside waiting to escort Nixon back to the Embassy and
off to his plane tomorrow morning.

Wednesday, February 26th
After the Nixon Cabinet last night I went back to the House and sat there on
the front bench in my evening dress to listen to the interminable discussion
on the Parliament Bill. It showed only too well what happens when you try to
run the House of Commons without the usual channels. The House only
functions because of the agreement on timetabling between the Government and the Opposition Whips and now our front-bench machine was
trying to run it without the co-operation of their front bench. We were
paying the price for breaking off the talks. That had given the Opposition the
let out. Their own back benchers hate them for having agreed to this
measure and now they are evading the responsibility for it, something that
became clearer and clearer throughout the night.

I went back to my room, did my work and came down again, to find
Callaghan in an extraordinarily bad temper, wanting to crush the people who
are wasting his time and at the same time agreeing that the Bill is no good. He
is in the most appallingly divided mood. At 3.0 a.m. we both went across to
his room and talked to the Chief and Fred Peart about the tactics to be

[1] Herbert Marcuse, Professor of Philosophy at the University of California at San Diego,
whose books, including *One-Dimensional Man* (Boston: Beacon Books, 1964; London:
Routledge & Kegan Paul, 1964) and *Eros and Civilization* (Boston: Beacon Books, 1966;
London: Sphere Books, 1969), had attracted a large following.

pursued. We all agreed that we must go ahead and that our best chance is perhaps to get a guillotine. If we lose it that's that but it's the best thing to go for. Then I was sent home to bed.

Thursday, February 27th

All last night the back benchers were saying, 'This bloody Government, we don't want this bloody House of Lords Bill, we don't really blame people for filibustering against it. Why don't the Government get a guillotine or drop the Bill? Something must be done to stop this intolerable business of staying up night after night on this boring, second-rate measure.' All this is directed at me because the Tories spent the night saying that nobody else apart from me really wanted the Bill. This morning I saw in *The Times* a long account of how the back benchers are demanding that the big Bill should be dropped in favour of a Bill on powers. Obviously this is utterly ridiculous. We have done sixty-one hours on the big Bill and got the three most difficult clauses through. If we were to drop this and go for a Bill on powers we should have the whole Tory Party against us and their front bench in open opposition. It would take seven or eight days to get through and then we would have the House of Lords fighting it line by line, something that would be far worse. I assumed that Callaghan had put this in *The Times* and that we should have a tremendous row in Cabinet.

Right at the beginning Harold allowed Dick Marsh to make a bitter complaint about a vicious little story which had appeared in the *Guardian* and the *Financial Times*, recounting how he had put forward his Green Paper on the highway system and Cabinet had forced him to rewrite it. The story had mentioned a particular road in the South-West which Marsh had been forced to reconsider. The conversation moved from there to an attack by Harold on the B.B.C. because young David Dimbleby had made a flippant commentary on the Nixon arrival.[1] Harold had made a formal complaint to the B.B.C. via the Chief Whip and demanded the text of Dimbleby's remarks. The net result, as Harold himself frankly admitted, was that he had made this the major story in the Tuesday press and entirely eclipsed the story he wanted of the historic Cabinet the night before. He is obsessed with the B.B.C., and this and his obsession with leaks are his most outstanding weaknesses as a leader.

Harold then asked Fred for a report on Lords' reform. After Fred, Callaghan came in. I was expecting him to launch into a speech saying we ought to give up the Bill, but no, he was far cannier than that. He said things were very, very difficult and we had our own side against us. He thought we ought to soldier on, knowing that this would take not five days but more like the fifteen or sixteen that the Social Secretary had prophesied. Then I made

---

[1] Eldest son of the famous broadcaster Richard Dimbleby (who had died in 1966). He was a reporter for B.B.C.'s 'Panorama' programme 1967–9 and was its presenter 1974–7. From 1969 to 1972 he was presenter of '24 Hours'.

my speech about the lack of collaboration between the usual channels and said that it seemed to me that we had got to face sitting on perhaps into the Whitsun recess or well into August. We had to remember that Arthur Balfour got his 1902 Education Act through by sacrificing everything else, sitting until the middle of August and then getting Royal Assent in December. These things did take time and the important thing was that our own back benchers shouldn't believe that we were going to drop it. Once they knew we were going to soldier on life would be very different. Nothing really happened. Harold was careful and he also seemed to think we should soldier on. Michael Stewart took the same view and nobody dared say 'Drop the Bill'. I know why this is. If we dropped it at this stage because thirty or forty people are making a nuisance of themselves, it would be only too easy to apply the same argument to the Prices and Incomes or the Industrial Relations Bill. I think this was the basic thing which kept the Cabinet so uneasily quiet. We decided to soldier on but this is something we can't do. Maybe it is true that we can't get a guillotine yet, although Eddie Shackleton tells me that the Opposition aren't absolutely against it. Maybe we must hang on for another week or two but I am pretty sure we shan't be able to get through this unless we really work all through August or unless we can reconstitute the relationships between the two front benches. It is a major parliamentary problem and we left it unresolved.

Monday, March 3rd
Eddie summoned me across to the House of Lords where I found George Jellicoe. Just like last year Carrington has gone off to Australia at a critical moment and George wanted to talk to me about the Bill. We discussed things quite amiably until I finally said, 'But you see, George, we shall only get it through if you face the fact that your people are absolutely failing to help. It's like running a Finance Bill without a voluntary timetable. We only have our Whips there, yours aren't functioning at all and though it is making life virtually impossible we are going to jolly well slog ahead.' George had asked if there was any chance of a deal. I said, 'There's no chance of a deal because there is nothing we can get out of it. We have nothing to deal with because your people say they are incapable of leading your party and so they've bloody well got to face it, we're going to plough on even if it means their losing their Whitsun holiday.'

Tuesday, March 4th
The papers are full of the result of the vote on Barbara's White Paper yesterday.[1] Fifty-five of our people (counting tellers), including four P.P.S.s, had voted against.

[1] The motion approving the White Paper was carried by 224 votes to 62. The Conservatives and some 39 Labour M.P.s abstained and 9 Liberals in addition to the Labour rebels voted against the motion.

We sat down at a meeting of the Ministers concerned with the House of Lords affair. It wasn't a meeting of the P.L. Committee but Callaghan was in the chair with Fred Peart, John Silkin, Eddie Shackleton and me. We discussed tactics. It was obvious that Jim was going to go for a guillotine and he railroaded through the view that this is what we must have. We all knew what the choices were. One, to soldier on, trying to get the Bill through and taking about ten to fifteen days over it, which he ruled out on the ground that the Party wouldn't take it. Two, he ruled out abandoning it. He didn't mention the short Bill which I know is his real desire so we were left with three, the guillotine, and he got the Committee to agree. I said, 'A guillotine is no good. What matters with a guillotine is getting some chance of success. You won't have a chance of carrying a guillotine unless you show determination to carry on. In fact, you won't be able to shorten the proceedings unless you really are prepared to get the Bill even with long proceedings.' I was pushed aside but it was obvious that though Jim was shoving hard neither the Chief Whip nor Fred Peart were convinced that a guillotine was really possible.

In the afternoon the Prime Minister sent for the House of Lords Committee. I was in the middle of a meeting but the others reported to him that we were going for a guillotine. The Chief was to inquire carefully what was possible and our representatives were to talk to the Opposition front bench about the likelihood of their supporting us. I got hold of Harold afterwards and we had an interesting half-hour. I said, 'Well, there's no doubt about it now, Jim wants the guillotine even if we are defeated on it. After the election, when we are in Opposition, his chances will be better if it's been defeated. You have got to face it, Harold, he is playing for high stakes.' We discussed this a bit and then I said, 'But you know, the real truth is that if we have a guillotine we shall have to carry on.' 'Oh,' he said straightaway, 'I don't think we will. It's what I thought last summer and I've come back to it again. We ought to do just the Bill on powers if we can't get the other one.' I then said, 'You've forgotten the argument I gave you. I keep telling you it and after five minutes you interrupt me.' He said, 'I remember, Dick, but I warn you that at present I am thinking in terms of the short Bill.' Although he didn't agree with me he trusted me, and I was able to say, 'Well, I'll spell it all out for you at Cabinet on Thursday.' We were sitting in his room in the House, drinking whisky, and in half an hour we got through quite a lot and into a very friendly state together, so I was able to say this to him.

Meanwhile, although our Committee had agreed that our three, Callaghan, Peart and Silkin, should meet the Tory three, Maudling, Whitelaw and Jellicoe, the meeting wasn't organized because Callaghan didn't want it. He merely talked to Maudling, who said there could be no question of the Tories helping us and that they would have a three-line whip against the guillotine. There was no life left in the Tory Party for this Bill and least of all would they support a guillotine on a constitutional issue. When I met Willie

Whitelaw in the Lobby this evening he took me aside and repeated this. He said, 'I don't often have a chance to talk to you, Dick, but I just want to make sure that you know there can be no question of this. I know John Silkin isn't always believed but we really are going to have a three-line whip on this. I may think it right or wrong, I am one of the few who wants your Bill but this is really it.' This was completely at variance with what we had thought yesterday when we had vaguely talked about the hope of getting some twenty or thirty Tories to abstain on the guillotine motion. It was now clear from what Whitelaw was saying that their lists would be carefully examined, that nobody would be able to stay away and there would be a real Tory vote. So we know before Thursday's Cabinet that the guillotine will end in a Government defeat by about thirty votes.

Thursday, March 6th
At Cabinet we first of all discussed the Parliament Bill and already the Ministerial Committee's proposition for a guillotine was out of date, unless we were prepared either to challenge John Silkin's figures or to accept a defeat. In a sense Jim Callaghan tried to do both and we saw that he didn't mind the Government's losing and Fred Peart or John Silkin's authority being undermined. He revealed himself far too openly and it knocked out his views. The notion of a guillotine was defeated not only because we thought we might lose it but also because to use it would almost certainly make the Lords also vote the Bill down.

But when we came to an alternative things weren't so clear. Harold Wilson duly put up the notion of the short Bill and I am glad to say it was defeated, not only by me. Four or five people almost immediately said, 'For heaven's sake, don't let's think of short Bills as all that easy.' Another proposal was to have a timetable for a Committee of fifty upstairs but this was also seen to be practically impossible because there we would have an even smaller majority and even more difficulty in getting it through. It was felt that we should try to get the Bill through on the Floor of the House without a guillotine just as we are trying to do, and the first requisite is for the Party to know that we intend to do it. This is where the difficulty comes in because so long as Callaghan is in charge of the Bill no one's going to believe that this is our intention because he goes round saying it isn't. We are in a circular trap. Roy Mason then spoke extremely well and started up a new train of thought. It wasn't merely a question of the Parliament Bill, he said, or the difficulty we have on a measure which our own supporters don't care about and the Tories hate. People are being difficult about this Bill because they are being difficult about our legislative programme as a whole. The Party's discipline is being undermined and the chronic opposition, the thirty Labour M.P.s opposing the Defence Estimates, the bloody-mindedness on *In Place of Strife*, the difficulty on almost every subject we touch, is all part of the same thing. 'If we lose the Parliament Bill,' he said, 'we lose Barbara Castle's Industrial

Relations Bill.' Barbara saw this absolutely clearly and again Jim Callaghan miscalculated and lost because it brought every member of Cabinet who wanted any legislative programme to realize that we must not only soldier on but take active dynamic steps to get the P.L.P. to fight the bloody Bill through. If we were prepared to fight without a guillotine we could conceivably get enough of our people to vote for a guillotine, and that is roughly speaking where we got to.

Sunday, March 9th

We have been having the most wonderful spring weather, sharp, thick, white hoarfrost, cloudless skies night and day, brilliant moonlight and brilliant sunshine all day yesterday and again today. Spring comes, just as it often does, late but in the nick of time. I have been pruning our willow tree today and cutting off its top to make it a real weeping willow once more. Wonderful weather for our walks, good food and good drink in our lovely warm house. Anne and I are dreading the arrival of the new furniture, two great new sofas and magnificent new chairs, on which we have spent the vast sum of £800, for fear they are going to spoil the drawing-room. Last time we dreaded it and now we have got used to our splendid new table. Patrick said to me at breakfast today, just before we started our last reading from *Gulliver's Travels*, the part about the Yahoos, 'Why doesn't home ever occur in your diary?' and I said, 'I think it does quite a lot, it's always there in the background.' Perhaps it doesn't appear enough to make a real picture of my life and perhaps I ought to put more in about the role of the family to show how important it is to a politician but I am not sure really that I wouldn't then be writing creative fiction rather than the sort of diary I want.

Here at Prescote I am reflecting on the week. It's been dominated by the Ford strike. The Company's seeking an injunction to stop the union's breaking the contract caused an almost universal strike, then the Company lost its case and now the situation is worse than ever. Do Jones and Scanlon want to smash the Company and get a huge wage rise without promising any productivity or accepting any discipline? We have to face it that the unions are getting more and more out of control and difficult to manage than ever before.

The second thing we have to face is the crisis over the House of Lords. We are now getting to a situation where the Government might find itself in such a fix that it might have to go for an autumn election because we have disintegrated. I have already described in this diary what a mess we got into over Barbara's White Paper *In Place of Strife* because of Roy Jenkins's extraordinarily lackadaisical agreement to rush through her package. By agreeing to this, Roy has lost his incomes policy legislation; that is obvious now, nobody even discusses it any more. The Government is clearly not going to have another Prices and Incomes Bill, and Callaghan has won *de facto*. We always assumed that in its place we would have Barbara's trade union reforms as our main policy and we thought that this was a more constructive, more suitable electoral theme, but now slowly, slowly over a period of weeks, the inner crisis about Lords' reform is deeply affecting all our legislative plans. Callaghan is schizophrenic on the Parliament Bill, which has been one of the major factors making it easier for the Tory front bench to opt out of any responsibilities they had. The Committee Stage is at a standstill and we are not doing anything about it next week. Perhaps we can be excused by saying that this is the period to get the Defence White Paper through but it is obvious that unless we can finish the Lords' Bill before the end of April we shall be in a first-rate crisis.

This brings me to something which I was reflecting on this morning at 7.15 when I came down to my study and got my tea. I have been trying to compare the Cabinet of today with the Cabinet we first had in 1964 and the Mark II version in 1966. Harold said to me yesterday week that he found Cabinet so much easier to manage now. Well, that's certainly true. He has the whole of foreign affairs, including Rhodesia and entry into Europe, completely under his control, along with his old buddies Michael Stewart and Denis Healey. Then he has the economic side tightly tied up, with discipline entirely under Fred Peart and John Silkin and very little consultation about that. It's true we have Parliamentary Committee, where we discuss political problems a bit, but S.E.P. has now become two-thirds of the Cabinet, doing just the kind of stuff we used to do in Cabinet itself. O.P.D. hardly meets and when it does it's on secondary issues and whenever Harold arbitrarily chooses to call it rather than because it's got a regular job of work. So Cabinet as a Cabinet is meeting less and is less effectively controlling policy than ever before but, as I have said, it really matters less because there is less policy to control. As usual the budget has all been tied up absolutely secretly and no doubt the main post-budgetary decisions will already have been taken. The main thing is that there is nothing much to be done since we are now set on course and we can't move off it. Somehow, then, we have a lightweight talented Cabinet and one that is no longer a team. Nixon apparently said after he had been to our Cabinet that it was one of outstanding ability and calibre and variety. This is true; it isn't simply that we have six Oxford Firsts (seven before we lost Frank Pakenham), it is that we are still quite an interesting gang of people.

However there are two big contrasts between our Cabinet now and our Cabinet of '64, one being loss and one gain. The gain in my view is that the economic group—Barbara Castle, Roy Jenkins and Tony Crosland, buttressed by Peter Shore and Tony Wedgwood Benn—are infinitely superior to the collection we had running the economy in 1964—James Callaghan, George Brown and Douglas Jay. There is no doubt that if we had had this group at the beginning we would probably have made far fewer economic mistakes. On the other hand, Cabinet is now terribly unbalanced on its class and its trade union side and this is directly related to our present disastrous relationship with the trade union movement. George Brown and Ray Gunter may not be very big fish in the trade union pond but in our world they were. Although I think Roy Mason is one of the most promising new members and one of the ablest, infinitely superior, for example, to Dick Marsh, one can't really say that Mason and Marsh make up for the loss of Brown and Gunter and Frank Cousins.

Let's just spell the Cabinet round. There is Harold in the middle, facing out towards Horse Guards Parade, next to him now sits Roy Jenkins, then me, Willie Ross, George Thomson, George Thomas, that lickspittle from Wales. Next the Chief Whip, Tony Wedgwood Benn, Ted Short, Peter Shore, Jim Callaghan, Michael Stewart, Gerald Gardiner, Tony Crosland and then comes Dick Marsh. We are now on the far right, along the Horse Guards side. We find on Harold's right Jack Diamond, Roy Mason, Tony Greenwood and Burke Trend. Now I think what Nixon said is true—quite a talented gang, but politically lightweight. The fact that there are so many people who don't weigh at all in Cabinet is extremely expensive.

The third thing is the sameness of the Cabinet bloc. In the centre of the Cabinet is Denis Healey, still running defence like a tight little monopoly and trying to stray into foreign affairs fields. We have Willie Ross, conscientious, hard-working, with that terribly braying voice, almost as bad as Alice Bacon's, but decent, honest and still miraculously surviving all the changes. Gerald Gardiner, the Lord Chancellor, is as utterly remote from the reality of politics as ever, and ineffective, though he could be a great influence from that position. He is as Quakerish and high-minded as ever but also Quakerish and ruthless in his determination to get his way. Then we have John Diamond, who wasn't in Cabinet before, but here he is now with just the same accountant's mind, and then Michael Stewart, to and fro either in Education or D.E.A. or the Foreign Office, absolutely dull but a brilliant debater, an important, doctrinaire right-winger at the dead centre.

That group is all exactly the same, so I turn to what has happened at the other levels. What about the make-weights, the people who are there just because Harold wants them in? Tony Greenwood has stayed the pace throughout, holding an important office extremely badly, and he is there as a vote for Harold. We have three other complete cyphers—Cledwyn Hughes, George Thomas and George Thomson not doing a stroke—all Harold's henchmen. I mentioned Benn and Shore as members of the economic team and they have of course a great role. They are not as close to the Prime Minister as they were because each of them has settled down and established himself in his own job. Benn has enormously improved at MinTech. after a ghastly start as Postmaster-General. He has obviously put himself over to British industry, a very easy thing to do because he has gone for only that research which is going to be commercially beneficial. He and Shore represent the interventionist side of Harold's mind, his belief in the I.R.C. and in investment grants.

Let me turn now to mavericks. There are always some of these. In the first Cabinet we had Frank Pakenham and now we really have two odd characters. There is Ted Short, who began with a brilliant press as a wonderful chap, but he is just a martinet headmaster, bleating for what he can get, with no wisdom and giving very little to the Cabinet. There is Dick Marsh, our Minister of Transport, brash, erratic, invariably swallowing the departmental line, preaching it, and otherwise expressing as the youngest member of the Cabinet the most reactionary views on things like votes at eighteen or the attitude to students. They really add very little.

I haven't yet mentioned Eddie Shackleton. Cabinet is greatly strengthened by having Frank Pakenham out and Eddie in. He is now the Minister of the new Civil Service Department, an addition to some extent to the economic side and to the solid Centre. I have also left out of account discipline, which is enormously important. The Bowden–Silkin regime of 1964 did extremely well in the first Parliament when things were relatively easy and there was a majority of three. Then came the second liberalizing regime of myself and Silkin, the reforming period that ended very abruptly when I quarrelled with Harold and demanded to get out. I was replaced by Fred Peart, who as Minister of Agriculture had been quite a force in his own right, a loyal Harold Wilson supporter, an anti-European, standing for a lot, right in the middle of the Cabinet. As I have said before, he is like the Duke of Omnium, a solid representative of the Labour Establishment, charming, nice, decent; I am fond of him. He hasn't got the intellectual substance which I had but he's a great deal more popular in the House and I think in the Party. Here his ineffectiveness is almost an advantage because they allow him to get away with the business of the week more easily. But he lacks authority on a thing like the Parliament Bill and the new crisis of discipline which is now threatening the Party. I don't think the Government can hold together for the rest of this Parliament with Peart and Silkin in charge of discipline, Peart because he lacks authority, Silkin because he has not developed a yard. He is still the Prime Minister's lap-dog. When he took over from Ted Short in the summer of 1966 he was very young, having only been in Parliament three years. He is a squashy, fat Silkin, anxious to please, and he does not assert any authority over the Prime Minister. John changes his mind whenever Harold's mind changes, to and fro he goes, talking differently to different people.

What about Barbara? She is the great new axis of strength. She has jumped from the bottom of the Cabinet to the top and she is really, though not the Deputy Prime Minister in title, the effective number two. She is the only person of Prime Ministerial timber in the Cabinet. She is very unpopular now and though the job she is doing is terrific it is unsuccessful. A dynamic prices and incomes policy attached to the person of the First Secretary is, I think, terribly damaging to the Party. But she is as nice as ever and as effective. She is a real politician. Barbara has risen and expanded as a person, whereas Roy Jenkins, after an early rise to fame, has settled down to being a rather narrow, conventional Establishment Chancellor, not much coming out of his shell, and being defeated when he tries to.

I must say the only other person who is in any way of the same stature as the Prime Minister or Barbara is, in my view, Jim Callaghan. He and I in a funny way are the two odd men out in the Cabinet. As Chancellor Jim was for some months psychologically out, clearly exhausted, nearly physically broken, and when he recovered he did an enormous take-over of the Home Office, building up his position as a plain-style man of the people who will have no nonsense. With great skill he has established himself quite consciously over the past nine months as the only man who is known to be opposed to Harold, known to have no particular support for this Government in its present form or for the prices and incomes policy, speaking out on behalf of the trade unions or anything else he likes, setting himself up fairly openly as an alternative to Harold Wilson. Not, of course, the alternative now but the other axis of attraction. There he sits, and there he knows perfectly well, as I do, that right up to the election there is no future for Jim beyond the place he occupies. It's after the election, leading the rump in Opposition, that he sees his chance will come. He is also a tremendous intriguer, a politician in the Daltonian sense, except that Dalton couldn't keep his secrets and his Machiavellianism to himself.[1] Jim can be two-faced, but his fault is perhaps that he does far too much talking for a really successful Machiavellian politician, round the smoking room, round the tea room, dashing away with all the boys. He is a tremendous chatterer with the press, especially the *Guardian* 'Miscellany' column, and he is as compulsive a communicator with the press as I am and a great deal more leaky. Most of what I chat about is stuff they don't want to print but I suspect that Jim is now a major source of embarrassing material.

What about me? Last of all, we come to the Social Services Secretary. I am still rated, and rightly, as an absolutely solid Harold man, never dreaming of challenging his authority. I am very free in my outspoken, objective criticism of him, which is not all that elevated, but saying quite clearly that whatever his deficiencies he is the only thing we've got and we will keep on having him. What else am I in Cabinet? Having given up my central position to Fred Peart, where I might have stayed as a general authority in Cabinet and in the House, I have now got right away to one side, on to the back of a huge Department in the Elephant and Castle where I rule my own roost. It is as big as Defence and in a way much nearer to public opinion. Then in the Cabinet I

[1] Hugh Dalton, Labour M.P. for Camberwell 1924–9 and for Bishop Auckland 1929–31 and 1935–59, was Minister of Economic Warfare 1940–2, President of the B.O.T. 1942–5, Chancellor of the Exchequer 1945–7, Chancellor of the Duchy of Lancaster 1948–50, Minister of Town and Country Planning 1950–1 and Minister of Local Government and Planning 1951. He became a life peer in 1960 and died in 1962. He wrote three volumes of memoirs which in their uninhibited candour are the nearest rival to Crossman's own. *Call Back Yesterday, The Fateful Years, High Tide and After*: London, Frederick Muller.

have my very downright, outspoken, utterly independent position as the one man who can really stand up to Harold because his loyalty is not in dispute. So here we have Jim, the one man who stands up to the Prime Minister because his loyalty is in dispute, I the one whose loyalty is not in question, the two big old men, so to speak. That is roughly what we are.

Monday, March 10th
This evening I had a great deal of reading to do. One of my three boxes last night was entirely devoted to the Ely Hospital near Cardiff. Brian Abel-Smith had reminded me that in October I had been told that I would soon have this appalling problem. Geoffrey Howe,[1] one of the ablest of the young Tory lawyers, had been Chairman of an Inquiry into an outrageous news-paper story that there had been cruelty and pilfering in the Ely Mental Hospital. Kenneth Robinson had established the inquiry in September 1967, and it had taken more than a year, submitting its report in September 1968, before I took over. The report had been 83,000 words long and straightaway the Ministry had said that there must be a confidential report in full for the Department and a shortened version for publication. 'Not on your life,' Geoffrey Howe had said, 'I must get out the essential facts.' For three months the Department and Howe had fought about the character of the report. We had three drafts, the full, unabridged 83,000 words, a much shorter version of some 20,000 words and a medium version omitting only one-twelfth of the original stuff. I was suddenly told that I had to agree this because it was necessary to publish the report of the Inquiry before March 31st, the date on which I hand over the control of Health in Wales to the Secretary of State for Wales. I was furious because it was outrageous to bring it to my notice on Monday night, giving me two days to agree with it when I could have seen it at any time in the last three months.

Tuesday, March 11th
This morning I summoned Miss Hedley,[2] the head of the Hospital Section, and Dr Yellowlees and said,[3] 'What the devil is this? I can't possibly decide it overnight.' I told them I would read it all tonight because time was really pressing. We would have a special meeting tomorrow morning and I would meet George Thomas on Thursday. I think I put the fear of God into them and I also warned them that I would then make the decision whether to publish in full or not but that in my view of the situation there was no alternative to publishing the full, unabridged 83,000 words. If I published

[1] Conservative M.P. for Bebington 1964–6, for Reigate 1970–4 and for Surrey East since 1974.
[2] Under-Secretary at the D.H.S.S. 1967–75, she had been Secretary to the Royal Commission on the Law Relating to Mental Illness and Mental Deficiency 1954–7.
[3] Sir Henry Yellowlees (K.C.B. 1975) was Deputy Chief Medical Officer at the D.H.S.S. 1967–72, Second Chief Medical Officer 1972–3, and since 1973 Chief Medical Officer at the D.H.S.S., the D.E.S. and the Home Office.

any less Geoffrey Howe would be entitled to go on television and talk about suppression.

So tonight I went to bed and read and read and it seemed clearer than ever that the whole thing had to be published. The report completely substantiated the *News of the World* story and I might as well make the best of it by outright publication. But I was also clear in my own mind that I could only publish and survive politically if in the course of my Statement I announced necessary changes in policy including the adoption by the Ministry and the R.H.B.s of a system of inspectorates, central and regional, such as there are in almost every other Ministry and such as the Health Service has never yet permitted itself.

Wednesday, March 12th
At 12.30 this afternoon we had the critical meeting on Ely in my room at Alexander Fleming House with about twelve people round the table. Bea Serota came. She has been extremely good and forced this issue through directly she took over from David Ennals, who had done nothing about it for two months. There we were with the retinue of officials. I started by saying that we had better face it that this report was not only a tremendous indictment of the Ely Hospital but of the Hospital Management Committee, which had failed to be aware of what was going on, and of the Regional Hospital Board and of ourselves, because we as a Ministry are responsible for our agents down there in the Health Service. Ghastly things had gone on for years at Ely. We hadn't known, for example, that two nurses had been dismissed because they had tried to expose the scandals. The officials were on the defensive and I discovered that they intended me simply to publish the report with a Statement deploring it. I said, 'Not on your life. If I do that there will be a whole series of investigations into hospitals all over the country'—because I had found during this week that there are no less than 250,000 people in long-stay, sub-normal, psychiatric or geriatric hospitals, cooped up in these old public assistance buildings with no adequate inspectorate—'and the inquiries might be able to find in many of the other ones equally scandalous things. It is a first-rate crisis for the Service.' This produced some consternation. They said my idea was quite impracticable. An inspectorate would have all kinds of difficulties. The doctors would demand that their affairs should only be inspected by doctors and anyway this decision couldn't possibly be taken between now and the publication of the White Paper.

Then we had a long, long argument about which version should be published and on that I simply won. At the end one or two of the officials said, 'Frankly, there doesn't seem to be any difference between the twelve-twelfths and the eleven-twelfths.' I pointed out that either we took the credit of publishing the whole thing or we would be at the mercy of one of the cleverest Conservative lawyers. One of the most dramatic moments of this meeting was when I referred to our not knowing anything about it and Bea said, 'Didn't we? You ask the Chief Nurse what she knows about it.'[1] Dame Kathleen said, 'Oh, yes. We used to have people going down there, regularly visiting.' I said, 'Did they report?' 'Yes.' 'When was the last report?' 'Three or four years ago.' 'Have you got it?' Bea had arranged to have it and she threw it across the table to me. It was a deplorable report, admitting scandalous conditions, bad nursing, the basis of all the *News of the World* revelations that Geoffrey Howe had confirmed. I asked what had happened to this when it came in and the answer was that it had gone on file. So the Ministry did in fact know and I am pretty sure they have a shrewd idea that there are a great number of unspecified long-stay hospitals with conditions not very different from those at Ely. I have to be careful of course, because the badness of the ghastly old buildings I have visited doesn't necessarily mean there is pilfering, torture and cruelty. That is a matter of staffing. Nevertheless staff do get utterly demoralized by bad buildings, bad pay, staff shortages, lack of domestic help and the two things are linked together. It was a tremendous meeting and I simply told them, 'I am going to see the Welsh Secretary tomorrow. I shall get his leave to publish. Not what you propose, just putting a copy of this in the Library and giving it to the press, but publishing a White Paper. We will bring it right out into the open and I want a draft Statement to be submitted to the Social Services Committee. Incidentally, I have talked to the Prime Minister already about it and he agrees.' This produced real movement.

Sunday, March 23rd
When I got my boxes yesterday I found at last a file on Ely, a businesslike action plan and a better draft, more like what I wanted. At last I'd got a concession that the inspectorate will be independent and reporting to me, so I won on that one. Altogether it was a serviceable job and I worked over the draft trying to sharpen it up. I rang up the editor of the *News of the World*, the paper whose sensational disclosures had started the whole thing off, and warned him what was happening, saying that I would give him an exclusive article. Wilfred Sendall, Political Correspondent of the *Daily Express*, who had scented something, rang up and wanted to know where the place was. I wouldn't tell him or give him anything about it except that there was a sensational report coming and I would be making a Statement next week. I have already seen George Thomas and shown him my draft paper and we've had an interesting discussion about linking things up with his office.

For the rest of the day Charles and Mary Woodhouse, my favourite sister and brother-in-law, came over from Oxford, and Charles spent the whole afternoon playing games with Patrick and Virginia, who adore him, while I

---

[1] Dame Kathleen Raven (D.B.E. 1968) was Matron of the General Infirmary, Leeds 1949–57 and Chief Nursing Officer at first the Ministry of Health and then the D.H.S.S. 1958–72.

took Mary and Anne for a walk in the bleak east wind, the sort of weather we always seem to have here in March. This is a bitterly cold month in North Oxfordshire. Our grass never seems to grow and there is always a shortage of food for the cattle and an anxiety about how we shall keep them going. When it hasn't been snowing it's been raining and flooding and the farm is really down. However, everything was fine for the children and we have now to make arrangements for the pool to be heated on Good Friday, ready for our Easter holidays, so that I can have at least a week of daily swimming whatever the cold outside. Life at home is as good as ever.

Monday, March 24th

I was able to have a special meeting of the Social Services Committee to report on my draft on post-Ely policy and formally get their consent. It is part of our Cabinet machinery that it is wise to get your Committee behind you and as I was introducing a new service and inspectorate which would require manpower and money, though of a limited amount, it was wise to do this. The Ministry are now calling the inspectorate a policy advisory service and in the draft it is clearly stated that the Director of the new service should be directly responsible to me. It was a very sympathetic meeting. Everybody seemed to admit frankly that they knew the whole treatment of mental health was inadequate. It was one of those occasions when each person could chip in as a human being, not as a Minister, for, except for the Treasury, there was virtually no departmental briefing. After this I cleared the redraft of the Statement with George Thomas. We had agreed that I would first announce this and take upon myself the responsibility of the scandal (which has taken place not only in a Welsh hospital but in his own constituency area of Cardiff). He has been tricky and jumpy but I have managed to carry him along.

Tuesday, March 25th

I reported on our meeting at Social Services Committee and Cabinet was pretty aghast. They thought, 'My God, another bloody scandal,' but really the interest to the Prime Minister lay in the fact that it was being announced on Thursday, the day of three by-elections.[1] It appalled him that I should have forgotten this and it was even worse when it was discovered that Fred Peart, who had given me written leave to make my Statement, had forgotten it as well. Harold wondered how it was possible that one should ruin the chances of people voting Labour by having this terrible story blurted out on the 6 o'clock news that very evening. It is quite true that neither Fred nor I

[1] At Walthamstow East on March 27th Michael McNair-Wilson regained the seat for the Conservatives with a majority of 5,479 on a 15·9 per cent swing from Labour. In the by-election at Brighton Pavilion, Julian Amery held the seat for the Conservatives with a 12,982 majority and a 17·9 per cent swing from Labour. At Weston-super-Mare, Alfred Wiggin held the seat for the Conservatives with a 20,472 majority on a 13·9 swing from Labour.

had remembered the by-elections when we fixed the date. We had wanted to have a Monday for it and we had put it back to the Thursday for the convenience of the Secretary of State for Wales. Nor would it have occurred to me that this could do us electoral harm. Indeed it was my deep conviction that it could do us only electoral good to be seen to be acting courageously, but that was not Harold's view and he sat and fretted until I finally made it clear that all the arrangements had been made and we couldn't go back on them. Anyway he was due to fly to Lagos on Wednesday night and I suppose he went away feeling, 'There's Dick, out of touch again.'

Thursday, March 27th
The actual day of my Report—and the whole of the morning from 9.0 to 12.0 I had a series of meetings. In the House of Commons Michael Stewart was answering Questions for Harold, who had set off for Lagos.[1] I had a considerable time to wait because my Office had slipped up. In order to speak before the Business Statement I would have had to answer a Private Notice Question but, as the Office hadn't put one on at the end of the list of Questions, my Statement on the White Paper had to follow the Business Statement. After Michael Stewart's Question, therefore, we had half an hour of the real heavy, idiotic House of Commons' humour that there is from 3.30 to 4 o'clock on Thursdays, ribbing the Lord President of the Council about the Parliament (No. 2) Bill, about Nabarro and everything else. The House got sillier and sillier and I felt a bit bleak and wondered whether I could switch their mood in the way I needed.

At last we got to the Statement. This must have been the ninth or tenth draft and I felt a great frog in my throat when I started because I really do care and feel righteously indignant about this. I launched in and in thirty seconds I knew I had gripped the House by admitting the truth of the allegations, the excellence of the Report and the need for remedial action. Tam had done well and briefed three or four Labour M.P.s so we managed to have questions from which all the points I needed were made thoroughly and effectively, about the preliminary clean-up which has taken place at Ely, the need for professional support on the Advisory Service, the need to get our priorities right within the N.H.S., not just to get extra money for mental hospitals but to get our balance right between these and ordinary hospitals. Nearly all of it came right and all the way through Ted Heath, Quintin Hogg and Iain Macleod sat on the Opposition front bench and approved. Although it had come after the Business Statement they stuck it out for the next half-hour. I sat down knowing I had brought off a success.

During the week before Easter the Government's difficulties on the Committee Stage of the Parliament Bill came to a head as back benchers continued to

[1] The Prime Minister had flown to Lagos, Nigeria in a vain effort to sit as a conciliator in the Nigerian Civil war. He later flew on to Ethiopia.

filibuster. The Party and the Government also continued to be deeply divided over the industrial relations policy. On March 26th the N.E.C. had voted against the First Secretary's plans by 16 votes to 5, the first occasion on which they had formally rejected a Government proposal since the 1964 General Election. James Callaghan, the Party Treasurer, appeared to be one of those opposing Mrs Castle's policy.

According to Mr Wilson's own account, while he was returning to London from Ethiopia he received en route, *on April 2nd, a telegram from Barbara Castle about the Chancellor's proposal for a short interim Industrial Relations Bill, to be announced together with the dropping of further prices and incomes legislation in the budget speech. The First Secretary saw some advantage in this course but stated that she had received advice that such a short Bill could not be prepared in time. On his return to London and after making a Statement to the House on his Nigerian visit the Prime Minister had a late meeting with Barbara Castle and Roy Jenkins and, to his surprise, the First Secretary 'was now confident that the Bill could be got ready'.*

On April 3rd the Cabinet met and the Prime Minister began by making it clear to Mr Callaghan and any other critics of the proposed trade union reform that they were free to resign. Cabinet unanimously reaffirmed both the decision to introduce an Industrial Relations Bill and also the obligations implied by collective responsibility. The Chancellor's proposal for the package was put to Cabinet and approved.[1]

Friday, April 4th–Monday, April 7th

This is a kind of part work, part holiday, pre-budget diary. The first thing to mention about Easter is the weather, which turned good last Wednesday. I came down yesterday evening and now we are having absolutely perfect cloudless days. There was a cold east wind at the beginning but the temperature is creeping up into the sixties and seventies and spring is slowly coming out of winter. When I got back, Anne Swingler had come over from Ilmington to take a few days off and to escape from a tiny cottage and a lot of relatives. I should have been more sympathetic to her when I arrived but I came in somehow keyed up. I was sure the swimming bath would be ready and heated but the *En Tout Cas* company haven't turned up from Leicester and there I was with my greatest anticipation frustrated. It made me more downcast than it should. Perhaps I was overwrought, perhaps I had had a long time in Parliament, but, oh dear, I felt that my Anne and Pritchett had let me down.

I have spent quite a lot of time on my island and quite a lot of money planting bulbs. I had been in despair because time after time they were flooded in this drenching winter but now there are scillas and young irises and daffodils. It's only a tiny beginning but the little patches of flowers on my

---

[1] According to Mr Wilson's own history the proposal was also put to Cabinet on April 14th. See *Wilson*, pp. 642, 626–7, 639–40.

island are my pleasure. By the end of the weekend my bad temper had quite disappeared.

Tuesday, April 8th
Over the Easter weekend I rang Roy and Barbara and we agreed to meet at Roy's this afternoon at 6.0.

In the evening I motored to East Hendred and there in the garden just as the sun was setting I found Roy with Barbara, who had arrived at 5 o'clock in time for tea and a long talk with Roy. We got down to business and began to discuss what our political strategy should be. I outlined my idea that we should drop the Parliament Bill in exchange for an immediate short Industrial Relations Bill this session. 'Well,' said Roy, 'we have been thinking rather differently. Barbara has proposed that in my budget speech I should announce that we are not reviving the 1968 prices and incomes legislation when it lapses at the end of the year and then some weeks later, just before the Whitsun recess, Barbara will announce her immediate short-term I.R. Bill. She would like us to do it in these two stages. She is reluctant to depart in any way from her principle of full consultation with the T.U.C. and she sees every kind of difficulty, but if she has to do it she would like to do it this way. I think we should do it all in one. I can't just announce the end of prices and incomes. I ought to announce in the budget speech both that and the immediate I.R. Bill at the same time as part of a single strategy.'

I immediately agreed with Roy, and said it had always been my view that the fatal flaw in Barbara's strategy was to have a White Paper in January and then ten months of bickering and so-called consultation before the Bill could be got ready. As a result she would have to make far more concessions than she wanted and I just didn't think it was practical politics. I then said, 'It is a bit difficult to know about this unless we know what is in the budget speech,' whereupon Roy pulled himself together and said, 'Let's go indoors and have a drink in my study and I'll tell you about the budget.'

Then he filled me in on the main proposals of the budget, what you might call the socialist proposal to make bank overdrafts no longer free of tax, the clauses removing the injustices of the Land Commission and on the taking of £¼ million out of consumption by relatively mild methods, including the increase of S.E.T.[1] We all agreed it would be the making of this humdrum budget to have a broad statement of our policy with regard to prices and incomes and trade union legislation. All this would therefore have to be said on the budget Tuesday, and at the party meeting on the Wednesday morning Harold would announce the dropping of the Parliament Bill in favour of the immediate short-term Industrial Relations Bill and the Merchant Shipping Bill. Barbara didn't like the idea, and was insistent at first, but she finally

[1] Selective Employment Tax, the brainchild of Lord Kaldor and introduced by Mr Callaghan in his May 1966 budget, was a payroll tax paid by employers, with refunds for manufacturing industry.

understood that the only way to get her Bill in the form she wanted was to shove it through this session, so that next September the Trade Union Congress will be presented with a *fait accompli*. Barbara said she and the Prime Minister were seeing the T.U.C. and that she would no doubt be told by them not to have a Bill. We told her that in that case it was most important to keep things open.

We discussed what we should say to Harold. We agreed to fill him in on the telephone tomorrow and we decided to meet again the day after tomorrow and ask Harold to see us.

Thursday, April 10th

Harold was coming back from the Scillies this afternoon, travelling up by train from Penzance to arrive in London at 4 o'clock, so this morning I took the 12.30 train up to London, the only one which would get me there in time to see Roy before Harold arrived. I went in and had tea with Roy and then Barbara arrived and we checked things over. The new fact was that in preparation for the meeting with the T.U.C. General Council tomorrow, Vic Feather had last night sent Harold a very friendly letter,[1] simply saying 'Let's settle this amicably in tripartite discussion with the C.B.I.' It was quite different from the threatening tone that, according to the morning papers, he was supposed to have adopted. This was however much more difficult to handle because it was so much more reasonable and at first sight it seemed that it would knock out the idea of an early Bill to be announced in the budget. How could Harold and Barbara meet the T.U.C. on Friday and blankly listen to them, knowing at the back of their minds that the following Tuesday we were going to announce the immediate Bill which they don't want?[2] But the more we reflected, the more we realized that the T.U.C. letter was chiefly tactical and that if we accepted it we would go on talking till kingdom come and there would be no Bill. What we had to do was to use Friday's meeting to warn them that we couldn't exclude the possibility of legislation and this was something we had to bring home to Harold.

We went from Roy's room through to No. 10 so the press outside didn't know we were there and found Harold, fat and bronzed, coming into his study, anxious to talk to us as though nothing had happened. He was full of fitness and life and he simply turned to Roy and said, 'Come on.' Roy, who had already explained it all to him on the telephone, started with a few sentences and then turned it over to Barbara. She is a curious girl when she

[1] Assistant General Secretary of the T.U.C. 1960–9 and General Secretary 1969–73. He became a life peer in 1974 and was Vice-Chairman of the British Waterways Board from 1974 until his death in 1976.

[2] The meeting was originally to take place on the morning of budget day, April 15th, but the Prime Minister felt that, since that meeting would be concerned with the Chancellor's announcement of the package in the budget speech, there should be an earlier meeting 'for them to make their formal representations on the White Paper'. A meeting was accordingly arranged for Friday, April 11th. See *Wilson*, p. 641.

talks, unwinding her skein of long, slow sentences, repetitious and rather trying to listen to, and to my surprise the package we had agreed on was not what she was describing. She started by saying that if it hadn't been for the letter we had received and the need to talk to the T.U.C. tomorrow she would have advised us to let Roy announce the Prices and Incomes Bill, then to make her own announcement three or four weeks later. She said, 'It would be less of an affront to the T.U.C. and would give them more time for consultations. Since they are now going to directly question us tomorrow, I think this is what we have got to do.' She had found herself a complicated new reason for lining up.[1] Harold listened and then jumped in before I could have a word, making it clear that he wanted the whole shoot right at the beginning. He immediately saw the case for instant politics and that instant it must be. I interrupted and said, 'Look, the most powerful reason for a package is the Parliament Bill. If Barbara has her way and we take this in two stages, we shall have another four weeks of the Parliament Bill. Now, either we push that Bill or we drop it and as we can't drop it without a good reason, what we need is a package with Roy making his announcement as we have planned, next Tuesday, and Harold making his announcement on dropping the Parliament Bill the day after.' 'Yes,' said Harold, thinking of something new. 'I can do it at 3.30 on Wednesday and put the blame on the Tories for breaking the all-party arrangement. This makes the whole difference, Dick's quite right. This is what is really important.' Then he was off again for a good half-hour's discussion with Barbara on his idea of how to get round the difficulty of fining unofficial strikers, cooking up the most elaborate alternative of a special levy on industry, and so on.

We then had a very interesting time listening to Harold discuss the reactions of the rest of Cabinet. Should the Chief Whip be told? Well, not too soon, he is fairly secure, but he talks. What about Denis? Roy said that he had already told Denis on the telephone to Washington. What about Tony Crosland? Roy had talked to him too and he was mainly concerned not about the merits of the plan, which seemed to him fairly sound, but about the procedures and the possibility that the inner group would be blamed for not consulting Cabinet in advance. Should Judith be told? 'She is a talker,' said the Prime Minister and we agreed that I should speak to her on Monday just before Cabinet. Tony Greenwood? 'He'll cut up rough but he's ineffective.' Short? 'Absolutely unpredictable and doesn't matter.' Willie Ross? 'He's all right,' said the Prime Minister. 'Cledwyn Hughes is bound to be all right and so is George Thomson.' Nobody mentioned Peter Shore or Gerald Gardiner, I realized afterwards; they didn't count in our calculations. Dick

[1] From Crossman's ambiguous account of the First Secretary's remarks it is impossible to tell whether she is saying that she still wished to 'line up' the two announcements in the same package or to separate them by three to four weeks. It seems from Crossman's account of the conversation and his own arguments that the First Secretary favoured the second, longer drawn-out course.

Marsh is unpredictable and he'll come down on our side and Mason will be loyal. I said finally, 'What about Jim Callaghan? Do we plan for his resignation? I think if we have this package and wrap it up tight, after the terrible press Jim has got he may be compelled to resign, not for reasons of courage but for reasons of cowardice. I wouldn't rate it as probable,' and I added something Roy had said to me minutes before, 'but highly possible. I'd rate the chance of his resigning as 40 per cent.' Harold said, 'I don't mind if he does.' We all agreed that it would be infinitely less damaging if he resigned now that we had taken the initiative than if he had resigned on the Thursday before Easter. All this had taken from 5 o'clock until just before 7 o'clock, when I strolled out across the park.

Monday, April 14th
The budget Cabinet went quietly. Roy explained his ingenious contraption at some length. It showed what you could do with a no-change budget.[1] We were carrying on the strategy exactly as before and only raising the minimum amount to see us through. He has added £340 million on taxation, out of S.E.T. and little bits on estate duty, wine and purchase tax, so ingeniously disposed that it won't hurt too much and will only increase the cost of living by ½ per cent. A masterly minor performance again, each item beautifully prepared by Roy and beautifully rehearsed. He has prepared his budget speech as carefully as I prepared my Ely announcement but it only marks the contrast with the flaccid, indecisive bungling of Harold's central direction.

From there I went at midday to the Industrial Relations Committee, where Barbara put before us the package she proposed for the short Bill. The Committee changed it tremendously. We firmly recommended the substitution of a section on inter-union disputes for the section on compulsory strike ballots and we also thought that attachment of wages was out as well and that Barbara should think of something else. We thought we had done pretty well and after that Barbara and I rushed off, ironically, to the Café Royal, right up to the top to a delicious flat where Charles Forte now lives.[2] He not only has a string of cheap restaurants including the motorway ones where Patrick and Virginia love to eat baked beans, sausages and chips, but he now owns the Café Royal and he has made it into a slap-up restaurant.

[1] In what was the third heaviest imposition on the taxpayer of any post-war budget the Chancellor raised the tax on petrol by 3*d.* a gallon, increased taxes on gaming and table wine, raised corporation tax by 2½ per cent to 45 per cent of net company profits, removed tax relief for interest payments on loans and bank overdrafts and raised from 37*s.* 6*d.* to 48*s.* a week the Selective Employment Tax paid by employers in the service industries for each adult male worker they employed. The only concession was an increase in income tax allowances, which abolished income tax for about 1 million of the lowest paid and reduced it for a further 600,000. The Chancellor also announced that in the autumn there would be an uprating of social security benefits, so that from November the basic pension for a single person would rise by 10*s.* to £5 a week and for a married couple by 16*s.* to £8 2*s.* a week.
[2] Deputy Chairman of Trust Houses Forte Ltd since 1970, Chief Executive 1971–5 and Joint Chief Executive since 1975. He was knighted in 1970.

He is a tiny, clever man, with a big voice and a long head, who has proposed that we should borrow his motor-yacht and crew at Whitsun. We decided to cruise from Rome down to Naples and we've booked our flights to Rome for four Crossmans and the two Castles. But will this be possible? The Parliament Bill is out of the way and so the main parliamentary obstacle to a full fortnight recess at Whitsun has been removed but will Barbara and I still be on the same side? I don't know.

I went straight into Cabinet and the question of the short Industrial Relations Bill. There was a good deal of complaint and not only from our old friend James Callaghan. Roy Mason, Dick Marsh and Tony Crosland were all upset at the sudden change of plan. Why should the Cabinet be rushed, why shouldn't we work out a package which the trade union movement as a whole could accept? On the other hand there was a deep feeling that a short Bill was the only practical thing and Tony Crosland was certainly influenced by the thought, although this wasn't allowed to be mentioned, that the dropping of the Parliament Bill was some compensation for this. Strangely enough, the thing which excited most alarm was the dropping of the Prices and Incomes Bill. There was a feeling that Part II of the present legislation was not sufficient, that we were shifting about and obviously being harried from pillar to post and that this would give a tremendous sense of weakness and disillusionment in the country outside. I am afraid that all this is true and that the situation is desperate, and Cabinet think this as well. I feel that in giving up the Prices and Incomes Bill now, and saying so in his budget Statement, Roy is asking for trouble because from now until the end of the year everybody will forge ahead with their wage claims while we are indulging in a fight with the unions about industrial relations which will almost provoke them into increasing wages if they possibly can. This point was well put by Peter Shore and also by Tony Wedgwood Benn, who was gravely anxious about the whole strategy. What about Mr Callaghan? When I had discussed this with the Prime Minister and Roy beforehand, they were quite certain he wouldn't resign, though I myself felt rather the opposite. I couldn't have been more wrong. His whole attitude at Cabinet was that his presence was essential to retain the unity of the unions and if he thought he saw, as I thought I saw, that we had dropped the idea of a compulsory strike ballot and were going to modify the clauses on attachment of wages he clearly felt that this justified him in staying and in adopting the line he was going to take. So he made a long speech about how we must now work together and how pleased he was at the decision. I got a little note from the Prime Minister, which I have kept, saying 'the most salubrious part of Cardiff will in future be called Paper Tiger Bay.'* It showed that Harold was still capable of a skilled wisecrack and I was delighted, as indeed I was on the whole delighted by the entire meeting.

* A reference to the fact that the very insalubrious dockland area of Tiger Bay is part of Jim Callaghan's constituency.

Sunday, April 20th

I was really cheerful earlier this week because I thought we were launching the new policy with reasonable success and that at least we had cleaned out the compulsory strike ballot and made one major, clear-cut concession to the trade unions. Now I find that in a speech in Scotland on Friday Barbara has announced that we haven't dropped the strike ballot but merely postponed it to the big Bill in the next session.[1] When I look back at Wednesday's Cabinet minutes, sure enough, I see that it has only been postponed for discussion till this coming week. Again, on the attachment of wages we have still found no way of not sending strikers to jail. This has all been mucked up, nothing is clear and we have come totally unstuck. What happened? At Easter we three met and after that Harold and Barbara saw the T.U.C. for two hours on the Friday and again on the Monday and nobody knows what they said. Tony Crosland thinks we understand one thing and they decided another. There is no inner coherence and we are blundering ahead with Barbara and the Prime Minister just as much a two-man show as ever they were. They launched this thing in December, pushed it through Cabinet by extremely unscrupulous means in January and, when we learnt what they were doing, got Cabinet to accept the Bill. They refused to give it green edges, decided to go ahead on the long-term plan and then, when it failed, as we predicted it would because they couldn't sustain consultations, we put on a short-term plan. Now we have agreed on this, we haven't any inner body to plan exactly how to put it through and what will be the form of our discussions with the trade unions, the N.E.C. and the Parliamentary Party. It now sticks out a mile that we are having a quarrel on a phoney issue.

I talked to Roy about the leadership yesterday on the telephone and we feel that we must now get Harold to have at least a little strategy group to plan for next year. Between our talk to him that Thursday evening after Easter and the implementation of our scheme nothing has been done about this. Harold has no chief of staff, no executive, and with Burke Trend away ill he just has his Marcia, his Gerald Kaufman and his new fellow Eric Varley.[2]

Harold lives in his lonely little place and doesn't do anything. We have got to get an inner Cabinet to restrain him and to see whether with that we can steer the Party through the terrible year that is coming. Harold has not reasserted himself. Indeed, something very strange, macabre and tragi-comic is now happening in the Parliamentary Party. The disillusionment of the Left, which has now broken for ever with Harold, has taken the form of a new cult of Crossman. Crossman, who took a reasonable line last January and has been relatively successful in the last two or three weeks, is being

[1] Mrs Castle was addressing the Annual Conference of the Scottish T.U.C., who were meeting at Rothesay.
[2] Eric Varley, Labour M.P. for Chesterfield since 1964, was Assistant Government Whip 1967–8, P.P.S. to the Prime Minister 1968–9, Minister of State at MinTech. 1969–70.

spoken of as the only person who can get us out of our difficulties. Tam is picking up this remark from all kinds of people and though I have told him from the start that it is sheer nonsense and that there is nothing to it whatsoever, when Tommy Balogh came back from Paris this week he said the rumour there was that Crossman was the man. Well, it wasn't Paris but what he picked up when he got home to Hampstead and had a gossip there. If it's true that this is being said in the Parliamentary Party, if only as a reaction against Harold, it is totally impractical for three reasons. One is that I don't want it and haven't the energy or the belief to do it. Secondly, it is far too late to do anything but pull the Party together a bit and prepare it for a less disgraceful election defeat. Thirdly, and most important, unless Harold falls down dead it won't happen. He will fight until his dying day and if he heard or suspected for a moment that I was countenancing anything of this sort it would do nothing but damage. It would turn him in on himself and make him even more conspiratorial, even more persecuted and even more devastatingly isolated.

Monday, April 21st
I went back to London depressed by Albert Rose, who had rung me up to say that he couldn't get more than twenty-five people to attend the constituency annual dinner and so we must call it off. I told this to Roy outside the Cabinet room before S.E.P. and he laughed and said, 'That has often happened to me in the last five years at Stechford. We don't take it too seriously.' Nevertheless Albert's news had cast me down.

Sunday, April 27th
Albert Rose ran up Anne yesterday to say that the moment he had cancelled the constituency annual dinner the applications began to pour in but this doesn't really satisfy me. I know that in a place like Coventry the industrial relations issue is terribly serious. It has been mounting up all this week. The whole trade union machine is going into action with conferences one after another, the calling of a special Congress and the possibility of a May Day demonstration with a maximum number of strikes.[1] Although public opinion is still vaguely but quite warmly on our side, a lot of the people who think there ought to be legislation are going to vote Tory anyway and the minority who think there oughtn't are the people whose votes and whose work we desperately need. There is a further difficulty that people in the movement have a deep suspicion that the Government is anti-trade union. It's likely, as Tony Crosland said, that around the country nobody has read *In Place of Strife*, and they just think that Wilson has got a massive trade union bug in him and that Barbara has gone bonkers. I think we may well have to face the fact that by next autumn there will be a unique kind of political crisis, a

---

[1] The special Congress was to be held at Croydon on June 5th.

situation where a Government with a majority of 100 and backed by a relatively united party has, however, lost so much authority that it is justified in demanding a dissolution, yet cannot go to the country for fear of a débâcle.

I think this is linked with the muddle-headed incompetence of the central direction of the party. The thing which worries me most of all is the failure of Barbara, Roy and me to get an inner Cabinet going. How often Harold has said he is agreeable to having an inner Cabinet and how often, the moment he has said it, he evades and sidesteps. This is what he has been doing all this week. We agreed that Roy should have a word with him on Friday and that Barbara and I should try to see him at Chequers this weekend, but the Italian President, Saragat,[1] is at Chequers today and the P.M. made it clear that he hadn't even got an hour for us.

'He is in danger of total disintegration,' Barbara said to me on the telephone today. It is a word that I have dared to use myself more than once in the last three weeks. Total disintegration! There is nothing left of him as a leader and a leftist. He is just a figure posturing there in the middle without any drive except to stay Prime Minister as long as he can. The other thing which I suspect has now begun to happen, beginning perhaps in the Scillies at Easter, is that he assumes that we can't win the next election. I noticed that in Cabinet this week he twice spoke on the assumption that the Tories would be taking over in the 1970s, whereas he has been scrupulously careful to avoid such talk in the past. This affects the whole of the conduct of the Government and means that everything the Government does is under question. It is more difficult to get anything sensible through and, equally, any weakness in a Ministry is mercilessly attacked. Barbara and I don't have any great hope of succeeding very far in our talk to him but we are prepared to go a long way towards saying that, frankly, we are not prepared to go on working under these conditions.

Tuesday, April 29th

At long last Barbara and I were to see Harold at 9.30. He started off straightaway by saying that he was going to let us have an inner Cabinet of seven and that he was thinking of sacking the Chief Whip. Barbara immediately said, 'Be careful. Who are you going to put in his place?' and Harold said, 'Well, it hasn't really got as far as that yet. I am only making overtures at present.' He played with Barbara in this way and pushed her off and then we discussed the committee of seven. I said, 'It all depends who is on it. Is Callaghan in or out?' 'What do you think?' he said, and Barbara and I both answered, 'If it is going to be a real group, an inner Cabinet of likeminded

---

[1] Giuseppe Saragat, founder of the Italian Workers Socialist Party (later called the Social Democratic Party) 1947 and a Member of Parliament 1948–64, was Minister of Foreign Affairs 1963–4 and President of the Italian Republic 1964–71.

people fighting to win and fighting to build you up, Harold, then it is no good having Callaghan. This is an acid test of your intentions.' He made it quite clear that he agreed with us and that Callaghan should be excluded. We talked about this at length and tried very hard to put over to him that what is wrong with his leadership is his lack of contact with us, with the Left, and with the Parliamentary Party. But it was a stiff interview, with a man very much on the defensive, handing to us the main thing we had come to ask for quickly, before we could mention it.

Back to the Ministry for hours and hours of sitting in the larger Ministerial Conference Room at a whole series of meetings. First of all I had a long meeting with the Joint Consultants Committee, a very high-grade committee of the eight leading men in the medical profession.

Next a briefing meeting with the Department on Regional Hospital Boards and then another meeting about post-Ely work, in the middle of which I was sent for by the Prime Minister. He wanted to tell me that he had just sacked John Silkin as Chief Whip and brought in Bob Mellish.[1] Bob was my old number two at Housing and I know him pretty well. He had been one of my worst enemies in the trade union movement and suddenly became a faithful, adoring lieutenant. We really liked each other. I think him a pretty good replacement for John, who has been getting idle and terribly two-faced and ambiguous in his relationships, far too friendly to the Left, and far too much the Prime Minister's poodle. Mind you, to be fair to John, the liberal regime did work fairly well after an appalling beginning but I think it is time for him to go. It is impossible to run a liberal regime under very great difficulties, with the increasing unpopularity of the Government, the decreasing success of Harold Wilson, and an amiable nonentity as Leader of the House. Liberal whipping requires authoritative leadership and my disappearance and Harold's decline have made John's position so impossible that a change was necessary. I talked this over with Harold, who said, 'I know Barbara will be upset.'

Just as I got upstairs Judith came in, looking very grey and seeming terribly upset about Bob Mellish. Next was Barbara, furiously angry at what Harold had done, taking it as a personal insult. I took her out to dinner and she fumed. After all, he had talked to us for an hour this morning and given us the impression that he was just thinking about having a new Chief Whip and then, under her nose, he swept John Silkin away and put in Bob Mellish, a *bête noire* of Barbara's, without consulting her and in the middle of her own negotiations with John about the conduct of her Industrial Relations Bill. She said it was intolerable, she would never forgive Harold, she was going to destroy him and finally I advised her to write him a really stinking letter. I

[1] On April 29th Robert Mellish was appointed Chief Whip, replacing John Silkin, who took Mr Mellish's post as Minister of Public Building and Works. The Parliamentary Committee was replaced by an 'inner Cabinet' of seven senior Ministers, who were to plan and co-ordinate long-term policy.

think she had every right to be angry. It is exactly this kind of conduct that makes Harold an intolerable, mean leader. When he does this he is a timid, awful little man who to avoid a scene lies and is evasive. So over dinner Barbara worked out the phrases for her letter and afterwards we went into Fred Peart's room to discuss the progress of the Bill with the new Chief Whip. She was fairly civil to him but it was a difficult evening we had there, trying to make sense of it all and to look forward to the future.

I went home and after midnight the Prime Minister rang me up. I have never in my life heard him so frightened. He had received Barbara's letter and wanted to read it aloud to me. 'No,' I said, 'it is a private letter to you but I tell you she is very upset. She isn't going to do what you think, though. She isn't going to resign. Don't try to speak to her tonight but arrange to see her early tomorrow and do for heaven's sake realize that you can't treat people in this way, Harold. But I assure you she isn't going to resign. You are all right.' He said, 'Thank you, Dick. At least I shall sleep tonight.' And that was Tuesday.

Thursday, May 1st

This evening Jimmy Margach came to see me with an astonishing story of how all the Commons' lobbies were seething with revolt against Harold and with talk of a round-robin sent by 100 Labour back benchers, some for Callaghan, some for Healey, a few for Jenkins, a few for me, but that they were mainly shouting against Wilson. So I was not surprised to have a message that I was urgently wanted by the Prime Minister at 10.15, along with Barbara.

It was a remarkable contrast with Tuesday morning. Then Harold had been his old, devious, bilateral self, keeping us where he wanted and at the same time facing us with the *fait accompli* of conceding the things we were about to ask for, but now, for the first time since I have known him, Harold was frightened and unhappy, unsure of himself, needing his friends. The great india-rubber, unbreakable, undepressable Prime Minister was crumpled in his chair. It was a touching evening for Barbara and me. We sat with him as old friends who wanted to help. Mind you, he had been spending the previous night boozing with the industrial correspondents, claiming that he had a stomach upset when he really had a hangover, but we saw at last that he was injured, broken, his confidence gone, unhappy, wanting help. Yes, he had agreed to the inner Cabinet last Tuesday, but reluctantly. Between Tuesday and Thursday something had happened to his self-esteem and the inflated gas balloon had been punctured. It became clear early on in the conversation that he had changed his mind about Callaghan's exclusion from the inner Cabinet and that he would be in after all. Harold tried to persuade himself that he had told us this, which was quite untrue because he had said the opposite. Anyhow, he had now seen Callaghan and told him that he was an essential member of the group. I don't think Harold is lying in these things and I don't think I blame him, except for once again changing his mind, twisting and turning and saying different things to different people. Barbara and I stood beside him and she said, 'My God, we want to help you, Harold. Why do you sit alone in No. 10 with Marcia and Gerald Kaufman and these minions? Why not be intimate and have things out with your friends?' We said, 'If you have to have Jim in the inner Cabinet, all right, but do also have your friends. We must be in and out of the house. For God's sake, realize that the inner Cabinet won't just meet once a week. It will be the seven people you call together for any crisis. You can't just call five one day, three another and six another, always varying them, creating new committees to keep us divided. We all want to help you and we want to put you back.' I was saying this all the evening from 10.15 till midnight, with all the more feeling because I knew, after what Jimmy Margach had told me, what was going on in the lobbies and what was likely to be reported tomorrow.

Friday, May 2nd
Sure enough, every newspaper reported the anti-Wilson ferment in the Parliamentary Party. Names weren't mentioned but I got them later – Brian Walden, John Mackintosh, the old independents, all turning against Harold and saying the only hope was to get rid of the leader. There was one article which I read with some interest, a report from Peter Jenkins, the *Guardian* columnist. It partly came from me. I had lunch with him last week and he had been clever enough to get a little from me and some more from Roy, so that the whole picture was of Callaghan insisting that Harold couldn't afford to leave him out of his inner Cabinet. It was probably true that Callaghan had brazened his way through and that Harold had funked what I had begged him to do on Tuesday night on the telephone, to have Callaghan in, talk to him straight and tell him either to be loyal or to get out. But, as the press made only too clear, that hadn't happened.

Sunday, May 4th
I have been reflecting on the reports of the anti-Wilson campaign boiling up in the P.L.P. and talking to people in Coventry, and I think I now appreciate the reasons for it. The truth is that not only have the trade union leaders written the Government off as finished and as a mere prelude to a Tory Government but most of the members of the Parliamentary Party itself are just fighting to keep up their morale. Deep underneath they know they can't win next time. This is what has undermined confidence because they then ask why we should even try to have our own Industrial Relations Bill, when the Tories are bound to introduce one. So we have had the mutterings of revolution and the open demand that Wilson must go and now I have started the fight back. I began it with a speech on Friday evening and the climax will come with Harold's May Day speech this afternoon.

Monday, May 5th

There was a splendid account of Harold's speech on the news last night. His phrase was, 'They say I'm going—well, I'm going on',[1] and it had come off. As I travelled up in the train this morning I read the speech and saw that he has had an immense success and that this is a turn for the good.

But when I got to the office I found waiting for me a Statement on teeth and spectacles. I knew this was a bit unpleasant. It had been postponed because of the Scottish local elections and then I had been too busy to deal with it, so it had come down to Prescote in my fourth red box this weekend. It was quite a trivial regularization to relate the charges for N.H.S. teeth and spectacles to the cost and I had corrected it last night and banged it in the box for the post office to collect at 9.30 p.m. when they send the boxes back to the office to be dealt with on Monday morning.

When I arrived I was mildly surprised to find this and I half realized it must be for today because I knew I had a few Questions and a Statement to deliver. I tidied it up a bit and forgot about it until lunch time, when I was talking to a B.B.C. correspondent at a little restaurant in Northumberland Avenue. He told me that the increased charges were banner headlines on the front page of the *Evening Standard* and I suddenly realized that I was going to be in trouble this afternoon. My God, the local elections! Tam, by the way, had gone off to Indonesia and hadn't been there to warn me and, because of a new procedure by which the Speaker puts up in the No Lobby at midday an announcement of any Statements which are going to be made, the lunchtime press was full of it. It was on the B.B.C. and the front page of the *Standard* and the *News*, and by 2.0 p.m. it was the news of the day.

By 3.30 the House was filled with people. There were a lot of Statements and then came my short Statement and my replies.[2] I did quite well, I was cool and controlled and sensible, but of course the Parliamentary Party didn't bother to listen to what I was saying. They hadn't realized that this was only a minor readjustment of the cost of teeth and spectacles; for them it was another breach of faith. By the time I got into the lobby at 6.30 for the first division on the Post Office Bill the wolves were howling and spitting round me. One can hardly blame them. They had been shattered by the row over Barbara's Bill, then they had Callaghan's sensation and the Prime Minister's come-back and now here was I, on the Monday before the local elections, bashing them with teeth and spectacles. I took the responsibility and said as they stood round me, 'It is my fault. I didn't realize until last night that the Statement was on today and the local elections weren't in my head at the time.' Perhaps I was unwise to say this but I did and within minutes they had

[1] Harold Wilson's actual phrase was 'I know what's going on—*I'm* going on.'

[2] Crossman announced a 25 per cent increase in charges for dentures and spectacles provided by the National Health Service. £3½ million was to be raised by a modest increase in the charge to patients, some £1 extra for dentures and 5s. for spectacles (and the decision had been published in the P E S C White Paper), but it provoked indignation in the Labour Party, particularly on the eve of the local urban and borough elections.

25 With his family at Prescote, May 1970.

26 Harold Lever, Paymaster General (left), with Tony Benn, Minister of Technology and Power, in conference, October 1969.

27 In April 1970, Roy Jenkins, Chancellor of the Exchequer, knows that he will have to take unpopular measures in his Budget to bolster the ailing economy and thereby risk seeing the Tories come to power later in the year.

all rushed out and were giving the press an account of this ghastly Crossman and his ghastly gaffe, and I, who for a few months had had quite a good reputation with them and had been talked about as a possible alternative to Harold, there I was a broken idol, smashed. Just a few hours after I had been dictating that complacent diary I was down at the bottom with the worst clanger, I suppose, in my political career since my *Mirror* article on the trade unions.[1]

Wednesday, May 7th

The big news was yesterday's Party meeting, which I had missed. It had been attended by very few people. Douglas Houghton had delivered an ultimatum warning the Cabinet that they shouldn't break with the T.U.C., speaking as Chairman of the Parliamentary Party, summing up the Party's point of view while the debate was still under way. It was headlined in every paper but whereas I got the blame on Monday for destroying our chances in the municipals Houghton got no blame at all.

Thursday, May 8th

By this morning I had simmered down. The press stories continued and I knew talk was going on inside the Parliamentary Party but it was no good fretting any more. I must now concern myself with what Jim Callaghan and Douglas Houghton were up to. I rang Barbara and Roy and said to them, 'We have Cabinet this morning. What are you going to say with Callaghan there? What is our situation? Here we are with Douglas Houghton saying the whole Parliamentary Party is against us and that we can't possibly get the Bill through, openly threatening us on behalf of the Party and siding with Callaghan. What are we to do?' But neither of them had much of an answer. We agreed to try to keep the subject out of Cabinet and to talk to Harold before the Management Committee,[2] so I telephoned the Prime Minister and pleaded with him not to try to talk too much. We agreed that we four would meet at 3.30 directly after Prime Minister's Questions and, having done this, we would then face Callaghan at Management Committee.

The main thing at Cabinet was the Industrial Relations Bill. Although this morning Barbara and Roy and I had begged Harold to stay off the subject he couldn't resist talking about it and, before we knew it, he had made a long speech about the constitutional point raised by Houghton's intervention. This opened up a full-length discussion. On the other side we had Dick Marsh saying much the same as Callaghan, asking why on earth we were destroying the party by getting into a conflict with the whole trade union

---

[1] In an article in the *Daily Mirror* on July 5th, 1957, Crossman had said that only four trade union M.P.s were serious candidates for key posts in a future Labour Government —and had made the mistake of naming them.

[2] The new inner Cabinet. Its members were the Prime Minister, Michael Stewart, Roy Jenkins, Richard Crossman, Barbara Castle, Fred Peart, Denis Healey and James Callaghan.

movement, and others saying that after all Douglas Houghton is speaking for
the P.L.P. and, constitution or no constitution, a Government has to keep its
majority in the House of Commons and the Chairman of the Party is entitled
to make this point. Harold was arguing on the constitutional position but
Callaghan was getting the better of the argument. He maintained that the
Prime Minister was quite wrong and that it was unrealistic to talk of constitu-
tionality. The issue was whether the Government could sustain its majority. I
finally got irritated with Callaghan and said, 'But look, we are not facing the
real issue, which is that Douglas Houghton has lined himself up with people
who are trying to get rid of the Prime Minister. That is the meaning of his
speech. He is prepared to see the Prime Minister go because he hopes to get
another Prime Minister who will drop the Bill. As I tried to say last Friday at
Yardley this is totally unrealistic and it would not be credible unless it was
believed that there was somebody in the Cabinet who held the same view. I
know and you all know that Roy Jenkins and Barbara Castle are as deeply
committed as the Prime Minister and that there is no sense in suggesting that
the Prime Minister could be got rid of. I detest these rats who are leaving our
sinking ship to climb on to another sinking ship. We have got to sink or swim
together.' At this point Callaghan said from the other side of the table, 'Not
sink or swim, sink or sink,' and I said, 'Why can't you resign if you think like
that? Get out, Jim, get out.' We had never had such a scene in Cabinet before
(I was told later on that it was a phenomenally dramatic moment) and there
was an awkward silence. Then Jim muttered, 'Of course, if my colleagues
want me to resign I'm prepared to go if they insist on my going.' He had been
punctured. He hadn't responded, he had crawled, and it was quite a moment.
We didn't get much further with that this morning.

Afterwards we four, Harold, Barbara, Roy and I, slipped out into his room
where he had his glass of brandy and we all settled down round the table.
Barbara said, 'The worst of it this morning was that your talk about the
constitution enabled Jim Callaghan to suggest that we should postpone the
Bill at least until after the Whitsun recess to give more time for discussion. I
think we ought to do this now because, after all, if we don't at least listen to
the Party and leave the Bill until after the Trade Union Congress, how can
we say that we have really been trying to reach agreement?' We rapidly
agreed that we should make this proposition and that if we postponed the
Bill until after Whitsun we should probably have to run into August. We
should also have to have my pensions up-grading Bill before Whitsun. At 4
o'clock we had to break off because the others were due to come in. Harold,
very characteristically, ordered the postponement of the Management
Committee for a quarter of an hour and said to us, 'Slip out so that nobody
notices you and come back as though we haven't met.' Although we had had
our inner inner Cabinet, Harold's fear that others would see the three of us
had been there and would think the worse of him made him contrive this
little piece of deception. When we came back, he greeted us with 'Hallo,

Barbara, how are you?' and 'Hallo, Dick, where have you been?', elabo-
rately trying to pretend that we hadn't been with him five minutes before. In
came the full Committee and we worked out the schedule, with Callaghan all
meekness and mildness and collaboration.

Friday, May 9th
We had the local election results.[1] In Coventry last year we only lost one seat
and had the best result in the country and now we are back in the rut like
Birmingham. Eight out of ten of our councillors had been defeated. I rang up
Albert Rose, who obviously felt that his Dick Crossman, with his teeth and
spectacle increases, was to blame. He was utterly disheartened. I then had to
run off to No. 10 for an eight-hour session of the N.E.C. Harold had
managed to prove to himself that these election results were a considerable
improvement on last year's, with less of a swing against us. I suppose
nationally this is true, in the sense that fractionally fewer people abstained or
fractionally fewer Tories voted, though it wasn't true in Coventry. We sat
around in that great big room at No. 10, just like the old days on the
Executive. We didn't fuse; though we were civil to each other we were
utterly remote. The eight hours were as boring as usual. Roy Jenkins started
with a good, powerful speech on the economic situation and then burbled
along a bit and Joe Gormley rose to say what a muck-up I had made on
health charges and how the Government must stop tearing the Party to
pieces and climb down on the Bill. Denis Healey made a serious, pro-
Government speech but the only dramatic remarks were from Jim Callaghan. We had all had a dressing-down from Harold at the previous Cabinet
and we had all agreed that we must speak on this big issue with absolute
collective responsibility—but not old Jim. He got up and gave us all a long
lecture, saying that of course Cabinets have the right to be authoritative but
they can't impose a Bill unless they are absolutely certain and have proof
positive that it is necessary. He lectured us and he lectured them and his was
the only speech which had no kind of applause whatsoever. After him
Barbara replied, looking neat and trim despite her tiredness. She was
immensely moving and everybody there cheered their redhead but it didn't
make the faintest difference.

Monday, May 12th
I had been told that we were to see the Prime Minister this evening, and, sure
enough, at 8.0 there were Barbara, Roy and I, the inner inner Cabinet,
sitting with Harold drinking brandy and discussing Jim Callaghan's future.[2]

---

[1] In the local authority elections, May 5th–10th, Labour lost 917 seats to the Conservatives
and retained control of only 28 out of 342 borough councils in England and Wales.
[2] The remarks that the Home Secretary had made at the N.E.C./Cabinet meeting on Friday,
May 9th, had leaked into the press and, as he appeared to be dissociating himself from the rest of
the Cabinet on the issue of the I.R. Bill, the Prime Minister decided that Mr Callaghan should be
excluded from future meetings of the Management Committee.

We were all clear that he couldn't stay on. Was it that he couldn't stay on during the negotiations with the T.U.C. or that he couldn't stay at all? We didn't want him in and it was decided that Harold should tell him not to attend the Management Committee tomorrow. Harold promised to do so but Barbara bet me half a crown[1] that he wouldn't carry out his promise and I was extremely dubious myself.

Tuesday, May 13th
However, this morning Callaghan was sent for at 9.30 and told he couldn't attend the meeting at 10 o'clock. So there we were without him and we spent the first hour discussing how this should be handled in the press. We finally decided that no reason should be given and the No. 10 habit of simply giving the names of Ministers who attended Committees should be continued unchanged. No. 10 should simply say that the six of us had a meeting with Harold and leave it to the press to notice that Jim was not there.

Wednesday, May 14th
The papers were absolutely dominated by the news of Callaghan's exclusion, and we got a fairly bad press for it with *The Times* saying that it was inefficient and that we couldn't really have an inner Cabinet without Jim. But the real reason for the bad press was the grave mistake Harold made in announcing the formation of the Management Committee as though it were a Cabinet Committee. It isn't a normal Cabinet Committee and this could have been presented in an invaluably useful way.

My problem today, however, was how to handle the special Party meeting at which they were to hear about teeth and spectacles. I rang up Barbara and Harold and, though I don't often do this, I asked them if I should tell the truth and explain how we had done it to help Ted Short over a difficult crisis with his comprehensive schools programme. Both Barbara and Harold thought it was much better to tell the Party the truth about what had really happened. I went along to the meeting.

I had a tremendous, high-minded harangue from Laurie Pavitt, as though I had introduced brand new prescription charges, and a great attack from Edith Summerskill, speaking for Shirley who was absent. She lashed me as clever, academic Crossman, psychological warfare Crossman, but rather funnily she got into a controversy with Norman Atkinson and suddenly rounded on him, saying in her dear, traditional, female sergeant-major way, 'Stand up, man. Stand up and say what you mean.' Within three minutes she lost the whole audience, leaving them feeling what a terrible woman she was. In the end I spoke as I had intended, explaining first that there was no principle of charges involved. I have been helped here by a Question John Dunwoody had asked on May 5th, which he now repeated. He had said that

[1] 2s. 6d. (12½ new pence).

many people were anxious that my suggestion that there should be an automatic relationship between the level of charges and the cost of the services concerned seemed to be introducing a new principle into the question of N.H.S. charges. I repeated all the assurances he required and I also tried to explain how this fitted in with our new idea of block budgeting and how we had adjusted our own estimates to help Ted Short. This flabbergasted them and they received it in a slightly bewildered silence, so I thought perhaps I had managed to bring it off.

Monday, May 19th
I had my Question Time and in fact I handled all the seventy or eighty Questions with pretty good skill. Nevertheless it was a balls-up! Paul Dean got up and said it was absolute folly to raise £3½ million more in health charges and then hand it over to the educational services.[1] I replied, 'It would be folly if it was done. But any Minister who attempted to do this would be forbidden to do it by his Permanent Secretary. Therefore I would advise the Hon. Gentleman not to believe in something it is said I did.' Then Shirley Summerskill got up, 'Would my Rt Hon. Friend bear in mind that he gives the impression of somebody whose left hand does not know what his other left hand is doing? Are we to take it as a precedent that the National Health Service now has so much money that it can afford to give it to another Government Department?' 'That', I answered, 'would be the wrong conclusion to draw from my answer to Question No. 33.' That was all I said, a glimpse of the obvious, and the only mistake I made was to say Permanent Secretary when I meant Permanent Secretary and Accounting Officer,[2] but there it was, I'd boobed again. I was in the middle of a typhoon of attack, egged on by the back benchers who immediately went out to feed the press.

All day after Questions I lay low. Fortunately this evening the Czech Embassy had invited me to see a travelling company doing a rather ingenious miming show with lights and shades, so I crept away and hid myself pretty thoroughly.

Tuesday, May 20th
Huge headlines in today's papers, Calamity Dick, Muck-up, Disaster. At Management Committee I was item number one. How was I to be rescued?

---

[1] Conservative M.P. for Somerset North since 1964. He was Parliamentary Under-Secretary of State at the D.H.S.S. 1970–4.
[2] The Permanent Secretary is the Accounting Officer for the Department and must show the Comptroller and Auditor-General's office and, if necessary, the Public Accounts Committee that funds have been spent on the programmes for which they were voted. At the end of Question Time, however, Stephen Hastings, Conservative M.P. for Mid-Bedfordshire, asked the Speaker for a Standing Order No. 9 debate to discuss Crossman's answer, which, he alleged, stated that Permanent Under-Secretaries could forbid Ministers to take certain courses of action. The Speaker refused the request. (*House of Commons Debates*, Vol. 784, cols 9–10.)

Considering the fact that my colleagues quite like seeing people in the soup, they were not unfriendly and I got some support. They had to admit that they had urged me to explain the thing to the Party and to try to educate them in the language of priorities and they agreed it had all come unstuck. But I had got a phenomenally bad press, Dick who always drops clangers, Crossman the intellectual who is always wrong, and I knew I had plunged even further into unpopularity.

Then we went on to the Industrial Relations Bill, where we had our first really frank discussion. I told Harold it wasn't good enough to say that the Government was going to do this and if the Party defeated us the Government would go down. It wasn't necessarily true, somebody else might be called upon to be Prime Minister, and that would give Callaghan his chance. Harold said, 'Brinkmanship is essential; we have to push it right up to the edge.' So we spelt out the five possibilities and they are all down absolutely clearly in the minutes. One: not to legislate in the current session. Two: to introduce a Bill containing penal clauses in relation to union disputes but omitting the conciliation pause and the fining of strikers. Three: to introduce a Bill containing the penal clauses about the conciliation pause but saying they would be deferred for a specified minimum period and could be further deferred as the T.U.C. proved itself capable of exercising its own authority. Four: to introduce in the current session a Bill to incorporate ...[1] Four and Five, however, were agreed to be impracticable.

After a long discussion we agreed that as we couldn't really stop the Bill, the only two possibilities were either, two, to introduce a Bill without the conciliation pause or, three, to introduce a Bill with the pause but with power to postpone its coming into effect. Harold, Barbara and Roy all wanted to go for number three. The Chief Whip and I went for number two. Bob Mellish, who is a yapping terrier, at least speaks up and he is coming out in his true colours. He just said, 'You won't get anything except a Bill without the conciliation pause because, after all when the unions have approved the T.U.C.'s new policy you will find that the penal clauses will seem to be a worse alternative and even on the merits of the case we wouldn't be able to persuade the Parliamentary Party to do it.' That was it. Michael Stewart, Denis Healey, Roy Jenkins, Barbara Castle and Fred Peart are all solid with Harold. I am not solid with Harold and neither is Bob Mellish.

Thursday, May 22nd

Today we went off on holiday,[2] though the children and Anne had been waiting and wondering whether we should be able to get away. Harold had insisted that Barbara should have her fortnight's holiday, although at

---

[1] Crossman appears to have decided that the fourth and fifth possibilities did not deserve description.

[2] A joint Crossman–Castle holiday taken aboard Sir Charles Forte's yacht in the Mediterranean—see above p. 537.

Management Committee he had made it clear that talks would have to go on while she was away and I rather thought she might be summoned back.

Friday, May 23rd—Friday, June 6th
All week there was a tremendous fuss about how Barbara was to get back. She had been given an elaborate code, with the Prime Minister, for example, as Lion and herself as Peacock and me as Owl and members of the T.U.C. General Council as different animals, all tremendous fun, no doubt, for the Civil Service. They only forgot one thing, to make any contact with the consulate at Naples, through whom all communications had to come. So at the very last moment on Saturday, May 31st, she rang the vice-consul and he was there on Sunday morning to help her off the boat on to a little, slow, trundling special plane, which had been sent out by the R.A.F. to Naples.

When she came back[1] I gathered that Harold and Barbara's talks on Sunday were with Scanlon and Jack Jones, plus John Newton,[2] Chairman of the General Council this year, and Vic Feather. It seemed that nothing happened except to confirm everything her critics had warned her of. Scanlon and Jones were perfectly clear that they were not prepared to co-operate in any way with the Government and would do everything possible to wreck it if we went ahead with any penal clauses whatsoever. So they confirmed the hard line. According to her, they were still friendly and pleasant but that doesn't matter. As I said to her, the point was that the Government had not been able to move them an inch. This meeting was just before the special T.U.C. Conference, where it was clear that the General Council would receive a far higher degree of support than anybody would have thought possible.

However, after the others had left, the Prime Minister and Barbara had had a word together. They decided to send Vic Feather a letter insisting on a tightening up of the T.U.C. General Council's position with regard to disciplining unofficial strikers. We then spent a lot of time drafting this letter and telephoning with our yachting code. The letter was to be sent before the Congress took place in an attempt to influence them. I thought it was impossible to make the T.U.C. consider this but it was what Harold and Barbara had already decided and virtually committed themselves to. The other thing we talked about was nerve. Barbara said to me that the greatest quality in politics is good nerves. I said, 'I'm not so sure, Barbara. I think it's good nerves and wisdom, because brinkmanship without any wisdom can bring you to catastrophe.' One of her troubles is that she thinks she has got to go right to the brink and then the T.U.C. will finally give way. Well, it is my considered opinion that over the last two months the T.U.C. has completely

---

[1] Mrs Castle returned to Italy on the evening of Monday, 2nd June.
[2] John Newton was General Secretary of the National Union of Tailors and Garment Workers until 1970.

out-manoeuvred the Prime Minister and Barbara. The T.U.C. have made concessions at the right time and put themselves in the right with the Parliamentary Party, and they can almost dictate their terms. I don't think Barbara and Harold have any bargaining position now because, if they ask us to pass a Bill which means a complete break with the T.U.C. and also with Transport House, I doubt whether they will have the P.L.P. behind them or even, in the last resort, the Cabinet.

Sunday, June 8th

Back on Friday in gorgeous June weather to Prescote, I went off on the 4.40 for this evening's critical Management Committee meeting and eventually reached No. 10 at 8 o'clock. We had a three-hour discussion of the new tactic Harold wanted. He believed that the thing to do was to insist that if we were going to have no legislation on a conciliation pause with penalties the T.U.C. itself must write the same enforcements into its rules and take it upon itself to compel trade unions to intervene in unconstitutional strikes. Barbara and he were hoping for this and we talked for a long time about it. I must say I was dubious the whole way through because I know we are missing a great opportunity. Last Thursday the T.U.C. approved by an enormous majority a new programme of action far and above anything we thought possible not only six months or six years ago but six weeks ago. Barbara and Harold had achieved this by their tactic of going right up to the edge. I felt this was the moment for them to say to the trade unions, 'You've done very well and with this we can drop the short Bill and the whole idea of penal legislation for a year. We'll push the Bill back for a year and see how things get on.' But there was no question of that. The P.M. and Barbara took the view that although the trade unions were giving us sufficient T.U.C. sanction on inter-union disputes, their attitude on unconstitutional strikes was vague, and that as Jack Jones and Scanlon clearly didn't want to do anything else, we had to come back at them. The letter Barbara had drafted in Italy had not been sent but its substance had been published on the Friday morning after the Congress, confirming the specific pressure that was being put on the General Council to increase its authority to take disciplinary action in the case of unconstitutional strikes. Moreover, even before Barbara returned to Italy on June 2nd the D.E.P. had come back to the unions with a statement and the P.M. had followed it up with a statement in a speech yesterday. Today they were at it again, pushing further towards the brink. I also doubted whether the T.U.C. could go any further than they had at the Congress or that we could extract from them further concessions that would have to be confirmed at their annual Conference in September.

I was out of sympathy with Harold and Barbara, but at the Management Committee five of my colleagues were backing the Prime Minister. Peart and I had been impressed by the Chief Whip's warning but the others were not so firm and were anxious for a settlement. We were clearly outweighed this evening and the Prime Minister got what he wanted for his meeting with the trade unions first thing tomorrow morning. Management Committee gave him agreement for further negotiations.

Monday, June 9th
At 2.30 Management Committee met again to consider what Harold had achieved with the trade unions this morning. It was quite clear that he had got nothing more than an agreement to negotiate further. Mellish was present and he strengthened my position a little as we considered the three possibilities. One: the T.U.C. rewriting their own rules. Two: strengthening our own legislation but removing the penal clauses, which is more or less what I thought we would get. Three: a cold storage Bill, i.e. penal clauses but not to be put into practice for at least a year, which I thought was out of the question anyway. We really had to decide between one and two.

At 4 o'clock the three possibilities were presented to Cabinet. Nobody spoke out at all because the Prime Minister was merely asking to be permitted to put these ideas to the T.U.C. and try to get them through. Since all this was on the clear understanding that there would be no Cabinet commitment Harold didn't find it difficult. Cabinet was very piano. He worked hard to extract opinions from everyone but me, which was unusual but characteristic, since he knew what my opinion was. He tried to get Cabinet support but what he got was acquiescence without enthusiasm. Denis and Roy were stalwart, Michael gave unqualified support to a strong line and then there were Barbara and Harold but, apart from these, nobody else was for the strong line. I kept my mouth shut and nobody outside Management Committee spoke. It was all long and all boring.

Thursday, June 12th
Management Committee met again for half an hour for another report. The Prime Minister had worked out in even greater detail the exact changes he wants in the T.U.C. rules and he and Barbara are now firmly committed to this. He came out with the view that if he could get the rules changed he would drop the penal clauses. I intervened at this point to say, 'That doesn't mean that if you don't get the change in the rules Cabinet is automatically committed to the penal clauses,' and, to my surprise, the moment I said this it was agreed, because I warned Harold that if he tried to commit us this afternoon to the penal clauses he would get a split Cabinet.

When Cabinet met Barbara and Harold played fair and left the question open, although they made it clear if the T.U.C. refused to agree they would expect strong support for a no-climb-down, no-surrender Bill. If T.U.C. policing is inadequate there must be Government policing as well. It was clear that the longer this conversation with the T.U.C. went on the more difficult it would be to bring the Parliamentary Party to support a Bill which would have to be forced through in defiance of the T.U.C. Once again we managed to get agreement because Cabinet was merely being asked to allow the P.M. to negotiate. We were given the three possibilities and told that Cabinet would only make up its mind on the Bill next Tuesday or Wednesday when we had heard the result of the negotiations.

This evening there were a lot of divisions and I was going through the lobbies a good deal. The people I met were more and more baffled. The T.U.C. have turned the rule change down flat. Cledwyn Hughes, who is a little twister and turner, said to me, knowing I was one of the people who was critical, 'Is it possible? Can Harold really drive us into a conflict with the T.U.C.?' Tony Greenwood certainly felt that way, and I would think, even Wedgy Benn. Harold and Barbara are now trying to find an alternative, which I know has got to be to strengthen the Bill without penal clauses, and this is virtually a come-down. I think we are going to have a great deal of bitterness, with Barbara and Harold believing Cabinet has let them down. There have been a great number of stories in the press about Callaghan, Roy Mason and Dick Marsh, Tony Crosland and me, as people who have been doubtful and critical. I haven't particularly been talking to the papers but I haven't disguised my view that we really must settle and that we can't afford a break with the T.U.C. now. We shouldn't go on with brinkmanship beyond this limit. Harold and Barbara think Cabinet should have given them absolute support so they could go right up to the brink and force the T.U.C. to climb down but I've always thought that the T.U.C., following Jones's and Scanlon's wishes, were not going to move from the position the Congress took on June 5th.

Monday, June 16th

I was working at Alexander Fleming House this morning, when Barbara, looking very distressed, put her head into my room and said she'd had a terrible weekend. She asked me to come and see her, so at 6.30 I went along. I knew that one of the things she wanted to talk about was a very unpleasant piece which Alan Watkins published in his column last week, saying that I had remained uncorrupted by a fortnight with Barbara on Charles Forte's luxury yacht. The secret that he was our host had at last leaked out, though ever since Barbara said she wanted a veto on the story the whole of our family has been religiously careful not to speak about it. Alan Watkins has never even approached me on this and I have an uneasy feeling that he must have known it all along. It's fully possible that weeks before Barbara told us this should be a secret I mentioned to one or two people that we had this wonderful offer and were thinking of taking it. Perhaps, for example, in all innocence I told Paul Johnson that I was going but I now felt very uncomfortable because Barbara disliked it so much. However she is a sporting girl and agreed that we should give Charles Forte a John Piper watercolour as a tribute and I am going to give Barbara a pair of silver sauce-boats for her silver wedding celebration.

She said how miserable and unhappy she was and how she hadn't been sleeping over the weekend. I was pleased that she asked me to go to see her because I was aware that we were both terribly at loggerheads about the crisis over the Industrial Relations Bill. I found her with Bob Mellish and naturally he and I were on one side and she was on the other. We spelt out to her what the situation was, how we couldn't possibly get the Bill through the Party and that this would mean that if we didn't withdraw it in time the Party would reject it. She was saying how she had thought all this out clearly and she would have to resign. 'But that', I said, 'would be playing into Jim Callaghan's hands.' We went all through the argument together and then she said she was thinking of further proposals which would avoid putting penalties on the workers but she could only tell us a little before I had to rush off to Gluck's *Orfeo* at Covent Garden. It was not an attractive production but nevertheless I saw the whole of it before rushing back for the 10 o'clock vote.

By then the news was out that Douglas Houghton and the Liaison Committee had met and sent a powerful letter to Harold, warning him that the Party would not endorse any kind of penal sanctions. After the vote, I went upstairs for a drink with Tony Crosland. He and I saw completely eye to eye. Like everybody else, we had said that it would be inconceivable that we should be rushed into this Bill and that there must be a climb-down. But I warned Tony that we were still miles away from a compromise. 'Look,' I said, 'I don't think that is Barbara's mood and I don't think it is Harold's. In my view, they are intending to try the supreme brinkmanship of threatening to resign in the hope that first Cabinet and then the Party won't accept their resignations. But in the last resort the Party will accept them. I am sure they are playing for the highest possible stakes. They believe the Bill will have to be presented to the Party, they have it ready with the penalty clauses and they are going to force it through Cabinet this week and then hope to carry the Party with them. This is what we have to fight, for the danger is that they'll come unstuck and get defeated at the Party meeting or, if not defeated, the minority will be so large that it will be like Chamberlain in 1940.' Tony and I discussed this at length.

Tuesday, June 17th
We started with Management Committee at 10.30 and it really was most extraordinary. Immediately we got there Barbara Castle said she had thought up a new idea. We would drop the penalties on individual trade unionists which she had been fighting for for six months and instead have a new system of penalties imposed on trade unions as such, to be paid by the trade unions. This would remove the sense of individual victimization and she thought it would be infinitely more acceptable to the unions. It was something, she said, that she and Harold had thought up late last night.

I must say that when she described this Management Committee was bewildered. She had a short document but it contained nothing more than what she had said. Here was, no doubt, quite a bright idea but it was yet another improvisation. The history of this Bill has been a history of improvisation. The White Paper was very largely rewritten when some of us criticized it and no Bill or anything near it emerged from that. Since then we have had a series of improvised measures from the parliamentary draftsmen, trying desperately to keep up with the modifications flowing from Barbara and Harold. That's all right for negotiation but it's not all right for the drafting of legislation. In this case it wasn't any good for negotiation either because, as most of us instinctively felt this morning, in their present mood the trade unions are not going to agree to being fined for failing to order their members back to work from unofficial strikes. That is a non-starter and in trying to put it forward at the last moment Barbara would merely decrease confidence in herself and Harold.

The other thing we discussed was timing and whether the aim now was to get Cabinet committed to a Bill with penal clauses before Harold and Barbara met the T.U.C. tomorrow morning. I made it quite clear that I thought this most unwise. But Harold and Barbara were both obviously worried and it was clear that they hoped to be able to go to the General Council tomorrow and say, 'It is either/or; we have full Cabinet backing. We tell you we shall publish a Bill tonight and it will be in the papers on Thursday morning. The Bill with penalties is ready; it has been through Cabinet.' I am quite certain it was their plan to get Management Committee to agree to this but they were unable to do it.

Cabinet started at 11.15. We only had an hour and a quarter because Golda Meir was coming in for a talk before lunch. Barbara embarrassed us straightaway by saying she had a bright new idea and that she wanted to hand round a paper on it. I spoke early because I thought it essential and said, 'Before we do anything in detail about this idea, let's get clear what you are aiming at. Do you want to get Cabinet backing for a Bill with penalties in it before you go to see the General Council tomorrow? Because if you do I am against it.' Everybody heard my challenge and everybody quietly knew this was what the P.M. and Barbara were after, but Harold is a clever chairman and didn't take up my challenge. His friends in Cabinet tried to avoid this discussion, so most of the morning was spent talking about Barbara's new idea. It was a thoroughly bad and unfortunate thing to have put forward and the more she was made to talk about it the less convincing the proposition appeared, though she continued to say that she was convinced that the trade unions would prefer it. It was certainly clear that Harold had a timetable.* He was going to get this through Cabinet this morning and put it to the Trade Union group of the Party at 7 o'clock this evening, telling them why he couldn't accept the T.U.C.'s terms. Tomorrow afternoon he was going to

* And I heard from a very good source that at the meeting of the Socialist International at Eastbourne yesterday Harold had let this be known through Gerald Kaufman.

present the Bill to Cabinet and announce the terms to a special Party meeting. He and Barbara had clearly made up their minds that now was the moment to force the issue and present the Bill as a further stage in their brinkmanship negotiations with the T.U.C.

This morning it became clear that the plan was coming unstuck. Harold was getting a bit rasped and he said, 'It's about time people pulled themselves together and faced their responsibilities.' Then came Peter Shore's intervention. Gripping himself, as members of the Cabinet do when they really have got to say something, Peter said, 'Right, if I am challenged, I will,' and he spelt out why in his view Harold had it all wrong. He said, 'The real thing wrong with Harold and Barbara is that they now say that an agreement under which we should be content with the advance registered at Congress, plus a declaration of intent, is a helter-skelter retreat. This is a complete misjudgment. So far from a retreat we have made an enormous advance and this would be to stablilize it.' Peter spoke with tremendous strength. Everybody in Cabinet agreed that it was the first time he had ever said anything which had a real effect. Somehow it summed up the real reason why Cabinet couldn't authorize Harold and Barbara to go ahead and threaten the T.U.C. with a Bill including penalties and it's got to be understood that this embittered Barbara all the more because Peter was the only member of the Cabinet who had been present at the Sunningdale Conference where, along with Tommy Balogh, Barbara and her civil servants had evolved the idea of *In Place of Strife* and devised the package that was put to us last autumn. Peter had been in on this deal from the start, even before Roy, and had fully sympathized with the whole thing. When he abandoned it this morning it was a tremendous blow for Barbara. I don't think there was any other speech that surprised me except for Gerald Gardiner, who said that there could be other penalties for the trade unions and he couldn't quite see why we should force this Bill through. Even he was not on Harold's side.

Throughout the morning Jim Callaghan behaved with an egregious smoothness and oiliness which was almost unbearable. He kept saying, 'Ah, but Prime Minister, we don't want to tire you too much, we want to enable you to save your resources,' and he significantly repeated, 'I believe that if the Prime Minister tries to force this through he will succeed.' I can't help feeling that Jim has come to the conclusion that the best thing to do is to let Harold and Barbara destroy themselves and that he may profit by their destruction. It's the only explanation I can give because Jim was completely contradicting what Bob Mellish told us. It was interesting that no report was made of Douglas Houghton's letter. Management Committee had been told about it in close confidence but anyhow Douglas had given it straight to the press. It had a tremendous impact but today Harold tried to keep it from Cabinet and it was never shown, never discussed, as though the episode had never actually happened. Although Harold refused to read the letter out, Bob Mellish was as firm and solid as ever. Each time I called on him from my end, saying, 'Couldn't we just hear the Chief Whip again?' Bob said, 'I tell you, I'm sorry, but you can't get this Bill through the House of Commons.' This view was naturally opposed by Barbara and Harold, who both said that they were convinced that with guts the Cabinet could, but it was very disturbing that Callaghan also denied it and said he believed we would be able to scrape the Bill through. It was an odious combination of Harold's enemies supporting him and his friends opposing him.

At 5.30 Cabinet started again, the most devastating Cabinet meeting I have attended. This evening Harold found people committing themselves in detail for the first time.[1] It had been a bad meeting in the morning and it was bad now. I said again, 'Look, the real issue we have to discuss is whether Cabinet should be committed today to a Bill with legal penalties and, if so, what are the penalties? Should we commit ourselves to this today before Harold and Barbara return to negotiate with the T.U.C. tomorrow morning and should they be empowered to tell the T.U.C. that either they should actually change their rules or we shall publish the Bill?' On this everybody cast their vote and gave their opinion and, apart from Cledwyn Hughes and George Thomas, everyone overwhelmingly turned Harold down. Person after person said no. Tony Wedgwood Benn said in his thoughtful way, 'We are in advance of the times. We only started talking about trade union legislation a year ago, and it is too early to talk about a statutory obligation when we haven't yet had a process of education,' so he turned it down. The Foreign Secretary was away on the front bench dealing with tanks for Libya, so Harold's only real supporter was absent. Roy Jenkins sat there aloof and detached, saying a few words but never committing himself, never helping Barbara.

It became clear that Harold's self-confidence, complacency, bounce and good temper were all breaking down. At one point he said, 'Well, you're all giving this up because it's unpopular. You're committed by Cabinet's decision on the White Paper. Cabinet has given the go-ahead on the short Bill. Everyone here is committed by that and you are abandoning your Cabinet commitments because they are unpopular. You're soft, you're cowardly, you're lily-livered. If you do that, why shouldn't I?' he said. 'Why shouldn't I suggest abandoning the National Insurance Bill, with its increase in contributions, or the teeth and spectacles changes? If you abandon yours, I abandon mine.' He repeated this theme of how cowardly we were and how we couldn't stick it and he finally said, 'I won't negotiate on your terms. If you order me to go back to the T.U.C. and say I'm to accept a declaration of intent I refuse to do it, because a declaration would not be worth the paper it is written on. I insist on getting the change of rules or on standing for the penal clauses. You can't deny me this.' He was a little man, for the first time dragged down on our level. It was painful because in a sense he was sabotaged and utterly nonplussed.

[1] See *Wilson*, pp. 656–7.

After all these disavowals Harold said, 'What is the Cabinet decision? What do you want me to do?' Jim Callaghan said, 'I could easily frame a decision if you wish: that we wish you to seek a settlement on the basis of a firm declaration of intent.' The moment Jim said this Harold scented danger and shied off, realizing that this would have bound him. He is very much aware of the force of Cabinet decisions. 'No, I won't accept that,' he said. 'Barbara and I must not be tied down. We must be free to negotiate as we wish and I warn you I shall certainly say what Barbara and I will do about the penal legislation if we don't get our way. Without a weapon to threaten them with we should be completely impotent.' (One of the themes which he and Barbara had used throughout the afternoon had been that unless, with the Cabinet behind them, they had an effective threat, the T.U.C. wouldn't give anything away.) The meeting ended with no Cabinet decision and with the Prime Minister summing up how he and Barbara would tomorrow morning seek to negotiate but with no Cabinet backing and no decision whatsoever.

So it was a victory for those of us who had said the one thing we were not going to give Harold today was the right to a Bill with penalties. We had won at the cost of the most searing, awful, bloody row I have ever had with Harold. It's very difficult to have a row with him. At one point I had said, 'Don't be mean, Harold. Don't attribute motives to us. Of course we are not lily-livered cowards, we just disagree with you. We think you are wrecking and destroying the movement. Do, for heaven's sake, see that your critics have the same principles as you have. They care about the party.' These were the kind of arguments we had all afternoon.

The meeting became more and more awkward because at 7 o'clock the Prime Minister was due to address the Trade Union group. He said, 'I've got half my speech written here, the half which says why I must insist on the rule change and why I can't accept a declaration of intent. I suppose all that is out of date.' We had to say, 'Yes, we're afraid you won't be able to deliver it.' 'What am I to say to these people?' By this time it was ten to seven. 'What shall I say to them?' and somebody suggested, 'Give the history of the thing for thirty-five to forty minutes. You can space things out.' He said, 'You mean you are asking me to be dull?' and everybody gave rather an embarrassed laugh and said 'Yes'. So there it was, a terrible exhibition in which the P.M. was rasped, irritated and thoroughly demoralized, really shouting I won't, I can't, you can't do this to me, terribly painful because he expressed a loathing, a spite and a resentment which is quite outside his usual character. Although I didn't see it, both Fred Peart and Roy Jenkins said afterwards that three large double brandies were handed to him out of the cupboard during the last half-hour. I have never seen the P.M. driven to drink in the course of an evening. And all the while beside him sat Roy. In the morning he had intervened at one point, saying, 'Aren't you leaving Barbara Castle in rather a difficult negotiating position? Shouldn't we just remember that?' but this afternoon he didn't say anything. He is letting Harold down. As

Peter Shore said, Roy's failure was perhaps the most dramatic feature of all this.

Wednesday, June 18th

At 11.30 I went across to see the Chancellor. I have had more time with Roy during the course of today and seen him at closer quarters and in a more interesting situation than ever before. I asked him about his remark at Cabinet yesterday morning about the difficulties of Barbara's position. 'Did you really want to give her anything?' He said, 'No, I was just filling in time at a rather awkward moment by saying something which sounded good.' How often does Roy reveal himself quite as clearly as that? He revealed himself as a man who consciously felt nothing except what was to his own advantage.

Now, you have to remember that this morning we had no idea what would happen. Harold and Barbara had talked in the wildest way about insisting on a Bill with penalties and Cabinet hadn't yet voted them down. That would have to be done this afternoon. This morning Roy started by saying, 'You appreciate that, though I agree with you that we can't have the Bill with penalty clauses, I am bound to vote with Harold and Barbara if the issue comes up. I expect we shall be voted down but that is that.' I said, 'But if you do that, Roy, if you vote with Harold and Barbara, you are doomed. You will be bound to resign with them when resignation comes.' I explained what I had been saying to Barbara on the boat about how we would sort this out and how my mind was clear, and I said, 'If we have to vote on the Bill and defeat Harold at Cabinet, this is the real issue. Probably we won't defeat him despite the 19 to 3. He might well win by a majority of one or two but if he wins with a majority of that size it won't make any difference if the Trade Union group is solid against and the Party votes him down. The crisis is upon us. I can assure you that, if he and Barbara resign, you will have to resign with them and Callaghan will come in your place. Do you really want to do this?' I urged him to make up his mind that he couldn't possibly vote with them and that, on the contrary, if this were put to us it would be his duty to get the meeting stopped as quickly as possible and say we must reflect on it overnight and then report back. We should say we couldn't take a decision on the Bill until tomorrow morning. We must have a delay, during which, as a last resort, Roy should go to Harold and throw his weight in, telling Harold that if he went on with this Roy would vote against him.

Roy said to me, 'You do appreciate, don't you, that I have kept my word to Barbara, though I really believe in the policy less and less. I have felt it my duty to keep my word to her rather than to Harold.' I said, 'Yes, but there come times when you have to decide on the future of the party and when you have to realize that if there is a possibility that Harold might go somebody has to take his place. You and I have to see that the party goes on running and that the machinery is put in motion for replacing the P.M.' So we spent a little time discussing the constitution of the party, how the Party meeting should be called and whether Roy could go to the Palace direct. All this we discussed and we made it quite clear that Roy would stand against Callaghan in the event of Callaghan's making a bid for the leadership.

Then I went through from No. 11 to No. 12 and had a long talk with the Chief Whip. He told me that yesterday evening he had been summoned very late to No. 10, where he found Harold pretty tiddly, and they had discussed the future far into the night. Harold had described to Bob the contempt he had for his colleagues, how they had betrayed him, how he would challenge them and fight the Bill through, and how, when the crisis was over, he would get rid of the lily-livered people and have a different kind of Cabinet, how Callaghan would have to go and that Jenkins was a coward. Bob said Harold didn't call me a coward because I had been fairly consistent on all this but that he had talked in this wild way as though he was prepared to see the break-up of the party as the price for getting his way. I found Bob pretty solid and both he and I, as Harold's close friends, agreed that if Harold and Barbara were to end the day like this we would have to have the vote postponed until tomorrow morning and try to get them defeated, to prevent Cabinet putting forward this Bill with penalties. It must be postponed until after the Party meeting at 7.0 tonight. I won't rehearse all the other chats and chivver we had waiting for the meeting at midday.

All day, however, Cabinet was postponed by half-hours and forty minutes, and finally, after hanging about all morning, and filling in the afternoon with a conference about heart transplantations, I strolled across to No. 10. Half of us didn't really believe Cabinet was on at last but there we were, with the whole General Council upstairs negotiating in the dining room. The door to the Cabinet Room was open so instead of standing outside as we usually do we filtered in one by one, Tony Greenwood, Judith, myself, Roy, and we all sat down rather sheepishly. In came Jim Callaghan and said, 'There is a settlement. I got it by telephone a few minutes ago.'

I was quite certain this was correct because I had heard it from the press half an hour before and, indeed, the longer the delay the more confident I had been that an agreement would be reached. Bob had been telling me how violent Harold was this afternoon and how he was talking about refusing to climb down but there was one very big difference. Last night he had been talking about resigning, refusing to be our negotiator, but he had obviously reflected during the night that this was not sound policy. Harold had said to Bob, 'I'm not going to resign. They won't chase me out, I'm going to stay,' and the moment I heard this I knew that he would settle. He was prepared to threaten to resign as long as he thought there was no chance of his resignation being accepted, but when he realized that Cabinet was solid against him he decided he must stay and settle. That, the view of the Cabinet combined with the view of the Trade Union group, is what forced Harold to go into the negotiations with the T.U.C. determined to get agreement and to survive as

Prime Minister, knowing his bluff had been called in advance. He had to leave Barbara in the lurch to save his own muttons and his own Prime Ministership. I have no doubt that this is the motive which drove him and of course there is nothing like the prospect of certain death to concentrate energy. This afternoon he had concentrated his energies on getting the best possible agreement.

In Mr Wilson's account of his meetings with the General Council of the T.U.C. on June 18th, he describes how he outlined, in the morning session, three possibilities: legislation on the lines the Government had proposed; legislation omitting the penal clauses but 'involving the statutory imposition of effective clauses in [the unions'] rule-books', to deal with indiscipline, with the sanction that unions failing to do so would lose the protection accorded to them by the 1906 Act; or a decision by the T.U.C. 'to alter their procedures on the lines we have suggested'. He told the T.U.C. that the second course had been considered and rejected. The General Council then proposed that the Prime Minister and Mrs Castle should meet the negotiating committee to discuss amendments to Rule 11. This group was firmly opposed to an actual rule change which, Hugh Scanlon pointed out, would be opposed by the National Executive of the A.E.U., bringing with it a defeat for the other procedural changes agreed at the Croydon Congress. Instead, the group proposed that the T.U.C. should make 'a solemn and binding' undertaking to scrutinize the Government's proposals, an undertaking that would, after Congressional endorsement, eventually become a 'rule of Congress'. During the lunch-time interval, Mr Wilson, Mrs Castle and her officials considered the proposal and the Prime Minister and Mrs Castle decided to draft, with the Attorney-General's help, an immediate statement to be accepted by the General Council as a binding undertaking. Meanwhile Cabinet, which had been postponed several times, was called for 4 p.m. In the afternoon the Prime Minister and Mrs Castle saw first Vic Feather at 2.15 and the General Council at 2.25. The General Council were left to consider the draft undertaking, while Cabinet waited, and eventually at 5 o'clock Vic Feather was able to assure the Prime Minister and Mrs Castle that the General Council was unanimous, that the draft had been accepted without amendments and that in the report to Congress the names of all the members of the Council would be appended to it. At 5.15 Mr Wilson and Mrs Castle delivered the report to the Cabinet.[1]

I shall try to find out from Victor Feather and the others how much the T.U.C. knew of the real predicament. They certainly knew of Douglas Houghton's position and they certainly got a picture from Jim Callaghan but I don't think they knew how desperately weak Harold's position was in Cabinet by last night. They certainly knew that if Cabinet got into conflict

[1] See *Wilson*, pp. 657–61.

with the Parliamentary Party it might well be defeated and this, I think, was the key issue which really moved the T.U.C. So I don't believe myself that Victor Feather and his colleagues were tremendously struck when Harold threatened that if he didn't get his way he would impose a Bill with penalties. I don't believe they thought he had the power to do so. We can't know this but maybe I will find out in conversation later on.

So there we sat about waiting, until Harold finally came in, very abrasive, very tough, very furious with Cabinet. Despite all the difficulties of negotiating from the worst possible position, he told us, we have a settlement and Barbara chimed in, 'Yes, and despite this morning's disastrous press we managed to get a settlement.' There it was, a solemn declaration, not a declaration of intent but an agreement by the General Council of its attitude, including what we had asked them to include. Well, they had been moved to go a little way. The one surprise was that when I said, 'I take it you have left open what you have in the big Bill?' Barbara replied, 'Oh, no. We have excluded the penal sanctions from the big Bill as well.' I don't quite know why but they had just chucked them all away.

Then we had a series of little odious speeches, with George Thomas congratulating the Prime Minister and Jim Callaghan soft-soaping and saying that despite all the difficulties we now had a chance of re-election and he would like to say that all his energies would be on the side of the Prime Minister. People were saying that we shouldn't leave too soon, or it would be supposed that Cabinet had no serious doubts, so we spun it out for a quarter of an hour until Harold went out again and then came back with the announcement. He and Barbara once more had the congratulations of the Cabinet and we were ready for the 7 o'clock meeting with the Parliamentary Party.

This was perfectly straightforward. Barbara came in looking white and drawn and sat down beside Harold. When he arrived there had been a moderate cheer, but no one stood up and there was no standing ovation after he had read his typed-out speech. The press, no doubt on Douglas Houghton's instructions, all reported that he got a hero's welcome. I don't think that's true. I think the Party was relieved and that they heard the speech with somewhat cynical disdain. They had got the climb-down they wanted but you don't greatly admire a leader who climbs down, even when it is you who have ordered him to do so. My God, we are out of the wood, we are not tearing ourselves to pieces and at the last moment we have got him off the hook but there is no enthusiasm. I had dinner with Michael Foot and we discussed it in detail. I really love talking to him, he is one of the people I can talk to freely. What a day it has been. Somehow throughout the day I had been confident that this would happen, because I judged that after Cabinet yesterday Harold Wilson would decide to hold his position, to fight for his life and rebuke us. It will not be over this crisis but later on that trouble will come.

Thursday, June 19th

I decided to write a long letter to Harold. I had all kinds of business in Alexander Fleming House which interrupted me but I finally got a minute written and put it on the file. I tried to sum up what I think and the key fact is not that Harold is a cautious, devious man, but a reckless, impulsive creature, and that we have had six months of unnecessary, misjudged, unsuccessful cliffhanging. Once again he has rushed into a thing, come unstuck and got out. I dictated the letter and got it into my box for tonight.

Friday, June 20th

I got into the train and found that by mistake I had slipped into my briefcase the text of my letter to the Prime Minister, so it would have to be sent back to London in a sealed envelope in time for him to get it in his weekend box. I therefore had a chance to withdraw and I wondered if I should send it after all. Anne had said, 'It sounds like a headmaster addressing a pupil', and I had said, 'Not exactly, it's like a senior housemaster addressing an unsuccessful headmaster'. I thought no, this was the most deplorable, catastrophic exhibition between a Cabinet and a Prime Minister and we shouldn't just let things slide. We have now got to get Cabinet right and the Management Committee right and get Harold to be a more sensible Prime Minister. Though I could have withdrawn my letter, I thought, what have I got to lose or to gain? I am sixty now, a senior member of the Cabinet and if I can't do this, who can? This is my function in life, to try to have things said to Harold which no one else will say and this, which I could never say to him, he will have to read, and I will have it for the record. It doesn't read too badly and on the whole I think it is right to send it.

Tuesday, June 24th

After a meeting in the Department on post-Ely policy and a quick interview for Thames T.V. on why we were delaying the implementation of the Seebohm Report, I had dinner with Brian Abel-Smith and Tommy Balogh until at 9 o'clock I had to break off to walk across to No. 10. There was Harold in his study, which is dominated by a big photograph of Attlee. He sat on the sofa a long way off on the other side of the fire and we got down to two enormous drinks and really chatted. He started quite simply, 'I got your minute. I thought out a reply and dictated it and as it has been typed out I may as well read it to you because it's going to be in my memoirs, not in yours. You can have your letter to me and I will have my letter to you.' (This is what actually happened.) He read aloud very fast a long, detailed reply, perfectly friendly, accepting that I had been consistent throughout, even in supporting him on the short-term Bill when I wanted the crisis overcome, and then he defended himself on my main charge of cliquiness on the ground that he couldn't trust the Management Committee with Callaghan in it. Out of this defence it clearly emerged that Harold was saying that he must have a Cabinet of cliques because there are always members he distrusts.

We got down to a long two-hour discussion of our colleagues. Harold has ruled out Jim Callaghan, who has been in cahoots with the T.U.C. throughout, who is playing double and is only concerned with getting the leadership. But Harold's wrath was now concentrated on two other people, Tony Crosland and Dick Marsh, who I believe he thinks are the chief sources of the leaks. He is probably right, these two do chat maliciously with the press and, while at Cabinet Dick Marsh always asserts his innocence, Tony Crosland is silent. The fact remains, however, that we will always have leaks from our Cabinet because Harold is the leakiest of them all. We talked this evening about the Sunday press and, when I said I thought Tony Howard in the *Observer* was very much better than anybody in the *Sunday Times*, Harold said, 'Yes, I did brief him and I briefed Margach. I put Gerald Kaufman on to put them straight.' Harold sees nothing at all improper in doing this, while he bitterly blames Crosland and Marsh for doing the same against him. I have no doubt that Tony and Dick have very different motives. Tony has never forgiven Harold for making Roy Chancellor and has never lost hope that if Roy goes he will be Chancellor in his place. His best chance would be the breaking up of this Government and Callaghan's taking over. Though this sounds a terribly remote possibility I can't help thinking that it has been at the back of Tony's mind during the course of the last six months, when he has switched from demanding stronger anti-trade union measures to being 100 per cent pro-Callaghan. Harold is right, Tony and Jim do see a lot of each other and I know it because my room in the House is on the same landing as theirs. They are in cahoots with Douglas Houghton, the Chairman of the Party, and it has been their triangle which has really endangered Harold in this crisis.

What else did he say about our people? He almost ran down the list. Yes, poor Peter Shore—he's out, not that he wasn't out before. He's admitted to be a failure. Harold said, 'I over-promoted him, he's no good.' He was short and sharp on him. On the other hand, Mason, in contrast to Peter Shore and Dick Marsh, is a solid success in Harold's view and so is Tony Wedgwood Benn, who also turned against Harold on that famous Tuesday. He is recognized as having really done his job and Harold said, 'Though he talks nonsense outside MinTech., when he's on the job he talks sense.' We discussed Roy at great length and his particular relationships with Harold and agreed that he sat on the fence. I said, 'You can't blame him because he and I both sat on the fence, Harold, on that Wednesday morning when we didn't know whether you and Barbara were going to bring back an agreement.' We agreed that Roy had remained canny and aloof and had looked after himself and mustn't be expected to expand but that, provided you accept his limits, he is a man of integrity and loyalty. It became clearer to me that Harold is steeling himself to try to get rid of a Cabinet which makes life intolerable and creates an atmosphere of no confidence in the Government. If he is really not going to have everything done by hole-and-corner methods in special little cliques of Ministers, he must have an inner Cabinet he can trust. His final conclusion on all this was, 'You know, you and Barbara and I ought to see even more of each other.' So the Management Committee is in a sense too big for him and now he's driven back to talking about his three old friends. At least he says that to me. One can never be sure with Harold that in talking to others he won't talk very differently. But his relationship with me was as good as ever and there was no discussion of my failings or my difficulties, which were all left to one side, except for the assumption that we would have to find some solution to the teeth and spectacles problem. There it was, a real old-fashioned gossip, a long discussion of scandal and success and failures and how the P.M. was looking forward to the reconstitution of the Cabinet. There was no great argument about winning the election but a great deal of discussion about unifying the Party and getting the leadership right.

Wednesday, July 2nd
At 4 o'clock I rushed over to No. 10 for the continuation of Management Committee. The only issue was the one I raised. Granted the economic tramlines and that we must continue roughly as we are, is the Chancellor right to say that in order to achieve a good budget next year with no increases in taxation we must accept yet another savage cutback in our plans to expand the social services? We all accept that this year's £160 million overspending has to be cut back. The question is whether we should cut £240 million beyond that, making a total of £400 million. A solid portion, some £160 million, would come from defence and savings in the investment plans of the nationalized industries, but the rest would have to be found from the civil programme. Is that necessary? Is it right that we should at all costs avoid higher taxation and put the whole burden on public sector expenditure? Roy's only defence is that he needs a cut in demand and, frankly, you cut demand more effectively by raising purchase tax or by other direct imports than you do by cutting public expenditure.

I raised this issue and then Barbara had her go, with a frontal attack on the tactical question of how large the cut in demand should be, whether it should be by public expenditure cuts or by actually cutting demand, and how far we still ought to rely on a prices and incomes policy. I must say I then pointed out that I didn't feel quite as shocked as Roy had been when he spoke of Reggie Maudling's gamble before the 1964 election.[1] I would like to see

[1] In the budget of April 1963 Reginald Maudling, then Chancellor of the Exchequer, had given £169 million in tax relief for 1963/4, of which over two-thirds had been in personal income tax, mainly at the bottom of the scale. Firms in areas of high unemployment were allowed to write off the costs of their capital equipment for tax purposes, and were also encouraged by a 30 per cent investment allowance. Mr Maudling's 1964 budget took only £100 million out of the economy, in taxes on tobacco, beer and spirits, but although in the summer months share prices continued to rise and the unemployment figures to fall the production index was stationary and the trade gap continued to widen.

something of a gamble. I know we couldn't repeat the Maudling policy but we might be able to take certain risks and we should also face the fact that cuts in public expenditure were much less effective and more painful than cuts in demand and might produce devastating effects. We have already been wringing a lot of water out of that flannel, running big programmes on small, worn shoestrings. If we went on doing this and, to avoid detection, simultaneously maintaining the size of the programme, we really could come unstuck.

The discussion was on the whole friendly and good-tempered. At the end Roy said severely, 'It's no good. It's not true that the Social Services Ministers can't get economies if they really want to. The fact is that they don't really want economies; psychologically they are spending Ministers.' He had to be reminded that we had already loyally carried out the economies he had asked for. We had been given a four-year programme and told that in 1969/70 there could be 3 per cent growth, so we had planned for that. It wasn't fair to say that we were not economical. We had kept within the margins that were given to us. 'You have changed your mind,' we said, 'and cuts us further and further each month.' By the end of the afternoon, Barbara and I had secured one major success. We persuaded Roy not to circulate his paper but to discuss this orally, 'on the basis of the medium-term prospects and the various economic documents', but without his specific project of a 2½–3 per cent cut, which we didn't want to see in the newspapers. Roy agreed to that and admitted that he must direct himself to the Cabinet more tactfully and not present us with this kind of unconditional ultimatum.

Harold asked Barbara and me to stay behind for a minute or two. I was surprised because we really had no time but he sat down with us and said, 'What do you think about a smaller Cabinet? Don't you think it is essential that I should have a reconstruction?' I said, 'Yes. We now have a contradiction in terms. We can't function as a Cabinet because you don't trust Callaghan, Crosland and Marsh. When you select your Cabinet in future the first requisite should be that you trust its members. Otherwise you not only behave badly to the three you distrust but you also upset all your friends by your hole-and-corner methods of consultation.' Harold talked as though he was determined to remove Callaghan, Marsh and Crosland from the Cabinet. He is infuriated by Crosland and I must say that Tony's behaviour at the Board of Trade has been more than usually irritating. He has been inefficient but nonchalant and cavalier, just not seeming to mind. He seems thoroughly browned off, sick at not being Chancellor, sickened by the Chancellor's policy and, having failed to become Chancellor, he now seems to have got into that peevish frame of mind which I believe is one of the bases of leaks. I find I am inclined to talk when I feel frustrated, left out, when I don't know things. This is ironical because then I start talking, feeling 'I haven't been consulted about this, therefore I am entitled to talk to the press about it because my guess is as good as anybody else's.' This is my view of

Crosland's psychology. Marsh is a bit different. He is brash, promoted far beyond his merits. He is not corruptible but Melchett and people can get at him easily and so can the press. His leaking is more like Gunter's used to be.

Harold added that he must deal with some other failures. He mentioned Peter Shore again and said how disappointing Judith had been. I said, 'You know, she would have done better to have stayed as Minister of Social Security outside the Cabinet,' and it looks as if this might be Harold's plan. Then he said, 'I shall cover this up by another big piece of departmental reconstruction,' and he hinted that MinTech. and the Board of Trade are to be fused under Tony Wedgwood Benn to make it seem that people are being not excluded but just pushed away. The great unknown is whether Barbara will stay in her present Ministry or whether she would go to the Home Office instead of Jim. I believe this would be the right thing since what's happening now indicates pretty clearly that she has completely lost control. One of the effects of dropping her short-term Bill has been a rash of unofficial strikes — dock strikes, Leyland strikes, G.P.O. and National Health Service threats. So it is possible that she might be moved and I think she should be. But the inner group remains clear enough. The P.M. feels at home with Barbara and me, he talks to us freely and says, 'At any rate, even if we disagree, Dick, you and I, you never quarrel or do the dirty on me as other people do.' Roy of course is perfectly in but he is not psychologically or personally in with us. He still remains aloof, the Chancellor in No. 11, biding his time, calculating, with his own friends, his own society.

Thursday, July 3rd
We had worked properly together at Management Committee and carefully thought out Roy's presentation to Cabinet this morning. Still, nobody's views were in any way inhibited. We disagreed in Cabinet in much the same way as in the Management Committee and Barbara and I were again the two chief disagreers. Once more Barbara projected her alternative policy and really got no support at all. I don't think anybody saw it as a serious possibility and Roy quietly demolished her, pointing out quite rightly that it was a policy which could only follow disaster and which would in no way obviate the need for the cuts in public expenditure or demand which he required. Barbara only got a little support from Tony Crosland, who once again wondered what had made our prediction of 3 per cent growth unjustified, what the imbalance in the economy really was and whether we had to accept the level of unemployment that the cuts required. He put this in his usual detached economist's way, exerting quite a powerful influence, but Roy had solid support from Denis Healey, Michael Stewart, Fred Peart and Gerald Gardiner. This time the Prime Minister was absolutely solid with Roy. They are obviously lined up on this policy and that's always so. Ever since I can remember the Prime Minister and his Chancellor have always come into a Cabinet meeting, even into Management Committee, fully

prepared in advance. The only people who were dubious were Judith Hart and Peter Shore. Peter was muted this time. I think they both know they are in the doldrums and are anxious not to cause any more trouble.

I, of course, did not put in full Cabinet the suggestion that we should take risks like Reggie Maudling and gamble a bit but I did put the simple thought that it was much more difficult than Roy seemed to imagine to impose these cuts undetected and just squeeze $2\frac{1}{2}$ per cent out of the Ministries with no changes of policy. I said that it was frankly impossible. We couldn't make cuts without declarations and in particular we couldn't impose their half of the cuts on the local authorities without a squeal.

We had some success, a great defensive victory. Roy didn't get Cabinet to agree to his cuts, only to agree to his having bilateral talks with Ministers, so that at next week's Cabinet he can present his cuts and we can then see whether they would be more painful than the increases in taxation which are the alternative. That's where we have got to this year on the July public expenditure crisis and we will see what happens next week.

Thursday, July 17th
Yesterday afternoon's Cabinet had got rid of the other items before the big Cabinet this morning, so now we turned to public expenditure. At the beginning some of us, Crosland and I, Barbara and Judith, all very carefully said that there wasn't any question yet of our having to agree that £350 or £400 million should be found by cuts. This was only one possibility; others were to find it by reducing investment grants or increasing taxation. Cabinet was merely going to listen to what the Chancellor put before it. This the Chancellor didn't like but he and the Prime Minister had to take it. Most of the morning was spent in the really unsensational story of the fix Roy had done with Denis Healey. Denis has a great margin with his £2,000 million and he made a tremendous speech about how once again he would have to cut but, after all, his job is to cut defence and if he can get it down further and faster presumably he ought to like it. He never admits that cuts are very different for those of us whose aim is to expand the social services. However, this morning we had them one after the other, the non-controversial Ministers, Defence, the nationalized Industries, the Transport people. For some reason Dick Marsh can once again be squeezed successfully and there was Barbara Castle being very virtuous and saying that she was contributing half a million by building two fewer new training centres this year. Then we got to Education, where Ted Short offered a 20 per cent cut in the minor works programme, starting with the provision of new classrooms in primary schools, particularly denominational schools, an enormous cut in the most sensitive and damaging area, with another 3*d*. on school meals, £5 million on charging people for school transport and small cuts for the universities. This package is dynamite. It could certainly not be implemented quietly because the school meals increase would need one announcement and the transport

charges would require legislation. Only the cuts in the minor works programme can be made without announcement and they on the whole are the most damaging and disastrous thing of all. At this point we had to break off.

When Cabinet resumed we had to deal with the really controversial parts of the public expenditure cuts, that is to say, education and health. It became clear that Cabinet was not going to tolerate the education cuts. All this was complicated by Barbara's complaint that the decision to raise school meals by 3*d*., instead of getting another £10 million by increasing the fees for further education, had not gone to Cabinet and that she couldn't possibly agree to it. This is a nice question. It was pointed out that since this was only a substitute device preferred by the Minister concerned, it wasn't something that would usually go to Cabinet. When it had come to me in Social Services I had advised Short not to take it to S.E.P. but to go straight to the Prime Minister and the Chancellor, so we had agreed it a bit hanky-panky and Barbara was now out for blood because she thought that raising the price of school meals would hit the lower-paid worker. There was something in what she said but I didn't know how we were going to get out of it. There was a long and ardent discussion with much the same line-up. Tony Crosland, of course, as an ex-education Minister, was for having no cuts and virtually everybody else supported Ted Short, saying that this was impossible and we ought to raise taxation.

So we got through that very well and then came Health. Here the Chancellor started by saying what his cuts were in my case and then handing over to me. I again made a mistake because I explained how I really needed £17 million extra but I was willing to absorb this revenue cut. Apart from that I would introduce a new charge on insurance companies to cover the cost of the hospitalization of accident cases, which I said would raise £9 million. The Minister of Transport was a bit surprised and said that was the first he'd heard of it, and it's true, but still I got it across as something bright and new which we could do. Then I turned to the hospital building programme and said if it was insisted I should have a cut I could postpone new starts for three months and save £9 million but I would have to announce it. There were great cries of 'Oh, nonsense, here is Dick deceiving us. He doesn't have to announce it. He can do it by slippage.' That's all right for me because I shall go back to Cabinet and say, 'Right, if I don't announce it, it will only be £5 million instead of £9 million,' so I shall get away with another £4 million. I didn't do too well on this, because as I am a big spending Minister with £6,500 million, and as there are cuts in Social Security, Cabinet was certain that some small amount could be taken out of the hospital building programme without being noticed. Of course it can, but whether it is to be £9 million is a different matter. That is about as far as we got. We are going to have a discussion again next Thursday to put the whole thing together and then we shall measure the advisability of accepting all these things. My suspicion is that Roy will be well over a £100 million short and that he should remain so. We shouldn't let him try to extract any more.

Thursday, July 24th
One of the things one really does learn is the effect on Cabinet of having to meet in the Prime Minister's room at the House of Commons, rather than the Cabinet room at No. 10. The Prime Minister's room, like the Ministerial Conference Room on the floor below, is said to be secure enough for meetings, although God knows what the difference really is, but it is so crowded that we can scarcely get round the table and some people have to sit on sofas and at little extra tables. The atmosphere is always bad-tempered. There is something slightly more relaxed about the Cabinet room, which is bigger. The table is longer, the room is higher and it gives more room to breathe and argue, relax and talk to each other as human beings.

This was the Cabinet for the great discussion of the cuts and it became clear that on Education Roy was going to have great difficulty, because item after item was challenged. It also became clear that the increases for school meals, transport, etc., would require a public statement and that there would be a major crisis in the Party. More and more people were saying that if we really had to raise an extra £10 or £15 million it would be better to do it by taxation than by this. However we didn't get very far before we broke off and I went along to 70 Whitehall for the second of my informal drinks with medical journalists.

At 5.30 we started Cabinet again, once more in Harold's room in the Commons. All this morning we had heard announcements about offers from Treasury Ministers and the nationalized industries—how much Roy Mason would offer, the reduction in gas and electricity investment, how much would be cut off the railways. This afternoon we turned back to the public sector and I was the part of the public sector where we had halted on the previous occasion. Instead of doing what he usually did, this time Roy turned to me and I began to explain the situation as I saw it. Within a matter of minutes there was a furious confrontation between us. I explained in answer to a challenge that in order to get the £9 million from hospital building cuts, I would have to make a Statement next week. I could confirm this because only £12 million of the building programme was under my control and the rest was under the control of the R.H.B.s, with a firm arrangement that in the course of this programme they could go straight ahead within the cost limits allowed. I would now have to instruct them to hold back artificially, so the story must come out.

I said Cabinet must be quite clear that there would either have to be an announcement about this, or I could only cut it back to £5 million and, before we knew it, we were in the middle of a terrible row. I had already said I would no longer ask for the £17 million and that I would try to contain that requirement by cutting my revenue expenditure, but this was regarded by

Roy not as a give-away but as proof that I had that amount of fat to take off. We got very heated and finally I simply said, 'If the Treasury insists, someone else can carry out the announcement of the suspension of the hospital building programme. It's absolutely crazy. I can only do it if it's part of a general announcement of a general cut and therefore it is all a question of publication and the package we present.' Unfortunately, in the course of all this argument I also said that Roy's officials had bullied my officials into consent, but as a matter of fact this was completely untrue. We had known Roy was going to ask for £23 million and we had gone to see him about it and showed him the choice between a six-month cut or a three-month cut and said that in either case we would have to have publicity.

It was perhaps the roughest row we have had but I have not forgiven him for his last budget, when he took from me all the nice things, the benefits, and, by refusing to announce the increased contributions for teeth and spectacles, caused endless trouble in the summer. I am not going to let him do it this time, now that he has already started preparing for a splendid budget next year, with reductions in taxation at the cost of making us cut back our programmes. Not bloody likely! From the start I had been determined to defeat him on this and bring Cabinet round to saying that rather than have cuts in Health and Education we would have increased taxation.

After this stormy meeting, with Harold trying to make peace and divisions interrupting us, the Prime Minister said, 'We must have some starred items. We shall have to put together all the items which are doubtful and look at them again next week and, then, when we come to our general decision, we can see whether we wish to do the job by increased taxation or by cuts in expenditure or by a different mixture of both.' I got my £9 million hospital capital building cut included in the starred items, so I have fended off the immediate danger. It's only £4 million I'm touting for now, to cut it down from £9 to £5 million. My other proposal, to introduce a levy on motor-car insurance companies to pay for the cost of accidents, has gone pretty well on the official level. We could get £10 million from this. It was only attacked by Dick Marsh and I was able to explain the principles behind it. I came out of that Cabinet meeting enormously elated, I must admit. After a bloody awful time I had got a little of my own back by asserting myself in Cabinet in a fairly decisive way and I had shown Roy where he could get off. I had been given solid support by Tony Crosland, which doesn't help me much since Roy regards him as an enemy, and I was also helped by all the social service people. Callaghan had been silent and judicious, but I had Ted Short, the Welsh and Scottish Secretaries, and even George Thomson. Yes, Roy was really pretty well isolated now, along with the standard supporters of Government policy, Michael Stewart and Denis Healey. This evening I could retire feeling that I had achieved something and I am looking forward almost with relish to next week's meeting.

Tuesday, July 29th

This was the day for the big Cabinet to which I had been looking forward so much last week and which, somehow, in retrospect I didn't enjoy. The morning session took from 10.0 till 1.0. First there was a statement by Harold and the Chancellor on what the situation was. Roy said he had asked for £400 million and that if he managed to get everything, including the starred items, he would have £304 million. If he didn't get the starred items he would have only £292 million, far less than he needed, because he wanted to have a neutral budget in which he would be able to prevent more working-class people coming under income tax. We went into the details of the problem and he carefully reserved the disputed education items and my item, the extra £4 million. To my surprise he said he must have the £4 million from Health because he had to have something flexible for new claims for extra money. There were four claims: for the Land Commission, which was a technical PESC claim, not really an increase; two claims from the Board of Trade, for the retention of the National Film Finance Corporation and for a national consultancy organization; and then one from the Lord Chancellor who wanted rather more money for legal aid. All these would add up to about £10 million and the Chancellor said it was for this he needed my £4 million. Now it is my impression, for what it is worth, that this very morning Roy and the Prime Minister had talked it over and knew they couldn't get the £4 million out of me, so I think they had pretty well agreed to drop that demand and concede most of the demands for minor extra things and that the whole day was a slightly put-up job. Anyhow the morning passed mainly in this detailed argument until lunch-time, when, as we got up, Roy said, 'What do you want, Dick? Are you going to have a big battle in this afternoon's discussion?' I said, 'I just want to stop you making a fool of yourself with the £4 million.'

We came back at 3.30 and went on to 5.30 and all the time I was very carefully holding my breath and saying, 'Let all the claims be made and then let us ask the basic question of whether we have got the priorities right and whether the Chancellor is right to say it is more important to have a neutral budget than it is to keep our public expenditure programme going.' But when it came to it I made a speech. Willie Ross told me I spoke for so long that I nearly lost it. I don't think that is true but I don't think I did myself any good. I said it was absolutely demented to be squabbling about £4 million from the Ministry out of a £17,000 million total. We had already had prescription charges and teeth and spectacles, and now the Chancellor wanted an announcement that we were cutting the hospital building programme as well, all for the sake of £4 million. I said I couldn't take it, it was just nonsense, I just wouldn't pay it. I was in a tizzy, I was too worked up and of course I didn't realize at the time that I made a bad impression. The backing I got was striking. Judith Hart supported me and Tony Crosland and everybody else looked awkward. Barbara never said a word and none of them wanted to take part in this gladiatorial fight between Roy and myself. Well, I won. Finally Roy gave in and the Prime Minister summed up. You won't find the summing up in the Cabinet minutes, but, let's be clear, the defeat took place. Roy didn't get his drastic cuts in either Health or Education. On Education he got the minor works, half a million off the school building programme, and 3d. on school milk, but he lost on school transport.

My own Department certainly hadn't expected me to win on this. Dick Bourton sent me his warmest congratulations afterwards but somehow I didn't enjoy it. We'd discussed it for six hours and I had perhaps been overwrought. I had in a sense shouted and abused my position too much, that's my own feeling. I thought, what the hell shall I do? It was a sweltering evening. Ben Whitaker was giving a party so I made Peter Smithson motor me up to Hampstead, where Ben has a magnificent house with a huge great garden behind. I walked into the main room and there was Roy. 'Ha,' he said, 'we have said enough to each other today,' and I felt the same and turned to the bar. After three or four hours I went home.

Wednesday, July 30th

Another Cabinet and Harold started by saying, 'Well once again we have full reports and details from the usual two, the *Guardian* and the *Financial Times*.' Tony Crosland said, 'I have read the reports. There is nothing in them, mere guesswork. All they know is that there was a PESC meeting and that people have been discussing their budgets with the Chancellor. There is nothing here to prove there has been any kind of leak.' Dick Marsh chipped in too, saying it was absurd, and of course it is absurd, and yet Harold was convinced that the press had been given real information. I watched him as he thought, 'Now I've got Crosland and Marsh.' He is determined to regard them as leaky and probably, in some way, to demote them but today there was no evidence whatsoever on which to base the belief.

The other important item was Northern Ireland. We were warned by Callaghan that we were coming up to a tremendous demonstration on August 12th by the so-called Apprentices of Derry, and there might be major catastrophes.[1]

Friday, August 8th

I remembered this morning that Harold was off to the Scillies, so I rang him up to say goodbye and that I was sorry I hadn't sent him across some notes for a speech on social services he is going to give at the T.U.C. Conference. I found he had already gone on the 12.45 p.m. train. I don't think it matters and though I felt it would have been pleasant and nice to have talked to him,

---

[1] The annual Apprentice Boys' March was a Protestant demonstration celebrating the relief of Derry on August 12th, 1689, after a 105-day siege by James II's Roman Catholic soldiery.

I must now try to do the work for him, because I feel that my position has begun to decline. Yesterday it was announced from No. 10 that Harold has selected the three members of the Cabinet to work with him on the Campaign Committee, Wedgwood Benn, Bob Mellish and Denis Healey. It's true that I am on the Management Committee, which Harold says will in effect have the real strategic control, but nevertheless he has not chosen me. I grant that if he had taken me and not Judith Hart it would have been terribly hard on her but I think he wants to keep her out of the new Cabinet. True, he wants to give a young image, and Denis and Tony Benn are younger people who are going to be in his next Cabinet, whereas I know deep down I am not. It is a mark that he thinks I am getting on, a senior member of the Cabinet who doesn't mind too much because I have no future. All that has an impact on Harold's estimate of me and I think he sees me as an old friend who is becoming a bit of a ruddy nuisance.

Monday, August 18th–Saturday, August 23rd
The only thing I need really record has been the big Cabinet meeting on Tuesday afternoon, where the main subject was Northern Ireland. There had been the sudden decision last week to put in the troops and now we had to evolve the policy to be presented to Chichester-Clark,[1] who was coming over to talk to the P.M. and Callaghan. Harold and Jim had really committed the Cabinet to putting the troops in and once they were there they couldn't be taken out again, so we had to ratify what had been done. I think it is fair to say that Callaghan wanted to put very strong pressure on Chichester-Clark and to extract from him an agreement that we should take complete control of the police force, that we should wind up the 'B' Specials, change the command and get ahead with the reforms, and that we should do all this without taking over, but with Chichester-Clark as our agent, and if he wouldn't agree we should have to be prepared to take on direct rule.

The only difference was between the Home Secretary, the civil authority, on the one side and the Minister of Defence on the other. Healey, representing the military, was rather more cagy and said on no account must we risk having to take over, so we must only push Chichester-Clark as far as he wanted to go. If there was any real danger of his giving up and our having to take over we would have failed. This is true in a sense, because a take-over would put the British soldiers under pressure from the Republicans and the Catholics. Callaghan and Healey both reminded us that our whole interest was to work through the Protestant Government. The Protestants are the majority and we can't afford to alienate them as well as the Catholics and find ourselves ruling Northern Ireland directly as a colony. We have also to be on the side of the Catholic minority and try to help and protect them against their persecutors.

[1] Prime Minister of Northern Ireland 1969–71.

There wasn't any tremendous disagreement. It was one of those Cabinets where Harold takes great trouble to make sure each Minister is consulted, going round the table for opinions from each. Nor do I believe there was much difficulty in deciding what to do. It was a case where in a sense our mind was made up by events. It wasn't so much deciding what policy to have as being able to excuse it and for the execution of this kind of policy the combination of Callaghan and Harold is quite good. Whatever his other deficiencies, Harold is a very competent tactical negotiator in the short run. So we gave him full power to negotiate with Chichester-Clark and to press him as far as he possibly could but it was certainly made perfectly clear that if Chichester-Clark jibbed at the transfer of power from the police to our military force, Cabinet was to resume later tonight, because the House of Commons would have to be recalled to pass legislation for direct rule. It wasn't a very exciting meeting because, as I say, it was the formal Cabinet acceptance of a *fait accompli*. We went on for three hours because we were questioning and investigating and testing, so afterwards there was only a break of about forty minutes before Harold and Jim sat down for their six-hour conference with Chichester-Clark.

Harold has always fancied himself as a negotiator and he thinks that this is all you need to be if you are Foreign Secretary. However in this case, because Northern Ireland isn't a foreign country but part of Britain with the same language, I had confidence that he and Jim would handle it fairly well, and this happened. Chichester-Clark gave them practically everything they wanted, indeed rather more in certain ways, because a complete take-over by the military had not been what we expected. We had expected the nomination of a new Head of the R.U.C. but, no, the military were to take over as well, and the 'B' Specials to be withdrawn, and towards the end of the discussion Chichester-Clark and Harold went on the ten o'clock news programme to announce the agreement. There was some uncertainty, though, and during the next two or three days there was a good deal in the Tory press about Harold's having cocked it up again, making an announcement on '24 Hours' which didn't square with what Chichester-Clark was actually intending to do in Northern Ireland. But it came out right for us, because these were merely the contortions of the Northern Ireland Government, who didn't like to admit how far they had surrendered. In fact what Harold said was true, we had made a take-over, British troops were in Belfast and Londonderry and the British Commander in Chief was in charge of the Northern Irish police. All this went on between the Tuesday and Saturday, by which time I had slackened off and had left for my holiday.

Friday, September 5th
At the end of July the Management Committee had decided to have a whole day at Chequers. Here today were Harold, Roy, myself, Fred Peart, Barbara, Michael Stewart, Bob Mellish, now regularly there, but not Denis

28 Fellow commuters complained about the Secretary of State reserving a whole first class compartment of the train between Paddington and Banbury while many had to stand. Crossman himself has the 'reserved' notice withdrawn and uses the crowded restaurant car in the morning. March 1970.

29 The General Election of June 1970 brought an end to the Labour Government. Crossman, after campaigning with his wife in Coventry East, the constituency he has represented for 25 years, learns that he has held his seat with a reduced majority.

30 His Party defeated at the polls after six years in government, Harold Wilson makes way at No. 10 for the incoming Tory Prime Minister, the musical Edward Heath. While Mr Heath has his piano delivered at the front door, workmen carry out Mr Wilson's harmonium by the rear.

31 As editor of the *New Statesman*, November 1970.

Healey, who was on holiday recovering from a hernia operation. It was another lovely September morning and I decided to motor down with Roy. His great Austin Princess drew up outside 9 Vincent Square at 8.55 and we were off punctually at 9.0. On the way down Roy was careful. He was interesting about Callaghan, though, saying, 'You know there is nobody in politics I can remember and no case I can think of in history where a man combined such a powerful political personality with so little intelligence.' I was a bit taken aback because I think Jim Callaghan is a wonderful political personality, easily the most accomplished politician in the Labour Party, and I think he is quite able as well. I said, 'He works hard.' 'Ah,' said Roy, 'yes, he is very conscientious with his briefs. I don't work nearly as hard as he does,' and I thought, 'My God you don't.' We talked a lot about the Cabinet reshuffle and exchanged notes. 'After Harold asked you and Barbara your advice,' said Roy, 'I asked Harold about it and he told me his intentions for Callaghan, Tony Crosland and Dick Marsh, which I was strongly against, and his intentions for Tony Greenwood, Judith Hart and Peter Shore, which I strongly approved.' We discussed the new industrial Ministry to some extent and the possibility of Harold Lever being promoted, finding that we had roughly the same story on that but that neither of us had heard anything at all recently.

When we got to Chequers we settled down not in the big room as usual, but in comfortable armchairs in the long lounge which stretches right across the side of the house. The Prime Minister began by saying how much the situation had improved, how much the polls were turning in our favour, and how Heath had a record bad result, so bad they couldn't publish it. I was interested because of course a major factor of political life since the beginning of the week has been the disastrous reaction of the T.U.C. to the Prime Minister's speech at the T.U.C. Conference. On Monday he had gone down to Portsmouth to make his oration, a stolid, dull speech with a lecturing tone to it, 'There can be no backsliding etc., etc.' and making too much of the agreement between himself and Victor Feather.[1] He obviously displayed an offensive, unsuccessful attitude which had been followed by the rejection of any kind of sanctions for a voluntary prices and incomes policy. Day after day the whole Congress had been anti-Government, snubbing, crushing, but Harold didn't seem unduly depressed. He recalled that last year they had had an even worse Conference and the Labour Party had an even better one as a result. Anyway, in his view the situation was improving economically and in terms of public opinion.

Bob Mellish, direct and narrow-minded, was asked to open the discussion

[1] For the 'strong meat', that he did not expect to be received with enthusiasm, see *Wilson*, pp. 699–701. The Congress not only declared that the Government should not renew the powers in Part II of the Prices and Incomes Act, allowing them to delay wages settlements, but also passed by 4,652,000 votes to 4,207,000 a resolution demanding repeal of the entire Act, including price controls.

and he simply said that the things that worried people were the cost of living, mortgages and unemployment, and these were the three things which we ought to consider. Roy Jenkins then came in with a very interesting statement that the balance of payments had improved enormously this year, and that we were going to have a good third quarter too, but accompanied by a very dicey situation for the pound.[1] Ever since the French devaluation and the publication of our latest trade figures the pound had been doing extremely badly. He then made a statement about the N.E.C. document on economic strategy, which includes a demand for a wealth tax and a whole series of other new taxes. What a disaster, he said, that this should give the impression that we have old-fashioned ideas of restriction and heavy taxation, when it is really taxation that is our difficulty. I must say Roy is right. Barbara and I rubbed in what Bob Mellish had said about mortgages and said that this was only one aspect of people's feeling that they are overtaxed. Roy lectured us, saying that we have gone beyond the limits of taxation, and it is true. One of the things which came out, I think, in this conference at Chequers was our agreement that we must get a neutral budget, one which does not actually increase people's tax burden. We can't have any stunts but we must simply go for the balance of payments because any other policy would be seen through and would fail. There are no gimmicks we can use.

Then Michael Stewart talked about the Common Market and how it was now likely that the French would lift their veto and that we might be invited to start negotiations. In that case he would want to make a positive statement in favour. Fred Peart doesn't add much to the conversation but he barged in and said we couldn't possibly do this, it would upset everybody. It is quite true that anti-Common Market feeling is now very strong in the country but Barbara and I both made it quite clear that we knew we couldn't possibly go back on our decision to seek admission. Both of us pointed out, though, that the question was of what posture we should adopt. We must seek admission but at the same time defend ourselves and consider the terms. Do we accept the Common Agricultural Policy without question? Do we sacrifice the sugar agreement and New Zealand? Barbara went so far as to say that she thought we couldn't afford to give too much away in the period of negotiation, but we couldn't afford to stall because if it went on next summer and we were forced to have an election this might be dangerous. Here we came to the interesting question of timing because Harold had assumed at the beginning of the meeting that we would be having an autumn election. Barbara strongly argued that there might be a great risk in holding out beyond May until the autumn and we might well lose by it. Autumn is always a difficult period economically and in terms of the pound. If the

[1] The current balance for July–September 1969 showed a deficit of only £7 million. There was a £40 million surplus on visible trade for the month of August, but June and July had shown deficits of £24 million and £37 million respectively.

difficulties of the Common Market might be added to this, we ought to be thinking of a spring or early summer election. Then Harold said, 'Even if it meant losing your Industrial Relations Bill?' and Barbara answered, 'Well, if we have started on it, that is all that matters.' I found this very interesting.

We sat there from 10.30 until at 1.0 we broke for lunch. After lunch, to my surprise, Harold gave a full account of his new reshuffle, practically the same as he had told Barbara and me before. He wants to cut down the size of the Cabinet but he doesn't think he is going to get down to fifteen or sixteen as he thought earlier. He then said that Callaghan had done well for himself and the party on Northern Ireland, he had played the game and it was time we brought him back into the Management Committee, but of course only if assurances were given that he wouldn't play hanky-panky with prices and incomes in the trade unions again. Harold is clearly implacable on this and thinks that he and Bob Mellish know the real story of the treacherous deals which were being done by Callaghan and Houghton with the T.U.C. General Council. Harold doesn't want that repeated in prices and incomes next year, though of course it is not likely to happen again now we have abandoned the policy and are only going to reactivate the Bill by an affirmative order. So Callaghan is not only to stay but to be brought back into the Management Committee. As for George Brown, he gave a press conference this week in his constituency, saying he had fully recovered and was back in politics, and it has been surmised that he is to return to the Government. It's true that Harold talked to him in July and also much more recently and George made it clear that he wanted to come back but only with the full status of Deputy Leader. Today Harold said, looking at Michael Stewart, that this was out of the question, so he wouldn't have George back now but that he might later on, just before the election, as a kind of mark of unity.

The general atmosphere was amiable. The Prime Minister is not now pretending that we are certain to win the election and he even talks as though there might be an interval before the next Labour Government. He is much more detached and relaxed, better able to face reality.

We sat there for two hours until 4.0 in the afternoon. It was easy going, it wasn't very profound, but I suppose that we each got a picture of the others' philosophy, and it was clear today that there is now no chance of a run-up to the election with a different policy, with a planned expansion, planned risk-taking. We are simply going to plough ahead on the present policy with no unexpected changes. As Roy quite rightly says, if we do anything else we shall risk another November, and looking back it was that sudden hitch last year, the sudden imposition of the regulator, that was the fatal thing. The Government can't take any risk which might lead to another crisis. The one thing that was clear to the five of us was that we were regarded by Harold as his big lot, he is content with us and with Callaghan as well, and we are going to be the powers which run this Party until Parliament ends.

Wednesday, September 10th

It was amusing to see in all the papers a statement that George Brown is not going to be a member of the Government. This occurred because yesterday morning Walter Terry of the *Mail* had announced that George was coming back.[1] No. 10 had obviously issued a denial within twenty-four hours, which I suppose is a tribute to Walter Terry as a journalist and to the importance of George and also showed me that the P.M.'s briefing at Chequers was correct and George was out. Harold hasn't changed his mind.

Thursday, September 18th

At the office I was mystified to see that I was booked for 'Cabinet photograph, Transport House', because the Cabinet photograph is taken in the garden of No. 10 and we had it a few months ago. A garbled message from my Private Office said I was wanted with the Lord Chancellor and one or two others and I thought it must be some election thing.

I was desperately keen to get to the meeting of the Local Government Committee at 10.30 and here was the photograph at the same time, with the Prime Minister insisting on my presence. So I got there at 10.20. Being early was no help; there was the photographer in No. 3 Committee Room in Transport House, trying to set it up as a mock Cabinet room with a curved table, and I learnt that a special selection of people had been summoned by the P.M., some ten or twelve of us, for a photograph of us working with him. He would have liked it in the Cabinet room itself but that would have been too difficult to arrange. As Fred Peart and Roy Mason came in, it suddenly struck me that if Harold needed a Cabinet photograph taken now, he could only have certain members because of the forthcoming reshuffle. It came out that Harold wanted the photograph for the first number of the *Daily Mirror* colour supplement, which appears in a fortnight, and he had very secretly got together a group of Ministers without revealing it to the rest, so it was of some interest to see who was there. On the far side of the table was Tony Wedgwood Benn, next to him Barbara and Roy, and on our side of Harold there were Fred Peart, myself, Roy Mason and Gerald Gardiner, an extra-ordinary lot. People I knew to be in London who weren't included were Peter Shore and Judith Hart. Tony Greenwood was in America so it was open about him and we were ostentatiously told that Michael Stewart couldn't come.

There was a great deal of joking and when Harold came in I said, 'We have come to the conclusion that we are the ten to whom you are saying goodbye before your St Bartholomew's Day massacre, before you do a Macmillan on us.' Harold looked very sheepish. He has great delight in playing about with reshuffles, and he didn't deny for one moment what it was all about.

[1] Walter Terry was Political Editor of the *Daily Mail* from 1965 to 1973 and of the *Daily Express* from 1973 to 1975, when he joined the political staff of the *Sun*.

Sunday, September 21st

This has been one of those good weeks in politics, good in the sense that the position of the Labour Party has improved a great deal. Last Thursday we published the best trade figures we have ever had and the Gallup Poll on Wednesday showed the Tory lead had dropped to $8\frac{1}{2}$ per cent.[1] We always have this annual improvement when Parliament isn't sitting and it has been a decent summer, with at long last a sense that the economic situation is improving. The newspapers are now full of discussions about the possibility of Labour winning the next election, or at least giving the Tories a run for their money, and Heath's unpopularity and the Tories' failure to cash in on our failures have improved our own optimistic tendencies a great deal. Meanwhile, though the Northern Ireland crisis is black in one sense, it has got a great deal better, partly because we have hung on. The British Army is gradually persuading people to take the barricades down, the take-over has been absorbed, and we have done all this without the Chichester-Clark Government either breaking with us or being broken by their own supporters.

Sunday, October 5th

In the evening came the news of this famous reshuffle which had been dominating Brighton.[2] I rang Barbara this morning, who said she knew nothing and had no contact with Harold about it even though she sat in Conference with him. What do we see when we compare it with Harold's great talk of July and early August of removing Callaghan, Marsh and Crosland? Callaghan is exactly where he was, stronger than ever as a result of Ireland. Crosland is promoted to the gigantic job of running Housing and Transport, with Tony Greenwood under him. The only man who is clean out is Dick Marsh. Harold has kept his word there. Benn has been promoted, as he thought he would be, to run the big industrial Department with several people under him. Benn and Crosland are now super-Ministers of industry and planning, the same level as Barbara and me. Judith is out of Cabinet and into the Overseas Department and Peter Shore is in Cabinet without a job, but I suppose he will be the Prime Minister's aide, as well as doing public relations. Kenneth Robinson, who has done a faithful job, is finally thrown out. This is a most extraordinary thing to do while leaving that wet Tony Greenwood at Housing. George Thomson is back in European affairs. I thought Tony Crosland would go to Europe but he is being put in charge of local government, which he knows nothing about. These are ups and downs and the shuffle is a great deal less drastic than Harold intended. He has got

[1] There was a £28 million surplus in the visible trade balance for September and seasonally adjusted figures showed an overall surplus of £214 million for the third quarter of 1969, compared with a £72 million surplus (revised figures) for the second quarter.

[2] The Labour Party Conference had taken place at Brighton from Monday, September 29th to Friday, October 3rd. Crossman, now off the Executive, spent only a day there.

his two ministerial groupings as we expected, but he has made very many fewer changes. There is no move for Healey or for me, of course, and Barbara and Roy are unchanged. Harold Lever has been promoted into Trade because Roy won't have an expert of that kind with him in the Treasury, more's the pity. These are my first impressions. The shuffle leaves the seven people at the top unchanged, it gives Benn a big leg-up and, to everyone's surprise, Crosland too. Peter Shore is left in the Cabinet quite undeservedly and Judith is out, I think rightly. Tony Greenwood and Roy Mason are out, I think rightly.* There it is. We are left with two fewer people in Cabinet.

Monday, October 6th
I went up to London and had only just time to go to the office before I was off to Eastbourne to address the Public Health Inspectors. I went down in brilliant sunshine, addressed a couple of thousand people, had lunch and then came straight back. Directly I got to Victoria I was whirled to St James's Square to a secret meeting with Barbara which we had arranged on the telephone yesterday. My office had told her office that if she and I didn't reach agreement I would be circulating a Cabinet paper advising against having only the Industrial Relations Bill this session and suggesting a White Paper. I got there a bit early, went into her room, and there she was with Denis Barnes and Alex Jarratt,[1] a grey-haired, distinguished gentleman, like a handsome American. She gave me a drink and we sat down together to discuss her Industrial Commission and my insistence that the doctors must be excluded. It was an interesting meeting because she put her case and then I put mine and then I said, 'I am sorry but the very announcement of the intention to have a Bill will force me to define to the doctors where we stand. There is no half-way house here. Either they must be completely out or we bring them right in and say their salaries will be dealt with by the new Industrial Commission, along with higher civil servants and everybody else, in which case there will be hell to pay and I can say goodbye to a revised Health Service.' She was resistant at first but then Jarratt and Denis came to my assistance and said, 'Frankly, whatever happens, no Government will dare to discipline the doctors.' They accepted my view that we had done extremely well under Kindersley, which had got the doctors to accept limits on their salary increases and the principles of the prices and incomes policy

* I made one mistake. I thought Roy Mason was out of the Cabinet but in fact he is in the Cabinet and actually promoted, I think. He is President of the Board of Trade, which is now really a Ministry for exports.
[1] Alex Jarratt, an Under-Secretary at the Ministry of Power 1963–7, was seconded as Secretary to the National Board for Prices and Incomes 1965–8. He was a Deputy Secretary in 1967 and then Deputy Under-Secretary of State at the Department of Employment and Productivity 1968–70 and Deputy Secretary at the Ministry of Agriculture 1970. In 1970 he joined the International Publishing Corporation as Managing Director, becoming the Chairman and Chief Executive of Reed International in 1974.

in a way that no Industrial Commission could have done. We have nothing to complain of in the Kindersley Committee except that it is not tidy and the doctors seem to be in a privileged position. We finally reached firm agreement. Barbara gave me a secret understanding that, provided I didn't press for special favours for the doctors and that I was easy with her when the thing came before the Management Committee and the Cabinet, she would give me a tacit understanding that when it came to the drafting of the Bill the doctors' position would not be affected in any way. Jarratt has put this in writing so I have got her tied up tight. She has bought me off but the price is a very high one and one for which I am bound to stay quiet because all I want is to keep the doctors out. I'm not in any way against her having the Bill.

Tuesday, October 7th

I reflected on our talk and wondered how often such secret understandings are arrived at between members of the Cabinet. There we were, me with my Permanent Secretary and her with her two officials, reaching a secret agreement. I took care to indicate to Burke today that Barbara and I had reached this understanding because he is in the centre of things and it is very important that he should realize what has happened. I didn't of course tell any politician about it but it was probably the most important thing I shall do this week.

Wednesday, October 8th

We had a first-rate meeting of the Management Committee, just six of us because Denis Healey and the Chief Whip were away, and this is the right number. Harold has always said that we must have Callaghan back, which would make a total of nine, but he is now wondering if we should add the other two super-Ministers, Tony Wedgwood Benn and Tony Crosland, making it eleven, in which case we already represent half the Cabinet. This is a real problem for Harold. I think he will probably enlarge it but if he does it will become a public meeting. I can see now that the size of these committees is all-important. If you can get down to fewer than seven important Ministers, something like a natural conversation takes place between fellow-politicians who are not just pontificating from briefs, on points and postures relating to their job. The whole point of a committee of this kind is to loosen one from one's job.

We discussed absolutely frankly the problems of Barbara's new Industrial Relations Bill and the Industrial Commission. Over the last week or two she has switched from saying she wants a small limited Bill to saying she is going to have a big Bill, even though this has the disadvantage of being wholly pro-trade union. All it has omitted from *In Place of Strife* are her three sanctions proposals, so the trade unions get everything they want. I accept her view that she can't afford to go without any Industrial Relations Bill and that it must please the trade unions and keep to the terms by having no sanctions. It may look like a sell-out but there is no choice, because if we were to put sanctions into it our own party would accuse us of breaking faith with the unions and their undertaking. We argued this out at length and, on the whole, I backed her, but of course I had my secret arrangement.

Thursday, October 9th

First at Cabinet we had Wasp helicopter exports to South Africa. At O.P.D. there had been a division, with Denis Healey, Tony Crosland, Eddie Shackleton and Roy all wanting to sell Wasps only on a replacement basis, but Harold had not liked this and had brought it back to Cabinet. He collected opinion all round the table and we had a clear majority saying we can't sell arms to South Africa, resurrecting the whole atmosphere of December 1967. I was pretty cowardly and, when I was asked my opinion, I said, 'I hear from John Diamond and Roy Jenkins that not to sell them will cause a disastrous political commotion and from Barbara Castle that if we do it will cause a disastrous political commotion, so I would like to hear from the Chief Whip which is true.' The Chief said, 'To sell them will cause a disaster in the Party.' I am not sure he was right but Harold got his way and prevailed against the sane rational views of Denis Healey and the others.

Then we had an interminable talk about Barbara's two Bills. She droned on and on and on at inordinate length, just thinking aloud and reading every clause of the Bill. Oh dear, what a bore! Everybody agreed that it was an untidy and incoherent Bill and she didn't know what she meant. The opposition, led by Tony Crosland, had all the best of the argument, yet it was felt Barbara would have to have the Bill as a substitute for the prices and incomes policy, to cover up the vacancy of it all. I know very well that if I had been tough and pushed hard I could have made it very difficult for Harold to interpret the Cabinet view as anything but an opposition to legislation this session but I kept my word. She rambled on until after 1 o'clock. In a way it was lucky for me because Cabinet had no time to hear my report on the abatement negotiations, so I slipped the scheme through. I must say I was pleased when Peart said, 'You said more in ten minutes than she said in forty.' I got an agreement and that was that.

Before Cabinet I had a frantic message that Tony Crosland wanted to lunch with me. I took him to lunch. (I don't know why he doesn't take me, perhaps because he doesn't have a club.)[1] So off we went to the Athenaeum where I gave him grouse and claret and he told me the following story, which rather confirmed something Roy told me. I had guessed that making Tony an overlord at Transport and Housing wasn't what Harold originally intended and it is certainly true that he was only offered this job about ten days ago, just before he made a voyage to Tokyo as President of the Board of Trade. He was offered it in vague outline and he came back on the day of the

[1] His entry in *Who's Who* gave his club as Grimsby Labour.

reshuffle to find that it had all been done in his absence. This shows he wasn't part of the original plan for this Ministry, which, I would like to bet, was that Healey should be moved into this world, and I think Roy has some evidence that Denis was offered this and turned it down. My suspicion is that, at the time when Harold was violently anti-Crosland, he intended to put Denis here and try to transfer Crosland from the cut-down Board of Trade to the job of Minister for Europe at the Foreign Office. Over lunch we discussed his role in his new super-Ministry or non super-Ministry. He has taken over the D.E.A.'s regional planning, but not the parts of the Board of Trade which deal with regional planning and industrial development certificates. I remember from being Minister of Housing that Douglas Jay's power to bitch up my housing plans was gigantic, because he could control the I.D.C.s and the permission for industry to move, and the chap who runs that controls the speed of development of the new towns. All this has gone to Tony Wedgwood Benn, and is still to be industry-dominated, so in this battle for power Benn already has powers far greater than Crosland. Benn's Ministry of Technology has also swallowed the whole Ministry of Power and a large section of the Board of Trade, whereas there has been no change in the relationship of Transport and Housing, the two very different Ministries under Crosland.

The poor man is in the position of an overlord but he won't run the Ministry, because, even more depressing for him, it has been publicly announced that the integration of his Department will take low priority, and his job now is to conduct negotiations for the Maud reforms and to deal with pollution. Although Harold has created this Department of Local Government and Regional Planning, he has left the two Permanent Secretaries at the Ministry level, one at Transport and Matthew Stevenson at Housing, and Tony with apparently no one at all. Tony said, looking rather shamefaced, 'Ten days ago I got the impression that I was going to get Matthew Stevenson, but now I come back to find that the Permanent Secretaries are to remain at Ministry level.' 'Well,' I said, 'you'd be crazy to let that happen. You must go back to Harold and fight your battle. Stevenson is a powerful man and, let me tell you, if you fail to get him you will be alone in the stratosphere.' I couldn't help remembering exactly what happened to me when I was Lord President and gave up the Leadership of the House for a general co-ordinating job in the Social Services, and the promise of a merged Ministry in due course, with in the meantime the two Ministers staying and my having supervisory powers. I found that my supervisory powers were completely ineffective. Even though the Civil Service knew that I was not only overlord but taking over a merged Ministry in a matter of months, they began to suspect the thing wasn't coming off and I had to press the P.M. to make announcements all the time in order to get any authority at all. In Tony Crosland's case it is known that there will be no merger before the election and in my view this is a disaster for him.

Sunday, October 12th

There is no doubt that, whether Harold intended it or not, one of the major effects of this shuffle is completely to reaffirm the dominance of the Treasury and of the Chancellor. The elimination of D.E.A. has taken away what Harold described as creative tension, at the time of George Brown and Callaghan,[1] and the removal of Tony Crosland from the Board of Trade and its transformation into a mere foreign trade organization under Roy Mason has removed a second post which was traditionally held by an economist who could stand up to the Chancellor.

A third but not insignificant factor is the character of Wedgwood Benn. Here is this inordinately large Ministry of Industry headed by Wedgy Benn, an intellectually negligible whizz-kid who simply can't stand up to Roy at all and won't have the staff or the time to deal with economics. Of course it may be said that Tony Benn has been strengthened by giving him as his intellectual adviser Harold Lever but that is really moving Harold away from things he understands, like liquidity, international affairs and currency, into industry, of which he knows very little. I know from that long talk which I had with Roy on the way down to Chequers that he doesn't really trust Harold and has been wanting to get rid of him. Harold Lever has been moved out of the Treasury because Roy is jealous of his expertise and the Treasury were glad to get rid of what they felt to be a dangerous, awkward customer. So in a sense this also enormously strengthens Roy, though at the cost of denying him powerful advice.

A final advantage to the Treasury is the continuation of the D.E.P. under Barbara and the extension of its power. We all know that when Barbara was put into D.E.P. or, rather, when D.E.P. was created out of the traditional Ministry of Labour because Roy refused to have her at the counter-balancing post at D.E.A., she tried to build up the Department constructively and keep in with Roy. She accepted his economic policy and he accepted her industrial relations and prices and incomes policy. Now her prices and incomes policy and Industrial Relations Bill have collapsed, she has nothing except to try to conceal the disaster and to build up some substitute to bolster her position. This really means that again it is the man with a clear-cut Ministry who has his position strengthened.

This is the last reshuffle we will have and it is obvious that there will be nothing but minor changes between now and the election. We have had two Cabinets this week and we've begun to settle down. My first impression, although it doesn't really agree with Roy's, is that it is a better Cabinet. Roy said our Tuesday discussion was awful but that wasn't really what I was thinking of. I suppose I am thinking more of the inner nine, the P.M., Stewart, Jenkins, Gardiner, Crossman, Castle, Callaghan, Healey, Peart. This is the established core of the Cabinet and I think it is fair to say that we have all learned a hell of a lot as Ministers and we are a good, competent,

[1] In 1964, when the D.E.A. was created as a counter-force to the Treasury.

hard core. Even the press has been obliged to admit this. More important, Harold has had to admit it by leaving those nine unchanged. It is obvious when you sit there that we are the ones who, in a sense, matter.

Tomorrow Parliament reassembles and we will sit from now until the end of July, except for a very short recess. Do I want it? No, no Minister does. By the way, I should add in an interesting talk I had with Jock Campbell.[1] He said to me, 'We would rather like to have you as editor of the *New Statesman*. We have told Paul Johnson, who wants to go. Could you take his place?' I said, 'No, I can't possibly do that because I am going to go right on till the election and then I shall be bound to fight it.' It's true that during the past week I have been thinking that I may want to go on but I will be sixty-two, and if I go on for another five years ... So I quickly made up my mind, because both Patrick and Virginia desperately want me a little more at home, and I thought, 'Well, that's it, the editorship of the *Statesman*. Let us see if we can get a compact to agree that immediately after the election I will take over.' It's apparently what Jock Campbell and the Board of Directors want. Isn't it ironical? I couldn't get it when I wanted it,[2] and now, after I have had this wonderful time as Minister, I am retiring to be the editor of the *New Statesman*. Shall I be too old? Yes, I'll have it for a few years and then a younger man will have to replace me but, by God, I can do something for the paper. It is an exciting thought for today.

Tuesday, October 14th
Cabinet started with Jim Callaghan. He is an astonishing phenomenon. As Home Secretary he has carried, I should think, 40 per cent of the main burden of the legislation of the last twelve months and he is now carrying it again. Yesterday he was the main speaker on Ulster and today he was to be the main speaker on the Seats Bill and our attempt to defeat the Tories' effort to force redistribution on us before the next election. Jim is going to triumph on this. He has managed to engineer a situation where the Tories are given the choice of either getting what they partly want, which is to have redistribution in London at least, before the election, or of accepting total defeat, and they are accepting total defeat rather than have any comprom-ise.[3] We have therefore done the job of actually making it impossible to redistribute the constituencies before this election. Certainly we have had to concede a redistribution before the next election but this has been a great

[1] Lord Campbell of Eskan, Chairman of the Statesman and Nation Publishing Company Ltd 1964–77. A former chairman of Booker, McConnell Ltd, he was a life-long socialist who had recently become a friend of Crossman's.
[2] In 1955 Kingsley Martin refused to promise Crossman the reversion on the *NS* editorship and Crossman left the paper to become political columnist for the *Daily Mirror*.
[3] On October 14th the Home Secretary ensured that the Commons rejected the Lords' amendment giving him another three months to lay the Orders. The Commons passed a Government amendment proposing that by March 1972 either a Boundary Commission should be reactivated or the 1969 recommendations laid before Parliament and the Bill was returned to the Lords for passage.

achievement and it has come out right because of the skilled work between Callaghan and Wilson. What are their relations now? They work closely on this kind of thing. This week Harold almost got himself to praise Callaghan for his achievements in Ulster. Almost. Harold brought himself to the point and said, 'Once again he has come back with success.' He didn't say how wonderful he had been but nevertheless they are getting on well together.

The main thing was the Queen's Speech and on the whole it is clear that we have got an electioneering speech. Things are being packed in that we can't possibly carry through even if we run into next October. Harold goes on talking as though we are running till next autumn, but if we did, and then had a September or October election, everything which was overspilled from next July might fall by the way. I am pretty sure that the election will be earlier than that, and I think that if it is at all possible Harold will have it in May. I am a bit concerned to get the Superannuation Bill published and put on the Statute Book in time.

Thursday, October 23rd

Cabinet met at 10.15 and we confirmed the tactic which we agreed last week for getting rid of the boundaries issue.[1] We agreed to have all the Orders put to the Commons and the trick would be to put them but not approve them, so that in one go we would negate the lot. Callaghan and Wilson have won. We have not been discredited because the ordinary public are convinced that both the Government and the Tories are concerned with boundaries for our own self-interest. Apparently our line has won, we have defeated the Lords and the Tories and killed the redistribution, so we shall be fighting the next election on the present boundaries.

The Foreign Secretary had his usual boring routine but this time reporting on something quite important, that Willy Brandt has become the Chancellor of West Germany.[2] We expected Kiesinger to win as he had been making a come-back towards the end, but, no, although the Christian Democrats were the biggest party, the Social Democrats plus the Free Democratic Party have now been able to form a coalition to keep the C.D.U. out. The Social Democrats have twelve members in the Cabinet including Helmut Schmidt and a number of people I know, and I expect they will be more anxious and

[1] The House of Lords had rejected the Commons' amendment and, under the terms of the 1947 Parliament Act, the Seats Bill was delayed for a year, which obliged the Home Secretary to lay the Orders. Mr Callaghan then adopted the ingenious device of laying the Orders before Parliament for affirmative resolution and requesting Labour M.P.s to follow the advice of the Whips to vote against him. When the Conservatives returned to office in June 1970 they announced their intention of proceeding with the implementation of the Boundary Commission's recommendations as soon as possible and the Orders were laid in October 1970.

[2] After the federal elections on September 28th, and the subsequent formation of the S.P.D./F.D.P. coalition, the new Bundestag elected Willy Brandt as its Chancellor on October 21st. Helmut Schmidt, previously the parliamentary leader of the S.P.D., became Minister of Defence.

more positive in trying to bring Britain into the Common Market, something I don't particularly want.

Then we had Barbara, who had to admit that the whole industrial field is in complete anarchy, with strikes in the motor-car industry, the whole of the coal mines on strike,[1] including the prosperous fields, and now this madness affecting the nurses, who are steaming up at their conference at Harrogate. We find this unrest and disarray everywhere in the public service, firemen, dustmen, local government officers. Barbara reported that everything was out of control. Heavens alive, here we are, we have taken it upon ourselves in the Queen's Speech to reactivate Part II of the prices and incomes policy and we know it is going to be completely meaningless. Barbara says quite openly that the policy is in ruins.

Wednesday, October 29th
The papers are full of the by-elections and the latest polls indicate that we might possibly lose Swindon and Newcastle-under-Lyme. The euphoric sense that we are bound to win has been suddenly shattered and people are terribly anxious because the polls are telling us that there is really a chance for the Tories.

Thursday, October 30th
It was the day of the by-elections and everybody was rather tense. The first thing was S.E.P., the first meeting of this central strategic and economic committee for a good long time. It doesn't do any economic strategy now, that is left to a much smaller group of Harold, Roy and Barbara. I'm not on that and don't even know the members but S.E.P. is a largish committee and as usual most of the Cabinet seemed to be there. A civil aviation White Paper was being presented and an important modification of S.E.T. but I wasn't interested in those because I was waiting for the third item, the motorists' levy to cover the costs of accidents. After Roy had bought the idea, Cabinet had agreed provided it was regarded as workable. I had the greatest difficulty in getting anybody to consider it workable and the more it was examined the more resistance there had been from the Ministry of Transport, who said we would have a bleeding row with all the motoring organizations, and also from the Treasury, which regarded the levy as merely another form of tax and therefore no real, genuine saving.

I had got it through my own Social Services Committee only by saying that

[1] On October 13th an unofficial stoppage began over a demand for a forty-hour week, inclusive of meal breaks, for surface workers. It began in Yorkshire and spread until 121,000 miners were involved. After three days of discussions between miners' leaders and Vic Feather, on October 24th normal working gradually resumed, but 979,000 days had been lost in what was the largest single stoppage in the coal-mining industry since 1944. A month's stoppage had begun at Vauxhall in September, at Standard Triumph International from late August to November, and labour relations in the motor-car industry were generally troubled. Firemen had threatened to strike on Guy Fawkes Night, November 5th, but their claim was settled and a strike avoided.

if we didn't get our £9 million this way, we would have to cut the hospital building programme, which would give us even worse publicity. Nevertheless, the new Minister of Transport, Fred Mulley, had reserved his position, so I took it to S.E.P. Here it got even worse treatment, more and more people objected, and the only way I made the thing acceptable at all was by saying that otherwise the £9 million would have to be raised by the cut in hospital building and it's now too late to do that without bringing the whole of this year's programme to a stop. It shows you how completely this awful PESC dominates proceedings and decisions. There it was and I was told to put a paper to Cabinet along with Mulley.

Immediately afterwards came Cabinet and a very extraordinary thing happened. The Prime Minister started with a longish talk about the political situation and the by-elections, in which he showed that he had suddenly lost his nerve. The euphoria had gone, he was scared stiff by the latest polls and said we might well have to face the loss of all five. If we did Cabinet should stick together and show the same reaction and he advised us all how to handle it. I have never heard him in that mood before. Up, and then right down. He was deeply depressed, trying to hold us for the catastrophe which was coming. To be honest, I have always been uneasy about these by-elections and his euphoria. He also went on to say that in this new situation we must hit back at Heath. He was deeply upset by Ted Heath's personal attacks on him and the thing we must do now is (and these were the words he used), 'Kick Ted in the groin; we must be rough with him.' I must say that at this point Tony Wedgwood Benn coolly and quietly said, 'This is a great mistake. It won't do you or us any good. If you kick Ted Heath in the groin you will build him up. You have done so very well over the summer because you have been attacked by the Tories and you have come through it. Why should we give Heath the advantage of treating him as a leader when they are really a leaderless party?' Person after person put this argument and Harold began to modify his tactics. He said, 'I don't want you to attack Ted Heath, only his policies.' Then I said, 'That would be a disaster. The biggest thing in the summer has been your recovery, Prime Minister, from a desperate position. Why should we harm that by reversing our attitude just when it is most successful?' I added, 'Of course you might say that, apart from attacking Heath, we ought to praise you more. Well, frankly, we all talk a lot about you.' At this point the whole Cabinet was convulsed with laughter. They were laughing because they thought this meant that they gossiped about him outside and to the press. It didn't upset Harold or me too much but it did reveal to me that Cabinet think I am a great, compulsive communicator about Harold Wilson and that I had caught myself out.

Friday, October 31st
When I arrived at Management Committee I found that for some extra-ordinary reason Burke had rearranged the cards and I wasn't sitting in my

usual place next to the Chancellor but opposite the P.M. and Roy, whom I saw worrying and fussing as we went through a whole series of items. The meeting started with Harold saying, 'We all got pretty nervous about the by-elections,'[1] and he was very candid about it. He said, 'It got worse and worse throughout the day yesterday and it was even worse in the evening when Transport House said we were certain to lose Paddington and Islington North.' However we were all jolly relieved and agreed that this was about the best result we could have had because it would neither discourage the Party nor make people over-optimistic.

Tuesday, November 4th
In the House I ran into Heath walking along the passage. For once we got into conversation and I said, 'Back at school. I always feel one can manage the Department nicely until Parliament starts.' 'Yes,' he said. 'Why on earth haven't you taken the opportunity to relieve yourself of that problem?' 'What do you mean?' I said. 'Why haven't you arranged to have Ministers outside the House of Commons?' I really was surprised. Ministers outside? 'Oh, no,' I said, 'I don't want that at all. I find it a strain but I wouldn't lose my position in the Commons for anything.' Heath pursed his lips and I suddenly realized he had let out something he really meant. He would like an American presidential system with Ministers outside the House and suddenly he had let his guard down and said something true about himself. He won't say anything to me again for five or six months, I know that very well.

Thursday, November 6th
Cabinet. Suddenly Vietnam was mentioned, and the Lord Chancellor woke up and said, 'I don't often speak but I have strong views on this. It is what I care about more than anything else. How can we possibly have a Statement from the Foreign Secretary this week approving of Mr Nixon's statement?'[2] I was a bit surprised because Nixon had made a statement saying he was trying

---

[1] At Paddington North Arthur Latham held the seat for Labour with a 517 majority, on a swing to the Conservatives of 11·4 per cent. At Islington North Michael O'Halloran held the seat for Labour with a 1,534 majority, on a 9·2 per cent swing to the Conservatives. At Newcastle-under-Lyme John Golding kept the seat for Labour with a 1,042 majority, on a 10·7 per cent swing to the Conservatives. At Glasgow, Gorbals, Francis McElhone held the seat for Labour but there was a Conservative swing of 7·8 per cent and the majority of 9,940 in 1966 was cut to 4,163. At Swindon the seat was won by a Conservative, Christopher Ward, who had a majority of 478 votes. The swing to the Conservatives was 12·8 per cent.

[2] Little progress had been made in the Paris talks but President Nixon was determined to reduce the strength of American forces in Vietnam. On November 4th he announced in a television broadcast that he had written to Ho Chi Minh, the North Vietnamese leader, suggesting that the time had come to negotiate a peaceful settlement, but that in a reply received three days before Ho Chi Minh's death on September 3rd this initiative had been rejected. Meanwhile the planned withdrawal of troops continued. The President had stated that 35,000 troops would return home between mid-September and mid-December and military activity was reduced. Nevertheless Americans at home continued to demonstrate and protest against the war.

to get out of Vietnam. Someone said so and Gerald Gardiner then said, 'The last time, we had a statement approving American bombing. Why can't we dissociate ourselves from those Americans?' He spoke like an innocent, young left-winger, with an amazing ignorance, and he hadn't actually read Nixon's statement. On the whole we had only picked out for praise the decision to withdraw but it was difficult to blame the Foreign Secretary for this.

Then we had the E.E.C. We had all recently received letters, one from Michael Stewart suggesting that all junior Ministers should now join the organization for stimulating the creation of the Common Market, some all-party organization we have allowed ourselves to get into, and then we had the Prime Minister writing to tell us all to be enthusiastic about the Foreign Secretary's policy and not to be obsessed by the terms of entry. I said I couldn't really see the point of these letters and I thought we had got our posture right. 'Yes,' said Harold, 'look at my Statement.' 'Yes,' I said, 'look at your Statement. But why, then, these letters telling us to show enthusiasm?' Michael Stewart very unwisely said, 'The fact is that we have to make all the pro-speeches and we would like more Ministers to join in.' 'Would you really like Fred Peart or me to join in?' I said. 'We will if you like but I shall take the proper posture the Prime Minister recommends, which is that we haven't changed our view that we should enter if the conditions are right because we are now strong enough to ensure they are right.' There wasn't much discussion. The P.M. looked a bit peeved and his face puckered. He doesn't like being treated in this way by me and he knew that in this discussion Cabinet was registering a check on him and Michael Stewart, who are still hell bent on getting the negotiations going as fast as they possibly can. The one thing which struck me was that when it was suggested that the negotiations couldn't get going until the New Year or even later, he added, 'Anyway, we can ensure that the election comes first before anything gets embarrassing.' I think myself he must be working to have a spring election if he possibly can.

Tuesday, November 11th
The big item today was the incident of Philip's broadcast.[1] I had missed this but on Sunday night Prince Philip appeared on a recorded T.V. interview in

---

[1] During an interview on American television on November 9th Prince Philip had been asked about the state of the royal finances and he had replied, perhaps with deliberate exaggeration, that the Royal Family would 'go into the red next year' because the Queen's civil list allowance, voted annually by Parliament, was 'based on costs of eighteen years ago' and was insufficient. Prince Philip's remarks annoyed those who felt that the matter should first have been raised at home, horrified those who believed that the Government had been neglecting the Queen's difficulties and embarrassed the Government, which was not only struggling to devise new prices and incomes legislation before the present Act expired on December 31st but was also preparing for a General Election.

In a Statement on November 11th the Prime Minister explained that for some time Government and Palace officials had been discussing the civil list, that the figure had been put at

America, making astonishing remarks about how hard up the Queen was, how they were going into the red and how they might have to sell Buckingham Palace. It had caused a major sensation. The Prime Minister had let it be known that he would make a Statement this afternoon. I don't think myself that this was any deep-laid plot by Philip to put pressure on the Government to increase the Queen's screw but simply a sheer piece of exhibitionism, showing off how good he was on T.V. We discussed it at length and here you see the real point of Management Committee. We couldn't have considered it in this way at Cabinet. First the Prime Minister told us about his text. He had it all ready and made it quite clear that it was his Statement and we couldn't try to redraft it. It was very adroit and revealed a whole mass of facts of which, though a member of the Cabinet, I had no notion. It revealed that discussions had been going on even before we took over and since then the Prime Minister and the Chancellor of the Exchequer had been making elaborate arrangements for other ways to carry more and more of the Queen's expenses. Despite the fact that the royal grant had been kept at the level fixed in 1952 she wasn't in the red and wasn't due to go into the red until next year. Some of her expenses had been transferred to various departments, for example the Ministry of Works was carrying the cost of the royal castles and all her royal tours abroad and expeditions in this country were being paid. A perfectly respectable story of what had been going on had very discreetly been put in the Statement.

We all agreed the Statement and began to discuss the situation when Barbara suddenly blew up and said what I had been feeling: 'I must say this is absolutely outrageous. We agree with your Statement, Prime Minister, but I think we should make some political capital out of this. Now that Prince Philip has put all this before the public, complaining about the Government as though we are being unfair to them, at least let's have a Select Committee to look into the private fortune of the Queen.' This is something I've thought about for many, many years. The Queen pays no estate or death duties, the monarchy hasn't paid any since these taxes were invented and it has made her by far the richest person in the country. Not only has the family accumulated pictures and riches, but their estates and actual investments must have accumulated and they are inordinately wealthy. Harold himself said, 'Most rich men feel that part of the job of a rich man is in spending a good part of his wealth for charitable and public purposes. It takes royalty to assume that all their private income is to be kept to themselves and accumulated and that they are not obliged to spend any of it on seeing them through their public

£475,000 p.a. in 1952 in order to produce an annual surplus of £70,000 to accrue against later deficit and that the accounts had remained in surplus until 1961, after which there had been increasing deficit. It was estimated that the reserve would be exhausted by 1970. The Prime Minister proposed the appointment of a Select Committee to review the Queen's income and stated that in the meantime arrangements had been made to cover any deficit from 'funds available to the Queen' from other sources.

life.' It was a fair point but Barbara, radical, determined to have a go, brought it out very clearly.

Barbara, Roy (which is striking) and I are republicans, we don't like the royal position, we don't like going to Court or feel comfortable there, and we know the Queen isn't comfortable with us. Fred Peart, on the other hand, was appalled. Not only did he think it was politically unwise to have any radical taint to what we do but he naturally adores being Lord President and gets on with the Queen just like George Brown and Callaghan do. Callaghan said, 'I am a loyalist. I wouldn't like to see the royal family hurt and I think Philip is a very fine fellow.' By God, Jim made a speech of such banality and appalling conventionalism, attacking the sentiments of middle-class intellectuals. He really is putting himself forward as the spokesman of the conservative working man, and his new role is growing on him. Harold also had apparently no sense of indignation with Philip, no anxiety to take the opportunity to get death duties applied to royalty or all the other things we naturally wanted to do. He is a steady loyalist and, roughly speaking, it is true that it is the professional classes who in this sense are radical and the working-class socialists who are by and large staunchly monarchist. The nearer the Queen they get the more the working-class members of the Cabinet love her and she loves them. Fred Peart and Harold adore public dinners and most of my working-class colleagues and their wives think of this as part of the perks of office. It's only Barbara, Roy, Michael Stewart and I who intensely dislike these occasions.

In the afternoon I went down in good time to sit next to Harold and hear his Statement. He had just had a very rowdy Question Time, scoring off the Opposition in his most brilliant party pugnacious way. He revels in the battledore and shuttlecock of parliamentary politics and he lives for it. Thank God the Statement was long and detailed, because while he was making it the mood of the House changed sufficiently for Harold to handle Heath. We had known this morning that Heath and Maudling and the Tories had decided to make a political issue out of this and to insist that a Select Committee be appointed immediately because of the desperate situation which Philip had revealed. Harold was able to say that there was no new situation, that it was all perfectly in hand, and he was able cautiously to reveal that he himself had already agreed to the Select Committee being appointed for the next Parliament. It was superb and it knocked out the Opposition. If Harold had mishandled it we should now be in a long unpopular row in which we should lose votes by seeming to be mean to royalty. He got over the fact that we hadn't been mean, that basically there was no case for having an immediate Select Committee that would bind a future Parliament and, above all, he got over the fact that Heath and Maudling were playing party politics with the monarchy and the constitution, while he was putting country and Queen first.

It was by far the best parliamentary performance I have ever seen, because

Harold was speaking without the snide, anti-Heath, knockabout party polemic which he loves to indulge in. At all costs he wanted to show restraint, reticence, real statesmanship, very like the way Baldwin with his instinct and closeness to the people handled the abdication crisis of 1936.[1] Why? Because Harold cares passionately about the Queen and the monarchy. It was astonishingly different from his normal performance and I thought, 'Oh God, Harold, if only you could behave like this on other issues and not always feel that everything is a matter of making party capital.'

Thursday, November 13th
At Cabinet we had an interesting discussion on the question of televising the proceedings of Parliament. Bob Sheldon has been lucky in the ballot and is proposing to move again my motion for a television experiment, the one that had previously been rejected by a single vote. After the experiment in the House of Lords inertia set in. Fred Peart is against both radio and television broadcasting of proceedings and he wanted to be able to intervene in the debate and show a neutral attitude. Discussion revealed that some of Cabinet who had not spoken on this subject last time had strengthened their views and the Prime Minister is now convinced of the importance of getting television accounts of Parliament. Maybe he thought how much he missed last Tuesday by not having his magnificent performance televised, because, though he did wonderfully and the whole public would have been impressed, there was no real account of his achievement in the newspapers, apart from the *Daily Telegraph*. I think Barbara, Roy and a number of others are quite keen on television now but the antis are as strong as ever, headed by Peart and Callaghan. Once again, curiously, intellectuals are lined up against the working-class. Anyway the situation is totally different now, so that when Fred Peart said, 'We had a Cabinet decision and we must carry it out,' we could say, 'No. The Cabinet decision was for the experiment which has already been done in the Lords. We have no Cabinet policy on this.' We finally decided that the front bench should not vote but everybody else should be allowed a free vote. What I think will happen is that there will only be about seventy or eighty people in the House and that closure will not be obtained. It will only be a little discussion.

   Then we had Fred Peart again on M.P.s' allowances. Fred and the Chief Whip are concerned with the morale of our own back benchers and simply say we have to give them something. At a previous Cabinet meeting we had resisted an increase in salary but had been driven reluctantly to agree that something had to be done about secretarial assistance. So Fred was able to rely on a Cabinet decision (this is always a sore point) and Harold pushed at this all the time, saying it was now only a question of how much and how it should be given. Fred's proposal was to allocate £750 a year to each M.P. as

[1] When Baldwin advised Edward VIII that he must abdicate if he wished to marry Mrs Wallis Simpson.

an additional secretarial grant, and he had agreed with John Diamond, the Chief Secretary, that in order to get this each must sign a pledge that he was really going to use it for a secretary and he must give the name of the secretary to the income tax authorities.

By jove, we got into confusion. We always get very excited in Cabinet about this type of thing. Barbara was terribly aware of the damage it would do. I think she is right, although Fred Peart and the Services Committee and Selwyn Lloyd himself are in favour of a grant of perhaps £500, £750, even £1,000 for secretarial assistance. I've no doubt it will be very unpopular with the public, just at the end of the incomes policy. Coming immediately after Prince Philip it shows that everybody is rooting for cash now including M.P.s, and when M.P.s want cash and get it they are the most unpopular of all. Barbara is right and, as Chancellor, Roy felt the same.

Fred made his proposal for £750 and then Harold Lever, who is a new member of the Cabinet and hasn't spoken yet, weighed in and said, 'This is just a gimmick, a way of giving an increase of salary without saying you're giving it. If you are going to do that give them a decent amount, £1,000.' Barbara said, 'No, only £500. More than that and the gimmick will be obvious.' Then I said, perhaps wrongly, 'Look, frankly, all they will have to do is give a name. If they haven't got a secretary they must give their wife's name.' Oh, what an uproar in Cabinet. That would be an absolute scandal but I said, 'A lot of us do it already. My wife *is* my secretary,' and Anne is, ever since Jennie gave up she has been doing all my constituency work. Ironically, it's true that all the better-off people who can already afford to have secretaries will be able to pay more of their secretary's salary and it will also pay them from the tax point of view. All those who actually have wives who are genuine secretaries will also gain by it and the rest, the poorer people, will have to pretend their wives are secretaries even though they are not. Cabinet was tremendously confused.

Harold finally said he would call for names and he went round for support for £500 or for £750. He said it was a tie but Roy, who always puts the names down too, said Harold had counted wrong and we voted again. There was chaos. It was eight for £500 and seven for £750. It was nearly 1 o'clock and Fred Peart said he just couldn't sell this to the House. So great was the confusion that Harold said we should consider this again at the next Cabinet.

Thursday, November 20th
At Cabinet came M.P.s' pay again. We had taken the decision for £500 and now the issue was whether this should be paid only on written guarantee or as part of the normal expenses. Harold Lever and I were able to prevail by saying, 'For God's sake, no special guarantee. Just raise the expenses part of an M.P.'s salary from £1,250 to £1,750 and apply it to the Lords as well. It will be profoundly unpopular with the general public but if that is the deal

...' Then Fred Peart made another great effort for an increase of £750. He said Jack Diamond had lied about Selwyn Lloyd, who had shown himself willing to go up to the higher sum, whereupon Jack Diamond said, 'You fixed him after the event.' Barbara looked across and said, 'But we don't say that to each other, Jack.' And we don't. One of the most extraordinary things about our Cabinet is how polite we are, how genteel, how very rarely we say what we really mean to each other, leaving the unpleasant truths unsaid, because we don't wrangle and fight. I suppose I am one of the very few people who blurts out. Everyone else is too refined, letting things go wrong rather than speak the truth. The P.M. finally asked, 'Does anybody want to change his vote?' Silence. 'Right,' he said. 'The Cabinet voted last time, I must take the vote unchanged.' So £500 it was.

Tuesday, November 25th
Cabinet and we dealt with Ulster. We have now passed the Act setting up the Ulster Defence Regiment, against tremendous opposition from our left wing. Bernadette Devlin has been saying we are setting up 'B' Specials in another guise and surrendering to right-wing reactionaries. The Labour Left kept the House up all night on this issue. I think myself it has been an extremely successful operation and that the Ulster Regiment is totally different. It's entirely under the control of British officers. I think it really is a cover under which Chichester-Clark can maintain his subordination to us.

The main contest this morning was between the Minister of Defence and the Chancellor. Denis had a long elaborate argument to show why, even after the withdrawals from East of Suez, we would have one or two expensive years. He said that other nations were now moving ahead and were using a higher percentage of their G.N.P. for defence than we were. We would be falling behind our allies. (That statement brought forth cheers from me.) I am not sorry to say he didn't stand a chance. The Defence Minister is now in a hopeless position and what he was saying was that he would have to have a fifth Defence Review if he didn't write in an increase in one of these two years. He was told that these figures in the White Paper were just as notional for defence as for anybody else's programme. They didn't absolutely mean a cut but there couldn't be a White Paper publishing an increase in defence expenditure as the net result of final withdrawal from East of Suez. I don't know how far Denis put this on as an exhibition piece. I suspect it was done in order to carry the chiefs of staff by showing how hard he fought for them before giving way.

Thursday, December 25th
I have been reflecting on this long period of illness.[1] I have certainly kept control over the Department and, indeed, Alan Marre apparently remarked

[1] Crossman was ill with 'flu and then pneumonia from November 26 onwards.

at the Ministry's Christmas party that in many ways I was more trouble when I was kept at home. I have had time to read and make minutes on everything and master all the departmental paper work, exerting a more detailed and continuous grip than when I am up and about with Cabinet and Parliament and public meetings. This last few weeks I've been running the Department more as I run it in the recess and, in addition, psychologically I've kept right out of the Cabinet team and certainly out of the Parliamentary Party.

As for my colleagues, I've kept in touch with the Prime Minister only because of the problem of Clifford Jarrett.[1] On Christmas Eve Roy Jenkins rang me up from his home in the country to see how I was doing and really to establish relations with me. He'd had very bad 'flu with a touch of pneumonia but had been forced to go back to make the winding-up speech on Prices and Incomes. Apart from these two, the only person who has made any contact with me is James Callaghan, who wrote me a letter in longhand, saying he hoped I would get well and that Cabinet was very different without me. Very characteristically he didn't say whether it was better or worse. I don't say he is two-faced, only that his feelings about me are ambiguous, but he does genuinely feel for me as a person. Otherwise I've had no contact with Cabinet. My effort to get hold of Tony Crosland failed and I spoke just for a moment to George Thomas to brief him about his speech in the debate on private practice. Barbara has not rung me up though I know she saw Bea Serota last Monday. I think Barbara's real trouble is that for the last ten days she has been so desperately busy with her own problems and her own frantic Prices and Incomes debate. She is very much aware that I am not on her side here, so I can't blame her for not making contact but I think I shall ring her up this weekend.

But it's a funny Cabinet isn't it, with each of us so inhumanly detached one from the other, where one member can disappear with nobody noticing? This is what George Brown and Ray Gunter felt when they walked out. They went, other people took their place, and that was that. One's colleagues are colleagues and no more. Harold Wilson too, hasn't otherwise been too desperately sorry to see me away. He urged me not to come back. He knew I wasn't keen on Barbara's Prices and Incomes, he didn't want me about and, anyway, from his point of view I'm not too successful a Minister now.

This brings me to something else, my unpopularity in these last few months. Take the Herbert Morrison lecture, which I took tremendous trouble to clear with all my colleagues.[2]

[1] The senior Permanent Secretary at the D.H.S.S. He had originally wanted on retirement to accept a job as President of the Corporation of Society of Pensions Consultants, and this—because of the Department's National Superannuation Bill—had caused Crossman some anxiety.

[2] Crossman had delivered the lecture, in which he sharply criticized insurance schemes for private medical treatment (naming principally the British United Provident Association), the previous June. But it only attracted attention when it was published as a pamphlet by the Fabian Society (*Paying for the Social Services*, Fabian Tract 399) in November.

Once again I was thought to have made an unnecessary blob. Harold was shown the script and thought it excellent and he doesn't really blame me for not noticing the trouble it would cause. However I have no doubt that he felt embarrassed. He and Mary are both members of BUPA. I wasn't, as a matter of fact, terribly worried about the newspapers. I had completely forgotten when I did the Fabian lecture and when I passed the script that Anne had insured herself and the children with BUPA and that we regularly pay the annual subscription. It's true that we have never used the insurance. Patrick had his tonsils out in the ordinary way through the N.H.S. and when Anne had her little operation she paid for the operation privately and never got around to claiming from BUPA. Nevertheless it would have been embarrassing if it had come out that I had attacked BUPA while at the same time my wife and children were insured with them. That would have been the end for me because I would have looked ridiculous. It didn't happen however. In the first week when I was very ill the *Express* was down here nosing round all the members of my own Dr Long's group practice. They went all round the hospital but they couldn't find anyone there who remembered me. Still, I am worried and edgy about the whole of this private practice story.

All this has also had a deplorable effect outside. Sir John Richardson wrote me a letter saying that the whole prospect of getting a decent relationship with the consultants had been imperilled by what they regard as an outrageous attack from the Secretary of State. Of course I haven't made an attack. I had merely said that private insurance was no substitute for taxation and was an inadequate way of paying for the N.H.S. Nevertheless it was interpreted as an attack and the phrase 'queue-jumping' was certainly disturbing. Sir John was terribly upset and when they all came down last Monday I got him to stay behind to talk the thing over. He said how embarrassing it was and asked whether we could help him at all, at least by ensuring that where there was a real need for private beds we shouldn't stop hospitals from providing them.

I said, 'Surely we have had to cut back the number of private beds by some 60 per cent in the last five years simply because they are not fully used?' 'Yes,' he said, 'but the difference is that in some parts of the country like Bournemouth or London you need a lot of them and in others like Doncaster you need none at all. Couldn't we at least allow enough of them in new hospitals to satisfy private demand?' I said, 'Yes, of course we could, if there is a genuine case and if they are fully used.' Maybe we shall get some good out of this but nevertheless it's shaken my self-confidence a great deal and I suppose this illness, combined with the ridiculous incident of the Herbert Morrison Lecture, has worried me more than I have worried about anything since teeth and spectacles. It has made me realize that I am right out as a member of the Government, unpopular with the local parties, detested by them. It's not uncharacteristic that, in one of those endless assessments of the 1960s that all the Sunday papers are printing, I appear with full marks as the most tactless Minister of the year. Tactless, Anne Scott-James has said,[1] first because of the announcement of the cost of teeth and spectacles three weeks after the budget (which only shows you how memories fail. She knew I had done something tactless but it wasn't the fact that it was three weeks after the budget but four days before the municipal elections) and then I showed my tactlessness once again by plunging into an attack on private practice. I have also had complaints from the Slough and the Greenwich parties about my misbehaviour in cancelling engagements. These have been brought to my attention by Bob Mellish. In all these ways I am failing now. This is serious. I'm failing, of course, because I wanted to. I gave up being on the Executive and in giving up—this is the interesting thing—you cease to try as much as you did before. In that sense I am on the way out, I know it. I am on the way out and I have made these arrangements to take over at the *New Statesman* directly after the next election.

But here I am having terrible second thoughts. In looking at the *New Statesman* and at the kind of writing which is fashionable now and at the modish way of dealing with things, I am square, absolutely out-of-date. Can I possibly be the editor at the age of sixty-three, with this illness behind me, with my decline? Am I in my decline? Well, I am sure that if I put that question to anybody in the Ministry they would be knocked backwards, because they would say, 'You kill yourself with overwork but you are doing two or three times as much as the others, Minister. You are enormously energetic and vital.' I know that to be true, yet on the other hand in the last twelve months I've been feeling in my bones my old age coming on me. Is it just that I am ageing or is it perhaps the strain of the fifth year of being a Minister? Or is it the strain of seeing one's children growing up and getting to an age when they feel you are old? Whatever it is, this illness has shaken me up a great deal, detached me even more from my colleagues but left me passionately keen on running the Department. Heavens alive, though, I am even keener on getting out.

---

[1] Women's Adviser to Beaverbrook Newspapers 1959–60 and columnist on the *Daily Mail* 1960–8, she has been a freelance journalist since 1968. In 1967 she married the cartoonist Osbert Lancaster, who was knighted in 1974.

1970

Thursday, January 1st
The first thing this morning was the New Year's Honours List, with Alan Marre to be congratulated on his knighthood, the Chief Nurse on her D.B.E.[1] and John Lewis, the Chairman of the Birmingham Hospital Board, on his knighthood. It is a not uncharacteristic, deeply Establishment, Harold Wilson list. He has failed to give Nicholas Davenport a life peerage but there are one or two things I like, including a life peerage for John Beavan, the chief political adviser of the *Daily Mirror*, though this could force him to resign his job straightaway. Most remarkable of all is the knighthood for Walter Adams, the head of L.S.E. Well, sometimes Harold is right in these things and sometimes he is wrong. Looking back I think he was right to give the Beatles their M.B.E.s. How respectable they seem now, how useful, how neat their hair-cuts and their dark blue suits, compared to the hippies of five years later. But whether he is right to side gratuitously with Walter Adams, who has been at the centre of the L.S.E. troubles, I don't know. It is very typical of Harold.

Wednesday, January 14th
For the whole of Management Committee this morning, some two and a half hours, we solemnly discussed electoral strategy. Everybody assumes that we will go to the country in October and I was fascinated to see how much Roy Jenkins wants to be the Chancellor who puts the balance of payments right, gets a £500 million surplus and keeps it. There should be no ugly rush to accept the avalanche of wage claims and then go to the country before their effects have worked out. Roy's theme is, 'We ought to keep the economy sound.' He was strongly supported by Barbara and there was no real opposition. Frankly, I don't see any chance of allowing an avalanche of wage claims which will make us popular and then fitting in an election before prices begin to rise. I don't think we can. This time is very different from 1966. We have a vast body of debt which we would like to reduce, and prices are already beginning to rise. It's clear that we shall only be able to go to the country on a policy of sanity, steady recovery and moderation. There will be no extremes, no dazzling ideas and all we can hope to say is, 'Well, we got the balance of payments right and we're on a sensible course'. We shall have, as one or two commentators are saying already, a deeply conservative policy. Our theme will be, 'Vote against the radical innovations of Heath and Powell, vote for Wilson and keep things going along as they are at present.'

Thursday, January 15th
I dropped in to see the Prime Minister for a minute or two this morning and I was able to congratulate him on his Nigerian success.[2] We talked a bit about

[1] An odd lapse on Crossman's part—see p. 529.
[2] The Nigerian Civil War had virtually ended with the fall of the Biafran capital, Owerri, on January 12th. The British Government had supported the victorious Federal cause.

electoral prospects and for the first time Harold seems to realize that we may have an honourable defeat. I didn't mention my own future but simply said that I was old and he said, 'Yes, but you are old with young children.'

Friday, January 16th

For most of the day I slaved away at my speech for the Second Reading of the National Superannuation Bill. Yesterday afternoon Peter Brown, whom I haven't seen for a long time, came into the office and asked me, straightaway, how the speech was going. I told him I was having to sweat it out from a vast brief. 'Oh,' said Peter, 'forget about all that. Do it impromptu. You have it at your fingertips and you can do it off the cuff. You must pick up all these details and then in a broad sweep make people enthusiastic about it.' I felt he was right, so I have been trying to reorganize the huge brief prepared by the Department to make it far more punchy, simple – rhetorical, if you like. It's a bit of a gamble but I'm fairly pleased with it and I think, under Peter Brown's influence, it may be a great deal more successful than it would otherwise have been.

Monday, January 19th

The afternoon began with Harold's Statement on our relief efforts in Nigeria. I assumed that he would steal most of my thunder because there was tremendous excitement. Harold handled himself with dignity and self-control and though his Statement was inordinately long, he didn't try to get too much credit out of it. Then came the debate. I had deliberately made my speech popular and partisan, challenging the Tories to oppose us and arousing our own people. It was fifty-five minutes long and I think in electioneering terms and in its intelligibility it was an able speech. I was right back at the top of my form, fully recovered, capable, rallying the Party not only to me but to the scheme.

I was followed by Balniel, who, to my amazement, quite unexpectedly came out with the outline of the Tory alternative. They have got off the fence and this is enormously important. The rest of the debate went perfectly all right for us. Houghton made a helpful speech with a characteristically unhelpful end to it and David Ennals made a rather dull but perfectly capable winding-up speech. It was a good team and at the end, on a three-line whip, we had a very good vote. There were two votes, one on a Conservative reasoned amendment and one on a motion clean against giving the Bill a Second Reading.[1]

Afterwards I checked with Balniel that the Tories intend the Bill to go on the Statute Book. That's quite clear, as they need the earnings-related contributions, but they're going to try to amend it. They're not simply opposing the Bill but opposing all the essential parts of the benefit scale, but

---

[1] The Conservatives' amendment was defeated by 307 votes to 236 and the Bill was given a Second Reading by 304 votes to 244.

their variant is one which will be extremely easy for us to score off and it's taken away a great deal of their manoeuvring power against us. I am greatly relieved that they have done this.

Thursday, January 29th
This morning was chiefly notable for the start of the Standing Committee on the National Superannuation Bill. I was able to attend because, as Harold is still flying back from America,[1] there was no Cabinet. All the newspapers have carried stories about the Tories fighting our Bill line by line but there were in fact no more than the normal number of amendments. I sat there in that great Room 9, horribly crowded, because I had insisted on a Committee of thirty members. I have to be away a great deal and we don't want just to have a majority of one or two. Against me are Balniel and Paul Dean and we have a strong number of people on our side. Our only nuisance is Tom Price,[2] aged, I should think, nearly seventy. He hates my guts, he is against our Bill and is going to be confoundedly difficult. When I saw his name on the list I insisted he should be taken off and David Ennals went down to the Whips. I was finally told that we couldn't take his name off because he had been promised membership of the Standing Committee in a deal to persuade him to do some business the Whips wanted and if his name were removed he would stand up in the House and object, delaying the proceedings. This is characteristic of the Whips' relationships. They like to run the Committees, to nominate the people and have the whole thing in their hands and they much resent Ministers interfering. So we had to carry J. T. Price, though we changed two other names. I did get as our Whip Walter Harrison,[3] a good friend, who was being kept by the Chancellor for his Finance Bill, and I also got Brian O'Malley. It's a jolly good team. We got quite a lot of business done but, though we couldn't possibly complain of any delay or filibustering, we calculated that if we go on at this rational pace, it will take 250 hours of Committee time to complete the Bill. Sooner or later we shall have to have three days a week of open-ended sessions and almost certainly a guillotine at the end.

Monday, February 2nd
No. 10 for Management Committee and another meeting devoted to tactics. The minutes say it was devoted to strategy but, heavens alive, we were not discussing strategic considerations but what could be done in the shortest

[1] From January 26th to 29th the Prime Minister visited Canada and the United States for talks with Mr Trudeau, President Nixon and U Thant.
[2] Labour M.P. for Westhoughton from June 1951 until his death in February 1973. He was an Opposition Whip 1953–64 and a Council member of the Association of Superannuation and Pension Funds 1937–68. He was born in October 1902.
[3] Labour M.P. for Wakefield since 1964, Assistant Government Whip 1966–8, a Lord Commissioner of the Treasury 1968–70, Deputy Chief Opposition Whip 1970–4 and Deputy Chief Government Whip since 1974.

term, between now and next October, to improve the situation. The Prime Minister started by referring to the Tories' Selsdon Conference as a great success. I have seldom heard Harold admit a success to the other side but he said this had depressed him and that they had pulled off a successful publicity stunt. He was also anxious about the build-up of Heath and we were asked to discuss how we could counter this. Were Ministers prepared to go into action to destroy the other side? Harold always asks this when the critical point comes and implies that only he does it.

The trouble about these meetings of Management Committee is that, though having eight or nine of us makes it the right size and we don't leak because we know and trust each other, nevertheless there isn't what I call a real argument. Partly as a result of Harold's leadership, people don't let themselves go nor do they disagree. We make little speeches to each other round the table and all the morning consists of is a five- or six-minute speech from each individual, with a few questions at the end of each one and the P.M. noting the points. That's one way of conducting a meeting but it's not really a way to raise the difficult and awkward issues. I've noticed this as one of the characteristics of Harold Wilson's Cabinet, particularly since the disappearance of George Brown and the end of the open rows we used to have between him and Callaghan. We are almost too mealy-mouthed. Only on quite secondary or departmental issues have we disagreed and the underlying potential clashes are not allowed to come to the surface. Harold would detest that and, indeed, even in a private talk with him he discourages any of us from raising basic issues. As a result there are very few really tense moments of real conflict and the underlying tensions are only hinted at.

Look at this morning. Here were Barbara and Roy disagreeing on a basic point. Towards the end of the morning Roy was saying, 'Frankly, we know we don't like the word consolidation but as a Government we are bound to have a conservative policy and to say, "You will be safer with us and you will find the Tories more frightening".' (One of the conclusions we had come to was that the only way to keep the Tories out was to say we were a lesser evil.) Barbara, though, felt passionately that this would be to sacrifice the whole of her left-wing tradition and that she must stand for new radical ideas and so must the party. Neither of them really brought this out into the open. Roy says we stand for a civilized society; we certainly stand for a civilized Cabinet, one which pulls its punches, which makes little speeches in succession but which doesn't really have it out across the table. So today each person listed the points they felt we ought to consider but we did all this only a few weeks ago and there wasn't very much more to be said.

Thursday, February 5th
At our second Cabinet we had a very interesting problem about abortion. In Legislation Committee yesterday we had dealt with a Tory Private Member's Bill on abortion that is down for Friday next week. It simply

consists of introducing into the present Abortion Act a single amendment to make it illegal to perform an abortion without there being a proper consultant gynaecologist present. When the Abortion Bill was going through, one of the last votes in the Lords was to reject this particular proposal, which I think had been put in by the professional gynaecologists. It had been turned down on the grounds that it was a wrecking amendment, which wouldn't reduce the misuse of the Act but would undoubtedly slow up the number of cases which could be dealt with. Anyway, yesterday I was able to argue that, whether the amendment was right or wrong, the Act has been in operation for less than two years and I didn't want it changed. I said that I merely wanted this Private Members' Bill to be talked out in the usual way. When this was raised at Cabinet today, the Chief Whip immediately said it was not so easy. It couldn't be talked out and there would have to be a free vote. I said, 'A free vote? But, look, I am administering the Abortion Act, and as Minister I say to you that I want the considered view of the Government to be that the Act should not be amended now but should continue to run. Therefore I would like the payroll vote of Ministers to be instructed to vote for me because to have the Government view defeated on a free vote would be intolerable.' 'Ah,' said the Chief Whip. 'You can't do that,' and Harold also said, 'You can't order Ministers to vote for abortion. Anyway, you certainly can't put the Whips on because if that were known there would be a tremendous fuss.'

This raised a most interesting constitutional issue, which Jim Callaghan was quick enough to see. 'There you are,' he said. 'I was against the Government allowing the passage of these Private Members' Bills on controversial and important matters.' We've legislated for the improvement of the law on homosexuals, on divorce, on abortion, all of which have been Private Members' Bills, passed with a lot of time and help from the Government. The Government remains technically neutral, so that the consciences of people like George Thomas and Willie Ross and, in the case of abortion, Shirley Williams, can be squared. We have got away with changes which were long overdue and which no Cabinet would ever make before because these matters of conscience would cause a Government split. When I was Lord President I evolved this technique, arguing that these were issues which the House ought to decide and, whichever way it went, that the Government should accept the Commons' decision. The difficulty arises because a Government which in a sense has no party authority for passing a Bill must administer the legislation and defy those who want to tamper with it. I think I was quite right to claim that constitutionally I ought to get Government backing but it was also politically clear, as the Chief Whip and Barbara said, that it would have to be on a free vote which we would have to win. It will be extremely difficult to run the Health Service when part of it can be chopped this way and that by a free vote, and that's something I certainly didn't think of when I was Leader of the House.

The last item was Harold's report on Washington. Roy leant across afterwards and said, 'You know, it's extraordinary how every word of Harold's reports of his foreign visits increases one's incredulity.' Roy is right. The Prime Minister started by saying this was by far the most successful visit he had ever paid to Washington. He added, 'You see, the President obviously feels the inferior intellectual capacity of the men surrounding him and he was impressed by the quality of the British Prime Minister and the Foreign Secretary. This is what gave warmth to our reception.' Here is a fantastic degree of complacency in Harold Wilson, a feeling that the Americans must really admire him and think how good he and Michael are. It was piled on and on.

Sunday, February 8th

Another week, and from the electoral point of view, still no progress at all. Since Heath came back from Australia[1] with his new self-confidence, the papers have been cracking him up, saying the tide has turned and that the Tory Opposition is now in a winning mood. This threat was clinched last weekend by the public relations exercise at Selsdon Park.[2] Suddenly Ted is described as a winner. I don't think he has changed much but I think it is what the newspapers were waiting for. Heath's new standing has come just at the right moment. I dare say what was said behind the scenes at Selsdon Park wasn't very important but I think it was of great importance to the Tories, to Heath's image and their image in the country. Now Harold has come out with a tremendous political speech against Heath and the Tories. He spoke on Friday, rumbustious, old-fashioned party propaganda which should arouse our own people, but which I suspect is very unwise unless he really has got an early election on his hands. But there it is, as we saw at Management Committee last Monday, this is Harold's mood. He has to hit back and we must all join in.

Mind you, I think Harold really is alarmed by the Tories' threat that they will make law and order one of their biggest themes. Harold didn't mention race at Monday's meeting but I thought much more frightening the Tory promise to put Commonwealth immigrants on a level with Germans and Frenchmen and, indeed, as Enoch Powell has said, the Southern Irish too. Harold is also worried that the Tories will attack us for failing to be compassionate. It's true that if the press and the Opposition work hard enough the Government can seem to lack compassion and this is even more credible when our own friends like the Child Poverty Action Group mercilessly attack us, as they have done in this week's New Statesman. All we have done

[1] Edward Heath had won the Sydney–Hobart yacht race with his boat Morning Cloud the previous month.

[2] A conference of senior Conservatives and their advisers had been held the previous weekend at Selsdon Park Hotel in Croydon. The general view was that its results represented a tilt to the Right—hence Harold Wilson's subsequent jibe 'Selsdon Man'.

on pensions and benefits and national superannuation is dismissed as utterly hopeless and, once we are denounced by our own side, the Tory stuff, odious as it is, becomes effective. These threats have seriously alarmed Harold.

Sunday, February 15th
In the middle of the farm dinner last night, Jennifer Jenkins rang up to ask the whole family to lunch today and I jumped to the conclusion that Roy wanted to talk to me privately. Off we went on a brilliant morning and as we sped along I read *Our Mutual Friend* aloud. We had a very good lunch with Roy and Jennifer and Edward, his youngest son, who is at a London grammar school, and afterwards, as we all sat together in the sitting-room, I waited and waited, thinking there would be a moment when Jennifer would say to Anne, 'Let's go out with the children for a walk.' But there wasn't.

Then Roy suddenly said, 'Well now, Dick, are you standing at the next election?' 'Yes,' I said. This was awkward because of course I have made my agreement with Jock Campbell for the *New Statesman*, but my reply came quite naturally. Next Roy asked me what I thought the chances were and I found he didn't want to talk to me about the budget as I had expected, or to brief me secretly, but just to chat about my ideas for the future and the reasons why I was standing. I found myself saying, 'You and I, Roy, are the only two who have an alternative career outside politics.' But he wasn't telling me anything, only trying always to find out what my view was of a summer or an autumn date, of our chances, of what we should do after the election. I made it clear that I didn't think there was much chance of winning and that it will depend entirely on what he can do in the budget, where I don't see much room for manoeuvre. But if we don't win I shan't have any great enthusiasm for political life afterwards. I didn't really tell Roy more than that.

During this conversation I thought, 'Why have I motored over? It's been a lovely drive and a lovely lunch but why has Roy brought me here?' When I got home I rang Nicky Kaldor, partly because I want to get him and Tommy over to hear their expert opinion on the economic prospects for the next six, nine and twelve months, but also to tell him a little about this conversation with Roy. Nicky said, 'I've been seeing Roy this week and I know Tommy is seeing him next week. There's something queer about this. It's unsettling. I think Roy feels that if he stays on he wants the leadership of the party.' An hour later Nicky rang me up again. 'Roy was trying you out. He wants to know whether you'd be there to support him.' I wonder if that is right. I've asked Nicky to come tomorrow evening and explain things further. This may all be imagination but I think there is something in it. It was very odd today. We had lunch and the family sat about. It was very boring for the children and out of it nothing came except chat about my prospects in the election. I suppose the real answer is that Roy is now making up his mind about his budget. He can be cautious and conventional and keep his reputation as

Chancellor, making an election defeat absolutely certain and keeping himself in a position to seize the leadership afterwards, or he can conceivably take the other risk and have a more expansionist budget, which could give us a chance of election victory but could also ruin his reputation if it went wrong. I wonder. I hope I didn't say anything which would influence him one way or the other.

Monday, February 16th

This evening Nicky came round to Vincent Square and we talked. He was very well-informed. He had been to see Roy last week to put to him a most ingenious plan for a massive income tax reduction for people below average wages, the cost to be carried by S.E.T. increases or increases in the employer's contribution. Nicky had seen Roy and the Inland Revenue and the Treasury and he described Roy's extraordinary coyness. Then he had lunched alone with Jennifer, Roy's wife, during the week and they had discussed Roy's future. In Nicky's view, the real difficulty was whether Roy wanted to win the election or not. Did Roy feel he wanted to take the risk of making the massive tax reductions which would be necessary to win the election or did he feel that he should be the Iron Chancellor and do the only correct thing, which couldn't possibly win, but with the hope that if we lost he might take Harold's place? Nicky had got out of these talks with Roy and Jennifer, as far as I could see, without committing himself to any firm opinion.

Wednesday, February 18th

In the evening Anne and I gave a dinner at Vincent Square. We haven't dined there for a long time but we got the house warmed up and Anne brought up the food and wine, and I brought over the gin and the sherry from my store in the Ministry. Peter Shore was there, Wedgy Benn, Barbara and Tommy Balogh, and we managed to give them all an extremely good time. Again, the whole discussion wasn't really about policy but about Roy, and this was right, because never has the Government been so wholly dependent upon one person as we are upon him. Roy has an absolute choice between being a stern, severe Chancellor who doesn't do much or of having a smashing budget which really gives us a chance of victory. I think it is true that his choice will largely depend on his calculation of what will happen after the election and that this explains why on Sunday he asked me about my intentions and thoughts after the election. I suppose it is also true that when I showed I was unlikely to go on in Opposition he lost interest because I guess that he was thinking to himself whether he could talk to me about his own chances afterwards. Now it's true that after a defeat the chances of a change of leadership are somewhat greater and Roy clearly feels that he has some chance of becoming leader. I also think he feels that if the election is a success, the whole thing will continue in the same way with Harold and Jim at the top and Roy as number three. Then he might join me in writing books. I believe that is what is in his mind.

The result of my talk with Nicky and my talks with Barbara and Peter and Tommy tonight were all the same. We decided that we had to persuade Roy that his future depends on a really good budget, that a high-minded, Iron Chancellor's budget would ruin his chances of the leadership of the party. This I think to be true. In one sense Roy is in such a weak position with the Party, so remote from it, that there would be a tremendous revulsion against him if he produced a budget which couldn't win the election. Barbara and I will no doubt speak to him and try to have a dinner for him next week or the week after and we shall have to see where he stands. But there is very little doubt, and we all seem to share the same view, that he is uncertain. Nicky feels that Roy hasn't yet revealed his intentions to the Treasury nor to the Inland Revenue, and that Jennifer is anxious about him and would like him to be all out for the Party and for a victory this time. I think the rest of us all feel the same about this strange, inscrutable young man, this extraordinary mixture of ingenuousness, feminine petulance and iron determination.

Sunday, February 22nd

Yesterday morning Harold made a big speech to a Labour Party rally,[1] a very balanced, skilful performance. I spent a lot of last week with Arthur Gavshon and David Watt telling them that Harold just wouldn't play double about Europe and that he still wanted to go in, but I also added that he would take full advantage of the situation. He certainly did so yesterday, demonstrating that whereas we were willing to go in only if the price was not too high, the Tories were prepared to pay the price whether we went in or not. This is one of his favourite phrases and he brought it out again today in a long interview after the 1 o'clock news. Heaven knows why he suddenly decided to do this. I suspect he wants to back-pedal on Europe.

In fact the only news he gave at lunchtime was that he wouldn't go to see the South African cricketers play this summer.[2] In a way this shows you the

[1] At Camden town hall in London. See *Wilson*, pp. 761–4.

[2] Opponents of apartheid, led by a young South African, Mr Peter Hain, had been demonstrating against the South African Springbok rugger team, as part of a campaign to stop the forthcoming visit of the South African cricket team, who were to play in the Test Matches. The cricket authority, the M.C.C., declared that politics should be kept out of sport, that a more effective way of ending apartheid was to encourage contact with South Africa and that the British Government had a duty to preserve the right of citizens to enjoy their private pleasures. However on February 12th the M.C.C. announced that the South African tour was to be cut from twenty-eight to twelve matches to be played on closely guarded pitches. The Conservative legal spokesman, Sir Peter Rawlinson, stated that the Government was acknowledging the licence to riot.

Later in the spring it became clear that if the South African visit took place other Afro-Asian countries would withdraw from the Commonwealth Games, to be held in Edinburgh in July, and on April 30th the P.M. appealed to the Cricket Council to think again. On May 21st the Home Secretary met leading officials of the Council and, explaining the Government's anxieties about the future of the Commonwealth Games and the possible threat to public order that the tour might provoke, he formally requested them to cancel it.

danger of T.V. and radio appearances. Harold went on the air to deal with Europe but he was asked a direct question about the cricket tour and now he has committed himself to the line that while we agree with the demonstrators that the tour shouldn't take place, we agree with the supporters of law and order that we must enable anyone who wishes to see it. I think myself that this is too subtle. It's not the position Jim Callaghan would adopt. Once again Harold showed that when he is challenged on a simple moral principle he stands by it.

Nicky Kaldor rang me this weekend and has added a little more. He is a tremendously pertinacious lobbyer is our Nicky and he had been to see Jim Callaghan, who told him that Harold was now wondering whether he shouldn't in the course of the summer retire Michael Stewart and put Denis in the Foreign Secretary's job. That would keep Roy's nose to the grindstone and remove the only slot he could possibly escape to. I found this an interesting comment of Jim's because it is so unconvincing. After all, if you do that to Roy it means that he can do what he bloody well likes to you. It is much more likely that Harold would allow Roy to believe that if he produced a really good budget he could be promoted to the Foreign Office. That would seem to me more likely and that Harold is leaving this job open in the summer so that he can give it either to Roy or Denis, neither of whom he likes or trusts but both of whom I'm sure want it, although both must be very clearly aware that it is very unlikely that the job will remain in Labour hands after the election. I rang Roy this morning to ask him to dine on Tuesday with Barbara and me, but I rather stupidly forgot that this was the first day of the Common Market debate,[1] and he is absolutely 100 per cent engaged. Soon enough, though, we are both going to have to talk to him.

Thursday, February 26th
Harold scored all the headlines this morning. Poor Roy had apparently made an absolutely first-rate speech, elegant, alpha-plus as an ardent European, but it got very little notice because Harold had come bashing in. It's true that Roy had done his positive best to upset Harold by saying rather primly that he was in favour of entry and wasn't qualifying this in any way. He couldn't have been more different in tone from Harold and I have no doubt that this was deliberate. There is growing tension between them.

At Cabinet we had Barbara on the settlement of the Ford strike, and whether we should refer it to the Prices and Incomes Board. How mad that would be! But she wasn't pressing very hard and she dropped the matter and turned to a speech Donald Stokes had made, attacking the madness of the

---

Mr Quintin Hogg, for the Conservative Party, described Mr Callaghan's intervention as 'a classic illustration of the inability of this Government to preserve freedom . . . or to maintain law and order'.

[1] The debate to take note of the White Paper on Britain and the European Communities (Cmnd 4289) took place on February 24th and 25th.

motor-car industry and saying it wasn't all management's fault. She wanted
to rebuke him for it. Barbara's arguments are getting worse and worse and
on this occasion she was at her most futile.

Then we had an extremely interesting item, Callaghan on drugs. At Home
Affairs Committee he had put up a proposal to have drugs reclassified into
three sorts, hard drugs, drugs of secondary danger, such as purple hearts and
cannabis, and drugs of tertiary danger.[1] We had agreed on this and that we
should reduce the penalties for possession of drugs in the second class but
enormously increase the penalties for trafficking. There was then an absolutely outrageous press leak saying that Callaghan had been overruled and
that the Government was going to go soft on drugs and make major concessions on cannabis. This was very awkward because it wasn't quite true.
Nevertheless Callaghan was coming back to Cabinet to say that, partly in
view of the leak and partly in view of public opinion, he now proposed to
have no reduction at all in any penalties on cannabis. This was unusual. One
usually only brings things to Cabinet where there is a disagreement at a
Cabinet Committee but he was asking for the advice of his colleagues on
whether the Home Affairs proposal was right or whether he shouldn't go
back to very heavy penalties.

As we discussed this it became absolutely clear that the issue was really
whether we should kowtow to public opinion or not. It was fascinating to see
that at this point we had for the first time a sociological vote, that is to say,
every member of the Cabinet who had been at university voted one way and
everyone else voted the other. Michael Stewart happened to go out but I
checked him on the front bench later and there was no doubt he would have
voted with the university people for maintaining a discrimination, reducing
the penalty for possession and increasing it on trafficking. Gerald Gardiner,
Barbara, Denis, Tony Crosland, Roy, Dick Crossman, Wedgwood Benn,
Peter Shore, Shackleton, Diamond and Harold Lever, we were all pro-
gressives. The antis, all saying public opinion was too strong for us, were
Willie Ross, Ted Short, Roy Mason, James Callaghan, Fred Peart, George
Thomson, Cledwyn Hughes and George Thomas, and also Harold Wilson,
who was on the side of Peart and Callaghan. But they were outvoted and

[1] The Misuse of Drugs Bill, published on March 11th, discriminated between hard and soft
drugs and, for the first time in British law, between drug trafficking and possession. The Bill
divided drugs into three categories. Class A covered injectable amphetamines and hal-
lucinogens, such as L.S.D., and these were subjected to the same controls as heroin, opium,
morphine, pethadine and other narcotics recommended for the strictest control by the United
Nations Convention on Narcotic Drugs 1961. Class B contained, in addition to cannabis and
cannabis resin, six narcotics, such as codeine and five stimulants such as benzedrine, dexedrine
and drinamyl (purple hearts). Class C covered nine named amphetamine-like drugs, which were
considered to be less dangerous. The maximum penalty for possessing Class C drugs was two
years and an unlimited fine, although trafficking in these could incur a five-year sentence.
Possession of Class A and Class B drugs could incur a maximum of seven and five years'
imprisonment, but trafficking and smuggling offences in drugs of these two categories could
attract a maximum penalty of fourteen years' imprisonment and an unlimited fine.

Harold gave the clear majority to us. Having lost this battle, however, Callaghan whipped in with another suggestion and we did in fact give him the major concession that we would make the maximum penalty for cannabis offences not the three years originally proposed but five. The discussion was particularly fascinating because no one really doubted the rightness of the tripartite classification of drugs, the reduction of the penalties for possession and the creation of a new crime of trafficking. Nobody denied this, they simply said that the public wouldn't understand it and that we now couldn't afford to alienate people on this issue.

Sunday, March 1st
I talked to Harold on the telephone about Roy. All last week Barbara and I were trying to get Roy to see us this weekend, and he still hasn't given us a time. I don't know, I've got an inhibition about ringing him up and haven't done so, but I have fixed that Barbara and I should see Harold next week. From our telephone conversation I learnt that Harold has been extremely worried because Roy has been feeding the *Evening Standard* and the *Financial Times* with stories about how he is going to be the Iron Chancellor, doing enough but not too much, and how he has alternative careers if we lose the election. The P.M. was extremely alarmed by the posture Roy was adopting. Harold said, 'Remember his attitude at that meeting of S.E.P. and how he turned down the suggestion that he might do a Maudling.' I talked to Nicky Kaldor too, as we have all been constantly talking to each other, because of course Roy is omnipotent now. Harold can only pressure him. I believe the only sensible thing to do is for Harold to say to Roy, 'Look, if you give me the right budget I will make you Foreign Secretary.' Would this be practicable? I shall certainly put it to Harold when Barbara and I see him next week because the whole future of the Government depends on Roy. The Chancellor is inscrutable and remote. He knows very well what everybody is thinking but he is in two minds. He is certainly under pressure from the Treasury this way and that way but so far he has avoided any possible decision.

I discussed all this with Bob Mellish who came down yesterday evening to the Banbury Labour Party dinner. Anne and I went along and brought him home afterwards. He had made, in his racy way, a long forty-minute speech full of funny stories, but the only interesting thing he told me concerned the leak about decimal currency last week. Bob had been anxious to take the matter up and he had become more and more puzzled about it. He had wondered whether it hadn't come from the No. 10 morning prayers meeting which is attended by the Chancellor, the Foreign Secretary, the Lord President, the Chief Whip and the Prime Minister. Bob had said to Harold, 'Surely, this has something to do with Walter Terry?' and the Prime Minister just evaded it, so it was quite clear that Harold knew the leak had come from Marcia talking to Walter Terry. That interested me. Bob also talked a great deal to Anne and gave her a picture of me as a ferocious man who didn't want the Ministry of Housing, who was miserable, rude and violent, and yet, on the whole, over a period of months got to be some good.

Friday, March 6th
I rang the Prime Minister to talk about Jimmy Margach, who came into my room on Thursday and said, 'I hear you are going to have a Chequers meeting this weekend.' I was really flabbergasted because I didn't at all want to be responsible for a so-called leak, knowing what Harold felt, so I replied, 'Oh, I don't know anything about that,' and tried to put Jimmy off, adding that anyway I thought it most unlikely that we would have it with the Chancellor so busy just before the budget. But Harold said this morning, 'It's all going to be official,' and I realized that No. 10 had already been telling the press that they could expect a Chequers meeting. All the papers are speculating, speculation which is being fed pretty steadily by John Harris on Roy's behalf and no doubt by a number of others.

I had also to tell the Prime Minister about a conversation I had with Roy last night. For the whole week my Private Office and Roy's have been fencing with each other about a meeting which Roy had promised would take place between him on the one side and Barbara and me on the other to discuss the budget. I finally fixed that Roy should come to dinner at Vincent Square next week but I also arranged to see him before then to talk about national insurance contributions. So after last night's vote on Defence, while the House was still putting on a disgusting display of shouting and booing, we had our talk. Roy was cool and charming as he sat there in his evening dress. He said, 'If you want a big increase, it will have to be paid not only by employers but also by employees.' I said, 'No, no. We are going into Europe. This is the employer's contribution.' He said, 'Surely there has to be parity?' and I said, 'No, not on the National Health side.' I then realized he didn't really understand what I was talking about because he wasn't briefed on contributions.

I have mentioned it again today and no doubt we shall discuss it again when Barbara and I see him next Wednesday but I don't think he knows enough about the contributory system. Indeed, he mystified me even more last night by looking up and saying, 'Can you promise me you won't have to have an increase in pensions and national insurance this winter?' 'Of course not,' I said, 'they are biennial. This is the year for supplementary benefits,' and Roy said, 'But I thought you might have to have national insurance this winter.' This bewildered me. One finds him with such gaps in his knowledge and they are so difficult to deal with. At this point the division bell rang again. Though Roy didn't want to continue the conversation I had already got a great deal of information—that he wasn't considering using contributions, that he didn't even know and therefore hadn't considered the possibility of deliberately paying for the Health Service out of the employers' contributions and that he was alarmed about pension increases. The Treasury had put some absolutely inane fears into him.

Sunday, March 8th

Ages ago we had decided to have a meeting of the Management Committee at Chequers and during the past week we had fixed a good many of the subjects to be discussed, and we had also considered whether we could afford to make it a Management Committee or whether it should be a private meeting. By making it a Management Committee in the morning with Burke Trend attending and a private meeting in the afternoon, we were able to come in our own official cars and,* incidentally, to announce that we had met.

For once I took a full note of the meeting and I intended to put down here what actually happened, but, and this is a funny thing, when I opened my box I found I had got Barbara's notes of the Management Committee and not my own, so I shall have to remember the morning's discussion as well as I can. First we dealt quite shortly with immigration and the problem of the figures. Then we went on from that to law and order, starting with the whole problem of how to handle university uproar. By and large Callaghan took the traditional view, saying, 'Naturally I must always permit people to demonstrate even if I disagree with them.' Barbara and I tended not to say this. 'I can't take quite such a simple line as that,' I said. 'I remember how the Weimar Republic went down and I think we are entitled to say we can't possibly give people the right to destroy democracy. As long as the enemies of democracy are weak we can let them demonstrate. The moment they become strong we must be resolute and attack them. It's true that in Britain they have been weak up till now but it's rather different in universities, where the opponents are strong relative to the strength of the university. We believe that vice-chancellors should have been much tougher in winkling out the ring-leaders and dealing with them.' There was disagreement here, with some people saying we would have made martyrs of the student revolutionaries, but Barbara and I replied, 'We're not talking about our doing it or the police doing it. We are talking about encouraging vice-chancellors to do it.' Everybody agreed that we shouldn't in any way meddle in the universities or take responsibility for them.

Then we came to the Springboks, where there is no doubt whatsoever that the demonstrators have terribly damaged their own anti-apartheid cause. They have strengthened racialism and turned sportsmen against them, and there will be more trouble when the South African cricket team comes in the summer. We have to oppose both the disruption of sport and apartheid and this double role is extremely difficult. Our policy of banning arms sales to South Africa is also very unpopular in the country and, in my view, we have

---

* This matters to me because I can't drive and if I can't use my official car Anne has to ferry me about.

in this respect been a puritanical, prim Government.

The next thing was a paper I had prepared listing social priorities, the goodies we could actually produce. Number one was more money for legal aid, which Gerald Gardiner wanted, and another raising of supplementary benefit next autumn, not by the minimum 5s. but by 6s., 7s., or 8s. We went through them all, Ted Short's increase of nursery classes, the introduction of the constant attendance allowance before the rest of the National Superannuation Bill in 1973 and increased widows' pensions. Roy was quite firm in saying that the only thing we needed this winter was a 5s. cost of living increase in supplementary benefit and no more. He was prepared to consider the possibility of helping the over-seventy-fives or the over-eighties but he thought that was all we could afford. That is really as far as we got in the morning and then, after a very good lunch and a lot to drink, we settled down to a solid session from 2.30 till 5 o'clock.

The Prime Minister started by going round the table asking everyone for their views of the date of the election. Here are my notes of what was said. Harold said one of the problems was the World Cup.[1] If it wasn't for that, he would favour the end of June, and was now trying to find out at what time of day the match was played, because he felt this was a determining factor. Denis Healey was then asked his opinion and in a nutshell he firmly declared for the autumn unless we could manage the end of June. Fred Peart pointed out that we have never had a June election, and he thought we wanted late September or early October. Wedgy Benn said that with a reasonable budget he would go for early June.

I said I had no desire for early June because I thought we wouldn't have got public opinion or our own Party woken up by then. I wanted early October. So did Crosland but since the Tories had a 7 per cent lead he would wait beyond that. Peter Shore said he wanted the earliest possible date and he emphasized that the Opposition were unprepared. Mellish said that he thought there was a very strong case for October but if there was a chance in June he would consider it. Jenkins said he thought we ought to have organizational planning for a June possibility and policy planning for October. Stewart said that, if it was an irrevocable decision, October, but if there was clear evidence of a big swing in public opinion he considered we should have it earlier. He said waiting for spring 1971 was a counsel of desperation.

Callaghan said we should have the election as soon as we felt we could win, subject to the World Cup, and that if the Tories' lead was 3 per cent or less the date should be June. Barbara made the point that saying we should have it when we could win didn't carry us very much further; the question really was whether we should have it when we had put most money into most people's pockets. That, if we could fix it, would be the best time to win.

---

[1] The World Cup soccer matches were to be held in Mexico in June. Britain, as the 1966 winner, held the Cup but was to be defeated by West Germany by three goals to two.

Then we were back to Harold. He said he had tried hard to work this out in January 1966 and at that time he had discussed an Easter date. Now autumn 1970 is the obvious date but that meant the Tories would pile up their propaganda and be ready for us and, again, the World Cup was crucial. The longer we go on, he said, the greater is the danger of our balance of payments being undermined. The Tories are well organized and from early June until September there would be a closed period in which they could do anything they liked, even causing a run on the pound. There could be strikes, endless hazards, he said, and clearly his mind was moving to June. Healey then said that the message should go out from this meeting that we are planning for a long haul. The optimum is either mid-June or early October. The risk of June is the World Cup, the risk of October is rising prices. The trouble is that no announcement made after June will do us any good. For instance, the knowledge of an increase in supplementary benefit in October is better announced in June. Harold added, 'In June the evenings are light right up to the close of the poll.' That was the end of that little discussion and it revealed quite clearly that Harold is anxious for an early election and he intends to have one.

I drove back through the snow to Prescote, depressed at two things, I suppose. One is my colleagues' blindness to the fact that they are staring defeat in the face unless they can basically change the situation. They think they have a good chance of victory if they don't stumble and fail. This is such a difference of outlook that I can feel very little sympathy with them. I am also depressed because I see no chance of getting the budget which I have been trying for and this is just another nail in the coffin of the Labour Government. The Government is going to get knocked on the head next October because neither Roy nor Harold is prepared to take the steps that are necessary now however risky they may be. Perhaps they wouldn't be a success, perhaps the budget can't do it but I know very well that a budget of the dimensions Roy and Harold are planning can't succeed. It certainly can't succeed in June and if we carry on until October we shan't get any real pull at our own people.

Wednesday, March 11th
I am having some trouble with John Mackintosh[1] because today I was urgently rung up by David Watt to say that an account had just been published of a lecture John had given to some learned society in Manchester. In this lecture he had given a sensational story about what happened last summer on the Industrial Relations Bill and how the P.M. had been forced to settle with the T.U.C. because Roy and I had gone to Harold and threatened to support Callaghan as P.M. This really was extremely embarrassing

[1] John Mackintosh, Labour MP for Berwick and East Lothian, had been asked by Crossman to help with the preparation of his Godkin lectures, due to be delivered at Harvard University at the beginning of April.

because Mackintosh said he had got it from an unimpeachable source, which could only have been me or Roy or Harold or somebody round him, and frankly he had got it from me. I had told John the story last week and explained that on the whole the crucial fact had been that Harold and Barbara's plan to threaten to resign had been defeated when Roy and I made it clear that if they resigned we would stay. That is true. What isn't true is that Roy and I went to Harold and gave an ultimatum. This shows the extreme difficulty of getting people to understand what goes on in Government. John Mackintosh has written a book on Cabinet Government, he is an experienced man, yet even he simplified and vulgarized what I told him. I suppose he actually drew the conclusion that Roy and I must literally have gone to Harold and presented him with a joint *démarche*, but it was much more subtle than that. Anyhow John had jumped to conclusions, made a simple, effective story out of it and so distorted it. In a way this made things easier for me because I was immediately able to deny the story, just as Roy denied it, but it was an embarrassment to me because I suppose I was suspected. I was very puzzled that John had given it to the press, but I now gather that he didn't know that the lecture would be reported. When he comes back from the South Ayrshire by-election I shall have to discover what actually happened. He isn't such a fool as to think that it could be published without being denied. Still, it has left a slightly awkward taste in my mouth.

Tuesday, March 17th

The first thing we had was a meeting of the P.M.'s Housing MISC. This device of setting up hundreds of MISCs simply to deal with specific jobs, instead of sending awkward subjects to the standard Cabinet Committee, is one of the strange features of Harold's method of running things. I am not on many of these committees now because I am out of favour and too busy to be one of the Cabinet members who are put on them to add weight but I do see how important they are for helping the Prime Minister to get his way. In the standing committees every important issue is appraised by a group of Ministers who have been carefully balanced for the purpose and there is a rule that what is agreed there doesn't go to Cabinet but now everything of real importance is pushed outside the normal channels and through special committees, specially packed, so the situation is very different and the Prime Minister can exert far more influence. Harold has circulated a very interesting personal minute on Cabinet Committe procedure, M 23/70.[1] I will set down an extract from it:

> ... it is clearly understood that Cabinet Committees operate by a devolution of authority from the Cabinet itself, and their procedure therefore follows the Cabinet's own procedure, particularly in the sense that it is the

[1] Compare Harold Wilson, *The Governance of Britain* (London: Weidenfeld & Nicolson and Michael Joseph, 1976), pp. 64–6.

chairman's responsibility at the end of a discussion to specify clearly the decision which has been reached, and that he does so, not by counting heads, but by establishing the general consensus of view around the table. [That is interesting.] Nothing in these arrangements derogates or should be allowed to derogate from the right of any Minister to dissent from the final decision of a Committee, or to reserve his position to say that he wishes to appeal to the Cabinet. This is the basic right of all Ministers, and it must be maintained. Nevertheless like all rights it can be abused, and the abuse will weaken both the right itself and the whole system, which exists to preserve it. If the Cabinet system is to function effectively, appeals to Cabinet must clearly be infrequent. Chairmen of Committees must clearly be free to exercise their discretion in deciding whether to advise me to allow them. It goes without saying that they must not be made lightly, still less for reasons of mere obstructiveness, and if they are made they must carry with them the full authority of the Minister concerned, and must be supported by very compelling arguments. It is for these reasons that I decided some time ago that I would not entertain appeals to the Cabinet except after consultation with the chairman of the Committee concerned.

The whole note is very interesting and if you had standing committees with permanent members who worked as a team, as a microcosm of the Cabinet, it would be satisfactory. But if half the awkward decisions are shoved outside into these special MISCs, Harold can get his way and in my view Cabinet Government can be frustrated.

Today's MISC was meeting for the final discussion on our interim housing policy. I don't know what Tony Greenwood thought he was about, because it is an absolutely futile policy, just building a few more houses and giving more 100 per cent mortgages. Tony Crosland and Tony Greenwood had put up a series of feeble suggestions, which wouldn't get a single extra house built before the election. I still don't understand how Harold could have consciously allowed the cut in the housing programme.[1] About six months ago he suddenly discovered how catastrophic the figures were, yet that knowledge was there all the time and he wouldn't alert himself to it. Now a feeble answer is to be made in the House tomorrow.

Thursday, March 19th
Brian Abel-Smith and I went out to dinner and I told him (the first person I have told) about my intention to go to the *New Statesman*. He was sharp and clear-headed and thought it was crazy. He said, 'You can either go on in government or you can retire and write a book but to go out of government and waste your energies on all that ephemeral journalism makes no sense at all.' He may be right. Making that promise to Jock Campbell may have been

---

[1] Housing completions were running at 365,000 p.a. rather than the 500,000 promised by the Government at the time of the 1966 election.

an idiotic mistake. My top secret intention is becoming more and more difficult now that there is some chance of the Government's winning the election because if we won it would be very odd for me to resign to go to the *Statesman*, unless I simply did it on grounds of age. And in that case to go to the *Statesman* would be just as odd. No, I think I am in rather a fix, because I have promised to do it. Paul Johnson has stayed on specifically to give me time and it would be a terrible thing to pull out now. Yet I feel unhappy about it. I also feel unhappy because as I read the weeklies I feel less and less sympathy with the *Statesman*. I actually prefer the *Spectator* now and, although I am told its style is hopeless, to me it seems readable. I am bored by the weeklies, bored by the Sunday papers, and in fact I now seem to be bored by most things—that is another worry.

Friday, March 20th
It was a good morning, with a 5½ per cent opinion poll, and then the South Ayrshire by-election result, the best result we have had since the General Election.[1] It has come at a critical moment and will steady everything in Scotland. Indeed, judging by Harold's attitude at Chequers, it may tip him into having an early election in June or July. Tam took a leading part in the by-election, organizing teams of canvassers, and obviously he cared about this more than anything else. I suppose I feel frustrated because I don't really care. Though I see things we can usefully do, I don't terribly want us to win the election and, if we do win, I don't think we will do particularly well. I am irritated with myself and in my relationship with Tam and I am also uneasy in my relationship with other members of the Party and of the Cabinet.

Sunday, March 22nd
Somehow I have felt bored, bad-tempered and frustrated all the week. I don't know what it is about this present period. I have even felt angry all week with darling Tam, who cooks my breakfast for me. We had a tremendous row about the South Ayrshire by-election because he wanted to be away for a whole week to help his friend Jim Sillars. The by-election has been an immense success, but nevertheless I personally despair. And then I have had this curious and unpleasant problem with John Mackintosh. After my denial of the story that appeared in his Manchester lecture, the poor man came along in a terrible tail-spin to see me, and he has also written a grovelling letter of apology. I found out that he had been addressing the Manchester Statistical Society just as his wife was about to have a baby and he was all het-up about her. Nevertheless it was a very odd episode and doesn't really explain why he wanted to append this footnote to a learned

[1] In the by-election, caused by the death in October 1969 of Emrys Hughes, James Sillars, an official of the Scottish T.U.C., retained the seat for Labour. He had a majority of 10,886 and there was a swing of 2·9 per cent to the Conservatives. In December 1975 Mr Sillars announced that he was forming a separate Scottish Labour Party—an enterprise in which he was joined by only one other Scottish Labour M.P.

statistical study of the Industrial Relations Bill. Whether he intended it to be published God only knows, but it has upset me and the more so because of our work together on the Godkin Lectures. We have been through the third draft of the first one and I shall have something I can show to Harold, even though they are not yet in my own style and I must modify them a great deal before actually delivering them at Harvard.

Monday, March 23rd

We started Management Committee with the Official Secrets Act. The editor of the *Sunday Telegraph* and one of his correspondents was being accused of violating the Act because he had published a document giving a sensational estimate of the strength of the Biafran Army. Ironically, it was published on the day the Army collapsed and as a result the *Sunday Telegraph* looked extraordinarily silly but nevertheless appalling ill-will has been caused by the fact that this was a secret document that came from our military attaché.[1] I suppose there was a very strong case for saying that people who purloin documents and pass them on to a paper should be punished but there are some puzzling aspects to this case. Hugh Fraser[2] has said he had a copy of the document but he hasn't been prosecuted. This I imagine is because he didn't publish it, which seems to be the crux of the matter. I felt very strongly that there couldn't be a worse time for us to have a row with the press like the one on D-notices, but the P.M., exactly as one would expect, said that he left all these things to the Attorney-General. It is quite clear that our Prime Minister's passionate spiritual and emotional commitment to our relations with the Nigerian Government makes him willing to do almost anything to help them and he sees this whole case in that light. I see it in the context of our relations with the press in an election year. Harold said, 'Of course, for all we know there may not be a verdict of guilty,' and I said, 'Well, that would be a good thing for us all.' 'Why?' asked Barbara Castle. 'Surely,' I said, 'you understand that what we most want is to get this case over with the minimum of fuss and without laying charges against the press.' But my view wasn't shared by the others, who were all deeply anti-press.

Then we had a general discussion of the effects of the by-election. The Prime Minister was indignant at the way the press was describing him as preparing to snatch a victory in June. Nobody could have been more cool, more detached, or less ready to jump to conclusions after the South Ayrshire

[1] The *Sunday Telegraph* had published an appraisal of the Nigerian civil war, allegedly prepared by the British Government's representative in the British High Commission in Lagos, and on March 17th the Attorney General had served summonses, issued under the Official Secrets Act, on Mr Brian Roberts, the newspaper's Editor, Mr Jonathan Aitken, a journalist and prospective Conservative candidate for Thirsk and Malton (and since February 1974, Conservative M.P. for Thanet East), and Colonel Cairns, the British representative on the international team of observers which the United Nations had sent to Nigeria. An account of the case is set out in Mr Aitken's book *Officially Secret* (London: Weidenfeld & Nicolson, 1971).

[2] Conservative M.P. for Stafford and Stone since 1950 and for Stone (Staffs.) 1945–50.

result, but Harold was clearly optimistic. We were all asked for our views, and Barbara said that in Blackburn things weren't quite as good as Harold might think. Callaghan declared that at his annual general meeting there had been a bigger turnout than ever before. I described the complaints and apathy I had encountered at the Coventry East annual constituency dinner last week but, broadly speaking, Barbara and I were the only two who were doubtful. Each man had his little story of enthusiasm. Roy said he never finds Birmingham quite as depressing as I find Coventry, but I remember Jennifer's remark when we visited them the other day. She said, 'You haven't canvassed there for twenty-four years.'

Thursday, March 26th

End of term today, with the adjournment debate in the House and the Prime Minister answering Questions at 11.45, so that Cabinet at 10.0 was in the P.M.'s room in the Commons. What did we do at that Cabinet? I had heard on the wireless this morning and noticed in the papers that Peter Shore had been addressing the Manchester Junior Chamber of Commerce and had made a remarkable speech on the Common Market.[1] He had been very much more critical, saying that there were formidable disadvantages to entry and that this was something which couldn't be decided by the politicians. The people must also make their decision and we mustn't go in unless it really paid us to do so. This is exactly what I felt and feel, an attitude which I think is shared by the vast majority of the people. The anti-feelings have been growing steadily for the last six months and something like two-thirds of the people in this country are against going in, though, like me, they are quite prepared to have a go and see whether the terms are tolerable or not. But Peter's speech was certainly a great deal more anti-Common Market than anything which had been said by a Government spokesman before and every newspaper had jumped to the conclusion that Peter Shore, the co-ordinator of home publicity and the P.M.'s ex-P.P.S., was speaking as the P.M.'s *alter ego*.

At Cabinet the Foreign Secretary went through a whole series of items in his usual boring voice, and then he suddenly said, 'There is one more thing I have to refer to, the Minister Without Portfolio's speech. This completely upsets the balance, Prime Minister, and I must insist that the balance is restored, because otherwise I shall not be able to explain this speech to Europe.' Harold said, 'I knew nothing about the speech. I see the papers say I did, but I had absolutely no notion it was being delivered and I have already made that perfectly clear.' Michael Stewart tried again to get the balance redressed. Peter Shore then said he saw nothing wrong with the speech, which he had made very carefully. He was offering his own point of view,

[1] Mr Shore had made a speech in Manchester on March 25th in which he said that Britain's decision to join the E.E.C. should not be left only to politicians but should be a matter for public debate.

whatever other people might think, and it was in accord with our policy. Then the P.M. said the speech hadn't given the whole balanced policy, only one aspect of it, and we had all told each other all the time that we must be careful to get the balance right, and in particular that we were making a real and serious bid for entry. It was that point which hadn't come out clearly in the speech. I don't know whether I helped at all, but I then said, 'Tell me, was this extempore? Were you reported straight or was there a press release?' Peter said, 'It was a press release. I only just had time to give it to Transport House. I didn't have time to show it to the Foreign Secretary.'

That really did take my breath away. To release it to the press without any previous consultation with the P.M. or the Foreign Secretary was an act of total recklessness and, curiously, I had absolutely assumed that such a thing could not have occurred. I had asked Roy if he thought Peter had talked to the P.M. Roy said, 'No, I don't think he did. I don't think the P.M. would go back on his agreement to that extent.' But Roy has a very poor opinion of Peter and he simply said, 'It shows again what a hopeless fellow he is.' To me it showed how impossible it is to interpret politics and be sure you are right. When I heard about the speech I would have said that Peter couldn't have made it without prior consultation of some sort. Of course I haven't yet had time to see Peter and find out whether, in his view, there was no prior consultation, or whether (with some encouragement) he was flying a balloon. What I do know is that the evidence so far is that he did it on his own and that the P.M. was able to show complete ignorance of the press release. Yet into battle in the House the Prime Minister had to go.

Within a few minutes the P.M. was on the front bench answering a Question into which all this was dragged in. He didn't disown Peter in any way but merely said he supported him loyally, though the speech should be seen as giving a single viewpoint. Harold also took care to make Peter give a press release for tomorrow morning's papers, saying that this was entirely his own personal view. The P.M. dissociated himself to that extent but he showed himself loyal to a friend, even though the friend had made his life extraordinarily difficult. So this afternoon there was Harold performing away, Heath and he, hammer and tongs at each other, accusing each other of being double-crossers and ratters, enjoying themselves no end, neither doing his own side much good.

Saturday, April 4th

At 9.15 I went in to the P.M., who looked rather white and puffy, as he does when he is tired. I said something about Michael Halls[1] but Harold only talked a little about Mrs Halls being upset and then we got down to work on the lectures.[2] I made some notes.[3] On the first page there was a story about

[1] The Prime Minister's Principal Private Secretary had died suddenly earlier in the week.
[2] These were the drafts which John Mackintosh had made. The lectures Crossman actually delivered at Harvard are published as *Inside View* (London: Cape, 1972).
[3] Mr Wilson gives his own account of the discussion in *The Governance of Britain*, p. 56.

the contrast between a day in the life of President Johnson, absolutely driven in his work because he is Chief Executive, and a day in the life of the British Prime Minister, who, as many of them have said, can relax because he hasn't got a Department. Harold didn't like this at all. 'Did I really say all this? I think Marcia may once have said it in your presence.' 'No,' I replied, 'you said it in a T.V. broadcast and I took it from there. You don't like this?' 'No,' Harold said, 'I don't think you ought to give that impression about me because in fact this is a full-time job. I can tell you this, I have never read a book in No. 10. At Chequers I've read a book but, unlike Sir Alec Douglas-Home, who used to go downstairs to the big room and read novels, I don't. I've got to cover everything. Take this morning's news, the Post Office charges.[1] I feel personally guilty because I have allowed the Tories a second bite of the cherry. The Postmaster-General announces it just before the recess and we get a bad effect on the G.L.C. elections. Now he gives the full details and the story is told for the second time. The third time will be when the Tories move a vote of censure. I ought to have seen to this. This is the kind of area, you understand, that I have to keep check of. That is the job of the British Prime Minister. He is on the go the whole time, covering everything. And then, you know, there is the strain of leading a team.' I said, 'Yes, of course, and with Ministers working away on their own I suppose keeping control is a great difficulty.' 'Yes,' he said, 'I must keep complete coverage of the Government.' But I never feel he does keep complete coverage of the Government, though I suppose the answer might be that he gives me a free hand. Still, it was an interesting point.

The next point that upset him was that I said that unlike the American President, the Prime Minister was relieved of a great deal of official ceremonial by the Queen and Prince Philip. Harold said that this would be a most unhappy way of putting it. 'I hope you won't say that. After all, let's be clear about it. Macmillan was an idle man, who just didn't work as Prime Minister, and Douglas-Home was idle. I am not an idle man, I have never worked harder than I do here.' Then he said he thoroughly approved of my contrast between the Prime Minister's attitude to Cabinet and the President's view of them as mere agents. He added, 'I was amazed at that story about your leaving out of your introduction to Bagehot that paragraph about Russia.' This had been a paragraph saying that the British P.M. had more power to sack people than the Russian P.M., and the publishers had advised me to take it out. Harold said, 'I didn't know publishers did that.' I said, 'They had

[1] On March 23rd Mr Stonehouse had told the House of Commons that the Post Office was considering increased telephone charges and, during the recess, he announced that there would be a rise of 20 per cent in charges, an 18 per cent increase in the connection charge, 25 per cent in domestic rentals and 50 per cent in business rentals. Mr Stonehouse had refused to be drawn on the question of increased postal charges but it was rumoured that the Post Office intended to raise to 7d. the charge for first-class letters and to 6d. the charge for second-class mail. A Conservative motion of censure, debated on April 21st, was defeated by 327 votes to 286.

a good reader who suggested that this was incredible. Of course the day on which the proofs went to the printers Macmillan sacked more than half his Cabinet, proving my point.' The P.M. said, 'No Russian Prime Minister can sack anybody. It's almost impossible. I don't know how anyone would ever think he could.' I just note this here as an interesting sidelight.[1]

But Harold was mainly concerned with the section about Cabinet minutes. This had been written not by John but by me and I had made the point that, because the P.M. alone approves the minutes after they have been drafted by the Cabinet Secretariat and because he is able to have the minutes written as he wants, the record of Cabinet discussion and decision can be slanted and this greatly strengthens the P.M.'s hand. I absolutely meant what I said and Harold said it was completely untrue. He said that very occasionally he might have seen the minutes, or very, very occasionally Burke might have consulted him before they were written, but rarely has he been consulted before they are issued and very rarely does he bother to read them afterwards. This is interesting. I have spent six years with Harold in his Cabinet and, having often talked to Burke, I am deeply convinced that the P.M. does approve the minutes, but no, according to Harold this is not so.

The other point was that I had said that Burke was Harold's grand vizier, and the Cabinet Secretariat his praetorian guard. Harold said, 'You know, Burke isn't all that close to me. He is such an Establishment figure and the Cabinet Secretariat is very much an independent force, standing on its own. I don't think you should describe it in this way.' But I *do* think Burke has been Harold's grand vizier, and in the first two years they were very close. I suspect that Harold has never trusted him quite so much since the D-notice mess, for which Burke was responsible, and that they have grown much more distant. Nevertheless I think that although Harold doesn't feel Burke is very close to him, Burke feels his first loyalty is to the Prime Minister and to strengthening his position, a loyalty which he doesn't feel to other Ministers. Harold was also critical of my observation that the way to the top of the Civil Service is via the Cabinet Secretariat. He thought this wasn't true at all and he said that the mark of the coming man was to spend some time as a Treasury official, although that isn't as true now as it used to be. In another passage about the Prime Minister's control over the Civil Service I pointed to his power to veto, at least, the appointment of every Permanent Secretary and Deputy Secretary. 'Yes,' Harold said, 'that is true but I have set up a new arrangement so that the names are discussed by a panel before they come to me. This has reduced my personal power,' and he then told me the history of this. The other thing he particularly wanted me to emphasize was the importance of the confrontation between the P.M. and the Leader of the Opposition at Question Time on Tuesdays and Thursdays. This is perfectly true and it's really quite a modern phenomenon. Until 1960 the P.M. took on Tuesdays and Thursdays Questions after Number 45, and Question Time

[1] See *Inside View*, p. 47.

was often finished before we could reach this point. Putting them on at 3.15, whatever the other business, has made P.M.'s Question Time an institution and we have a twice-weekly confrontation whenever Parliament is sitting. In this sense Parliament is still a better forum for a confrontation between the party leaders than anything the Americans have.

These were Harold's main points and he was obviously concerned, as he often is, that he shouldn't be quoted out of context and anxious, in case it upset us in the election, that the Labour Party shouldn't be described as having totalitarian discipline. But Harold was free-and-easy and his relations with me were apparently absolutely spontaneous. We seemed to behave naturally towards each other but of course we now keep a certain distance. He knows me very well, I know him very well, neither of us says everything to the other, nor says what he thinks of the other and frankly I wonder if he wants me to stay on after the election. Does he think that it would be a convenient moment for me to retire? I have no idea and maybe when I come back from America I will ask him.

Saturday, April 11th[1]
During the flight home I slept for two and a half hours and when I woke up I saw England and Wales with a brilliant covering of white snow on the Black Mountains. We swooped down on London Airport at 9.30 in the morning and there I found Robin Wendt,[2] who had motored over to give me all the news. I felt very pleased to see him. It was sunny at Heathrow but as I drove through the Chilterns it began to cloud over. I stopped at Watlington to see Jennie Hall, who was wonderfully kind. She and Gil and Jessica had been out into the woods and had collected for me a box full of bluebells in their own earth for my island. I was back at Prescote by 12.30 and, while I was getting myself shaved Anne told me that the swimming bath had been cleaned and was heating up, so tomorrow I shall be able to dive in for my first bathe of the year.

My only contact with Britain during my Sabbatical week in Cambridge, Mass., was on Thursday last, when I was rung early in the morning by the Consul, who had received a telegram from the Prime Minister. I thought, 'Oh, my God, what is this?' The message simply said that there was a sensational story in that morning's *Daily Mail*, in which Walter Terry had asserted that Harold Wilson and George Brown had planned to intervene in the Israeli Six-Day War, but by the second day Harold had become less keen on the plan and it was dropped. This was a strange story and I know how it had come about. Just before I left London, the *New Statesman* had asked me to review Patrick Gordon Walker's book,[3] and I had noticed that the

[1] From Monday, April 6th, to Friday, April 10th, Crossman was at Harvard.
[2] Crossman's third and last Principal Private Secretary at the D.H.S.S.
[3] *The Cabinet* (London: Cape, 1970; rev. edn 1972). The description of the imaginary Cabinet meeting appears on pp. 153–67 of the revised edition and the author indicates that it is partly based on three debates held in Mr Wilson's Cabinet in May 1967.

fictitious meeting he had described was remarkably like one of the Cabinets where we discussed the closing of the Strait of Tiran and the British role. Walter Terry had apparently deduced from this passage that it revealed a secret. I was very amused because I had discussed Gordon Walker's book with Harold, who told me that the text had been cleared by Burke Trend, so this very passage had in fact been approved by the Secretary to the Cabinet. Harold had now specially telegraphed to tell me not to give any public or private interviews about this and that further directives would follow. When the airmail edition of *The Times* arrived, there on the front page was a formal denial from No. 10, giving maximum attention to the story. I gather that next Monday there is to be a debate on the Middle East, so no doubt this will come up again. Ha, ha! It is true that I had discussed Patrick's book at Harvard and there was always, I suppose, a danger that I could be cross-examined on it, but it was amusing that all Harold could think of was to stop me talking about the story.

Monday, April 13th

Traditional Cabinet meeting on the day before the budget. There is no agenda so there are no red boxes and Harold always says, 'I don't want any notes taken and if they are taken I don't want them taken out of the room.' We sat very quiet and listened to Roy describing his budget. I would call this a spineless Cabinet but it is an election year when none of us want to break things up, so perhaps that's why there wasn't any real discussion. Jim Callaghan was the only man honest enough to say, right at the end of the meeting, that the budget was an anti-climax but he also rather touchingly added that he was deeply impressed by Roy's mastery of the international monetary situation, which is really the basis of the budget. Of course, after two and a half years Roy's got the job in hand, just as each one of us has learnt the rigmarole and mastered the ideology and arguments of his Ministry. Roy has got this at his fingertips and he can talk the Treasury language to us. His budget was exactly what I had predicted. Instead of the £400 million income tax remission which Nicky Kaldor had planned, Roy had limited it to half that amount, which meant that he didn't have to offset another £200 million by raising money from an S.E.T. increase or an increase in employers' N.I. contributions. This is the correct, prim and proper thing to do and it is also positively socialist, because the remission only applies to people with incomes between £16 and £19 a week.

Tuesday, April 14th

This morning I drove up to St James's Square to see Barbara. We had to talk about another batch of wage claims, including one from the hospital laundry managers, a very militant group. These claims are mostly consequential on the nurses' award and I wanted Barbara's authority to go above the 15 per cent to which the P.I. Committee had limited me. I explained that, if I could go to at least 15½ for the first offer, it would enable me to do some restructuring for the laundry men but I might possibly want to go to 18 per cent. She consented to this with a good grace. Then I turned to the Kindersley Committee and it was clear that Barbara was going to urge us to accept the recommendations and phase the award but to take this opportunity to put the consideration of doctors' and dentists' salaries under a central commission, just as we are doing with judges' salaries. I must admit that there are very powerful arguments for this, though I know I shall have a hell of a row with the doctors and that my Department is against it.

I rushed back to the House just in time to squeeze myself on to the front bench at the end by the Speaker's chair. I must admit I fell asleep during Roy's budget speech, which was pretty heavy going, especially the international part.

Thursday, April 16th
I had to go out early to see David Ennals, who was concerned about a speech he is to deliver to the Child Poverty Action Group's annual conference this coming Sunday. I still feel unhappy about the way I fell into a bitter argument with Peter Townsend, when he came to represent the C.P.A.G. a few weeks ago. In this respect Roy's budget is a relief to me because it does give some money to the lowest possible income groups, and to this extent we should have spiked the guns of the C.P.A.G. and of Peter Townsend and his friends. David had brought me a long, intricate defensive speech and we struggled over it with Brian before I went to Management Committee at 10.30.

This is turning out to be very useful. As Patrick Gordon Walker quite rightly says in his book, the Prime Minister has to have a very large Inner Cabinet because at least eight people are too important to be left out and he has less freedom in choosing his Inner Cabinet than his main Cabinet. The problem with the Parliamentary Committee was that it both limited the Prime Minister's freedom and infuriated those non-members who found that decisions were being taken in their absence. But the Management Committee meets merely as an informal discussion group, exactly as it should. Though we leave firm decisions to the Cabinet, the initial discussion brings us into line with each other or else reveals differences, so that at Cabinet itself it is much easier to get a decision.

This morning I had to report to Kindersley and see that we didn't take the recommendations to the P.I. Committee, which would leak, but to a special MISC headed by Barbara. I also had to clear the raising of the supplementary benefit increase, which I had set for S.E.P. next Tuesday. These two items were dealt with in fifteen minutes. Otherwise we discussed, as we always do, the local election results and the prospects before us and we talked about decimalization and the future of the sixpence, and whether we should write a series of pre-election articles for *The Times*.

Immediately afterwards we had Cabinet and the first reactions to Gordon Walker's book, which was published this morning. Last week while I was away Cabinet had discussed the fantastic story about Suez and this morning members of Cabinet were asked not to permit the meaning of Gordon Walker's reference to be elicited from them. Harold was as fussy as ever but he was unable to do anything about the book, and he didn't mention that I had agreed to review it.

We then came to a most interesting item, a Top Secret paper from the Home Secretary on the case of Colonel Ojukwu, the former head of the Biafran rebel regime, who had been overthrown by General Gowon and had fled to the Ivory Coast, a French colony. It seemed likely that Ojukwu would seek refuge here and, as that would create a real breach between the British and Nigerian Governments, Harold had decided when we first discussed this before Easter that there must be full Cabinet backing to stop him. Our friend Callaghan was his usual uncertain self, behaving on this rather as he has done on drugs. He almost asked Cabinet to prevent him from doing as the P.M. and the Foreign Secretary wanted and he said that he couldn't do anything unless Ojukwu actually got here, though a watch would be kept at Customs and if Ojukwu were spotted he would be shipped back on the next plane. When Jim had made his case, I said, 'Look, last time we discussed this I asked what precedents there were and I was told that nobody knew. Since this paper does not mention any precedents, I assume that none exist. So we are proposing that the Home Secretary should take an unprecedented action that is a departure from the long tradition that there is a right of asylum in this country. Liberty is very unpopular. It is an unpleasant, difficult thing, but let us at least be clear about what we are doing.' The Solicitor-General confirmed that banning Ojukwu would be an unprecedented action and Callaghan leant across and said, 'Are you opposing it?' I said, 'Well, you must know your business, you and the P.M.,' and that was that. The thing went through and the minutes didn't even have a reference to my remarks. Afterwards, as we were getting up, Callaghan said to me, 'Of course, if you had opposed that I would have gone along with you,' and Roy said, 'Yes, if you had opposed it I would have supported you as well.' It was a shock. What had happened to me? Why hadn't I opposed Harold and Michael Stewart and split the Cabinet? I knew the Home Office proposal was wrong and I believe I could have carried the majority with me. I suspect that it was because I have lost the spirit, the dynamic, for taking such a stand. Am I a member of Cabinet at all? Or am I just sitting there watching? Years ago I would have done it, but now I am a senior member and carry more weight I don't act. It shook me a good deal.

I gave Nicky a slap-up dinner at the Garrick. He's a man who is always preoccupied by a single idea at a time, and he'd only one thing to say to me. A fortnight ago he had published in the *New Statesman* an article saying that the E.E.C. agricultural policy is hopelessly reactionary and terribly expensive and that from every point of view, that of the members and of the world, the E.E.C. is a hopeless organization, and there is no reason whatsoever for us to join it. It was a most expert article and very powerful. Nicky said this evening, 'Now that you have failed in your budget, which will neither win nor lose you any votes, you have to get another election-winning instrument. What you must do this summer is to choose your time and then say, as a Government, "Unless the E.E.C. changes the Common Agricultural Policy we won't go in." You, Dick, you alone, could put this forward to Cabinet with any chance of success.' This made me recollect what happened at Cabinet this morning. If I were to choose my time and insist on doing as Nicky suggests, I think Harold, Michael and Roy would find it difficult to refuse me and I would have people like Barbara and Fred Peart supporting me and, I suspect, Ted Short and Peter Shore as well. But I had to say, 'Nicky, I don't want to do this. I don't want to split the Cabinet. I have done that once before when I fought Harold, Barbara and Roy on industrial relations. I don't want to fight Roy, Harold and Michael on this. I am too old, too divided and anyway I don't want Labour to win the election. I want to be out writing my book.' He said, 'This is discreditable.' I said, 'Yes, it's only half my attitude.' I went away disturbed and uneasy about myself and my role in Cabinet, and I am still brooding. Would it be all right, should I do it? I had better hurry up because there isn't very much time.

Monday, April 20th
As I was waiting outside the door before Management Committee, Roy came up and said, 'By the way, I wanted to mention that I shall be raising the issue of the Kindersley Report.' I noticed that he had a long speech written out and I realized that he was going to cause trouble. After the first item, he started trying to make a great speech but I was able to stop him, saying, 'Look, this is ridiculous. Most people here haven't seen the Report. The Chancellor is away next week, so if he is anxious about this, let us postpone consideration of the Report, even though it's a bit of a nuisance, because it will mean that we can't deal with it before the B.M.A. meet on May 8th.' This nonplussed Roy, who had been determined to do me down by having it all discussed in detail today and having it knocked out in one. But even if you are Chancellor you can't do that.

Our main discussion was about the legislation programme and whether we should plan for a normal new session after the summer recess or whether we should carry over the existing session until the election in spring 1971, assuming we weren't going to the country this September. All the arguments suggested that it would be impossible to start a new short session in the autumn and that we should run the present session through until March, giving us time to complete Barbara's Bill and various other things. However, the more we discussed it the more obvious it was that we no longer have that option. Only a devaluation threat or some ghastly disaster could force us to

carry on. We really have only one date for the election and that is October
10th. It is either that or bringing it forward to June but, as Bob Mellish has
discovered, June is clearly impossible because no Member feels he is ready
and nobody is going to consider that possibility until we have seen the results
of the municipal elections. Who is going to tell me that we will have such a
triumphant result in May that we can have a snap election? No, we realized
today that autumn is the only time.

Towards the end of the meeting I raised the problem of the Common
Market. Nicky had rung me on Saturday night to make me read his *New
Statesman* article, and he had convinced me that I must do something. I
managed to say, 'Look, let us discuss the programming of our Common
Market attitudes. Would the P.M. tell me something about this? Are we
planning to open negotiations or not?' Of course I have been reading the
telegrams but the fact that I asked this shows how little I know about these
things and how departmentalized we are. It emerged that in July we are to
have what Harold described as 'a Victorian family portrait'. He said, 'That is
what Willy Brandt has called it, a family portrait, with all the members of the
E.E.C. and all the applicants coming to record their official positions.' I said,
'Marvellous. It would suit us very well to have that in July. But, in that case,
Prime Minister, you must appreciate that we are hoping you will be able to
use it for electoral purposes because, after all, the only thing wrong with
Peter Shore's speech was that Peter Shore said it. If you had said it, from
your central position, it would have been O.K. What I am expecting of you is
that in July you will be able to make a speech about food prices and the cost
of entry and of the C.A.P., and you could suggest that Britain isn't going to
join. With that you would win the election. As we have given up the idea of
an election-winning budget, we are left with the E.E.C., where Heath is
suspect. We are depending upon you to do it.'

We discussed this for thirty-five minutes and, although Harold continued
to say we couldn't discuss the Common Market without Michael Stewart
(the Foreign Secretary is in Turkey at the moment), we were obviously doing
so. There was not even a denial from Roy, who might have said that
appearing to manoeuvre in this way would be very dangerous, and that we
shouldn't exploit the Common Market in the election. Denis and Fred Peart
also sat silent, merely smiling. Barbara and I made it clear that in the summer
we would expect the P.M. to make our negotiating posture an election-
winning issue. We reached a general agreement that Michael Stewart had
been wrong to urge members of the Cabinet to do their share of speaking on
the Common Market and that only the inner three should do so. The
minority would express their view by remaining silent and any speaking I
were to do would be misunderstood. Harold and Michael are ardent Common Marketeers now, more I would say than Roy who, as Chancellor, sees
the real difficulties and is certainly prepared to postpone if demanding
higher terms would win us the election. The other ardent marketeers are

Tony Crosland and Denis Healey, who certainly wasn't before but now, I think, feels that he has to be in favour of entry if he is ever going to become Foreign Secretary. As for the rest of Cabinet, Barbara and I are willing to try but not on terms that are too high, Fred Peart is firmly opposed, Bob Mellish is a sort of Marketeer and George Thomson is infatuated because he is at the F.O. Nobody else is very enthusiastic one way or the other.

Afterwards as Burke was using his key to get the two of us into the Privy Council offices, I said to him, 'We had better not have any of that in the minutes.' He said, 'No, I agree with you. It was a useful discussion but not one we will mention.' Sure enough, no minute of this discussion is to be found.

Thursday, April 23rd

I rang the P.M. this morning because I was worried about my review of Gordon Walker's book. I had sent a draft across to No. 10 on Monday, explaining that it had to go to press on Friday, and I had mentioned it to Burke at Management Committee and at S.E.P. Burke had said yes, he knew about it, he was quite impressed and he would get it into the P.M.'s box. But Harold had been away at Oban addressing the Scottish T.U.C. and today he told me hadn't had time to look at my draft. I said, 'Well, I am off to Winchester tonight. Could you possibly read it in the course of the afternoon?' It was difficult to talk to him about it when his whole mind was obviously full of his success with the Scottish T.U.C. and the improvement in the polls, and he probably felt that Dick needn't and shouldn't be messing about with a ridiculous little thing like this. However he was pleasant and he promised to read my article.

At the beginning of Cabinet Harold spent a great deal of time on the question of what help the Opposition should be entitled to have. It was clear that a number of us had given the Opposition some access, although as Harold made clear, only on matters of machinery. For instance, I had allowed the officials to discuss not the policy of Health Service reform, but Health Service reconstruction and its consequences. We all automatically understand that an Opposition which might take over must be allowed to discuss the machinery of government, just as George Brown was permitted to do on the whole question of the establishment of a Department of Economic Affairs.

Harold now ruled that we must make the following distinction: the Opposition must be permitted to discuss the machinery of government with our civil servants but, if they want to discuss a matter of policy and brief themselves for the speeches they are going to deliver against us in the Commons or the country, they must not go to the civil servants but must see us. The Common Market is a very good example. If the Conservatives were to demand, as apparently some of them are doing, that they should be allowed to find out from the Foreign Office what our negotiating position is or what sticking-point we are proposing, we could not permit it. It is true that we must allow a simple, straight, effective switch-over after an election and it is important that an Opposition should be briefed in an appropriate way but there should be nothing beyond that.

It was interesting to discover how little we had asked for help before 1964. True, one was entitled to be briefed by Foreign Office officials when one went abroad but that was a well-established practice, and our Defence people also had a little briefing, mainly by the chiefs of staff and by the Ministers rather than the officials concerned. But as a Shadow Government we had not really expected contact with officials and certainly I didn't expect it. Harold himself admitted that his chance only came on the last day of the 1963/4 parliamentary session, when he was able to talk to the key officials. Today Harold was extremely careful to lay down the line.

This afternoon I was having a highly technical meeting of Coventry shop stewards when Robin Wendt came down to the House to say that the Prime Minister urgently wanted to see me. I rushed up and found him sitting in his room (I rarely go there now) and I saw he had in front of him my review, with another long piece of paper attached to it. Harold said, 'Now this is quite a thing. It seems to me that first of all we have Gordon Walker on *The Cabinet* and then Macleod's review of Gordon Walker, then Crossman on Macleod and now Burke Trend on Crossman.' He threw across a five-page review of my article from Burke Trend's office. It was the most extraordinary stuff, a kind of public school, prim, pious critique of Crossman as an easy-going person who didn't appreciate the meaning of collective responsibility. It was a picture of the non-loyal member of the team, who is using his position in an improper way, and about whom nothing can be done.

Among this there was a proper criticism saying that I had mentioned three times that members of the Cabinet had got away with writing books violating the Official Secrets Act. Harold said this was highly embarrassing not only because this week such a prosecution is going on, but also because Ministers can't be prosecuted in this way. He said, 'For God's sake, can't you get the Official Secrets Act out and substitute "collective responsibility"?' I said, 'Of course I can't. It doesn't fit.' But to my amazement I found it did. I had learnt something staggeringly important. Burke and Harold admit that the Official Secrets Act, which is really the only threat against a Cabinet Minister, doesn't operate.[1] No one can be prosecuted under it, so there is therefore no sanction against a Cabinet Minister at all. He must be allowed to have access to the documents, he writes what he likes and then it is a matter of whether the Secretary of the Cabinet and the Prime Minister of the day can manage to persuade him to leave out things they think improper. In fact it is a question of whether sufficient sense of collective responsibility is instilled into you to ensure that, after you leave office, you will in your book-writing still feel enough of a member of the team, a part of the Cabinet

[1] It was never, in fact, invoked even in the legal proceedings against these *Diaries*.

system, to behave properly. That is all they rely on. It may sound obvious now I have said it but I certainly hadn't known it before. I had thought the ultimate sanction was the threat of prosecution.

It made me realize that Burke can be two-faced. He has never indicated in any possible way that he disapproves of me but I know that he does. He actively distrusts me, mainly because I am not a reliable member of the team and when I get the chance I am liable to write a book which will say more than should be said and which he therefore won't approve. Burke knows this and I now think it is quite right that I should do it.

These were some of the points which came out in the course of our discussion. Harold said, 'I don't know. I stand somewhere half-way between you and Burke Trend. I don't hold all that Burke holds but I do think you are wrong about the Official Secrets Act. Couldn't we get that bit right?' Then he went right through my review and made a number of drafting suggestions, introducing far more clever propaganda into it than I wanted. I took very careful notes of each point. Towards the end I said, 'Look, Harold, what about my future after the election?' He said, 'What do you mean?' I said, 'You'll be making changes. I assume that Michael Stewart will be retiring.' 'Oh,' he said, 'not retiring, I think, but he has certainly got to have a change.' I said, 'What about me? Do you think at sixty-two I am ready to retire from the Cabinet?' He said, 'I have never thought of such a thing,' and he obviously hadn't. I remarked, 'Well in that case you'll want me to stay at my present job but with enlarged powers?' 'That's it,' he said, and I realized that he couldn't conceive that I should want to retire. Harold's main anxiety was that I wanted to be Foreign Secretary and was competing for promotion. There are only three jobs I could get. I could become Minister of Defence, not that this is much promotion, Chancellor or Foreign Secretary, and obviously Harold heaved a sigh of relief that I wanted to stay where I was and have my powers extended. Now I didn't say I didn't and I didn't tell him anything about my own intentions.

We sat side-by-side at the table in his room in the House of Commons and chatted about the election and what was going on on the front bench, about Burke Trend and Roy and his budget and his success. An anodyne chat it was but I had learnt something of Harold's thoughts about my future. It doesn't make life any easier, because the more I think about this the more I realize that after six years I've had enough. In a curious way this conversation with Harold has confirmed it. I know where I am. Now I know I can go on if I want to, I know I don't want to. Writing this review has taken me a stage further towards resigning and going back to journalism and my books. Perhaps the most amusing thing was that when Harold talked about his own book-writing he said, 'When I retire I shall be the youngest retired Prime Minister for 100 years and I shall have time for plenty of writing. I have got my plans clear. The first part will be my three- or four-volume memoirs and the big job will be the twenty-volume memoirs I shall leave for posterity.' I remember his

saying something of this sort at least once before. One improves one's
remarks by trying them out and he now said it with such complacency that it
seemed to have been rounded and finished.

Wednesday, April 29th

At Management Committee we talked about electoral prospects. Burke and
his staff were absent and Harold gave us a special warning that the meeting
was secret.* He started by saying, 'This is your meeting and I'm not going to
say anything, I'm leaving it to-you.' Then he spoke, and I timed him, for
twenty-five minutes. These days Harold is becoming more and more verbose
and he talks more and more prosily as his personality sinks further and
further into his image. His face is getting greyer and he becomes more a part
of his suit. He began, of course, by saying that one had to consider all the
practical possibilities and at inordinate length he discussed the timing of
the South African cricket tour, the timing of the Wakes Weeks, the timing of
the Coventry shut-down week, not forgetting the World Cup at the end of
June. All this had been worked out to show there was really only one election
date, the third week of June, unless we were to look forward to October. He
then talked about the pros and cons. Wage inflation is continuing and in the
country there is a wild sense of unreality, far worse than in 1966, when we
got in before things busted and wage inflation won us the election. This time
people fear that boom will be followed by bust and we may as well get in first.
Harold was supported by Bob Mellish, who said that when he took the straw
poll of M.P.s it was 2:1 for October, but since then there has been a change in
the Parliamentary Party and everybody was now telling him, 'The P.M.
knows things we don't know. Trust the P.M. If he wants to go in June, we are
ready to go then.' Fred Peart and, to my surprise, Michael Stewart, both
favoured June and only Barbara and I were firmly for October.

Let me make a note for the record. In the spring of 1966 Harold was
deciding election dates absolutely on his own, perhaps consulting a small
circle of Marcia, Gerald, Peter, Tommy and me, but virtually no one else.
Now he sits around with nine of his colleagues at Management Committee
perfectly prepared, apparently, to see this as a matter for consultation, first
with us and then with the N.E.C. on the 18th (when I shall be in Malta). As
Gordon Walker says in his book, all this formalization indicates a weakening
of the P.M.'s position. Harold really has got an Inner Cabinet round him and
now we would all question his right to decide the election date by himself. As
P.M. he has grown in stature in the last ten years and he's back on top of his
form and his popularity. When electioneering he is in his element. Yet his
Cabinet colleagues who used to be unknown and inexperienced have now
won themselves some position in the party, in Parliament and in the public
eye, and the balance of power is very different from what it was.

* Next day Harold felt entitled to say he had not discussed election prospects with the Cabinet
or with any of his ministerial colleagues, though he had in fact spent two hours doing so.

This evening Nicky Kaldor came to dinner with me. By this time the whole House of Commons was brimming with rumours that tomorrow's opinion poll would show a 2 per cent lead. The moment has arrived when one can sense a great lift of desire for a June election. I tried to get from Nicky an objective estimate of what the situation was likely to be in October but the economists can't be sure. There has never been a time when things have been so unpredictable because America is totally unpredictable, particularly after Nixon's vast gamble in Cambodia. We should have a clearer picture before the summer is out.

Tuesday, May 5th
At Cabinet we were concerned with Cambodia, and Michael Stewart started by outlining the speech he wished to make to the House this afternoon. It was a dry, detached defence of the Americans, theoretically right in certain ways but in a form which would antagonize the whole of the Left and also the whole liberal opposition among the British public. The Prime Minister immediately came in without waiting for anyone else. He said, 'That isn't good enough. Somehow we must avoid this position of total neutrality and move to the position of a friend who is warning and advising an ally.' Harold outlined this in twenty minutes, warming up Michael's remarks and adding a sop to our own back benchers. Then the fat was in the fire. Barbara broke out and said this was totally impossible. A completely new situation had arisen, the Americans had now apparently abandoned the whole of their plans to withdraw from South-East Asia and Nixon was in the hands of his generals. I spoke with passion too. All this stirs me from the bottom of my heart and I said, 'It's no good. We put pressure on Johnson to stop the bombing of the North, supported him in the withdrawal policy and we have supported Nixon. Since it seems that Nixon is abandoning this policy, we must say to him, "If this marks your abandonment of the policy of withdrawal or, even worse, if you still intend to keep to the policy but are becoming so deeply involved that you can't withdraw this summer, we have reached the parting of the ways."' I said the test of Michael Stewart's speech was whether he could say that the Americans' action might have been a dangerous and tragic miscalculation and for this I was sternly rebuked by Jim Callaghan, who was staunchly for the Americans.

It went round the table and there was an interesting line-up. Roy Jenkins was sitting there making notes and he threw across to me one that said, 'Here is the spectrum of the Party as I see it.' The spectrum ranged from Harold Lever on the extremest pro-American right, saying this was a tactical manoeuvre for getting out and that we must stand by them. Along with him were Michael Stewart, George Thomson, Roy Mason and Shackleton. On our side were Barbara and me, Peter Shore and Tony Wedgwood Benn. Tony put in an admirable contribution, saying that it wasn't the content of the speech that mattered but the style and that we must show sympathy with the liberal forces in America. If we were going to bring youth to our side we mustn't seem to be supporting age against youth.

We also had, rather surprisingly, Ted Short and Cledwyn Hughes, Fred Peart in a sort of way, and Bob Mellish, not because the last two felt very strongly, but because they knew the Parliamentary Party required it. Roy was trying to get the best of both worlds, as he often does now. He and Harold were very unsatisfactory but they knew the Cabinet was split and they were trying to hold it together. Denis Healey stayed woodenly in the middle, trying to ease the situation but basically siding with Michael Stewart. Harold finally summed up. Cabinet minutes are fairly truthful here, though they don't express the strength of the support for the switch Barbara and I wanted. Michael Stewart was told that his speech wasn't good enough and that he must take a position of detachment, so that he could still play his role as co-Chairman. We all hoped that something had been achieved, though I didn't have much confidence that anything we had said had made the faintest impact on the Foreign Secretary.

Towards the end of Cabinet Harold had said, 'I think I shall have to wind up this afternoon.' (The Chief Whip had mentioned that the P.M. might have to do it.) I jumped in and said, 'Certainly,' because we all thought, 'My God, if Michael's going to be like this, we mustn't have the final speech made by George Thomson who would be worse, but by the Prime Minister, who might improve things a little.'

I had to go out to a meeting with the local authorities but I came back in time to hear the Prime Minister make a tremendously valiant effort. But of course he was tied in by Michael, whom he couldn't repudiate. Harold went as far as he possibly could to put the issue in a more reasonable frame and, indeed, I should think he held ten or twenty votes at the end. Harold is a brilliant tactician and his speech was sufficiently different from Michael's to split the Tories, a lot of whom had wanted to go into our lobby but now refused to do so and in many cases abstained. The debate ended in a terrible schemozzle. There were 68 votes against, of which 59 were Labour and if Harold hadn't split the Tories successfully, we would have heard nothing but a tale of Labour splits. As it was, appalling damage had been done and the Party was furious. I was white with anger. I told the Chief Whip how impossible it was and we fumed together. When I went upstairs there was Brian O'Malley looking green, saying that as a junior Minister he hadn't approved of Michael's speech. I said, 'My God, *you* didn't approve. Do you think I did?'

Monday, May 11th
As I went up in the train I reflected on all the inconvenience that an early election would cause me. I had already made it only too clear to Management Committee that I should be the person who loses a major Bill,[1] which

[1] Crossman's National Superannuation Bill, still at its Committee Stage.

would then take another six months to put on the Statute Book. It's sad for me because I shan't be there to carry it through or to deal with my other two big projects, the White Paper on the reform of the National Health Service and the preparation of a White Paper on mental handicap. All these will be left half done for my successor to finish. I have privately asked Tam, Brian and Tommy whether it wouldn't be possible for me to stay on for a year or even six months to see the Superannuation Bill through, but to prepare the two White Papers and the draft legislation would, of course, require a three- or four-year stint. I tend to think that I can't go back into the Cabinet and then get out and in any case I am beginning to feel ready to move. Moreover, I have promised Jock Campbell that I will be ready to take over at the *Statesman*. We haven't spoken to each other yet about the election date but that I suppose is the next thing I ought to do.

Thursday, May 14th

Management at 9.30. Harold said, 'We needn't, of course decide anything yet,' and then he made a twenty-minute speech. The most interesting point was that he had got Roy's certificate that it would be just as safe to have the election in October as in June. Nevertheless Roy had decided that in the circumstances June was right. 'Basically,' Harold said, 'I really decided this a month ago.' That is right. He made up his mind a month ago, he wanted June and waited for the facts to come his way. Perhaps we could have dragged him back but events have been on his side. Harold has got his way and he has done so by being an election Prime Minister, creating the atmosphere and the news, working up the fever, making postponement impossible. We then discussed whether we shouldn't announce the date after today's Cabinet. Many papers were expecting this but Harold wanted to wait until next Monday. We heard some of the detailed mechanics—how Harold had warned the Queen before she went off on her New Zealand trip and how all the arrangements had now been made for him to talk to her on Monday.[1] It became clear that the Prime Minister didn't want the announcement before next Sunday's joint Cabinet–N.E.C. meeting at No. 10. If an announcement were made they would sit down to write the manifesto, which Harold wants to do himself with Peter Shore. He intends to leave the N.E.C. in suspense, which means the meeting will be a sheer waste of time. Thank God I won't be there.

It was quite easy-going. I wanted to know about timing and whether one could go away on holiday. Harold said that if necessary he wanted us all to come back. Judith, who would be touring by car, would have to clock in by telephone every day. I said, 'Well, I shall be in Malta.' There was a bit of surprise and then Harold said, 'I excuse the halt, the lame, the blind and the old.' I said, 'I qualify in all four categories,' and there was a hearty laugh. It is

[1] The Queen, the Duke of Edinburgh, Princess Anne and Prince Charles visited New Zealand and Australia from March 30th to May 3rd, to take part in the Cook bicentenary celebrations.

interesting that Harold is allowing me some time off and it is more evidence that he may not be utterly surprised when I bring him my news. But I don't know.

Meanwhile Cabinet was waiting outside and after forty-five minutes in they came. They were just told that there was still no decision but that it was most important to say there had been no discussion. Then we arranged the business for the first week in June but all this will fall to the ground, because in fact Parliament will be brought back a week early, on the Tuesday after the Whitsun bank holiday, and after three days it will be prorogued, so that we can go right into the campaign. The election will be on June 18th, the date Harold has always wanted. Barbara was eagerly saying she must get her Equal Pay Bill through but I told her, 'That doesn't matter, we can have it again. What matters is to get the Seebohm Bill through, because that has an appointed day and delaying it would hold up the whole of local government reform.' Old Barbie always tries to get everything for herself. Then we were told there was to be another inquiry into the B.B.C.[1] I asked why colleagues weren't consulted and Harold said some colleagues were. Here is another instance of a major decision being privately taken by Harold and a few others.

By this time the newspapers were blazoning the results of the polls. The Tories were six points down in Gallup and 3·5 in N.O.P. and it was obvious that everybody knew we were going to have an early election.

Friday, May 15th

At 9.30 we had a short meeting of Management, where Roy and I raised the matter of the Kindersley Report. We pointed out that we should decide whether to publish it or just suppress it and announce that we would decide on doctors' pay after the election. After a working lunch with the P.U.S.s and the Ministers, I went off to Heathrow to catch the 5 o'clock plane to Malta.

Tuesday, May 26th

I flew back today, leaving the family behind for the rest of their second week. Before going round to the Elephant and Castle I called in at Transport House, because the Private Office had made a mistake and thought that a joint meeting of the N.E.C. and the Cabinet was taking place there this morning. I looked through the door and there only seemed to be about twelve people in the room. Tony Wedgwood Benn said, 'Hallo, Dick, what are you doing here?' and I told him that I thought there was a joint meeting to draft the manifesto. 'No, no,' he said, 'this is a drafting Committee but do

---

[1] The Prime Minister announced that a Committee to inquire into the future of broadcasting was to be set up, with Lord Annan as Chairman. After their election victory the Conservatives announced that no Committee would sit but when Labour returned to power in 1974 Lord Annan was once more asked to undertake the inquiry and a Committee was appointed. It eventually reported in March 1977.

come in. We have just reached your bit on social services.' A curious coincidence. I sat down and read it, tidying it up as much as I could. I realized that poor old Peter Shore must have had a very tough time trying to draft this without me. But in fact my presence wouldn't have made the faintest difference, because they had been given a ruling that the Chancellor must not be committed to any extra expenditure. As there is nothing we can do which doesn't cost money, the only pledge is the thoroughly bad one to reform the House of Lords. So all they could do was write the manifesto shortly or at length and I don't think I had missed a great deal.

I went up to the Elephant and Castle to sort things out before going over to the Athenaeum for a quick lunch by myself and to prepare for this afternoon's departmental meeting on the final draft of the Social Services Committee on mental handicap, the preliminary to the White Paper. But after lunch I learnt that the meeting had been scrubbed and that I was to see Harold straightaway about the doctors. A letter had just been received from the B.M.A. with a sensational press release saying they were so angry and fed up that, unless we published the Report by the end of the week, the B.M.A. action committee would advise the Council to advise the profession to take the first steps of protest, i.e. to break off all contact with the Government and stop signing sickness benefit certificates. Pretty hot stuff; with no warning, their General Secretary and officials were blowing the thing up into a sensation.

This letter was handed to me the moment I walked into Harold's room. He was about to tell me that postponing Kindersley was no good. The doctors' indignation was mounting and we had to publish. I said, 'But if you publish after seven weeks' delay, it will look much worse. People will want to know why we couldn't make up our minds and meanwhile the doctors will use the Report to put pressure on every parliamentary candidate. I see no advantage in publishing, Harold.' 'Well,' he said, 'I assure you that we have to give way now. You don't understand the opinion that is building up in the country.' I replied, 'We certainly can't publish at the very moment when they are threatening strike action. This has given us a great chance. I have already summoned the doctors to see me at 5.30 and I suggest that we simply reply that I am not prepared to surrender to strike action. We can certainly say that, though you and I were considering publication last week, there is no question of our doing so in the face of this threat.' 'Yes,' Harold said, 'that's right. Draft a statement on those lines and we will have Management Committee at 4.30.'

So I brought a draft statement into Management Committee but nobody seemed to like it very much. Indeed, Harold once more made it clear that he thought it a great mistake not to publish, despite the fact that last time this had been brought up at Management he had capsized within four minutes and agreed not to publish. Barbara also thought we ought to publish and to publish our decision as well. Roy immediately supported her and I realized

that, if we had to publish, it was certainly a lesser evil to publish the Report
and the decision together and that to do this in an election atmosphere would
not be such a bad thing, because the doctors' demand for 30 per cent across
the board and their outrage at getting only 15 per cent would seem extremely
greedy. I also saw that if we published now I could perhaps get 15 per cent
flat-rate payment on account, plus the full amount for the junior doctors, so I
straightaway switched to support Barbara and Roy. This discussion went on
until 5.20 and I was due to see the doctors at 5.30. I said, 'I must tell them
that the Prime Minister and I will agree to see them this week.' Harold said,
'All right, I'll see them but not tomorrow or Wednesday because that would
spoil the press for the manifesto. If I see them on Thursday it will get into the
Friday press.' We agreed to see them on Thursday morning in No. 10.

Thursday, May 28th
The first thing was the meeting with the B.M.A. at No. 10. I got there a
minute or two early and went in the back way to join Harold. Then they all
came in—Dr Gibson, Dr Cameron, Dr Stevenson with his assistant secretary, and two dentists. They were on the far side of the table, facing Harold
and me. The P.M. did practically all the talking and started by being very
strong to them, as he had promised, and rather offensive about their threats
of industrial action. Then he said, 'Let's put a veil over the past,' and
announced that we had conceded publication next week. That was the
soonest they could have it, both in terms of printing the document and of
getting our decisions ready. The meeting was tough and there were a great
many speeches. They kept saying, 'It's impossible, you must publish this
weekend or the whole thing will blow up. Our relations with the Government have been put back ten years.' They made the wildest claims but we
insisted that they could only have the Report in a week's time.

Then they demanded that we must guarantee that the Government
decision would be nothing less than the whole recommendation. Harold and
I said that it was absurd to ask this. A Government doesn't say these things,
doesn't automatically grant everything a Report recommends. We hadn't
finished considering it yet and we couldn't possibly give such an assurance.
They said, 'Without it the whole profession will be in chaos.' As a matter of
fact, all these predictions were quite wrong because the B.M.A. which was in
session today, agreed to wait for a week and the junior doctors and everybody else agreed, although there were mutterings that if the decision wasn't
satisfactory they would proceed with strike action.

Thursday, June 4th
My first job was to see Lord Kindersley himself. He turned out to be a
genteel, faded man of some seventy years old, with a kind of club-foot. It
turned out that his review body consisted of completely reactionary economists and vice-chancellors, whom we hadn't bothered to change, and from his

attitude after he had read our report it was clear that he was against me. I told him not to resign. I said, because I had persuaded Harold this morning to agree to it, 'The Prime Minister would like to see you as soon as possible, you and your members, so for heaven's sake don't do anything drastic without seeing him.' But I was uneasily aware that Kindersley wasn't all that amenable.

Meanwhile I had received a vigorous message from the ten B.M.A. delegates, who had arrived at 9 o'clock in order to have time to study the Kindersley Report, which they had received last night with our accompanying statement. They were waiting in Alex Baker's room along the corridor and their message said that unless they could come along pretty soon they would leave. It was only 10.25 and we had asked them for 10.30. I thought this was a bad sign. However I went downstairs to Cabinet Room A and they were brought in. Gibson, a nice fellow, the doctor from Winchester, started by saying, 'I don't know why we should stay here at all, let's go out,' but he was restrained by one of the G.P.s and a consultant. I presented them with the Report, and they couldn't have been more hostile or violent. All last night, while we were preparing the papers, and the day before, we had been discussing what the B.M.A. were likely to do. The C.M.O. had said that on balance there was just a chance that they might, not accept, but acquiesce in the Report, but I had never thought there was much chance of that. On the other hand, I didn't expect them to be quite so ferocious.

The meeting took about an hour. They said they were utterly opposed to us tooth-and-nail, that they were not prepared to collaborate in any way, that they were going to meet the B.M.A. Council on Saturday and there was little doubt of the advice they would give. We just had time to go round to Admiralty House for the press conference. No drinks now. There was one serious question, and then in a very undramatic way I presented to the press the generosity of the deal and all its ingenuities. I said that it was worth £55 million as against £87 million of the Kindersley recommendations, that it was money on account and that the cheques would go out on July 1st, backdated to April 1st. I told them that we were not rejecting the Report only submitting it for a second opinion. I did the best I could but I was well aware that it was relatively easy to present my case to the press in a way that I couldn't to the doctors.

Friday, June 5th
I had to decide what to say in reaction to the announcement of the review body's resignations, but first of all I went to a meeting of the *Statesman*'s Board. We made the arrangements and they told me that I ought to be out of the House in a matter of days. I explained that I couldn't possibly do this because it would depend on my constituency and the size of my majority, and anyway I hadn't talked to Harold about it. We had a long argument about the communiqué but it was all perfectly amicable.

I got out in time to rush back to the Elephant and Castle to talk to Clifford Jarrett about the payment of sickness benefit in the event of a doctors' strike and to have one more go on the Green Paper. Then I did 'The World At One' and rapidly dictated my reaction to the review board's resignation before I was off in the car to Buxton, where I was to address the Personnel Management Society's annual conference, taking Barbara's place. It was perfect summer weather and we had the most beautiful drive through the Peak District until we came to a vast hotel, where I got into a bath and thought about a speech on equal pay, something I know nothing about. There were endless excitements just before the Conference dinner, with the B.B.C. saying they wanted me to go down to Stockport later on to answer questions from Robin Day in London on the storm of indignation which the doctors had aroused. So I ate the dinner, made my speech fairly satisfactorily and then drove off with Peter Brown to Stockport, where we found an enormous empty hall with broadcasting facilities. I had to look at a tiny little television set and though I couldn't see Robin Day and Reg Maudling I heard them through a damned thing in my ear. I found that the questions were not about doctors' pay but entirely about the economic situation and I discovered that something I had said in my secret talk with the doctors had caused great alarm and despondency. They had apparently rushed out and complained that I had said the reason why we couldn't accept Kindersley in full was because the instability of the economy had put the nation in peril. This has been one of the great Tory lines, which fitted the doctors' line, and I had to spend my time denying it.

Sunday, June 7th
When we got back to Prescote there were more endless telephone calls about the doctors. The B.M.A. had met and decided on a partial strike but fortunately for us the junior hospital doctors' breakaway union had come out on our side, and so had the Medical Practitioners' Union. We have at least succeeded in splitting them that much.

So here we are at the end of the first week of my last election campaign. Apart from doctors' pay, the only other sensation has been Tony Wedgwood Benn. He made a sensational speech, not attacking Enoch Powell but asserting that Heath was really a cover for Powell, who was the real power in the Tory Party. Tony made some very wild remarks about Belsen and Dachau, delivering himself into Tory hands, so that Heath was able to demand that Harold should repudiate such extremism. Harold went as near repudiation as anybody could and, ever since, the Tories have been mounting an attack on Wedgwood Benn. So now we have two extremes, with Powell and Benn somehow cancelling each other out.

I talked to Harold on the telephone about this, and he said, 'As a matter of fact, the Campaign Committee had decided they wouldn't play up Enoch Powell and now Benn has gone completely against the directive.' Harold was furious. Still, I don't think it's been disastrous, just as I don't think the tremendous row which is now building up between the Government and the doctors is in any way disastrous for us. Indeed, the Tories may well have discredited themselves by automatically jumping on the doctors' bandwagon within a few hours of the publication of the Kindersley Report and announcing that every penny of the £85 million award should be paid.

I suppose my main impression of this campaign is that it has been masterminded by Harold and this new fellow William Camp.[1] The P.M. has evolved a new technique of being televised and photographed with party workers and this has brilliantly contrasted him with Heath. Harold is the easy-going, nice fellow, while Heath is making boring, serious speeches. Harold has got the bit between his teeth and he is fighting the election in his own individual style. He has dispensed with practically all policy and there is no party manifesto because there are no serious commitments at all. In that sense we are fighting a Stanley Baldwin, 'Trust my Harold', election, or a 'Doctors' Mandate' election, call it what you like. The Tories are fighting a scare election, simply and solely on the threat of rising prices, of a wage freeze and the imminent breakdown of the economy. Their theme is, 'If you put Labour in there will be another crisis,' and to make it effective they have been searching out ministerial statements which indicate that we think there will be a wage freeze after the election.

Monday, June 8th

This afternoon I.T.N. demanded that I do something for their news programme on 'economic peril' remark. 'Oh,' I said, 'that old story. I wouldn't have thought people would want to hear any more about that.' But I discovered that I.T.N. had a guilty conscience because they felt they had been giving too much attention to the doctors and too little to me. This news item would restore their balance. So I looked in on the way to Euston and in an excellent three-minute interview I corrected the record again. Mind you, this business goes on and on. I suppose it's done me a certain amount of harm but at least this evening I was able to say that Dr Stevenson was spending more time on Conservative propaganda than he was on the good of the B.M.A.

Let me get the story absolutely straight. As I was describing to the doctors the possible repercussions of clamping an £85 million claim into the economy, I had said it was a perilous situation. Three or four minutes later one of the doctors had said, 'You said we are in economic peril.' I had said, 'No, I didn't. I told you that the impact it would produce would be a perilous situation.' 'No,' he had answered, 'I heard you say the other.' Then, and this was probably a mistake, I had said, 'If you heard that I withdraw it and

---

[1] Public Relations Adviser to the Gas Council 1963–7. Director of Information Services at the British Steel Corporation 1967–71. He was on unpaid leave as Special Adviser to the Prime Minister during the 1970 General Election.

substitute what I have told you, because that is the real reason.' They had gone off and immediately talked to the Tories.

Sunday, June 14th

Today I took a complete rest. There are just four days to go and so far it has been one of the easiest campaigns I've known. I think I can best sum up the mood by saying that it most reminds me of the 1959 election, the 'You never had it so good' election, when the Tory Government had no real programme. This time we are in a very similar situation, though of course the real resemblance is not between Wilson now and Macmillan then but between Gaitskell then and Heath now. Heath is nicer-looking than Gaitskell was, but they both have that lock-jaw effect, that remoteness and glazed eye. In Hugh it was beginning to rub off as he learnt a bit about being less detached and intellectually superior (and became as a result somewhat dogmatic), but Ted Heath hasn't learnt even after four years. He is still a waxwork, stiff and tense, and, poor man, during this campaign he has been subjected to a most merciless press.

As in 1959, the Opposition are fighting a fine weather mood and a sense of complacency, yet I have to record that we can't say the electorate has never had it so good. Macmillan could point to five years of economic expansion and a tremendous rise in living standards, five years of Tory easy-going. We have given them three years of hell and high taxes. They've seen the failure of devaluation and felt the soaring cost of living. Yet Harold Wilson is running the election in this Macmillan-like way and he has suddenly found that the mood is on our side and that people are good-humouredly willing to accept another six years of Labour Government.

I think this is a result of most unusual circumstances, in which three separate factors have converged. The first, quite simply, was the end of the prices and incomes policy, following on the dropping of the Industrial Relations Bill and our decision to rely on the T.U.C's voluntary effort. This has allowed the official trade unions to be friendly with us again and it has permitted Jack Jones and Hugh Scanlon to feel it was time to end the animosity which was wrecking local parties. The abandonment of the policy brought about the second factor, that for some months now wages have been rising faster than prices. Everybody knows, of course, that prices will catch up within the next twelve months but at this particular moment, as in the spring of '66, the British elector feels good and, though he knows this won't last long, it changes his attitude to the Government. The third thing which actually crystallized the feeling of lift and the sudden transformation of our chances was the Tories' announcement of their carefully contrived exercise at Selsdon Park. It came as a shock to have this tough, strong picture of Selsdon Man leading a virile, capitalist, anti-trade union revival, and suddenly people thought, 'My God, if that is the alternative, there is something to be said for dear old Harold now that he has learnt his lesson.' I think this is what has given us such an easy election. The country isn't in the mood for Cassandra prophesying doom nor does the electorate want, or have any confidence in the effectiveness of, Heath's reconstructed, reactionary Toryism of free enterprise and anti-trade unionism.

Monday, June 15th

Today's trade figures show us £31 million in the red and this evening, watching a dusky television set, I saw Iain Macleod spiriting disaster out of Aladdin's cave. Then I watched Harold addressing a huge meeting in Hammersmith and making jokes about half the deficit being due to the purchase of jumbo jets. That sums up the campaign, but still Harold was more effective than spooky Macleod. It is now clear that the only thing which the Tories have to hang on to is the rise in the cost of living and its effect on the pensioner and the housewife. I am not sure whether there will be a large Labour abstention or how many pensioners and housewives will switch to the Tories but it won't win them the election.

Thursday, June 18th

A perfect polling day, warm and sunny with not a drop of rain. We began our formal journey round the polling stations, ninety-eight of them in the whole constituency. I suppose we went to about seventy or seventy-five, more than I have ever done before, because there was really nothing else to do. Winnie Lakin[1] went tootling ahead, her little car covered with posters, with Anne and I driving slowly behind. So the day went on in an absolutely inane routine of driving to the polling stations, getting out, looking inside, saying how do you do to the polling clerks and asking how much had been polled. The candidate has the right, I don't quite know why, to go in and talk to the returning officers and ask them for the number of votes that have actually been cast. I took notes all the way round, so I felt able to form an opinion and from 6.30 onwards it was obvious that something was going very badly wrong. The poll was only just over 50, 52, 55 per cent, even in our safest, biggest wards, and by 9 o'clock it was only 60 per cent. I was sure that I had found in microcosm what we were going to discover in macrocosm.

In the evening Winnie Lakin, Albert Rose, Anne and I all went to the Craven Arms Hotel in the centre of the town for a rather solemn, good meal, and in the middle of it a young man, someone who was doing a technical training course at the Lanchester Polytechnic, came up and insisted on standing us a most inappropriate bottle of champagne in which to drink our health. Then we went over to the Police Hall for the count and stood about until the ballot boxes arrived at about half-past ten. The count took three and a half hours, an appallingly slow process, but it wasn't long before we

---

[1] Crossman's agent in Coventry East.

began to suspect that things were not going well. Albert became terribly nervous and told me that the boxes were showing 50/50 Labour and Tory. We very soon discovered that we were getting 3,000 votes to 2,000, 4,000 to 2,000, not at all the proportion we expected. At a count you are supposed to be cut off from the outside world but somebody had brought in a little transistor radio and we heard the first result from Guildford, a swing of 5·3 per cent to the Tories.

Then came the news that Enoch Powell had increased his majority, with an 8 per cent swing in Wolverhampton, and a 9 per cent swing against Renee Short in the other part of the town. Within an hour I knew we had comfortably lost the election. There were of course redeeming features. By 1.0 a.m. we'd learnt that Bill Price had retained Rugby with an increased majority, Bill Wilson was back with a somewhat reduced majority in Coventry South and there was a rumour that we ourselves were probably going to have less than a 10,000 majority. Finally, after an interminable time, at 2.10 a.m. we had our result and our 12,000 majority. What I had learnt between 7.0 p.m. and 9.0 p.m. reflected not only our own polling stations but the whole town.

Afterwards we all went off to watch television. The end wasn't quite as bad as the beginning. They'd talked about a Tory majority of 100, but the figure fell to 45 and then to 39.[1] Suddenly it was 4.30 a.m. and Anne and I motored home in the cool, delicious dawn of an exquisite morning.

Friday, June 19th
At 4.0 I was driven up to Downing Street in a pool car, because Peter Smithson is away on holiday in the South of France, confidently expecting to come back and drive me again. I found a great crowd shouting 'Out, out,' with a few bystanders who were sympathetic and in a political way quite friendly. Then I was inside. There was poor Tony Wedgwood Benn looking white and drawn, appalled by the result, and Michael Stewart, who'd lost his voice from so much public-speaking. Roy breezed in, Harold arrived and we drifted into the Cabinet room for the last time. Barbara told me later that she wasn't asked to this meeting but in fact they couldn't find her. Denis Healey came in a little late and there we were, a smallish gathering without Fred Peart, Bob Mellish or Tony Crosland. We chatted about the election and the future. Harold said that when the Queen's Speech was presented we must make only formal opposition. We must give the Tories a honeymoon period but maybe within two years we should find an opportunity for attack. Then I think it was Roy who said, 'We might have some meetings, because the party's morale will need bolstering a bit,' and somebody else added, 'They ought to be private meetings.' I observed, 'If they're private, you'll be having

[1] The Conservatives gained 74 seats and lost 6, Labour gained 10 and lost 70, the Liberals lost 7. The final figures were: Conservatives 330 seats; Labour 287; Liberals 6; Scottish Nationalists 1; Welsh Nationalists 0; Independent Labour 1; Protestant Unionist 1; Unity Party 2; Republican Labour 1.

inquests about the election,' and Michael Stewart said, 'We can't afford to have any inquests about the election; it would be terrible to disagree.' Denis Healey put in, 'I hope that in public we can all say the same thing. I've been doing a bit of morale-building on I.T.N.,' and I thought to myself, 'You may hope there will be no inquest, but there will be, because the party will indeed be asking how it was that we were forced into June, how it was that we were given the illusion that we were winning and how it was that we were let down. There will indeed be a reaction and the *New Statesman* will have something to contribute.' But I didn't mention the *Statesman*, although just before the meeting I had rung Harold to say that I would have to make my decision and see the *Statesman* today.

It was a desultory meeting, pleasant and friendly, and Harold was cool, collected and apparently self-possessed. At one point, while I was getting myself some iced water from the decanter at the end of the room, I looked out and saw thirty or forty packing cases. I said, 'What is that?' Harold said, 'Those are our files.' I asked, 'Is that your twelve-volume book?' and he said, 'No, they include my constituency files as well. We ought to be out of No. 10 today and we're still packing. By the way, I shall be living near you. We have taken 14 Vincent Square for three months while Mary is house-hunting. She wants to live in the centre of London rather than going back to Hampstead.'

We discussed where we should meet in future and arranged that Management Committee should meet again, because until the Shadow Cabinet is elected we remain in control. Harold will then appoint those whom he wishes to lead the new Opposition. He said he thought that Bob Mellish should continue as Chief Whip and it was also agreed that we hoped Harold himself would be automatically re-elected to the leadership but that there should be a re-election for the Deputy Leader. In the presence of both Callaghan and Roy, we were all far too discreet to ask whether this would be a contested election. I would have thought that since Callaghan is Treasurer of the party, it would be tactful to let Roy be Deputy Leader to allow him to be a member of the Executive, but it won't happen like that and I think the two of them will probably fight it out in the Parliamentary Party.

Throughout the discussion I was thinking of my forthcoming meeting with Jock Campbell, Paul Johnson and the three members of the *N.S.* staff who had been invited. I got to Vincent Square just after five to find them all waiting, among a vast number of bottles, because all my surplus drink had been brought across in red boxes from Alexander Fleming House and unloaded on the floor. So we settled down to our first *New Statesman* meeting. We decided that the press release should be issued at 6.0 p.m. tomorrow, and that I would brief the Sunday press, spelling out that the whole thing had been fixed well before I knew that the party had lost and that Paul Johnson was unwell and wanted to resign. Paul and Jock then drifted off leaving me with Tom Baistow, the Deputy Editor, Anthony Thwaite, the

Literary Editor, and a fellow from the management, and we sat quietly over a drink and chatted about the future of the paper. It was all natural and spontaneous and I tried to create the feeling that I was coming home to the *Statesman* and that they were going to have an editor who belonged to their traditions.[1]

---

[1] Crossman's contract as Editor of the *New Statesman* was abruptly and prematurely terminated by the paper's Board in March 1972.

Index